RABINDRANATH TAGORE

ALSO BY KRISHNA DUTTA
  Rabindranath Tagore's *Glimpses of Bengal* (translator)
  Rabindranath Tagore's *Selected Short Stories* (translator)

ALSO BY ANDREW ROBINSON
  Satyajit Ray: The Inner Eye
  The Art of Rabindranath Tagore

ALSO BY BOTH AUTHORS
  Noon in Calcutta: Short Stories from Bengal (editors/translators)

RABINDRANATH TAGORE
The Myriad-Minded Man

Krishna Dutta and Andrew Robinson

St. Martin's Press ✺ New York

Endpaper art: *Self Portrait*, Rabindranath Tagore, 1935
(Rabindra Bharati Museum, Calcutta)

ISBN 0-312-14030-4

First published in Great Britain by Bloomsbury Publishing Ltd.

First U.S. Edition: January 1996
10 9 8 7 6 5 4 3 2

To the Best of Bengal

'Languages are jealous sovereigns, and passports are rarely allowed for travellers to cross their strictly guarded boundaries.'

Rabindranath Tagore, 1935

'I never had the feeling of grappling with an alien culture when reading European literature, or looking at European painting, or listening to western music, whether classical or popular.'

Satyajit Ray, 1982

'The West is still, after half a century, groping in the half-light to discern the features of Tagore's genius.'

E. P. Thompson, 1993

Contents

Illustrations

All illustrations are identified from left to right. Normally only those people mentioned in the book are identified. The name of the artist or the photographer, where known, is given first in roman, followed by our source in italics (*RB* stands for Rabindra Bhavan, Shantiniketan).

Frontispiece Rabindranath Tagore, 1926 (Bula Mahalanobis/*RB*)

Between pp. 48 and 49
 1 'Prince' Dwarkanath Tagore, grandfather of Rabindranath, 1845/46 (Baron de Schwiter/*RB*)
 2 Maharshi Debendranath Tagore, father of Rabindranath (*RB*)
 3 Sharada Devi, mother of Rabindranath (*RB*)
 4 Two elder brothers of Rabindranath and their wives: Jnanadanandini and Satyendranath, Jyotirindranath (*seated*) and Kadambari (*RB*)
 5 Jnanadanandini Devi, in Karwar (near Goa), 1883 (Jyotirindranath Tagore/ *Twenty-Five Collotypes From the Original Drawings by Jyotirindra Nath Tagore*)
 6 The house of the Tagores, 6 Dwarkanath Tagore's Lane, Jorasanko, north Calcutta, today:
   a main entrance seen from lane (Suman Datta)
   b prayer hall and main courtyard (Samiran Nandy)
 7 *The Familiar Black Umbrella*, 1916 (Gaganendranath Tagore)
 8 Rabindranath, in England, *c*. 1879 (*RB*)

Between pp. 112 and 113
 9 Rabindranath, 1882 (*RB*)
10 Rabindranath and his nephew, artist Abanindranath, 1892 (*RB*)
11 Rabindranath, *c*. 1881 (Jyotirindranath Tagore/ *Twenty-Five Collotypes From the Original Drawings by Jyotirindra Nath Tagore*)
12 Rabindranath reading, 1892 (*RB*)
13 Rabindranath and his brother Jyotirindranath composing, *c*. 1892 (*RB*)

Acknowledgements

Writing about Rabindranath Tagore is extremely stimulating and utterly draining. We are lucky to have had the support of three people, Anita Desai, Amartya Sen and the late E. P. Thompson, each interested in a different facet of Tagore. This book is indebted to them.

Satyajit Ray has been with us throughout. Rarely can two great artists have had such an affinity as Ray and Tagore.

Nirad C. Chaudhuri, both in his writings and through our personal contact with him, has been a bridge to a vanished world. His long chapter on Tagore, 'The Lost Great Man of India', in the second volume of his autobiography (1987), was an inspiration to us. It presented a uniquely honest picture of Tagore's ambivalent relationship with Bengali society; it also provoked us to attempt to rescue Tagore from the limbo so brilliantly described by Chaudhuri.

Prashanta Kumar Paul, currently writing a multi-volume biography of Tagore in Bengali, published as far as 1913/14, impressed us with his devotion, fair-mindedness and attention to detail under difficult conditions. We salute him.

Alex Aronson in Israel shared his knowledge of Tagore's university and Bengal from his stay there more than half a century ago. Dipali Ghosh of the India Office Library and Records in London enthusiastically excavated documents. Uma Das Gupta in Calcutta was hospitable and helpful in numerous ways. K. G. Subramanyan in Shantiniketan, India's finest living painter, reminded us of Shantiniketan as it was in Tagore's lifetime. Howard Young in California generously made available his expert knowledge of Juan Ramón Jiménez, Tagore's Nobel prize-winning Spanish translator. The London Library was an invaluable and accessible resource, particularly of memoirs and biographies.

We wish to thank the following people in Britain: Frank Anderson, Kenneth Ballhatchet, Sir Isaiah Berlin, Richard Blurton, John Boulton, Vicky Bowman, Robert Bradnock, Simon Brandenburger, Judith Brown, Kathleen Cann, Lionel Carter, Andrew Cook, Margaret Drabble, Ronita Dutta, Warwick Gould, Diana Harris, Dominic Hibberd, Richard Hoggart, Michael Holroyd, Brian Josephson, Nasreen Munni Kabir, Eivind Kahrs, Robert Knox, Kalyan

Kundu (of the Tagore Centre), Brian Lapping, Christopher London, Sarah Lutyens, Gopa Majumdar, Peter Marshall, Ian Mayes, Partha Mitter, Ray Monk, V. S. Naipaul, John Rosselli, Dilip K. Roy, Peter Salinger, Jacqueline Sen, Lord Skidelsky, Duncan Spiers, Jon Stallworthy, Marjorie Sykes, Anne Taylor, Dorothy Thompson, Anthony Valsamidis, Ronald Warwick and Michael Yeats. In Dartington, the institution inspired by Tagore, we are grateful to Peter and Bobbie Cox, Maggie Giraud, Mary Bride Nicholson and Michael Young; also to Lucy Bartlett.

In Shantiniketan, the late Sanat Bagchi, Martin Kämpchen and Supriya Roy provided much-needed help. We also thank Nemaisadhan Basu, Sabyasachi Bhattacharya, Anathnath Das, Indrani Das, Mira Ghosh, Sankha Ghosh, Ashis Hazra, Samiran Nandy, Ajit Podder, Sibnarayan Ray and Gourchandra Shaha.

In Calcutta, the following people were of assistance: Nirmalya Acharya, Dwijendranath Basu, Samar Bhowmik, Samir Kumar Bose, Ashin Das Gupta, R. P. Gupta, Dipankar Home, Russi Mody, Indrapramit Roy, Manasij Sen Gupta; elsewhere in India, Indrani Majumdar, Siv Ramaseshan and Sumita Bahadur Singh.

Worldwide, our thanks go to: Dmitri and Lena Antonov, S. C. C. Atukorale, Nancy Baxter, Kenneth Blackwell, Fritjof Capra, Henri Cartier-Bresson, Subrahmanyan Chandrasekhar, Michael Coe, Gherardo Gnoli, Elisabeth Heisenberg, Elisabeth Higonnet-Dugua, Julian Crandall Hollick, Pico Iyer, the late Stella Kramrisch, Dan H. Laurence, Roger Lipsey, Jagdish Mehra, Claude Mignot-Ogliastri, Erin O'Donnell, Asko Parpola, Kai Pfähler, Thomas Pinney, Ilya Prigogine, Annette Pringle, Mary de Rachewiltz, Helmut Rechenberg, Anne and Arthur Row, Robert Schulmann, S. D. Serebriany, Aida Sofjan, Rebecca Timbres Clark and Mya Thein Tint.

And of course we thank Liz Calder, our eclectic editor at Bloomsbury Publishing, Joy Press, our copy editor, and Mary Tomlinson.

Andrew Robinson received a fellowship from the Leverhulme Trust in 1993, and small grants from the British Academy, the Harold Hyam Wingate Foundation, the Society for South Asian Studies, the Society of Authors and the Spalding Trust.

ABOUT THE TRANSLATIONS

A vast amount of Tagore's writings has been translated into English, mainly by Bengalis. Where a satisfactory translation exists, we have generally used it (duly credited in the Notes) – except in the case of Tagore's poetry. Most of the poetry we quote we have translated ourselves, with an attempt to preserve, in as many cases as possible, the rhymes in Tagore's original. We need hardly say that we are not fully satisfied with the results, but we take some comfort from the fact that Nirad C. Chaudhuri and Satyajit Ray, brilliantly bilingual in Bengali and English, both thought Tagore's poetry virtually untranslatable.

THE SPELLING AND PRONUNCIATION OF BENGALI

We have tried to use Bengali names and words sparingly, to avoid overloading the reader unfamiliar with Bengal. The transliteration of such names and words in English is a tricky and unsatisfactory business. Rabindranath is pronounced 'Robindronath', for example, Satyajit – 'Shottojeet'; Tagore is an anglicized form of Thakur, Banerji of Bandopadhyay, Chatterji of Chattopadhyay, Ganguli of Gangopadhyay. Many names and places mentioned here have no widely agreed spelling, e.g. Chandernagore/Chandannagar, Shelidah/Shilida, Santiniketan/Shantiniketan, and we have adopted one that is commonly used or reasonably consistent and, if possible, not too off-putting for a non-Bengali reader. All Bengali words we have spelt without scholarly but cumbersome diacritical marks, and have tried instead to use a spelling that reproduces the sound not the orthography of Bengali. In the case of 's', almost every 's' in Bengali is pronounced 'sh'. This means that, rather than employing the conventional but confusing 's' and 'sh' to represent the three Bengali letters for 's', we have transliterated all three letters as 'sh' – except where there is an established spelling, as in the word sari, the name of the Tagore house, Jorasanko, or the name of Tagore's brother, Satyendranath.

RABINDRANATH TAGORE

Introduction

I have this paradox in my nature that when I begin to enjoy my success I
grow weary of it in the depth of my mind.

letter to Edward Thompson,
Shantiniketan, 1921

This is an ambivalent book. It has to be, whichever way one views
Rabindranath Tagore, more than half a century after his death. Seen from
the West, Tagore appears to have come out of nowhere in 1912 and collected a
Nobel prize without the least effort; to have travelled the world and enjoyed a
worldwide homage for over two decades not granted to any other writer this
century; and then to have evanesced until he is barely more than a name. But
seen from Bengal he looks very different. Before 1912, Rabindranath was
rejected by many, perhaps the majority, of Bengalis as being a product of western influence; for the rest of his life he experienced a unique blend of vilification
and homage; and only after his death in 1941 was he canonized as Bengal's
greatest creative artist and raised to the Olympian pedestal he now occupies. No
writer, living or dead, is today more actively worshipped in Bengal than
Rabindranath Tagore.

From his own point of view, Tagore's predicament was even more contradictory. As an idealist – which he remained to the last – he reserved his highest
admiration for the humane spirit of the West he had first encountered in the liberalism of nineteenth-century English literature and politics. 'Whatever may be
the outward aspect of Europe's power, I have no doubt that at its core is the
power of the spirit', he said before leaving Bengal in 1912. Like some other
highly educated Bengalis of his time, until about 1920 Tagore believed British
rule in India to be providential, necessary for the reform of a moribund, degen-
erate society. But as a patriot, particularly after 1900, he needed to believe in the
persistence of ancient India's spiritual values in contemporary India. In 1912,
through his poems *Gitanjali* (*Song Offerings*), translated by himself, and
through his personal presence in England – where people were even reminded
of Christ – these two beliefs became harmonized in his mind. For a few brief

years he brought East and West into receptive emotional and intellectual contact. Thereafter, with the First World War, the upsurge of the Indian nationalist movement, its suppression by the imperial government, and the popularity of the non-cooperation movement led by Gandhi, neither belief proved tenable. Both, however, continued to coexist in Tagore's mind. As a direct consequence, he found himself obliged to defend Indian spirituality when abroad, and the spirit of the West when in India. Not surprisingly he felt inwardly torn and often tortured.

But before we delve further into his own ambivalence, here are three stories of Tagore's one-time fame in the West, each illustrating a different aspect.

In August 1920, while he was in England, Tagore received the following letter from an Englishwoman:

Dear Sir Rabindranath
I have been trying to find courage to write to you ever since I heard that you were in London – but the desire to tell you something is finding its way into this letter today. The letter may never reach you, for I do not know how to address it, tho' I feel sure your *name* upon the envelope will be sufficient. It is nearly two years ago, that my dear eldest son went out to the War for the last time and the day he said Goodbye to me – we were looking together across the sun-glorified sea – looking towards France with breaking hearts – when he, my poet son, said those wonderful words of yours – beginning at 'When I go from hence, let this be my parting word' – and when his pocket book came back to me – I found these words written in his dear writing – with your name beneath. Would it be asking too much of you, to tell me what book I should find the whole poem in?

The writer was Susan Owen, mother of Wilfred Owen. The verse was from *Gitanjali*. That Wilfred Owen truly did cherish it, is shown by the fact that he wrote it on the back of a message form in early 1917, eighteen months before he said goodbye to his mother in August 1918. [pl.33]

The second story was told in 1961, the centenary of Tagore's birth, by the German playwright Carl Zuckmayer, who, like Owen, fought in the First World War. He heard the story from a friend, a sergeant in the German army's medical corps. An Indian soldier in a Gurkha regiment of the British army had been taken prisoner and wounded in both legs. Only amputation of one of the legs could save the soldier's life – and the chief surgeon wanted the man's consent or at least some sign of trust. But neither the Indian soldier nor the German medical officers had much command of English; and the soldier of course spoke no German. The more they tried to talk to him, the more anxious and scared he became – he had probably heard frightful stories about enemy treatment of prisoners. At last, Zuckmayer's friend thought of the only Indian words he knew. Bending down to the sweating soldier he whispered: Rabindranath Tagore! Rabindranath Tagore! Rabindranath Tagore! 'After he had said it three times the Indian seemed to understand. His face relaxed, a shy little smile came into his eyes, then he closed them, his fear was gone, and he nodded weakly his consent and confidence to the enemy doctors.'

The third story dates from the Second World War. It happened in the Warsaw Ghetto, in an orphanage headed by the writer and educator Janusz Korczak. Despite offers from friends, Korczak refused to leave the ghetto without 'his' children. On 15 July 1942 he produced his last play with them, ignoring SS orders forbidding Jews to perform works by Aryan authors. It was *The Post Office*, Tagore's most famous play (which Radio France had broadcast in June 1940, the evening before Paris fell). The central character is a dying boy, bedridden on doctor's orders, who is made to believe that a king will visit him and grant his dearest wish. When after the performance Korczak was asked why he chose this play, he answered that 'eventually one had to learn to accept serenely the angel of death,' in the words of Bruno Bettelheim. In August 1942, Korczak and the children were taken to Treblinka and gassed: today their grave is marked by a rock, the only rock among all the rock-graves of Treblinka to bear a human name.

The Owen story may be said to show the power of Tagore in person; the Zuckmayer story the power of his name; the Korczak story the power of his writing. A biography of Tagore must take into account all three aspects of Tagore's reputation and their ramifications. These can be astonishing. In 1935, for instance, Tagore received a letter from Count Michael Tolstoy, a son of the writer, which began: 'You were my father's friend and shared his way of thinking. Knowing how highly my father valued and respected your literary and philosophical work and achievement, I venture to write to you . . . ' But Leo Tolstoy, who died in 1910, never read Tagore, far less corresponded with him; and Tagore felt no particular affinity for Tolstoy's works!

Almost all Tagore's contacts with writers and others outside India are marked by this air of unreality, to a greater or lesser extent. They were 'imperfect encounters', to borrow the title of Tagore's thirty-year correspondence with Sir William Rothenstein, the artist who introduced Tagore to literary London in 1912.

The most celebrated of these encounters was undoubtedly with W. B. Yeats. In his Introduction to *Gitanjali*, Yeats wrote ecstatically:

these prose translations . . . have stirred my blood as nothing has for years . . . These lyrics . . . display in their thought a world I have dreamed of all my life long. The work of a supreme culture, they yet appear as much the growth of the common soil as the grass and the rushes.

He had just spent some weeks helping Tagore to revise his translations for publication.

But by 1917, after giving further assistance, Yeats was writing to Macmillan, Tagore's publishers:

> After *Gitanjali* and *The Gardener* and *The Crescent Moon* (exhaustively revised by Sturge Moore), and a couple of plays and perhaps *Sadhana* [philosophical lectures delivered at Harvard University in 1913], nothing more should have been published except the long autobiography . . . , a most valuable and rich work . . . These later poems are drowning his reputation.

And in 1935, a few years before his death, in a letter to Rothenstein Yeats delivered this broadside against Tagore:

> Damn Tagore. We got out three good books, Sturge Moore and I, and then, because he thought it more important to see and know English than to be a great poet, he brought out sentimental rubbish and wrecked his reputation. Tagore does not know English, no Indian knows English. Nobody can write with music and style in a language not learned in childhood and ever since the language of his thought. I shall return to the question of Tagore but not yet – I shall return to it because he has published, in recent [years], and in English, prose books of great beauty, and these books have been ignored because of the eclipse of his reputation as a poet . . .

Yeats never did return to Tagore, but he published seven of Tagore's poems (five from *Gitanjali*) in *The Oxford Book of Modern Verse* the following year.

His ambivalence was shared by the poets who have translated Tagore, who included three subsequent Nobel laureates, André Gide, Juan Ramón Jiménez and Boris Pasternak. Jiménez, his Spanish translator, dropped Tagore in the early 1920s after twenty-two books and became sensitive to suggestions that Tagore had influenced his own poetry. But in later life, walking one day on a beach in Puerto Rico, his self-exiled home, Jiménez bent down and scooped up the foam from a wave. 'These are Tagore's ashes,' he said. 'Why could they not have come here from the Ganges flowing along the waters of the world? For it was my hand that helped to give our Spanish form to the rhythm of his immense heart.'

Anna Akhmatova, while translating Tagore into Russian in the mid-1960s, made caustic gibes at the poems. But having finished, she declared: 'He's a great poet, I can see that now. It's not only a matter of individual lines which have real genius, or individual poems . . . but that mighty flow of poetry which takes its strength from Hinduism as from the Ganges, and is called Rabindranath Tagore.'

Tagore himself, it must be said, was fully – painfully – aware of the difficulties of translation, and of his incapacity to tackle them properly. He said so again and again to literary friends whose first language was English. An early instance was his letter to Ezra Pound of February 1913. (Pound had come to know Tagore through Yeats and was for some months even more enthusiastic, comparing Tagore with Dante in a weighty review of *Gitanjali*.) Tagore had sent Pound some translations – later to form part of *The Gardener* (the book after *Gitanjali*) – and Pound said he had detected in them a whiff of didacticism that would soon put him off Tagore's works. Tagore replied:

> I had my misgivings . . . But I must say they [the poems] have not been purposely made moral, they are not to guide people to [the] right path. They merely express the enjoyment of some aspects of life which happen to be morally good. They give you some outlook upon life which has a vastness that transcends all ordinary purposes of life and stirs imagination. I am sure in the original there is nothing that savours of pulpit. Perhaps you miss that sense of enjoyment in the English rendering and bereft of their music and suggestiveness of language they appear as merely didactic.

While this last sentence is certainly true, there was much more to the collapse of Tagore's reputation in translation than languages and their atmospheres. Behind language lay the daunting disparity in cultures. In 1913, Occident and Orient were more distant than today. For some readers of *Gitanjali*, such as Yeats, this provoked curiosity; for others, such as André Gide, it was a matter of active indifference. 'What I admire in *Gitanjali* is that it is not encumbered with mythology . . . it is not at all necessary to make preparations for reading it', wrote Gide in his preface. 'No doubt it can be interesting to discover in what respects this book belongs to the traditions of ancient India; but it is much more interesting to consider in what respects it appeals to us.' Besides *Gitanjali*, Gide translated into French only *The Post Office* – nothing else by Tagore. When Tagore's autobiography *My Reminiscences* appeared in English in 1917, Gide read it and noted in his journal: 'But that Indian Orient is not made for me.' For Yeats, by contrast, this book was 'most valuable and rich' – an opinion he persisted in until his death.

Over the years a peculiar, unique situation developed. For many readers, Tagore became an honorary European who wrote in English – or even Spanish.

(In Spain and South America, and even sometimes in England, he is pronounced
'Tagoré'.) His *Collected Poems and Plays*, published by Macmillan in 1936 and
still available, contains not the merest hint that the contents are translations, let
alone that they were written in Bengali. A well-known biography of T. S. Eliot,
published in 1984, states curiously that Eliot was 'the sixth Briton' to receive
the Nobel prize – Kipling, Tagore, Yeats, Shaw and Galsworthy being his predecessors. And in 1993, in a British parliamentary debate, a speaker asserted
confidently that the English language was 'not only the language of Shakespeare
and the Romantic poets, but also the language of James Joyce, Rabindranath
Tagore and of Hemingway, and many African writers today'!

Tagore in person was less easy to annex. Sometimes he was treated as a
European; more often as a representative of mystic India; seldom as a Bengali.
George Bernard Shaw 'Europeanized' him, joking to William Rothenstein's
wife in 1913: 'Old Bluebeard, how many wives has he got, I wonder!' Jacob
Epstein 'Indianized' him, sculpting a lugubrious bust in 1926 and remarking
cattily in his memoirs that Tagore in person contradicted his *Gitanjali*: 'I am he
that sitteth among the poorest, the loneliest, and the lost.' Actually, said Epstein
(who had grossly misquoted the original poem), Tagore 'was conducted about
like a holy man . . . and if he needed anything only one word of command
escaped him to his disciples . . . It has been remarked that my bust of him rests
upon his beard, an unconscious piece of symbolism.' William Rothenstein, who
drew an exquisite series of pencil portraits of Tagore both in India and in
London, felt quite differently to Epstein [pl.31] – but his friend Max
Beerbohm, prefacing a book of Rothenstein's Tagore portraits, struck a note of
criticism similar to Epstein's, if more subtly condescending:

> Most men are not at all like themselves. The test of fine portraiture is in its
> power to reconcile the appearance with the reality – to show through the sit-
> ter's surface what he or she indeed is. I take it that Tagore was for
> Rothenstein a comparatively simple theme.

Shaw's comparison with Bluebeard, though amusing, was misjudged – as
Shaw realized when he met Tagore again in later life. Nor was Tagore some sort
of precursor of Bhagwan Shri Rajneesh, as Epstein implied, though he could on
occasions appear to be so. (In this case, he perhaps instinctively distrusted the
acerbic Epstein, and wore a mask over his real self.) A glance at some of the
many self-portraits that Tagore painted in old age, gives an inkling of his inner
complexity. In one series, he has over-inked his own sage photograph, beard and
all, to make twelve transmogrified faces, several of them distinctly zany, one a
kind of monster (a touch of Bluebeard), another a woman. None of the twelve

suggests either the tranquillity of Rothenstein's drawings, or the spiritual vanity of Epstein's bust. [pl.44]

'The West sees an ineffective dreamer, v dignified and calm. Reality sees a restless, versatile spirit, of feminine contradictoriness', complained a frustrated Edward Thompson, Tagore's first major western biographer, who had known Tagore in Bengal, writing to a Bengali friend in 1920.

'There's no literary news here,' wrote the poet Philip Larkin from Hull to a poet-friend in London in 1956, 'except that an Indian has written to ask what I think of Rabindrum Tagore: feel like sending him a telegram "FUCK ALL LARKIN".'

'But why should the West care?' asked Satyajit Ray in 1963, speaking of western attitudes to Indian cinema in general, and, by extension, his own film adaptations of Tagore. Twenty years later Ray added: 'the cultural gap between East and West is too wide for a handful of films to reduce it. It can happen only when critics back it up with study on other levels as well. But where is the time . . . ? And where is the compulsion?'

The only valid counter to Ray's doubts is the one given by Rabindranath Tagore's grandfather, 'Prince' Dwarkanath Tagore, a century and a half ago. In 1846, he was staying in Paris in the best suite of apartments in one of the best hotels. Here the young Friedrich Max Müller, later the most celebrated Orientalist of the nineteenth century, sought Dwarkanath out. Having discussed their shared taste for European music, Max Müller made a repeated request to hear an authentic specimen of Indian music. At last Dwarkanath yielded, played a piece on the piano and sang; but Max Müller could find in the music neither melody, nor rhythm, nor harmony. When he said so, Dwarkanath replied:

You are all alike; if anything seems strange to you and does not please you at once, you turn away. When I first heard Italian music, it was no music to me at all; but I went on and on, till I began to like it, or what you call understand it. It is the same with everything else. You may say our religion is no religion, our poetry is no poetry, our philosophy no philosophy. We try to understand and appreciate whatever Europe has produced, but do not imagine that therefore we despise what India has produced. If you studied our music as we do yours, you would find that there is melody, rhythm, and harmony in it, quite as much as in yours. And if you would study our poetry, our religion, and our philosophy, you would find that we are not what you call heathens or miscreants, but know as much of the Unknowable as you do, and have seen perhaps even deeper into it than you have.

Dwarkanath Tagore was a remarkable man. In Calcutta, a city of merchants second only to London in the British Empire, he was the leading businessman and philanthropist, India's first industrial entrepreneur. In Europe, he was 'the Oriental Croesus', welcomed by Queen Victoria, King Louis-Philippe and Charles Dickens, and granted the Freedom of the city of Edinburgh. But neither in Europe, nor, more significantly, in Bengal, is Dwarkanath now much remembered. He has been consciously written out of the Tagore story by Bengalis. And the first to do so was the Tagore family itself.

Rabindranath in mid-life was said to have burned most of his grandfather's personal correspondence. Certainly references to Dwarkanath in his voluminous works are extremely rare. The charge against him, though never clearly articulated by his grandson, seems to have been that he was far too commercial in outlook; and secondly that he was a lackey of the colonial authorities. He dealt, for instance, in opium, sending it in clippers to China; and he paid a fulsome tribute to the East India Company when in London. But in disowning Dwarkanath, Rabindranath not only did an injustice to his grandfather (who was a complex figure, definitely no toady), he also distorted his own relationship with both Britain and Bengal. Too often, against his own instincts and experience, Rabindranath deluded himself that Britain was essentially commercial in outlook and Bengal essentially spiritual. He thus tended to divide English people into a handful untainted by commercialism, such as Rothenstein and Yeats – and the rest, shopkeeping John Bulls anxious only for profit out of India. He never fully accepted that even in his high-minded friend Rothenstein, there was, so to speak, a touch of Larkin.

In Bengal, the delusion brought him approbation when he boosted Bengal abroad, but vituperation when he tried to make Bengalis live up to his ideal. His speeches and writings on this subject were never less than direct, often satirical and sometimes ferocious. In 1917, he told a Calcutta audience (in Bengali):

We all live in the same town, under the same municipality, but with this difference: the Indians acquiesce, while the Europeans do not . . . We . . . throw up our hands, sigh heavily, and say, 'The Master's will be done'. We give the Master a thousand names, such as father, elder brother, police inspector, priest, pundit, Sitala [goddess of smallpox], Manasa [goddess of snakes], Olabibi [goddess of cholera], Dakshin Ray [tiger-god], and the heavenly bodies, Sani, Mangal, Rahu and Ketu. We smash our own power into a thousand bits and cast them to the winds . . . National self-respect is making us turn our faces forwards to the world and demand political authority, but it is also making us turn our faces backwards to our country and demand that in all religious, social, and even personal matters we do not move one step against the Master's will. This is what I call the revival of Hinduism. National self-respect is ordering us to perform an impossible task: to keep one of our eyes wide open and the other one closed in sleep.

Thousands of Bengalis were turned away from this lecture for lack of space. When it was repeated in a large theatre, mounted police had to be called because the crowd was so great. Rabindranath's Bengali audiences probably seldom agreed with his lectures – but they were never indifferent to them. A section of the press kept him under constant fire, frequently descending into mud-slinging; one newspaper even alleged that Rabindranath had syphilis. 'Few writers have been more scurrilously abused [than Tagore]', wrote Nirad Chaudhuri, the leading critic of modern Bengal. It was this abuse, in part, Chaudhuri claimed, that forced Rabindranath to look westwards for appreciation in 1912.

Today, in Calcutta (and elsewhere in Bengal), the attacks have been replaced by eulogies. In the public prints, and often in private too, Rabindranath is now a god. Even intellectuals worship him. 'It is perhaps true to say that no man in the whole range of known history can rival his all-comprehending genius, equally splendid in thought, in creation and in action.' This statement by a prominent Bengali scholar appeared in a 1967 biography of Tagore written in English. But actual experience of today's Bengal proves – another Bengali scholar honestly admitted – that 'the average Bengali's first-hand acquaintance' with Tagore's work 'is generally limited to his songs.' One is frequently tempted to agree with Chaudhuri that Tagore, in Bengal, 'has become nothing more than the holy mascot of Bengali provincial vanity.'

He is found everywhere in Bengali life – and yet he is lost. This is literally true in the case of his family mansion, located in the old and congested Jorasanko district of north Calcutta, which in 1961 became a museum and university. To get there, ask not for the Thakur Bari (Tagore House), the museum's Bengali curator quietly advises – ask instead for Ganesh Talkies, the nearest cinema hall.

The condition of the Jorasanko house is dismal. A vital portion, originally constructed for 'Prince' Dwarkanath's dazzling receptions and later the home of India's first modern art movement, was demolished in the 1950s to make way for a nondescript building in Tagore's memory. Though efforts to restore the remainder, the major portion, have been made for three decades, both nationally and internationally (by UNESCO), the condition remains unworthy of a building that stands in relation to modern Indian history somewhat as Blenheim Palace does to British history or Monticello to United States history. The main reason in recent years would appear to be that Tagore was not a Communist: the government of Bengal, Communist since the mid-1970s, has therefore dragged its feet about restoration.

The neglect reflects Tagore's ambivalence too. Though he was born in the Jorasanko house, lived there until he was almost thirty, and wrote vividly of his childhood and youth there, he disliked both the building and the city and left them both when he had the choice, settling finally in a poor rural area about a hundred miles north-west of Calcutta. Here, at Shantiniketan (the 'Abode of Peace'), on an almost bare tract of land, he founded a school (in 1901) and, twenty years later, a university and an 'institute for rural reconstruction' in a nearby village. In 1951, ten years after his death, the institutions were taken over by the central government of independent India, which continues to run them.

Not even the kindest critic of Tagore's institutions could deny that they have faults. Whatever their past achievements under Tagore himself – and those were substantial, in painting and music and in the study of oriental languages, in the training of workers in rural development and in the education of some remarkable individuals (such as Satyajit Ray and Indira Gandhi) – today the institutions cannot be taken seriously in any field. While the spirit of Rabindranath is still perceptible in the beauty of the setting, it has utterly deserted his institutions. Even while he lived, it was a will-o'-the-wisp.

As a founder of institutions Tagore was ambivalent. 'I do not put my faith in any new institutions, but in the individuals all over the world who think clearly, feel nobly and act rightly', he wrote at the very time he started his university. One of these individuals was (Sir) Patrick Geddes, the Scots pioneer of town and regional planning. Geddes was in India for a while and offered his help to Tagore. In 1922 Geddes requested him to define his dream more clearly. Tagore replied:

> I find it rather difficult to answer your question because my . . . work in Shantiniketan has been from first to last a growth, which has had to meet all the obstacles and obstructions due to shortage of funds, paucity of workers, obtuseness in those who were called upon to carry out my ideal . . . In writing my stories I hardly ever have a distinct plot in my mind. I start with some general emotional motive which goes on creating its story form very often forgetting in the process its . . . original boundaries. If I had in the commencement a definite outline which I was merely to fill in, it would certainly bore me – for I need the constant stimulation of surprises . . . The same thing happened with my Shantiniketan Institution. I merely started with this one simple idea that education should never be dissociated from life.

This was good as a principle, springing as it did from Tagore's abhorrence of almost all formal education in India – including his own in Calcutta in the

1860s and 70s (he never matriculated, let alone took a university degree); but less good when applied to a large institution. A steady stream of distinguished visitors made their way to Shantiniketan from 1913 onwards (starting with Ramsay MacDonald); indeed Mahatma Gandhi insisted to foreigners visiting him in India that they see Shantiniketan. Most of them went away impressed by the idea, but unconverted by the actuality.

One who was there in 1945, four years after Tagore's death, was E. M. Forster. To his hosts Forster said charmingly: 'I am not here to pass any verdict on India nor do I fortunately carry the white man's burden on my shoulder. All that I carry round my neck is the pleasant light burden of a lovely garland of marigold, which, I feel, is the symbol of your love and friendship.' To an English friend he was more frank: 'we went over for a night to [the] Shrine. It was less shriney than I expected, indeed there were some sensible remarks about the Passed Master. Much kindness, and my two companions (Muslims) were moved, as was I. I am afraid that the place does not cut much ice now, except as through the elderly and theosophic. The educational side of it is too casual.'

Of course Forster could not meet Tagore. Indira Gandhi, who was at Shantiniketan in 1934–35, shared Forster's scepticism about the educational standard – as did her father Jawaharlal Nehru – but she felt compensated by Tagore's presence. Looking back from an English girls' public school a year and a half later, she wrote to her father: 'In the very atmosphere there, his spirit seemed to roam and hover over one and follow one with a loving though deep watchfulness.' Then she added (rather precociously for a nineteen year old), 'And this spirit, I feel, has greatly influenced my life and thought . . .'

Both Nehru and his daughter, each of whom was for many years the chancellor of Tagore's university, were genuinely affected by Tagore's spirit – much more than by his writings, which they read in English translation. (Nehru almost never quoted them; Indira Gandhi only occasionally.) It probably encouraged Nehru in his greatest political blunder: his profound conviction of Indo-Chinese unity (which Tagore had believed in), prior to India's war with China in 1962. But it may also have nagged at Indira Gandhi's conscience during her suppression of Indian democracy in 1975–77. As she once informed the Convocation at Shantiniketan: 'If democracy is to survive, we need a large body of mature individuals who are bound together by great objectives, voluntarily accepted.'

This is a concise definition of the ideal Tagore dedicated much of the second half of his life to instilling into his fellow countrymen. But, as usual with Tagore, the ideal and his instinct were at war. His temperament was aristocratic, his personal relationships, even with Bengalis, constantly strained; in fact he had few friends, those he had were not lifelong, and his family life was, for the most part, tragic. Whatever his ideals, as a human being Tagore was a 'ferociously egocentric individualist', as Nirad Chaudhuri put it. Satyajit Ray, who knew Tagore personally as a student at Shantiniketan in 1940–42, found him unapproachable: 'You could never get close to him.' When talking, 'he never used a wrong word. If you recorded his normal conversation it would sound like a prepared speech – the choice of words, the intonation, the inflection, everything was so incredibly perfect.'

The sheer volume and diversity of Tagore's oeuvre in a creative life of over sixty years is enough to make one gasp. In Bengali, there are twenty-eight large volumes consisting of poetry, dramas, operas, short stories, novels, essays and diaries; and a similar number of (slimmer) volumes of letters, still being edited and published. His songs, separately published, number nearly two and a half thousand, his paintings and drawings over two thousand. A large fraction of all this is still read, performed and studied in Bengal.

In translation, only a small fraction of this fraction can give pleasure comparable to that of great literature in the reader's own language. The best of the short stories, letters and essays (including Tagore's memoirs) lead the field, with a handful of poems – perhaps as many as fifty – in the second place, one or two novels (notably *The Home and the World*) coming a poor third, and the plays as non-starters, with the possible exception of *The Post Office*. The best of the paintings – several hundred – are powerfully appealing (and suggestive of the untranslatable delicacies in the poetry). As Tagore remarked in Germany in 1930, 'My poetry is for my countrymen, my paintings are my gift to the West.' His songs, which have the deepest hold of all on Bengalis – not to mention India's film industry: Tagore could have made a fortune as a composer of film songs – do not really transplant to foreign soil. Their greatness lies in their perfect fusion of words and melody.

Overall, to quote William Radice, the British translator who in the 1980s gave some of Tagore's poetry a new lease of life in English, we can say that

> Tagore's art is a vulnerable art. Nearly all his writings are vulnerable to criticism, philistinism or contempt, because of his willingness to wear his heart on his sleeve, to take on themes that other writers would find grandiose, sentimental or embarrassing, and his refusal to cloak his utterances in cleverness, urbanity or double-talk.

This is true of his Bengali writings, and, *a fortiori*, of translations.

The fundamental ideas that Tagore expressed in lectures before large audiences in the world's greatest universities between 1913 and 1930 survive both translation and, frequently, the severest scrutiny. 'More than any other thinker of his time, Tagore had a clear conception of civil society, as something distinct from and of stronger and more personal texture than political or economic structures', wrote E. P. Thompson in 1991, introducing a new edition of Tagore's *Nationalism*.

He was not an analytical thinker, always an intuitive one who preferred a poetic analogy to a prosaic argument. Sometimes his thinking was inchoate, on occasions he could be chauvinistic (especially around the turn of the century), but without exception he was courageous. In 1916, speaking in Japan and across the USA, he eloquently warned each nation about the dangers of militaristic nationalism, unbridled commercialism, and the love of technology for its own sake. In 1919, by repudiating his knighthood, he became the first Indian to make a public gesture against the massacre at Amritsar. In the 1920s he stood up to Gandhi and the non-cooperation movement with pungent rationality, and earned from the Mahatma (a title Tagore first popularized) the grudging sobriquet, 'Great Sentinel'. 'I regard the Poet', Gandhi said, 'as a sentinel warning us against the approach of enemies called Bigotry, Lethargy, Intolerance, Ignorance, Inertia and other members of that brood.'

When Rabindranath was born in 1861, notions of racial inferiority and superiority were engrained in educated minds eastern and western. By the time he died in 1941, such ideas were no longer respectable in democratic societies. Tagore was among the pioneers of that global sea change in attitudes.

In foreseeing the need to apply western scientific expertise in what we would now call 'Third World development', Tagore was perhaps at the head of the field. His earliest efforts date back to the turn of the century and took place on the Tagore estates in East Bengal (now Bangladesh). In 1921, with money from the American heiress Dorothy Whitney Straight and unstinting effort by a young British agricultural economist, Leonard Elmhirst (who later married Straight), Tagore started a farm, the nucleus of his 'institute for rural reconstruction' near his university. Although the institute had limited success, it influenced many in the government of independent India; it inspired the Elmhirsts to buy Dartington Hall in England and to found the Dartington Trust; and it left a legacy that became the orthodoxy in successful development aid half a century later. In Tagore's scheme of development, the developer must strive to be in sympathy with the developing – imposed solutions and imported technology do not last. 'It was not the Kingdom of the Expert in the midst of the inept and ignorant which we wanted to establish – although the experts' advice [is] valuable', Tagore chided Elmhirst in 1932. 'The villages are waiting for the living touch of creative faith and not for the cold aloofness of science which uses efficient machinery for extracting statistics'.

Tagore insisted that science, which he studied and wrote about from an early age, must, in its application to society, serve society, and *not* vice versa. This was a conviction with a philosophical basis. In 1930, talking to Albert Einstein in Germany, Tagore told him: 'This world is a human world – the scientific view of it is also that of the scientific man.' Though Einstein did not agree, some distinguished scientists now see Tagore's point. One of them, Ilya Prigogine, a Nobel laureate in chemistry, claimed in 1984: 'Curiously enough, the present evolution of science is running in the direction stated by the great Indian poet.'

Tagore's faith in the unity of man and nature informed everything he did. Dwelling on Shakespeare's plays, he commented that despite Shakespeare's 'great power as a dramatic poet', there was in him a 'gulf between Nature and human nature owing to the tradition of his race and time. It cannot be said that beauty of nature is ignored in his writings; only that he fails to recognize in them the truth of the interpenetration of human life with the cosmic life of the world.' A fascinating letter Rabindranath wrote to his niece Indira in 1892 goes further:

> I feel that once upon a time I was at one with the rest of the earth, that grass grew green upon me, that the autumn sun fell on me and under its rays the warm scent of youth wafted from every pore of my far-flung evergreen body. As my waters and mountains lay spread out through every land, dumbly soaking up the radiance of a cloudless sky, an elixir of life and joy was inarticulately secreted from the immensity of my being. So it is that my feelings seem to be those of our ancient planet, ever germinant and efflorescent, shuddering with sun-kissed delight. The current of my consciousness streams through each blade of grass, each sucking root, each sappy vein, and breaks out in the waving fields of corn and in the rustling leaves of the palms.
>
> I am impelled to give vent to this sense of having authentic ties of blood and affection with the earth. But I know that most people will not understand me and think my idea distinctly queer.

'No biography, however laboriously written, could ever give an adequate picture of such a complex personality as his', wrote Tagore's scientist son Rathindranath in 1958. Tagore himself wrote famously, while reviewing a biography of Tennyson in 1902, that you cannot find a poet in his life-story. The comment appears as a kind of motto on the jacket of the latest Bengali biography of Tagore, a work in progress. The biographer, Prashanta Kumar Paul, has so far produced six densely-printed volumes, and, as of writing, has reached only 1913/14. A colossus such as Rabindranath Tagore deserves no less. But a biographer of Tagore writing in English must have a different readership in mind, somewhat as Tagore himself did when he translated his works into

English. One can aim primarily at non-Indians, or at Indians who are not Bengalis, or at the large number of Bengalis who like to read seriously in English. What one cannot do is to give equal attention to the interests of all three groups. We have therefore had to make a choice. This book is for non-Indians, for Indians who are not Bengalis, and for Bengalis – in that order.

There have been many biographies of Tagore in English. However, only two are generally regarded as significant. The first, by Edward J. Thompson, a Wesleyan missionary in Bengal, later lecturer in Bengali at Oxford University, appeared in England in 1926, was revised in the mid-1940s, and was republished in India in 1991. Entitled *Rabindranath Tagore: Poet and Dramatist*, it is essentially a critical study of the poems and plays. Enlivened by interviews with Tagore, quotations from his letters, some good translations and brilliant *aperçus* from the author (who was a poet), it is vitiated by Thompson's focus on the least translatable portion of Tagore's writings (i.e. poems and plays), his desire to discuss every major work regardless of his own preferences, and by an element of cultural blindness that allowed him to propose, in all sincerity, that 'European music may yet do for Indian music' what European literature had unquestionably done for modern Bengali literature. As E. P. Thompson aptly wrote in 1993, his father's book took shape within 'an extraordinary flux of negative and positive feelings'.

The second book, *Rabindranath Tagore: A Biography*, by Krishna Kripalani, who worked with Tagore in the 1930s and married his granddaughter, first appeared in England and the United States in 1962, and was revised and republished in Bengal in 1980. Though it connects Tagore's life with his literary and artistic creations (which Thompson's book barely does), the primary focus remains the oeuvre rather than the life. Here it can be useful. But the book has two fundamental weaknesses, besides factual errors: a tendency to deify Tagore, and a glorification of Indian nationalism typical of the immediate post-Independence years in India. According to its introduction, Tagore's 'personal life was as harmonious and noble as his verse is simple and beautiful.' This is both misleading and grotesque (besides being sanctimonious); Kripalani, as a member of Tagore's immediate circle, must have been acutely aware of the falsity but too loyal to admit the truth.

Our primary focus is the man, not the oeuvre. We discuss Tagore's writings and other artistic works frequently, occasionally extensively – but only in so far as they illuminate his state of mind from year to year, month to month, sometimes day to day. We quote substantially only where we ourselves enjoy the work in translation. We omit numerous works that a longer book would no doubt have included. It is Tagore's *personality* – a favourite word of his – in all its 'myriad-mindedness' (Oxford's fine word when giving Tagore a degree in

1940), that intrigues us as biographers; not his works *per se*, and certainly not his relics. As so often with Tagore, he has himself encapsulated our feelings:

> Ordinarily research scholars seem to ignore the fact that the past is of interest to us only in so far as it was *living* and that unless they discover it for us in such a way as to make us feel its life, we may admire them for their patience and industry but will not be the wiser for their labours. I have often felt sad that so much human talent and industry should disappear in the publication of matter where bones keep on rattling without forming for us an outline of the figure that once moved.
>
> *London, December 1993*

1 The Tagores and 'Prince' Dwarkanath

'I was born in what was once the metropolis of British India,' Rabindranath Tagore told an audience at Oxford University in 1930, when he was almost seventy years old.

> My ancestors came floating to Calcutta upon the earliest tide of the fluctuating fortune of the East India Company. The unconventional code of life for our family has been a confluence of three cultures, Hindu, Mohammedan and British. My grandfather belonged to that period when amplitude of dress and courtesy and a generous leisure were gradually being clipped and curtailed into Victorian manners . . . I came to a world in which the modern city-bred spirit of progress had just triumphed over the lush green life of our ancient village community. Though the trampling process was almost complete . . . , something of the past lingered over the wreckage.

The Tagore family was always Hindu, but at the edge of the Hindu pale from the start of their recorded history. Like some other well-known families of Calcutta, they claim descent from five orthodox Brahmins said to have been invited into Bengal by a Hindu king after he had taken Bengal from a Buddhist ruler, possibly around AD 1000. But unlike these other families, the Tagores became tainted by contact with Muslims – or so goes the most widely accepted story of their ancestry.

It all began with a joke, some time in the fifteenth century when the Delhi Sultanate controlled Bengal, before the rise of the Mughals. During Ramadan, when Muslims fast, two brothers, Brahmins, were sitting in the court of Mohammed Tahir Pir Ali, the vizier of the governor of Jessore. (Jessore lies roughly half-way between Calcutta and Dhaka, and is now in Bangladesh.) Pir

Ali, though a Muslim, had been born a Brahmin; he had converted to Islam in order to further his career and because he was in love with a Muslim girl. As they talked, a gardener appeared with a large lemon, freshly plucked. When Pir Ali held it to his nose and exclaimed, 'How fragrant!', one of the Brahmin brothers remarked that Pir Ali had violated his fast – for smelling is half eating according to the Hindu scriptures, which Pir Ali had once obeyed. The taunt provoked Pir Ali to get his revenge. He invited the brothers to a meal, ensured that they smelt beef being cooked, and forced them to taste it. Subsequently converted to Islam, the former Brahmins were given land near Jessore.

Their relatives were still Hindus, however, and deemed by Hindu society to be polluted. From one of them came the ancestors of the Tagores. Known from then on as 'Pirali' Brahmins, they were unmarriageable by orthodox Hindus. This ostracism was so serious that, around 1802, an orthodox Brahmin who ate with a Pirali Brahmin had to pay 50,000 rupees – a king's ransom – for readmission to caste; and in 1852, when the nephew of a leading Brahmin married a cousin of Rabindranath Tagore, the boy was expelled from his family.

The taint did not bother the fishing folk of Govindpur, a small village on the river Hooghly (a branch of the Ganges), south-west of Jessore. Here a descendant of the clan, Panchanan Kushari, having left Jessore for reasons unknown, settled in the late seventeenth century. He was revered as a Brahmin and addressed as Thakur, meaning holy lord. His move was shrewd commercially too, because Govindpur became one of the nuclei of Calcutta, when British merchants landed thereabouts in 1690. Thus Panchanan Thakur was in at the beginning of the second city of the British Empire. The East India Company merchants addressed him as Mister Thakur, or rather Mister Tagore, since they could not easily pronounce his Bengali honorific.

The Tagores flourished as middle-men. Panchanan's sons collected revenue for the Company, built the Maratha Ditch to protect Calcutta from the Maratha raids in the 1740s, acquired land, houses and a fortune. Among his four grandsons, one became the first Indian to know English well; another supervised the rebuilding of Fort William in Calcutta following Clive's victory over the Muslim power at the battle of Plassey (1757); the remaining two, Nilmoni (the great-great-grandfather of Rabindranath) and Darpanarayan, constructed a mansion on the Hooghly at Pathuriaghat where they lived together until 1765. In that year, Nilmoni accepted Clive's offer of a lucrative position away from Calcutta. His savings were sent home to Darpanarayan, who meanwhile looked after the family's affairs in Calcutta and also traded on behalf of the French Company up-river at Chandannagar (Chandernagore).

Some time after Nilmoni's return to Calcutta, the family developed a rift. The cause was money. Around 1784 (the year before Warren Hastings left

Bengal), Nilmoni walked out of the family house at Pathuriaghat accompanied by his three sons and a daughter, holding in one hand, so they say, the *shalagram* or sacred image of his household deity, and in the other hand a bag containing one lakh (100,000) rupees. On a plot of land at Jorasanko, a little away from the river, he began to build the house where Rabindranath would be born three quarters of a century later. From then on, especially during the high noon of Empire in India after 1857, the two branches of the Tagores at Pathuriaghat and Jorasanko would have little to do with each other.

Rabindranath Tagore never once referred to this split directly. (There was not even a hint of it in his memoirs.) It surfaced instead in a moving short story he wrote in 1911, 'Rashmani's Son' – though the parallel is in the pathos of the underlying situation, not in the plot. A missing will, obviously removed from a safe by one branch of a wealthy 'joint' family living in the country, is the instrument that divides the family. Eventually the shrewd branch abandons the family seat and goes to live in the town, where it flourishes. The other branch of the family remains in the village and steadily declines in prosperity. Years later two descendants, one from each branch (unknown to the other), now students in the big city of Calcutta, are reunited by the power of natural affection triumphing over the gulf of difference in wealth. But Tagore did not write a happy ending: the indigent scion dies of illness contracted in grinding poverty. The missing will is mysteriously returned to his grieving parents – but it arrives much too late to heal the breach.

Rabindranath was undoubtedly repelled by the materialism of the Pathuriaghat Tagores descended from Darpanarayan. While behaving as comparatively orthodox Hindus (though remaining inevitably Pirali Brahmins), they were intimate with the imperial authorities of Calcutta during the British Raj. Such contradictory behaviour was typical of many rich Bengali families at this time, but it was anathema to the Jorasanko Tagores who succeeded Dwarkanath. 'Do you really maintain that we are more materialistic than the West?' an Indian interviewer questioned Rabindranath on his return from Europe in 1926. He replied: 'Yes, in the broad sense of the term. What is materialism, if it is not the formalism that dominates our religion? The belief that external observances have spiritual meanings, is that not a materialistic view? Is it not materialistic to believe that sin can be washed away by water, or dust from people's feet?'

A grandson of Darpanarayan was the leading Bengali jurist until his death in 1868, with a command of English equal to that of London lawyers. He became one of the earliest Indian members of the council of the lieutenant governor of Bengal. (Nevertheless he disinherited his only son for becoming a Christian.) A great-grandson was created a maharaja in 1877 after Queen Victoria became empress of India; earlier, he had been honoured by the government as the head

of a family 'great in the annals of Calcutta . . . conspicuous for loyalty to the
British Government and for acts of public beneficence.' His brother was a musi-
cologist and composer of considerable significance, who was awarded a
doctorate in music from Oxford University in 1896 (the first Indian to receive
an honorary Oxford degree), Sourindromohun Tagore. His compositions
included 'Victoria-Gitika, or Sanskrit Verses, celebrating the deeds and virtues
of Her Most Gracious Majesty, Queen Victoria, and her predecessors', and
'Fifty Stanzas in Sanskrita in Honour of H.R.H. the Prince of Wales', which
even a British commentator found embarrassing: 'the generous exaggeration of
a loyal poet, especially when the poet is an Oriental, must not be counted a
fault.' Sourindromohun's nephew represented Calcutta at the coronation of
Edward VII in 1902, thanks to the viceroy, Lord Curzon. 'I shall ever remember
with deep gratitude this special mark of favour shown to me personally', he
informed Curzon when the viceroy retired. Given this background of
Pathuriaghat Tagore sycophancy, one can understand why Rabindranath seems
to have asked that all mention of Sourindromohun be deleted from his own
citation when he received an honorary Oxford doctorate in 1940 (the next to be
awarded to an Indian).

Dwarkanath, the grandson of Darpanarayan's brother Nilmoni, and the most
flamboyant of all the Tagores, was on the surface similar in attitude to the
Pathuriaghat branch of the family. But inside he was much more ambivalent
towards the British. There was 'nothing of the flunkey in his composition',
wrote his Bengali biographer in 1870.

Born in 1794, Dwarkanath died in 1846. He therefore witnessed almost the
whole of India coming under British rule. In Bengal the Company's rule was
already consolidated: the 1793 Permanent Settlement had created the system of
landowning known as zamindari that would persist through Rabindranath
Tagore's lifetime; and Calcutta had already become the City of Palaces, with
splendid mansions mushrooming in both the White Town, the European quarter, and in the Black Town, the native quarter, where stood the Jorasanko house
of the Tagores.

Nearby, in the Chitpur Road, was a school run by a Mr Sherbourne. Here,
until the age of sixteen, Dwarkanath had his formal schooling. Sherbourne was
an unusual figure, said to have been born of an English father and a Brahmin
mother, who described himself proudly as 'a Brahmin grandchild'. He had
many pupils from wealthy Hindu families who brought him gifts which he
accepted in the manner of a traditional guru. Later, when Dwarkanath became
wealthy, he settled a life pension on Sherbourne.

In 1811 he married. The girl, a beauty, was a nine-year-old Pirali Brahmin
from Jessore. This was usual in the family; less usual was her addiction to ritual.

An idea of what this entailed, and continued to entail in orthodox Hindu families a century later, can be found in Tagore's story, 'Match-Making', written in 1917. It is an exquisitely ironic account of an eligible but independent-minded bachelor's failure to find himself a satisfactory wife. Here he describes a girl he felt obliged to reject:

> [She] was like a small and beautiful doll. She appeared not to have been designed in the usual way; someone seemed to have stuck in place every strand of her hair, painted her eyebrows, and modelled every inch of her by hand. She could recite Sanskrit hymns to the Ganges. Her mother even washed the cooking coals in Ganges water and shrank from all contact with the world, since Mother Earth included all races. In fact most of her rituals involved water, because aquatic creatures could be trusted not to be Muslim, and onions, a favourite Muslim food, do not grow in water ... She was taught to worry about certain people's shadows that might pollute her. She bathed in the Ganges from inside a palanquin; indeed the eighteen ancient *Puranas* prescribed and circumscribed her whole world.

Dwarkanath's wife died fairly young – from a chill caught through excessive bathing, apparently. In her later years she had shunned all contact with her husband because of his intercourse with Europeans.

In stark contrast, Dwarkanath's world constantly expanded. Having taken over his late father's estates in 1812, he worked hard to understand the intricacies of zamindari law arising from the Permanent Settlement. His teachers included a renowned British barrister and an American missionary, who put him in contact with various British merchants, besides improving his command of English. Soon he was advising other zamindars and earning substantial fees for his expertise in the law combined with his capacity to draft petitions in Persian, Arabic and English (as much as two guineas a line for translation into English).

He had inherited a zamindari that straddled the districts of Jessore and Pabna in East Bengal and included a town which was an important centre for trade and for indigo and silk manufacturing. There were also inherited estates near Cuttack in Orissa, down the coast from Calcutta. In 1830 and 1834, Dwarkanath purchased two more zamindaris in East Bengal. Besides managing these four estates, he bought other estates speculatively and at times also acted as the general manager for the whole of the Tagore family estates scattered in every district of lower Bengal. Altogether, he managed one-fifteenth of the total land revenue of the lower districts. Sixty years later, his poet-grandson took over the job in the four estates and became known as the most enlightened zamindar in

Bengal. Not a single word about his grandfather crept into his copious writings about the estates.

What kind of zamindar was Dwarkanath? The record is not flattering, though no worse than that of the average zamindar. In 1833, for instance, the ryots (peasants) in one estate petitioned Lord Bentinck, the governor general, against their 'stoney-hearted zamindar', Dwarkanath Tagore, after he had tried to raise their customary rents illegally. 'He imprisons some and corrects others,' but 'on account of the said zamindar being affluent' the collector, commissioner, and magistrate 'paid no attention to their pitiable condition'. According to a modern economic historian, Blair Kling, 'As a zamindar Dwarkanath was mercilessly efficient and businesslike, but not generous . . .[He] must be included among those zamindars who contributed to the oppressive nature of the indigo system.'

It was his other activities, as a businessman, patron and philanthropist, that made Dwarkanath interesting. They foreshadow something of the diversity, vision and mercurial spirit of his grandson's life and achievements.

In 1828, while he was serving as a revenue agent for the East India Company, Dwarkanath launched the Union Bank, independent of any commercial house and of the Company. Over the next two decades, until its crash after his death, the bank was 'the keystone of the commercial structure of Calcutta.' The directors were primarily wealthy Bengalis but the secretary, an independent merchant, was an Englishman, William Carr. In 1834, he and Dwarkanath (who now resigned from Company service) formed Carr, Tagore and Co. Through the new company Dwarkanath bought a coal mine in 1836 which became the heart of his empire; it was located, ironically, not far from Shantiniketan, where Rabindranath would settle in 1901. He pioneered tea-growing in Assam, and sent the first shipment of tea to London in 1838. He had interests in indigo, salt and sugar production. He also promoted the Calcutta Steam Tug Association to help ships navigate the dangerous mouth of the Hooghly up to Calcutta; the Steam Ferry Bridge Company to provide a vital bridge between the two banks of the Hooghly at Calcutta (not permanently bridged until 1943); the India General Steam Navigation Company to create a proper steamer service for the lower Ganges; and he supported a railway company, the Great Western of Bengal, which planned to build a line running from Calcutta through the coal-fields, to a point near Varanasi (Benares). Though several of these ventures failed, largely through a waning of interest from Dwarkanath, and the mismanagement of others, they nevertheless made him the chief of Calcutta's business world.

His entertainments added to his reputation. They took place at Belgatchia, his villa outside Calcutta on the way to Dum Dum, which had been fitted out by an English architect in an entirely European style. Emily Eden, the lively sister of Lord Auckland, the governor general, visited Belgatchia more than once in 1836. She called Dwarkanath 'the only man in the country who gives pleasant parties', and wrote home that

> all Calcutta got greatly excited, because the Governor-General was going to dine with a native. The fact of a native dining with a Governor-General is much more remarkable, and Dwarkanath is one of the very few that would even sit by while we were eating . . . Dwarkanath talks excellent English, and had got Mr Parker, one of the cleverest people here, to do the honours; and there were elephants on the lawn, and boats on the tank and ices in the summerhouse, and quantities of beautiful pictures and books, and rather a less burning evening than usual, and so it answered very well . . . we hear he gives remarkably good dinners to everybody else.

Indeed, he did, not excluding his countrymen, often to the accompaniment of a magnificent display of fireworks, and dancing, music, mummery and other amusements. But it was said that, in deference to his mother's wishes, until her death in 1838, Dwarkanath abstained from eating at the same table as his European guests. When everyone had departed, he would wash with Ganges water, change his clothes and eat alone.

His philanthropy was remarkably free from prejudice, as well as open-handed to a fault (which would cause problems for his son Debendranath after his death). He donated to good works, especially the new medical college, to the establishment of a liberal newspaper, to the arts (particularly the theatre, which he adored), to charitable activities and to religious institutions (less so to Christian missions); and the recipients included both the celebrated and the unknown, both the Bengalis and the British. Once he gave a lakh of rupees (£10,000) to the District Charitable Society; on another occasion he was kind to a young East India Company military officer in dire straits who approached him in his office at the Union Bank. Having blurted out his story in front of a native with some embarrassment, the officer received a small chit from Dwarkanath torn off the newspaper he was reading. 'Pay Rs.10,000/-, D.T.' The officer thought he was being mocked, but the cashier paid up as requested, and Dwarkanath turned down the proffered IOU. Smiling, he said, 'Look, if you are a gentleman, as I have no doubt you are, a note of hand is not necessary, for you will surely honour the debt. If, on the other hand, you are not a man of honour, a mere note of hand will have no value.'

On the eve of his first departure for Britain in 1842 (sailing to Suez in his own steamer, *India*), the Baptist-run *Friend of India* – no particular friend of

Dwarkanath – editorialized: 'To describe Dwarkanath Tagore's charities would be to enumerate every charitable institution in Calcutta, for, from which of them has he withheld the most liberal donations?'

He loved travelling and kept a vivid and concrete diary of his grand tour through Europe, quoted by his 1870 biographer but now lost. In Rome, he was presented to the Pope and apologized for keeping on his pugree (turban), explaining that in India this was a mark of respect to a dignitary. He saw the Colosseum, was impressed, but commented that it had once 'resounded with the shouts and groans of thousands'. (Eight decades later, thirty thousand Romans would greet his grandson Rabindranath there.)

In London he was treated almost as royalty – in fact he was given the unofficial title of 'Prince'. He met the prime minister Sir Robert Peel, and was presented to Queen Victoria. At her invitation – the first of many – he attended a grand review of the troops, where he was seated with the Queen, Prince Albert, the duke of Wellington and other members of the aristocracy. The evening before, he had dined with the directors of the East India Company; a month later, he was the guest of honour at the lord mayor's banquet; and at Edinburgh, he became the first Indian to receive the Freedom of the city.

Dwarkanath moved in other circles too. He met radicals and social reformers, one of whom, George Thompson, a firebrand opponent of slavery, agreed to come to Calcutta with him. He went north and visited the coal mines around Newcastle and the steel industry in Sheffield, where, ever-intrigued by technology, he purchased a many-bladed knife 'with a pencil at one end'. In Glasgow he was present at a march of Chartists and the unemployed. He wrote home: 'They may talk of the starvation of the Hill Coolies in India, but I see around me still more distress.'

And he met writers. It was Count D'Orsay, the close friend of Charles Dickens, who recommended Dwarkanath to Dickens. Dickens called on him in 1842 shortly before he sailed to Calcutta; in 1845/6 they met again several times. Dwarkanath held a dinner, attended by Dickens, D'Orsay, William Thackeray, Douglas Jerrold, Mark Lemon and Henry Mayhew, all but D'Orsay celebrated contributors to *Punch*. It was an animated occasion.

Exactly what Dickens thought of Dwarkanath was not clear. In 1842, before they met, he wrote to D'Orsay in response to his letter of introduction: 'A Tiger with such a name as Dwarkanaught Tagore, is not an everyday animal. Can a pinch of salt be dropped upon his tail?' After some more fooling, he continued:

Dwarkanaught Tagore! What does the postman think of him – what does a long-stage coachman say, when he has him on the Waybill – what does his washerwoman call him, when she mentions him to her friends – who gave him that name – had he godfathers and godmothers – or did some old Maniac of a Brahmin, drunk with the spirit of Rice, invent it? . . . I have spelt it backwards, but it makes no less tremendous nonsense that way. He is a live hieroglyphic. I give him up.

Three years later, having just called on Dwarkanath at his hotel, thanked him 'heartily' for his donation to a sanatorium, and invited him to supper, Dickens wrote a brief note to D'Orsay. This time he referred to Dwarkanath by his Bengali honorific 'Baboo' (roughly, Esquire): 'I saw the Baboo yesterday, and engaged him to dine here . . . The B (I am afraid to write Baboo again, for I am always going to put an N after it) wants to hear all about the Paper; and I told him I would ask [to supper] the Gentleman who is going to India, and two of the Proprietors – my printers.' Years later, long after Dwarkanath's death, Dickens noted in *All the Year Round* that 'Dwarkanath Tagore' (now correctly spelt) 'was called "the Oriental Croesus," and was well known in England.'

Dickens' mixture of facetiousness and respect is curiously reminiscent of George Bernard Shaw's attitude to Rabindranath Tagore ('Old Bluebeard') in the next century. And this was not entirely accidental, for Rabindranath resembled his grandfather in character much more than is generally acknowledged.

The only explicit comparison Rabindranath himself allowed was with his grandfather's dislike of routine and rigid plans, which he shared. Rabindranath used to joke to his family circle, 'Babu changes his mind often' – referring to a despairing comment on Dwarkanath sent home to Calcutta by a young Bengali member of his grandfather's entourage in England. Certainly there were sharp and essential differences between grandson and grandfather, most obviously Dwarkanath's commercial shrewdness, his lack of pity as a zamindar and his desire to industrialize India. But the similarities are striking: both were drawn to music, theatre and literature; both were generous; both revelled in travel, often staying at the best hotels; both loved to meet the best minds and enjoyed the company of beautiful women; both had a keen sense of national pride; both believed in the energy and discipline of the West; both shared a vision of East and West meeting in cooperation; and both were caught in the contradictions of this vision. One might almost say of Rabindranath in 1912 (his *annus mirabilis*) what was truly said of Dwarkanath in 1846 by his biographer Blair Kling:

In Calcutta he was the bold and uncringing political leader trying to whip up support for political action. In England he was the urbane diplomat, emissary from the people of India, playing the 'Grand Mogul', surrounded by his retainers, and exchanging gifts, courtesies, and hospitality as an equal . . . At bottom, however, he believed [that] . . . the East India Company had exploited and robbed his people. On the other [hand, he knew that] in the contemporary world the British alone could provide the best possible government for India.

2 Maharshi Debendranath

Everyone knows that my grandfather used to invite English officials to his Belgatchia villa, but I have heard that he issued instructions to my father – do not sup with the English!

My Reminiscences (unpublished draft)

Dwarkanath Tagore died in London on 1 August 1846, aged fifty-two. Less than three months before, he wrote a letter to his eldest son Debendranath, then aged twenty-nine, admonishing him for neglecting the estates: 'Your time [is] I am sure being more taken up in writing for the newspapers and in fighting with the missionaries than in watching over and protecting the important matters which you leave in the hands of your favourite Amlas [office clerks] . . . I hear of nothing going right. We are losing every Lawsuit.'

Until he was twenty-one, Debendranath had been little more than the spoilt son of a fabulously wealthy father. Married at the age of twelve to an eight-year-old girl from Jessore, he led a gilded, hedonistic youth, which he would describe with amusement to his son Rabindranath. For a while, he recalled, the height of fashion had been to wear one's exquisitely fine Dacca muslin with the border torn off, to avoid irritating one's supremely sensitive skin. He himself had once ordered a pair of slippers studded with diamonds and other precious gems, so coruscating that they compelled even the rajas of society to stoop before his feet.

The only serious contrary influence on Debendranath was Raja Rammohun Roy, a former servant of the Company who had made good in business, and who was, according to Rabindranath, 'the best friend of my grandfather'. In 1830, before any other Bengali of note, Roy visited Britain, where he was widely welcomed and died in 1833. (There is a blue plaque where he stayed in London's Bedford Square.) Controversial at the time, Rammohun Roy continues to polarize Indian opinion. Unquestionably, he was a phenomenal linguist who drew upon sources written in Sanskrit, Arabic, Persian, Hebrew, Greek, English, French and of course Bengali (one reason for the continuing lack of a satisfactory biography of Roy). He was also the greatest Indian intellectual of the nineteenth century. But he was further, and less convincingly, hailed as the Father of Modern India. 'When most Indians lived a frog-in-the-well existence, [Rammohun Roy] acquainted himself with the great intellectual forces at work in Europe – the ideas of the Enlightenment, the concepts of liberty and equality, and the method of inquiry which the pioneers of science had promulgated . . . [His] is the vision of the Universal Man', said Indira Gandhi in 1972. But to Mahatma Gandhi, never one to be over-impressed by western ideas, Rammohun Roy was a 'pygmy' among the great Indians.

Rabindranath placed Rammohun without hesitation among the greatest Indians. Beginning in 1885, Tagore lectured repeatedly on Rammohun's life and work. In 1895, for instance, he said that Rammohun in his dress and manners was an 'out-and-out Bengali', whose mastery of ancient Indian learning was 'without peer' and whose advocacy of Bengali had 'laid the foundations' of mother-tongue (as opposed to Sanskrit, Persian or English-language) education – and yet whose 'fearless strength', 'practice of truth and benevolence', and 'inflexible determination and self-reliance', were 'very close to the great men of Europe'.

Today, at least in the West, Rammohun is known mainly for his stand against *sati* (suttee), widow-burning, which was finally banned by the British in 1829. More generally, he aimed to rid contemporary Hinduism of what he could demonstrate to be inauthentic traditions. After years of debate with Christian missionaries in Calcutta (who wished to claim Roy as a Unitarian), he founded, around 1830, the Brahma Sabha, a monotheistic Hindu society implacably opposed to the ubiquitous idolatry, rituals and belief in caste. For the Brahma Sabha, idols, rituals and caste were blasphemous – at least in theory. It took its beliefs from Rammohun's interpretation of the *Vedas*, Hinduism's earliest scriptures. Within a few decades of his death, this society became a movement, the Brahmo Samaj, the most influential, rational movement of religious and social reform in nineteenth-century India. One of its pillars was Dwarkanath's son, Debendranath Tagore.

Debendranath did not formally become a Brahmo until 21 December 1843, a date that would become a red-letter day in the calendar at Shantiniketan. But he had been pondering it for more than five years, since the death of his beloved grandmother in 1838. She passed away, as was customary, on the banks of the Ganges, accompanied by her grandson. The night before she died, as the funeral chant began, Debendranath experienced an epiphany. He described it in the spiritual autobiography he wrote in extreme old age (admired by many, including E. M. Forster): 'a strange sense of the unreality of all things suddenly entered my mind. I was as if no longer the same man. A strong aversion to wealth arose within me. The coarse bamboo-mat on which I sat seemed to be my fitting seat, carpets and costly spreadings seemed hateful, in my mind was awakened a joy unfelt before.'

His father Dwarkanath spent nearly 50,000 rupees on the *shraddha* (funeral) for his mother, which was celebrated with great and orthodox pomp – no nonsense about rejecting idolatry here. The District Charitable Society was promised twice that sum of money, a lakh of rupees, given in memory of the deceased woman.

A restlessness now took possession of the young man. Having rejected any Hindu *shastra* (scripture) containing idolatrous preachings, Debendranath came to believe that all *shastras* were idolatrous. Then, one day, while in this depressed state of mind he happened to see a page from some Sanskrit book flutter past. Asking a pundit-friend to decipher its meaning, he went off to the Union Bank where it was his job to assist the cashier. He came home early, eager to know what the page said. But the pundit, an orthodox Hindu, could not make sense of it. 'This is what the Brahma Sabha talks about,' he said. And so a scholar from the Brahma Sabha was called; he declared, 'Why, this is the *Isopanishad.*'

The verse from the sacred *Upanishads* made a deep impression on Debendranath, and subsequently on Rabindranath and on Gandhi. It meant (in Tagore's translation): 'All that is changing in this changeful world, know that it is enveloped by Him who is the Lord of all things. Therefore take your enjoyment in renunciation. Never covet wealth.'

It is the same root idea that inspires Rabindranath's haunting little song:

The flower says
Blessed am I
Blessed am I
Upon this earth . . .

The flower says
I was born from the dust
Kindly kindly
Let me forget it
Let me forget it
Let me forget.

Of dust inside me there is none
No dust at all inside me
The flower says.

The idea of God's immanence in all things recurs throughout Tagore's works. But though Rabindranath, like his father, revered the *Upanishads* as the summit of Indian philosophical achievement, unlike Debendranath he found them 'incomplete in their answer to the complex longing of the human soul.' In 1938, introducing a translation of several Hindu scriptures, including the *Vedas* and the *Bhagavad Gita*, Tagore said of the *Upanishads*: 'Their emphasis was too intellectual, and did not sufficiently explore the approach to Reality through love and devotion.'

Debendranath was now in his mid-twenties. Over the next few years, his new-found Brahmo faith was severely tested. The Tagore family's idolatrous rituals continued unabated in the house at Jorasanko, culminating every September/October in the Durga Puja, still Calcutta's leading festival (equivalent in importance to Christmas), when gigantic many-armed images of the goddess are worshipped for days and then taken in noisy procession to be immersed in the Ganges. To avoid this detestable spectacle, Debendranath took to travelling. In due course he would journey through much of northern India, and be away from his family house more often than he was at home. He was up-river in mid-1846 when news of his father's death in London reached him.

It put him in a quandary. As the eldest son, he was expected to perform the funeral rituals at his father's *shraddha* in Jorasanko. But as a Brahmo he knew he could not go through with it. In the end, his younger brother agreed to perform the ceremony. The Tagore family were split on the issue: Debendranath's uncle, first cousins and four of his aunts supported him; the rest boycotted the feast on the day after the ceremony. The head of the (more orthodox) Pathuriaghat Tagores (the jurist) sent a message: If Debendra never acts thus again, we shall all accept his invitation. Debendranath's reply is recorded in his autobiography: 'If that could be, then why should I have made all this fuss? I can never again join hands with idolatry.'

A year or so after this incident, Carr, Tagore and Co. closed its doors, the final blow being a bill for Rs. 30,000. Debendranath was thirty years old, his two brothers twenty-seven and eighteen. They were all protected by Dwarkanath's foresight: in 1840 he had put in trust for them his four principal zamindaris (in East Bengal and Orissa). Notwithstanding, Debendranath volunteered the trust properties to the creditors in settlement of the firm's debts. They were already favourable to the memory of Dwarkanath; this gesture by his eldest son touched them further. As a result, an arrangement was made whereby the brothers gave up the villa at Belgatchia but kept the house at Jorasanko, and gave up the estates in exchange for an annual allowance of Rs. 25,000. Soon the management of the estates was permitted to revert to the family.

Debendranath, for all his spiritual unorthodoxy, had inherited some of his father's business shrewdness, and a little of his hard-heartedness, even in family dealings. As a zamindar he was not 'stoney-hearted' like his father, but neither was he enlightened. So thriftily did he manage the properties – as Rabindranath would discover when he became manager under his father's eye during the 1890s – that by 1905, when Debendranath died at the age of 88, the zamindari income had increased threefold.

Dwarkanath's numerous personal debts – all, it seems, to fellow Bengalis – were less easy to discharge than his business debts. But Debendranath was extraordinarily scrupulous in honouring them. 'Not until he was quite old did he pay off the last creditor and at his death he left one lakh of rupees he had managed to save as a legacy to the blind', according to Rabindranath.

Such cast-iron probity of behaviour, combined with his continuing spiritual search – which led him into the Himalayas like the *rishis* of old – laid the foundation of Debendranath's awesome reputation in late nineteenth-century Bengal. Dwarkanath had been known as Prince; his eldest son became Maharshi ('Great Sage'), soon after Rabindranath's birth in 1861. Reviewing the Maharshi's autobiography in 1914, E. M. Forster remarked that Brahmoism was 'not so much a creed as an attitude of mind, and would particularly appeal to a spiritual rebel.' While this was true, Brahmoism could easily turn sectarian, puritanical and somewhat ridiculous: a mixture of Sunday school earnestness, Victorian prudishness and old-fashioned vicarage tea-party. The stereotype of a Brahmo among more orthodox Bengalis became, as it still is, the one-time behaviour of the principal of the main Brahmo college in Calcutta. He was walking in the street when a man asked him the way to the Star Theatre. 'I don't know,' he replied shortly and walked on. Then, realizing that he had told an untruth, he ran back to the man and said, 'I know, but I won't tell you.'

The heyday of Brahmoism coincided with roughly the second half of Debendranath's life and the first half of Rabindranath's: 1860 to the first decade of the new century. Nirad Chaudhuri, who was born in 1897, was not a Brahmo, but imbibed Brahmo values as a child. He wrote that in this period, under Brahmo and related reforming influences, the Hindu middle-class showed 'greater probity in public and private affairs, attained greater happiness in family and personal life, saw greater fulfilment of cultural aspirations, and put forth greater creativeness' than at any time in recent centuries. A Bengali of the next generation, Satyajit Ray, whose family were prominent Brahmos, though he himself was not, also admired the period (as reflected in one of his finest films, *Charulata*, a Tagore story set in 1879/80). Brahmos of that time, said Ray, were 'very powerful figures, very demanding figures with lots of social fervour in them: the willingness, the ability and the eagerness to do good to society, to change society for the better.'

This was not likely to make them popular with orthodox Hindus, who naturally formed the vast majority in Bengali society. Weddings were a particular focus for hostility. In 1861, Debendranath broke with Hindu tradition by marrying off his second daughter using a Brahmo ceremony for the first time. A report appeared in Britain in Dickens' magazine *All the Year Round* under the heading 'A Curious Marriage Ceremony'. It noted that the Brahmo wedding 'retained much of its Hindoo character; we think, wisely, because if it were made too European, there would be no possibility of rendering the improvement popular, and a powerful opposition would be aroused among the gentle sex.' In fact, Debendranath's relatives were greatly embittered. When he repeated the ceremony for a son, in 1863, police had to be called to control the anti-Brahmo feeling.

Debendranath, 'spiritual rebel' though he was, was fairly conservative in social matters and acutely aware of conservative forces pressing on the Brahmo Samaj. He knew too how controversial would be any attempt to dismantle caste barriers. A fellow Brahmo – in fact the writer of the report for *All the Year Round* – had proposed in a moment of inspiration that Brahmos should cease to wear the sacred thread, chief symbol of Brahminhood. When this man's orthodox father heard of the proposal, he immediately tried to stab himself in the heart with a knife.

That was in 1845, only two years after the formation of the Brahmo Samaj. In 1864, the issue was raised again by one of the young and advanced Brahmos, Keshubchandra Sen, a favourite of Debendranath. Keshub insisted that 'no minister or preacher of the Samaj should retain any mark of caste or sectarian distinction whatever.' The Maharshi was unable to agree: 'You must remember that the zeal and patience of the old class of Brahmos have paved the way for the reforms advocated and adopted by yourselves . . . What I desire is simply this: that the old and the new members of the Samaj do combine their forces, so that their united strength may sustain the Institution and that your examples may strengthen and encourage those that are lagging behind.'

It was a forlorn hope. Keshub left the Brahmo Samaj and formed his own movement in 1866 (though he remained a devotee of Debendranath); and in 1878 there was a second schism, forming a Low Church to Debendranath's High Church. Most of the reformist energy admired by Nirad Chaudhuri and Satyajit Ray came from this Low Church rather than from Debendranath's group. When, in 1884, Rabindranath took over as secretary of the original Brahmo Samaj, he found Brahmins with sacred threads still very much in charge. When he asked if he might introduce ministers other than Brahmins, his father unhesitatingly agreed. But the new secretary found himself unable to carry the congregation with him – as Debendranath himself had long since discovered when attempting reforms. 'Until the right man arrives, any form is better than none – this, I felt, must have been my father's view', Rabindranath commented in his memoirs. 'But not for a moment did he try to discourage me by pointing out these difficulties.'

In matters of social custom, neither father nor son was by nature an iconoclast, unlike grandfather Dwarkanath, who dined with the sahibs, drank alcohol and bluntly refused to make public atonement for crossing the 'black waters' between India and Europe. The Maharshi wore a sacred thread until he died and invested Rabindranath with one in 1873; and Rabindranath in turn invested his son Rathindranath in 1898. But whereas Debendranath, like most men, became more conservative with age, Rabindranath in later life became more and more radical. The first part of Tagore's life was undoubtedly dominated by his father's austere spirituality – but the second part, which made him world-famous, owed as much, if not more, to the influence of his worldly, pleasure-loving grandfather.

3   The House of the Tagores

*In those days devils and spirits lurked in the recesses of every man's mind,
and the air was full of ghost stories.*

                                  My Boyhood Days

The mansion in which Rabindranath was born on 7 May 1861, No. 6
Dwarkanath Tagore's Lane, Jorasanko, lay in the heart of the Bengali section of Calcutta. [pl.6] The lane was virtually a cul-de-sac: at its head, hardly
more than a stone's throw away, ran the Chitpur Road, the original north–south
artery of Calcutta; and less than half a mile beyond that were the river and the
bathing and burning ghats. Turning north out of the lane, after travelling not
much over a mile, one reached the ruin of the once-magnificent Black Pagoda, a
Hindu temple built by a notorious zamindar in the days of Dwarkanath's great-
grandfather, regarded roughly as the city proper's northern limit. Turning
south, after less than a mile one found oneself in the heart of government: the
Writers' Buildings (of the now-defunct East India Company), Government
House (home of India's governor general), Esplanade Row, and beyond these
the green Maidan, Calcutta's Hyde Park, stretching south towards Fort William
and the Eden Gardens beside the river. On either side of the Chitpur Road
stood mansions similar to the Tagores', set in gardens, built after the European
fashion and inhabited by wealthy Bengalis and Europeans (the latter living
towards its southern end); in between them lay spacious bungalows (the word
derives from Bengal), humbler dwellings thatched and tiled, shrines and the
occasional temple, and rows of shops forming a famous bazaar. What is nowadays a claustrophobic, airless and hellish mêlée of dwellings, shops, pavement
stalls, Hindu shrines and the occasional mosque, tram-cars, motor-cars and
rickshaws, goods, people and animals – all stewing in north Calcutta's fumes,
garbage and racket – was in those days a rich and appealing scene, much
painted by British artists.

    There were no electric lights then and, of course, no motor vehicles. Looking
back from 1940 Tagore remembered that, 'when the day was over whatever

business remained undone wrapped itself in the black blanket of night and went to sleep . . . Outside the house the evening sky rose quiet and mysterious. It was so still that we could hear, even in our own lane, the shouts from the grooms of the carriages of fashionable people returning from taking the air in the Eden Gardens by the side of the Ganges.' In other words, a mile and a half away.

Perhaps he could catch some other sounds too that he preferred not to put in print. For at the back of the Tagore house lay a celebrated prostitutes' quarter. (In fact, after Tagore's death prostitutes were living in the rear of the house itself; they had to be evicted when it became a museum and university in 1961.) The boy Rabi must have overheard the tinkling bells, soulful singing and plangent instrumental accompaniment of the nautch girls and courtesans as they quite openly entertained the wealthy baboos of north Calcutta. (It was even recorded, in a survey of Calcutta conducted in 1806, that 'a member of Dwarkanath Tagore's family' owned a brothel in Bow Bazar Street, not far from the Tagore house.)

A classic Bengali lampoon published in the early 1860s, *Hutom Pyanchar Naksha* (roughly, 'What the Screech-owl Saw') gives a picture of night-time Calcutta somewhat different from Tagore's:

> The church clock chimed – tung-tang-dhong, tung-tang-dhong. It's 4 a.m. The rakes are returning home . . . There's a light breeze. The cuckoos have begun to sing from the balconies of the whore-houses . . . One or two groups of women have just come out for a dip in the Ganges. The butchers of Chitpur are carrying bags of mutton. The police sergeants, inspectors and constables and other such enemies of the poor are squeaking back to their posts after having finished their rounds; everyone has his pocket jingling with coins and packed with rupees . . .

The Tagore mansion actually consisted of two main houses. Debendranath and his descendants occupied No. 6; his younger brother and his family lived in No. 5, another three-storeyed building, now demolished, which had been constructed by Dwarkanath for entertaining outsiders (in addition to his villa at Belgatchia). After the death of the younger brother in 1854, it was home to his two sons and later to his grandsons, the artists Gaganendranath and Abanindranath.

This younger brother was the one who had agreed to perform the idolatrous funeral ceremony for Dwarkanath when the eldest son, Debendranath, refused. He had also taken charge of the household deity brought to Jorasanko by Nilmoni Tagore in 1784. No. 5 was thus more orthodox in religious matters, idol-worshippers, compared to the Brahmos in No. 6. Nevertheless, genial relations subsisted between the two houses. The young Rabindranath's memories of his childhood belong almost as much to No. 5 as they do to No. 6; in fact he draws no definite distinction between the neighbouring houses in his two memoirs, *My Reminiscences* (1912) and *My Boyhood Days* (1940).

While this was probably a true reflection of the family history overall, Tagore's extreme reticence concerning any of the tensions of 'joint family' life in these writings (he was somewhat franker in his letters) was misleading. His short stories, novels and poems were, after all, preoccupied with the family – not to speak of his many essays on social problems.

V. S. Naipaul's moving and comic masterpiece of Hindu family life, *A House for Mr Biswas*, gives the western reader some idea of the emotional currents and undercurrents that flowed within the Jorasanko mansion. Most of the tension centred around the women. Rabindranath's eldest sister Saudamini recalled an occasion, for instance, when an orthodox uncle who lived in No. 5 'felt ashamed' at seeing his nieces walking about freely on their roof. He complained to Debendranath who replied (perhaps a shade regretfully), 'Times have changed.' But the women themselves were in many cases very reactionary. Dwarkanath's wife we know shunned him in later years. A sister-in-law of Rabindranath remembered in old age that as a new bride fresh from Jessore, she had been scrubbed with potions by maidservants at the instruction of her mother-in-law (Debendranath's wife Sharada), in the hope of lightening her complexion. (Tagore women were often very fair, so much so in the case of Saudamini that she was once detained while going to school in her palanquin by the police, who thought she was an English girl who had been kidnapped.) Another sister-in-law, Rabindranath's favourite, suffered severely from the backbiting of other women, as we shall see. In general the Tagore women, when compared with other relatively well-educated Bengali women of their time, could not be said to have been especially enlightened.

Contact between the Tagores and Europeans was another area of family tension. The Pathuriaghat Tagores cultivated it; the Tagores of Jorasanko were ambivalent, even hostile. Debendranath as a young man had contact with English-men through his father's business and entertaining, but no friendships. After his father's death and the collapse of Carr, Tagore and Co., these contacts stopped. For the rest of his life, the Maharshi, who never travelled to the West (though he did go to China), kept the British and other Europeans at arm's length. He avoided writing in English and refused to use it when writing to Bengalis. 'On one occasion when some new connection by marriage wrote my father a letter in English it was promptly returned to the writer', Rabindranath recalled in *My Reminiscences*. This particular policy became almost a rule in the family.

Debendranath avoided politics, but he supported a political-cum-cultural festival, the Hindu Mela, started in Calcutta in 1867 by an ardent nationalist

Brahmo. It aimed to boost national pride by turning the attention of city-dwellers to indigenous rather than imported (British-made) products, and to the tradition of village handicrafts in particular. With Tagore family help, including Rabindranath's, it became an annual event and a precursor of the Indian National Congress (founded in 1885). But its execution was decidedly confused. The presence of senior British officials was keenly solicited, and the chief organizer had surprising views as to what constituted genuinely 'indigenous' painting. The eldest brother of Rabindranath, visiting the fair, was horrified to find a large, specially commissioned 'nationalist' work on display, 'depicting the people of India in an act of supplication before the figure of Britannia'! He remonstrated with the organizer and had it turned round so that other visitors – including British high-ups – could not see it.

This brother, Dwijendranath, born in 1840, was an interesting and gifted figure. So were four others of the thirteen surviving children of the Maharshi: Satyendranath, born in 1842, Hemendranath, born in 1844, Jyotirindranath, born in 1849, and a daughter Swarnakumari, born around 1856. Rabindranath, who was the youngest, far outshone them all, but he owed much to their stimulus in childhood and youth – particularly to Jyotirindranath. These five, plus two sister-in-laws and two elder cousins living in the other house, together with the cream of Calcutta's artists and intelligentsia as visitors, generated an atmosphere in Jorasanko of variety, vivacity and celebration of eccentricity virtually bound to nourish any seeds of talent.

Dwijendranath was the most intellectual and the least worldly of the siblings. Deeply immersed in the study of Indian philosophy, mathematics and geometry, he also revelled in folding complex paper boxes and was responsible for inventing the first Bengali shorthand and musical notations. These interests he liked to share with others, however unlikely they were to understand them. Once a visitor to Jorasanko, passing the door of Dwijendranath's room in the company of Rabindranath, expressed a desire to meet his eldest brother. With a look of mock horror Rabindranath said, 'If Bara Dada [elder brother] gets hold of you now, you will be done for!'

But fortunately for Rabi, Dwijendranath was also a poet. The composition of his chief poem, *Swapnaprayan* (Dream Journey), took place on a comfortable cushion in the south verandah of No. 5, seated before a low desk and attended by one of the cousins and the young Rabi. In *My Reminiscences* he recalled:

[My cousin's] immense capacity for enjoyment helped poetry to bloom like the breezes of spring. My eldest brother would go on alternately writing and reading out what he had written, his boisterous laughter at his own conceits making the verandah tremble. He wrote a great deal more than he finally used in his finished work, so fertile was his inspiration. Like the flowerets that carpet the feet of the mango groves in spring, the rejected pages of his 'Dream Journey' lay scattered all over the house. Had anyone preserved them they would have made a basketful of blossoms to adorn today's literature.

Dwijendranath was more of a nationalist than his younger brothers. His indignant reaction to the painting of Britannia and her Indian subjects was characteristic; later he was the first Tagore to recognize Gandhi's leadership. He differed greatly from the next brother, Satyendranath, who was the most westernized of Debendranath's children. [pl.4] In 1863, Satyendranath became the first Indian to break into the Indian Civil Service (ICS), having travelled to London to study and sit the exams. His entire career was served away from Calcutta, but from the first he insisted on taking his wife with him – an unheard-of step, of which the Maharshi and his wife definitely did not approve. (It was this girl who as a new bride was scrubbed to try to lighten her skin.) Not only did she speak no English, she had no clothes suitable for travel: Bengali Hindu women of the time wore only a sari, no blouse or petticoat. Rejecting European clothes, she responded to the challenge by adopting the Parsi (Bombay-style) fashion of wearing a blouse with a sari, but she altered the actual mode of draping to suit Bengal. (In time, after much opposition, all Bengali Hindu women followed suit.) Later, in 1877, Satyendranath took another unprecedented step: he sent his wife to England alone with their young son and daughter, joining her the following year with the teenage Rabindranath in tow. As his daughter said of Satyendranath long after his death: 'nothing gave Satyendranath greater pleasure than to see social restrictions for women and barriers like purdah being broken down.'

His attitude to Europe was not simple admiration, however. In a letter to an English friend written years after he retired from the ICS, Satyendranath spoke of 'the fiery ordeal of service'. He did not adopt the purely western dress, or the sola topee, retaining instead the small turban known as the 'Pirali' pugree; he agonized over the requirement upon him as a judge to hand down sentences of hanging; and he experienced some prejudice from fellow British officials. Although his command of English was perfect – as suggested by his translation of the Maharshi's autobiography – his real literary achievements lay in Sanskrit and Bengali, not English.

Jyotirindranath, the tall and debonair mentor to Rabindranath in his teens and early twenties, had the most artistic temperament of the family (excepting Rabindranath). With it went a daredevil streak bordering on craziness; and indeed two of his brothers suffered from mental illness and spent much of their lives in asylums. This side of his character Rabindranath caught affectionately in his autobiography when he described the secret and not-so-secret activities of a patriotic society founded by Jyotirindranath:

> My brother . . . began to busy himself with a costume for all India, and submitted various designs to the association. The dhoti was not deemed business-like; trousers were too foreign; so he hit upon a compromise which detracted considerably from the dhoti while failing to uplift the trousers. That is to say, the trousers were decorated with the addition of a false dhoti-fold in front and behind. The even more fearsome thing that resulted from the combination of turban and sola topee even our most enthusiastic member would not have had the temerity to call an ornament. No person of ordinary courage could have dared to wear it, but my brother unflinchingly wore the complete outfit in broad daylight, passing through the house of an afternoon to the carriage waiting outside, indifferent alike to the stare of relation or friend, door-keeper or coachmen. There may be many a brave Indian ready to die for his country, but there are few, I am certain, who even for the good of the nation will walk the streets in such pan-Indian garb.

William Rothenstein thought Jyotirindranath Tagore India's finest living artist and in 1914 arranged the publication in London of a book of his brilliant pencil portraits of the Tagore family and friends. [pls5,11] Satyajit Ray, marvelling at his songs and his ability to play several musical instruments, called Jyotirindranath a 'born musician'. He also wrote historical plays and farces in Bengali which attracted crowded houses in Bengali theatres (unlike the plays of Rabindranath), he acted on stage, and he translated into Bengali Sanskrit dramas and French literature, including Molière's plays and the short stories of Maupassant. No wonder his shy teenage brother called this dashing elder brother's companionship 'as necessary to my soul . . . as the monsoon after a fiery summer.'

It was Jyotirindranath and his wife Kadambari (another bride from Jessore who was almost Rabindranath's age) who most encouraged the young Tagore's interest in Bengali literature. This was an exciting time for literature in Bengal: English (and to some extent Continental) literature had at last penetrated the hearts and minds of Bengali writers and begun to transform the idealized images, simple poetic metres and Sanskritized diction of centuries. The period 1850–80 saw the creation of the first blank-verse epic in Bengali by Michael Madhushudan Datta, based on an episode in the epic *Ramayana* and much indebted to Milton and Homer; some bold experiments with colloquial Bengali, such as the already-quoted lampoon *Hutom Pyanchar Naksha*; and the triumphal arrival of the Bengali novel, with the work of Bankimchandra

Chatterji, the so-called 'Scott of Bengal', the most famous nineteenth-century Bengali writer. (The first Bengali woman novelist was Rabindranath's elder sister Swarnakumari.) At the same time, essayists such as the scholar and reformer Iswarchandra Vidyasagar, revered by Rabindranath second only to Rammohun Roy, wrote on social matters in powerful and precise language that harmonized the classical and the vernacular.

All these writers were steeped in Sanskrit (as was Rabindranath). The influence of Sanskrit on Bengali, wrote J. C. Ghosh in *Bengali Literature*, 'was similar to the influence of Latin on English, but much greater, because Sanskrit was not a foreign tongue and was alive at the time when Bengali was born', i.e. during the three or four centuries before the Muslim conquest of Bengal around AD 1200, after which Sanskrit ceased to be a living language. The conquest introduced into Bengali many Persian, Arabic, and Turkish words, chiefly relating to administration – an influx that increased after 1576 with the absorption of Bengal into the Mughal empire under Akbar. (The word '*zami*ndar' derives partly from the Persian for 'land', for example.) Two centuries later, with the rise of the European empires in India, English words (and a few Portuguese, French and Dutch words) infiltrated Bengali. Today a little over three per cent of the Bengali vocabulary is of Persian origin, a little over one per cent from European languages.

Tagore referred frequently to Sanskrit literature, less often to European literature and hardly at all to Persian literature in his memoirs of his early years (though he did read some Persian literature). Like all Hindu children in India, now as well as then, he enjoyed retellings of the great epics, the *Ramayana* and *Mahabharata*, in his own language; later, in his teens, he read them in their Sanskrit originals.

Kalidasa, the greatest Sanskrit poet, stirred him especially: 'Once, on the roof terrace of our riverside villa, at the sudden gathering of clouds my eldest brother repeated aloud some stanzas from *The Cloud Messenger* by Kalidasa. I could not understand a word of the Sanskrit, neither did I need to. His ecstatic declamation and the sonorous rhythm were enough for me.'

He also loved Jayadeva, a court poet of the last Hindu king of Bengal before the Muslim conquest. Jayadeva wrote the erotic *Gita Govinda*, the best contribution to Sanskrit poetry by a Bengali. As a boy Rabindranath found a copy belonging to his father. Even though he knew no Sanskrit, he could still 'read' the book because it was printed in Bengali script and so – like a Latin text in the hands of someone who knows English but not Latin – many of its words were familiar to him. The *Gita Govinda* has been called the Indian 'Song of Songs'. It is a high point of Vaishnavism, the worship of the god Vishnu in the form of Krishna that became especially developed in Bengal. There the divine love of Krishna and Radha, which was known throughout India (and today throughout the world, courtesy of the International Krishna Consciousness Movement), was expressed at its most intense. The combination of physical passion, sensuous imagery and verbal music in the best Vaishnava poetry is almost unrivalled in world literature. The Tagore family, being Brahmos, somewhat disapproved of it. But Rabindranath was definitely influenced. There can be no doubt that Vaishnavism was a well-spring of the imagery in *Gitanjali* that would overwhelm W. B. Yeats in 1912.

Being 'sheer word-music', in J. C. Ghosh's phrase, the best Vaishnava poetry does not translate fully into English. Still, there have been some worthwhile attempts. In a song by Govindadas, perhaps of the seventeenth century, Radha, separated from Krishna, wishes that she might die and her body dissolve into the five elements:

Let my body become the dust on the path my lord treads.
Let it become the mirror wherein he beholds his face.
May the conflict between separation and death be over. May death unite me
   with Krishna.
Let my body become the water in the pool where he bathes.
Let it become the gentle breeze that fans his body.
Let my body surround him like the sky wherever he roams, a blue cloud.

Vaishnavaism has been both the glory and the bane of Bengal. Bengali literature, even as it celebrated Krishna and Radha, sometimes mocked the sentimentality and hypocrisy endemic in the Krishna cult. (In a 1930s poem, Tagore refers to the wet clothes of a dreamy office clerk caught in the monsoon as 'oozing and lachrymose' like 'the thoughts of a pious Vaishnava'.) Bengali painting did the same, notably in the sensuous colours and startling caricatures of the Kalighat paintings, comparatively familiar in the West – with their bloated *babus* (baboos) pawing ineffectually at the feet of curvaceous courtesans – and, less familiarly, in the equally vital caricatures of Gaganendranath Tagore. So, in recent decades, did the films of Satyajit Ray.

But despite this countervailing critical strain, emotionalism predominated in Bengali life. It made the Bengalis of Tagore's youth sensitive mainly to the passion in English literature, not as attuned to its intellectual side. Bankim Chatterji's novels, which overwhelmed Bengal (Rabindranath included) in the later nineteenth century and were even translated into English, followed a code of love borrowed from English romantic novels, but presented their heroes and heroines within a framework of Brahminical values. 'His depictions of love rivalled the dithyrambs of the great Romantic exponents of love in Europe', wrote Nirad Chaudhuri. 'This seemed so strange to traditional Bengalis, and yet took such a strong hold on the young, that Chatterji was accused of corrupting the youth of Bengal.' Or, in the words of Rabindranath himself, looking back a shade wistfully to that period in his memoirs:

> Our literary gods were Shakespeare, Milton and Byron and the quality in their work which stirred us most was strength of passion. In English social life passionate outbursts are kept severely in check; for which very reason, perhaps, they so dominate English literature. Its characteristic is the suppression of vehement feelings to a point of inevitable explosion. At least this was what we in Bengal came to regard as the quintessence of English literature.

4 Rabi
(1861–1873)

Looking back at my childhood I feel the thought that recurred most often
was that I was surrounded by mystery.

My Reminiscences

My Reminiscences is certainly among Rabindranath's most enchanting (and
quotable) prose writings. W. B. Yeats called it a 'most valuable and rich
work'. But as a guide to the events of that period in Tagore's life it must be read
with caution. As Yeats once said to a friend when writing about *his* boyhood:
'Inaccuracies don't worry me, so long as the phrase is beautiful.'

Rabindranath himself was conscious of the fact. He called *My Reminiscences*
(and by the same token *My Boyhood Days*) 'memory pictures', adding: 'To
regard them as an attempt at autobiography would be a mistake.' Pursuing the
pictorial analogy, he made some nice observations about memory which seem to
foreshadow the bold chiaroscuro and distortions of human and animal figures
that are integral to his paintings. He wrote:

I do not know who has painted the pictures of my life imprinted on my
memory. But whoever he is, he is an artist. He does not take up his brush
simply to copy everything that happens; he retains or omits things just as he
fancies; he makes many a big thing small and small thing big; he does not
hesitate to exchange things in the foreground with things in the background.
In short, his task is to paint pictures, not to write history. The flow of events
forms our external life, while within us a series of pictures is painted. The
two correspond, but are not identical . . .

There is no event in my reminiscences worthy of being preserved for all
time. Literary value does not depend on the importance of a subject however.
Whatever one has truly felt, if it can be made sensible to others, will always be
respected.

Judged by his own account, the chief impression of those childhood years is of a rather solitary boy bereft of luxuries and affection, longing to connect his acutely sensitive inner world with the generous artistic atmosphere of the adults. That was how Satyajit Ray showed Rabi in his documentary film *Rabindranath Tagore* made for the Tagore birth centenary in 1961. A beautiful dreamy-looking boy clutching a flute is seen dawdling in the wide verandah of the house at Jorasanko. From adjacent rooms along the verandah come overlapping clashing sounds tantalizing the boy's ears: someone is mellifluously reciting from one of the 'literary gods', Shakespeare's *Hamlet*; someone else (Jyotirindranath?) is picking out a tune on a piano; another voice is practising scales in a syncopated classical Hindusthani style; the beats of a *tabla* are also heard. The house is a hive of artistic activity. But all that young Rabi can do is turn away.

In *My Reminiscences* he said of himself and the other children in the house (of whom there were surprisingly few for so large a family as the Tagores): 'We were too young then to take part in these doings, but the waves of merriment and life to which they gave rise came and beat at the doors of our curiosity.' Sometimes the sounds came from No. 5 Dwarkanath Tagore's Lane rather than from his own house. A burlesque written by Dwijendranath was once rehearsed in the big drawing-room of No. 5. 'From our place against the verandah railings of our house we could hear, though the open windows opposite, roars of laughter mixed with the sounds of a comic song'. They could also catch sight of 'extraordinary antics' by one of the actors, a friend of the family. But neither the words nor the gestures were clear enough to follow, alas.

'In our boyhood we beheld the dying rays of the intimate sociability characteristic of the last generation', Tagore apostrophized in 1912.

> Since then everything has become much grander, but hosts have become unfeeling, and have lost the art of indiscriminate invitation. The indigently clad, or even bare-bodied, no longer have the right to appear without a permit on the strength of their smiling faces alone . . . Our predicament, as I see it, is that we have lost what we had, but lack the means of building up afresh on the European standard, with the result that our home life has become joyless. We still meet for business or for politics but never for the pleasure of simply being together, with no purpose in mind than good fellowship – that has vanished.

This says as much about Rabindranath, perhaps, as about Bengali society. Western influences undoubtedly had curtailed older Bengali habits of leisure, but if there was one thing for which people in Bengal had remained famous (as they still are), it was for their love of meeting 'for the pleasure of simply being together' or, to use the Bengali word, 'to do *adda*'. Bengalis seem always to have gathered in groups for no particular reason and at almost any time of the day or night, in order to gossip on every conceivable subject. That is the definition of *adda*. Plays, novels, stories and films have been built around it. *Addas* have, it is true, fallen markedly in standard of wit and intellect within the lifetimes of middle-aged and older Bengalis today, let alone since the palmy days of the late nineteenth century. But even then, when Rabindranath was young, he himself was by no means addicted to *adda*. He could be sociable, but frequently he took part in a social occasion because he had been invited to lecture, recite, sing, act or produce one of his plays or operas. When he wanted to be idle, more often than not he preferred his own company, or at most one or two friends or family members, rather than a party.

In other words, in his two memoirs Rabindranath tended to substitute emotional truth for facts. That was why, for example, his grandfather Dwarkanath was omitted from these books, though he was definitely sociable in the old manner approved by his grandson. And it was why Tagore several times stated that, as a boy, he lacked good clothes. For instance: 'Luxury was a thing almost unknown in my early childhood . . . On no pretext might we wear socks or shoes until we had passed our tenth year.' (*My Reminiscences*) And: 'We wore the very simplest and plainest clothes . . . it was a long time before we even began to wear socks.' (*My Boyhood Days*) Yet according to the Tagore family cashbook, two dozen pairs of socks were bought for Rabi in January 1865, when he was not yet four, along with pairs of shoes in 1864, 1866 and 1868. In March and April 1865 alone, two dozen *kurtas* (loose shirts) were bought for him, a dozen of them being of an expensive variety. There is even a pencilled note in the cashbook: 'Will the Governor [i.e. the Maharshi] approve?' The overall picture is of a boy who, while not spoilt like his father when young, was not deprived either.

It is likely that, rather than clothes, affection was what was lacking and (as suggested by Prashanta Paul) this lack of love was transformed into a lack of clothes in Rabi's imagination. Again and again in his memoirs Tagore spoke of the unbridgeable distance between the children and the adults in Jorasanko. They were, he said, 'kept apart as strictly as men and women with their separate apartments.' This was not very surprising in the case of his remarkable brothers, given the difference in ages: Jyotirindranath was twelve years older than Rabi, Dwijendranath old enough to be Rabi's father. The remoteness of his parents calls for a little more explanation.

Sharada, his mother, was already the mother of twelve living children (seven sons and five daughters) when Rabi was born. [pl.3] Several of them had wives or husbands living in the house, for whom Sharada felt responsibility. In addition her health was not strong. Her husband Debendranath was constantly away from the house, travelling in northern India and elsewhere. Indeed Sharada's thoughts were preoccupied with ways to encourage him to return. Mostly she relied on priests, offerings and astrology. (She never entirely shook off orthodox Hindu behaviour, despite being married to a devout Brahmo.) Once, though, as a last resort she enlisted Rabi's help, when he was around eight or nine. These were the early days of the so-called 'Great Game' between the Russians and the British on the borders of India (the backdrop to Kipling's *Kim*). Sharada had heard a rumour of a Russian invasion of the Himalayas, where the Maharshi was travelling, and had become alarmed. Unable to stir up the rest of the family she turned to Rabi and begged him to write his father a letter. As Rabindranath recalled: 'I did not know how to begin or end a letter, or anything at all about it. I went to Mahananda, the estate *munshi* [secretary]. My resulting form of address was doubtless correct enough, but the sentiments could not have escaped the musty flavour inseparable from correspondence emanating from an estate office.' His father replied, asking his son not to be afraid; 'if the Russians came he would drive them away himself.'

On the occasions when the Maharshi did return to Calcutta, it was almost as if he had not, so distant did he remain from Rabi during his first ten or eleven years. Partly this was the way of a Victorian paterfamilias, in Brahmo Bengal as much as in Britain, but it was also the product of the Maharshi's religious turn of mind. Rabi's archetypal image of his father at this time was the one he saw from a favourite hiding place on the roof of the house. Across the roof lay his father's room: 'The sun had not yet risen, and he sat on the roof silent as an image of white stone, his hands folded in his lap.'

Almost all of Rabi's direct experience then lay within the walls of the Tagore house. He was forbidden to leave it (except for school) – or so he said. In this case it was probably literally true. Debendranath Tagore would hardly have wanted his son mixing with Europeans or shopkeepers in the Chitpur Road, less still with the denizens of the streets behind the house. The result: 'Beyond my reach stretched this limitless thing called the Outside, flashes, sounds and scents of which used momentarily to come and touch me through interstices. It seemed to want to beckon me through the shutters with a variety of gestures.' Rabindranath meant this more than figuratively. Not only did he crave open space throughout his long life, he also personified nature in his writings to a degree rare among western writers (if fairly common in Sanskrit literature).

A similar feeling imbues his often haunting paintings. Trees, for instance, appear often to conceal a tenebrous presence. Ghosts seem just out of sight. Significantly, ghosts were firmly excluded from *My Reminiscences*, which was written years before Tagore began painting, but they surface in the much later

1 'Prince' Dwarkanath Tagore, grandfather of Rabindranath, 1845/46 (*Baron de Schwiter*)

2 Maharshi Debendranath Tagore, father of Rabindranath

3 Sharada Devi, mother of Rabindranath

4 Two elder brothers of Rabindranath and their wives: Jnanadanandini and
Satyendranath, Jyotirindranath (*seated*) and Kadambari

5 Jnanadanandini Devi, in Karwar (near Goa), 1883 (*Jyotirindranath Tagore*)

6/The house of the Tagores, 6 Dwarkanath Tagore's Lane, Jorasanko, north Calcutta, today:
top – main entrance seen from lane (*Suman Datta*)
below – prayer-hall and main courtyard (*Samiran Nandy*)

7 *The Familiar Black Umbrella*, 1916 (*Gaganendranath Tagore*)

8 Rabindranath, in England, *c.* 1879

My Boyhood Days. There Tagore remembered a ghost that must have frightened him a good deal as he watched the outside world from the roof, especially at twilight. It was linked with a thick-leaved almond tree at the western corner of the mansion. 'A mysterious Shape was said to stand with one foot in its branches and the other on the third-storey cornice of the house. Plenty of people declared that they had seen it'. Nor could he escape ghosts by going downstairs away from the roof. In the dark rooms of the ground floor, rows of giant clay water jars stood filled with a year's supply of drinking water. (There were no water pipes then.) 'All those musty, dingy, twilit rooms were the home of furtive "Things" – which of us did not know all about those "Things"? Great gaping mouths they had, eyes in their breasts, and ears like winnowing fans; and their feet turned backwards.' The whole atmosphere of the house was so ghost-obsessed that Rabi could not put his feet into the darkness beneath a table without getting the creeps.

The water jars are gone today, but the poky rooms are still there at the back of the Jorasanko house, shabby and broken down. It is easy to see how depressing (and spooky) they must have been to a sensitive young boy. And Rabi spent a substantial proportion of his early years in and around these rooms under the charge of the family servants. In *My Reminiscences* he termed this period a 'servocracy', adding wryly that 'In the history of India the regime of the Slave Dynasty was not a happy one.' Again, his picture was probably not much exaggerated, since it is supported by the experience of children in other wealthy Bengali families of the time and by the many convincing details of life under the rule of the servants – not all tyrannous – supplied by Rabindranath.

The water jars, for example, came in handy for the servants. 'How well I recall their attempts to suppress our wailing by cramming our heads into [these jars].' So did the food cooked for Rabi and the other children. When they sat down to eat, a wooden tray would be placed in front of them with a quantity of *luchis* heaped upon it. A few of these fried wafers of bread would be dropped gingerly on to each child's platter by the chief servant. Then would come an enquiry as to whether anyone would like to have more. Rabi knew which reply would 'most gratify' the questioner and – unlike Oliver Twist – he did not ask for another helping.

The *Ramayana* too was useful to the servants. Shyam, a country boy from Jessore second-in-command of the servants, would place Rabi in a certain spot, trace a chalk circle around him and warn him solemnly with raised finger not to transgress this circle. 'Whether the danger was physical or mental I never fully understood.' But he did not disobey because he had read in the *Ramayana* of the tribulations of Sita in the forest after she disobeyed a command not to step outside a magic circle drawn around her cottage. (She was tempted out of it by the words of a wandering hermit – really the Demon-King Ravana in disguise – and kidnapped.)

The same Shyam told blood-curdling stories of dacoity – gang robbery. Dacoities were quite common in Bengal in the 1860s, commonplace in the time of Dwarkanath Tagore. Indeed many zamindars made a profession of it. There was a story of one whose gang returned on a new moon night carrying the severed head of a victim, in order to make a puja at the temple in honour of the blood-thirsty goddess Kali. But when the zamindar saw it, he cried out, 'What have you done? It's my son-in-law!' In another story, told by Shyam, a woman succeeded in 'robbing the robbers' by dressing herself as Kali, complete with heavy curved blade, appearing dramatically before the dacoits and claiming their devout offerings.

One day some ex-dacoits turned up in Jorasanko and gave a display of wrestling. Tagore remembered it well in old age. One dacoit got another dacoit

> to grasp him by his shaggy hair, and then whirled him round and round by a mere turn of his head. Using a long pole as support and lever, they leaped up to the second storey. Then one man stood with his hands clasped above his bent head, and others shot through the aperture like diving birds. They also showed how it was possible for them to manage a dacoity twenty or thirty miles away, and the same night be found sleeping peacefully in their beds like law-abiding citizens.

The technique was to use stilts, which meant a dacoit could run faster than a horse. Thirty or forty years later, when he founded his school in Shantiniketan, Rabindranath would encourage his pupils to try stilt walking.

It seems like a bizarre scene for the courtyard of the highly respectable Maharshi Debendranath. But the Tagores of that time were never far removed from the harsher realities of Bengali life, physically and mentally. The Tagore women mostly hailed from villages in East Bengal; the men had seen the hard life on the family estates at first hand; and the Jorasanko house stood cheek-by-jowl with the poverty and low life of north Calcutta. The Tagores were never typical of the Calcutta *bhadralok* – a term much used by historians which translates more or less as 'gentlefolk', and connotes (now as it did then) the class of Bengalis who revere intellectual work of any kind, even clerking, and despise practical and manual activities, no matter how mentally demanding. One would not know it from such works as *Gitanjali* or even *My Reminiscences*, but Rabindranath Tagore cultivated his physique as well as his mind. He could swim the Padma (Ganges) at the Tagore estates, or walk 25 miles in the hills at a stretch. He also introduced judo into India. As a child, wrestling was part of his home-based education.

The latter was the responsibility of Hemendranath Tagore. This brother was keen to impart to Rabi a much wider range of subjects than was taught in Calcutta schools. He believed too that learning should be in Bengali not English – not at all the done thing among the gentry in the 1860s and 70s. Rabindranath never ceased to be grateful to him. At the time, though, his brother's programme seemed a stiff one. Up before dawn and clad in a loincloth, Rabi had a bout or two with a wrestler. Then, slipping a *kurta* over his dusty body, it was straight on to lessons in literature, mathematics, geography and history. Then off to school. On his return, more lessons in drawing and gymnastics. Last of all, in the evening by lamplight, came lessons in English. Between 4 a.m. and 9 p.m. he barely stopped. Most Sundays he had a singing lesson and a science lesson. Finally, he was taught anatomy using a skeleton, and the rules of Sanskrit grammar by rote. 'I am not sure which of these, the names of the bones or the *sutras* of the grammarian, were the more jaw-breaking. The latter probably took the palm.'

English was his least favourite subject, and he would never acquire complete confidence in it (especially the grammar). His interest developed only later, almost entirely through reading literature. Until the time he translated *Gitanjali*, he wrote in English very rarely. In general Tagore, like many people with a highly developed feeling for their own language, found other languages difficult to learn (Sanskrit excepted). 'The discovery of fire was one of man's greatest discoveries so we are told,' he wrote in *My Reminiscences*. 'I do not dispute it. But I cannot help feeling how fortunate the little birds are that their parents cannot light lamps in the evening. They have their language lessons early in the morning – how gleefully everyone must have noticed. Of course we must not forget that it is not English they are learning!'

For the first publication of this memoir, Gaganendranath Tagore painted a charming black-and-white scene. Entitled 'The Familiar Black Umbrella', it shows Dwarkanath Tagore's Lane seen from the verandah of No. 6. [pl.7] Rain is lancing down, the lane is flooded (it still floods during a heavy shower), and a male figure clad in a dhoti is picking his way towards the house beneath a large umbrella. Rabindranath explained:

It is evening . . . Our lane is under knee-deep water. The tank has overflowed into the garden, and the shaggy tops of the *bel* trees are standing guard over the waters. Our whole being is radiating rapture like the fragrant stamens of the *kadamba* flower. Our tutor's arrival is already overdue by several minutes. But nothing is yet certain. We sit on the verandah overlooking the lane, waiting and watching with a pathetic gaze. All of a sudden our hearts seem to tumble to the ground with a great thump. The familiar black umbrella has turned the corner, undefeated even by such weather. Could it not be somebody else's? No, it could not! In the wide world there might be found another person, his equal in pertinacity, but never in this particular little lane.

Possibly if the English lessons had been scheduled for the mornings, Rabi's aversion might have been less extreme. But this is doubtful because he early on developed a deep dislike for conventional teaching of any subject. Towards his formal schooling outside the Jorasanko house his antipathy was almost heroic. 'Rabi went to four schools and hated them all', said Satyajit Ray in his film – with perfect truth. Everything Tagore would subsequently say on education – a vast number of essays and lectures to audiences in almost every major nation, perhaps more than he said on any other subject – was rooted in his own experience of school. He summed up both the strength and the weakness in his approach with this comment:

> The main object of teaching is not to give explanations, but to knock at the doors of the mind. If any boy is asked to give an account of what is awakened in him by such knocking, he will probably say something silly. For what happens within is much bigger than what comes out in words. Those who pin their faith on university examinations as the test of education take no account of this.

Meanwhile, around the age of eight, he became a poet. 'Like a young deer which butts here, there and everywhere with its newly sprouted antlers, I and my budding poetry made a nuisance of themselves.' A slightly older brother – not one of those destined to be remembered for any achievement of his own – encouraged Rabi. He insisted on trailing him around the Jorasanko house and having him recite. One of their early victims was the same Brahmo nationalist who organized the Hindu Mela, who was also editor of a Brahmo newspaper. They nabbed him as he stepped into the house on business. There and then, at the foot of the stairs, in a high-pitched voice, Rabi read his poem.

'Well done!' the editor said with a smile. 'But what is a *dwireph*?' Rabi was nonplussed. He had probably got the word from a dictionary and, liking its sound in his poem, had chosen it instead of the ordinary word *bhramar*. Both have two syllables and mean 'bumble-bee', but the first is Sanskritic, unlike the second: it would translate better as 'twin-proboscidean' than as 'bumblebee'. Hence the editor's smile.

The poet never read his poetry to this particular man again. 'I have added many years to my age since then,' he wrote in his memoirs, 'but I have not been able to improve upon my test of who is and who is not a connoisseur ... the word *dwireph*, like a bee drunk with honey, remained stuck in position.' Already, Rabindranath was showing signs of the boldness with Bengali to come.

5   A Journey to the Himalayas
(1873)

Just as he allowed me to wander the mountains at will, so [Father] left me
free to select my path in the quest for truth.

My Reminiscences

1873 was an important year for Rabi. It brought him into close contact with
his father for the first time. It also took him out of the house at Jorasanko for
a few months on his first major expedition.

But before that he had to pass through a ceremony, *upanayan* – the
investiture of the Brahmin's sacred thread – which marked the transition of a
Brahmin boy to adulthood. The Maharshi believed in this custom, however
unorthodox his spiritual beliefs. So did Rabindranath, however self-mocking he
was in describing the rituals. These began with Rabi and two other boys of the
family learning from the Maharshi how to chant the *Upanishads*. Next, after
some days of chanting, with shaven heads and gold rings in their ears the three
'budding Brahmins' went into three days' retreat in a portion of the top storey
of the house. Here, instead of meditating, they had fun. The earrings were a
good handle for pulling each other's ears. A small drum that chanced to be in
one of the rooms was another opportunity. Whenever a servant appeared down
below them they rapped a tattoo. First the man would look up, then he would
avert his eyes and beat a hasty retreat.

I am convinced that boys like us must have been common in the hermitages
of old. If some ancient document has it that the ten or twelve-year-old
Saradwata or Sarngarava [two novices mentioned by Kalidasa] spent the
whole of his boyhood offering oblations and chanting mantras, we are not
compelled to put unquestioning faith in the statement; because the book of
Boy Nature is even older and is also more authentic.

Once more, Rabi was called into his father's presence. How would he like to
accompany him to the Himalayas? How? 'I would have needed to rend the skies

with a shout to give some idea of How!' Apart from the excitement of the trip, he had been worrying about the reaction to his shaven head of the Eurasian boys at school: their reverence for Brahmins was minimal, as he well knew. It was a great relief to avoid their jeers.

Father and son (the latter wearing a gold-embroidered velvet cap on his hairless head and 'newly sacred-threaded' in the sarcastic phrase of an anti-Brahmo Bengali newspaper) left Calcutta by train on 14 February. They travelled on the line that some thirty years previously Dwarkanath Tagore had hoped to build. (He died too soon.) That same evening, after a journey of a hundred miles or so, they reached Bolpur station in the district of Birbhum. Close by was Shantiniketan. Rabi was about to set foot in the place that would eventually become linked with his name worldwide.

It was, however, his father who discovered it. The purchase of the land – nearly seven acres – dated from 1863. Maharshi Debendranath bought it from a local zamindar named Sinha, a friend of his. The story goes that he stopped his palanquin there in order to meditate under a pair of *chhatim* trees, and fell in love with the spot. (A marble prayer seat was later constructed under the trees.) A gang of dacoits were said to have come up, seen the Maharshi and been so affected by his still poise that they left him alone and in due course even took up service under him. [pl.25]

The place was already called Shantiniketan ('Abode of Peace'), possibly after a small hut known by that name. The hut and the *chhatim* trees apart, there was nothing else there: just denuded red soil and the plain of Bengal stretching beyond a line of distant palm trees towards infinity. This utter bareness was what first appealed to Debendranath. Soon afterwards he brought good soil, trees and plants and established a mango grove. In 1866 a house was started, which would gradually be extended during the coming decades. But in 1873 there were barely two habitable rooms. [pl.26]

Rabi probably knew nothing of all this. Instead he had been fed a story by a mischievous nephew, and had believed everything he was told. Getting into the palanquin at Bolpur at twilight he shut his eyes, so as to preserve the wonders mentioned by his nephew until dawn. As he remarked ruefully forty years later, reading the *Mahabharata* and *Ramayana* was not a good training for determining 'the line between the possible and the impossible.' He hunted without success for a path from the house to the servants' quarters which, though not covered, 'did not allow a ray of sun or a drop of rain to touch anybody passing along it.' And he searched in vain for the cowherd boys said to be frolicking in the fields of ripening rice. But there was a marvellous compensation: 'What I could not see did not take me long to get over – what I did see was quite enough. There was no servant rule, and the only ring which encircled me was the blue of the horizon, drawn around these solitudes by their presiding goddess. Within this I was free to move about as I chose.'

It was a significant episode. Shantiniketan, in Rabindranath's mind, from the very first meant freedom, a realm where ordinary rules were suspended. His school and later his university would be projections of this boyish imagining onto the physical world. A bare tract of land in a poverty-stricken district of Bengal became, in his mind, a utopia. But in taking concrete steps to realize the dream as an adult, Rabindranath risked breaking his spell. Only if one could preserve one's faith in magic could the dream and the reality of Shantiniketan coincide.

After happy weeks there father and son crossed India by train and stopped at Amritsar in the Punjab (near what is now the border with Pakistan). For about a month they settled in a place not far from the Golden Temple of the Sikhs. The Maharshi was drawn to the temple by the rousing worship in the middle of the sacred lake, and Rabi went too. Sometimes the Maharshi joined the hymns. No Sikh ever objected. Here was a prime lesson in religious tolerance. For the rest of his life Rabindranath regarded Sikhism (along with Buddhism and Brahmoism) as a reforming movement within Hinduism, not as a separate religion. In 1937, aged seventy-six, he informed Gandhi:

I do not find anything in their [the Sikhs'] religious practices and creeds which hurts my human dignity. My father often used to offer his worship in Amritsar Gurdwara where I daily accompanied him but I never could imagine him at the Kali's temple in Calcutta. Yet, in his culture and religion he was a Hindu and in his daily living maintained a purer standard of Hinduism than most of those who profess it by words of mouth [*sic*] and pollute it in their habits.

Here in Amritsar, aged eleven, Rabi composed his first song. He also began to sing for his father. Evening was their time. The Maharshi would sit on the verandah facing the garden. 'I can see the moon risen; its beams, passing through the trees, falling on the verandah floor; and I am singing in raga *Behag*':

You are my friend in all difficulty and doubt
And companion in the darkest passage of life.

'My father with bowed head and clasped hands listens intently. I recall the evening scene quite clearly.'

They also read together in Sanskrit and in English. One of the books was

Proctor's *Popular Astronomy*. Debendranath explained it in easy language which Rabi then rendered into Bengali; thus began his lifelong interest in the science of the heavens, which influenced all his writing including his poems. Another book was a biography of Benjamin Franklin. The Maharshi, according to his son, thought the book would be both entertaining and instructive. But not far in he became disillusioned with Franklin. 'The narrowness of his calculated morality disgusted my father.' Sometimes while reading Franklin Debendranath would burst out in denunciation. For himself he had had sent from Calcutta the twelve volumes of Gibbon's history of the Roman Empire. Rabi looked at them and wondered why adults should ever feel the desire to read such dry tomes.

Come mid-April, when the plains of Punjab begin to burn, they and their servants set off for the Himalayas. Their destination was Dalhousie, a sparsely populated hill-station on the borders of Kashmir at 7,500 feet, where they had taken a house on the highest hill-top, Bakrota. To get there from the plains in the 1870s meant a long trek carried in a litter known as a *jhampan*, staying each night at bungalows. Rabi drank in the new sights, so utterly alien to Calcutta, Shantiniketan or the Indian plains: the climbing road, the gorges beneath, the great forest trees clustering together at bends in the road, at their feet small waterfalls and streams babbling over black moss-covered rocks. Years later he commented:

That is the great advantage of a first vision: the mind is not aware that there are many more to come. When this fact penetrates that calculating organ it promptly tries to make a saving in its expenditure of attention. Only when it believes something to be rare does the mind cease to be miserly. In the streets of Calcutta I sometimes imagine myself to be a foreigner, and only then do I discover how much is to be seen.

While on the move his practical education began. Without any fuss the Maharshi transferred his cashbox – a good prize for any hill dacoits that might have been about – from Kishori, its normal custodian, to Rabi. Every night Rabi had to make it over to his father. Once, when he forgot, he was reprimanded. And on arrival in Bakrota, the Maharshi took over the role of Hemendranath, Rabi's home-educator, too. Lessons began in the chill before dawn with the memorizing of Sanskrit declensions. The Maharshi would be up already, sitting at his devotions in a glazed verandah, while outside, way beyond the house, the snow peaks could be seen shimmering dimly in the starlight. Sometimes a half-awake Rabi would see him pass softly by, wrapped in a red shawl with a lighted lamp in his hand. Then, after he had dozed off, his father would nudge him – 'an excruciatingly wintry awakening from the caressing warmth of my blankets!' Next, when they had taken a tumbler of milk together (which Rabi always tried to evade), as the sun rose over the Himalayas they stood and chanted the *Upanishads*. After that came a walk, an hour of English and at ten o'clock an ice-cold bath, an old practice of Debendranath when travelling in the mountains. Later, after a midday meal, lessons were supposed to begin again. But, the adult Tagore recalled, 'This was more than flesh and blood could stand. My outraged morning sleep *would* have its revenge and I would be toppling over with uncontrollable drowsiness. But no sooner did my father take pity on my plight and let me off than my sleepiness was off likewise: the Lord of the mountains was calling!'

Remarkably, the Maharshi never tried to stop Rabi wandering in the mountains. No one accompanied him, a boy not even in his teens; all he had was a staff in his hand. Even allowing for a little later exaggeration by Rabindranath, his father's attitude was questionable, verging on the foolhardy. But his son always honoured him for it. In every area of life, Rabindranath insisted long after the Maharshi's death in 1905, his father had encouraged him to develop self-discipline, independence of spirit and dislike of domineering behaviour. 'He held up a standard, not a disciplinary rod.' Yet to an outsider, it will often seem that Debendranath's influence inhibited his son, both as a man and as an artist, until the last decade or two of his life. For the moment here is Tagore's moving tribute to Debendranath spoken at Shantiniketan in 1936:

The impression on my mind of my father in those days is that of a man who, though shouldering all the responsibilities of a large family, always kept his spirit free, unaffected by worldly affairs, soaring in its spiritual detachment. The picture of the supremely beautiful Kanchanjungha peak of the Himalayas, which is unique in its grandeur and spotless aloofness, rises at once before my mind's eye when I remember Debendranath. Or, as the *Upanishad* would say, he stood 'like a tree established in heaven.'

6 Adolescence
(1873–1878)

Boys are less bold and far more self-conscious than girls.

My Boyhood Days

After a month or two in Dalhousie, Rabi returned to Calcutta in the company of a family servant, leaving his father in the hills. He had just turned twelve and was full of knowledge and experience. Very soon he found himself in demand at his mother's *adda* on the roof terrace in the evenings, where the ladies of the house gathered to gossip. Gone was the physical separation of son from mother of his first decade. He recited with great charm verses from the simplified versions of the epics in Bengali, which he had picked up from the servants. He also declaimed scraps of other poetry taken from his books on Bengali prosody and rhetoric. And he regaled his listeners with titbits of astronomy from Proctor's book and from school. One of his favourite facts was that the sun, though small to the human eye, is actually thousands of times bigger than the earth. The name Rabi means 'sun' in Bengali, so this therefore appealed to him all the more: 'I at once disclosed it to my mother.'

Eventually his boasting got him into trouble. One of the Sanskrit books he had been reading with his father was Valmiki's *Ramayana*. He mentioned this proudly to his mother, who could not read Sanskrit. Immediately she wanted to hear him recite from it: to her Valmiki's version seemed as superior to the Bengali version as the Authorized Version of the Bible might seem to a reader who knew only the modern English version. Rabi was in a fix. He knew that he had read a mere extract and had not fully mastered that. Moreover, when he looked again at the extract, he found his memory often hazy. But he lacked the courage to admit he had forgotten it. Somehow he managed to give a garbled rendering. Then came the bombshell. 'You must read this to Dwijendra,' his mother said excitedly. There was no escaping her wish. His elder brother was sent for, duly came, listened to a few verses and then, with his famously preoccupied air, remarked simply, 'Very good,' and walked off.

Dwijendranath's *Swapnaprayan* (Dream Journey) was in full flow at this time, and perhaps he wanted to get back to the poem. Untranslatable as the poem is, one appealing verse is worth giving in rhymed Bengali with a rough English rendering. Into it Dwijendranath contrived the names of eight Tagores: the six brothers, Satyendranath, Hemendranath, Birendranath, Jyotirindranath, Somendranath and Rabindranath, cousin Gunendranath and Maharshi Debendranath.

Bhate jatha *satya hem* mate jatha *bir*
Gun jyoti hare jetha maner timir
Shab shobha dhare jetha *shom* ar *rabi*
Shei *deb*-niketan alo kare kabi.

Where truth [*satya*] shines golden [*hem*] and a hero [*bir*] plays
Where virtue [*gun*] and light [*jyoti*] chase gloom with their rays
Where moon [*shom*] and sun [*rabi*] in all their glory goeth
In that abode of the gods [*deb*] O behold this poet. [i.e. Dwijendra]

When the poem was finally finished, Dwijendranath read it to the family circle, including his old nurse. At the end – so it was said – she bowed down to the ground, thinking the poem to be a hymn to the gods.

Meanwhile Rabi's first published poem appeared – anonymously. It was entitled 'Abhilash' (Yearning). Perhaps he wrote it during class hours. Having tasted freedom with his father in Shantiniketan and beyond, he was finding his return to school even more crushing. At the end of 1873 his family took him away. Following a year at home he attended St Xavier's School, run by Jesuits, in 1875. (His name appears in the register as 'Tagore, Nubindronath'.) But this was not a success and he left after two and a half months. St Xavier's was his fourth school, and his last.

Tagore recalled one happy memory of St Xavier's, a teacher named Father DePeneranda. One day during class, seeing Rabi's pen not moving, he stopped, bent over him, gently laid a hand on his shoulder and enquired tenderly: 'Are you not well, Tagore?' 'It was only a simple question,' Tagore wrote in 1912, 'but one I have never been able to forget . . . I cannot speak for the other boys, but I felt in him the presence of a great soul'. (Twenty years later he learnt that the father was a Spanish count who had given up everything when he entered the Order, and who was an excellent pianist, mathematician and astronomer. He came from Andalucia and his family was known to Juan Ramón Jiménez, Tagore's Spanish translator.)

Although the family permitted Rabi to leave school, some of them were critical. His brothers fairly soon gave up on him; after all, none of them except Satyendranath had bothered themselves overmuch with formal education. His elder sister Saudamini said: 'We had all hoped Rabi would grow up to be a man, but he has been our biggest disappointment.' Though Rabi was stung, he could not bring himself to return to what seemed to him 'a hideously cruel combination of hospital and jail'.

He did make one more attempt to receive formal education, Calcutta-style, as he recalled over sixty years later while giving the Convocation Address at Calcutta University – the first ever in Bengali. For just one day he ventured into the first-year class at Presidency College, then the acme of English-style education. But his appearance 'was greeted with a gust of suppressed laughter' which made him feel an acute misfit. He could not muster the courage to return the next day; after that, he said, he had never expected to enter the portals of a university again.

His attitude to academe would be a mixed one throughout his life. Abroad he would meet many university scholars, a few of whom he would persuade to lecture at his university. But he became intimate with none. In Bengal and in India generally he did much to encourage the best minds in most disciplines, but he scorned the majority of Indian scholars. Though he was tactful about this for the most part, those he scorned were aware of his true feelings. As a result, his relationship with Calcutta University was at best uneasy. In 1936 Tagore told an audience at Shantiniketan: 'Our country provides numerous instances of persons with dead minds ascending to the highest peaks of academic success.' The charge was entirely fair – but it was not calculated to win him friends in Indian academe.

So now Rabi was casually educated at home. Literature predominated; with the help of teachers, and increasingly on his own, he read works in Sanskrit, English and Bengali. (He also tried Dante in English translation, and Goethe in the original, but without much pleasure.) His Sanskrit tutors took him through Kalidasa's *Birth of the War-God* and *Sakuntala*, translating them into Bengali as they went along. In English he read Byron's *Childe Harolde's Pilgrimage*, Moore's *Irish Melodies* and Shakespeare's *Macbeth* and *The Tempest*. Some of these he translated into Bengali, the entire play in the case of *Macbeth*. 'I was fortunate enough to lose this translation and so am relieved of the burden of my karma to that extent', he claimed in his memoirs. Actually, the 'Witches' Scene' was published in 1880 in the Tagore family magazine, and it is still a good read. One can see why one of Rabi's home-tutors wanted to show off his prodigy to the great Pandit Vidyasagar, scholar and social reformer (whose name meant 'Ocean of Learning'). 'My heart thumped as I entered the great pundit's study, packed full of books; nor did his austere visage help to revive my courage.

Nevertheless, as this was the first time I had had such a distinguished audience, the desire to win renown was strong within me.' He was a hit.

But it was less elevated writing than Shakespeare that made the biggest impression, and in Bengali not in English, which remained a struggle. There were the farces of Dinabandhu Mitra, for instance, then delighting Calcutta theatre audiences with their 'crude and crazy mirth' (J. C. Ghosh). The titles give an idea of the plays' contents: *Shadhabar Ekadashi* (Forced Widowhood of a Married Girl, 1866), *Biye Pagla Buro* (Old Man Mad for Marriage, 1866), *Jamai Barik* (The Barrack for Son-in-Laws, 1872). Mitra's first play, a tragedy called *Nil Darpan* (The Mirror of Indigo, 1860), caused a sensation when it was translated into English and published by the Reverend James Long, an Irish missionary. Long had criminal proceedings brought against him by the indigo planters in Bengal, backed by the European business community in Calcutta, and he was fined and imprisoned.

Rabi had to obtain these plays surreptitiously because the family did not consider them suitable for a boy of his age. There was no such difficulty with the compilations of old Bengali poetry that were then appearing for the first time. With Bankimchandra Chatterji's novels, then being serialized in Bankim's own monthly *Bangadarshan* (The Mirror of Bengal), the problem was different: Rabi's elders held on to each issue for themselves. Bankim's impact on Bengal, in the 1870s and 1880s especially, was tremendous. In Tagore's words, Bankim took the Bengali heart 'by storm':

Nowadays anyone who wishes may swallow the whole of *Chandrashekhar* or *Bishabriksha* [The Poison Tree] at a mouthful. But the process of longing and anticipating, month after month, of spreading over wide intervals the concentrated joy of each short reading, of revolving every instalment over and over in the mind while watching and waiting for the next; the combination of craving and satisfaction, of burning curiosity with its appeasement: those drawn-out delights, none will ever taste again.

During this period Rabi grew very close to his brother Jyotirindranath, to whose heterodox influence he would often pay tribute. His brother never forced him in anything. If he had, said Rabindranath at seventy-one, 'I would have moulded myself into something satisfactory to society, but it would not have been anything like me.' Music was their first common bond. Looking back nostalgically, Tagore recalled an enchanted tableau:

At the end of the day a mat and pillow were spread on the terrace. Nearby was a thick garland of *bel* flowers on a silver plate, in a wet handkerchief a glass of iced water on a saucer, and some fragrant *pan* [betel] in a bowl. My sister-in-law would bathe, dress her hair and come and sit with us. Jyotidada [elder brother Jyoti] would come out with a silk *chadar* thrown over his shoulders, and draw a bow across his violin, and I would sing in my clear treble voice. For providence had not yet taken away the gift of voice it had given me, and under the sunset sky my song rang out across the house-tops. The south wind came in great gusts from the distant sea, the sky filled with stars.

Jyoti, Rabi and a friend spent days at the piano. 'Showers of melody would stream from his fingers,' the middle-aged Tagore remembered, while he and his friend sat on either side, busily fitting words to the tunes, so as to help hold them in the memory. 'This was how I served my apprenticeship in song composition.' Among the many influences on the group were the humorous, often topical and sometimes ribald songs of the *jatra* (operatic) performers enjoyed by the less respectable classes. From the start of his career as a composer Rabindranath drew on every kind of musical style, with less and less inhibition – one reason for the immense popularity of his melodies, not just in Bengal but India-wide.

Some time in 1875–76, ignoring family doubts, Jyotirindranath took Rabi out of Calcutta to the Tagore estates in East Bengal, of which he was then manager. For the first time Rabindranath saw Shelidah, the unmapped village at the confluence of two great branches of the Ganges that would be his headquarters during some of his most fruitful periods as a writer. (Here in 1912 he began the translations that won him the Nobel prize.) As manager himself in the 1890s he would have the run of a substantial and handsome estate house built in the 1880s. [pl.23] But when he and his brother came, they stayed in the old house that had belonged to an indigo planter. The planter was said to have been Mr Shelley, after whom the tiny village was named.

Downstairs, where the indigo factory had once been, was now the zamindari office of the Tagore estates. Upstairs was the zamindar's living quarters with a very large terrace, and beyond that tall casuarina trees which had grown in tandem with the increasing prosperity of the planters. But where were the sahibs now? Like many old buildings in India, the disused factory felt as if it were haunted. In due course its ruins were swept away by the changing course of the River Padma that has devoured so much of East Bengal's history. In 1940 Tagore pondered:

Where is now the indigo factory's steward, that 'messenger of death'? Where the troop of bailiffs, loins girded up and *lathis* [truncheons] on shoulder?

Where is the dining hall with its long tables, where the sahibs rode back from their business in the town and turned night into day? The feasting reached its height, the dancing couples whirled round the room, the blood coursed madly through the veins in the swelling intoxication of champagne – and the authorities never heard the appealing cries of the wretched ryots [peasants], . . . [Today] the high casuarina trees bend and sway in the wind, and sometimes at midnight the grandsons and granddaughters of the former ryots see the ghosts of the sahibs wandering in the deserted waste of garden.

What Tagore did not mention, but must have brooded on, was the role in all this of his grandfather Dwarkanath – that 'stoney-hearted zamindar' who had dealt so profitably in indigo a century before.

In Shelidah Rabi learnt to ride, on a pony provided by his brother. He was also taken tiger-hunting, once on foot and once by elephant; Jyotirindranath was a good shot with a rifle. And of course the isolation was ideal for writing poetry. Rabi took a fancy to the idea of writing verse in ink made from pressed flowers. He designed a machine with a cup-shaped wooden sieve and a pestle revolving in it via an arrangement of ropes and pulleys. With his brother's co-operation and the skills of a local carpenter, the device was built – and proved an utter flop. 'This was the only occasion in my life on which I tried my hand at engineering . . . from that time I have not so much as laid hands on any kind of instrument, not even on a sitar or an *esraj*.' (Astonishingly for someone so musical, Tagore never played an instrument of any kind.)

Back in Calcutta, Jyotirindranath encouraged Rabi's patriotism. He formed a secret society which met in a tumble-down building in an obscure Calcutta lane. The meeting was held in darkness, the talk was in whispers and the watchword was a Vedic mantra; the centrepiece was a copy of the *Vedas* wrapped in silk with two skulls on either side containing candles (representing the eyes of dead India). Much hot air was generated. Rabi's most revolutionary *act* was to read one of his poems at the Hindu Mela in 1877. It contrasted the glitter of Lord Lytton's Durbar in Delhi, celebrating Queen Victoria's accession as empress of India, with the skeletons then scarring the land as a result of a terrible famine. (It was at this Durbar that a Tagore from the 'loyal' branch of the family became a maharaja; while Maharshi Debendranath was sent a certificate from Queen Victoria honouring him as 'Son of the Late Esteemed Baboo Dwarkanath Tagore' and 'Head of the Conservative Brahmoo'.) In 1912, Rabindranath remarked self-mockingly: 'although my poem lacked none of the fire appropriate to my age, there were no signs of consternation in the ranks of the authorities from commander-in-chief down to commissioner of police. Nor did any letter to *The Times* allude to apathy among the men on the spot in dealing with such impudence and go on in tones of sorrow more than anger to predict the downfall of the British Empire.'

His literary idol was then Biharilal Chakravarti, a poet in his forties known for his exquisite lyrics (today unread). Rabi began to visit his house at all times of the day and evening. He would listen to Biharilal reciting from his two favourites, Valmiki's *Ramayana* and the writings of Kalidasa. Once, after declaiming a sonorous description of the Himalayas by Kalidasa, he told Rabi: 'The succession of long "a" sounds here is not an accident. The poet has deliberately repeated this sound all the way from *Devātmā* down to *Nagadhirāja* as an aid to realizing the glorious expanse of the Himalayas.'

Kadambari, Jyotirindranath's wife, admired Biharilal Chakravarti's poetry passionately. She also admired her brother-in-law Rabi, who was almost the same age as she was. (Kadambari was about nine when she married Jyotirindranath in 1868 and came to Jorasanko.) But in order to keep Rabi's vanity in check, she pretended *not* to admire either his poems or his looks; indeed at the beginning she discouraged contact of any kind. In a poem written in 1939, clearly auto-biographical, Tagore wrote:

Hesitantly I tried to come a little close
  To her in a striped sari, my mind in a whirl;
But there was no doubting her frown – I was a child,
  I was not a girl, I was a different breed.

During the 1870s, a highly affectionate, teasing, somewhat childish relationship grew up between Kadambari, who remained childless and somewhat lonely, and the budding poet Rabi, especially after the death of his mother Sharada in 1875. Without doubt, Kadambari was the deepest female influence on Rabindranath's youth.

Whereas music drew him to Jyotirindranath, with Kadambari literature was the first bond. She seems to have read almost anything Rabi wrote as soon as he wrote it. And she liked to hear him read the work of others, particularly the novels of Bankim. When a new issue of Bankim's *Bangadarshan* reached Jorasanko, it came first to Kadambari. She would immediately send for Rabi and abandon her usual midday nap. 'There were no electric fans then, but as I read I shared the benefits of my sister-in-law's hand fan', he delicately recalled when he was eighty. (This is the charged, semi-erotic atmosphere, so wonderfully captured by Satyajit Ray in *Charulata*, his film based on Tagore's 1901 novella *Nashtanirh*, that described himself, Jyotirindranath and Kadambari.)

Rabi named Kadambari Hecate, after the Greek goddess associated with the night. She may have returned the compliment by naming him Bhanu, meaning 'sun' (as does Rabi). At any rate he adopted Bhanu Singh as a pseudonym when he published his first significant poetry in 1877. His reason was that Bhanu Singh sounded like some old Vaishnava poet – which suited Rabi's purpose. He had become intrigued by the story of Chatterton, the eighteenth-century English boy-poet who had passed off his poems as the work of a fifteenth-century monk, been ostracized when the deception was revealed, and committed suicide. What Chatterton's poetry was like, his Bengali imitator had no idea, but the 'melodramatic element' in the story fired Rabi's imagination: 'Leaving aside suicide, I girded my loins to emulate young Chatterton.' He pretended to discover the work of an old Vaishnava poet, Bhanu Singh, while rummaging in the Brahmo Samaj library. A friend who read the manuscript was ecstatic and declared that it must be published. When Rabi revealed the truth – that he was the author – his friend's face fell and he muttered, 'Yes, yes, they're not half bad.' The poems were published pseudonymously in *Bharati*, the family magazine started in 1877. A Bengali close to the Tagore family then in Germany read them and apparently included Bhanu Singh in his PhD thesis on the lyric poetry of Bengal, giving him a 'place of honour as one of the old poets, such as no modern writer could have aspired to' – to quote Tagore's wryly amused words. (The PhD was duly awarded.)

Although Tagore preserved these pseudonymous poems in his collected works, he did not think highly of them. In his memoirs he swore that he himself would not have been deceived by them, because their sentiments did not pass muster, whatever their felicity of style. 'Any attempt to test Bhanu Singh's verse by its ring would have revealed base metal.'

As a literary critic he was now reading voraciously in Bengali and, less confidently, in English. *Bharati* offered a platform, and he eagerly filled its pages. His maiden contribution was an attempt to reveal base metal in Michael Madhushudan Datta's blank-verse epic of the 1860s, an attack that Tagore later condemned as 'impudent'. Other articles, published in 1878–79, included 'The Anglo-Saxons and Anglo-Saxon literature', 'The Normans and Anglo-Norman literature', 'Petrarch and Laura', 'Dante and his Poetry', 'Goethe', and 'Chatterton'.

Some of these pieces were written on the other side of India, at Ahmedabad. In early 1878, the Maharshi had decided that his wayward youngest son should go to England, in the hope that he would train as a barrister. His second son Satyendranath, the ICS officer, was due for leave in September in England, where he had already sent his wife and children; Rabi would accompany him. But he needed to have some preparatory contact with the thinking and customs of the West. And so in May Rabindranath had been despatched to his brother in western India.

Satyendranath was then a judge, and his quarters were magnificent. He lived in the Shahi Bagh, a seventeenth-century palace constructed by Prince Khurram, later the Mughal Emperor Shah Jahan, builder of the Taj Mahal. In front of it was a broad terrace stretching down to the Sabarmati River, only knee-deep in the summer, meandering over an ample bed of sand. (Close by, curiously enough, Gandhi would establish his first ashram in India in 1915, just after leaving Tagore's ashram at Shantiniketan.) Here and there along the terrace were stone-built water-tanks. When his brother went off to court, Rabi was left absolutely alone in the vast expanse of the palace with only the cooing of the pigeons for company. He wandered curiously and compulsively from room to echoing room and imagined that the stones of the tanks held wonderful secrets of the luxurious bathing-halls of the Mughal begums. In his thirties the conceit inspired one of his best-known stories, 'The Hungry Stones', based on the Shahi Bagh.

Inside his brother's chamber, within niches in the wall, he discovered books. One was a gorgeous edition of Tennyson, with large print and numerous dramatic drawings by Gustave Doré. Rabi's English was not yet fluent: 'That book, for me, was as silent as the palace, and in much the same way I wandered among its coloured plates. I could make nothing of the text, but it nevertheless spoke to me in inarticulate cooings rather than words.' This was no frilly figure of speech: Tagore's entire view of England, and of Europe as a whole, was then highly romanticized. Half-grasping Tennyson's poetry in a Mughal palace was bound to produce a puzzling distortion of English reality. As long as he lived, Tagore never entirely shook off a tendency to idealize the West. He spent two or three months in this grand solitude. Then his brother dispatched him to Bombay to stay with a Marathi friend, in order to give him less bookish contact with things western. Atmaram Turkhud was a well-known physician and social reformer, not a Brahmo but highly sympathetic to Brahmo ideals. But it was his sixteen-year-old daughter Anapurna, recently returned from England and an extremely sophisticated girl, who affected Rabi deeply. There is not a word about her in *My Reminiscences* – his discretion was total – but in his sixties and seventies Tagore spoke and wrote more openly.

Clearly Ana was bowled over by Rabi. Once, after she had listened to him singing a song in the *Bhairavi* mode of early dawn in which he had entwined his special name for her, Nalini, she said: 'Poet, I think that even if I were on my death-bed your songs would call me back to life.' Another time she asked him 'very particularly' to remember one thing: 'You must never wear a beard. Don't let anything hide the outline of your face.' Rabi, however, was so innocent of women – Kadambari was the only one he knew well – and so extravagantly dreamy, shy and self-obsessed, that he failed to understand her intentions fully.

Later he laughed at his naivety, but he never laughed at Ana's love for him. In old age he told a Bengali friend:

I could never insult her memory by putting a common label on her love for me. I have passed through various experiences of fire and shadow, the warp and woof with which Providence weaves its strange webs of human personality. But one thing I can say with honest pride: that I have never made light of the love of a woman no matter how she had loved me. I have always been grateful for it all, always looked upon it as a grace – a favour . . . Her gift of blooms may fade with time, yes, but the memory of their fragrance, never.

7 England
(1878–1880)

Before I came to England, I supposed it was such a small island and its inhabitants were so devoted to higher culture that from one end to the other it would resound with the strains of Tennyson's lyre.

letter,
England, 1878/79

The seventeen year old from Calcutta who reached England in early October 1878 had hardly met an English person, let alone made friends with one. [pl.8] What he knew of England was at one remove (or more) from reality: learnt from English literature, from 'England-returned' Indians like Ana Turkhud and from his anglophile brother Satyendranath, who worked amongst Englishmen. In those days, Tagore recalled half a century later during his last visit to England, 'We believed with all our simple faith that even if we rebelled against foreign rule we should have the sympathy of the West.'

The contrast with his worldly, wealthy grandfather's first visit to England in 1842 could not have been greater. Dwarkanath dined with Queen Victoria, the prime minister and the greatest writers of the day; Rabindranath with general practitioners, private tutors and other Bengalis. Dwarkanath stayed at the best hotels; Rabindranath lived in lodging houses, as a paying guest and with his family. Dwarkanath toured the country, including Scotland; Rabindranath saw central London, Brighton, Torquay, Tunbridge Wells and little else. Most of all, Dwarkanath relished life in England; Rabindranath was much more divided.

This emerged graphically from the letters he wrote home, which contained passages of detailed observation of western life never subsequently bettered by him. Shot through with sharply-expressed opinions both for and against, they were a piquant travelogue. How utterly different would have been Tagore's reception in London in 1912 if he had offered these letters for English consumption, instead of his serenely disembodied *Gitanjali*!

As an adult Tagore suppressed parts of the letters, and they were never translated into English in his lifetime. They were published in *Bharati* in 1879–80 and as a book in 1881, *Yurop Prabashir Patra* (Letters from an Exile in

Europe). But in *My Reminiscences*, when Tagore was fifty, he wrote:

> Now it is beyond my power to call them back. They were nothing but the
> outcome of youthful bravado. At that age the mind refuses to admit that its
> greatest cause for pride is in its power to understand, to accept, to respect;
> and that modesty is the best means of enlarging its domain. To admire and
> praise becomes a sign of weakness or surrender, and the desire to cry down
> and hurt and demolish with argument gives rise to a kind of intellectual
> fireworks. These attempts of mine to establish my superiority by revilement
> might have amused me today, had not their want of straightforwardness and
> common courtesy been too painful.

There were, it was true, certain passages in the letters that might have justified
this, but on the whole Tagore's later self-criticism told more about the tone he
adopted for his translation of *Gitanjali* in 1912 than it did about the tone of his
teenage letters.

His letters and memoirs remain the best source for Rabindranath's sixteen or
so months in England. There is also a third source: the memories of his niece
Indira, daughter of Satyendranath, who, as we know, had been dispatched to
England in 1877 with her brother Suren and her remarkable mother. Later
Indira became one of her uncle's confidantes in the family (and among the most
beautiful of the Tagore women, surpassed perhaps only by her mother). In 1878
she was just five years old (and Suren was a year older). Nevertheless, decades
after, she retained fresh memories of Rabi Kaka (Uncle Rabi) in the family
house at Medina Villas, between Brighton and Hove, where he settled for
several months. She recollected music most of all, which would be the strongest
link between uncle and niece for over sixty years. [pl.18]

Her vivacious uncle sang fashionable Victorian songs, for instance, such as
'Won't you tell me Mollie darling', and 'Darling, I am growing old'. (Back in
Calcutta, Indira accompanied him on piano when he sang 'Come into the
garden, Maud', 'Goodbye sweetheart, goodbye' and 'In the gloaming'.) He also
had a comic style of singing a particular Hindi song. 'He would start singing in
common time. Then gradually the tempo would get faster and faster until his
lips became a mere trembling line, and we would rock with laughter.' And he
liked to set to tunes – à la Gilbert and Sullivan – the initials of well-known
Indian railway companies, E.I.R. (East Indian Railway), G.I.P.R. (Great Indian
Peninsula Railway) and so on.

This last was an apt expression of the adult Tagore's feeling about the root
differences between eastern and western music. The railways were of course a
western import into India; they had absolutely no connection with the cultural

traditions of the subcontinent. Their initial purpose was wholly utilitarian, though later they acquired their own romance – in the minds of Europeans in India at any rate. To Tagore, western and Indian classical music belonged in compartments as separate as those of railways and religion in India – an opinion he would hold with deepening conviction as he aged. In his memoirs he wrote:

> European music seems to be intertwined with the material life of Europe, so that the text of its songs may be as various as life itself. If we attempt to put our tunes to the same variety of uses they tend to lose their significance, and become ludicrous; for our melodies are meant to transcend everyday life and carry us deep into Pity, high into Aloofness: to reveal the core of our being, impenetrable and ineffable, where the devotee may find his ashram, or even the epicurean his paradise, but where there is no room for the busy man of the world.

His visit to England first imprinted this distinction on his mind. In Brighton and in London he heard the cadenzas of a prima donna, in some of which she imitated bird cries with extraordinary skill. Rabindranath found the experience comical and pointless. (Perhaps his grandfather Dwarkanath had once felt the same, judging from his comments to Max Müller in Paris, quoted in the Introduction; but he persevered, and came to love opera, even taking singing lessons in Italian.) 'Music should capture the delight of birds' songs, giving human form to the joy with which the bird sings. But it should not try to be a representation of such songs', Tagore told Romain Rolland in 1930. Indian rain-songs did not attempt to imitate the sound of falling raindrops, he noted; instead they conveyed something of the feeling associated with the rainy season. In a poem he wrote in the 1890s, 'Gan Bhanga' (Broken Song), a king, who is a musical connoisseur, requests an old court singer to 'give us a song as songs ought to be' – not like the song that he has just heard, which is 'all tricks and games, like a cat hunting a bird', sung by a pyrotechnical young singer. 'In our country a correct and artistic exposition of the melody is the main object, all effort is concentrated upon it', Tagore asserted in *My Reminiscences*. 'Our connoisseurs are content if they hear the song; in Europe, they go to hear the singer.' Whether Tagore was correct or not, western and Indian music – and their incompatibilities – would be a leitmotif of his entire English visit.

After spending a short time in a school in Brighton and Christmas with his family, he was taken away to London by a friend of his elder brother, who felt he was making little progress towards becoming a barrister. There he would stay during most of 1879, with a break to visit Devon, where his sister-in-law had taken a house, and, most probably, time spent with some cousins living in

Tunbridge Wells. (They were from the Pathuriaghat branch of the family, daughters of the Tagore who had been disinherited for converting to Christianity.)

According to *My Reminiscences*, London was a grim and solitary experience until the last few months. But judging from the letters he wrote home, he was sometimes gregarious. There is quite a discrepancy between Tagore's two accounts. The middle-aged Rabindranath seems to have disavowed the gay young Rabindranath, ignoring altogether the parties and dances and fashionable ladies that preoccupied the letter-writer.

Undoubtedly London did have its hard and lonely side. Rabindranath had been living in a home from home, looked after by his sister-in-law, with two delightful children to fuss over and no studies. Now he was stuck in one stuffy, sparsely-furnished room in Regent's Park in bleak midwinter, having to fend for himself. 'Sometimes Indians would come to see me and, though my acquaintance with them was but slight, when they rose to leave I wanted to hold them back by their coat-tails.' Later he lived for a short time in the house of an exam-coach called Barker, a former priest with a pet dog which he kicked at the slightest provocation. He and his mild little wife quarrelled quietly and monosyllabically over the most trivial matters, such as the number of potatoes he should have with his meat, while an embarrassed Tagore looked on. 'Once Mrs Barker was playing the piano to me and Mr Barker came in and said, "When are you going to stop?" "I thought you had gone out," said Mrs Barker. She stopped playing. After that, whenever I asked her to play the piano, Mrs Barker would say, "I'll play to you whenever that horrible man is out of the house."'

But around the same time he also attended a fancy-dress ball. One girl there was dressed as a snow-maiden, her whole body covered with sparkling snow-white beads. Another was dressed as a Muslim girl, with red flowery trousers, swathes of silk above them, and a sort of topee on her head. Yet another was wearing a sari and bodice with a *chadar* around her shoulders – very fetching, thought Rabindranath. And yet another was dressed as an English maidservant – 'and her looks were such that only servant's clothes would have suited her.' He went in the costume of a Bengal zamindar, clothes and pugree made of velvet stitched with gold thread. Some friends had persuaded him to wear the typical beard and moustache too, and one or two ladies had complimented him on the choice prior to the ball. (Obviously they did not agree with Ana Turkhud.) But at the ball itself he was ostracized. No women would acknowledge him in his beard and moustache. They shook hands with everyone except him: 'Any that I approached shied away.' He was so 'enraged and grieved and mortified' that he there and then tore off the offending facial hair and stuffed it in his pocket. 'Things went better after that . . . '

Rabindranath had only just come to accept that he was attractive to women. Kadambari, his sister-in-law in Bengal, with her deliberate disapproval, had convinced him he looked ordinary. When English girls complimented him, he began to worry about the apparent divergence in standards of taste between England and back home. (The idea popped up some years later in his amusing short story about an unscrupulous Bengali trying to become a barrister in London, who secretly acquires an English wife in addition to his Bengali wife.) He wrote chirpily to Calcutta about one girl, a Miss Scott:

You perhaps find it hard to believe that any person with good eyesight could fall for anyone with a face like mine. But that is just prejudice on your part. I can see the effect of my face in the mirror of her pretty face. Not bad, eh? I daresay none of *your* heads would turn at the sight of my face – but maybe you haven't got heads.

He was flattered, but he was critical too. He was drawn to the freedom and energy of some women he met – though perhaps a little frightened of them – but Victorian fashions, flirting and obsession with physical beauty did not much appeal to him. Again and again in his letters (though not in his graver memoirs) he expressed his irritation, tinged with disapprobation and a certain pity for the women. 'I really cannot bear this posing and posturing, this draping of arms and legs, this refining of the voice, this sweetening of the laugh . . . all to catch men!' At one dance he found himself pulled 'like a magnet' towards the only dark-skinned face in the room, 'marked with the sweet, demure character of our Bengali girls' – only to be told by someone that she was in fact English. After that, he did not have the nerve to introduce himself.

His first impressions of the men were generally unfavourable, though he modified them somewhat as time went on. Mr Barker, the coach, was one such. He also got to know a middle-aged general practitioner, Dr M– (he did not give his surname), and his brother. Both of them patronized him as a 'complete ignoramus'. The brother stopped outside a shop window and proceeded to explain that these things called photographs were made by machine, not drawn by a human hand. A crowd gathered, and Rabindranath was very embarrassed. In a watch-shop the brother took the trouble to explain what wonderful inventions watches were. Dr M– himself, a full-blown Little Englander, roused sarcasm in the eighteen-year-old letter-writer:

He is so lacking in imagination that he cannot believe that those who do not subscribe to the Ten Commandments are not going to lie without compunction. This is his main argument against the morals of non-

Christians. A non-Englishman, a non-Christian – he is absolutely foxed by such an extraordinary creation! He cannot imagine how it could be called human. His motto is 'Gladly would he learn and gladly teach', but though I can see that he has much to learn, he doesn't seem to have much to teach. He knows remarkably little about the literature of his own country: all he does is read a couple of journals each month and pick up a bit of superficial knowledge that way. I have gradually realized that he thinks of us as uneducated, because he cannot imagine that an Indian *can* be educated. In winter the women here stick their hands into a round article called a muff; when I first arrived in England I asked Dr M— what that unfamiliar article was for. He practically fell through the floor at my question, he couldn't believe that I didn't know what a muff was. How uneducated could I be!

Tagore concluded devastatingly: 'Dr M— must have thought, "It's quite absurd that someone who doesn't know what a muff is has read Shakespeare!"'

But his most scathing criticism Rabindranath reserved for his own countrymen in London. He called them by a name coined by his brother Dwijendranath in Calcutta: *ingabangas*, a barely translatable expression meaning anglicized or England-knowing Bengalis – anglomaniacs. One of his letters dissected their 'lifestyle' (as it would now be termed) with gleeful satire. The same tone would appear constantly in the short stories he wrote about *ingabangas* from the 1890s onwards. Coming from most Bengalis in England then, the tone might have been hypocritical, but in Rabindranath's case he did not share any of the traits of the species he was satirizing – nor did he aspire to. He understood his targets extremely well from personal experience, even had some sympathy for their predicament, but he could genuinely stand back from them, observe and analyse.

To know the *ingabanga* truly, one must observe him in three situations. One must see how he behaves with Englishmen; how he behaves with Bengalis; and how he behaves with fellow England-knowing Bengalis. To see an England-knowing Bengali face to face with an Englishman is really a sight to gladden your eyes. The weight of courtesy in his words is like a burden making his shoulders droop; in debate he is the meekest and mildest of men; and if he is compelled to disagree, he will do so with an expression of extreme regret and with a thousand apologies. An England-knowing Bengali sitting with an Englishman, whether he is talking or listening, will appear in his every gesture and facial movement to be the acme of humility. But catch him with his own countrymen in his own sphere, and he will display real temper. One who has lived three years in England will regard himself as infinitely above one who has spent a mere one year here. Should the former type of resident happen to argue with the latter, one may observe the 'three-year' man exert his prowess. Each word he utters, and each inflection he gives it, sounds like a dictum personally dictated to him by the lips of Goddess Saraswati. Anyone who dares to contradict him he will bluntly label 'mistaken', or even 'ignorant' – to his face . . .

In such an atmosphere, it took some courage and aplomb for an Indian to state the truth about India to an English audience. This was what Satyendranath Tagore did, watched by his brother, at a meeting of the National Indian Association in February 1879. The association was composed chiefly of 'old India hands' and English people interested in India with a sprinkling of natives, who met to hear lectures and hold discussions aimed at improving understanding between Britain and India. Satyendranath's speech was mild and low-key, but it was not pious. Addressing himself to the English living in England, he said that they could have no idea of the wide gulf that separated the two peoples in India. One reason for this gulf, he said, was that the Englishman in India felt himself to be a member of the ruling race, and from this point of view looked down upon the natives. Another was 'the insular habits of John Bull and his refusal to forego his customs and habits'. In England, Satyendranath added – with more hope than strict accuracy – there was 'no trace' of the feelings between the races that existed in India.

There was no argument afterwards – but the minutes of the meeting suggest that the speech was not exactly welcomed. Sir William Muir, K.C.S.I.*, replying, admitted the great obstacles between Englishman and Indian in India, but 'trusted that those mentioned by Mr Tagore were by far the least.' In Muir's view, the chief obstacle was that Englishmen were not permitted to get close to the families of Indians – because of the restrictions on Indian women.

Later that year Rabindranath quoted his brother's talk in an essay he wrote for an appreciative Henry Morley, the educator and contributor to Dickens' magazines, whose classes in English literature Tagore attended at University College. Otherwise he had little to do with politics as such, apart from spending some time in the Visitors' Gallery of the House of Commons. His impressions of Parliament were mixed. The rowdy behaviour and name-calling by MPs astonished him. He noted a general antipathy towards the Irish MPs. In a debate on Indian affairs he spotted not more than nine or ten members in the chamber until it was time to vote. Party spirit was usually the deciding factor in a debate, he decided. 'Conservatives are blindly dogmatic. Liberals seem

*Knight Commander of the Order of the Star of India

reasonable – they do what they consider to be right. That is why they have such differences of opinion among themselves', he wrote home.

The two speakers who impressed him most were John Bright and W. E. Gladstone. He heard Bright speak both inside and outside Parliament. Sixty-two years later, in 1941, in his last lecture Tagore said: 'The large-hearted, radical liberalism of those speeches, overflowing all narrow national bounds, made so deep an impression on my mind that something of it lingers even today'. Gladstone, he saw, could fill the chamber. Rabindranath contrasted him with an Irish member in one of his letters. The Irishman gesticulated and spoke fast, thereby making an impression but not a permanent one. Gladstone emphasized a point by bending forward with both fists clenched 'as if he were wringing out each word.' Such words entered people's minds by 'breaking down all the doors and windows.'

The Houses of Parliament were almost the only great institution described by Tagore in his letters. He was never a sightseer, but his lack of curiosity about London's other great sights – he wrote not a word about Westminster Abbey, the British Museum, or Trafalgar Square, for instance – was surely significant. In later life, he would write not a single detailed description of any building, whether sacred or secular, seen during his worldwide travels; and only rarely would he write about those in India.

More surprising was his lack of reaction to the glories of the English countryside, given his obsession with nature in Bengal. It is not true that Tagore never wrote about them, as Nirad Chaudhuri claimed – but he did so infrequently. He was thrilled, for example, by the flower-covered meadows, shady pine woods and rocky coastline around Torquay – and deeply grateful to escape the smoky air of London, which made him feel 'as if a seam of coal [had] formed in [his] head'. He wrote a poem, 'Magnatari' (The Sunken Boat), sitting on a slab of rock overhanging the ocean. (Later he wished he had drowned it at birth.) Love of Devon was what made him suggest Devon to Leonard Elmhirst forty-five years later, as the site for his educational experiment at Dartington.

This digression was in the summer of 1879. Subsequently he was obliged to return to London where in November he enrolled at University College. One consolation was Henry Morley's classes, in which he read and enjoyed *Antony and Cleopatra*, *Coriolanus* and the *Religio Medici*; another was a classmate, Loken Palit. He was the son of Satyendranath's friend who had taken Rabindranath from Brighton to London in January. They immediately got on well and remained friends in Bengal, where Palit joined the ICS and served up-country in the *mofussil*, the boondocks of Bengal. There, miles from civilization, Rabindranath would sometimes meet Palit and talk until dawn. 'Many an extraordinary flight of imagination began in his bungalow in the remote *mofussil.*' The earliest of these tête-à-têtes was in London, in the University College library, where Palit would burst forth in laughter at the least provocation. In mid-life Tagore remembered half-repentantly the girl students sitting near the two of them, a 'multitude of reproachful blue eyes which vainly showered disapproval on our merriment.'

It was Palit who helped him in a matter close to his heart: Bengali versus English. Rabindranath had agreed to teach his landlord's daughter Bengali in return for her help in correcting his English. When he started out he confidently assumed that Bengali spelling was far more regular than English spelling. But he quickly realized that 'force of habit had blinded me to its transgressions.' His friend Loken, to his surprise, cleverly discerned rules in Bengali orthography.

By now he was living with the Scotts, a doctor's family, at 10 Tavistock Square in Bloomsbury, within easy walking distance of University College. The doctor had six children, two sons and four daughters, two of whom were only small. There were also three maids in the house and a dog called Toby, old and blind in one eye. When the daughters heard that a strange Indian was about to enter their home, two of them went off to stay with a relative. They returned only when the third daughter, the eldest, informed them 'that I was harmless.'

These few months in the Scott house greatly improved Tagore's impressions of the English. This was clear from his letters; in his memoirs he dwelt on it:

> Mrs Scott treated me as a son, and the heartfelt kindness of her daughters was something rare even from one's own relations . . . One thing struck me when living in this family: human nature is everywhere the same. We are fond of saying, and I also then believed, that the devotion of an Indian wife to her husband is something unique, not to be found in Europe. But I at least was unable to discern any difference between Mrs Scott and an ideal Indian wife.

Much later, he confessed to a Bengali friend, speaking of the doctor's two attractive daughters: 'I have not a vestige of doubt that they had both fallen in love with me. How I wish I had the moral courage to face up to it when there was yet time!' Instead he wrote a poem when he returned to Calcutta, the last two lines of which he omitted from the published version:

> And O the regret and shame of it!
> I came for two days to this land – only to break a gentle heart!

One of the games he and the girls played was a table-turning seance. They all placed their fingers on a small tea-table, and it went capering about the room.

Soon everything they touched began to quake and quiver. Mrs Scott, as a good Christian woman, did not quite approve but tolerated the fun – until, that is, they laid hands on Dr Scott's chimney-pot hat. 'She could not bear the idea of Satan even momentarily having anything to do with her husband's headgear.'

Music was the chief link between Rabindranath and the daughter called Lucy. She played the piano and he sang in a fine tenor voice; sometimes she sang too. In such romantic circumstances he swiftly picked up and came to like a string of English songs. But when he sang them to his family in Calcutta, they found them comical (somewhat as he found western operatic singing). Some of these songs were later transmogrified by him into songs for operas and dramas.

He did not say if (like Dwarkanath with Max Müller in the 1840s) he tried to introduce Lucy Scott to Indian singing. But he did mention some excruciating occasions when he had to sing an Indian song in company. He deeply resented being mocked in this way – as he rightly saw it – but had to give in out of politeness. The worst instance, which became a long-running farce during his visit, was with the overbearing India-returned widow of a high official, who liked to address him as 'Ruby'. 'An Indian friend of hers had composed a doleful poem in English in memory of her husband', and had indicated that it should be chanted in the raga *Behag*. Each time Ruby met the lady at a social gathering, out would come printed copies of this composition and the unavoidable request to sing after dinner. Just before Rabi left London she sent him a pressing telegram and he felt obliged to journey into the suburbs in bitterly cold, snowy and foggy weather to see her for the last time. After misadventures with the train and meagre hospitality from the widow, the following morning he found himself standing on the landing of her staircase, facing a closed door, and giving voice to the dreadful dirge. Inside the room, invisible to Rabi, lay one of the widow's guests who, feeling poorly, would not come out. When Rabindranath finally returned to Tavistock Square he had to take to bed himself. 'Dr Scott's girls implored me, on my conscience, not to take this as a sample of English hospitality: it was surely the effect of India's salt.'

In February 1880 the time came for him to leave. His brother's furlough was over and he and his family were returning to India. Originally Rabindranath was to have stayed on in London and acquired a qualification, but now the Maharshi sent instructions that he should come back. The tone of Rabi's letters seems to have worried the conservative patriarch: was Rabi not in danger of forgetting himself in his new-found admiration for western women? Dwijendranath, the eldest son, certainly thought so, for he published critical comments on some of Rabi's later letters in the family magazine *Bharati*. Dwijendranath said, Look at the women of Japan and Bombay/Maharashtra (e.g. Ana Turkhud) – how emancipated they are, yet how traditional. If a woman really loves her husband, she will surely not want to make friends with other men. And anyway, if the writer (i.e. Rabindranath) likes white women so much, why did he feel elated when he set eyes on a dark one? (a reference to the girl Rabindranath thought was Indian, who was actually English). Such was the drift of the eldest brother's not-very-cogent thinking.

As an adult, Rabindranath was by no means immune to such arguments, in fact his whole life would be full of ambivalence towards female independence. He had unstinting sympathy for the plight of Indian women in his writings and other works, but in his life he loved to receive their unswerving devotion. These two attitudes did not necessarily contradict each other, but in practice they often did.

The same may be said of the greatest ideal of his life, the *synthesis* of East and West, which formed in his mind very early. He wrote of it well before his visit to England, in an essay 'Bangalir asha o nairashya' (The hope and despair of Bengalis):

The European idea in which freedom predominates, and the Indian idea in which welfare predominates; the profound thought of the eastern countries and the active thought of the western countries; European acquisitiveness and Indian conservatism; the imagination of the eastern countries and the practical intelligence of the West – what a full character will be formed from a synthesis between these two.

His first visit to the West, for all its awkwardnesses and irritations, had not dented that ideal in his mind, rather it had inflated it. He had come to feel, not unreasonably, that 'East and West [had] met in friendship in my own person.' He continued to believe in this ideal implicitly until his last decade, when India began fighting in earnest to be free of British rule. Even then he would retain much of his youthful faith.

8 Renaissance in Bengal
(1880–1883)

We wrote, we sang, we acted, we poured ourselves out on every side.

My Reminiscences

The four years in Bengal following Rabindranath's return from England and culminating in his first major bereavement, set the pattern for the rest of his life as a creator. Rather than specializing in, say, poetry, he began to produce diverse works in a variety of forms. There were poems, of course, but there were also musical dramas/operas, songs, a novel and essays, not to mention letters. Though most of these works were immature and do not bear comparison with his later works, some are still read and performed.

The first book to appear (though not Tagore's first published book, which had appeared in 1878) was *Bhagna Hriday* (The Broken Heart), poems written partly in England. Afterwards Rabindranath excluded it from his collected works, and when efforts were subsequently made to republish it, he wrote 'Rubbish' on the proofs. (He was always his own best literary critic in Bengali.) Commenting on the book in his memoirs, he quoted a letter he had written when he was thirty:

When I began to write *Bhagna Hriday* I was eighteen – neither in my childhood nor in my youth . . . The curious part . . . is not that I was eighteen, but that everyone around me seemed to be eighteen also; we all flitted about in the same baseless, substanceless world of dream, where even the most intense joys and sorrows seemed insubstantial. There being nothing real against which to weigh them, the trivial did duty for the great.

Nevertheless, the poems brought him a certain celebrity. In 1882, the private secretary of the maharaja of Tripura, a princely state on the eastern border of Bengal (today still part of India but sandwiched between Bangladesh and Burma), came to see Rabindranath at Jorasanko. His wife had recently died and the maharaja had found *Bhagna Hriday* a great consolation. He wished to invest the young poet with the title 'best poet'. It was an auspicious start to a lifelong relationship between Tagore and the rulers of Tripura, who would give Tagore's school financial backing at a crucial stage in its development.

Among the Calcutta literati he began to be known as the Bengal Shelley. (Michael Madhushudan Datta was the Milton of Bengal; Bankim Chatterji was the Scott; someone else was the Byron.) 'This was insulting to Shelley and only likely to get me laughed at.' Even less welcome to him was another cognomen, the Lisping Poet – though in his memoirs Tagore admitted the justice of the name. Looking back on himself at twenty with the hindsight of fifty he wrote:

My attainments were few, my knowledge of life meagre, and in both poetry and prose the sentiment exceeded the substance. There was nothing on which anyone could base praise with any degree of confidence. My dress and behaviour were of the same anomalous description. I wore my hair long and indulged in what was probably an ultra-poetical refinement of manner. In a word, I was eccentric and could not fit myself into everyday life like an ordinary man.

One other thing about *Bhagna Hriday* was significant: its dedication. Translated from Bengali it meant 'for Lady Hé'. In later life Rabindranath admitted in conversation that 'Hé' stood for Hecate, the name he had given to Kadambari.

His relationship with her and with her husband Jyotirindranath was at its most intimate during these two or three years. Soon after his return he and his brother plunged into musical composition, as they had before he went to England – but now both of them were full-fledged composers. [pl.13] The result was an opera, *Valmiki Pratibha* (The Genius of Valmiki), that quickly took its place in the repertoire. It is one of the few dramas by Tagore with an immediate and authentic appeal outside Bengal. There is vigour and variety in it, a vivacity, spontaneity and wonderful gamut of styles and emotions missing from his later dramas.

The story is simple. Valmiki, the author of the *Ramayana*, is said to have been a dacoit-chief. Moved to pity by the grief of one of a pair of cranes after the other had been shot by a hunter, Valmiki broke into verse and composed the epic. In Rabindranath's version, Valmiki is moved by the piteous cry of a young girl caught by his followers, who plan to sacrifice her to the goddess Kali. Valmiki disbands his gang and becomes a wanderer in search of his vocation. Now the goddess Saraswati reveals herself to him: it was she who had taken the form of the young girl. As a boon in reward for his awakened sense of humanity, she gives Valmiki the gift of song, saying: 'Your voice shall resound from land to land and many poets will echo your songs.'

The importance given to both words and melody in *Valmiki Pratibha* had its roots in the special genius of Bengali music. Unlike the words of the songs in classical Hindusthani music (in, for instance the style known as *thumri*), the words in Bengali songs are often fine poetry. The generic name for such songs is *kirtan*, which means celebration, narration. Most *kirtans* concern the loves of Radha and Krishna – it was Vaishnava composers who brought *kirtan* into existence in the sixteenth century – but there is also Kali-*kirtan*. Searching for an analogy, Tagore compared *kirtan* to the classical Hindusthani style. He wrote that the latter was like a collection of jewels in cases: 'It is for the master jeweller, the virtuoso, to open them out and display their contents to the best advantage, with dexterous twists of his expert hands, so as to bring out to the full the sparkle of the gems, the finish of their setting, the beauty of form which has its final value in its own perfection.' The *kirtan*, by contrast, 'is a jewelled garland round the neck of Beauty. The lover has no eyes for the separate values of the adornments of his beloved. The living beauty has absorbed the beauty of each of the ornaments.'

He also compared *kirtan* to the rivers of Bengal, the many tributaries and mouths of the mighty Ganges: 'Its freedom from intricacy of musical phrasing made the *kirtan* an elastic vehicle for the mingling of the voices of emotion, broad as the plains of Bengal herself, wherein the numerous rivers coursing southwards and eastwards in quest for the one Sea, meet and mingle in a network of speaking waters.'

Rabindranath and his brother took the majority of the songs in *Valmiki Pratibha* from this tradition, embellishing it with their own ideas. In addition two English tunes were borrowed for the drinking songs of the dacoit band, and an Irish melody was used for the lament of the wood-nymphs. In February 1881, the first performance was held at Jorasanko with Rabindranath as Valmiki and his niece, Pratibha, in the part of Saraswati. So good was her performance that Rabindranath punningly changed the title from 'Valmiki' to *Valmiki Pratibha*. [pl.14]

Shortly after this, in the same month of 1881, he gave a lecture and wrote an essay that showed how he could branch out in disparate directions simultaneously. The lecture was on 'Music and feeling'. In it he tried to argue, using many examples sung by himself – which must have been a delight to hear – that the chief aim of vocal music was to aid the expression of the meaning of the words. Later, in his memoirs written in 1912, he disagreed with himself and said that melody had taken too submissive a role in Bengali songs. It should, he said, 'follow the example of wives in our country who formally obey their husbands but actually rule them; music, while professedly in attendance on words, should in fact dominate them.' But in the best of his own songs, he did not apply either theory: words and melody are in unique balance.

His essay, by contrast, was entitled 'The death traffic'. It was actually a review of a German book in English translation on Britain's opium trade with China. Rabindranath was scorching: perhaps, in addition to being genuinely outraged, he was settling a score with the shade of his grandfather. Dwarkanath, as we know, had been among those who had shipped Indian opium to China in the early days of Chinese addiction. No doubt his grandson also had in mind some of the bluntly unimaginative Englishmen he had met in the mother country. 'A whole nation, China, has been forced by Great Britain to accept the opium poison – simply for commercial greed', he wrote. 'In her helplessness, China pathetically declared: "I do not require any opium." But the British shopkeeper answered: "That's all nonsense. You must take it."' Tagore cited the example of an Englishman who went into an opium den and spoke to a smoker who confessed that he spent 80 per cent of his income on the drug. When the Englishman told him that he came from England, 'The reply was: "What sort of person is this Queen Victoria? We send her the finest silk and tea; and she sends us instead this poison to kill us." That is the way in which the Chinese people think about the English', Rabindranath commented indignantly.

Such powerful feelings may have played a part in Tagore's cancellation of his second visit to England in April 1881. He and a nephew got as far as Madras on a boat for England. There they turned back, the nephew claiming to be seriously ill. Rabindranath suspected he was simply missing his new wife, but he himself was happy enough to abandon a second attempt at starting a legal career in London. Luckily the Maharshi was sympathetic.

Instead he went to stay with his favourite brother and sister-in-law at Chandannagar (Chandernagore), the French settlement a short way up-river from Calcutta. In 1881, industry, notably jute mills, had not yet established itself on that stretch of the Hooghly (Ganges): the banks were not 'desecrated by cloven-footed commerce', in Tagore's strong words of 1926. He whiled away a happy summer in a riverside villa at Chandannagar known as 'Moran's Garden' (named after an indigo planter, like Shelidah). In the woods he and Kadambari spent hours collecting berries. He went swimming in the river, while she watched and shivered. He composed songs, as well as articles and poetry, reflecting their shared interests. And sometimes he and his brother would drift along in a boat, one singing, the other accompanying on his violin, gradually altering the raga with the time of day as prescribed by the purists: 'Beginning with raga *Purabi*, we went on varying our ragas with the declining day, and saw, on reaching raga *Behag*, that the western sky had pulled down the shutters on its storehouse of golden playthings, and the moon had risen in the east.' Then the three of them would sit out on a quilt spread on the terrace above the river, and be bathed in silvery peace. [pl.11]

Rabindranath was, formally speaking, Kadambari's *debar*, which means her younger brother-in-law and, from Sanskrit, her 'second husband'. This Hindu family relationship was customarily a special one, even in a family as unorthodox as the Tagores. Convention permitted an intimacy not allowed between other in-laws, with an element of danger: 'the possibility that a relationship of a rather deep nature might develop', in the words of Satyajit Ray. His film *Charulata*, based on Rabindranath's own relationship with Kadambari, caught the nuances of this unwestern bond: unmistakably erotic and passionate, but not consciously sexual.

There is also an immaturity in it, as expressed in the poems of *Charulata*. One of these, 'Light of the Moonless Night', concocted by Ray, is the work of the budding poet Amal, the character based on Rabindranath, who is extremely proud of it – as the eighteen-year-old Rabi was proud of *Bhagna Hriday* (The Broken Heart). His own poetry was at that time chock-full of facile conceits, deep on the surface. (Later in the film another character, maturer and more prosaic than Amal, groping for the title of the fictional poem, gets muddled and calls it 'Night of the Moonless Light'.)

Bearing this in mind, how much significance can be attached to an actual poem by Rabindranath, full of obscure anguish, that was probably written in the villa at Chandannagar? The title translates as 'Suicide of a Star'. Not long before this, Kadambari was said to have attempted suicide: there is no evidence, only the statement of a Bengali biographer who knew Tagore. Were it not for the repeated use of the word *jyoti* (light, lustre), the poem could be dismissed as the product of an overwrought twenty-year-old's imagination, like 'Light of the Moonless Night'. But would Rabindranath have made such a pun on Jyotirindranath's name when writing about such a serious subject as suicide? Was he trying to jolt his maverick brother, his favourite, into an awareness of future danger?

The poem was published in *Bharati* and then, in July 1882, in Tagore's first worthwhile volume of original poetry: *Sandhya Sangit* (Evening Songs). Though called songs, the poems were in fact lyrics. They brought him two admirers who had dismissed *Bhagna Hriday* as juvenile. One was Priyanath Sen, a well-read man some seven years older than Rabindranath, who became a friend and critic for many years, besides acting as a go-between for Tagore concerning financial loans and the marriage of one of his daughters. The other was Bankimchandra Chatterji, no less, the grandest figure in Bengali letters. About three weeks after publication, Bankim and Rabindranath were present at a wedding. When the host placed a garland of welcome on Bankim, he took it and placed it round the neck of Rabindranath, saying: 'The wreath to him . . . ; have you not read his *Sandhya Sangit?*' When his host said no, 'the manner in which Bankim spoke of some of the poems was ample reward', Tagore recalled. [pl.9]

Not long after this, following a suggestion of Jyotirindranath, Rabindranath tried to draw Bankim and other distinguished writers into an Academy of Literature. The idea was to compile authoritative technical terms for Bengali and generally to assist the growth of the language. But the reality was a flop: leading writers took little interest. Pandit Vidyasagar refused to join and told Rabindranath: 'My advice to you is to leave us out – you will never accomplish anything with bigwigs; they can never be got to agree with one another.'

Some of the poems in *Sandhya Sangit* were written in a house rented by Jyotirindranath, in the European quarter of Calcutta. (He perhaps wanted to get Kadambari away from gossip in the Jorasanko house.) Here Rabindranath had a remarkable visionary experience. He was up at dawn, as usual, watching the sun rise through the leafy tops of some trees:

As I gazed, all of a sudden a lid seemed to fall from my eyes, and I found the world bathed in a wonderful radiance, with waves of beauty and joy swelling on every side. The radiance pierced the folds of sadness and despondency which had accumulated over my heart, and flooded it with universal light.

That very day the poem 'Nirjharer Swapnabhanga' (The Fountain's Awakening) gushed forth and coursed on like a cascade. The poem ended, but the curtain did not fall upon my joy.

Less loftily, he spent much time with his other sister-in-law and her two children, Indira and Suren, who, returned from England, had found life in the Jorasanko house impossible and had eventually settled in a house in central Calcutta. (Satyendranath, her husband, was back at his post on the other side of India; the children had to be educated in Calcutta; he and his wife therefore spent long periods apart from each other.) 'My mother', Indira wrote later, 'had the quality of centrality, that is the power of attracting people around her'. Rabindranath was most certainly one of her admirers; this sister-in-law, who had the unpronounceable name Jnanadanandini, was the only female Tagore of whom the most famous Tagore was perhaps a little frightened, even in old age. Her house was a lively and artistic one, which had been nicknamed the 'Ingabanga Samaj' by eldest brother Dwijendranath and his conservative circle in Jorasanko, because most of those who gathered there had been partly educated in England.

For two months in the autumn of 1883, Jnanadanandini, the centre of this group, her children Suren and Indira, Rabindranath, and Jyotirindranath and his wife Kadambari, went south. They joined Satyendranath in his spacious bungalow at Karwar, a small town on the western sea-coast just below Goa at the mouth of the Kalanadi River. It was a secluded place, ravishingly beautiful and pregnant with romance for a young poet. Not only were the hills above known to him from Sanskrit literature as the place where the cardamom creeper and the scented sandal tree grew, they were also dotted with old hill-forts built by the great Maratha chieftain Shivaji in the seventeenth century. Below, the crescent-shaped beach, fringed with a forest of casuarinas, 'flung out its arms around the open sea exactly as if eagerly striving to embrace the infinite.'

Here Rabindranath wrote a verse drama, *Prakritir Pratishodh* (Nature's Revenge). The hero was a sannyasi, an ascetic, who was striving to conquer the seductions of nature in order to arrive at a true knowledge of himself. Somewhat as in *Valmiki Pratibha*, a girl, very young, restores the sannyasi to the world 'from communion with the infinite and into the bondage of human affection', as Tagore described it.

Then the sannyasi realizes that the great is to be found in the small, the infinite within the bounds of form, and the eternal freedom of the soul in love. Only in the aura of love does every limit merge with the limitless . . . *Prakritir Pratishodh* may be seen as an introduction to the whole of my future literary work or, rather, to the subject on which all my writings have dwelt: the delight of attaining the infinite within the finite.

And then – to come down to earth in the extremely abrupt words of *My Reminiscences* – 'Shortly after my return from Karwar, I was married. I was twenty-two years old.'

9   Marriage and Bereavement
(1883–1884)

Emptiness is a thing man cannot bring himself to believe in: that which is *not*, is untrue; that which is untrue, is not.

My Reminiscences

Tagore never referred to his wife in *My Reminiscences*. 'I was married': that was all he wrote. Such reticence was not due to delicacy about her feelings, since she had died some ten years before. Nor, on the other hand, was it in the least unusual among men of his time in India: even today, distinguished Indians maintain silence about their wives in print. But coming from Rabindranath Tagore, who broke nearly every other literary convention, it calls for explanation.

The root cause lies in something much stronger than literary convention: social convention. Debendranath, the head of the family, sometimes radical in his religious beliefs, was (as we know) rarely so in matters of social behaviour. Every one of his children was married to someone unknown to him or her, and in the case of his sons, the wives were all child brides. The feelings of the son or daughter in question, though not ignored by the Maharshi, were a minor factor. The question of love was not even considered. [pl.15]

In early 1879, while Rabi was enduring a London winter, Atmaram Turkhud, social reformer of Bombay, visited Calcutta with his two daughters, one of them Ana. Almost certainly he paid a call on the Tagores at Jorasanko and met the head of the Brahmo Samaj. What passed between them was not recorded, but it seems highly likely that marriage between Ana and Rabi was mooted by Atmaram – and rejected by Debendranath. Ana's own feelings may be gauged from the fact that after her marriage (to a Scotsman), she continued to use Nalini, the name Rabindranath had given her, as a literary name: and that one of her nephews was named Rabindranath. Ana died young in Edinburgh in obscurity. It is difficult not to feel a pang of regret that we shall never know what turn she might have given to Rabindranath's life.

There is no record of when the Tagore family's search for Rabindranath's bride began. In old age he told an amusing story about an early expedition.

Word came that the ruler of a principality in the southern presidency of Madras had a suitable daughter. Rabindranath, accompanied by Jyotirindranath, set off to see her. There, in the ruler's palace, they met two young women, one extremely attractive, the other exceedingly plain. Their hopes rose – only to be dashed when they learnt that the first lady was the stepmother of the girl 'on offer'.

In June 1883 the ladies of Jorasanko seem to have taken a hand in the search, as they had with the elder brothers. The hunting party consisted of Satyendranath's wife Jnanadanandini Devi*, Jyotirindranath's wife Kadambari Devi, Rabindranath's young niece Indira, his brother Jyotirindranath, and finally – and probably least significant – Rabindranath himself. They went to Jessore in East Bengal, the favoured source of Tagore brides of Pirali caste. (Both of the sister-in-laws in the party were from Jessore.) Indira, a city girl through and through, had a good time in the village, she remembered. But they found no one suitable to marry Uncle Rabi.

In early September Rabindranath received a letter (in Bengali) from his father, who was then, as so often, in the hills:

Dearest Rabi
   You must come here and see me at once. I would be very happy to see you after such a long while. You had better bring some bedding and a blanket. Show this letter to Jyoti and get your expenses paid from the estate account. Get a second-class return ticket. Accept my affectionate blessing. Sri Debendranath Sharman.

Again there is no evidence of what the Maharshi said to his son. Within three weeks, however, with Rabindranath back in Calcutta, arrangements for his wedding were put in hand. Presumably Debendranath had asked others in Jessore to look out for a bride. Someone – a great-aunt on his late wife's side – had suggested the daughter of an employee on the Tagore estates. She was a Pirali Brahmin, about ten years old, quite thin, not good-looking and almost illiterate; her name was Bhabatarini, which was old-fashioned even in 1883. Rabindranath appears to have accepted his father's choice without meeting her.

The wedding took place at Jorasanko on 9 December 1883. This was unusual in itself for not being held in the bride's home. Moreover there was amazingly little ceremony by Indian standards. Rabindranath had sent out a few invitations to close friends such as Priyanath Sen, in which he wrote obliquely that 'his intimate relative Rabindranath Tagore is to be married' – implying that the real Rabindranath was detached from the event. (Maybe he was also

*Devi was then the Bengali honorific for a married woman, similar to Mrs.

embarrassed.) Of his immediate family, his father, brother Satyendranath and sister Saudamini were definitely *not* present; while Jyotirindranath was present, as was Kadambari. The rituals were naturally those of the Brahmo Samaj. Rabindranath wore a silk shawl from Varanasi (Benares) consecrated for weddings by family tradition, and at one point he sang a song written by his sister Swarnakumari, while eyeing his bashful bride. There was no pomp of any kind.

Bhabatarini stayed about a month in Jorasanko. Her name was changed to one more euphonious: Mrinalini (roughly, 'lotus-like') – suggested not by Rabindranath but by his brother Dwijendranath. On 26 December the Maharshi arrived in the mansion, presented four gold *mohurs* to the newly-weds, conducted prayers for the Brahmo Samaj and departed again five days later. Then Mrinalini was dispatched from Jorasanko to stay in central Calcutta with her much older sister-in-law Jnanadanandini, the centre of the Ingabanga Samaj. The idea was that she should start to be educated. (She was sent to Loreto House, a well-known convent school.) She did not return to live in Jorasanko for more than six months.

There are very few direct clues as to Rabindranath's reaction to this ten-year-old stranger. For rather more than a year after his marriage, he appears to have lived almost entirely separately from his wife. To his friend Priyanath Sen, who had written that he did not want to interrupt the honeymoon, he quipped that since the moon always has phases the question of interruption did not arise. At an exhibition opening in the Indian Museum, where his wife appeared for the first time in public with Jnanadanandini, he caught sight of her while he was passing with a tray of sweetmeats, noticed that she was looking chubbier, and once more embarrassed her by singing 'You make the flowers bloom in the garden of my heart.' (This was reported many years later by a gossipy sister-in-law, not by Rabindranath.) Otherwise, silence.

On the one hand Tagore knew that he was simply following all his brothers in the family tradition, on the other he must have compared Mrinalini unfavourably to Ana Turkhud and the girls he had met in England. Perhaps his silence, then and ever after, reflected the impossibility of resolving this deep conflict in his mind.

He would have seen his wife at Jnanadanandini's house, where he was spending more and more time. There, before his marriage, he wrote the poems published in February 1884 as *Chhabi o Gan* (Pictures and Songs). These he dedicated to Kadambari. One of them was particularly striking. Entitled 'Rahur Prem' (The Love of Rahu), it concerned Rahu, a popular demon in Hindu mythology. Rahu is a bodiless planet in love with the moon; Rahu eternally chases her and occasionally swallows her in an eclipse. The parallel with sexual desire is obvious (though it would not have been obvious to its writer, three or four decades before Freud became known in India). Here is a paraphrase of part of the poem in which Rahu speaks:

I am your companion from the beginning of time, for I am your own shadow. In your laughter, in your tears, you shall sense my dark self hovering near you, now in front, now behind. At the dead of night when you are lonely and dejected, you'll be startled to find how near I am seated by you, gazing into your face.

Wherever you turn I am there, my shadow sweeps over the sky and covers the earth, my piteous cry and my cruel laughter echo everywhere, for I am hunger never appeased, thirst never quenched. I am always there, a dagger in your breast, a poison in your mind, a disease in your body.

I shall chase you like a terror in the day, like a nightmare in the night. Like a living skeleton in a famine I shall stretch my hand before you and pester you to give and give and give. Like a thorn I shall prick you day and night, like a curse I shall haunt you, like fate I shall follow you – as night follows day, as fear follows hope.

Two months after publication, Kadambari Devi committed suicide, aged about twenty-five. On 19 April 1884 she poisoned herself, possibly with an overdose of opium, and died, probably on the morning of 21 April, with eminent doctors in attendance. The police were informed but the body was not sent to the morgue; instead a coroner's court sat at Jorasanko. The report appears to have been destroyed, along with a rumoured letter in which Kadambari explained her reasons for suicide, and all her other letters – presumably on the orders of Debendranath, to avoid scandal. There was no report in the newspapers; in the family account book there was an entry: 'Expenses towards suppressing the news of the death to the press Rs. 52.'

For Rabindranath there could be no suppression. Kadambari's death was the first of a person he had deeply cared for. Though he wept when his mother died in 1875, the impact had not lasted. Over the years death would become his constant companion, living with him on terms of understanding: so much so that quotations from Tagore head each chapter of the classic study *On Death and Dying* by Elisabeth Kübler-Ross, who believed that no one had thought more deeply on death than Tagore. But in 1884, at the age of twenty-three, the experience was world-shattering.

That there could be any gap in life's succession of joys and sorrows was something of which I had no idea. I had seen nothing beyond life, and accepted it as the ultimate truth. When death suddenly came, and in a moment tore a gaping rent in life's seamless fabric, I was utterly bewildered. All around, the trees, the soil, the water, the sun, the moon, the stars, remained as immovably true as before, and yet the person who was as truly there, who, through a thousand points of contact with life, mind and heart, was so very much more true for me, had vanished in an instant like a dream. What a perplexing contradiction! How was I ever to reconcile what remained with that which had gone?

The terrible darkness disclosed to me through this rent, continued to lure me night and day as time went by. I would constantly return to it and gaze at it, wondering what was left to replace what had departed. Emptiness is a thing man cannot bring himself to believe in: that which is *not*, is untrue; that which is untrue, is not. So our efforts to find something where we see nothing are unceasing . . .

Yet amid unbearable grief, flashes of joy sparkled in my mind on and off in a way which quite surprised me. The idea that life is not a fixture came as tidings that helped to lighten my mind. That we are not forever prisoners behind a wall of stony-hearted facts was the thought that kept unconsciously rising uppermost in rushes of gladness. What I had possessed I was made to let go – and it distressed me – but when in the same moment I viewed it as a freedom gained, a great peace fell upon me.

The all-pervading pressure of worldly existence is compensated by death, and thus it does not crush us. The terrible weight of eternal life does not have to be endured by man – this truth came over me that day as a wonderful revelation.

Three, probably four, of Rabindranath's books were dedicated to Kadambari while she lived. After her death he dedicated at least two more. In 1901 he portrayed her almost directly as Charu in *Nashtanirh* (the basis of *Charulata*). For the rest of his life he wrote about her in his poems. In his paintings a mysterious woman's face appeared again and again: he admitted to an artist-friend that she might well be Kadambari, whose 'glowing eyes present themselves before my sight not unoften' when painting, he said. Her presence can also be felt in his songs. (No remotely comparable claim can be made for his wife Mrinalini, to whom he never openly dedicated a book and about whom he wrote only a very few poems explicitly.)

What could have prompted Kadambari to take her own life? Indira, Rabindranath's niece, who was best placed to find out, stated years later that she never knew the reason. But she may have said this simply to dampen speculation. Any answer is bound to be complex and unverifiable. Perhaps it is best to consider four probable contributing elements in turn: the personalities of Jyotirindranath, Rabindranath and Kadambari, and the Tagore family atmosphere as a whole.

Around this time Jyotirindranath was both preoccupied and foolhardy. For one thing his plays were a success on the Bengali stage and with his dashing figure he was a centre of attention. As an actor he was in contact with several actresses, and this might have upset Kadambari. (She was said to have discovered a letter or letters from one of them in his pocket.) More important, following a patriotic impulse he had bought a steamer hulk at auction for 7,000 rupees, had it rebuilt, and started a steamer service in East Bengal, in the Ganges delta downstream from Shelidah. Later he added three more steamers, and expanded the service. Unfortunately for him he was in competition with an experienced British-run company. His patriotic spirit was not enough to save him from his unbusinesslike self. (At one time his line carried passengers free and even offered light refreshments gratis; Indira recalled gorging herself on sweets.) Eventually, in September 1885, one of his steamers fouled the pontoon bridge across the Hooghly at Calcutta and sank, and Jyotirindranath lost a lot of money. Presumably his wife was concerned about the whole venture – not only financially but socially. Rumour had it that she had become depressed after he failed to fetch her for a party at the steamer.

Rabindranath too had moved away from her orbit, both physically and mentally. Gone were the days when they would sit out as a threesome on the roof terrace at Jorasanko or above the river at Chandannagar; Rabi was now living for substantial periods with his other sister-in-law in central Calcutta. Gone too were the poetic outpourings of emotion that they had shared in his teens and in *Bhagna Hriday* (The Broken Heart). Now he was capable of writing a virile poem such as 'Rahur Prem'. What impact might it have had on her impressionable mind, nurtured on the passions of Bankim's novels? She must surely have wondered whether Rabindranath was not casting her, partially at least, in the role of Rahu to his moon. This is certainly how Satyajit Ray visualized Charu in the later stages of *Charulata* as she begins to buckle under the force of her passion for Amal, her handsome poet brother-in-law. Charu does indeed become almost demonically possessed in her desire to hold on to him. Though in theory she tries to help her husband to marry off young Amal – as Jyotirindranath tried (ineffectually) to find a wife for Rabindranath – in practice Charu resents the idea of Amal marrying, because it will take him away from her. Perhaps in reality Kadambari failed to find Rabindranath a bride in Jessore because she did not want him to marry. That she committed suicide within a few months of his marriage was surely more than a mere coincidence.

Kadambari was also childless, unlike her sister-in-laws (but like Charu). As a result she had 'adopted' the youngest daughter of Swarnakumari, Rabindranath's sister. At the end of 1879 this girl died, aged only five; Kadambari was probably badly affected by the tragedy. At any rate, from June 1883 we know she suffered from an unspecified illness. There is no firm evidence that it was a mental illness. However, there was considerable mental illness in the Jorasanko mansion and one or two other cases of suicide in the family. In such a hot-house atmosphere, any such tendencies would have been exacerbated.

Direct family criticism of Kadambari most probably added to her mental imbalance. There was her childlessness after fifteen years of marriage, for one thing. She was very fond of reading poetry and novels, for another, a habit the orthodox considered unsuitable for a woman, even seditious of domestic harmony. And she tended to keep herself aloof. The women of the house would readily have carped at her for all three failings, as they would have regarded them. That may have been why Jyotirindranath took Kadambari away from Jorasanko so frequently, to Chandannagar, to Darjeeling and to other houses in Calcutta.

Perhaps, in the end, all Kadambari's problems combined to crush her. As a woman in a patriarchal society who was not herself an artist, she was largely denied any outlet for intense emotions. Thirty years later, Rabindranath himself had a period of suicidal depression. His faith in his powers as an artist seems to have pulled him through.

Whatever its causes, the death of Kadambari unquestionably improved and deepened Tagore's work. It took him a long time to assimilate its full meaning, but its effect was fundamentally creative. A mere month afterwards he gave vent to these contradictory feelings in a light-hearted account of his brother's patriotic steamer venture: 'When clouds gather in your heart, their shadow falls on your writing. Your innermost words fall like a shower in *Shraban* [the monsoon month]. But nobody will like a piece of rainy-season writing. Whatever may be in my mind, I don't want it to block my readers' sunshine.'

10 Peripatetic Littérateur (1884–1890)

I was tormented by a furious impatience, an intolerable dissatisfaction
with myself and all around me. Much rather, I told myself, were I an Arab
Bedouin!

My Reminiscences

Two days before his wedding in December 1883, Rabindranath received a
letter from his father. It asked him to prepare himself to take over the management of the family estates. The way to do this, the Maharshi suggested, was
to spend some time in the estate office: scrutinize the accounts, make a summary of them each week and show it to him. He would explain the figures, and
when he was satisfied as to his son's 'efficiency and foresight' he would let him
live at Shelidah up-country, 'in the *mofussil*'. He concluded: 'without knowing
the nature of the work, simply living in the *mofussil* would be of no benefit.'

This suggests that Rabindranath had shown some desire to leave Jorasanko
and live at Shelidah. But during the 1880s, curiously, nothing came of the
proposal. Not until 1889 did Tagore follow up his teenage stay on the estates
with a further visit. And not until late 1890, seven years after his father's letter,
did he take over as manager.

Instead he spent the decade searching for himself in Calcutta and in various
places in India, winding up in London in September 1890. A restlessness got
hold of him which would never let him go, but would rather intensify with age,
until, in old age in Shantiniketan, when he could no longer travel far, it could be
satisfied only by moving within the Abode of Peace from small house to small
house, each built according to the poet's whim.

The restlessness was never merely frenetic, always (or at least nearly always)
productive. The poems, dramas, prose fiction, essays and songs continued to
flow, culminating in his first mature poetry, *Manashi* (The Lady of the Mind),
published in late 1890. To them he added a spurt of translation from English
into Bengali and – a new venture for him – the editing of a children's magazine.
This was started at the initiative of his sister-in-law Jnanadanandini and was
called *Balak* (The Boy); in 1886–87 it published serially Rabindranath's second

novel based on an episode in the history of the rulers of Tripura (whose maharaja had so appreciated his poetry). Although Rabindranath did not edit *Balak* for very long, like Dickens he found the editor's role interesting; in the 1890s and after he edited various magazines.

In addition he took his first steps into public life by writing and lecturing on controversial subjects. And he tried to found a school at Jorasanko. Nothing came of it – perhaps because he did not yet have the need to educate children of his own, as he would have a decade or so later. He also became secretary of the Brahmo Samaj, or rather the 'High Church' wing of the Samaj headed by his father. Rabindranath felt that new life was needed in the movement, which in January 1884 had lost its most charismatic leader, Keshubchandra Sen, Debendranath's erstwhile disciple who, after his difference with the Maharshi in the 1860s over the use of the sacred thread, had founded his own wing. (In the early 1880s there were thus three wings of the Brahmo Samaj: 'High Church', 'Low Church' and Keshub's 'New Dispensation'.)

Rabindranath's appointment to secretary coincided with the first issue of a magazine *Nabajiban* (New Life). Actually there was little that was new about it; it was an attempt to dress up the new (western) knowledge of the late nineteenth century in ancient Hindu garb, a vehicle for the ideas of the Hindu revivalist Pandit Shashadhar. The pundit sought to justify every Hindu practice – from child marriage and widow-burning to the most trivial of superstitions – by reference to the Hindu *shastras*, bolstered with pseudo-science. He claimed to find the roots of all scientific knowledge in Hinduism and dismissed western civilization as inferior. (His Hindu equivalents today claim that space flight and atomic energy were known to ancient India on the basis of the *Vedas*.) Shashadhar's ideas obviously had an immense appeal to many Bengalis bruised by the colonial encounter. But Brahmos, with their respect for western ideas, found the bogusness of Shashadhar intolerable. Bankim Chatterji, the novelist, who was a fine polemicist too, did not support the theories of Shashadhar. But he did lend his prestige to the Hindu revivalist movement of the 1880s. (In the 1890s this gathered force under the celebrated Swami Vivekananda, the Bengali disciple of the mystic Ramakrishna, guru of Christopher Isherwood and many other westerners.) A clash between Bankim and his admirer, the twenty-three-year-old Rabindranath, was almost inevitable. The argument began when Tagore criticized Bankim for being a 'preacher' in one of his novels, which he said made the characters unreal. It escalated into a debate between the orthodox Hindu, Brahmo and English views of truth and lies. The debate was a confused one, and both men wished they had not entered it. 'At the close of this period of antagonism Bankim Babu wrote me a letter, which I unfortunately lost', Rabindranath recalled much later. 'Had I not, the reader could have seen with what consummate generosity Bankim Babu took the sting out of that regrettable episode.'

No such rapprochement was possible between Tagore and the mass of the orthodox. In time the gap became wider not narrower, Rabindranath's invective sharper not milder, and the response of the orthodox correspondingly more malign. Tagore took his inspiration from Rammohun Roy (the founder of the Brahma Sabha, about whom he wrote for the first time in 1885), who had been largely ostracized by his countrymen and died in England.

Within the Brahmo Samaj Tagore's efforts were hardly better appreciated. He tried, as we know, to introduce some non-Brahmins as ministers – and failed. Later on his attempts to reunite the two wings of the Brahmo Samaj and to argue that Brahmos were part of the Hindu fold, not a separate religion, were bitterly resented. Many in the 'Low Church' Samaj were strongly opposed to Rabindranath's being admitted even as an honorary member. Only his devotional hymns were universally appreciated by Brahmos (and even by revivalist Swami Vivekananda, who sang them to Ramakrishna). In January 1886, at the Brahmo festival equivalent to Christmas, Rabindranath sang before three thousand Brahmos in the Jorasanko house. His father was so delighted by the hymns that he gave his youngest son a large cheque, his first literary prize.

To most Bengalis, and to all non-Bengalis, these dirge-like compositions are the least appealing part of *Rabindrasangit*, Tagore Song, with a few exceptions. If Rabindranath had composed nothing else, he might have pleased the Brahmo puritans – but today he would barely be remembered as a song-writer. But he went on to compose songs expressing almost every mood, including some verging on the erotic. They were so irresistible to Bengalis that even Brahmo sectarians who wanted to deny the composer honorary membership were pleased to sing Tagore's songs during their services.

His latest volume of poetry certainly shocked the puritanical in 1886. (Vivekananda later termed it 'erotic venom' – one wonders what the Maharshi thought.) Its title was *Kari o Komal* (Sharps and Flats). It included translations into Bengali from Shelley, Mrs Browning, Christina Rossetti, Hood, Moore, Swinburne, Victor Hugo and an unnamed Japanese poet – but the shock came from the frankness of Rabindranath's poems. Their keynote was in the following lines of the opening poem:

This world is sweet – I do not want to die.
I want to live within the stream of humanity.

Later Tagore told Edward Thompson: 'There *is* sensuality [in *Kari o Komal*]. I am willing to admit that there is an element which is carnal. But there is also the reaction, very strongly expressed in the later poems of the series, the trouble to escape from the same sensuality.'

He meant the group of sonnets in praise of the poet's mistress: her breasts, arms, feet, body, smile, her nakedness, her kiss and the act of love. By comparison with Vaishnava literature, such as the graphic *Gita Govinda*, which revels in the love-making of Radha and Krishna, *Kari o Komal* was not at all frank. But by the standards of Bengali literature in the late nineteenth century it was. Unfortunately Rabindranath's poems lacked both the erotic charge and the literary delights of the earlier masterpiece. 'Chumban' (Kisses), for instance, which was among the best, was nevertheless 'a morass of conceits' (Thompson).

Leaving their homes, two loves have made
a pilgrimage to the confluence of lips.
In the law of Love two waves have swelled,
breaking and mingling on two lips.

(The idea of confluence is more expressive and sensual in Bengali than in English, because in India pilgrims journey to the confluence of great rivers, such as Allahabad; and the word for confluence also means sexual intercourse.) And here are the opening lines of 'Bibashana' (Her Nakedness):

Throw off your robe, Love – discard it all.
Wear only the raiment of your naked beauty
Like a heavenly nymph robed in light.

Despite the inflated language, there was no doubting the desire; and the object of the desire. Rabindranath's first child, a daughter Madhurilata (Bela), was born in October 1886; his wife Mrinalini was then about thirteen. Strangely he did not mention the event in any of his letters at the time, so far as we know. Judging by a lecture he gave on 'Hindu marriage' in 1887, his inner struggle about his own marriage was as strong as ever. The lecture was a reasoned appeal, moderate, even cautious, for the abandonment of child marriage, several decades before the idea was generally accepted in educated Bengali society.

Tagore argued that rather than quoting a few scriptures out of context to glorify child marriage as the orthodox did, one should attempt a historical analysis of Hindu marriage as an institution. If, as some claimed, the ideal of Hindu marriage was the union of one man and one woman, how could polygamy, common among a certain class of Brahmins, be accepted? If, as others claimed, the ideal was a spiritual union, how could Bengali society sanction, as it did, sexual intercourse between a wife and her brother-in-law when her husband was unable to produce a child? If the well-being of society was actually the greater ideal, then was it not incumbent on society to think dynamically about marriage, so as to keep changing it in step with other social norms that had been influenced by foreign ideas? If so, the opinion of medical science was relevant. Doctors had stated that a child mother could not bear a sound child 'just as a baby with its first set of teeth cannot chew bones'. Even if one ignored their opinion and tried to solve the problem by raising the marriage age of boys, leaving girls as they were, men would die before their wives, with a resultant increase in widows – and ultimately a need to lower once more the marriage age for boys.

Thus far Tagore probably carried his orthodox audience with him. But then he made two observations that were highly controversial in 1887. If Hindu marriage truly was a union higher than the merely procreative, surely before marrying both partners needed education and some experience of life? This was impossible with child marriage. He was aware, he said, of doubts about how older girls would adjust to the demands of a 'joint family'. But child marriage could not be supported just for the sake of the 'joint family' system. The fact was, he asserted, the 'joint family' was now on the decline, like child marriage. Both institutions had proved themselves restrictive of the individual's personal development.

Supreme individualist that he was, Rabindranath was chafing at his bonds – familial, marital, financial and artistic – in the mid-1880s. A Bengali friend recorded an interesting vignette of Tagore in Jorasanko. They were sitting talking when a visitor was announced. Tagore was 'greatly put out', explaining to his friend that the visitor was a wastrel from a collateral branch of the family in the habit of pestering him for money. Though he could not afford it, he had already helped the man on various occasions and was not willing again – but he disliked having to confront him with the fact. He was about to leave the room when his friend persuaded him to stay. The visitor was shown in. Luckily for Rabindranath, the presence of his friend restrained the relative from importuning. After a few minutes he left, and Tagore was let off the hook.

In general he was itching to escape his surroundings. He conceived the idea of travelling the entire Grand Trunk Road, from Calcutta to Peshawar in Afghanistan. He would go either by bullock cart or on foot, he said, accompanied by two or three friends. They would travel very light, carry little money and take their chances. When he spoke to his father, the great traveller, the Maharshi offered only encouragement and stories of his own adventures on foot and horseback. But the bohemian plan eventually fizzled out.

In late July 1887 he wrote from Calcutta to a friend:

I have reached my twenty-seventh year. This fact keeps intruding on my thoughts – nothing else seems to have happened in the last few months. But is having reached twenty-seven a trifling thing? – to have passed the meridian of one's twenties on one's progress towards thirty? Thirty. Maturity: the age at which people naturally expect fruits rather than green shoots. Alas, where is the promise of fruit? When I shake my head it still feels full of frivolity, without even a kernel of philosophy.

People are beginning to complain:

Where is that which we hoped of you? For quite a while we have been expectantly watching the tender green of the unripe state and it has pleased us, but we cannot put up with immaturity forever, you know. It is high time that we learn what we may extract from you. We require an estimate of the amount of oil that an unblinkered unprejudiced critic can squeeze out of you.

My old excuse will not wash any longer . . . But what am I to do? Words of wisdom will not come! I am incapable of satisfying the general public. Beyond a snatch of song, some tittle-tattle and some harmless fun, I have been unable to advance. Those who had high hopes for me will undoubtedly turn on me; but did anyone ever beg them to nurse such expectations?

His next volume of poetry, *Manashi* (The Lady of the Mind), would be his answer to his critics. It took him nearly four years to write: in 1887–89, he published no book of poetry, only dramas, essays and his second novel. Meanwhile, he travelled with his small family. Much of 1888 was spent in retreat at Ghazipur on the Ganges not far from Varanasi (Benares). Tagore chose the place for its romantic associations: besides the presence of the river, it was a centre for growing roses (used to produce perfume), and it had old Mughal buildings. Here he may have grown the beard he would keep for the rest of his life. He also for the first time translated one of his poems into English to satisfy the curiosity of the local British civil surgeon. In October, after many months, he left the place to attend a family gathering at Shantiniketan. This was the official founding of the ashram, which now consisted of a large house, a mango grove and other trees and shrubs in the midst of the bare plain – but scarcely any residents. At the ceremony he sang. Afterwards he returned to Calcutta for the birth of his son Rathindranath at Jorasanko.

During part of 1889 he and his family stayed with Satyendranath in Solapur, a historic town about half-way between Bombay and Hyderabad. Then, in November, he at last went back to Shelidah, accompanied by his wife and nephew. The new estate house had come up in his absence. The setting awakened inklings of the feelings that would produce some of his greatest writing. A letter he wrote to his sixteen-year-old niece Indira in Calcutta captured both the terror and the beauty latent in the riverine landscape of East Bengal. His wife and nephew, ignorant of the river's ways, had vanished while out walking in the dusk. Eventually, after much searching with lanterns and many echoing shouts, they were located, trapped by the tide on a sand-spit, from which they had to be rescued by boat. Otherwise they would probably have drowned. This was the terror, inconceivable in Jorasanko. The beauty too was 'something easy to forget in Calcutta', he wrote:

When the sun sets each evening behind the peaceful trees along this small river, high above the boundless expanse of sand thousands and thousands of stars suddenly appear – you have to see it happen to grasp its wonder. At dawn the sun gradually turns the page of a great book, beginning in the east, and then at dusk turns it back again – in the grandest, most exclusive and least noisy schoolroom in the universe. But enough of this. Over there in the Capital it is bound to sound like poetry with a capital P, but here such words are not at all misplaced.

Within a year he would be back in Shelidah on his own, as manager of the estates with ample time to reflect on nature. [pl.21] But before that he returned to Europe, this time with no ulterior purpose. His brother Satyendranath and friend Loken Palit (whom Rabi had first got to know in London in 1879) had planned the trip; Rabindranath decided to go along 'for the ride'. He seems simply to have been curious and restless for another change. Whatever his motives were, the visit soon palled. Here was a syndrome Tagore would show over and over in travelling after 1912: in Bengal he would yearn to escape, but as soon as he had done so he would be desperate to return.

Just before reaching Aden he wrote to his wife, then pregnant with their third child, from the ship:

On Sunday night I felt my soul leave my body and go to Jorasanko. You were lying on the edge of the big bed, Beli and Baby by your side . . . I caressed you a little and said 'Little wife, remember that I left my body on Sunday night and came to see you – when I get back from Europe I shall ask you whether you saw me.' . . . Then I kissed Beli and Baby and came back.

In Italy he enjoyed the grapes and the sight of Italian girls. From the top of the newly-erected Eiffel Tower he sent Mrinalini a postcard. (Typically he said nothing original about the tower in his diary; engineering and technology rarely touched him.) In London he immediately went to Tavistock Square – and found to his disappointment that the Scotts had moved, no one knew where. Surprisingly he had not kept in touch in any way: perhaps he was uneasy about writing letters in English, perhaps he felt embarrassed about his relationship with the Scott daughters, or perhaps Calcutta was just too far away and too alien a world to explain in a letter. Maybe too, in his self-centredness he had somehow expected the London he knew to be preserved in aspic, so that he could take up again where he had left off in February 1880. [pl.22]

He was now at somewhat of a loose end in the capital of the Empire. He accompanied his brother and Loken on various visits and outings and met some new faces, none of whom seem to have made much impression. A Miss Mull took a fancy to him and flirted, as recorded in his diary (and deleted from the published version). But he much preferred a distant view of a girl in a box above the stage at the Lyceum. The play was an adaptation of Sir Walter Scott's *The Bride of Lammermoor* with Ellen Terry. Rabindranath, however, had eyes only for the dainty creature with a plait, the contour of whose face was lit exquisitely by the stage lights against the dark background of the box. 'While the show went on I was watching the play of emotions on her face. She too had looked at us through her opera glasses, but doubtless she did not get as much pleasure as we did.'

He also saw and enjoyed Gilbert and Sullivan's *The Gondoliers* at the Savoy Theatre and an exhibition of French art. This included a female nude that seemed to provoke in him the same feeling of wonder and excitement as his wife's body had in *Kari o Komal*. He told his diary that the work was of such beauty he would not have minded viewing it with his daughter, had she been older (a remark also excised from the published version).

Against these pleasant experiences he was laughed at in the street when he wore his pugree (turban). He noted in early October: 'If we black chaps wear western outfit, people don't find it strange. When girls laugh at me in the street my pride in my appearance just vanishes. Today is the 5th! Five more weeks to go.' Again, not a comment that survived in print.

Already Tagore was irritated by England and the English, more acutely than as a teenager ten years previously because he now had more pride, both in his achievements and in his looks (handsomely bearded). What's more he was married, for better and worse. Condescension or ridicule from English women, especially pretty ones, was galling. It must have reminded him of the ladies' smiles, suppressed and otherwise, when he had been forced to sing Indian songs during his first visit. He longed for home. On 6 October he noted astringently: 'When a mind is inert it can be activated by external stimuli, but when one's mind is continually working, actively cogitating, in love with itself, such stimuli are harrowingly confusing.'

What had put him in such a state of antagonism to London? Was there a major incident not recorded in the diary? Perhaps. But more likely was an accumulation of small pricks and a driving desire to prove himself as a writer in Bengal by publishing his latest poems, completed before he left for London. It is never easy to guess his thinking, some of which was not clear to him, by his own admission. What is certain is what he did. On 9 October 1890, a month early, he boarded a ship and sailed for Calcutta, leaving his brother and his friend behind. He would not come to the West again for more than twenty years.

11 *Manashi*, The Lady of the Mind (1890)

My poems had now reached the doors of men's minds.

My Reminiscences

Manashi (The Lady of the Mind) was published on 24 December 1890, some seven weeks after Rabindranath's return from Europe. He was then just short of thirty, the crucial age he had mentioned in his letter to his friend in 1887. During Tagore's birth centenary seventy years later, a Bengali critic and poet admired by Tagore, Sudhin Datta, said of this seminal collection:

> No poet before Tagore knew how to extract music out of Bengali consonants; and if at times our lyrical needs made us rebel against the tyranny of the fourteen-lettered line called *payar*, we either resorted to forms borrowed from Sanskrit, and thus unreadable by the rules of Bengali pronunciation, or, like Biharilal Chakravarti [Tagore's idol as a teenager] reduced the use of closed syllables to a minimum, imparting to our verse a sort of spineless elasticity. *Manashi* ruled such compromises out of existence, restored our measures to ordered autonomy, and broke with the past so sharply that ever since its appearance most of our previous poetry has seemed not only imperfect rhythmically but also metrically defective... Though the technical skill of its author never ceased to grow, his next basic contribution to the poet's craft occurred when, at seventy, he set about bridging the gulf between verse and prose.

Even to the non-Bengali unable to enjoy it in its original language, *Manashi* can still be startling in its range and power. Gone was the Lisping Poet whose sentiment exceeded his substance: clearly Tagore had taken note of this criticism. In his place had come a poet of many moods, from the tender to the fiercely satirical, and many subjects: nature and love, of course, but also ancient India and contemporary social and national problems. Certain poems seem haunted by memories of the dead Kadambari (as the book's dedication hints). The title *Manashi* is nicely ambiguous: it means both 'conceived by the mind, fancied', and 'a sweetheart of one's fancy'. It is also a common name for Bengali women.

One of the best nature poems is 'Shindhutaranga' (Sea-Waves). Unusually for Tagore, nature is presented as merciless, death-dealing, utterly scornful of human feelings. There is none of the 'interpenetration of human life with the cosmic life of the world' so characteristic of classical Indian drama and poetry. The poem, written in June 1887, was inspired by the sinking of a ship in May that year containing 735 pilgrims on their way to the great Jagannath [Juggernaut] Temple at Puri; the ship was hit by a cyclone in the Bay of Bengal. Edward Thompson called it the 'grandest sea-storm he ever did':

> On the breast of the shoreless sea Destruction swings and sweeps,
>   In dreadful festival.
> The indomitable wind is roaming, ungovernable in strength,
>   Beating its thousand wings.
> Sky and sea in one are reeling together in vast confusion;
>   Darkness veils the eyes of the universe.
> The lightning flashes and threatens, the foam-fields hiss,
>   The sharp white terrible mirth of brute Nature.
> Eyeless earless rootless loveless,
>   The mad forces of Evil
> Rush to ruin, without direction, they have cast off all restraints.

And here is the peak of the poem:

> Lifting the ship, the Storm, an ogress, shouts
>   'Give! give! give!'
> The sea, one massed foam, clamours with its million upthrust arms,
>   'Give! give! give!'
> Wrathful at the delay, foaming and hissing,
>   The azure Death grows white with mighty anger.
> The tiny bark cannot bear the great weight,
>   Its iron breast will burst!
> Above and Below have become one, they seize this tiny toy,
>   Seize it for their sport!

In absolute contrast is 'Meghaduta' (The Cloud Messenger). It was Rabindranath's tribute to Kalidasa, whose classic *Meghaduta* had first stirred him as a child, before he knew any Sanskrit, when his brother had gravely recited some stanzas 'at the sudden gathering of clouds'. Kalidasa's poem describes the voyage of a cloud across India in a little over a hundred stanzas and 'seems to contain the quintessence of a whole culture', as A. L. Basham wrote in *The Wonder That Was India*. Various later poets were inspired by *Meghaduta*, including Jayadeva, author of the *Gita Govinda* that Tagore admired. Now here was Rabindranath, destined to be India's greatest ever poet, on the threshold of his fame, sitting in Shantiniketan on a cloudy, rainy day in late May 1890, dreaming of Kalidasa's ancient world. 'As Dante looked across the centuries and hailed Virgil as master, as Spenser overlooked two hundred years of poetical fumbling and claimed the succession to Chaucer, as Milton in his turn saluted his "master Spenser", so Rabindranath turned back to Kalidasa', wrote Thompson.

Tagore's diction is deliberately Sanskritized, making it even harder to translate. Nevertheless, here is the opening stanza of 'Meghaduta' followed by a later stanza (Asharh is the Bengali month corresponding to June–July, when the monsoon usually begins):

Master Poet, in some unremembered year
On some forgotten first day of auspicious Asharh
You imagined your *Meghaduta*! Each sonorous stanza
Contains for grief-struck lovers a thrilling cadenza;
Like majestic rain-clouds, rumbling with gongs,
The verses accumulate, tier upon tier, thronged with song.
. . . In India's easternmost realm
I have my seat, in viridescent Bengal
Where too the poet Jayadeva one rainy season
Saw the horizon darkly fringed with *tamal* trees
Blue-green, under a caressing cloud-capped sky.

Later in the poem come lovely images, in which man and nature 'interpenetrate' with the jewelled exquisiteness of a Rajput miniature painting:

By the banks of some unknown stream
Jasmine-wood-frolicking belles wander and roam,
Their cheeks flushed, their ear-lotuses limp,
Desperately in need of the cloud's cool damp;
Village brides they are, no artifice in their frowns,
As they gaze at the sky, each face upturned
Towards the dark-blue cumulus, their eyes suffused

Pools of deep and flawless blue.
. . . There in the dead of midnight
Fretful amours forgotten, on house-turrets
Doves are sleeping; only distracted women
Have ventured out to await their love-trysts
In the impenetrable gloom of the city's highway
Pricked by infrequent forks of lightning.

But instead of being sublime, love could also be ludicrous in *Manashi*. Consider this, 'The wedding night', the opening scene of a poem with the deliberately ponderous title 'Nababanga Dampatir Premalap' (Loving Conversation of a Newly-wedded Bengali Couple). The bride is of course but a child:

Groom:
Life unto life   union with a wife;
     naught can compare with such grace.
Come, forget thy days   let us lift our gaze
     and glance, we two, at t'other's face.
Soul unto soul   in bashful whirl
     we are joined together in this place.
As if in swoon   we suck honey from one bloom
     forgetting ourselves without trace.
Since my birth   the fire in my hearth
     has produced only ashes, no peace.
Into thine ocean   of fathomless emotion,
     I have come – to find a consoling space.
Tell me once, Mine   'I am truly thine,
     None other do I wish to embrace.'
But – but what's this?   Where do you go, my bliss?
Bride: (tearfully)
     I am going to sleep with my nurse.

Rabindranath wrote this poem in Ghazipur in July 1888 when staying with his wife and daughter. Very likely it described his own experience of marriage three or four years earlier. He was mocking both himself, the pretentious twenty-three-year-old sentimentalist, and his situation, a grown man yoked to a girl who was barely more than a child. The mockery is gentle; in a further poem on child marriage in *Manashi*, it is savage:

Playing our flutes, let us bring home a bride of eight years. Let us snatch and tear open the bud of childhood, let us force out the sweet youth! Pressing a weight of Scriptures on the new expanding life, let us make it one with the dust of the wrinkled ages!

In another 'social problem' poem, 'Dharma Prachar' (Mission-Work), the savagery was allied with satire. This poem was based on a reported incident in 1888 in which some Bengalis, Hindu revivalists, launched a cowardly assault on a Salvation Army preacher. At the time such British preachers dressed as sannyasis (Hindu ascetics) and adopted Indian standards of life. Ironically, by doing so, they both attracted the ire of 'true Aryans' (i.e. Hindu fundamentalists who saw themselves as descendants of the Aryan invaders of ancient India), and deprived themselves of the protection afforded by European dress. Until the policy changed, many lives were needlessly sacrificed in these attacks. Although Tagore had little sympathy with Christian missionaries as a group, he had not a grain of sympathy for their Hindu assailants. Here, having heard the preacher's call, the captain of the patriots speaks:

Listen, Brother Bishu!
Outside – 'Victory to Jesu!'
Can you bear to hear that name,
Scion of Aryans you!

Vishnu, Shiva, every god
All will soon be undertrod.
If India worships Jesu,
Hindu texts will lie unread.

Brother, I hear that every mage
Every Indian saint and sage,
Vishnu, Harit, Narad, Atri
Weeps and dies in rage.

Where's our mighty karma?
Where the eternal dharma?

Then, having broken the preacher's head with their *lathis* (staves), the patriots catch sight of the police:

'Look out Shibu, look out Haru,
Look out Nani, look out Charu,

It's no time to watch the fun –
Save your skins, hurry hurry!'

'Police are coming, batons raised,
Run like streaks of flame!
Blessed be the Aryan faith!
Blessed Bengal's sacred name!'

They take to their heels, run home, brag of their 'victory' and, because their food is not ready in a hero's welcome, they beat and kick their wives.

The best of the 'social problem' poems is 'Duranta Asha' (Wild Hopes). Here, said Edward Thompson, 'His scorn has wings, has sweep and vigour.' The wild hopes in question are those of Bengalis who believe that they can achieve anything they like, should they deign to try – but who actually do nothing at all:

While in our hearts wild hopes hiss like snakes, thrashing the bonds of fate in futile anger let us dress respectably, polish and set out the hookahs with great care, and shuffle the grubby cards vigorously – for who can say when we may have to fight a game! Let us club together, all perched on one charpoy, a dozen of us rice-fed, milksop offspring of Bengal.

Then the poet bursts out in a line that became famous in Bengal:

Much rather would I be an Arab Bedouin!

But, after some fantasy on the delights of solitary desert life, he concludes that a quiet life combining obsequiousness to society with braggadocio in speech seems to content most Bengalis; he may as well accept his fate. Writing about himself to his niece a few years later Rabindranath repeated the line and said:

But I am a Bengali, not a Bedouin! I sit in my corner, moping and worrying and arguing. My mind is like a fish being fried – first this way up, now the other – blistered by the boiling oil on one side, and then on the other . . . Enough of this. Since it is impracticable to be uncivilized, I had better try to be thoroughly civil – why foment a quarrel between the two?

After *Manashi* was published, a friend (and shrewd critic) told Rabindranath that he had found in the poems 'a mood of despair and resignation'. Tagore's reply was remarkably frank and apposite, though he could not know it, to the entire course of his life. He wrote:

I sometimes detect within myself a battle-ground where two opposing forces are constantly in action, one beckoning me to peace and cessation of all strife, the other egging me on to battle. It is as though the restless energy and the will to action of the West were perpetually assaulting the citadel of my Indian placidity. Hence this swing of the pendulum between passionate pain and calm detachment, between lyrical abandon and philosophizing, between love of my country and mockery of patriotism, between an itch to enter the lists and a longing to remain wrapt in thought. This continual struggle brings in its train a mood compounded of frustration and resignation.

12 The Shelidah Years (1891–1901)

The fact is that here, away from Calcutta, in my inner world, time may be stretched or compressed and clocks do not work in the usual way.

letter to his niece Indira,
Shelidah, June 1894

Now, at last, Rabindranath took over the management of the family estates full time. He had to, whether he wanted to or not, because his brothers could not do the job: Dwijendranath the philosopher was temperamentally unsuited, Satyendranath the civil servant was employed on the other side of India, Jyotirindranath the eccentric had been badly burned by the collapse of his steamer company. Although Rabindranath was somewhat reluctant to begin with, the move turned out to be one of the most fruitful of his life. It gave him freedom from Calcutta at will, without cutting him off from the city; Shelidah was only half a day's journey from Calcutta by train and boat. Although he would be based at the estates for a decade, he would visit Calcutta constantly to conduct estate and publishing business, to give lectures and performances and attend meetings, and to see friends like Priyanath Sen and of course his family and his father, who required the estate accounts read to him every month. Family and others would make the journey in the opposite direction to Shelidah, including his wife, son Rathindranath and his other children; but not until 1898 did the whole of his immediate family join him in Shelidah and make it their home. [pl.17]

His motto in the Shelidah years was perhaps the short poem he wrote in 1896:

Whoever wishes to,
May sit in meditation
With eyes closed
To know if the world be true or false.
I, meanwhile,
Shall sit with hungry eyes,
To see the world
While the light lasts.

The results of his observations were prodigious. The two Bengalis who have done most to interpret them to the world since Tagore's death are Nirad Chaudhuri and Satyajit Ray. Chaudhuri was born in a village in East Bengal and wrote about it with unique vividness in *The Autobiography of an Unknown Indian*. Of Tagore's stay on his estates Chaudhuri later observed:

Calcutta was wholly outside the true Bengali landscape in which the blue of the sky, the green of the vegetation, and the grey of the waters mingled to create a vast expanse of tender stillness. Thus it happened that it was during his stay in his country estates, often floating in his houseboat on the rivers, that Tagore wrote some of his best work both in poetry and prose. Even his letters he wrote from this region to his relatives, and more especially to his favourite niece Indira . . . , are great works of literature. They also reveal his character and personality with unadorned truth.

Satyajit Ray, by contrast, was born in Calcutta. But he made two short films based on rural stories written by Tagore in the early 1890s, as well as the documentary film *Rabindranath Tagore*. One of the short films, *The Postmaster*, is among the most poignant films in cinema, and in the documentary the scenes dealing with the Shelidah years are the finest in the film, with a lyrical beauty equivalent to the untranslatable lyricism of Tagore's poetry in these years. To quote Ray's commentary:

With a worldly wisdom unusual in a poet but characteristic of the Tagores, Rabindranath in later life set about in a practical way to improve the lot of the poor peasants of his estates, and his varied work in this field is on record. But his own gain from this intimate contact with the fundamental aspects of life and nature, and the influence of this contact on his life and work – are beyond measure. Living mostly in his boat and watching life through the window, a whole new world of sights and sounds and feelings opened up before him.

The Shelidah years were fecund in poems, plays, songs, musical dramas and essays, many of them published in a new family magazine *Sadhana*, of which Rabindranath was chief contributor and later editor. But to these forms Tagore now added a new form, the short story. Between 1891 and 1901 he wrote fifty-nine short stories, set in both the villages and towns of Bengal and in Calcutta, and dealing with characters at every level in society. The best have a pathos and/or an ironic humour which is inimitable. Edward Thompson, having translated a number of them, was convinced that they were among the world's great short stories; and many others have felt similarly (Chaudhuri and Ray included).

However, the transition to the estates was a wrench, despite Tagore's reconnaissance in the winter of 1889–90. There was no trace of lyricism in the letter the poet wrote to his wife in Calcutta in December 1890. He had reached a village, the northernmost headquarters of the estates, sixty or seventy miles from Shelidah as the crow flew, much further when travelling by boat on the winding tributaries of the River Padma.

This river has no current. Slime floats on the surface, with clumps of weed here and there and an odour like that of a stagnant village tank, and I expect there will be plenty of mosquitoes at night. If I find it too much I shall run away straight to Calcutta. I felt like going home immediately when I read my sweet Belu-rani's [his four-year-old daughter's] letter. She misses me, does she? With her tiny little mind, however can that be? . . .

They tied the boat in a stuffy place last night and drew down the curtains. The closeness woke me up and on top of it some people started to sing at about 1 or 2 in the morning. 'How much longer will you sleep? Awake, awake, beloved!' . . . The boatman stopped them singing but the words went on ringing in my ears 'Awake, awake, beloved!' till I felt ill. Finally I raised the curtains and fell asleep towards dawn . . . I may be able to leave here after a fortnight but I am not yet certain.

In time the boat became almost a part of Rabindranath. It had been built by his grandfather 'Prince' Dwarkanath and been kept moored on the banks of the Hooghly near Calcutta. Maharshi Debendranath had used it regularly for his trips up-river; very likely he was living in it in mid-1846 when the message of his father's death in England was brought from Calcutta. Rabindranath named it *Padma*, after the great river on which it would spend the rest of its days. The design was of a kind to be found only in Bengal, flat-bottomed and with a wide beam, the combination being ideal for moving in the shallow and fickle rivers of the Ganges delta and for providing the ample accommodation required by a zamindar. These lumbering keelless barges were known as *Daccai bajras*, after Dacca (Dhaka), the centre for their construction. The British called them budgerows. [pl.23]

Rathindranath, Tagore's son, who travelled in the *Padma* with his father in the 1890s, later described the life of a zamindar on arrival, in his budgerow, at one of his several estate headquarters. 'What with the firing of guns by quaintly dressed guards, and the blowing of conch-shells by veiled women, the arrival . . . reminded one of the Middle Ages.' If it happened to be the annual occasion

9 Rabindranath, 1882

10 Rabindranath and his nephew, artist Abanindranath, 1892

11 Rabindranath, *c.* 1881 (*Jyotirindranath Tagore*)

2 Rabindranath reading, 1892

13 Rabindranath and his brother Jyotirindranath composing, *c.* 1892

Rabindranath as the dacoit-chief Valmiki in *Valmiki Pratibha*
(The Genius of Valmiki), 1881

15 Rabindranath and his wife Mrinalini Devi, soon after their marriage, *c.* 1883

Four of Rabindranath's five children: Samindranath (d. 1907), Renuka (d. 1903), adhurilata (Bela, d. 1918), Mira (d. 1969)

17 Rabindranath, in Shelidah, *c.* 1890, served by his niece Indira *(second from right,* his brother Jyotirindranath)

18 Rabindranath with his niece Indira and nephew-translator Surendranath, *c.* 1886

for rent collection, the Zamindar Babu (i.e. Rabindranath) would be taken in a palanquin to the office building and placed on a raised platform beneath a *shamiana* (awning). There the tenants would be conducted to him one by one, the elders and headmen of the villages first and then the commoners. Each would give his rent, generally a token payment only, and receive blessings with bowed head. Afterwards there would be a feast for several thousand people organized by the tenants according to a strict social etiquette; the fare itself would be of the simplest, consisting mainly of parched rice and sour milk.

Tagore himself said rather little about this side of his estate life in his wonderful letters to his niece Indira, which were later published in Bengali in 1912 as *Chhinnapatra* (Torn Leaves) and in English in 1921 as *Glimpses of Bengal*. These letters, he told W. B. Yeats in 1918, 'cover those very years which were most productive for me and therefore they act like a footpath in my life history, unconsciously laid by the treading of my thoughts. I feel sure these letters, when published, will present to you pictures and ideas concerning me and my surroundings more vividly and truly than anything that I have yet written.'

The *Padma* – both the boat and the river – were integral to the letters. At times they seem as much characters as the people Tagore described. Besides eating and sleeping on board, he wrote and read copiously there too. But most of all he watched life on shore. It might be a ferry endlessly loading and unloading villagers for market; or a group of boys raucously rolling a log along the bank until stopped by a disgusted small girl; or a tiny cowherd prodding a gigantic docile buffalo for no good reason; or a line of women in dripping saris weaving gracefully homewards with water-jars on their hips; or a free-spirited village belle sailing away to another village leaving behind a crowd of tearful well-wishers; or a gypsy woman boldly giving a high-handed police constable a piece of her mind; or, less pleasantly, a woman well-wrapped against the cold bathing a small naked boy and clouting him when he shivered and coughed.

Nothing, no matter how trivial, escaped Tagore's gaze. Everything was imbibed and stored until the moment was ripe for a poem or story or play or song to express it afresh. And of course the moods of nature – ranging from storms that wreaked dreadful havoc to nights of mirror-like tranquillity – influenced him constantly. 'All of a sudden I realized how hungry for space I had become and so now I am taking my fill of it', he wrote from the estate headquarters at Shahzadpur:

Here I am sole monarch of these rooms and have thrown open all the doors and windows. I feel the mood and the will to write here as nowhere else. The living essence of the outside world floats in freely in verdurous waves of light and air and sound and scent that mingle with my bewitched mind and mould it into story after story after story.

The intoxication is especially strong in the afternoons. Heat, hush, solitude, birdsong – particularly the cawing of crows – and languid, limitless leisure together remove me from reality.

I believe, though I have no proof, that the *Arabian Nights* came into being upon such sun-baked afternoons, in Damascus, Samarkand and Bokhara . . . Such a prodigiously grand and mysterious setting in such a far-away country was bound to lead to a thousand tales – credible and incredible – of the deepest hopes and fears of mankind.

Noontime in Shahzadpur is high noon for story writing. It was at this time, I recall, that my story 'The Postmaster' took over my thoughts. The light, the breeze and the movement of leaves on all sides combined and entered my writing.

'The Postmaster', written in 1891 (and filmed by Ray in 1960–61), was among Tagore's earliest stories. Its main character is a bored, desperate Calcutta boy, posted to the back of beyond – i.e. somewhere like Shahzadpur – to run a post office. As Rabindranath made clear in another letter, a real postmaster existed who used to tell him 'the most improbable things in the gravest possible fashion'. What was more, a second letter revealed that the real postmaster read the story, recognized himself and bashfully referred to the fact. Though he was not from Calcutta he shared the fictional postmaster's disdain for the locals and his yearning to escape. Tagore liked the man: probably a part of himself – the part that needed Calcutta life – identified with the postmaster's predicament.

The schoolmasters of Shahzadpur got shorter shift – or at least that was Tagore's intention. They came on a courtesy call, but the zamindar could not find a word to say to them. 'Every five minutes or so I managed a question, to which they offered the briefest of replies; and then I sat like a dunce, twirling my pen and scratching my head. At last I ventured a query about the crops, but being schoolmasters they knew nothing of this subject whatsoever.' Finally they left after an hour and a half: it might as well have been half an hour or twelve hours, wrote a disgruntled Rabindranath.

His tenants, by contrast, evoked his pity, with their devotion to him and their age-old plight. He wrote of watching their boats passing his houseboat, laden with paddy cut before its due time because of monsoon flooding, and of hearing the wails of the despairing cultivators. 'Within the workings of nature there must surely be some place for pity, otherwise why do we feel it?' But neither lamentations nor pity seemed to have the slightest effect. 'It is all beyond human understanding; we must simply accept it. And yet there *is* pity in the world, and there *is* justice – that too is vital to understand.' Then he took himself to task for quibbling and reminded himself that want and sorrow exist because Creation is incomplete.

Were Creation not so, it would be God, and then our cavils would cease. Do we dare pray for such a thing? The more we dwell on it, the more we come back to the beginning – why this Creation at all? If we cannot resolve to reject existence itself, it is futile to object to the fact of sorrow.

The plight of a visiting magistrate also moved Tagore, whatever his reservations about British officials in India as a class. In one of his most amusing letters to Indira (who much later described herself as 'half-English'), her uncle wrote of getting dressed up in the heat of midday to call upon this young Englishman in order to invite him to dinner, and finding him in the midst of dispensing justice from the verandah of his tent. The invitation was declined on the grounds that the magistrate was due elsewhere to arrange for a pig-sticking party: so Tagore went back to his estate house. Soon a tremendous storm blew up. Unable to read or write, he was pacing restlessly back and forth when suddenly he remembered the magistrate camped outdoors. He dispatched an invitation to shelter and only then discovered that his spare room was squalid. A detailed description now followed, written with almost Dickensian relish:

For a moment I was overwhelmed with dismay; then it was a case of – send for the manager, send for the storekeeper, the cashier and all the servants, get hold of extra men, bring a broom, fetch water, put up ladders, unfasten ropes, pull down poles, take away bolsters, quilts and bedding, pick up broken glass bit by little bit, wrench nails from the wall one by one. Why are you people standing there staring? – take hold of those and try not to break them. Bang, bang, crash! – there go three lamp-holders – pick them up piece by piece. I myself whisk a wicker-basket and a mat encrusted with the filth of ages off the floor and out the window, dislodging a family of cockroaches that scatter in all directions, to whose business I have been unwitting host as they dined off my bread, my treacle and the polish on my shoes.

The soaked sahib arrived, not a moment too early. The zamindar went to greet him in the drawing-room, trying to look like a gentleman who had been reposing there all afternoon. 'I shake the sahib's hand, converse and laugh without apparent concern; but inside I cannot stop thinking about his sleeping accommodation. When at last I showed him his room, I found it passable; he should have had a night's rest – if the homeless cockroaches did not tickle the soles of his feet.'

The blend of practicality, sensitivity and self-mockery here was typical of Tagore in his letters to Indira. But so too was a very Indian preoccupation with the illusory nature of human endeavour. Nearly every letter was introspective, many of them profoundly so. 'I have been here just four days', he wrote from Shelidah in June 1894,

but already I have lost track of time. If I were to return to Calcutta immediately I feel I should find much of it transformed.

It is as if I am now standing in a place outside the current of time, unconscious of the gradually altering set of the world. The fact is that here, away from Calcutta in my inner world, time may be stretched or compressed and clocks do not work in the usual way. Duration is measured by intensity of feeling; the emotions of the moment seem endless. Where the outside world with its flow of incident is not constantly employed in checking on my daily activities, moments become hours and hours moments, as in a dream. And then it seems to me that the subdivisions of time and space are figments of my mind. Each atom is immeasurable and each moment infinite.

A month or so later, Tagore wrote of being woken by a 'violent bubbling' of the river in the middle of the night. He opened the shutter of the boat and saw the current surging drunkenly between dim banks drowsy with slumber, the water streaked with starlight like a 'gash of agony'. Yet the following morning it was as if all he had seen was a dream. He compared the experience with European and Indian music:

The day-world calls to mind European music with its various concords and discords, orchestrated into a great, purposeful ensemble. And the night-world is like the sphere of Indian music with its unadulterated melody, sombre and poignant. Both move us, though they are in striking contrast. But why should that disturb us? Pairs of opposites lie at the very root of creation: king and queen, night and day, unity and diversity, the eternal and the evolving.

We Indians are under the rule of night; we are besotted with the eternal, the One. Our melodies are intended for the solitary individual; European music is for the multitude. Our music removes us from the domain of everyday joys and sorrows to a region devoid of company, as aloof as the universe; the music of Europe revels in the perpetual oscillations of the human condition.

The plangent boatmen's songs of the rivers of Bengal, known as *bhatiali*, exactly express Tagore's meaning – and indeed considerably influenced his own songs and poetry, including *Gitanjali*. (The haunting songs that float through the riverside window of Apu's bedroom on his fateful wedding night in Satyajit Ray's *The World of Apu* are *bhatiali* songs.) Here are the words of one such song, sung by poor illiterate boatmen on their way to the city before sunrise, their sails set to catch the wind that blows before the dawn:

> I am a lamp on the water; at what ghat didst thou place me on the stream? Where is the ghat where thou setst me afloat?
>
> In the dark night speaks but the garland of waves, and under it ever flows the stream like a flowing deep night. My only companion is the little flame, and no bank and no end is near . . .
>
> . . . O Ocean, in which all rivers find their destination, Friend, End of all endless movement, how many bends are there still? and then, with what call wilt thou reveal thyself to me? Thou wilt take me from the water, and there, under the protection of thy arm, near to thy heart, wilt extinguish the burning of the whole long journey.

*

Part of Rabindranath, the Bengali part so to speak, was content to feel like this. But the European side of his personality yearned for contact with artists, thinkers and doers. The tragedy was not that there were none on his estates – this was hardly surprising – but that there were so few in Calcutta or indeed anywhere in Bengal. Tagore often referred to this dearth in his letters to his niece. In August 1894, for instance, he wrote asking what she thought of the Goethe biography they had both read. 'One thing you must have noticed – although Goethe was in some ways a detached kind of person, he did not lack contact with men; as a matter of fact he was engrossed in them.' He mentioned the court at Weimar and some of the thinkers contemporary with Goethe, such as Schiller and Kant. 'We, luckless writers of Bengal, feel in our bones the lack of this living touch . . . If a person like Goethe needed the fellowship of Schiller, how much more do persons like us have need of the life-giving company of a man of true feeling and understanding!' [pl.12]

Most of his time on the estates Rabindranath was alone, except for his tenants, boatmen and servants. One of the servants prompted a poem from him in 1896, 'Karma' (The Worker), that gave a sharp picture of his quotidian existence:

No sign of my servant this morning
The door stood unlatched   my bath-water was unfetched
    The rascal didn't turn up last night.
Where my clean clothes were   I had no clue
    Nor where my meal was coming from.
Time passed, the clock ticking   I sat, irritation pricking –
    I would really tell him off, I would.
At last quite late he came   greeted me in the same way
    As usual, palms pressed meekly together.
I was seized by a fit   I cried, 'Go, get out,
    I do not want to see your face!'
He heard me like a dunce   as if stunned for once,
    He searched my face in surprise.
Then he said, 'Last night – '   he choked, 'at midnight –
    My little girl, she died.'
So saying, in haste   cloth on shoulder he went to face
    His daily chores alone.
And, as on any other day,   he cleaned, polished, scrubbed away,
    Left not a single task undone.

In the story 'The Postmaster', Tagore took a similar situation and expanded it, deepening its significance. Like all his best village stories, it has the same mixture of detached observation and emotional empathy as in the poem, infused with melancholy and touches of fantasy. Nirad Chaudhuri offered *The Wind in the Willows* as the nearest work in English literature; and 'The Postmaster' does indeed share the seeming simplicity of language, tremulous pathos and mingling of the animate and inanimate integral to Grahame's classic novel. Instead of the poem's zamindar and his bereaved male servant, in the story we have the postmaster from Calcutta, a fish out of water, and his village servant Ratan, a wispy little girl not yet a woman, without either father or mother. She cooks and cleans for her master, fetches his water (which he persists in storing in pitchers for his bath as people do in Calcutta, rather than risking a dip in the village pond), stokes his hookah, and nurses him when malaria strikes. She is vital to his survival in the village.

Without much to do, the postmaster feels forlorn and bored. It is the monsoon:

The rain-soaked foliage danced and shimmered in the wind, and the sunlit clouds piled themselves in layers like survivors from the vanquished storm – truly a sight to behold. The postmaster reflected: if only, right now, someone dear to me were here, one human companion I could love. Gradually the idea came to him that the solitary bird was saying the same thing, over and over again, and that the murmuring leaves of the shade trees were repeating the same message to the midday sun. No one would have believed, or been able to comprehend, that such an idea could occur to an underpaid postmaster of a village in the back of beyond, during the secluded siesta hours.

On an impulse he begins teaching Ratan to read and write and she responds very eagerly. Soon she lives for his call. To him, however, she is a pastime.

The attack of malaria is what finally drives him to resign his service and leave. He tells Ratan of his decision. 'For some time neither of them spoke. The lamp flickered, and at one point in the room rain dripped steadily from the decrepit thatched roof into a clay saucer placed on the floor.' Then, abruptly, the innocent little Ratan asks him – will he take her away with him? The postmaster laughs, 'What a notion!' Later, out of pity, he offers Ratan money he can ill afford, saying – quite unconscious of any irony – 'Ratan, I've never been able to give you anything.' She bursts into tears and runs away.

The time comes for him to depart. In the film the postmaster walks very slowly towards the ghat, following his luggage, and meets, coming the other way, the diminutive Ratan lugging a large bucket of water for his replacement. He tries to offer her a rupee – but she will not stop or even glance in his direction. It is a heart-rending finale. (As the hard-bitten *New York Times* film critic said: 'It says almost all that can be managed about the loneliness of the human heart.') In Tagore's ending the postmaster boards the boat and it casts off:

the rain-swollen river struck him as tears flooding up from Mother Earth. He felt as if a boundless sorrow had pierced his heart and overwhelmed him with a vague, all-pervasive grief. The face of an insignificant village girl hovered in his mind. Just once he thought: I'll go back; I'll bring that poor forsaken soul away with me. But then the wind filled the sail, the keen monsoon current bore swiftly on, the village dropped out of sight, and its cremation ghat came into view. In the hardening heart of the detached traveller there dawned this fundamental realization: life is full of parting, full of death – so what is the point in retracing one's steps? Which of us can ever know who belongs to whom in this world?

'But no such philosophy arose in Ratan's mind', Tagore concludes the story. Instead Ratan keeps alive a faint hope that the postmaster will return.

Alas for the foolish human heart! It cannot avoid making such blunders. Logic is slow to penetrate it. It distrusts proofs, however absolute, clutches at false consolations, until they sever all its arteries and suck its life-blood. Only then, finally, does the mind become aware of its errors; but the heart continues eagerly to fall into further nets of entanglement.

This, the mood of the closing paragraphs of 'The Postmaster', was also the mood of what are perhaps Tagore's most famous poems of the Shelidah period: 'Shonar Tari' (The Golden Boat) and 'Jete Nahi Dibo' (I'm Not Letting You Go). Both were published in *Shonar Tari*, the 1894 collection that was Tagore's first popular success. In the first poem, which is relatively brief, the poet sits, 'sad and alone', on the riverbank, sheaves of cut paddy waiting beside him (or her). A boat approaches, piloted by a mysterious figure – probably female, again the poem does not specify – who agrees to load the paddy. The person on the bank parts with it all and then asks to be taken on board too. But there is no room. 'Loaded with my gold paddy, the boat is full':

On the bare riverbank, I remain alone –
What I had has gone: the golden boat took all.

'Jete Nahi Dibo', a much longer poem, was directly autobiographical. As in 'The Postmaster' there is a grown man and a young girl. This time they are Rabindranath and his young daughter Bela at Shantiniketan in the summer of 1892; in the background, tearful, hovers Mrinalini, his wife, busy piling his luggage with indispensable pots and pans and saucers, bottles and bedding and boxes, until eventually the narrator (Rabindranath) protests, 'Let me leave a little behind and just take a bit!' The moment of parting has come: Rabindranath must return to the estate, 'back to the grind-stone'. Instead of a boat he must board a train to Calcutta and thence travel to Shelidah. But Bela will not budge.

Outside on the doorstep, preoccupied,
Sat my four-year-old daughter. By this time
She should have been washed and bathed,
And, whilst being fed, have her eye-lids drooping
With approaching sleep; but today her mother
Hadn't seen to her; it was getting quite late
And she was still unbathed. All morning she'd been
Following me about like a second shadow,
Gazing with inscrutable eyes
At the signs of impending departure. Now weary,
On the doorstep she'd fallen quiet as a mouse.
'Bye, sweetheart,' I said finally. Her face was doleful.

'I'm not letting you go,' she replied.
She remained sitting, where she was.
She did not grasp my hand, nor bar the door.
She only claimed her right to love,
With – 'I'm not letting you go.'
And yet our time was up, like it or not.
She had to let me go.

The rest of the poem develops this small incident into a cosmic truth in the same spirit as the conclusion of 'The Postmaster' (though it lacks the condensed emotion of the story). This became a common trait in Tagore's work that to a sceptical mind could easily seem mere philosophizing. But the philosophy was lived, embedded in the Bengali soil, fertilized by centuries of poets, singers and religious minds; Tagore, in a sense, merely gave it new form. Once, he recalled, on a visit to a small village inhabited mostly by poor Muslim peasants he had seen the animated, entertaining performance of a *jatra* (opera) belonging to a Hindu sect no longer in existence. Its subject was the different elements, material and transcendental, that constitute the human personality: the body, the self and the soul. One of the dialogues was between a person who wanted to reach *Brindaban*, the Garden of Bliss, and the garden's watchman (St Peter, so to speak), who had accused him of theft. It turned out that inside his clothes the person was secretly trying to smuggle into the garden the *self*, rather than surrendering it to God. Tagore remarked:

Under a tattered canopy held on bamboo poles and lighted by a few smoking kerosine lamps, the village crowd, occasionally interrupted by howls of jackals in the neighbouring paddy fields, attended with untired interest, till the small hours of the morning, the performance of a drama that discussed the ultimate meaning of all things in a seemingly incongruous setting of dance, music and humorous dialogue.

Most of Tagore's tenants were Muslims. Experiences like this one, crossing religious boundaries, formed the foundation of his attitude to Hindu–Muslim relations. Though he fully recognized the barriers between Hindus and Muslims – and, it must be said, had relatively little intellectual contact with Islam and educated Muslims – he always believed in the syncretic religious traditions of Bengal. (And of other parts of India: the mystic Kabir, a Muslim weaver deeply influenced by Hinduism who wrote in Hindi, was an especial favourite.)

He was also conscientious, generous, imaginative and above all active as a zamindar. [pl.24] During the 1890s he set up a complete judiciary on the estates, a parallel system to that of the government courts which eventually received unique recognition from the government. Cases were taken to the headmen of the villages, on appeal to a court of five headmen appointed from the entire estate, and, as the final court of appeal, to Rabindranath himself. According to his son Rathindranath, who took over as manager around 1910:

> This system prevailed for many years and not a single tenant ever filed a suit in the magisterial or munsiff courts nor did the Government ever object to the legal powers assumed by us. In one of the estates a complete system of self-government was introduced by Father, and it worked wonderfully well. Was not the Maharshi right in putting his youngest son in charge of the estates, even if he was a poet and a visionary?

So far as he could, Tagore protected his tenants against police callousness and corruption. One of his briefest but most powerful stories, 'Durbuddhi' (A Lapse of Judgement), showed with bleak irony that he was fully *au fait* with the grim reality of police behaviour in the lower ranks. But Tagore could not protect the tenants against themselves. 'It was so difficult to help them', he said much later, 'because they did not have much respect for themselves. "We are curs," they would say; "only the whip can keep us straight."' Once, for instance, he had a road built from the estate house at Shelidah towards Kushtia, the nearest railhead. He told the villagers living close to the road that its upkeep was their responsibility: they should get together and repair the ruts caused by the wheels of carts that put the road out of use during the monsoon. They were unwilling: 'Must we look after the road so that gentlefolk from Kushtia can come and go with ease?' He commented: 'They could not bear the thought that others should also enjoy the fruits of their labour. Rather than let that happen, they would put up with inconveniences.'

It was his work on the estates that bred in Rabindranath two unshakeable convictions: that Indians must help themselves, not wait for the government to help them; and that India could not regenerate itself without regenerating its villages. The first led him to found various small businesses in the 1890s, which all failed (Rabindranath was no Dwarkanath), but nevertheless became the seed for India's first modern patriotic movement, the Swadeshi Movement of 1905, which Tagore helped to lead. The second conviction underlay his experiments in rural development in the first decade of this century and later the founding of his 'institute for rural reconstruction' near Shantiniketan in 1921. In both convictions Tagore was ahead of his time, even of Gandhi.

*

For the Bengali elite of Calcutta, the *bhadralok*, especially the more anglicized of them, Tagore's ideas were truly revolutionary. At Bengali political and social gatherings in the 1890s, not a word of the speeches would be in Bengali, and everyone would dress impeccably in the English manner. Rabindranath, who was regularly called to sing at such occasions, brazenly challenged these conventions.

Once he and three of his nephews set off for a party dressed in dhoti and *chadar* with long-nosed Punjabi sandals on their feet. However, they were wearing the socially acceptable stockings. But barely had they started out when Rabindranath pulled off his stockings saying, 'Why keep them? Let us be really nationalistic.' The party was at its height when they arrived. Everyone looked grave, many old family friends turned stiffly away. 'It was bad enough turning up in Indian clothes but to appear with bare legs was really too much! Especially before ladies!' one of the nephews, the painter Abanindranath, recalled with amusement. 'Afterwards everyone copied us.'[pl.10]

That English was superior to Bengali was a belief far more resistant to change: today in Bengal there remains a gulf between those Bengalis comfortable in speaking English and the rest. The best Tagore could manage was a shaky compromise. At the 1897 Bengal Provincial Congress, as the political leaders orated in polished English imitating Gladstone, Rabindra Babu gave a running translation in Bengali. Afterwards one of the best known politicians, W. C. Bonnerjee, a Bengali truly 'more British than the British', twitted Rabindranath: 'Rabi Babu, your Bengali was wonderful, but do you think that your *chashas* and *bhushas*' – meaning peasants and common people – 'understood your mellifluous language better than our English?' [pl.19]

Around this time Tagore wrote a satirical short story 'Rajtika' (The Raj Seal) that dissected the pretensions of almost every Bengali politician to represent the interests of his country. The story details the twists and turns of a 'loyal' Bengali with no talent of any kind save as a flatterer of the British, who finds himself transmogrified, willy-nilly, into a patriot – and who then decides that he rather likes the praise of his nationalist followers:

The moment he set foot in Calcutta he was mobbed by Congress supporters; they danced around him as frenziedly as if the end of creation was nigh. There were eloquent speeches and encomia without end. The chorus was, 'Without heroes like you working for the country, the country has no hope.' Nabendu could hardly deny the truth of this, and so, all of a sudden, among all this hue and cry he found himself a national leader. When he entered the conference hall everyone rose to their feet and loudly shouted such queer foreign greetings as 'Hip hip hooray!' The Motherland blushed to the tips of her roots.

Perhaps the politicians could laugh at this story with slightly shame-faced self-recognition. No such response was possible when Tagore became blunt in his criticism. In 1895 he uttered some of the most flaming of his many burning words in Bengali on the subject of national degeneracy. The occasion was a memorial meeting for Pandit Vidyasagar, the great social reformer, who had died in 1891.

It is hard to see how such an outstanding example of manliness as [Vidyasagar] came to be born in this degraded land of ours. The cuckoo sometimes lays its eggs in a crow's nest; so providence must have assigned to Bengal the task of rearing [Vidyasagar] to manhood.

He was a lonely man, with no kindred soul among the people of his race. He was an exile in his own homeland, for there was none to share his ideals and his work. In the men around him there was not even a trace of his own authentic humanity, and so he was far from happy. He did good to others and received ingratitude and lack of cooperation in return. He saw day after day that we begin but never finish; we make a show but do nothing concrete; we do not believe what we set out to do; what we believe we do not carry out; we can spin out words without end, but cannot make the smallest sacrifice; we feel pleased with ourselves by exhibiting our pride, but never think it necessary to be worthy; we depend on others for everything and yet rend the skies finding fault with them. We take pride in imitating others, we feel honoured to receive their favour, yet we try to throw dust in their eyes and call it politics; and the main object of our lives is to make clever speeches that fill us with intense self-admiration. Vidyasagar had infinite contempt for this weak, mean, heartless, lazy, arrogant, argumentative race of men. He himself was apart from them in every way. Even as a mighty tree grows little by little until it thrusts its head skywards far above the undergrowth at its foot, so Vidyasagar, as he grew older, rose to a calm and solitary eminence far above the unhealthy thicket of Bengali society. He gave cool shade to the weary and fruits to the hungry, but he held himself aloof from the chattering, the endless speechifying, of the numerous mushroom societies and assemblies of the time.

There was a general rise in the emotional temperature of most of Tagore's essays at this time, whether he was lambasting his own people or attacking the arrogance and coarseness of the British in India. It was intensely painful to him to see how the weaknesses of his own people encouraged an overweening attitude in the foreign rulers, against their own best traditions in Britain.

When in mid-1898 the government of India brought in an Act to suppress 'seditious' speeches and writing in the newspapers, Tagore delivered an impassioned, hurt lecture at the Calcutta Town Hall, 'Kantharodh' (The throttled). Bengalis, he said, had been educated at English schools, had imbibed English literature and had adopted English leaders as ideals to emulate; now they were suddenly to be deprived of speaking their minds about the failings of the government. Was this the right way to end the two-hundred-year relationship between Bengal and Britain? Around the same time, he helped some of the braver Bengali politicians to collect money for the defence of the Bombay nationalist leader Bal Gangadhar Tilak, charged with sedition. Most of the donors preferred to remain anonymous; and the barristers of Bombay refused to take the brief. Calcutta sent not only money (nearly Rs.17,000) but also legal help: two British barristers, assisted by a Bengali barrister.

But politics, fundamentally, did not interest Rabindranath. In tandem with his patriotism grew the deepest of all his social convictions: that faulty education was the cause of most of India's ills. He hated the system's monotony, of course, its alienation from life and nature, its utilitarianism, its emphasis on English virtually excluding the mother tongue and, most of all, its joylessness. The whole approach and atmosphere, he felt, was unhealthy. He did not want his children – Bela (12), Rathindranath (10), Renuka (7), Mira (4) and Samindranath (2) – to endure what he had suffered as a child. [pl.16] So in the autumn of 1898, the whole family left Calcutta and settled with him in Shelidah. From now on he would educate them himself.

13   Family Life
(1898–1901)

If you and I could be comrades in all our work and in all our thoughts it
would be splendid, but we cannot attain all that we desire.

letter to his wife Mrinalini,
Calcutta, December 1900

Tagore was ambivalent about family life. He was devoted to his wife and
children, but he increasingly saw them less as individuals than as part of
the greater cause to which he felt his life was dedicated. The result for all concerned would be much unhappiness, even tragedy.

In 1896 he wrote a poem that expressed this tension. This is his own translation, revised by W. B. Yeats:

At midnight the would-be ascetic announced:
    'This is the time to give up my home and seek for God. Ah, who has held
me so long in delusion here?'
    God whispered, 'I,' but the ears of the man were stopped.
    With a baby asleep at her breast lay his wife, peacefully sleeping on one
side of the bed.
    The man said, 'Who are ye that have fooled me so long?'
    The voice said again, 'They are God,' but he heard it not.
    The baby cried out in its dream, nestling close to its mother.
    God commanded, 'Stop, fool, leave not thy home,' but still he heard not.
    God sighed and complained, 'Why does my servant wander to seek me,
forsaking me?'

The period of late 1898 to mid-1901 was the only one in which
Rabindranath, his wife and all his children lived as a family. Before that he lived
in Shelidah, they in Calcutta. Later, one of his daughters (Bela) married and
moved away. The following year, 1902, his wife died. Even in 1900–01 Mrinalini
spent long periods in Jorasanko; she did not share Rabindranath's love of
Shelidah and the rivers of East Bengal. (She had grown up in a village in

Jessore and was, it seems, glad to have escaped it.)

For the eldest son Rathindranath it was a magical period, which he described sixty years later in his often vivid, notably unpretentious memoirs, *On the Edges of Time*. He was then ten years old – the same age as Rabindranath when his father took him to the Himalayas – and responsive to education in the widest sense.

For English, mathematics and Sanskrit, the children had teachers living in the estate house – teachers trained by Rabindranath, who sometimes took over the lessons himself. 'Our teacher of English was an Englishman of a rather interesting type', wrote Rathindranath. His name was Mr Lawrence. He was given a bungalow near the house where he lived with thousands of silkworms. On Sundays he would discard all his clothes, wrap himself in old newspapers and lie amongst the caterpillars, which would crawl all over him. 'He was very fond of them and used to say they were his children.' (Later, in Shantiniketan, he took to drink and had to be sacked.)

Bengali was taught by Rabindranath. Often he would take up one of the poems he was writing and explain it in great detail to Bela and Rathindranath, paraphrasing and analysing every sentence, discussing every word but never calling the subject 'grammar'. He never used any of the graded readers written for schools. 'He did not like to make children feel that because they were immature they must read only that kind of silly stuff written specially for children by people who had little conception of their mental aptitude or capacity.' The two children quickly memorized whole books of poems and pieces of descriptive prose by well-known writers in Bengali, Sanskrit and English.

The *Mahabharata* and *Ramayana* were given particular importance by Rabindranath. But he felt the lack of versions suitable for children that kept only the main story and omitted the manifold digressions. He therefore persuaded his nephew Surendranath (Indira's brother) to prepare an abridged edition of the *Mahabharata*, and his wife an abridged version of the *Ramayana*; and he insisted that Mrinalini should consult the original Sanskrit and not depend upon Bengali translations. (One is reminded of his own mother's desire to hear the twelve-year-old Rabi read the Sanskrit version.) 'This was difficult for Mother,' Rathindranath remembered, 'but undaunted she read the *Ramayana* with the help of a Pandit'. Mrinalini began the writing but did not finish it before she died. Rathi and Bela used to read her manuscript avidly.

She also trained the two children in the household arts. Every Sunday she gave the servants the day off. Then the children did the cooking supervised by her. Rathindranath acquired considerable skill as a cook. In adult life he would be noted more for his practical abilities and craft skills – in total contrast to his father, to whom machines were a baffling mystery – than for his literary or intellectual capacity.

The River Padma and the *Padma* were great educators too. One evening Rathindranath and his father were sitting on the deck of the houseboat when Rabindranath's worn old slippers fell overboard. 'Without a moment's hesitation he dived into the river and swam after them, fighting with the swift currents.' The rest of the evening passed happily with the salvaged but now useless slippers drying in front of their owner.

On another occasion, after a tremendous storm in which the boat managed to take shelter from the river in an inlet, Rabindranath spotted a body floating down the middle of the river with a mass of dark hair rising and falling with the movement of the waves. Immediately he ordered the men to take a lifeboat and rescue the drowning person, who was undoubtedly a woman. The boatmen were unwilling to go. Rabindranath got annoyed and jumped into the boat himself. Then his old Muslim cook began to abuse the boatmen for being cowards. Ashamed, they followed the zamindar into the boat and compelled him to get out. Then they set forth. 'It was thrilling to watch the frail little boat being rowed across the boisterous waves,' said Rathindranath, 'the men pulling heftily for all they were worth, led by the encouraging gesticulations of the cook who had assumed command.' Darkness had fallen when the party returned with the woman. She had beseeched them not to rescue her: being an expert swimmer she had been unable to drown herself. She would not give her name, but Rabindranath discovered she was the wife of one of his tenants. 'The husband was sent for, and after Father had spoken to him, not only did he take his wife home but – so goes the story – never again did he give her cause to feel unhappy.'

Rabindranath in the prime of life took pride in being able to swim across the Padma. (He taught his son to swim by throwing him one day into the river from the deck of the houseboat.) Through remarkable self-discipline he acquired a high degree of control over his body. In a letter written in 1899 he told his wife that a scorpion once bit him while he was asleep in the Jorasanko house. By sheer will-power, he said, he could regard the pain as a doctor would have regarded it – as something external to himself. Though physically suffering acutely, he had been able to fall asleep once more.

Some of the visitors to Shelidah made a permanent impression on Rathindranath. His mother invited a friend, a lady from Calcutta who was unusually tall and rather manly in appearance. But she had a sweet soprano voice. Whenever she came Rabindranath would be roused to compose songs which she would pick up from him by ear. Then, in the evening, his son remembered,

> after a hurried dinner the whole family would tumble into an open boat and, rowing out into the middle of the river, keep it anchored there. Amaladidi and Father would take turns and song after song would float across the water

uninterruptedly until midnight. I would, of course, often be lulled to sleep on my mother's lap long before the party broke up. The river would be deserted and there would be nothing to disturb the stillness of the night except the gurgling of the eddies as they rushed past the boat. The moon would shine like silver over patches of water ruffled by the wind and occasionally belated fishing boats would be silhouetted against the light as they glided down on the current . . . A more romantic setting for music cannot be imagined.

The Padma dominated all their lives. In old age, Rabindranath remembered this period in a wonderful poem:

Once I lived on her sandy moorings
        Isolated, far removed from men.
Waking at dawn I saw the morning star
At night I was watched by the Great Bear,
        Asleep on the roof of the boat.
The myriad thoughts of my solitary days mingled
        with the margins of her aloof current –
The way a traveller passes by
        domestic bliss and sorrow, near yet far.

In the dry season during winter, when the Padma shrank to a comparatively narrow stream, the whole family would decamp from the estate house to live in houseboats moored on one of the gleaming white, spotlessly clean sandbanks known as *chars*, that stretched for mile after desolate mile. A cluster of bamboo huts would be erected for the servants, and a temporary bath-house jutting right out into the river, which the children loved. Wandering over these undulating *chars*, Rathindranath recalled, you would receive a sudden agreeable surprise: 'a crystal-clear lake or a meandering offshoot of the river inhabited by thousands of wild duck, or a coppice of stunted casuarinas – the favourite haunt of wild boars and jackals.' There were also the turtle tracks, 'parallel prints running like railway lines' – and sometimes a lumbering turtle, which could easily be captured by turning it on its back. The meat was excellent, as were the eggs buried in the sand. Another of the family's regular visitors, the scientist (Sir) Jagadishchandra Bose, taught the young Rathindranath how to locate the eggs; and caused him secretly to vow he would become a scientist himself when he grew up.

Bose was a significant figure, then on the threshold of international celebrity. He was the first Indian scientist to be taken seriously in the West and in 1920 became the second Indian F.R.S., fellow of Britain's Royal Society. Besides physics and physiology he was interested in literature and prodded Rabindranath into writing some of his short stories. In 1900 Bose made the earliest attempt to have one of the stories published in the West in English translation. (*Harper's Magazine* rejected it, on the grounds that 'the West was not sufficiently interested in Oriental life'.) He and Tagore were intimate for a few years around the turn of the century, indeed it would barely be an exaggeration to say that Bose was the only Bengali (perhaps the only person) ever to understand Tagore's personality 'in the round' – however briefly. In the late 1910s and 1920s, until the rise of Gandhi, Tagore and Bose would often be cited in the West as the two outstanding Indians who had disproved the prevalent western belief in Indian inferiority.

In mid-1900, in Paris, Bose demonstrated some of his amazingly sensitive experiments (concerning electric currents in frogs' eyes) at the International Conference of Physicists. The scientific response, initially sceptical, was sensational, though Bose knew it would not last without extensive further experiments. In an excited (Bengali) letter to Tagore from London, he described his reception, adding that he was in despair because he had no support from his countrymen for carrying on his work. 'The moment a new discovery is made here it is put to use . . . How long can races so inert and inactive as ours hope to survive? . . . Your poor champion is almost at his last gasp, but you may be sure he will not run away from the battle.'

Rabindranath replied:

There I was, quietly turning the pages of a French grammar, when your letter arrived and made me palpitate with excitement like a dead frog connected to an electric current. I was itching to show the letter to Loken [Palit] and Suren [his nephew], but both of them are far away; I'm sending it to them today.

Yes, declare battle! Do not spare anyone – whichever wretch fails to surrender, cut him down on his home ground with the logic of your arguments, be merciless like Lord Roberts: from the way you have deployed your strategy so far against the assembled company, I am firmly convinced you will be in Pretoria for Christmas. Then, afterwards, when victory is yours, we too – all of us Bengalis – will share in the honour and the glory. We don't need to understand what it is you have done, or to have given you any thought, time or money; but the moment we hear the chorus of praise in *The Times* from the lips of Englishmen we shall lap it up.

Bose's predicament sent Tagore into a flurry of unselfish fund-raising on behalf of his friend. In 1901 he managed to obtain a sum of money from the maharaja of Tripura which was sufficient for Bose to continue his work in London. Bose now published prolifically in western scientific journals, encountered both appreciation and some unscrupulousness from several physiologists, and eventually returned to Calcutta to found the Bose Institute. Today his work as a physicist has historical importance – it paved the way for Marconi's invention of radio – but his much bulkier physiological work is forgotten. (The physicist C. V. Raman, India's first Nobel laureate in science, called the latter 'mumbo-jumbo'.) There is a parallel with Tagore's western reputation, and one suspects that Bose's entire *oeuvre*, too, requires a sympathetic scientific 'translator' to sort out the wheat from the chaff.

Behind the wry humour of Tagore's letter lay an ardent patriotism, bordering on chauvinism. Around the turn of the century he became dissatisfied with his life as a zamindar, disenchanted with the West (despite his respect for science) and determined to start up 'national' institutions in parallel with the government's. In Shelidah, on 31 December 1900, he wrote a poem whose Bengali title translates as 'The Sunset of the Century'. It began: 'The sun of the century is setting today in clouds of blood – at the festival of hate today, in clashing weapons sounds the maddened, dreadful chant of death'. And it concluded:

Awakening fear, the poet-mobs howl round,
A chant of quarrelling curs on the burning-ground.

Tagore had in mind the suppression of the Boxer Rising in China and the Boer War in South Africa; and the effusions of imperial poets like Rudyard Kipling.

He also published a poem, 'Shastra' (What the Scriptures Say), the first stanza of which read:

After fifty thou'lt walk to the forest,
  so our scriptures say.
But we say a forest retreat
  is better in the youthful days.

He was about to turn forty, the mid-point of his life. Increasingly his thoughts turned to the idea of moving to Shantiniketan, to the 'forest retreat' founded by his father in 1863, there to start a school. It would, he decided, be a school in the tradition of the *tapoban*, the ancient forest ashrams mentioned by Kalidasa in such works as *Sakuntala*: dedicated to the ancient principle of *brahmacharya*, continence, later espoused by Mahatma Gandhi. In Tagore's imagination he would train students in the solitude of Shantiniketan, far from the disturbances and fleshpots of Calcutta. 'I wish to keep them away from all the luxuries of European life and any blind infatuation for Europe and thus to lead them in the ways of the sacred and unsullied Indian tradition of poverty', he informed the Tripura royal family with pious enthusiasm in April 1902. This austere mood would last until about 1908, when he began again to welcome western influence in India.

The mood made him take a radical step in his family life. There were other reasons too, such as constant financial worries brought about by the collapse of his *swadeshi* businesses in the late 1890s, his strong dislike for the family atmosphere at Jorasanko, and, perhaps, the illness and seemingly imminent death of his father, the Maharshi – eighty-four years old in 1901, a vast age in India (older than Queen Victoria, who died in January that year). Whatever the precise combination of factors was, in quick succession Rabindranath married off both his older daughters; the dowries and wedding expenses were paid by the Maharshi. Bela was then about four months short of fifteen, her sister Renuka was a mere ten and a half years old. Both girls were married to men they had never met.

By 1901 there was no social pressure for early arranged marriages in Brahmo circles, rather the reverse. Many Brahmo girls were marrying in their late teens: Indira, Rabindranath's niece, left marriage until she was twenty-six. In Bela's case his decision was perhaps just excusable, at least as far as her age was concerned, but in Renuka's it most certainly was not. The only mitigating factor was that Renuka's husband was immediately sent abroad (at Tagore's expense) to study medicine; Renuka therefore continued to live with her parents. Bela, on the other hand, had to leave her parental home and live near Patna in Bihar, the state west of Bengal. (Her husband was a lawyer, the third son of Biharilal Chakravarti, Rabindranath's one-time poet-idol.) In July 1901 Rabindranath took Bela by train to her in-laws and on the way back stopped at Shantiniketan, where he wrote to his wife in Calcutta.

> I have just come after leaving Bela in her new home. It is not what you may imagine from a distance: Bela is quite contented there. There is no doubt that she likes her new way of life. We are now no longer necessary to her.
>
> I have come to the conclusion that, at least for a short period immediately after marriage, a girl should keep away from the company of her parents and give herself unrestricted opportunity for uniting with her husband in every way . . .
>
> If Rani [Renuka] too goes far away after her marriage, it will be good for her. Of course she will be near us for the first couple of years but, after that, as soon as she is old enough, she should be sent entirely away from us for her own good.

The education, tastes, customs, language and way of thinking of our family are different from those of all other families in Bengal; that is why it is all the more necessary for our girls to remove themselves from us after marriage . . .

Think of yourself. If I had lived in Fultala [Mrinalini's village in East Bengal] after marrying you, your nature and your behaviour would have been quite different. Where one's children are concerned, one should entirely disregard one's own happiness. They were not born for our happiness. Our only happiness consists in their welfare and in the fulfilment of their lives . . .

Arriving in Shantiniketan today I am steeped in peacefulness . . . Surrounded by the limitless sky and the wind and the light, I am, as it were, nursed in the arms of the primal mother.

The most sympathetic description of this letter would be a monumental piece of self-delusion; the most honest would be rank hypocrisy. Either way it reflects badly on Rabindranath. Was this the same Tagore who attacked early marriage and the 'joint family' in 1887? Or were there two Tagores – the reformer and the human being – who were as disconnected as the proverbial left and right hand? As the tolerant Rathindranath remarked long after his father's death: 'It has occurred to me that very often Father did not want to admit even to himself his innermost feelings and convictions. It was therefore difficult even for those who were nearest to him, to know the reasons which made him act in a particular way.'

The most plausible motive was that in 1900–01 Tagore felt an irresistible urge to move to Shantiniketan and found a school. Call it patriotism, call it destiny, call it ego, or call it – as Tagore often did – his *jiban-debata* (literally 'life-god'): he had to follow the call. And so he felt he must disencumber himself of other commitments, such as his daughters. In the process he managed somehow to convince himself that he was acting in his daughters' own best interests.

What was bizarre was that Tagore wrote and published his controversial novella *Nashtanirh* (The Broken Nest) during the very same months of 1901 in which he was negotiating the marriages of Bela and Renuka. This, we already know, was the story of his own relationship with Kadambari and Jyotirindranath twenty years before (the basis of *Charulata*). So there he was: in his fiction portraying the searing agony of an arranged marriage between an older man and a barely-more-than-child bride ruptured by the passion of the grown woman, while in his life he was condemning his daughters to precisely the same relationship with the same potential for disaster. Was he conscious of the grotesque contradiction – or did the two activities dwell in distinct mental compartments? There is no way of knowing. In later life, however, Rabindranath betrayed many guilty feelings about the marriages of his three daughters.

Such self-delusion was to be a key element in his institutions at Shantiniketan. And perhaps anyone who attempts to turn a dream into reality must deceive himself about the difficulties to some extent. Initially Tagore could carry very few people with him in his vision of a school. Most of the family were definitely uncooperative; only the Maharshi gave the idea his unconditional blessing. (He had already made provision for a school in the trust deed of the ashram.) This was in August 1901, at the time of Renuka's wedding. Within two months, Mrinalini and the four children, Rathindranath, Renuka, Mira and Samindranath, had moved to Shantiniketan. Soon after, Rabindranath returned to Shelidah for a sort of last look at the place. He would live there again many times for weeks and even months at a time, sometimes with his children – but he would never again regard Shelidah as his home. He wrote from the estate house to his wife in Shantiniketan:

I find it very poignant to be back here . . . I associate Shelidah with both happy and sad memories – but more of them are happy than sad. This is not, though, the best time to be here. Everything is soaked in dew, there is mist until eight o'clock in the morning, and in the evening there is fog. The water is rotten in the well and in the pond – malaria is widespread. We were right to leave Shelidah: the children would have fallen ill if we had stayed. [Shantiniketan] is much purer and healthier. But what masses of roses are in bloom! Huge, beautiful roses. And there's a lovely smell of acacia flowers all around. Your old friend Shelidah sends you a few acacia flowers with this letter.

14   Small Beginnings in Shantiniketan (1901–1905)

I wish to keep my students away from all the luxuries of European life and any blind infatuation with Europe and thus lead them in the ways of the sacred and unsullied Indian tradition of poverty.

> letter to the prince of Tripura,
> Shantiniketan, April 1902

Nearly forty years had passed since Maharshi Debendranath had bought the almost bare land at Shantiniketan, nearly seven acres of eroded red soil a mile or two from Bolpur's railway station and about a hundred miles north-north-west of Calcutta, in order to establish a place for meditation – an ashram. Soil, plants and trees were imported from the 1860s onwards and a house begun in 1866. In 1867 a pond was dug but later abandoned: water would remain a constant problem for the institution. In 1888 a trust deed for the ashram was drawn up by the Maharshi and inaugurated with a gathering of Tagores and leading Brahmos. By then the house, somewhat resembling the estate house at Shelidah, was complete: here Rabindranath and his family stayed for periods in the 1890s – his 1892 poem 'I'm Not Letting You Go' concerned this house. [pl.26] The trust deed provided for the foundation of a school and library and the celebration of an annual country fair (*mela*) on 21 December, the day of Debendranath's initiation into the Brahmo Samaj in 1843. It also banned meat, fish and alcohol within the precincts of the ashram. In 1891 a striking prayer hall was completed, a sort of mini-Crystal Palace built out of plain and coloured glass on an ornamental wrought-iron framework with a marble floor. It was known as the Mandir, a word meaning temple. [pl.26] Here, in 1898, the young Rathindranath, after learning passages of the *Upanishads*, received his sacred thread – and then went to live at Shelidah for three years.

Thus the place that Rabindranath would now regard as home for the rest of his life had become something of an oasis in the midst of a hot, barren and poverty-ridden land. But what a staggering contrast between this area in West Bengal and the East Bengal landscape of Tagore's thirties! It was as if he had moved from the everglades of Florida to the semi-desert of southern California.

Tagore loved both landscapes and both infiltrated his work, but, according to his son, 'there is no doubt that his first and deepest love' was for the rivers, sandbanks and wild ducks of East Bengal.

In Shantiniketan Tagore lived even closer to the elements than in Shelidah, and in intimate touch with infinitude. Satyajit Ray, a student there in 1940–42, called Shantiniketan

> a world of vast open spaces, vaulted over with a dustless sky, that on a clear night showed the constellations as no city sky could ever do. The same sky, on a clear day, could summon up in moments an awesome invasion of billowing darkness that seemed to engulf the entire universe . . . If Shantiniketan did nothing else, it induced contemplation, and a sense of wonder, in the most prosaic and earthbound of minds.

Rabindranath wrote to his niece from Shantiniketan on the same subject in May 1892: 'The world is full of paradoxes and one of them is this: that far horizons, vaulted skies, black storm-clouds and profound feelings – in other words, where infinitude is manifest – are most truly witnessed by one person; a multitude makes them seem petty and distracting.'

Three weeks later he described a storm to Indira in sharp detail. He and two guests had gone out for a walk and had travelled about a mile when they realized that a beautiful line of clouds they had seen on the horizon to the north had 'swollen and darkened and was making for us with regular flashes of lightning.' Unanimously they decided to get back to the house – but too late:

> the storm, with giant strides over the open ground, was upon us with an angry roar . . . Dust made the sky so dark that we could not see beyond a few paces. The fury of the storm continued to increase, and grit driven by the wind stung our bodies like shot, while gusts took us by the scruff of the neck and thrust us along and drops of rain slapped and whipped our faces.
>
> Run! Run! But the ground was not level; it was deeply scarred with watercourses, and not easy to cross at any time, much less in a storm. I managed to get entangled in a thorny scrub, and as I was trying to escape, the wind grabbed me and practically threw me to the ground.
>
> We had almost reached the house when a host of servants came hurrying towards us with a hullabaloo, and fell upon us like a second storm. Some held our arms, some beat their breasts, some eagerly showed the way, others hung on our backs as if fearing that the storm might carry off their master altogether. We had a job to evade the attention of this retinue and get into the house, panting, hair dishevelled, skin dust-caked and clothing drenched.
>
> Still, I had learnt one thing; never again to write in a poem or story a

description of the hero, the image of his lady-love imprinted on his mind, passing unruffled though wind and tempest. The idea is quite false.

In this extreme and stimulating environment, on 21 December 1901, Tagore's school was inaugurated. There were five pupils, all boys and all Bengalis: four of them from Calcutta and the fifth the founder's son Rathindranath. At the opening ceremony in the Mandir they were given red silk dhotis and *chadars*. Satyendranath Tagore (now retired from the ICS) conducted the prayers. Rabindranath composed a song, 'Mora Shatyer Pare Man' (We Dedicate Ourselves to Truth).

Of the five teachers, three were Christians, two of them Roman Catholics. This, in a school that was supposed to be reproducing in modern form the glories of the ancient Indian *tapoban* (forest hermitage)! Among the Christians was Lawrence, the caterpillar-loving Englishman from Shelidah. One of the Catholics was a charismatic and muscular Bengali, a Hindu converted by reading Cardinal Newman, who spoke superb English but a few years later (after leaving Shantiniketan) started an extreme anti-British newspaper in Bengali 'of a Hitlerian type' (to quote Rathindranath); he was prosecuted by the government but died prematurely. It was he who first called Rabindranath 'Gurudev' – as Tagore himself would later be among the first to call Gandhi 'Mahatma'. Nevertheless he did not last long at Shantiniketan because he was a disciplinarian – 'the kind of discipline learnt on the cricket field' (Rathindranath again) – and also he believed strongly in the virtues of caste, despite (or perhaps because of) his conversion to Catholicism.

Such discipline held no appeal for Rabindranath, who had started his school precisely to avoid educational rigidities, but a belief in caste *was* influential in his thinking in these early years. For a long time at Shantiniketan – in fact until Gandhi stayed there in 1915 – the Brahmin boys dined separately from the others; and a Brahmin boy did not touch the feet of a non-Brahmin teacher. Rabindranath did not fully subscribe to the customs of Brahminism but he held with the superiority of Brahminical *ideals*, as interpreted by himself rather than by the Brahmin priests. (Recall his boyish rejection of ritual when receiving his sacred thread in 1873 – but his liking for some of the sacred texts.) Throughout his life he was, by training and temperament, an aristocrat not a democrat, an individualist never a willing member of a group. This led him to clash frequently with Gandhi and the Indian nationalist movement after 1920. Sometimes too it led him to mistake authoritarianism – both of the Left and of the Right – for altruism.

But more than religion he emphasized simplicity of living in Shantiniketan. The cultivation of beauty, for which the place would become a byword, was a later development. In the beginning life there was primitive. The vegetarian meals were 'comparable to jail diet in their dull monotony', Rathindranath recalled. No one wore shoes or even sandals, 'toothpaste or hair oil was taboo.' It was a great trial for his mother Mrinalini when his father insisted that Rathindranath live in the school boarding house. She would try to console herself by often inviting the teachers and the students to the main house, where she would feed them with delicacies cooked by herself. 'Naturally she did not resent it when surreptitious raids were made on her pantry.'

It is easy to imagine the reputation of such a school among the Calcutta *bhadralok*, the professional elite. For several decades Shantiniketan was regarded as a kind of reformatory, to which ne'er-do-well sons might be dispatched. Everyone there was thought to be a little touched: the typical Calcutta reaction to any mention of Shantiniketan would be, at best, a patronizing smile at a poet's impractical fantasy. Living in huts, learning under the trees, at the mercy of the seasons, bad food and water shortage: Shantiniketan was no place for those with worldly ambitions.

For the right personality the freedom was exhilarating, however. There was the poet Satishchandra Roy, for instance, whom Rabindranath thought to be the most gifted teacher he ever attracted to Shantiniketan. At the age of twenty-one he could recite for hours freely from Virgil, Dante, Goethe, Shakespeare or Kalidasa – his favourites being Browning and Rabindranath. The fourteen-year-old Rathindranath was deeply grateful for Roy's generosity. During the scorching sun and hot blasts of April 1903, with the summer holiday just beginning, the two of them sat during the day in a cool dark corner of the library and read the classics. Often they spent the whole night lying out on their backs on the bare ground, 'watching the constellations dip one after the other into oblivion', while Satishchandra recited Bengali poetry. In mid-April, on the last day of the year in the Bengali calendar, there was a storm. Rathindranath described it:

As we stepped out, a glorious sight took us completely by surprise. Black, inky clouds had gathered in the northwest sky and kept advancing like the deep cavernous mouth of an angry monster, ready to swallow the earth . . . its path was marked with clouds of red dust mountain-high. We stood awe-struck on the verandah and watched its rapid progress across the open ground, until it flung itself upon the Ashram with deafening peals of thunder and blinding showers of rain. At the same time Satish Roy's voice rang out with the opening stanza of 'Barsha Shesh' [(Year's End), by Rabindranath]:

Thou comest, New Year, whirling in a frantic dance
amidst the stampede of the wind-lashed clouds

and infuriate showers,
while trampled by thy turbulence
are scattered away the faded and the frail
in an eddying agony of death.

According to Rathindranath,

[Roy's] voice never faltered . . ., and kept even pace with the storm till the last line. I do not know whether I listened to the words that were uttered or merely watched entranced the speaker whose every movement seemed inspired. Before we realized what had happened Satish Roy had vanished into the storm. Afterwards a search party found his battered and half-dead form lying under a tree.

Tragically the young poet died the next year, 1904, of smallpox. (The school had to be temporarily moved to Shelidah.) Death hit Rabindranath hard in this period. He lost two close nephews in 1899 and 1902, his wife in 1902, his daughter Renuka in 1903, his father in 1905 and his youngest son Samindranath in 1907. The death rate in Bengal at this time was twice that of Britain and rising rather than falling as in Britain. Even so, Tagore was unlucky.

His wife Mrinalini was only thirty. She fell ill in Shantiniketan and was brought back to the Jorasanko house. The doctors were unable to diagnose what was wrong and she gradually faded. The last time he saw his mother Rathindranath said she could not speak; instead tears rolled silently down her cheeks. Significantly Rathindranath did not mention his father's reaction during the illness. Rabindranath did not nurse Mrinalini for two months day and night, as loyally claimed by his biographer Kripalani, he remained absorbed in the running of the school, often away from Jorasanko. After she died on 23 November, he showed no visible emotion and soon returned to Shantiniketan. There his feelings came out in a series of poems written in December, *Smaran* (Remembrance), bearing the austere dedication '7 Agrahayan 1309' (i.e. 23 November 1902). His grief was notably impersonal and generalized, with the exception of one or two poems where he spoke, for instance, of having found a few of his old letters secretly hoarded in his late wife's room:

Who will provide them with a place of rest?
They belong to no one here, yet they exist.
Just as once you guarded them with your affection
Mustn't someone now be giving you protection?

He, on the other hand, did not bother to keep his wife's letters. The harsh truth was, Rabindranath did not much miss his wife, either after her death or in later life.

Renuka was not yet twelve when she contracted tuberculosis in late 1902, before her mother's death. In May 1903, Rabindranath took her entirely away from Shantiniketan (leaving Rathindranath with Satishchandra Roy) to a hill-station, Almora, near Naini Tal. He stayed there until August and wrote the series of poems *Shishu* (The Child) that became known as *The Crescent Moon*, in order to entertain the motherless children. Here is the first verse of one:

> Supposing I became a *champa* flower, just for fun, and grew on a branch high up that tree, and shook in the wind with laughter and danced upon the newly budded leaves, would you know me, Ma?

The small child spends the entire day concealed as a flower, scenting his mother's prayers and swaying his tiny shadow on her book as she reads – all unknown to her – and then:

> When, come evening, you would light a lamp
>> And would make your way to the cowshed
> Then would I, finished as a flower-scamp
>> Drop down, gently alight on the ground ahead.
> Once more I'd become your little boy.
>> 'Story time!' I would command you.
> You would reply, 'Naughty, where have you gone?'
>> And I would say, 'That I won't let on.'

What Renuka and Sami thought of these poems Rabindranath did not say. Although he wrote much for children with charm and sometimes with real empathy, he never produced any classic work because he could never quite escape his adult mind. He admitted this in old age in a poem about a wild-natured ten-year-old boy who prefers the company of animals (a stray dog especially) to people:

> A poet who is truly of the boy's world
>> Would put the dung-beetle into so vivid a rhyme
> He would not put it down.
> Have I ever managed to reach the heart of a frog
>> or caught the tragedy of that piebald dog?

Rabindranath took the two children back to Calcutta and there, in mid-September, Renuka died. Though married, she was still a child. Very little is known of her character. Probably there was something of her in a poem Tagore wrote nearly thirty years later:

When Amala's mother died
Amala was only seven years old.
Some kind of fear took hold of me,
That perhaps she would not live long.
There was a pathos in her whole look,
As if the shadow of an untimely parting
Was cast backwards, refracted from the future
Onto her huge dark-rimmed eyes.

His father's death, aged eighty-seven, on 19 January 1905, was the end of an era. The Maharshi had been the leading Brahmo for over half a century. His funeral briefly united the various branches of the Tagore family and the three branches of the Brahmo Samaj at the cremation ghat, where the crowd was immense. The pyre was composed entirely of precious sandalwood; Dwijendranath, as the eldest son, lit the fire. 'Vedic hymns were chanted as the flames did their work and it was late in the evening when the elements were dissolved and dust returned to dust', in the words of the *Bengalee*. Rabindranath was of course present but only as one of the many shaven-headed mourners. He would not be without his beard again until the medical operation just before his own death.

The family estates had already been divided under an arrangement formalized by Debendranath in 1896. Now the 'joint family' itself split up. Rabindranath and Satyendranath had already moved out; over the next year or two Dwijendranath and Jyotirindranath and other family members left No. 6 Dwarkanath Tagore's Lane. Later Dwijendranath would settle with Rabindranath in Shantiniketan. The occupants of No. 5 Dwarkanath Tagore's Lane, Gaganendranath, Abanindranath and the third brother, stayed put.

The Maharshi's will left Rabindranath – the only son to be an executor – a monthly income worth Rs. 1,250–1,500, a regal sum for a Bengali writer in 1905 but by no means sufficient to develop a school – especially if the school did not charge fees, which Shantiniketan did not initially. (Later a charge of fifteen rupees per month was introduced.) The only outside income at this time was from the maharaja of Tripura. The rest had to come from Rabindranath's resources. Before his wife's death he sold all her jewellery. He also sold (to his sister) his gold watch and chain, and his bungalow by the sea at Puri. And in

1904 he licensed an edition of his works for the paltry sum of Rs. 2,000. The edition ran to 1,300 pages and contained short stories, novels, plays, songs, essays and letters – in that order – and cost just over one rupee. There were no poems, since these had been published in a collected edition in 1903. The difference in print run of the two editions was significant: 10,000 copies of the 1904 omnibus were printed, ten times the print run of the poems. (1,000 copies was the typical print run of a first edition by Rabindranath for most of his life.) So even at this relatively early stage in his career, Tagore's poetry was not his most popular writing. Not that Rabindranath would ever earn much money out of *any* of his writing in Bengali. What was clear, though, was that he was now his country's most celebrated living writer.

15 The Swadeshi Movement (1905–1907)

As the stream of village theatre, song festivals and story-telling parties gradually dwindles, sandbanks are emerging where formerly the waters of feeling flowed through our village life.

Introduction to Bengali folk tales,
Thakumar Jhuli (Grandma's Storybag), 1907

In mid-1905 a storm of patriotic feeling blew up in Bengal: the Swadeshi ('Our Country') Movement, a Bengali Sinn Féin. The immediate cause was the long-anticipated announcement of the government, under Lord Curzon, that it intended to partition Bengal into two states; but the real causes lay much deeper. In 1915, reflecting critically upon the Swadeshi Movement, Tagore would write his best-known novel in English translation, *The Home and the World* (which Satyajit Ray would film in the 1980s). But in 1905 he too was gripped by the excitement and for a few months became one of the leaders.

He had expressed his patriotism as far back as 1877, when he read his poem attacking the Delhi Durbar. His letters from London in 1878–80 extended his range. During the 1880s and especially in the 1890s he gave vent to some sharp criticisms of the British – his comments on the opium traffic with China and the Sedition Act, for example. In a letter to his niece he summarized his growing antipathy for Bengali dependence on the government. He had just listened to some English singing and himself sung to the sahibs in reply. Each party had duly applauded the other, but Rabindranath suspected the English response. 'Can such people ever enjoy what I truly love? And if they do not like something, is that thing therefore worthless?' He continued, in a mode similar to that of his grandfather Dwarkanath speaking to Max Müller in Paris in 1846:

If we begin to rate the applause of Englishmen too highly we shall come to reject much that is good in us, and adopt much that is bad from them. We shall grow ashamed to go about without socks, for instance, and cease to feel shame at the sight of their ball dresses. We shall have no hesitation in throwing overboard our manners, and cheerfully emulating their customary lack of them. Our *achkans* will be cast aside as unsatisfactory apparel, but we shall replace them on our heads with hats that are hideous. In short, consciously or unconsciously, we shall have altered our lives and trivialized them, according to whether we are clapped or not.

The founding of the ashram at Shantiniketan in 1901 was one outcome of this feeling, as were Tagore's attempts to found businesses in the 1890s; another was his decision to revive Bankim Chatterji's journal *Bangadarshan* (Mirror of Bengal) that had been the literary sensation of his teens. He edited it from 1901 for five years. There he enthusiastically reviewed *Letters from John Chinaman*, a book published anonymously in Britain in 1901 purporting to be letters from a Chinese government official criticizing the British in China. (In fact the author was Goldsworthy Lowes Dickinson.) He also replied to Lord Curzon's suggestion in a speech in 1902 that the East was prone to 'exaggeration or extravagance'. This was rich coming from a viceroy who was in the thick of planning a Mughal-style Durbar at Delhi to celebrate the coronation of Edward VII. Rabindranath pointed out that there was exaggeration in every language, including English – what about words like 'awfully, absolutely, immeasurably' or a phrase such as 'for the life of me', he asked? More significantly he cited the *Arabian Nights* as an example of eastern exaggeration about the East, and Kipling's just-published novel *Kim* as an instance of western exaggeration. No one expected literal truth from the *Arabian Nights*, but from Kipling, a clever writer, the reader (or at least the British reader) was led to believe that he was getting 'a true description of the real India'. Lord Curzon's Durbar would be similarly deceptive, Tagore said. There would be masses of pomp, as in the days of the Mughals, but no heart, no true generosity and beneficence. How could these be present when a writ had been served on each maharaja commanding him to provide a certain number of elephants, horses and followers? 'Such occasions cannot be carried off with one eye on the purse and the other on imitating the Badshahs.'

It was a quintessentially Tagorean view. A sceptic might well have replied that the history of the Mughal Empire did not suggest that it functioned on love and goodwill between ruler and vassal. But then who could – or can now – deny that the Mughals had grace, charm and aesthetic integrity and brilliance in their art, while British rule had little of these qualities? Instead of the Taj Mahal, the British Raj produced the Victoria Memorial in Calcutta. (The latter was a pet project of Curzon – who, it should also be said, was responsible for preserving and renovating the Taj Mahal.)

In mid-1904, in *Bangadarshan*, Rabindranath developed this line of thinking in a lecture, 'Swadeshi Samaj' (Society and state). 'To establish a personal relationship between man and man has been India's constant endeavour', he said. For instance, a Bengali retained contact even with distant relatives; parents and children retained close ties even when children grew up; and there were many ties of kinship with neighbours and others in a village, irrespective of caste or wealth. These ties, said Tagore, were not 'prescribed by the scriptures, but those of the heart.' Hence the fact that people close to a person in Bengal, but not actually related by blood, were often tagged as 'father', 'brother', 'auntie'.

> The moment we come into contact with a person, we strike up a relationship with him. So we do not slip into the habit of looking on man as a machine, or as a tool for the furtherance of some interest. There may be a bad as well as a good side to this; at any rate, it has been the way of our country; more, it has been the way of the East.

As an example of the 'bad side', Tagore cited Congress political meetings he had attended where the entire energy of the organizers seemed to be spent in giving hospitality rather than in discussing national work. He appealed for this to stop, not because the hospitality was bad in itself but because it was interfering with national work and unity. But then, rather than going on to appeal for a little less sustenance of the individual and a little more inculcation of group loyalty – in other words the willingness to accept 'man as a machine' to some degree – Tagore characteristically appealed to Bengalis to 'invest a strong personality with leadership and rally round him as our representative'. By 'strong' he presumably meant moral rather than manipulative or violent. His prescription was eventually applied with the rise of Gandhi fifteen years later. The Swadeshi Movement turned out to be the precursor of Gandhi's movement; it failed to develop, partly because in Bengal there was no one capable of wearing the mantle of leadership. Tagore was the only one who might have done; but when it lay within his grasp, he felt unable to take it up and escaped to Shantiniketan.

At the time his lecture was given, July 1904, everyone already knew that Lord Curzon wanted to partition Bengal into a western and an eastern portion (as would happen again in 1947, with the creation of East Pakistan, now Bangladesh, though along a somewhat different boundary). The official reason was administrative – the existing province of Bengal was too unwieldy – but the Partition was also an attempt by British officials to disrupt the incipient politics of Hindu Bengal. The first public announcement had come a year earlier, in June 1903. A year later, on 19 July 1905, the proclamation was gazetted, and 16 October was set as the date for the Partition's coming into effect. In between, during August 1905, its chief architect Curzon suddenly resigned as viceroy over a wholly different matter (his dispute with Kitchener).

Thus during the monsoon and autumn of 1905 in Calcutta there was a curious spectacle: 'loyal' Indians paid fulsome tribute to the retiring Lord Curzon, while in the streets thousands of 'seditious' Bengalis marched and sang in protest against Curzon's vivisection of their country. Curzon later published the letters and telegrams he had received. They included one from the head of the Pathuriaghat branch of the Tagores and another, confusingly, from one 'R. Tagore': 'Kindly convey to Their Excellencies a sincere and ardent admirer's and his family's feelings of great sorrow, for we are losing the great man and our greatest ruler. Beg leave to follow Their Excellencies to their next brilliant career, and pray for their long life, health, and happiness.'

Rather than writing encomia for the departing viceroy, the real R. Tagore – the famous one, that is – was composing rousing patriotic songs. Over a month from mid-September he composed twenty-three songs. They caught on instantly in Calcutta and many other parts of Bengal. Nirad Chaudhuri, as a boy in East Bengal, sang them. Nearly half a century later he wrote in his *Autobiography*:

Even now I cannot read the words of these songs, far less whistle the tunes, without instantly bringing back to my ears and eyes all the sounds from the soft rumble of the rain on our corrugated-iron roofs to the bamboo pipe of the cowherds, and all the sights from the sails of the boats on our great rivers to the spreading banian tree – the sounds and sights which embody for me the idea of Bengal.

Chaudhuri was thinking of a slow-moving song like 'Banglar Mati Banglar Jal' (The Soil and Waters of Bengal):

Let the soil and the waters and the air and the fruits of Bengal be holy, my Lord! . . .
Let the minds and the hearts of all the brothers and sisters of Bengal be one, my Lord!

Another popular hit, but with a more energetic rhythm, had a first line that translated as – 'You think you are strong enough to break the bonds that destiny has tied?' There was also a song later loved by Gandhi, 'If no one answers to your call, walk alone walk alone'. Tagore's songs avoided jingoistic sentiments (unlike some other songs that were popular too): he emphasized the beauties of Bengal, the revival of her greatness, and the need for inner strength – rather than hatred of the British. On 16 October, Partition Day, he provided a poetic gesture of protest by adapting an ancient Hindu festival ritual; each Bengali, he said, should tie a thread (*rakhi*) around the wrist of another Bengali as a symbol of brotherhood. Thus Curzon's Partition Day became *Rakhibandhan* (The Tying of the *Rakhi*). A great crowd took to the streets singing 'Banglar Mati Banglar Jal'. Tagore himself, along with some bolder family members, walked from Jorasanko to the river for a ceremonial dip followed by the tying of the *rakhi* on everyone nearby. On the way to the river crowds gathered, ladies scattered rice over them and blew conch-shells, and a great-nephew of Rabindranath with a powerful voice sang the already-famous song. On the way back they saw ostlers at work in a local stables. Rabindranath plunged in and tied the thread around their wrists; the rest of the party hung back, afraid of a row since the ostlers were Muslims. But nothing happened. After that the poet tied *rakhis* even on the wrists of the mullahs in the main mosque on the Chitpur Road. They smiled.

Later in the day there was a procession singing the song about the bonds of destiny, followed by a mass meeting in north Calcutta. Here Tagore gave an impassioned call for money to be donated to a National Fund. An astonishing sum was collected, at least Rs. 50,000 – about half Tagore's Nobel prize money and far more than Rabindranath would generally attract in the years to come when fund-raising for his university. [pl.20]

But Tagore was not sucked into the movement like the many Bengali political leaders. For one thing he stayed in Shantiniketan avoiding the first month or so of meetings and demonstrations after the Partition proclamation on 19 July. He did not speak publicly in Calcutta until 25 August, and he attended only five meetings up to 16 October, Partition Day. Many of his patriotic songs were written away from Calcutta in a calmer atmosphere. So, even at the crest of the Swadeshi Movement, Rabindranath stood apart.

The *swadeshi* activity that interested him much more than politics was education. He wanted to help set up institutions independent of the government, like his school. There was widespread support for the idea in Calcutta, and students immediately wanted to boycott the government institutions. This won over a group of radical politicians, but not Rabindranath. When a crowd of young students came to see him at Jorasanko and eagerly told him that they would leave their schools and colleges if he gave the order, Tagore emphatically refused. The students went away angry, doubting the sincerity of his patriotism. (Later he put a similar confrontation into *The Home and the World*, and it was stirringly dramatized by Satyajit Ray.) According to Tagore's son, who was a student in 1905, 'the genius in him was fundamentally creative' – boycotts held no appeal. In 1921 Tagore explained his thinking to an English friend: 'the anarchy of emptiness never tempts me, even when it is resorted to as a temporary measure. I am frightened at an abstraction which is ready to ignore living reality. Those students were no mere phantoms to me.' Hence the fact that Communism never got a real grip on Rabindranath, in contrast with so many of his fellow Bengalis.

Instead he put his formidable energies into a National Council of Education. He raised money, wrote a syllabus of studies, gave a systematic course of lectures on literature, and even considered affiliating his school to the new body. In this way he and others started off what became Jadavpur University in the 1950s. But Rabindranath was fast disillusioned and abandoned the council. One reason was that it suffered from faction fighting, the bane of Bengali public life. More important, he had realized that the rest of the members did not share his dream of founding something original: they wanted to establish a rival to Calcutta University, an imitation of all that Tagore thought was wrong with Bengali higher education – but under their control rather than the government's. The only major difference was that they wanted to create a bias towards technical education. Tagore's desire that the new university be more Indian and less imitative of the West was ignored, as his own university would be ignored by the majority of Bengalis during his lifetime.

His call for *swadeshi* work in the villages fell on ears deafer still. Calcutta politicians wanted to incite the villagers but had little interest in their welfare. Rabindranath had suggested that a band of workers be organized to give new purpose to village fairs (*melas*) with travelling theatre, songs, magic lantern shows, even bioscopes; to deliver lectures on sanitation; to hold exhibitions of home-made goods and agricultural produce; and generally to discuss with villagers their real wants concerning schools, roads, water supplies, pasture land and so on. From his own long experience he warned that no one should expect fame or praise from such work, or even gratitude from those being helped – their opposition was more likely.

Failing to stimulate interest in the city, Tagore decided to go it alone on his estates. He had already set up a judiciary there; during the Swadeshi Movement he started a Benevolent Society on one of the estates, involving 60-70,000 people and 125 villages. Its funds were entirely administered by elected officials drawn from the villages. Part of the money came from the estate, the rest was from a tax proposed and levied by the members themselves. It was spent on establishing and maintaining schools and dispensaries, constructing roads, filling up stagnant pools, re-excavating tanks and other public welfare projects. The success of the society was remarkable, and it continued to exist even after the estates were taken over by the government of East Pakistan with Independence and Partition in 1947.

But 'there was one problem which the [Benevolent Society] could not very well solve', Rathindranath Tagore wrote in 1961.

Most of the villagers were heavily in debt and were paying usurious interest to a flourishing breed of money-lender . . . A bank which could lend money on the security of the holding of the peasants was undoubtedly needed. But [Father] did not have any capital at the time. He borrowed some money from his friends and started an agricultural bank . . . Relief was immediate. Money-lenders began to shift their business outside the estate and the demand on the bank increased rapidly. Father had to pay 7 to 8 per cent on the money he had borrowed. The bank, therefore, could not charge less than 12 per cent, since it had to cover losses due to defaulters. Even this 12 per cent rate of interest was a pittance compared to what was extorted by the money-lenders. Father could not find any other capital for the bank until he got the Nobel prize in 1913. The prize money amounting to approximately Rs. 110,000 was donated to the Shantiniketan School with the suggestion that the money be invested in the . . . Agricultural Bank. A double purpose was thus served: the school steadily drew an annual income of Rs. 8,000 and the Bank had an additional capital to advance agricultural loans to the tenants.

In 1905 Rathindranath was seventeen years old. Naturally he was swept up in the Swadeshi Movement. But soon he became part of his father's longer-term plan for village development. In early 1906 Rabindranath decided to send Rathindranath abroad – not to London, as he himself had been sent in 1878, or to Oxford and Cambridge, favourite haunts of the Bengali well-to-do – but to the USA, to study agricultural science. 'R. N. Tagore Jr' would be among the earliest Bengali students in the United States. After a series of adventures on the way – including arrival at the smoking ruin of San Francisco, just after the terrible earthquake – he and a fellow-student from Shantiniketan ended up in the Corn Belt of the Midwest, at Urbana-Champaign south of Chicago. (No one met them at the station as they had hoped: a cable they had sent to the secretary of the local YMCA asking him to meet 'two students from India' had been corrected by the telegraph girl to read 'two students from Indiana'!) There Rathindranath studied until 1909.

In 1907 he was joined in the USA by his latest brother-in-law. Rabindranath had high hopes for Nagendranath Gangulee both as an agricultural scientist in the villages and as a husband for his youngest daughter Mira, aged thirteen. They were married in Shantiniketan on 6 June; but Gangulee turned out to be the worst choice of the three husbands selected by Rabindranath. In later life, when he settled in Britain (and traded on his relationship with Tagore), Gangulee showed some modest talent as a writer and editor and even received forewords from H. G. Wells and T. S. Eliot. Essentially, however, he embodied almost everything that Rabindranath struggled against in his educated male contemporaries in Bengal: he was spoilt, spendthrift, undisciplined, cynical, incapable of understanding villagers, addicted to things western (including alcohol) and, to cap it all, foul-tempered. Eventually, in the 1920s, after much agony, he and Mira separated and she went to live in Shantiniketan with her father. Looking back to their wedding day, Rabindranath told Rathindranath:

> I dealt the first blow to her life – without thinking and considering properly I arranged her marriage . . . On the night of the wedding I remember a worrying incident . . . When Mira went to the bathroom, a cobra reared up with its hood fully-blown – today I think that had it bitten her, it would have relieved her.
>
> There is a wild barbarity in Nagen that Mira always dreaded. If, in spite of the lack of love between them, they could have lived together in reasonable understanding, that would have been good. [A reference, surely, to his own marriage to Mrinalini.] But there is no possibility. Mira is incapable of deception and Nagen cannot control his temper.

Less than six months after Mira's wedding Tagore received the keenest of all the blows in his personal life. On 23 November 1907, the day he had lost his wife five years before, his youngest son Samindranath died of cholera. He was only eleven, a beautiful boy who had already shown signs of being the child who would take after his father. He lingered for a few days trying repeatedly to assure his father that he was free from physical suffering. Nearly thirty years later, writing to console a bereaved mother, Tagore called Sami's death 'the most poignant sorrow of my life':

> When his last moment was about to come I was sitting alone in the dark in an adjoining room, praying intently for his passing away to his next stage of existence in perfect peace and well-being. At a particular point of time my mind seemed to float in a sky where there was neither darkness nor light, but a profound depth of calm, a boundless sea of consciousness without a ripple or murmur. I saw the vision of my son lying in the heart of the Infinite and I was about to cry to my friend, who was nursing the boy in the next room, that the child was safe, that he had found his liberation. I felt like a father who had sent his son across the sea, relieved to learn of his safe arrival and success in finding his place. I felt at once that the physical nearness of our dear ones to

ourselves is not the final meaning of their protection. It is merely a means of satisfaction to our own selves and not necessarily the best that could be wished for them.

By now he had completely withdrawn from political involvement in the Swadeshi Movement. He felt able to support those non-violent patriots who were willing to go to prison for their principles: indeed, writing to Rathindranath in the USA he called a jail term 'a recognized hallmark of humanity in our country', presciently foreseeing the mass jail-going from the 1920s until Independence. But he was disgusted by the useless emotionalism of the crowd and the callousness of the political leaders, and horrified by the intimidation and violence that erupted from 1907 onwards, with Hindu–Muslim riots and bombs killing British officials. By 1910, he told his son, now back in Bengal as manager of the estates, that he felt ashamed of his drum-beating in 1905 on behalf of the National Fund and the National Council of Education. The fanfare had been followed by national humiliation, he said. He was now utterly convinced that the only way for Bengalis to succeed in national enterprises was to start small, out of the public gaze, and slowly nurture the enterprise.

This was what transpired with the Hindusthan Cooperative Insurance Company, whose secretary was Tagore's nephew Surendranath and whose office was on the ground floor of Rabindranath's portion of the Jorasanko house. Another example was the Benevolent Society on the Tagore estates, which he regarded as more important than any urban enterprise. The villages, he thought, were the heart of the civilization of India. In 1939, speaking for the last time at his 'institute for rural reconstruction' near Shantiniketan, he said:

> I cannot take responsibility for the whole of India . . . If I can free only one or two villages from the bonds of ignorance and weakness, there will be built, on a tiny scale, an ideal for the whole of India . . . Fulfil this ideal in a few villages only and I will say that these few villages are my India.

His vision had little appeal in Calcutta. Most Bengalis, including some of Tagore's friends, could see only that Rabindranath, having inspired the Swadeshi Movement, had rejected it. They therefore rejected him; and the writers and journalists of Calcutta, envious of his literary fame and comparative wealth, with a vengeance joined the majority. 'Tagore challenged all [the majority's] political, social, cultural, and religious superstitions, and was therefore regarded as an apostate. This gave to those who attacked him out of jealousy an appearance of respectability which otherwise they would not have had', wrote Nirad Chaudhuri. The Swadeshi Movement had fixed the pattern of Bengali response to Tagore for the rest of his life: encomia, escalating with his increasing years and honours, cheek by jowl with vituperation for not being 'one of us'.

16   The Voice of Bengal
(1908–1912)

The present unrest in India . . . is to me one of the most hopeful signs of
the times.

letter to Myron Phelps,
Shantiniketan, January 1909

During the 'Swadeshi Years' Rabindranath had published numerous essays,
but hardly any important poetry and fiction. In the next few years, by contrast, before his historic visit to the West, he produced some of his most famous
fictional works: poetry (*Gitanjali*), a novel (*Gora*) and a play (*Dak Ghar*, translated
as *The Post Office*). These years also saw the publication of his memoirs *Jibansmriti*
(*My Reminiscences*), his wonderful letters to his niece written in the 1890s,
Chhinnapatra (*Glimpses of Bengal*) and, not least, some further powerful essays.

The deaths of so many close to him and the failure of the Swadeshi
Movement deepened Tagore's thinking in every way – religious, educational,
social and political. The trenchancy of his criticisms of his countrymen
increased, and so did the index of their hostility, particularly among the
orthodox. At the same time he came into increasing contact with western
visitors to India, and began to throw off the self-imposed limitations of his
narrowly nationalistic phase, 1900 to 1905. The idea of India as a land with a
genius for the synthesis of East and West, which had been present in his writing
as far back as 1878, grew to dominate his thinking. He had never been
interested in the dynastic history of India and its violent political struggles:
always in writing about Indian history he stressed what he saw as its spiritual
unity, incarnated in the Buddha. In Tagore's eyes, Buddha combined both
contemplative spirituality and active spirituality – East and West so to speak.
From the 1890s onwards there were more and more references to him in
Tagore's works. In his seventies he would hail the Buddha as 'the greatest man
ever born on this earth'.

Rabindranath gave vent to this great theme of synthesis in two lectures
delivered in Calcutta in 1908 in quick succession. They were sparked by the
early terrorist acts of Bengali youths against government officials, both British

and Bengali, that launched a bloody history of terrorist outrages and government repression in Bengal lasting for the rest of Tagore's life and beyond. Tagore could never support such violence, though he did admire the courage of some of the terrorists (as he would show in *The Home and the World*). The impact of terrorism on the average Bengali he thought harmful. In his first lecture on 25 May, 'Path o patheya' (Ends and means), a month after a bomb assassination of Europeans, he argued:

> just because Bengalis have long been branded with the shameful stigma of pusillanimity, the present events have created in the Bengali mind a secret satisfaction, transcending considerations of right and wrong, at the removal of a long-standing slur on the national character.

He went on:

> Many of us have the illusion that our subjection is not like a headache, an ailment pestering us from within, but like a load on the head, pressing down on us from without in the shape of the British Government; and that relief will be ours as soon as we can shake off that load by some means or other. Well, the matter is not so simple as all that. The British Government is not the cause of our subjection; it is merely a symptom of a deeper subjection on our part.

This psychology he then analysed in words that foreshadowed his disagreement with Gandhi and non-cooperation in the 1920s:

> Some of us are reported to be of the opinion that it is mass animosity against the British that will unify India . . . So this anti-British animus, they say, must be our chief weapon . . . If that is true, then once the cause of the animosity is gone, in other words when the British leave this country, that artificial bond of unity will snap in a moment. Where, then, shall we find a second target for animosity? We shall not need to travel far. We shall find it here, in our country, where we shall mangle each other in mutual antagonism, athirst for each other's blood.

He concluded that in India 'men from all quarters of the globe have been endeavouring, consciously or unconsciously, to build a most wonderful temple of humanity out of the fusion of diverse races and religions and sciences. Let us join that noble endeavour, dedicating to it all the energies of our mind concentrated into a single energy of creation.'

This call he forcefully reiterated in the conclusion of his second lecture, 'Purba o paschim' (East and West), delivered in July 1908:

At every turn – in her laws and customs, in her religious and social institutions – India today deceives and insults herself. That is why the meeting of East and West on our soil fails to attain fulfilment. The contact yields nothing but pain. Even if we succeed in pushing out the British by one means or another, this pain will be there; it cannot go until an inner harmony between the two is achieved . . . Then alone will the present chapter of India's history come to its end and a new one start – one of the noblest in the story of man.

Tagore's own painful and ignoble position was demonstrated by two incidents in the months following his lecture. The government was prosecuting a Bengali writer of a 'seditious' book dedicated to Rabindranath (without his permission). The police had intercepted a letter from Rabindranath to the author in which he wrote that he could not condone incitation to violence. Subsequently the police for the first time opened a file on Tagore, while the government had called him as witness. But he refused to help the prosecution. In court he said that he found a young man's desire to write songs and poems calling for the freedom of his country natural, and that since he was not a lawyer, he could not judge what level of language would be regarded as seditious. The writer received eighteen months' imprisonment. Rabindranath seems to have resented the behaviour of both the police and the patriots – and not for the last time in his life.

Then in March 1909 a terrorist, Ullaskar Dutta, was tried and sentenced to death. The *Bengalee* – a newspaper run by a Bengali (in English) but certainly no supporter of terrorism – carried a report of the trial that is still strangely moving:

Before the court sat, in fact before the clattering of the hand-cuffs and creaking of boots were stopped, a voice, at once melodious and powerful issued forth from the prisoner's dock . . . All the 'golmal' [hubbub] in the room – even on the verandah – was at once hushed into perfect silence. Even the European sergeants – to whose ears an Indian tune would not naturally sound very sweet – adopted the posture of attention and began to listen with undivided attention.

The song was of course by Rabindranath. The newspaper printed the words, probably the first published translation of a Tagore song:

Blessed is my birth – for I was born in this land.
Blessed is my birth – for I have loved thee.
. . . I do not know in what garden,
Flowers enrapture so much with perfume;
In what sky rises the moon, smiling such a smile.
. . . Oh mother, opening my eyes, seeing thy light,
My eyes are regaled;
Keeping my eyes on that light
I shall close my eyes in the end.

In this charged atmosphere Tagore wrote a play in which he created an ascetic
who advocated passive resistance to an unjust ruler – an unconscious prototype
of Mahatma Gandhi. He also wrote his longest and most elaborate novel, *Gora*.
Its genesis was interesting. The novel's basic situation concerns a fair-faced boy
(*gora* means fair-faced), brought up as an orthodox Hindu, who rejects the
Brahmo Samaj but falls in love with a Brahmo girl; caught between worlds, he
finally learns that he is not a Hindu at all but an adopted son whose real father
was an Irishman killed in the Mutiny of 1857 and whose real mother died in
childbirth. The idea seems to have occurred to Tagore in 1904; at any rate he
told the story during the close of 1904 at the request of a European visitor in
Shelidah. But with an important difference: in 1904 he said that when the
Brahmo girl discovered Gora to be of European extraction, she refused to
marry him – whereas in the published novel the girl accepts Gora.

According to Tagore, in 1904 he wanted to make a point about the strength of
orthodox prejudice to his European guest. She was a Hindu convert, an
Irishwoman, Margaret Noble, who took the name Sister Nivedita ('the
dedicated') and worked with Swami Vivekananda, the disciple of Ramakrishna,
in Calcutta. She was a ferocious champion of Hinduism, celebrated in her time
both in India and in Britain. Tagore admired Sister Nivedita's devotion to India
and her love for Indians, but found her narrow-minded. She, for her part, was
angry with his story, telling him that he did wrong to Hindu women. Perhaps
that was why he changed the ending when he published *Gora* in 1910 – but as
likely a cause was the intervening Swadeshi Movement of 1905 and after, when
Tagore had seen many Bengali women come out of purdah and begin to make
more decisions in their lives. (This awakening became the crux of *The Home and
the World*, written in Bengali in 1915.) As a result, Tagore may have altered his
own comparatively conservative perception of Bengali women and so elected to
alter the plot of his novel.

For most western readers *Gora* presents major problems, unlike *The Home
and the World*. Its setting is completely alien and Tagore makes no concessions

to a reader not familiar with Bengal of that period, the mid-1870s. On top of that the novel is preoccupied with debates about caste, sectarianism and religion: Hinduism, Brahmoism and, much less, Christianity. When in 1924 it appeared in an unsatisfactory English translation, most readers found it simply tedious. (The translation was the fault of the publisher, not Tagore, who tried to have it corrected.) One of the exceptions was Leonard Woolf, critic, former Ceylon civil servant and husband of Virginia Woolf. He was drawn to the novel's content rather than to its style, and noted pertinently that '*Uncle Tom's Cabin* . . . had considerable merits, but they were not those of a work of art.' He wrote: 'The subject of *Gora* is intensely interesting to me, and Mr. Tagore's handling of it kept me absorbed throughout the book. His thesis is the social, political, and psychological problems which confront the educated Bengali in Calcutta today.'

Woolf was totally wrong in one sense. Not knowing anything about Bengal, he took the period to be contemporaneous, i.e. the 1920s. (Tagore made the date clear to Bengalis with a reference to an event in 1873.) But in another sense, perhaps more important, Woolf was not mistaken. For *Gora*, at bottom, *is* about the Indian predicament: whether modern India, under the impact of the West, can be anything but an imitation of the West. That debate is as alive today as it was in 1924 or in 1873.

The Brahmo Samaj from its inception in the 1840s to its fading away a century later was riven in all directions on the question of western influence. Many Brahmos were barely distinguishable from Hindu society; others cut themselves off altogether, dressed like the British, and wrote and spoke mainly in English. 'They want to sever all connection with Hinduism without discrimination, lest outsiders should mistakenly think they condone also its evil customs,' says an older Brahmo in *Gora*, who often seems to speak for Tagore.

Such people find it difficult to lead a natural life, for they either pretend or exaggerate, and think that truth is so weak that it is part of their duty to protect it by force or by guile. The bigots are those whose idea is, 'Truth depends upon me. I do not depend upon truth.'

The key issue was marriage and, underlying marriage, caste. Tagore was divided on it: in the marriages of all his children, including Rathindranath in 1910 (the last), he maintained caste. And in 1909, writing to an American correspondent Myron Phelps, a lawyer in New York with a sympathy for India, he partly defended caste in a thought-provoking way. (The letter was, incidentally, among his earliest to be written in English.)

It has ever been India's lot to accept alien races as factors in her civilization. You know very well how the caste that proceeds from colour takes elsewhere a most virulent form. I need not cite modern instances of the animosity which divides white men from negroes in your own country, and excludes Asiatics from European colonies. When, however, the white-skinned Aryans on encountering the dark aboriginal races of India found themselves face to face with the same problem, the solution of which was either extermination, as has happened in America and Australia, or a modification in the social system of the superior race calculated to accommodate the inferior without the possibility of either friction or fusion, they chose the latter . . . The great problem which from time immemorial India has undertaken to solve is what in the absence of a better name may be called the Race Problem.

In 1911–12, Myron Phelps visited India and was among the first European visitors to the school at Shantiniketan. He also visited Shelidah and was impressed with the farm started there by Tagore's son using his training in agricultural science in Illinois. Rathindranath was now the manager of the estates, having returned from the West in the autumn of 1909, aged twenty-one. His father had immediately taken him off to Shelidah for a tour in the houseboat. There father and son became intimate in a way that had never happened before and would not happen again, according to Rathindranath.

Successive bereavements and particularly the loss of Sami[ndranath] had left him very lonely and he naturally tried to pour all his affection on me . . . As we drifted along through the network of rivers so familiar to both of us, every evening we sat out on the deck and talked on all sorts of subjects . . . Father must have been hugely amused to hear me prattle and glibly repeat copybook maxims on agronomy, genetics, evolution and such subjects as were still fresh in my mind.

Most of the time he listened patiently to his son. When he did talk, he spoke about the social and economic conditions of the peasants and his own experience in trying to change them. He seldom talked about literature, 'probably thinking that my training in the sciences barred me from appreciating the arts.' (A number of the songs in *Gitanjali* came out of this stay on the estates. They were published in 1910, in the Bengali *Gitanjali*, but we shall come to them later, when they appear in their English translation.)

When father and son returned to Calcutta Rabindranath arranged his son's marriage. The wedding took place at Jorasanko on 27 January 1910; one of Rathindranath's presents, from an aunt, was his father's inscribed gold watch that had been sold to raise money for Shantiniketan. His bride Pratima was a Tagore: she belonged to the family of Gaganendranath and Abanindranath, the more orthodox side of the family, who lived in No. 5 Dwarkanath Tagore's Lane. Though caste was observed, several other rules were broken: the bride was not a Brahmo, and she was a widow, the first widow in the family to remarry. Rabindranath was beginning to escape from the social conservatism of the dead Maharshi. But the marriage was not destined for success. Nevertheless, unlike Tagore's daughter Mira and Nagen Gangulee, Rathi and Pratima did stay together while Tagore lived; they separated later. There were no children. Almost from the start Pratima devoted herself to her father-in-law in the Hindu tradition. Though Rathindranath was too loyal ever to say so in print, he must have resented this. It is difficult not to suspect that Tagore chose Pratima with this expectation in mind (whether consciously or not), knowing that he now had no wife of his own to look after his needs. [pl.27]

With Rathindranath and his wife now settled in Shelidah, managing the estates and running a farm, Rabindranath's thoughts turned back to Shantiniketan. But he seemed unable to settle there (or, of course, in Calcutta). Throughout 1911 there were signs of his restlessness, becoming stronger and stronger as the months went by. They were evident in all his major works of this year. He concluded *My Reminiscences*, for instance, by writing with some bitterness and poignancy:

In other parts of the world there is no end to the movement, clamour and revelry of life. We, like beggarmaids, stand outside and look longingly on. When have we had the wherewithal to deck ourselves and join in? Only in a land where an animus of divisiveness reigns supreme, and innumerable petty barriers separate one from another, must this longing to express a larger life in one's own remain unsatisfied. I strained to reach humanity in my youth, as in my childhood I yearned for the outside world from within the chalk ring drawn around me by the servants: how unique, unattainable and remote it seemed! And yet, if we cannot get in touch with it, if no breeze can blow from it, no current flow out of it, no path be open to the free passage of travellers – then the dead things accumulating around us will never be removed, but continue to mount up until they smother all vestige of life.

Shortly after this, he wrote a pointed satirical play, *Achalayatan* (The Institution of Fixed Beliefs), that depicted the inmates of a vast lunatic asylum: orthodox Hinduism. Then, in September, came *Dak Ghar* (*The Post Office*). This brief play would come to occupy a special niche in Tagore's worldwide reputation. It was performed in Dublin and London in 1913 at the behest of

W. B. Yeats; in Berlin in 1921 with a boyish-looking actress Elisabeth Bergner in the central role; on French radio in June 1940, in Gide's translation, the evening before Paris fell; and, of course, in the Warsaw Ghetto in 1942 by Janusz Korczak. Today it is the only play by Tagore in translation that is still regularly performed.

The plot is simplicity itself. Amal, a young boy, is gravely ill, dying. The doctor insists officiously that he stay indoors away from light and air, and his prudent, wealthy stepfather agrees. From his window Amal sees various villagers – a girl collecting flowers, a curd-seller, a watchman and also a wandering fakir – and they talk to him. He yearns for their freedom. Beyond he can see a big building with a flag flying from it: the King's post office. The watchman says that one day there may be a letter for Amal from the King; and the fakir concurs. Amal is thrilled. He imagines the journey of the King's postman,

> coming down the hillside alone, a lantern in his left hand and on his back a bag of letters; climbing down for ever so long, for days and nights, and where at the foot of the mountain the waterfall becomes a winding stream he takes to the footpath on the bank and walks on through the corn; then comes the sugar-cane field and he disappears into the narrow lane cutting through the tall stems of sugar-canes; then he reaches the open meadow where the cricket chirps and where there is not a single man to be seen, only the snipe wagging their tails and poking at the mud with their bills. I can feel him coming nearer and nearer and my heart becomes glad.

When the village headman hears of this fantasy, he is incensed and has the King anonymously informed of the boy's presumption. But instead of punishment, at night there arrive the King's herald and the state physician, breaking down the outside door. At the physician's command the doors and windows of the room are thrown open; the starlight streams in. Amal drinks in the sight, then drifts off into sleep. The girl Shudha now comes bringing the flowers she has promised him. She places them in his sleeping hand. It is she who has the final word. 'When will he be awake?' she asks the physician. 'Directly the King comes and calls him.' 'Will you whisper a word for me in his ear?' she persists. 'What shall I say?' says the physician. 'Tell him "Shudha has not forgotten you".'

Clearly the play treads the finest of fine lines between sentiment and sentimentality. Almost all its power depends on the actual performances. In 1917, when it was staged in a large room in Jorasanko, Amal was played by a boy from Shantiniketan, Shudha by the youngest daughter of Abanindranath Tagore, who himself acted the parts of headman and physician while his brother

Gaganendranath appeared as Amal's father (and designed the perfect stage setting). Rabindranath played – who else? – the fakir (and the watchman). Only one performance for a small and select audience was scheduled but the demand was so great that seven were given, the last in the presence of Gandhi and other Congress leaders. [pl.37]

When the play was performed in Berlin in 1921, Tagore was in the audience. He was struck by the difference in interpretation, which he could not define. A German friend hit upon it: the German version, he said, was suggestive of a beautiful fairy tale, whereas the Bengali interpretation emphasized the spiritual. Afterwards, Tagore tried to explain the meaning in a letter:

> Amal represents the man whose soul has received the call of the open road . . . But there is the post office in front of his window, and Amal waits for the King's letter to come to him direct from the King, bringing him the message of emancipation. At last the closed gate is opened by the King's own physician, and that which is 'death' to the world of hoarded wealth and certified creeds brings him awakening in the world of spiritual freedom.
>
> The only thing that accompanies him in his awakening is the flower of love given to him by Shudha.

He was writing to an English friend. In 1911, when the play was written, Tagore had no English friends. But his personal contacts with foreigners were increasing. Many were attracted to Jorasanko by the presence in No. 5 Dwarkanath Tagore's Lane of his nephews Gaganendranath and Abanindranath, both of them gifted painters and also collectors of Indian art. These two had rejected the mimetic naturalism of western academic art, then predominant in India. Abanindranath had borrowed instead from Mughal miniature painting and from classical Indian mythology and had founded what soon became known as the Bengal School of painting. Among his foreign friends were Okakura Kakuzo, the Japanese pioneer in reviving the Japanese people's interest in their own artistic heritage, and Ananda Kentish Coomaraswamy, of mixed Ceylonese and British parentage, the well-known pioneer in the study of Indian art and its interpretation to the West.

Okakura became friendly with Rabindranath and influenced him towards seeing Indian culture as part of a civilization common to Asia: an East, however diffuse and subtle, which could be meaningfully opposed to a West that was all too powerful in Asia. 'Asia is one', wrote Okakura famously. Tagore would never entirely relinquish this supposed unity.

Coomaraswamy and Tagore were never as close, but each recognized the quality of the other's mind. In 1911, with the help of a master at Shantiniketan,

Coomaraswamy translated some of Tagore's poetry and published it. These translations were among the first in English to attract attention.

Another friend of Abanindranath Tagore was William Rothenstein. In the winter of 1910–11 Rothenstein paid his first (and only) visit to India, in order to paint. Each time he went to Jorasanko, he found himself attracted to an uncle of Abanindranath, who would sit listening while others talked. He asked whether he might draw him, for he had discerned in him 'inner charm as well as great physical beauty', as he wrote twenty years later in his memoirs. 'That this uncle was one of the remarkable men of his time no one gave me a hint.'

Rothenstein and Rabindranath established a rapport. 'Yourself I shall always allow myself to regard with reverence and affection, and I hope you will . . . perhaps remember that I shall be grateful for any translations of poems or stories which may appear at any time', Rothenstein wrote to Tagore just before he left India. Back in London his interest was further aroused by reading a Tagore short story published in Calcutta's *Modern Review*. Rothenstein wrote to the family asking for more stories; he also offered his hospitality to Rabindranath, should he visit London as was expected. But instead of short stories, Rothenstein received an exercise book of poems translated by Coomaraswamy's Bengali collaborator, Ajit Chakraborty. The poems struck him as being 'highly mystical' and 'still more remarkable than the story, though but rough translations'.

One wonders what would have happened to Tagore's later reputation, had more short stories been sent instead of poems? By 1911–12 a fair number of Tagore's short stories had been published in English translation in India (the first one as far back as 1901), without making much impact on English readers – but hardly any poetry. What poetry was in print was unquestionably inferior to the short stories. It would seem, then, that the 'highly mystical' element was required to lift Tagore beyond the small circle of English people interested in India. Presumably Tagore's instinct told him this, and hence he suggested sending poetry to Rothenstein, instead of short stories.

The interest of Rothenstein, Coomaraswamy and others was like a tonic to Rabindranath. His physical health, so robust by Bengali standards, had started to give way. He had started to suffer badly from piles. A trip to Europe would give him both the chance of medical treatment and an opportunity to meet lively minds such as Rothenstein's. He began to feel intensely restless. When should he go? A passage was booked for him, Rathindranath and his wife in October, but various factors forced him to cancel; he tried again in March, and fell ill; he did not finally depart until the end of May 1912.

Curiosity was the positive part of his urge to travel (apart from the desire for medical treatment). There was also a negative aspect. In late 1911 and early

1912 he was particularly oppressed by his countrymen. Orthodoxy – Hindu and Brahmo – was up in arms over his novel *Gora*, his satirical play *Achalayatan* and a lecture to Brahmo sectarians in which Tagore stated provocatively: 'How can we utter this great lie that only what is dull and lifeless is part of Hinduism, whereas its ideal and its striving towards freedom are things which belong to the world but not to the Hindus?' And jealousy of his position as a writer, recognized by a unique fiftieth birthday reception for him at Calcutta's Town Hall in January 1912, added fuel to the attacks of the bigots (Hindu and Brahmo). Furthermore a confidential government circular sent out by the education department had described Shantiniketan as 'altogether unsuitable for the education of the sons of Government servants'. Bengali education officials had already refused Rabindranath's books in schools, because his Bengali was considered too unorthodox; now his own school was under surveillance by the police and boycotted by 'loyal' Bengalis (some of whom had no doubt attended his birthday reception).

The tangle around Tagore in Bengal was perfectly illustrated by an incident in December. 'Jana Gana Mana' is today India's national anthem, selected in the 1950s and composed by Tagore in late 1911. Officially it was written for the meeting of the Indian National Congress in Calcutta in December 1911, where it was sung for the first time. Most probably it was really composed for the occasion of George V's coronation at the Durbar held in Delhi in the same month – but not sung at the Durbar because it was insufficiently 'loyal'. There the head of the Pathuriaghat Tagores held an umbrella over King George; perhaps he and the Bengalis on the national reception committee had hoped that Rabindranath could manage a song in the same spirit as the umbrella. If so they were disappointed. The following year in London one of Tagore's Bengali friends explained how the song came about to W. B. Yeats, who told Ezra Pound, who then passed the story on to his father in the USA, calling it a joke 'worthy of Voltaire':

The national committee came to Mr Tagore and asked him to write something for the [Delhi Durbar]. And as you know Mr Tagore is very obliging. And all that afternoon he tried to write them a poem, and he *could* not. And that evening the poet as usual retired to his meditation. And in the morning he descended with a sheet of paper. He said 'Here is the poem I have written. It is addressed to the deity. But you may give it to the national committee. Perhaps it will content them.'

To escape Bengal and its contradictions for a while had become imperative for Rabindranath. On 27 May 1912 he, his son, his daughter-in-law, and a

companion from the princely family of Tripura, boarded a liner at Bombay.
With him went a manuscript, translations of various poems he had made over
the previous month or two while recuperating from a collapse in the quiet of his
beloved Shelidah. Whenever his mind became restless on the high seas, he
would sit in a deck-chair and translate one or two more poems. He had no
inkling of the unprecedented fate that would befall these fragile little verses in
the heart of the British Empire.

17 England and the USA (1912–1913)

When, in spite of all obstacles, something seemed to impel me to come to this country I never dreamt it was for this that I was taking my voyage.

letter to W. B. Yeats,
London, September 1912

The first thing Tagore and his party did on reaching London on 16 June was to lose the only manuscript of the translations that became *Gitanjali*. It happened on the Underground going from Charing Cross station to their hotel in Bloomsbury. None of them had ever travelled by tube and they were completely bewildered. Next day, when Rabindranath wanted the translations, his son could not find the attaché case. Luckily it turned up at the Left Luggage Office.

London was alien to them. More than twenty years had elapsed since Rabindranath had left the city after barely a month's stay, thoroughly dissatisfied and yearning to be back in Bengal. His son had visited more recently, on his way back from the USA in the summer of 1909, but his stay had been comparatively brief and superficial. Neither father nor son had any close friends in the city.

A few months later, writing in Bengali for home consumption, Tagore described his immediate feelings on arrival at the hotel. Typically he stressed the anonymous, active, mechanical impression made upon him by London life:

Although I do not need to look at it, I pull out my watch like everybody else, snap it open and then quietly put it back into my pocket. When the time is neither meal-time nor time to retire, the hotel looks like a moored boat, and one is at a loss to explain one's presence in it . . . As I stand by the open window I find streams of people running in various directions. They seem to me like so many tools in the hands of an invisible mechanic . . . I stand outside this giant engine and see the living pistons, propelled by the steam of hunger, moving up and down with an indomitable energy . . . If I shut my eyes for a while and try to form an idea of all the labour and movement that constitute this city of London, what terrible persistence! Nobody knows the goal of this incessant drive, what latent power is in the process of being manifested.

The tone was similar to that of *Nationalism*, Tagore's indictment of power politics and commercialism delivered four years later during the First World War. It seems also to foretell the mood of T. S. Eliot's (post-war) poem *The Waste Land*. Perhaps Tagore was voicing a feeling already subliminally present in the minds of those who were overwhelmed by *Gitanjali* that summer.

The first of these was of course William Rothenstein. It was Rothenstein who initially read Tagore's manuscript, exulted in the poems, contacted Yeats, introduced Tagore to writers, artists and thinkers, and arranged for the publication of the book by the India Society and then by Macmillan. In addition he looked after Tagore's material needs. Fittingly, *Gitanjali* was dedicated to Rothenstein. [pl.29]

His biographer Robert Speaight wrote that 'William's conception of friendship was almost oriental in its serious intensity, and Tagore was among the few who shared it.' In Rothenstein's own words to Yeats that fateful summer:

What the poems are he is. For years I have believed this to be a necessary relation between the artist and the work of art, & have suffered greatly both in my own struggles & because it has been difficult for me to accept much that is admired by many good men. When I first met Rabindranath it was like a personal reward, & the renewal of intimacy has been one of the prizes of my life. Above all, the poems have nothing in them which any man must feel it necessary to reject, as is the case with so much of the great mystical poetry of the world, where here and there are stated things which offend that perfect balance of visions which great art must show.

To Tagore, Rothenstein had 'the vision to see truth and the heart to love it. This is the quality that . . . has made him dear to me.' [pl.30]

Tagore never entirely lost this emotional intimacy with Rothenstein. But there were strains in the friendship from an early stage, that after an incident in 1921 became irreparable, as we shall see. Its effect was that Tagore, speaking to his biographer Edward Thompson in 1921, gave a distorted account of his encounter with Rothenstein in London in 1912. Rabindranath did not downplay the artist's crucial role in launching *Gitanjali* – how could he, even supposing he wanted to, given the evidence – but he *did* downplay his own eagerness for recognition in English. Rothenstein, Tagore told Thompson airily, had not been expecting him in London and did not know him as a poet at all, only as a member of the Tagore family. It was only after Rothenstein had settled him in a rented house in Hampstead, said Tagore, that 'one day' he showed interest in reading a poem or two. From then on, Tagore implied, events assumed charge of his insouciant translations and took them out of his hands.

In actual fact Rothenstein was fully expecting Tagore, had already planned a dinner for him and was involved in efforts to obtain an Oxford doctorate for him. Further, we know he had read and admired the manuscript translations of Tagore's poetry sent by Ajit Kumar Chakraborty, the schoolmaster at Shantiniketan; and he had heard all about Rabindranath as a poet from two Brahmo friends of Tagore who visited London in mid-1911. The result was, according to Rothenstein in his *Men and Memories*, written in 1932, that the moment he met Tagore in June 1912, he was handed a notebook containing translations. 'He begged that I would accept them.'

The disparity in the accounts would not matter much if it did not show in microcosm Tagore's ambivalence about his western success – perhaps all success. It also illustrated the inextricable mixture of humility and vanity that was Rabindranath Tagore. His intelligent western friends found themselves inspired and exasperated by this unique blend at one and the same time. But those who did not know Tagore personally, or knew him at a remove, tended either to worship or to debunk. No one understood him in the round, not even Leonard Elmhirst, who worked intimately with Tagore as both rural developer and secretary – and definitely not William Rothenstein, who never saw Tagore in his own setting at Shantiniketan.

On 27 June, at Rothenstein's behest, Tagore and Yeats met for the first time, over dinner. On 7 July there was a soirée at Rothenstein's where Yeats read some of *Gitanjali*. On 10 July a dinner was held in Tagore's honour at the Trocadero Restaurant, organized by Rothenstein with Yeats proposing the toast and reading three poems. Present were seventy people, among them Yeats' friend Maud Gonne, Cecil Sharp, Ralph Vaughan Williams and H. G. Wells. Rothenstein told Yeats the next day: 'I have I think never been present at a dinner where the minds of the diners were less bent on a thousand things & more centred upon the object and subject of the occasion'. That same night, Arthur Fox Strangways, one of the organizers, wrote to Rothenstein: 'I simply loved [Yeats'] Irish "friend" and the like, and the mystic waving of arms over the victim of the evening'. As a result Fox Strangways became Tagore's unofficial literary agent.

Within a week or so Yeats was at work selecting and arranging the poems and making pencilled corrections for Tagore to consider. Then, having written an Introduction, he sent it to Rothenstein in early September. He commented:

In the first little chapter I have given what Indians have said to me about Tagore – their praise of him and their description of his life. That I am anxious about – some fact may be given wrongly, and yet I don't want anything crossed out by Tagore's modesty. I think it might be well if somebody compiled a sort of 'Who's Who' paragraph on Tagore, and put after the Introduction a string of dates, saying when he was born, when his chief works were published. My essay is an impression, I give no facts except those in the quoted conversation.

This suggestion, a sensible one, was for some reason not taken up. The essay appeared in isolation. A little of it is in our Introduction. Some more is worth quoting here, so as to feel the full impact of Rabindranath Tagore on William Butler Yeats:

> I have carried the manuscript of these translations about with me for days, reading it in railway trains, or on the top of omnibuses and in restaurants, and I have often had to close it lest some stranger would see how much it moved me . . .
>
> If the civilization of Bengal remains unbroken, if that common mind which – as one divines – runs through all, is not, as with us, broken into a dozen minds that know nothing of each other, something even of what is most subtle in these verses will have come, in a few generations, to the beggar on the roads . . .
>
> A whole people, a whole civilization, immeasurably strange to us, seems to have been taken up into this imagination; and yet we are not moved because of its strangeness, but because we have met our own image . . .

The enthusiasm, however misinformed about Bengal it was, was infectious. On 2 October Yeats' friend Ezra Pound dined with Tagore. The following day he spent the whole afternoon with him, discussing prosody, watching Rothenstein do his portrait and listening to him read and sing. Tagore made Pound feel 'like a painted pict with a stone war-club', he wrote to a friend on 4 October. A month later he repeated exactly the same image while discussing the newly-published India Society edition of *Gitanjali* for the *Fortnightly Review*, and boldly asserted: 'Briefly, I find in these poems a sort of ultimate common sense, a reminder of one thing and of forty things of which we are over likely to lose sight in the confusion of our Western life, in the racket of our cities, in the jabber of manufactured literature, in the vortex of advertisement.'

Almost his only note of doubt in a critique running to nearly nine substantial pages – including a worthy attempt to analyse the metre of the Bengali originals (unique in the contemporary reviews) – was that the 'general reader' might find

the poems too pious. Pound rejected the criticism: 'I have nothing but pity for
the reader who is unable to see that their piety is the poetic piety of Dante, and
that it is very beautiful.'

Rothenstein's friend Paul Nash, not yet the well-known war artist, agreed,
and put his reaction more straightforwardly:

> One feels about them [that] they are the thoughts that come to *our* minds in
> moments of deep feeling, to some of us quite often to others rarely, written
> down for us in the simplest way. And so they delight me: for everywhere I am
> glad to find my confused thoughts and feelings expressed so clearly and so
> beautifully that I have sometimes laughed for joy, sometimes felt tears come.
> There is certainly a music in some of the poems but most of that I suppose is
> lost in translation. As to style, beauty of language, craft of any kind I am not
> bothered by it. I would read *Gitanjali* as I would read the Bible for comfort
> and for strength.

And the same was felt by the *Times Literary Supplement*, if more equivocally:

> As we read his pieces we seem to be reading the Psalms of a David of our own
> time who addresses a God realized by his own act of faith and conceived
> according to his own experience of life . . . If we cannot share the Indian
> poet's faith, we must at least acknowledge that he has not sacrificed his reason
> to it. He plays neither an artistic nor an intellectual game. As a poet should
> be, he is so simple that anyone can understand him; yet this does not mean
> that there is little to understand.

The truth of this last comment – that anyone could understand Tagore, or at
least thought he could – was proved by the copyright page of the Macmillan
edition of *Gitanjali*. First published in March 1913, *Gitanjali* was reprinted ten
times *before* the award of the Nobel prize on 13 November.

Gitanjali still repays reading, but only in fits and starts. In its 103 verses,
there are many individual sentences and longer sections that remain affecting.
For instance the first lines of verse ninety-six that moved Wilfred Owen: 'When
I go from hence, let this be my parting word, that what I have seen is
unsurpassable.' Or the lines from verse sixty-three that Ezra Pound admired
and that Tagore quoted in his telegram thanking the Swedish Academy for the
Nobel prize: 'Thou hast made me known to friends whom I knew not. Thou
hast given me seats in houses not my own. Thou hast brought the distant near
and made a brother of the stranger.' There are the lines from verse sixty chosen
by Yeats to conclude his Introduction: 'Children have their play on the seashore

of worlds. They know not how to swim, they know not how to cast nets.' Or the much-quoted opening of verse seventy-three: 'Deliverance is not for me in renunciation. I feel the embrace of freedom in a thousand bonds of delight.' Lastly, there is a line from verse thirty-nine loved by Mahatma Gandhi: 'When the heart is hard and parched up, come upon me with a shower of mercy.'

A few verses are compelling in their entirety. This is verse thirty:

I came out alone on my way to my tryst. But who is this that follows me in the silent dark?

I move aside to avoid his presence but I escape him not.

He makes the dust rise from the earth with his swagger; he adds his loud voice to every word that I utter.

He is my own little self, my lord, he knows no shame; but I am ashamed to come to thy door in his company.

And here is verse one hundred and two, deeply autobiographical:

I boasted among men that I had known you. They see your pictures in all works of mine. They come and ask me, 'Who is he?' I know not how to answer them. I say, 'Indeed, I cannot tell.' They blame me and they go away in scorn. And you sit there smiling.

I put my tales of you into lasting songs. The secret gushes out from my heart. They come and ask me, 'Tell me all your meanings.' I know not how to answer them. I say, 'Ah, who knows what they mean?' They smile and go away in utter scorn. And you sit there smiling.

Finally, here is verse sixty-seven, slightly edited by Robert Bridges for *The Spirit of Man*, his wartime anthology of poetry from all periods and civilizations, and later reprinted by Yeats as one of the seven Tagore poems in *The Oxford Book of Modern Verse, 1892–1935*:

Thou art the sky and Thou art also the nest.
O Thou Beautiful! how in the nest thy love embraceth the soul
    with sweet sounds and colour and fragrant odours!
Morning cometh there, bearing in her golden basket the wreath of beauty,
    silently to crown the earth.
And there cometh Evening, o'er lonely meadows deserted of the herds,
    by trackless ways, carrying in her golden pitcher cool draughts
    of peace from the ocean-calms of the west.

But where thine infinite sky spreadeth for the soul to take her flight,
    a stainless white radiance reigneth; wherein is neither day
    nor night, nor form nor colour, nor ever any word.

Such verses, especially the last one (exquisite as it is), have little in common with the short stories and novels of Tagore, or indeed most of his essays and letters and much of his other poetry. The Tagore of *Gitanjali* was not the Tagore of 'The Postmaster', *Gora*, 'East and West', 'Letters from an Exile in Europe' or 'I'm Not Letting You Go'. But by virtue of being published first in English along with Yeats' ecstatic imprimatur, *Gitanjali* fixed Tagore's image in the western mind irrevocably. He would be seen as basically a mystic, a Wise Man from the East, 'an ineffective dreamer, v dignified and calm', to repeat the disappointed comment of Edward Thompson. Tagore unquestionably encouraged this impression through his subsequent English translations and sometimes by his personal behaviour in the West. At the same time he regretted it.

But saying this does not account for *Gitanjali*'s and Tagore's phenomenal impact in 1912 and immediately after. Was it just a fashion, even a mirage born of a thirst for the exotic? Today it is fashionable to say so. The whole notion of a 'universal' poet is now treated with suspicion or worse. Think of Philip Larkin's reaction to Tagore: aggressive indifference. Yet the greatest writers have always crossed national boundaries. They have to leave baggage at home, particularly if they are poets; nevertheless much gets through if the translator is an inspired one. Are we to dismiss as ephemeral and even misguided the enthusiasm for Tagore of poets such as Yeats, Bridges, Gide, Saint-John Perse and Jiménez, and also Ezra Pound, Wilfred Owen, Edward Thomas, Hart Crane and Robert Frost? To say yes is truly to indulge in 'the enormous condescension of posterity' – E. P. Thompson's comment in another context.

The answer to the question of Tagore's impact is surely more interesting and subtle. Though it has many aspects and many levels, at root it harks back to Yeats' comment on *Gitanjali*: 'we are not moved because of its strangeness, but because we have met our own image'. Tagore's western admirers saw the humane spirit of Christianity, venerated in theory but ignored in practice, reflected back at them from *Gitanjali* in a pure form. Jesus Christ was an Oriental, Tagore emphasized; and his own idea of Indian spirituality had a strong affinity with that of the New Testament. Hence the reaction of Charles Darwin's granddaughter Frances Cornford, on meeting Tagore in Cambridge in July 1912. 'I can now imagine a powerful and gentle Christ, which I never could before', she told Rothenstein (whose fine drawings of Tagore expressed the same emotion). Others felt similarly, without making the comparison as explicit. 'Tagore brought back the ideal of the first beatitude transfigured, that is to say, without any painful abnegation and asceticism, and endowed with joyous peace', Nirad Chaudhuri explained much later.

In addition to poets and artists, the ideal was bound to have particular appeal to wealthy Edwardian Englishmen, satiated with luxury and privilege, who within two or three years would go gladly to the battlefields of the Western Front. Some of them appreciated Tagore's poetry. The irony of this – given Tagore's passionate pacifism – was as deep as the delusions of some who fought. One must assume that what they had seen in peacetime was indeed unsurpassable (to recall *Gitanjali*). Only a hero's death seemed able to cap it. Though Wilfred Owen was not part of this set, he seems to have absorbed its ethos. It is a pity that we shall never know what Owen really saw in *Gitanjali*. The strangest fact is that his interest survived, and even intensified, through the writing of his own bitter poetry during 1917 and 1918. One is tempted to recall another line from *Gitanjali*: 'From the words of the poet, men take what meanings please them, yet their last meaning points to thee.'

For all the enthusiasm, there were many more measured assessments, even at the outset of Tagore's English career. The poet and editor of Everyman, Ernest Rhys, an early and lifelong admirer of Tagore who wrote the first English biography of him (published in 1915), mentioned 'a famous English critic' who said 'half humorously', 'I have met several people, not easily impressed, who could not read that book [*Gitanjali*] without tears. As for me, I read a few pages and then put it down, feeling it too good for me. The rest of it I mean to read in the next world . . . ' The poet Thomas Sturge Moore, who had been present at the soirée on 7 July 1912, wrote to a friend:

> Yeats and Rothenstein had a Bengalee poet on view during the last days I was in London. I was first privileged to see him in Yeats' rooms and then to hear a translation of his poems made by himself and read by Yeats in Rothenstein's drawing room. His unique subject is 'the love of God'. When I told Yeats that I found his poetry preposterously optimistic he said 'Ah, you see, he is absorbed in God.'

Bertrand Russell (who had met Tagore in Cambridge, introduced by Goldsworthy Lowes Dickinson) paid him a back-handed compliment in mid-November. He had read the India Society edition of *Gitanjali* 'with the very greatest interest', he said: '[the poems] have some quality different from that of any English poetry – if I knew India perhaps I could find words to describe it, but as it is I can only say that I feel it has a value of its own, which English literature does not give. I wish I could read them in their original language.'

*

Tagore was by then in the USA, having spent some four months in England, three of them in London and one in the countryside, staying first in a vicarage in Staffordshire (arranged by another of his new friends, the missionary Charles Freer Andrews, also present at the 7 July soirée), later with Rothenstein in Gloucestershire. Having departed England on 19 October, he settled in Urbana, Illinois on 1 November, the day of publication of *Gitanjali* in London.

He had gone to Illinois to rest, and perhaps receive medical treatment for piles; also for the sake of his son. Rathindranath wanted to resume his studies at the university and work for a doctorate in biology, following the degree he had obtained in 1909. None of these intentions was to be fulfilled.

Although his reputation had not preceded him from London to this Midwestern backwater, Tagore was quickly in demand. 'The people of this country are quite crazy about lectures,' he wrote to his daughter Bela. They had put him in a quandary. In spite of the attention showered upon him in England, he had not lectured there. He had a real fear of appearing comical speaking in English. But he gave in just ten days after arriving in Urbana because the request came from a small club of Unitarians. Over the next three weeks he spoke five times from his discourses at Shantiniketan, which became the basis of his lectures at Harvard University in February 1913 and in London the following May and June. Later, after being revised by Ernest Rhys, they were published as *Sadhana: The Realisation of Life*.

Meanwhile Ezra Pound had been busy. He was the foreign correspondent of the new magazine *Poetry*, published from Chicago. On 24 September, after talking to Yeats but before meeting Tagore, he wrote to *Poetry*'s editor Harriet Monroe: 'I'll try to get some of the poems of the very great Bengali poet Rabindranath Tagore. They are going to be *the* sensation of the winter.' In October, now under Tagore's spell, he trumpeted, 'This is *The Scoop*. Reserve space in the next number for Tagore . . . I've known for weeks that he was *the* event of the winter.' In December's *Poetry*, the third issue of the magazine, six poems of *Gitanjali* were published, with a brief appreciation by Pound. This was Tagore's maiden appearance in American print.

But Harriet Monroe had as yet no idea that the 'very great Bengali poet' was living just over a hundred miles from her. She came to know it when Rathindranath (signing himself 'R. N. Tagore Jr.') wrote to her requesting two copies of the December issue of *Poetry*. (An editorial in the *Chicago Tribune* welcoming the poems seems to have alerted the Tagores.) Immediately she invited Tagore and his party to Chicago. Rabindranath was hesitant: 'I feel great reluctance in visiting big towns, where I am likely to be drawn into all kinds of engagements, which bewilder me . . . I am afraid, I have grown awkward, and I am not fit for social ceremonies.' That was on Christmas Day 1912. On 4

January he was softening: 'I think it is only my inertia that makes me feel reluctant to suddenly wrench myself from the little habits of living in retired corners.' On 13 January he sent her some new translations of love poems for *Poetry*. At last, on 22 January, he arrived in Chicago.

He spent nearly three weeks there on and off. Harriet Monroe in her memoirs recalled sitting around a hearth fire listening to him 'chanting his lyrics' and talking of 'Oriental creeds', making her feel as if she was 'sitting at the feet of the Buddha'. *Gitanjali* she described as 'those sacred songs of praise which were chanted everywhere in his native India.' (One wonders if Tagore ever contradicted this common howler.) She noted his 'satirical-humorous observations of Western civilization', his 'bitter' attitude to British subjection of India, and the fact that 'His English was more perfect than ours'. But overall it was the 'serenely noble Laureate of Bengal' that struck her, not Tagore's other selves. Whether she saw what *Gitanjali* had predisposed her to see, or whether Tagore himself consciously projected this pose, or whether there was a symbiosis between her predisposition and his pose, is hard to discern from her memoirs and letters. More than most men, Rabindranath Tagore was a chameleon.

She also introduced him to the person who became his closest American friend. Harriet Moody was the widow of William Vaughn Moody, the poet and playwright who died young in 1910. Over the years she was to be a friend of several well-known American poets, some of whom stayed in her spacious house. It was around her hearth fire that Tagore held court; he and his son and daughter-in-law, though complete strangers to Mrs Moody, were invited to stay. Later, she accompanied them to New York and Harvard, and they stayed in her flats in New York (Washington Square) and London (Cheyne Walk). The benefit was mutual, since she was lost after the death of her husband and other personal tragedies. According to *A House in Chicago*, the biography of Harriet Moody, 'Tagore's visit set the machinery of her life, her true life, in motion again.' Tagore himself wrote to Rothenstein: 'I feel I have been of help to her – for she was gradually drifting towards a vague region of Christian Science and its allied cults which are in vogue here and which are so destructive of spiritual sanity and health.'

The invitation to lecture at Harvard had come from the professor of Indian philosophy there, James Houghton Woods. The original suggestion, though, had come from Goldsworthy Lowes Dickinson in Cambridge, England, to A. Lawrence Lowell, the president of Harvard (and brother of Amy Lowell). But when Woods put the idea to the Boston Brahmins of the philosophy faculty, they were not very responsive, having apparently suffered from *swamis* making inroads into American spiritual life (following Swami Vivekananda's triumph at

Chicago in 1893). Woods prevailed however, and in February Tagore spoke thrice to Woods' philosophy class, and once each to the Philosophical Club and the Divinity Club.

Despite these reservations and Tagore's own doubts about calling himself a philosopher, the lectures were a definite success, the first of many for Tagore in the world's great universities. Woods himself wrote later to Tagore:

> I am still exhilarated by the influence of your visit. And on your return very many of us hope that you will consent to give the remaining three of your lectures . . . It seems to me that you have penetrated deeper and more resolutely in the evil of life than any of us.

He urged Tagore to have the lectures printed, and he even, it seems, offered to print an American edition of *Gitanjali* at his own expense and give the proceeds to Shantiniketan.

Another enthusiast was Ellery Sedgwick, editor of the *Atlantic Monthly*, who was taken to meet Tagore by his former teacher at Harvard, the Idealist philosopher Josiah Royce. 'I gained that night an impression of the wisdom of the East and West such as I have not had before or since', Sedgwick told Tagore in 1926. He immediately commissioned an article on Shantiniketan which was published during 1913, and in 1927 published another article by Tagore, despite its excoriating criticism of some fundamental aspects of American life.

One non-enthusiast was T. S. Eliot, a student of Woods. He appears (like Kipling) to have maintained an absolute silence about Tagore, though he did agree in 1951 to write a preface to an anthology of 'thoughts for meditation' that included Tagore. One might perhaps have expected Eliot to put Tagore down, as he did Goethe and as Pound would do several times both in private and in print after 1913. He would have reacted against Tagore's links with American Unitarianism, the religion Eliot had rejected in his own family, and he would have distrusted Tagore's interpretation of Indian spirituality. But perhaps Eliot was in some way touched by the man (he did attend one of Tagore's lectures), and decided to hold his peace on Tagore. One of Eliot's fellow students at Harvard, R. F. Rattray, who looked after Tagore in 1913, implied this in a 1940 letter to Tagore in Shantiniketan: 'it may be that it was impressions of you that worked into [Eliot's] poem *The Waste Land*: "Shanti! Shanti! Shanti!"' Tagore replied: 'I am interested to read what you say about Mr. T. S. Eliot. Some of his poetry [has] moved me by [its] evocative power and consummate craftsmanship. I have translated . . . one of his lyrics called "The Journey of the Magi".'

Tagore in person certainly touched a consummate craftsman of an earlier generation, Robert Bridges, England's Poet Laureate. Bridges attended a lecture taken from *Sadhana*, 'Realisation in love', given by Tagore at Manchester College, Oxford in late May 1913, some six weeks after his return from the USA. Remembering the occasion a year later in a long letter to Tagore, Bridges, who was not given to uttering platitudes, wrote: 'your presence there gave reality to the honest but vain profession of the University to be a home for all creeds and nations.'

He also invited Tagore to tea at his isolated house on Boars Hill outside the city, along with an Oxford student from Bengal, a Muslim, whom Bridges liked, Shahid Suhrawardy. Fortunately Suhrawardy produced a vivid portrait of these two most picturesque but dissimilar poets together:

> no poet in England was so indigenous as Bridges, so unexotic, so classically free from the touch of the Orient. And Tagore in my eyes represented the melody, the abundance, the grace of the East; to him Beauty came as she flowed down streams or awoke on the sprays of the breeze-tossed corn; she came to him naturally as the cherished one to her lover. Whereas to Bridges she was a burden; with him there was a constant struggle to reduce the conflict to the counterpoints of harmony, to force Beauty into the fierce shackles of tone and rhythm.

Tagore departed Boars Hill before Suhrawardy. He went by hansom-cab back to Oxford; Suhrawardy wanted to walk.

> After [Tagore] had left, Bridges excitedly spoke how that evening, more than he could from his works, he had come to understand Tagore's wise spirit. Then turning brusquely he added: Tagore is an extraordinarily good-looking fellow. There is something unreal about him, something Assyrian, Old Asiatic. Do you think he puts gold in his beard? When I suggested that it was the colour of the sunset that had been playing on their faces, he broke into a loud schoolboy laughter and said: You cannot know the vanity of poets. And striding to the mirror on the wall of his vast study he carefully combed with his fingers his hair and beard tousled by the wind.

Bearing this impression in mind, it is possible to feel what effect Tagore might have had, even on a sceptical Oxford audience, when he read a passage from his lecture such as the following:

> One day I was out in a boat on the Ganges. It was a beautiful evening in autumn. The sun had just set; the silence of the sky was full to the brim with ineffable peace and beauty. The vast expanse of water was without a ripple,

9 Rabindranath (*centre, standing*) with leaders of the Indian National Congress, in Calcutta, 1890: W. C. Bonnerjee (*left, seated*), Pherozshah Mehta, president (*right, seated*)

0 Rabindranath as patriot, Swadeshi Movement, 1905/06 (*Sukumar Ray*)

21 Rabindranath, in Shelidah, 1890

22 Rabindranath, in Europe, 1890

23 Shelidah/East Bengal:
top – the Kuthi Bari, estate house of the Tagores
below – the *Padma*, houseboat of the Tagores

24 Rabindranath as zamindar, on his estates in East Bengal

25 Shantiniketan: Chhatimtala, the original meditation spot of Maharshi Debendranath Tagore, today (*Samiran Nandy*)

Shantiniketan:
[above] – the original house, started in the 1860s
[below] – inside the Mandir (prayer-hall), completed in 1891, today (*Samiran Nandy*)

mirroring all the changing shades of the sunset glow. Miles and miles of a desolate sandbank lay like a huge amphibious reptile of some antediluvian age, with its scales glistening in shining colours. As our boat was silently gliding by the precipitous riverbank, riddled with the nest holes of a colony of birds, suddenly a big fish leapt up to the surface of the water and then disappeared, displaying on its vanishing figure all the colours of the evening sky. It drew aside for a moment the many-coloured screen behind which there was a silent world full of the joy of life. It came up from the depths of its mysterious dwelling with a beautiful dancing motion and added its own music to the silent symphony of the dying day. I felt as if I had a friendly greeting from an alien world in its own language, and it touched my heart with a flash of gladness. Then suddenly the man at the helm exclaimed with a distinct note of regret, 'Ah, what a big fish!' It at once brought before his vision the picture of the fish caught and made ready for his supper. He could only look at the fish through his desire, and thus missed the whole truth of its existence.

It is our desires that give rise to sin, Tagore concluded, 'For sin is not one mere action, but it is an attitude of life which takes for granted that our goal is finite, that our self is the ultimate truth, and that we are not all essentially one but exist each for his own separate individual existence.'

This is *Sadhana* at its most beguiling, unsententious and concise. But too much of these lectures was ponderous, pontifical and imprecise. The weakest sections were, as so often with Tagore, the most abstract ones, especially when delivered unedited by the skilled hands of a native-speaker such as Ernest Rhys. Dean Inge, the dean of St Paul's Cathedral, heard one of them in London in June, 'The realisation of Brahma' (published as 'The realisation of the Infinite'). He noted in his diary: 'It was a beautiful exposition of pure mystical doctrine, but I could not help feeling that there was no concrete filling of the idea of Brahma. The Absolute may be perilously near to zero, if all determinations are denied to it.' Nevertheless, commented Goldsworthy Lowes Dickinson, *Sadhana* had put forward 'a mysticism which does, at least, endeavour to allow for and include what I have called the [West's] Religion of Time. To [Tagore], and to other mystics of real experience, I must leave the attempt to reconcile Eternity and Time.'

Sceptics and atheists were less forgiving. The two most celebrated whom Tagore met were George Bernard Shaw and Bertrand Russell. They rank as the most imperfect of all Tagore's 'imperfect encounters' with famous westerners, epitomizing the mutual attraction and repulsion of Britain towards India, West towards East, and vice versa.

Shaw we know regarded Tagore with a puzzling mixture of respect and ridicule. At dinner in Rothenstein's house, he treated Tagore with absolute solemnity, and then, after he had gone, made jokes about him, including the crack about 'Old Bluebeard'. At the end of a concert at the Queen's Hall by the violinist Jascha Heifetz (then on his first European tour, aged twelve), Shaw appeared suddenly out of the crowd, caught hold of Tagore, quietly announced, 'Do you remember me? I am Bernard Shaw', and walked away. But just before Tagore left London, Shaw wrote about him to a friend: 'He had made an extraordinary number of deeply interested friends during his visit; and I am one of them.' Later he wrote to his friend, the critic and playwright William Archer, about the need 'to get to the truth regardless of shattered ideal[s] and ripped-up Rabindranaths' – this, by strange coincidence, at the very same time that Tagore repudiated his knighthood as a protest against shattered British ideals in India; and Shaw named an off-stage character in a playlet, a poet, 'Stupendranath Begorr'. But in 1931, after a long talk with Tagore in London, he seems to have realized the value of Tagore's efforts to create understanding between Britain and India. When Tagore died in 1941 it was Shaw who asked Sir Kenneth Clark, then director of the National Gallery, to hang portraits of Tagore (one of them by Rothenstein).

Tagore's relationship with Bertrand Russell is more puzzling still, almost as baffling as the infamous echo in the Marabar Caves. Theirs was a clash between two antithetical conceptions of what constitutes wisdom and the true philosopher.

There is no doubt that Tagore first met Russell in Trinity College, Cambridge, in July 1912. Lowes Dickinson, E. M. Forster's friend, took Tagore to Russell and wrote about it in 1923. It was a summer evening and they sat out in the glorious college gardens. Tagore sang some of his poems, 'the beautiful voice and the strange mode floating away on the gathering darkness.' (Shades of Professor Godbole singing mystifyingly of Krishna in Forster's soon-to-be-started novel.) 'Then Russell begins to talk, coruscating like lightning in the dusk. Tagore falls into silence. But afterwards he said it had been wonderful to hear Russell talk. He had passed into a "higher state of consciousness", and heard him, as it were, from a distance. What, I wonder, had he heard?'

When pressed further by Lowes Dickinson, Tagore was said to have replied: 'I do not remember a word of what the Professor said, though my ears listened intently, and appreciated [the] facility in his method. But it was all entirely irrelevant to the important matters of life and devoid of scientific discernment of demonstrably accessible fact.'

Now compare Tagore's son's account of the first meeting of Rabindranath and Russell in his memoirs. The scene is a London boarding house in South Kensington. Rathindranath recalled:

One more visitor was Bertrand Russell. He also turned up suddenly and had to introduce himself since Father had never met him. He told Father that he had come down from Cambridge specially to see him, and then without any further attempt at conversation abruptly asked him, 'Tagore, what is Beauty?' The question came so suddenly that Father kept silent for a minute and then explained his ideas on aesthetics . . . I could not judge whether Father's exposition satisfied Bertrand Russell because after listening with rapt attention he left just as suddenly as he had come.

Perhaps there was a case of mistaken identity and Rathindranath Tagore was describing a different Russell. It is *just* possible to believe this. When Bertrand Russell was shown Rathindranath's account in 1960, he was mystified, and said categorically: 'Tagore visited me three times, but I never visited him. When we met, no conversation remotely resembling [this account] occurred. I cannot imagine how this story came to be invented.'

And when he was shown Lowes Dickinson's 1923 account in 1963, Russell remarked:

. . . I recall the meeting of which Lowes Dickinson writes only vaguely. There was an earlier occasion, the first upon which I met Tagore, when he was brought to my home by Robert Trevelyan and Lowes Dickinson. I confess that his mystic air did not attract me and I recall wishing he would be more direct. He had a soft, rather elusive, manner which led one to feel that straightforward exchange or communication was something from which he would shy away. His intensity was impaired by his self-absorption. Naturally, his mystic views were by way of dicta and it was not possible to reason about them.

Russell was himself factually incorrect on three counts. There was only one meeting with Lowes Dickinson and Tagore (in July 1912); Russell met Tagore four times, in 1912, 1913 (twice) and 1926; and – what is really important – Russell *did* visit Tagore, in London, when Tagore gave a lecture. The fact comes from Russell's own letter. On 19 June 1913 he wrote to Ottoline Morrell from London, after hearing 'The realisation of Brahma' (from *Sadhana*):

Here I am back from Tagore's lecture, after walking most of the way home. It was unmitigated rubbish – cut-and-dried conventional stuff about the river becoming one with the Ocean and man becoming one with Brahma . . . The man is sincere and in earnest, but merely rattling old dry bones. I spoke to him before the lecture [Perhaps he asked him 'Tagore, what is Beauty?' as written by Rathindranath?] – afterwards I avoided him.

Then, in the very next paragraph Russell stated: 'All that has gone wrong with me lately comes from Wittgenstein's attack on my work – I have only just realized this.'

Obviously the super-rational Russell had been brooding while walking back from Tagore's supra-rational lecture – and the result was this Larkinesque outburst against the Orient. The connection with Ludwig Wittgenstein is rather intriguing. For Wittgenstein had launched his 'attack' – a turning point in Russell's life – on the identical article by Russell that Tagore had greatly admired, 'The essence of religion', published in October 1912 just before *Gitanjali*. Wittgenstein felt, according to Russell, that 'I had been a traitor to the gospel of exactness, and wantonly used words vaguely; also that such things are too intimate for print.' Tagore, by contrast, felt that Russell had touched something vital and congratulated him with a verse from the *Upanishads*: 'From him words, as well as mind, come back baffled. Yet he who knows the joy of Brahman (the Infinite) is free from all fear.'

In 1931, Russell wrote of Tagore: 'of what he has done for Europe and America in the way of softening of prejudices and the removal of misconceptions I can speak, and I know that on this account he is worthy of the highest honour.' Presumably he was speaking of the man rather than the mind. In 1967, Russell published in his *Autobiography* Tagore's 1912 letter of praise for his article on the essence of religion – without comment. But when asked his opinion of the letter he wrote: 'I regret I cannot agree with Tagore. His talk about the infinite is vague nonsense. The sort of language that is admired by many Indians unfortunately does not, in fact, mean anything at all.' This was Russell's last observation on Tagore: he dismissed him as a thinker (preferring a humbug like Sarvepalli Radhakrishnan) – and yet he could not quite shake off the feeling that, compared with himself, Tagore might have superior insight.

As a final twist to this perplexing story, *Wittgenstein* later (in the 1920s and '30s) became a devotee of Tagore. In Vienna, discussing philosophy with the Vienna Circle of logical positivists, Wittgenstein would sometimes lose patience with their certainties, turn his back on them and read from Tagore's poetry. He also much liked a Tagore play. It is tempting to draw a parallel between Wittgenstein's most quoted statement, the last sentence of his *Tractatus Logico-Philosophicus*: 'Whereof one cannot speak, thereof one must remain silent' – and Tagore's quotation to Russell from the *Upanishads*.

In general, it was the poets who understood Tagore best on his visit to the West in 1912–13. Yeats, Pound, Bridges, Sturge Moore, Rhys and Saint-John Perse were all moved by the work and touched by the man. Sturge Moore became a particularly loyal and perceptive friend, who was responsible for recommending Tagore to the Swedish Academy. After seeing Lady Gregory's production of *The Post Office* in London in July 1913, arranged by Yeats, Moore wrote to Tagore:

> I watched your lovely little play towards the end through my tears. I think it was more of a success than you have been given to understand, the first act genuinely delighted all those round me, the least rich and the most susceptible part of the audience, and was loudly applauded . . . No doubt Rothenstein who has seen real Bengalee villagers felt the timid and vague easternness in which the actors moved to be colourless, but for those who like myself have no previous knowledge this faintness realized the remoteness which is necessarily part of the charm for us.

Just before Tagore sailed for India on 4 September, Rothenstein and Yeats arranged a small and convivial dinner in his honour. Afterwards they asked Rabindranath to sing 'Bande Mataram', Bengal's nationalist song. He hummed the tune but could not remember more than a few words. Then, in succession, Yeats attempted the Irish anthem, Rhys the Welsh national anthem and Rothenstein 'God Save the King'. Each stumbled. 'What a crew!' said Rothenstein.

Over twenty years later, in his last letter to Yeats, Tagore wrote: 'Though I had already left behind me half a century of my life when I visited your country I felt that I had come to the beginning of a fresh existence young with the surprise of an experience in an atmosphere of kindly personalities.'

One of these was undoubtedly Ernest Rhys. Three weeks after the dinner, and two months before the Nobel award that would change so much in Tagore's life, Rhys wrote memorably to Rabindranath in India:

> We have so clear a sense of your having been among us, that we do not care now to make too much of your having gone . . . For myself, you have quickened my whole feeling for the sun, the light . . . you have brought back the old fond belief of my youth in the ideal life that is behind the real.

18   The Nobel Prize
(1913)

To deprive me of my exclusion is like shelling an oyster – the rude touch
of the curious world is all over me.

letter to Harriet Moody,
Shantiniketan, January 1914

The fact that he had won the Nobel prize reached Rabindranath in the late
afternoon of 14 November 1913. There was no telephone in Shantiniketan,
so a cable was sent from Calcutta. By an extraordinary coincidence Edward
Thompson, his future biographer, was paying his first visit to the school that
day. Posterity is indebted to him for recording Tagore's immediate reaction to
the astounding news. But first Thompson congratulated Tagore with confidential glee. 'Earth has nothing more for you now, Rabi Babu. You must commit
suicide this night. Only first let us settle what you are to do in your next incarnation.' Then –

> The boys went mad. They didn't know what the Nobel prize was, but they
> understood that the gurudev they adored had done something wonderful, as
> indeed he was always doing. They formed ranks and marched round the
> ashram singing their school song 'Amader Shantiniketan'. Rabi and I were
> sitting on the sofa, and they went past when they saw that. But they would not
> go past the second time but gathered at the door. I went and looked at them.
> They had gone wild. I called to Rabi, 'You'd better come.' He came. Then a
> frenzy of worship seized them and they, one after another, threw themselves
> down and touched his feet. That saint of a man stood deprecating, with his
> hands to his face, palms together, begging pardon. When his superintendent
> came he tried to stop him from homage. But all, masters, boys, servants, did
> homage. I could have done it myself almost, but I am an Englishman and have
> stern contempt for the fools who pretend they are easterners.

Tagore and Thompson went inside. The boys dispersed, made a huge bonfire
and went on shouting far into the night. Tagore said to Thompson:

I shall get no peace now, Mr Thompson. I shall be worried with appeals, all kinds of people will be writing to me. Do you know, Mr Thompson, sometimes I feel as if it were too much for me, as if I could bear it no longer. When I reached Bombay [six weeks before], I saw a lot of people with garlands. I thought they were waiting to garland some official. My heart sank when I found that they were waiting to make a public show of me there.

Even before the news, Shantiniketan had attracted its first foreign devotees. They were Charles Freer Andrews and William Winstanley Pearson, two British missionaries serving in India who had met Tagore in London in 1912 and were both, from the first, happy to touch his feet in the Indian manner. [pl.28] Now, post-Nobel prize, foreign and Indian visitors began to come in a regular stream and in some cases to stay for long periods. (Among them were Ramsay MacDonald, MP and future prime minister, and Will Lawrence, brother of T. E. Lawrence, who both visited briefly in December 1913.) Shantiniketan would gradually become less of a shelter for Rabindranath and more of a show-place. Which did he want for it, and for himself – obscurity or publicity? He could not make up his mind as long as he lived.

Four days later he wrote to Rothenstein a now notorious letter:

The very first moment I received the message . . . my heart turned towards you with love and gratitude . . . But, at the same, it is a very great trial for me. The perfect whirlwind of public excitement it has given rise to is frightful. It is almost as bad as tying a tin can at a dog's tail making it impossible for him to move without creating noise . . . I am being smothered with telegrams and letters for the last few days and the people who never had any friendly feeling towards me nor ever read a line of my works are loudest in their protestations of joy . . . Really these people honour the honour in me and not myself. The only thing that compensates for this is the unfeigned joy and pride that the boys of my school feel at this occasion.

As a tiny pinprick in the larger picture mentioned by a frustrated Tagore take the encomium he received from one J. R. Tullu 'of Municipal Camp, Poona' (still preserved in the 'Nobel Prize' files of the Tagore archives at Shantiniketan). Dated 19 November 1913 and inscribed in English on notepaper embossed with a red rose, his verses salute Tagore as 'Ind's Kipling!' (complete with exclamation mark).

On 10 December Rabindranath wrote again to Rothenstein: 'My friend, my days are riddled all over with interruptions, they are becoming perfectly useless to me . . . I was watching a calf this morning, tired of browsing, basking in the sun on the grass, supinely happy and placid; it made my heart ache with the desire to be one with the great life that surrounds this earth . . . Perhaps you will smile and think this mood of mine . . . absurdly oriental – but still it has its truth which must not be overlooked.'

And then a third time on 16 December:

My ordeal is not yet over. I still have dinners to attend to, and listen to speeches in praise of my genius, and to answer them in a becoming spirit of modesty. This has brought me to Calcutta and kept me in our Jorasanko lane, while the mustard fields are in bloom in Shilida [Shelidah] and wild ducks have set up their noisy households in the sandbanks of the Padma. I have already raised a howl of protests and vilifications in our papers by saying in plain words what was in my mind to a deputation who had come to Bolpur [Shantiniketan] to offer me congratulations. This has been a relief to me – for honour is a heavy enough burden even when it is real but intolerable when meaningless and devoid of sincerity. However, I must not complain. Let me patiently wait for the time when all this tumult will be a thing of the past and truth will shine and peace will come even to a man whom West has thought fit to honour.

Tagore was not exaggerating one iota. Something seemed to snap inside him when he saw the crowd of five hundred Calcutta citizens defiling his beloved ashram on 23 November. A few were his close friends, but the majority were strangers; and not a few had maligned him in print and by word of mouth, criticizing him for (amongst other things) being under western influence. Now they had come to hail him for receiving western approbation. 'What a strange people we are! We have so little of reverence in us', the schoolboy Subhashchandra Bose had written in September 1912 to his brother in London on reading in the Bengali press of Tagore's welcome there. If in late 1913 the Calcutta crowd had kept its distance, probably Rabindranath would have held his peace. But, bearded by it in his own home, he let fly with his contempt:

The calumnies and insult from the hands of countrymen which have fallen to my lot have not been trifling. Till now I have borne all that in silence . . . Today Europe has placed its garland of honour on me. If that has any value it lies only in the artistic discrimination of the arbiters of taste there. There is no genuine link between that and our country. No literary work can have its quality or appeal enhanced by the Nobel prize . . . Therefore how can I shamelessly appropriate to myself the honour of which you are making a present to me as representatives of the general public of the whole country.

This day of mine will not last forever. The ebbtide will set in again. Then all the squalor of the muddy bottom will be exposed in bank after bank.

This was from the extracts of the speech printed in Bengali in Calcutta. (In the recollection of a Bengali present among the crowd, who was infuriated by the speech, Tagore also employed the tin can and dog analogy he had written to Rothenstein. It was excised from the printed extracts as being too insulting.) The public reaction was strong. However, one well-known Bengali politician, Bipinchandra Pal, defended Tagore: 'Rabindranath would not have been what he is if he had failed to administer this salutary rebuke to those who evidently looked up still to European appraisers for the determination of the intellectual or moral values of their national efforts and achievements.'

The prejudices among Bengalis were curiously mirrored among the British in India. In October 1913, before the Nobel prize, Lord Hardinge, the viceroy of India, ordered that an honorary degree be conferred on Tagore by Calcutta University. He had been encouraged in this by C. F. Andrews, who had given a lecture on Tagore in May at a viceregal 'At Home' in Simla, the government's summer capital – thereby making Tagore pukka among the more enlightened high officials. But lower down the hierarchy there was distinct opposition to the idea. Hardinge overruled it. 'I do not care', he told Lord Carmichael, the governor of Bengal, 'whether the Criminal Intelligence Department give him [Tagore] a bad character or not. I am determined to give him an Honorary Degree . . . ' On 26 December the degree was conferred on Tagore, along with the eminent French orientalist Sylvain Lévi, later to be the first foreign lecturer at Tagore's university. Hardinge, as chancellor, seems to have had some idea of Tagore's true feelings because he said, 'I can only hope that the retiring disposition of our Bengali Poet will forgive us for thus dragging him into publicity once more and recognize with due recognition that he must endure the penalties of greatness.'

Honorary degree or no honorary degree, Nobel prize or no Nobel prize, Calcutta University remained unforgiving towards the man who had scorned any academic qualification in his youth. In 1914, in the Bengali-language paper of the University's matriculation exam there appeared a passage from Rabindranath – or rather a clever pastiche of his style. The examinee was asked to rewrite the passage – in 'chaste and elegant' Bengali!

In such an atmosphere it was easy for rumours to get afloat. The most popular one, that even today has some currency, was that Yeats had rewritten Gitanjali. A British correspondent connected with The Times, (Sir) Valentine Chirol ('an old Anglo-Indian reactionary hack', said E. M. Forster), more or less openly accused Tagore of taking credit for Yeats' work. 'Naturally such rumours get easy credence among our people who can believe in all kinds of miracles except genuine worth in their own men,' Tagore told Rothenstein wryly.

Yeats himself gave some support to the idea, though only in private correspondence. In 1917 he told Macmillan, 'William Rothenstein will tell you how much I did for *Gitanjali* . . . It was a delight . . . and at my request Tagore has made no acknowledgement.' But Rothenstein specifically discounted the rumour in his memoirs: 'Yeats did here and there suggest slight changes, but the main text was printed as it came from Tagore's hands.' And in Pound's excited commentary on Yeats, Tagore and *Gitanjali* in 1912, there was not a single reference to Yeats as *reviser*, nor in his later correspondence when he wrote of his disenchantment with Tagore. According to a Bengali scholar who has examined Tagore's original translations, Yeats amended about one-fortieth of the original text. Perhaps Tagore himself described the truth most clearly when he wrote to Edward Thompson in quite another context on 18 November 1913 (before the rumour started): 'I think the method that Yeats followed while editing my book was the right one in selecting those poems that required least alterations and rejecting others in spite of their merits.' In other words, Yeats' role was vital in the *selection* of *Gitanjali*, less so in its revision.

A second rumour, started in Sweden, was that the Swedish Academy had chosen Tagore under pressure from Prince William of Sweden, who had visited Calcutta not long before. In late 1913 the prince published an account of his travels in Asia written in Swedish. He described an encounter with Rabindranath Tagore and his family. He noticed how their eyes, lit by proud patriotism, blazed as they gave him a history of each antique in Jorasanko. A musician performed for him. The music, the prince noted, was the lament of a whole people, now slaves, filled with hatred of British rule. 'In all my life, I never spent moments so poignant as at the house of the Hindoo poet Rabindranath Tagore.'

Tagóre read the prince's account in English translation and mentioned it to Thompson with dry humour:

> But the beauty of it is that I never met him and the flashes of fire in my eyes which he considered dangerous for the British Government were under observation of the detectives of the Criminal investigation department somewhere behind my back. We are not allowed firearms and if any little fire is left playing in our eyes it should not be brought before the notice of our authorities.

A remarkably imperfect encounter this!

The deliberations of the Swedish Academy had a far sounder basis than the rumour, but still there were elements of misunderstanding bordering on comedy. What precisely *had* prompted 'that mysterious committee of international judges' to 'crown' a Bengali poet 'with bank notes'? – as Robert Bridges mused ironically in a letter to Tagore in June 1914. After all, they had already considered and passed over Tolstoy, Ibsen, Zola, Strindberg, Shaw and Yeats. In 1913 they would ignore Thomas Hardy in favour of Tagore – to the chagrin of the Royal Society of Literature in London, whose candidate Hardy was. (He never received the prize.)

The initial proposal came from Thomas Sturge Moore, a Fellow of the Royal Society. It was of course based on *Gitanjali*. Later in 1913 the Nobel committee would have access to the just-published *Gardener*, *Sadhana* and to a defective translation of Tagore's short stories not approved by Tagore. That was all. One member of the Academy, Esaias Tegnér, grandson of the poet Tegnér, knew some Bengali. Whether he had read any Tagore in the original was not clear. (He seems not to have taken Rabindranath very seriously, for he told a Swedish academic, later a member of the Nobel committee, that with a Bengali grammar and two or three weeks' study he would be able to read Tagore in the original.)

The chairman of the committee was doubtful as to how much of *Gitanjali* was Tagore's personal creation, as opposed to being an imitation of classical Indian poetry. What could not be doubted was *Gitanjali*'s idealism – which was crucial since Alfred Nobel's will stipulated that prize-winners must have an 'idealistic tendency'. This condition dominated the thinking of the selection committee in the early period of the Nobel prize and was responsible for the rejection of some of the great names mentioned above. In those days the condition was taken to mean that work must be morally good and supportive of social institutions. Later on a letter from a close friend of Nobel was discovered asserting that Nobel 'was an Anarchist: by idealistic he meant that which adopts a polemical or critical attitude to Religion, Royalty, Marriage, Social Order generally.' Partly for this reason, the first interpretation of 'idealistic tendency' was abandoned.

Obviously the Nobel committee of 1913 had not the foggiest notion that in far-off Bengal Tagore was a polemical critic of religious, social and political orthodoxy, and by no means friendly to Government. If they had read his Bengali essays, they would not have given him the Nobel prize. (Today, by contrast, his prose writings would more likely have secured him the prize than his translated poetry.) As it was, several members of the committee fell for *Gitanjali*. The decisive contribution came from Verner von Heidenstam, a Swedish poet now almost forgotten who won the Nobel prize in 1916. He wrote:

Just as a selection of Goethe's poems could well convince us of Goethe's greatness, even if we were unfamiliar with his other writings, so we can say quite definitely of these poems by Tagore, which we have had in our hands this summer, that through them we have come to know one of the very greatest poets of our age. I read them with strong emotion, and I can say that in the course of decades I have not met their like in poetic literature. The hours they gave me were special, as if I had been allowed to drink from a fresh and clear spring. The loving and intense religious sense that permeates all his thoughts and feelings, the purity of heart, and the noble and unaffected elevation of the style – all amount to a total impression of deep and rare spiritual beauty. There is nothing disputable and disturbing, nothing vain, worldly, or petty, and if it can ever be said of a poet that he possesses the qualities that make him deserving of a Nobel prize, then it must be Tagore. No one else now alive can in that respect, so far as I know, compete with him.

Heidenstam concluded less loftily by pointing out two other reasons for giving Tagore the prize. First, Nobel's will wanted the prize to go to a book published in the previous year. Secondly, the committee now had the opportunity of discovering a great name, he said, 'before it has already spent years haunting the newspaper columns.' In the words of Per Hallström, a Tagore convert on the committee, writing to Tegnér on 1 November: 'What Nobel in his innocence believed that we could do each year – present a new genius to the world – is something we are now free to do, for once.'

Inevitably opinion in the world outside the Swedish Academy was divided. Outside England, the only western country where Tagore and his works were known, there was praise and dispraise, and considerable confusion. Race, politics and religion entered in immediately. Misspelling the name as 'Babindranath', the *New York Times* commented on 14 November: 'It is the first time that this prize has been given to anybody but a white person.' (No American had yet won it.) Next day, seeking to repair its liberal image, the paper shot itself in the foot: 'Babindranath Tagore, if not exactly one of us, is, as an Aryan, a distant relation of all white folk.' In Vienna, a well-known liberal newspaper asked: 'Has the award of the prize been due to the exotic Buddhistic fashion or has England's policy in India been, perhaps, in favour of the crowning of the Bengali poet? This will remain the secret of the judges in Stockholm.' In Paris, a journalist approached Sylvain Lévi, since he was a Jew, asking for an interview about 'le Rabbin Tégoro'. (Possibly the first example of a persistent misapprehension about Tagore, who would become sometimes an Aryan and at other times a Jew.)

In England the press coverage was copious and laudatory, but perhaps less enthusiastic than might have been expected on the basis of the rave reviews of *Gitanjali*. In the literary world a reaction had already started, fuelled by disappointment that Thomas Hardy had been passed over. *Punch* printed some (quite good) parodies of *Gitanjali*; the *New Statesman* remarked waspishly, 'The unjustified boom we have always with us.'

'I am often angered when references to you catch my eye in the papers now for there is an itch about them to treat you unjustly as before they were fulsome in praise', Sturge Moore told Tagore in January 1914. Recalling his first months in England, Tagore replied from the heart: 'I would have gladly sacrificed my Nobel prize if I could be left to the enjoyment of [that] strong friendliness and true-hearted admiration.' But the Indian summer of western liberalism was almost over.

19   Never at Rest
(1914–1916)

To the open road! I have fled away from my school and am going to take my shelter with the wild ducks, the belated stragglers who are still lingering [on] the sandbanks of the Padma.

letter to Edward Thompson,
Calcutta, February 1914

The year just past had been a productive one for Tagore as a writer in translation. Besides *Gitanjali*, Macmillan had published *The Gardener* and *The Crescent Moon*, and *Sadhana*; the India Society had issued the play *Chitra* (republished by Macmillan in 1914); and there was also the defective translation of short stories published in India. But in Bengali not a single new work by Rabindranath had appeared.

His two and a half years in India, 1914–16, between his return from the West and his departure for Japan, would more than compensate for the hiatus in his literary career. They produced not only one of his best volumes of poetry, *Balaka* (Wild Geese), but also the novel *The Home and the World*, besides short stories, essays, a drama and songs.

His time in the West had given a kick both to his mind and to his works. Always restless, he was now seldom stationary for more than a month or so at a time. The distances and discomforts of subcontinental travel meant nothing. *Wanderlust* took hold of him rather as it had once taken hold of Maharshi Debendranath. On 1 January 1914 he wrote to Edward Thompson from Jorasanko that he had just come from Shantiniketan and was just off to Shelidah for a boat trip 'to have a little rest which I need very badly'. The rest of 1914 continued in this fashion: his focus remained Shantiniketan, but there were spells of wandering in northern India, interspersed with periods in Calcutta and Shelidah. During much of January he was on his boat. The first half of February saw him back in Shantiniketan, the second half back in Shelidah. Then back to Shantiniketan. In early May, with the furnace of summer beginning, he left for the foothills of the Himalayas near Naini Tal, and remained there until June. Then back once more to the Abode of Peace for three months or so. But he did not stay put in the ashram; he went into retreat at a house two miles away, in the village of Surul. He was in a strange and severe mood of depression and wrote few letters, having told Thompson, who wanted to visit him, 'I shall don the magic garment which will make me invisible'. In early October he reappeared in the ashram – not for long, however. During October and November he returned to Bodh Gaya, where the Buddha received enlightenment, and also visited Darjeeling, in the Himalayas; then he went down into the plains to Allahabad and Agra on a visit to the Taj Mahal that prompted his famous poem 'Shah Jahan'. Finally, back in Shantiniketan at the end of December, he told Rothenstein he would shortly be on a boat to Japan! No wonder his school suffered.

'Tagore has not really found peace', Rothenstein told Ernest Rhys around this time, ' – it is because he hasn't, because he feels the same impossibility of reconciling action with thought that there is so much reality and passion in his songs. Perhaps he feels more strongly than most men the need for peace, but he has found no road where he can walk safely'. [pl.32]

Whatever the specific causes of Tagore's turbulent frame of mind, which we shall come to, there was a more general tension in him between his roots in Bengal and his recent experiences abroad – a tension dramatized by the award of the Nobel prize. On 1 May, with school over, he read at one sitting a new book by Sturge Moore, *The Sea is Kind*, and immediately wrote him a highly perceptive letter:

> It will be difficult for you to imagine this blazing summer sky of ours with hot blasts of air repeatedly troubling the fresh green leaves of a tree whose name will be of no use to you. This is as unlike the climate and the country where your poems were written as anything could be. I feel your environments in your poems. There is in them the reticence of your sky, the compactness of your indoor life and the general consciousness of strength ready to defy fate. Here in the East the transparent stillness of our dark nights, the glare of the noonday sun melting into a tender haze in the blue distance, the plaintive music of the life that feels itself afloat in the Endless, seem to whisper into our ears some great secret of existence which is uncommunicable.

Just about all the difficulties facing a translator of Tagore's poetry are suggested in these few sentences. The amazing thing is, that despite the gulf he described, his *Gitanjali* did communicate to a poet like Sturge Moore. But *what* it communicated was much more doubtful. Tagore, better than anyone else in 1914, knew the fragility of the interest his work had evoked in London. He knew that of all his literary friends there, perhaps only Rothenstein had the potential, born of artistic sensitivity and first-hand knowledge, to appreciate Bengali life in all its alien intricacy. That was why he chose to translate poems that dealt with universal emotions and then, having chosen them, to strip them of what local habitation they had. *Shimul* and *palash* trees, silky white and blazing red, the glory of Shantiniketan in April/May; *alta*, the red lac-dye used to paint a woman's feet; the bagpipe-like *shehnai*, with its reedy ear-piercing note played at weddings; even the sound of baying jackals at night – to mention just four everyday experiences in rural Bengal – would these have meant anything at all to an English mind in 1914, even without their unfamiliar names? Tagore thought not.

But he believed that all great literature had a communicable, 'universal', core, and he cited to Sturge Moore as an example of eastern literature communicating with the West, the Bible:

> It has added to the richness of your life because it is alien to your temperament. In course of time you may discard some of its doctrines and teachings but it has done its work – it has created a bifurcation in your mental system which is so needful for all life growth . . . Western literature is doing the same with us, bringing into our life elements some of which supplement and some contradict our tendencies. This is what we need.

He recognized that much was bound to be lost or even mangled in translation, but he believed that the gains outweighed the losses:

> It is not enough to charm us or surprise us – we must receive shocks and be hurt. Therefore we seek in your writings not simply what is artistic but what is vivid and forceful. That is why Byron had such immense influence over our youths of the last generation. Shelley, in spite of his vague idealism, roused our minds because of his frantic impetuosity which is born of a faith in life. What I say here is from the point of view of a foreigner. We cannot but miss a great deal of the purely artistic element of your literature, but whatever is broadly human and deeply true can be safely shipped for distant times and remote countries. We look for your literature to bring to us the thundering life flood of the West, even though it carries with it all the debris of the passing moments.

Tagore did not mention Shakespeare, but he certainly thought of him in broadly the same way. In *Balaka* (Wild Geese), he paid tribute to Shakespeare's power to communicate with Indians in a short, simple, lyrical poem written in Shelidah in 1915 at the request of the Shakespeare Tercentenary Committee in

Britain. It was published in Bengali beside Tagore's English translation by the Oxford University Press in 1916. This is our translation:

When you arose, world poet, from behind the unseen
England found you within her horizon
And embraced you; took you to be her own,
Hers alone; she kissed your shining brow,
Clasped you a while within her sylvan arms, dandled
You a while hidden in her mist-mantle
In flower-covered dewy-green meadows
Where faeries played. As yet the isle's groves
Were not awake to hymn the poet-sun's true reckoning.
Then, gradually, at eternity's silent beckoning
You left the horizon's lap and through centuries ascended
To that zenith for which you were intended,
Your radiant throne at the centre of heaven,
Illuminating all minds; Hear how, after an aeon
The palm-groves on the shores of the Indian Ocean
Rustle their fronds and murmur their paean.

'Shah Jahan', a much longer poem also in *Balaka*, makes an interesting contrast. As might be expected of a writer generally hostile to the might of rulers, Tagore was altogether more complex and critical in his attitude to Shah Jahan, the Mughal emperor, as compared with Shakespeare. Indeed he admitted that there could be valid but conflicting interpretations of the poem. A few years before, he told an organization wanting his advice on how to perpetuate the memory of a particular (minor) Bengali poet: 'Great poets raise Taj Mahals to their memory out of their own works.' But, he said, he was not opposed to the idea of erecting a stone statue too – whether he meant for poets in general or for this particular poet because he was too minor to be remembered by his works alone, Tagore did not indicate. Clearly though, his analogy suggested his respect for the Taj Mahal; he did not regard Shah Jahan as having built in vain. (Recall that Rabi as a seventeen year old had thrilled to the Shahi Bagh palace in Ahmedabad, which Shah Jahan had built.) When pressed to paraphrase his poem on Shah Jahan by an English visitor to Shantiniketan many years later, he said: 'I say to Shah Jahan – you knew that grief however poignant is mortal; so you had the conception of imprinting in marble a teardrop on the cheek of eternity.' In other words, Tagore felt that a tomb, however much inspired by love and however miraculous in design, could not capture life; and yet he knew that this tomb, the Taj Mahal, *had* stimulated new life in his own mind. Both Shakespeare *and* Shah Jahan live on, he implied: the one through words, the other through marble.

Translation of 'Shah Jahan' is not satisfactory; Tagore's own version was so mutilated compared to the Bengali original that it was dropped from his collected works in English. Nevertheless here is the opening stanza in our translation:

> This fact you knew, Emperor of Ind, Shah Jahan,
> That Time's stream carries off life, youth, riches, renown.
>   Only your heart's grief
> Could be eternal, that was your majesty's true belief.
>   Your royal might, adamantine,
> Would fade into oblivion like the crimson of the setting sun;
>   Simply one great sigh
> Would stay, forever-impassioned, rending the sky,
>   That was your prayer.
>   Diamonds, pearls, rubies glisten
> Like the trickery of a rainbow on the empty horizon,
>   Soon to vanish like mist
>   Shedding just
>   One tear droplet
>   On the cheek of Time, shining and undefiled –
> This Taj Mahal.

And these are Tagore's concluding lines:

> Today his chariot
> Rides to the invocation of night
> To the music of the spheres
> Towards dawn's Lion Gate.
> I remain behind, burdened by the past:
> He is released, no longer here.

Undoubtedly the poet was speaking of himself, burdened with responsibilities and fame, and weighted with memories of all those dear to him who were now dead. *Balaka* contains a whole poem about Kadambari Devi, inspired by his coming across a picture of her; and the 'wild geese' of the title poem, written in Kashmir in 1915, are compared by him to migrating souls.

Nikhil, the zamindar in *The Home and the World* (*Ghare Baire*), who is plainly Tagore, feels similarly oppressed by his duties and memories. *Ghare Baire* was written at the same time as *Balaka* and published serially in 1915–16. Its patchy English translation, made by Surendranath Tagore, appeared in 1919. Still, it was immediately admired by Rothenstein, also by Yeats and Lady Gregory, and in Germany became one of Tagore's best-known books. 'You simply *must* read [it] – the finest novel I've read for a long time', a friend told Albert Einstein in mid-1920. Hermann Hesse, reviewing it, referred to its 'purity and grandeur'. Bertolt Brecht noted in his diary: 'A wonderful book, strong and gentle'. But the Marxist critic Georg Lukács attacked Tagore for putting himself 'at the intellectual service of the British police' in his 'libellous pamphlet', 'a petit bourgeois yarn of the shoddiest kind' containing 'a contemptible caricature of Gandhi'. (How little Lukács must have known of Gandhi and India to make this ludicrous comparison.)

Today the novel still has some power and charm, assisted by the film version made by Satyajit Ray in 1984. A contemporary Russian scholar finds it reminiscent of Dostoevsky's *The Possessed*. Anita Desai, who introduced an English edition in 1985, wrote:

In spite of the predominance and suffocating weight of so much polemic, there are extraordinary flashes of light and colour, as if created by the striking of flints, as well as touches of tenderness and childishness which lighten the lowering clouds of the prevalent mood of disaster and give the novel variation and vivacity . . . It is a dramatic tale, yet not particularly dramatic in the telling.

A small book could be written on the meaning of the novel's triangle – between the idealist zamindar Nikhil, his college friend Sandip, now turned *swadeshi* leader and seducer, and Nikhil's wife Bimala, torn between the two men. Into this flawed novel Tagore packed all his tangled emotions about the 1905 Swadeshi Movement transmuted by his extraordinary western reception in 1912–13. The 'home' and the 'world' referred to his own mind divided against itself, to himself versus his school, to Shantiniketan versus Calcutta, to Bengal versus India, to India versus Britain, to the East versus the West: there are elements of all these clashes. Nikhil states the theme beautifully:

During the day I forget myself in my work. As the late autumn afternoon wears on, the colours of the sky become turbid, and so do the feelings of my mind. There are many in this world whose minds dwell in brick-built houses – they can afford to ignore the thing called the outside. But my mind lives under the trees in the open, directly receives upon itself the messages borne by the free winds, and responds from the bottom of its heart to all the musical cadences of light and darkness.

No knowledge of Bengal or of Shantiniketan, where Rabindranath wrote the novel, is needed for this passage. Nor is any knowledge of Bengali history essential for following the story as a whole (in contrast with *Gora*). One can respond to it as English literature and ignore the specifically Bengali elements. This was what E. M. Forster (who disliked Bengal) tried to do in a review, a little condescendingly, and found himself warmly admiring some passages but being disconcerted by the 'babu' English of others. Tagore, Forster concluded, 'meant the wife to be seduced by the World, which is, with all its sins, a tremendous lover; she is actually seduced by a West Kensingtonian Babu, who addresses her as "Queen Bee", and in warmer moments as "Bee".'

The translation, it should be said, was partly to blame for this judgement. Bengalis also criticized Sandip, however; they too found him uncomfortably westernized and, unsurprisingly, a slur on the true patriotic leaders of the Swadeshi Movement. And what about Bimala, the wife – would a lady from an orthodox Hindu home be capable of such scandalous behaviour? Surely, Bengali critics said, she must be from a Brahmo home. (There is nothing in the novel to prove the point one way or the other.) Rabindranath's patriotism was once more in question; he suffered much criticism for writing *Ghare Baire*. More than two years after publication he defended himself vigorously:

> Unfortunately, in Bengali, the criticism of literature has resolved itself into a judgement of the proprieties which are necessary for orthodoxy . . . how far Sakuntala is the perfect Hindu woman and Dushyanta the perfect Hindu king – these are the questions seriously discussed in the name of literary criticism . . . There are a crowd of heroines in Shakespeare's dramas . . . [but] even the most fanatical Christian theologians desist from awarding them marks, in order of merit, according to their degree of Christianity . . . If one must indulge in this absurd mania for classification, even in literature, then at least it should follow the line of human nature as much as possible, instead of being arranged on the wooden shelves of what is Hindu, and what is not.

The Home and the World was among Tagore's darkest works. It concluded with Hindu–Muslim riots, armed robbery, the flight of Sandip, the utter humiliation of Bimala and the injury of Nikhil, probably fatally. The plot was based on the terrorist violence of 1907 and after, but the mood came out of Tagore's depression in 1914. Many of his contributions to a journal started in 1914, *Sabuj Patra* (Green Leaves), (edited by the husband of his niece Indira), shared this anguish. The depression attacked him unexpectedly in late May while he was staying near Naini Tal, lifted from his mind in June, returned in

July and lasted for long periods during the rest of 1914. Letters he wrote to C. F. Andrews gave vent to it; he also wrote a poem in July that spoke of the sudden destruction of the earth. According to Andrews the mood came long before any news had reached Shantiniketan about the impending war in Europe. Andrews therefore concluded that 'the Poet's highly sensitive nature had made him feel dimly beforehand the tragedy which was about to happen. In no other way can I account for his intense mental suffering.'

Maybe so, but several other explanations of Rabindranath's breakdown offer themselves (apart from physiological causes). He was not giving as much time to his zamindari as he knew it required. The school was in a mess financially, as he told Thompson in February. 'I have to be careful and strain all my resources to extricate myself from this tangle.' Constant criticism of him had taken its toll. 'A man who has grown up under abuse becomes obsessed with himself, as if rejecting his own nature', said a character in a short story he published at this time, who is unmistakably Tagore himself. And he was tortured by thoughts of his own failure to live up to his ideal, which he believed made him an inadequate father. 'I am ashamed of myself', he told his son. 'I have always favoured the idea of independence, but of late, in strange contrast, I am imposing my ideal on you.' He admitted to Rathindranath later that, back in May, the month the depression began, 'I felt I had not achieved anything, I wouldn't be able to do anything – my entire life was useless – I had no confidence or trust in anyone. My conscience was pricking me for not performing my duties to my school, zamindari, family and country.' He was haunted by a death wish; often, he said, he had contemplated suicide.

His son and daughter-in-law were now living in a large house at Surul, the village near Shantiniketan where in the 1920s Rabindranath would establish his 'institute for rural reconstruction' with Leonard Elmhirst as director. Rabindranath had bought the house in 1913, sight unseen (he was then in London), from the Sinhas, the local zamindar family who had sold the land at Shantiniketan to his father Debendranath in 1863. But the house had turned out to be less of a bargain than he hoped, and the area had a severe malaria problem. Nevertheless, at his request Rathindranath had agreed to leave his house on the estates at Shelidah, which he liked, and move into the Surul house in April 1914, which had been fitted up as a laboratory for him. He did not stay there long; within a few years he had moved to Shantiniketan proper. But his father often lived at Surul in years to come when he wanted to isolate himself from the ashram and its demands. (He wrote *The Home and the World* there, for example.)

At approximately the same time, C. F. Andrews and W. W. Pearson joined the ashram, having visited in 1913. Both men, Andrews in particular, became associated with Tagore in the mind of the Indian public more closely than any other foreigners. Andrews acted as an intermediary for Tagore in many matters, educational, social, political, literary and financial. Andrews' friendship with Gandhi – shown in the film *Gandhi* – and his good relationships with several viceroys and senior officials of the British Raj were especially useful. Pearson, besides teaching successfully at Tagore's school, wrote a book about it published by Macmillan in 1917. He also translated some of Tagore's writings from Bengali, including *Gora*. And in 1916–17 and 1920–21, Pearson acted as an effective secretary for Tagore on his tours of Japan and the USA. [pl.28]

Yet both men are now totally forgotten in Britain. Although both kept in close touch with England, they somehow belong exclusively to Anglo-India and are irredeemably historical figures. As for their personalities, one admires their courage (which enabled them to confront imperial racism in South Africa and Fiji) but not their judgement; and their emotionalism is often embarrassing. In July 1913, for instance, Pearson wrote to Tagore about his settling at Shantiniketan: 'I can never think myself worthy and it is of no use my waiting for the time when I can *feel* worthy, for that time will never come. So now I stand ready, faulty and sinful, but clear as to my call and with these two gifts to offer, my love and my need.' And in December 1914, after some months staying at Shantiniketan, Andrews wrote to an absent Tagore: 'Now I see that you were really asking all the while for something far deeper and truer and more manly from me than the weak, emotional and almost selfish love which I was offering.' (The biography of Andrews is appropriately called *The Ordeal of Love*.)

Both confessions were absolutely typical of these two lapsed missionaries. Tagore knew this, sometimes welcomed it, at other times was exasperated by it (with Andrews more than with Pearson). Part of him, the idealist part, regarded Andrews and Pearson as the highest form of Englishman: just, humane and fearless. Another part, the sharp critical faculty that all great artists must have, looked in vain for the reserve and restraint of some of his truly gifted friends in England. But whatever the conflict between his subjective and objective feelings towards these two friends, above all else Tagore valued their sincere loyalty to his unloved fledgling institution.

It was Andrews who first brought together Tagore and Gandhi. Andrews suggested to Tagore that Shantiniketan should look after Gandhi's students when they left the Phoenix ashram in South Africa in 1914 and returned to India. They settled in Shantiniketan in November. There was immediately a marked contrast between them, with their austere disciplined ethic of self-help, and Tagore's students. (In 1914 Shantiniketan still had very much the reputation among parents of being a kind of reformatory for difficult children.) Tagore at first criticized Gandhi's boys in letters to Andrews, but revised his opinion of them a few days later: 'I think they are very lovable, though I cannot get rid of my misgivings about their system of training.'

Gandhi himself turned up for a few days in February 1915, while Tagore was away (deliberately?), and returned again in March for another few days. By then Tagore was back. Almost immediately Gandhi suggested to all the boys and teachers that they do without cooks and cook the food themselves. Rabindranath was agreeable if the teachers were favourable. Most were willing, and the boys welcomed the novelty. Then, wrote Gandhi in *My Experiments with Truth*, 'Pearson began to wear away his body in making the experiment a success.' Although it was abandoned after some time – lacking leadership from Tagore – it survived as a token annual day, 10 March, 'Gandhi Day', when the ashramites gave the servants the day off.

'Our stay in Shantiniketan', Gandhi noted in 1930 with his inimitable plain-speaking, 'had taught us that the scavenger's work would be our special function in India'. (The scavenger, usually an Untouchable, cleaned latrines.) One wonders what the founder of Shantiniketan made of this bizarre remark: Indian habits of defecation were one of the few subjects on which Tagore remained silent in his hundreds of essays. The remark captures the peculiarity of Gandhi's friendship with Tagore from its beginning in 1915 to its end in 1940, when at Tagore's request the Mahatma agreed to nurture Shantiniketan after his death. To Gandhi, the bowels mattered almost as much as the mind mattered to Tagore. There was not one word in Gandhi's *Experiments* about the arts in Shantiniketan, nor any report of a conversation with Rabindranath. As Tagore remarked in 1937 to an American journalist friend who wanted him to write an 'intimate' profile of Gandhi, 'though I hold Gandhiji dear and cannot but feel the force of his personality, I can hardly be said to know him intimately. We have never lived together or worked together for any length of time. *What understanding and appreciation we have of each other is more or less intuitive.*' [our emphasis]

In 1915 Tagore's relationship with British officials was considerably warmer than that with Gandhi. Nine days after the Phoenix party left Shantiniketan Tagore received Lord Carmichael, the first governor of Bengal to visit the ashram; and in June he received a knighthood. For a few years, until the Amritsar Massacre of 1919, Tagore was able to exert some influence for good in the councils of the Raj. Several times he appealed privately for enquiries into the cases of young Bengalis held for 'sedition'. In May 1915, for instance, he asked Lord Carmichael to drop charges against someone who was losing his mind; Tagore promised to look after him in Shantiniketan. Carmichael agreed and wrote that 'between ourselves' it had been difficult to persuade the government. 'It is not easy all at once to get people anywhere to give up their prejudices; and here, where there is no really effective public opinion to teach our local rulers to see things in true proportion, it is particularly hard.' He added hopefully that he thought the war was bringing Englishmen and Bengalis together.

But in early 1916 there was a serious incident at Calcutta's Presidency College. Some Bengali students beat up one of the British professors, E. F. Oaten, in retaliation for some provocative remarks. (Among them was Subhashchandra Bose, though at the enquiry he denied being present.) Tagore immediately wrote an article which was translated into English as 'Indian students and western teachers' and sent by him to Lord Hardinge, the viceroy, and Lord Carmichael. It was a heartfelt effort to be fair to both sides. Both sides received it coolly.

Tagore wrote:

Let us, then, frankly acknowledge the natural difficulties of a European professor in dealing with Bengali students. We sometimes quote the instance of the relations of Oxford and Cambridge Dons with their undergraduates. But the cases are not parallel. There, the relationship is natural. Here, it is not. So it appears as if this vacuum in nature has to be filled up with brickbats of 'discipline'.

He continued:

Because the Bengali has become a mere adjective to the Englishman, signifying dislike, it has become difficult for the latter to feel our reality. I had hoped that Bengali youths might have been taken as volunteers to serve in this present war. If we could sacrifice our lives – so I thought – in the same cause with the English soldiers, we should at once become real to them, and claim fairness at their hands ever after.

The war was dividing the races, rather than bringing them closer. Carmichael gave Tagore an introduction letter to the British ambassador in Japan before he departed in May 1916. When the new viceroy Lord Chelmsford learned this fact later, from letters sent by Andrews (who was with Tagore) and opened by the Censor, he objected strongly. Chelmsford had no idea what Tagore's mission in Japan was but he suspected it as a matter of principle, and his officials had warned him against Andrews, who had been friendly with the liberal-minded viceroy Hardinge. Chelmsford sent a message to the British ambassador in Japan asking him to keep an eye on Tagore's party. To the secretary of state for India in London he wrote stiffly:

Tagore is, as you know, a poet and must have a poet's licence accorded to him. I don't think anyone attaches too serious a meaning to his lucubrations. Andrews is an eccentric with an unlimited capacity for enraging himself over the iniquities perpetrated by his mother country. He is perfectly honest and sincere, but very easily sees red. Men of his type are not unknown in England and, though he should be watched, I do not believe he would knowingly lend himself to anything like real sedition.

What Chelmsford did not mention – though he presumably knew – was that in May 1915 a man claiming to be P. N. Tagore, a nephew of the poet, had left India for Japan, supposedly in connection with the forthcoming visit by Rabindranath. The man was in fact Rashbihari Bose, a leading terrorist who had organized the throwing of a bomb that had almost killed Hardinge in 1912. In Japan, much to the indignation of the British, Bose was sheltered by ultra-Right nationalists until the Second World War. He also became friendly with Rabindranath.

Chelmsford was a mediocre viceroy by general consent. It was not surprising that he should have somewhat mistrusted Tagore in 1916 and much more so once he began to speak openly against the British Raj in 1917. But his attitude was significant of a larger phenomenon that was beginning to undermine Tagore's literary reputation. Artistic and literary circles in the West were not immune to the feeling; even Rothenstein had become nationalistic. D. H. Lawrence, who could hardly have been less similar to Chelmsford (or even Rothenstein), told Ottoline Morrell in May 1916: 'I become more and more surprised to see how far higher, in reality, our European civilization stands than the East, Indian and Persian, ever dreamed of . . . this fraud of looking up to them – this wretched worship-of-Tagore attitude – is disgusting.' From now on, Tagore would find himself increasingly sailing against the prevailing wind.

20 Japan and the USA (1916–1917)

My life commenced on the eastern horizon and will terminate on the western horizon.

letter to his daughter Mira,
Chicago, October 1916

Despite the war, Tagore wanted to travel. He had been to the West, now his thoughts turned to the East. Okakura Kakuzo, his main contact with Japan, died in 1913, but a final request Okakura made to Rabindranath that he visit the Far East had lodged in his mind. Hardly more than a year after his return from London, Tagore was booked to leave for Japan in January 1915. The trip was postponed till July 1915, then once more cancelled. He did not actually depart until May 1916. [pl.36]

Shortage of funds was one reason for the second postponement. Another was the threat of famine in his estates. But perhaps the uppermost reason was Japanese militarism. In June 1915 Tagore wrote to C. F. Andrews: 'I have given up Japan. I feel more and more sure it is not the country for me.' A month later he commented: 'I gave up Japan but Japan is insistent.' A deputation of Japanese gentlemen had been to see him, he said, and he had agreed to stick by his promise.

> But I am almost sure that Japan has her eyes on India. She is hungry – she is munching Korea, she has fastened her teeth upon China and it will be an evil day for India when Japan will have her opportunity . . . Japan is the youngest disciple of Europe – she has no soul – she is all science – and she has no sentiment to spare for other people than her own. If ever things go wrong with England everything is beautifully made ready for Japan.

Over and over in Tagore's lectures in Japan, and afterwards in the United States, such attitudes would surface. With one part of his mind, Tagore truly believed, following Okakura, that 'Asia is one'. But a different part, grimly prescient, totally contradicted this. Tagore never abandoned 'Asia is one' altogether, but in the 1930s he increasingly saw India and China as an entity, with Japan having sold its soul to western-style nationalism.

It was a telegram from the USA in mid-April 1916 that finally determined him to go. It came out of the blue from Keedick, an agent in New York, offering Tagore $10,000 and $3,000 in coast-to-coast travelling expenses for a forty-lecture tour in the USA. Tagore's star was riding high there. Macmillan in New York was begging him for translations of his short stories. George Brett, his publisher, had written independently of Keedick to suggest late 1916 for a visit. Barring war with Germany or in Mexico, Brett said, the moment was auspicious. 'The country is extremely prosperous and there is more interest in literature and culture and the life of the spirit than I have seen here for many years past.'

On 19 April, an excited Rabindranath told his daughter Mira: 'After repeated examinations and tests, I have clearly realized that God has not created me for a householder's life. I suppose that is why, from my very childhood, I have been constantly wandering about and have never been able to establish a home anywhere.' While this was true, as Mira well knew, Tagore was also frustrated at the criticism of his recent work (such as *The Home and the World*) and his article on the Presidency College incident.

Even so he turned down Keedick's offer. Besides requiring his travelling expenses to and from the USA, he did not want to give so many lectures and he wanted most of them to be at universities. Keedick tried to entice Tagore by saying that Shackleton, Baden-Powell and Amundsen, among his lecturers, had received the same terms. In the end he lost Tagore to another lecture agency arranged by Macmillan after Tagore had reached Japan.

They sailed – Tagore, W. W. Pearson, C. F. Andrews and a young Bengali art student – on a Japanese cargo boat calling at Rangoon, Penang, Singapore, Hong Kong and finally Kobe. With relatively few passengers on board besides themselves, and no snooty Anglo-Indians, it was a relaxing time when Rabindranath could ponder his forthcoming lectures. One might have expected his thoughts to turn to literature and the arts; instead – maverick that he was – he homed in on the war then raging in Europe, the cult of nationalism and its partner, industrialization. The seeds were already there in his remarks about Japan to Andrews in 1915; perhaps now they germinated as he observed the colonial ports along the way. These reminded him constantly of the commercial rape of the Ganges above Calcutta during his lifetime (we know this from his travel diary). The blatancy and uniformity of the ports' ugliness shocked his aesthetic sensibility and roused his dormant dislike of Trade. Perhaps they reminded him too that he was retracing the route taken in the 1830s and 40s by his grandfather Dwarkanath's opium clippers.

Japan's contrast between traditional beauty and imported ugliness was almost more than Tagore could bear throughout his three-month stay. He was enchanted by the women he met and wrote epigrams on their fans (some of which were later published in Bengali and in English as *Fireflies*). And on the way to Tokyo by train, nearly two weeks after arrival in Kobe, he was greeted at the station in Shizuoka by about two dozen Buddhists who had come to pay their respects. None could speak a word of English, so they stood with joined hands in a reverent attitude before the carriage window while their leader requested Rabindranath to place some incense in a burner; after which they all bowed solemnly and stood in silence as the train pulled out. At that moment, Tagore said later, 'for the first time I had the feeling that I was really in Japan, and I was so happy that tears of joy came to my eyes.' But when he reached Tokyo station, Tagore was immediately encircled by reporters and photographers with exploding magnesium flashes. They followed him and his group along the platform and through the subway, eventually leaving him nearly blinded and deafened. Afterwards, from the house of the Japanese artist where they were staying Pearson wrote to Tagore's son in Calcutta: 'The contrast is so striking that it is difficult to understand how a people with such an inherent love for beautiful things can copy our Western ugliness and feel that they have got something which is worth having.' [pl.34]

Among those who saw the photographs was a seventeen-year-old boy still in school, Yasunari Kawabata. In 1968 he became the second Asian to win the Nobel prize for literature. Soon after the award, lecturing on 'The existence and discovery of beauty', Kawabata said of Tagore:

> I remember even now the features and appearance of this sage-like poet, with his long, bushy hair, long moustache and beard, standing tall in loose-flowing Indian garments, and with deep, piercing eyes. His white hair flowed softly down both sides of his forehead; the tufts of hair under the temples also were long like two beards, and linking up with the hair on his cheeks, continued into his beard, so that he gave an impression, to the boy that I was then, of some ancient Oriental wizard.

Kawabata did not hear any of Tagore's lectures in 1916, but speaking in 1969 he singled out a remark by Tagore at that time. 'It is the responsibility which every nation has to reveal itself before the world . . . [Japan] has given rise to a civilization which is perfect in its form, and has evolved a sense of sight which clearly sees truth in beauty and beauty in truth.' 'We may rejoice,' Kawabata commented, 'and yet at the same time be saddened, by the thought that [our] very ancient *The Tale of Genji* fulfils the "responsibility of a nation" to which

Tagore referred, much more brilliantly than any of us can do today, and will very likely continue to do so in the future.'

Tagore put his finger on this feeling of loss, from the very beginning of his visit to Japan. On 13 June, the high point of his official reception in Tokyo, he told the prime minister, mayor, president of the Imperial University, minister of education, eminent Buddhist scholars and more than two hundred other dignitaries assembled at the Kaneiji Buddhist Temple: 'I sincerely hope that the Japanese people will not forget the old Japan. The new Japan is only an imitation of the West. This will ruin Japan.' He spoke in Bengali. Replying, the aged prime minister Count Okuma apologized for not understanding English, which caused some amusement, and then thanked 'the sage of India for his timely visit and for giving a very sound warning' to his country 'at the parting of the ways in her inner life'.

The reception cooled within days. Most Japanese felt themselves to be part of a nation ascending in wealth, power and education; they had no desire to hear what seemed a backward-looking message from a representative of a defeated nation. The nationalism that Tagore forcefully decried as western in origin and inimical in spirit to Japan was serving Japan well in Korea and China, they felt. Official invitations to Tagore soon ceased.

On Tagore's two subsequent visits to Japan, in 1924 and 1929, the response was cooler and cooler still. Tagore was in no doubt about the reasons, though mortified. The Japanese people, he told the Indian community in Japan in 1924 with blunt truth,

felt nervous. They thought that idealism would weaken their morale; that ideals were not for those nations who must be unscrupulously strong; that the Nation must never have any feelings of disgust from the handling of diplomatic filth, or of shrinking from the use of weapons of brutal power. Human victims had to be sought, and the nation had to be enriched with plunder.

The United States in 1916 would prove more receptive to his message. This was partly due to Tagore's agent, the J. B. Pond Lyceum Bureau. Its founder James B. Pond had in his heyday been P. T. Barnum's only rival. Now his son was running the show. In 1915, he had toured John Masefield; for 1916 his list included Harley Granville Barker, Edgar Lee Masters and, with top billing, Sir Rabindranath Tagore. 'I am of opinion that Sir Rabindranath's tour could be made one of the biggest in lecture history', Pond informed Macmillan in New York. In the event it did not fall far short. When Pond finally went bankrupt in 1933 during the Depression, he recalled Tagore's tour as one of his most successful. While Robert Frost, writing to a poet-friend about a reading fee in

1923, joked: 'Suppose we make it Chesterton and Tagore's figure – one thousand dollars.'

Half-way through the tour, the *Minneapolis Tribune* called Tagore 'the best business man who ever came to us out of India': he had managed to scold Americans 'at $700 per scold' while pleading with them 'at $700 per plead'. There was some truth in this gibe, as Tagore himself soon came to feel. Although every cent he earned was for his school – something unaccountably omitted from Pond's publicity – still he had to admit he was making money by attacking materialism. This fundamental ambivalence, verging at times on hypocrisy, would always beset him in the West, particularly in the USA.

Yet he did not deviate, which he could easily have done. Pond, understandably enough, seemed to expect mainly art, religion and readings of poetry, plays and stories from his Nobel laureate. In fact Tagore lectured mostly on nationalism, with occasional other lectures and readings. It was probably less paying from the business point of view – and, as we shall see, less wise from a political angle too – but it was what Tagore wanted to tell Americans.

He landed in Seattle on 18 September and left the USA from San Francisco on 17 January 1917. In between he visited twenty-five major towns and cities across the continent including New York in mid-November, where he spoke at Carnegie Hall. His sponsors were generally wealthy private groups, such as the Sunset Club of Seattle; cultural organizations such as the Drama League of America; Unitarian churches; and small colleges and large universities such as Yale, which presented him with the Yale Bicentennial Medal.

Probably his greatest success was on the West Coast, where he had not gone in 1912–13. 'The cult of Tagore,' wrote the San Francisco *Examiner*, 'which has stirred the intellectual world as the thoughts of no other contemporaneous writer have done, has taken San Francisco by storm.' It put Tagore in serious danger. Indian revolutionaries living in the Bay Area – mainly Punjabis and Sikhs, not Bengalis – regarded Tagore, ironically enough, as an agent of the Indian government preaching against Indian nationalism in the USA. One of them published a letter in the *Examiner* stating that, 'The heart of India is in the Anti-British revolutionary movement . . . But Mr. Tagore stands aloof from this movement just as Goethe stood aloof from the German war of liberation a century ago . . . The Hindus are justly proud of the poetic achievements of Tagore, but they do not care for his social-political philosophy.' A plot to assassinate Tagore was hatched. It failed probably because the two conspirators who had gone to his hotel fell out in the lobby over whether to go through with the murder. Tagore, unaware of its seriousness, was given police protection until the following morning when he left for Santa Barbara. Speaking in Los Angeles two or three days later he scoffed at the whole notion of assassination.

But the newspapers loved the story: 'Hindu Savant Safe After Wild Flight Under Body Guard', headlined one. He would have no more trouble of this kind during the trip. But in 1918, when he was back in India, the incident would have disastrous repercussions.

For the next few days he was in a particularly good mood. After giving a lecture ('Nationalism') in Santa Barbara, he spent a day relaxing on the beach and some hours sitting in meditation under the fragrant groves of orange trees around Los Angeles; of the Californian women he declared to a reporter: 'It is a pleasure simply to watch them.' To his son Rathindranath, writing on 11 October, he dreamed:

I have it in mind to make Shantiniketan the connecting thread between India and the world. I have to found a world centre for the study of humanity there. The days of petty nationalism are numbered – let the first step towards universal union occur in the fields of Bolpur. I want to make that place somewhere beyond the limits of nation and geography.

This was the earliest recorded glimmering in his mind of Visva-Bharati, his university-to-be. It was both fitting and curiously poignant that such a utopia should have struck him first in southern California, in the vicinity of Hollywood – and just days after some of his countrymen had thought to murder him.

The rest of the tour was less exhilarating. Tagore found the publicity wearisome. At Denver, asked which American marvel had impressed him most he replied tersely, 'The American newspaper reporter.' In Salt Lake City, two reporters succeeded in entering his hotel room by posing as 'a local citizen of prominence, with the vice-consul of the British Empire'. Another reporter published an interview (moderately accurate) with a photograph of Tagore at his most far-fetched and the memorable caption:

Sir Rabindranath Tagore, Hindu Poet, Winner of the 1913 Nobel Prize in Literature, and Apostle of Universal Brotherhood Among Nations, Snapped in Native Garb on His Arrival at the Union Depot in Denver This Morning. Tagore, a Master of Seventeen Languages, and Considered by Many the Most Commanding Personage in Contemporary Literature, Is on a World Tour. 'The Spirit of Peace' Permeates His Writings, While He Would Delete the Word 'Hate' From the Dictionary.

There were also many cranks, Theosophists being especially tenacious. Pearson, as Tagore's secretary, had to fend them off. One salesman wanted to show Tagore how to double his efficiency. He gave Pearson a demonstration of acrobatic exercises in the hotel lounge. When Pearson described the man to Rabindranath he said he would gladly have seen him – had he offered to halve his efficiency instead of doubling it.

And there were the trials of hotel and train living. Tagore never liked eating in public, and besides, he wanted to save money for Shantiniketan. 'We get quite a lot of amusement out of our secret meals in hotel rooms with imported provisions such as Boston Baked Beans!' Pearson wrote to Rathindranath. Rabindranath ate vegetarian food for some weeks but at Cincinnati he started to take fish and meat, 'with the immediate result that he's feeling ever so much stronger and does not get over-tired'. In Portland, Oregon, there was a real crisis for the harassed Pearson:

He woke me up in the train in the early morning telling me that he had tipped his set of teeth [down] the lavatory basin where he had carefully placed them the night before! . . . Fortunately a Japanese dentist had made a set at Yokohama, which Gurudev had with him in his bag, and these are really better for the purpose of speaking than the other set . . . so your father is quite reconciled to the loss.

Sixteen years later, James B. Pond remarked that only once had he seen Sir Rabindranath Tagore in a rage. 'That was when his wardrobe became dispersed and he was forced to give a lecture in a silk shirt and tweed trousers.' It is a hilarious thought.

'I am like a show lion in a circus now', Tagore wrote to Harriet Monroe from San Francisco. 'All my life I have been used to an amplitude of leisure and sky, therefore for me this tightfit arrangement of my day's programme is neither healthy nor comfortable. However, I shall try to look cheerful and go on dancing to the tune of your American dollars.' To their mutual friend Harriet Moody, with whom he snatched some days in Chicago in October, he wrote simply: 'Ich bin müde.' This was from New York on 23 November, after speaking at Carnegie Hall. The contrast between this visit and his peaceful visit to her house in 1913 could not have been greater. Three weeks later, he suddenly decided to cancel the tour, which was originally to have terminated in April 1917.

No doubt he was tired as he had told Mrs Moody. But other factors too were at work. Sales of his books were booming; there was a 'furore' over Tagore, his US publisher Brett wrote to Maurice Macmillan in London. At the same time he was being subjected to severe criticism in the press, both for his views on nationalism and for his poetry. War was in the air, especially on the East Coast with its European sympathies. Two distinct views of Tagore had crystallized.

The first, and the more widely held, at least for a while, was that of the *New York Times*. On 10 December a critic reviewing at length all ten volumes of Tagore's work concluded:

> if he is not the greatest secular figure in the world, he is the one that is most worthy of our attention and our reverence today. At a time when man and man, nation and nation, ideal and ideal is [*sic*] so tragically divided he comes forward to tell us that not in power but in comprehension is the fulfilment of man's existence.

But in the *Nation* Paul Elmer More, the journal's former editor and a Sanskritist, was almost savage in condemning Tagore. He printed a number of verses of his poetry and compared them with verses from the *Bhagavad Gita*, which More knew in the original.

> Whatever Tagore may be, and whencesoever he draws his inspiration, he is in essence everything that ancient India, philosophically and religiously, was not . . . In place of Tagore's delight in the waves of change, the alternations of birth and death, there was in the heart of the ancient Hindu a yearning to escape into a region of unchanging peace . . . And, above all, in place of this effeminate feeling of defeat, this pacifistic waiting by the roadside and puddling in sentiment, there was a manly call to battle in the everlasting fight of life . . . Mr. Yeats speaks by the card, and those who, like him, feel their blood stirred by this sort of spiritual pap – why, let them congratulate themselves for their supersensitiveness. As for me, if any one cares for my opinion, in these days when the devil is unchained, I look to get what consolation and hope I can from philosophers who at least have the advantage of being virile.

This long critique appeared on 30 November. Though Tagore did not say so, we can be certain he read it and read it carefully, since he particularly admired the *Nation*. And we may be almost as certain that it hurt him. An irritable tone appeared in most of the interviews he gave in early December before he cancelled his tour, and indeed afterwards before he left the USA in late January. He seems to have had a premonition that the American nation was about to join the war in Europe and he must have sensed that his anti-nationalist message would soon be distinctly unwelcome to most Americans. [pl.35]

To judge by two private comments in letters of the time, Tagore's instinct was well-honed. J. B. Yeats, the father of W. B. Yeats, heard Tagore on 'The cult of Nationalism' at Carnegie Hall on 21 November. He wrote to his son: 'his gift of expression is marvellous. But he is too much abreast of the times. I like a poet to be a little reactionary. His ideas are vaporously philanthropic, like Whitman and every *one else* . . . "Cut out the magnanimity," said Keats, "and fill every rift with ore."' Ezra Pound, to whom Tagore had been the new Dante in 1912, was cutting:

> Tagore got the Nobel Prize because, after the cleverest boom of our times, after the fiat of the omnipotent literati of distinction, he lapsed into religion and was boomed by the pious non-conformists. Also because he got the Swedish Academy out of the difficulty of deciding between European writers whose claims appeared to conflict.

Against these reactions there was the enthusiasm of a poet like Hart Crane, who met Tagore in Cleveland in November and whose poem 'The Bottom of the Sea is Cruel' was influenced by *Gitanjali*. Orson Welles' mother Beatrice was another enthusiast, oddly enough; she liked to include in her performances recitations of Tagore to piano accompaniment. And no doubt thousands of Americans who heard Tagore speak or read him as a result of the 'furore', shared the feeling of the *New York Times* critic.

It is not easy to estimate his effect, personal and literary, on the United States in late 1916. What one can say is that he somehow chose a peculiar moment in modern US history to visit. The Democrat Woodrow Wilson was re-elected in November 1916 on the strength of his slogan 'He kept us out of war.' On 6 April 1917 he took the USA into the conflict. Tagore's idealistic message found an echo in the feelings of that fleeting interim period. As Pearson suggested jokingly to C. F. Andrews in mid-November from Detroit, perhaps California had gone over to Wilson because Tagore had just spent six weeks lecturing there on nationalism? If he had been in New York instead, no doubt Wall Street would have reacted the opposite way, Pearson said. The election had been a knife-edge result, California the deciding factor; for some hours a Republican victory had been generally conceded. Who knows, perhaps Tagore and his message did play a part?

21 Anti-Imperialist
(1917–1919)

What is radically wrong with our rulers is this – they are fully aware they
do not know us, and yet they do not care to know us.

letter to W. W. Pearson,
Shantiniketan, March 1918

When Tagore returned to Bengal in March 1917, he still believed that
British rule in India was providential. By the time he left India's shores
again three years later, he had forsaken this belief. Indian politics in 1917–19, in
which he would play an important role, seemed to leave him no alternative.

But immediately after his return, it was not politics that preoccupied him but
culture. He was pleased to discover that in his absence abroad a club had been
established in his portion of the Jorasanko house. The moving spirit was his son
Rathindranath, supported by his nephew Surendranath (who had also been
preparing the translation of his memoirs, *My Reminiscences*) and his artist-
nephews Abanindranath and Gaganendranath. It was called the Vichitra
('multi-coloured') Club. Its activities were as diverse, not to say diffuse, as its
name. There were banquets in a downstairs room that was decorated each time
in a different style, for instance to resemble the red and gold interior of a
Chinese pagoda. There were literary evenings by well-known Bengali writers,
to which Rabindranath contributed readings from his unpublished works.
There were displays of art and craft collected from the villages of Bengal:
embroidery, pottery, basketry and *alpana*, the delightful white designs painted
by women on floors and walls using a liquefied pigment of rice-powder. Most
significant of all, there was a kind of art school held during the day, the style of
the paintings being mainly that of the Bengal School started by Abanindranath.
After 1919, some of the Vichitra Club artists moved to Shantiniketan; there
they founded an art school proper that became the leading department in
Tagore's university.

At the same time the Bengal School was attracting the patronage of the
British. Two successive governors of Bengal, Lords Carmichael and Ronaldshay,
gave it their support and became friendly with Gaganendranath and his

brother. Their interest was partly aesthetic and partly, as Ronaldshay admitted, political. By supporting harmless expressions of Bengali nationalism Ronaldshay hoped to undermine aggressive nationalism. The mythological and historical paintings of the Bengal School, pretty, insipid and safe, were ideal candidates. The same could not be said of the brilliant and savage caricatures produced by Gaganendranath from 1917, which were the visual equivalent of Rabindranath's early letters from England, his satirical short stories (such as 'The Raj Seal') and his polemical essays attacking orthodoxy. Some of this art had the ferocity of George Grosz. In the main it excoriated wealthy Bengali society – with its bloated, lascivious *babus*, parasitic priests and *ingabanga* imitation-Englishmen – but occasionally it took swipes at the British. The caricatures were not among the works shown in exhibitions of Bengal School art sponsored by the Bengal government; nor have they been given their proper due by Indian art historians.

'[They] are falling like bombshells in the reactionary camps', Tagore's son wrote excitedly to a friend in Chicago in August 1917. Earlier in the letter he described how his father had given a devastating lecture which had to be repeated, such was the public demand. The second time, Rathindranath wrote, mounted police had to be called to disperse the crowd.

He [Rabindranath] spared neither the Government nor the people; from no one else would the public have gulped down such scathing criticism of their social institutions. Father couldn't have chose [a] better time to give his message to Bengal. After the Swadeshi movement, there had been a strong revival of orthodox Hinduism – an orthodoxy that was desperately attempting to adjust itself to the advances made in the thoughts and ideas of the present century. An inevitable reaction had set in against this neo-Hinduistic movement. This was just the time to hit, and hit hard.

Rathindranath was referring to the speech quoted in our Introduction, in which Rabindranath had told his audience: 'National self-respect is ordering us to perform an impossible task: to keep one of our eyes wide open and the other one closed in sleep.'

The trigger for Tagore had been the Indian reaction to a government order interning Annie Besant in June 1917. The Theosophist leader and former Fabian socialist maverick had openly called for Home Rule in India. Instead of protesting against her internment, politicians in Bengal had allowed themselves to be cowed into silence by government threats. 'The weak are as powerful enemies of the strong as the strong of the weak', Rabindranath told his audience – an idea later quoted by Indira Gandhi.

Tagore had no regard for Besant personally and a well-justified distrust of Theosophy. What then persuaded him to issue a statement of unequivocal support for her in July? (His lecture came nearly a month later and made no reference to Besant by name.) In doing so he stepped directly into the political arena for the first time since 1905 and soon became embroiled in a mess. Why did he not stick to building up Shantiniketan after his return from abroad and to lecturing on more general subjects, such as he had in Japan and the USA?

The fact of Besant's internment had touched a chord in him. Hundreds of young men were then interned without trial in Bengal. Some of them were personally known to him through his school and in other ways. His heart was skewered by their suffering. At examination time he knew well that the police liked to take down his pupils' names as a matter of course and he knew better still what a disastrous effect police taint could have on the prospects of a boy. 'Even that most desperate of creatures, the Bengali father with an unmarried daughter to get rid of – to whom neither ugliness nor vice, nor age nor disease is a bar – even he refrains from sending the matchmaker to him.' Writing in April 1918 to Edwin Montagu, the liberal secretary of state for India then touring India to research his forthcoming reform policy, Tagore said candidly (thinking of the young Britons then dying in Europe):

Our young men in Bengal know that they are not trusted by their Govt. – they are spied upon, they are harassed, their field of employment is narrowed, they suffer for those very qualities which are encouraged in the country of their rulers. When they dedicate their lives for the welfare of their country, independent of Govt. help, their very success is looked upon with misgivings.

'In this crisis', he told an English editor and acquaintance, who had been surprised by his turning political, 'the only European who has shared our sorrow, incurring the anger and derision of her countrymen, is Mrs Besant.'

There was a new note of bitterness in Tagore. It bleakly presaged, both in general and in its specifics, the political disaster of 1919 at Amritsar, which is often regarded as the beginning of the end of the British Raj.

But before that, he himself, following Annie Besant, briefly became the subject of suspicion and attack in early 1918. This complex episode showed with unusual clarity the strengths and limitations of Tagore as an international figure, involving as it did five major countries – the USA, Britain, Germany, Japan and India – and their political elites.

The roots of the incident take us back to October 1916, when Tagore was nearly assassinated by Indian revolutionaries in San Francisco for supposedly being an agent of the Indian government. Before he left the USA in late January, he requested Macmillan to approach President Wilson on his behalf, as he wished to dedicate *Nationalism* to Wilson. On 9 April, three days after the USA declared war on Germany, Wilson declined. He wrote to Macmillan:

> Will you not express to Sir R. Tagore my warm appreciation of the motives which prompted him to make this request and my regret that it seems unwise for me to comply with it, not because of any lack of sympathy on my part for the principles which he so eloquently supports in his book, but because just now I have to take all sorts of international considerations into my thought and must err if I err at all on the side of tact and prudence?

Behind this statement lay some advice from the British. (Sir) William Wiseman, chief of British intelligence in the USA, had successfully manoeuvred the police into making a raid on Indian plotters in New York in March. Papers seized from them implicated Tagore in their conspiracy to foment revolution in India with German money. Tagore was said to have had talks with German officials while he was in the USA and to have accepted money from them. Wiseman therefore recommended to Colonel House, Wilson's friend and chief personal adviser, that the president should not accept the dedication.

During 1917 the wartime US government cracked down on the conspirators. A trial began in San Francisco in November and lasted until 23 April 1918. The government had indicted 124 persons of various nationalities; thirty-five were actually tried, including the former German consul-general at San Francisco and others in the consulate. (Count von Bernstorff, the former German ambassador to the US, was also implicated.) Besides prison sentences for the leading conspirators, on the final day of the trial the chief Indian conspirator Ram Chandra was shot dead in front of the jury box by a fellow Indian conspirator, who was then himself shot dead by a US marshal. (Chandra was probably the one responsible for masterminding the failed attempt on Tagore's life, though he publicly denied it in 1916.) At one point in the trial a letter was produced in which an Indian in Washington DC stated that Tagore had come to the United States 'at our suggestion' and implied that Tagore had tried to enlist support for the conspiracy when he met Count Okuma, the prime minister of Japan. At another point a telegram from an Indian living in New York to one in San Francisco was introduced as evidence that Indian revolutionaries approved of Tagore's speeches. (No mention, surprisingly, was made of their assassination attempt on Tagore.) The counsel for the defence objected, 'Tagore is not one of the defendants?' and the prosecuting attorney replied facetiously, 'No, he is not. We overlooked him in our haste.'

Rabindranath knew nothing of this until early May, when he was shown some foreign newspaper reports in India. They could hardly have arrived at a worse moment. In addition to his bitter feelings about official attitudes in India, he was in the midst of making plans for another fund-raising tour in the USA and his eldest daughter Madhurilata (Bela) was gravely ill with tuberculosis. On 16 May she died in Calcutta at her husband's house, aged thirty-two. To make matters still worse, father and daughter had hardly seen each other for more than five years since he had gone to England in 1912. Nothing can be said for certain, but apparently Bela felt aggrieved by Rabindranath's indulgence of her spoilt, irascible brother-in-law Nagendranath Gangulee (the husband of her sister Mira), whom Bela and her husband found intolerable; and so out of hurt pride she had cut herself off from her father. As the end approached Rabindranath saw Bela regularly and may have nursed her – accounts differ – but on the day she died, he could not bear to look at her face. According to Rathindranath, Bela was his 'favourite child'.

This private tension and tragedy may have contributed to the vehemence with which Tagore reacted to the events in San Francisco. He fired off a cable to President Wilson and followed it with letters to Wilson, Okuma, the viceroy Lord Chelmsford, George Brett of Macmillan, and finally American friends such as Harriet Moody. The letter to Wilson combined respect with trenchancy:

> Though I feel certain that my friends in America and my readers there who have studied my writings at all carefully can never believe such an audacious piece of fabrication, yet the indignity of my name being dragged into the mire of such calumny has given me great pain. It is needless to tell you that I do not believe in patriotism which can ride roughshod over higher ideals of humanity, and I consider it to be an act of impiety against one's own country when any service is offered to her which is loaded with secret lies and dishonest deeds of violence. I have been outspoken enough in my utterances when my country needed them, and I have taken upon myself the risk of telling unwelcome truths to my own countrymen, as well as to the rulers of my country. But I despise those tortuous methods adopted whether by some Government or other groups of individuals, in which the devil is taken into partnership in the name of duty. I have received great kindness from the hands of your countrymen, and I entertain great admiration for yourself who [is] not afraid of incurring the charge of anachronism for introducing idealism in the domain of politics, and therefore I owe it to myself and to you and your people to make this avowal of my faith and to assure your countrymen that their hospitality was not bestowed upon one who was ready to accept it while wallowing in the sub-soil sewerage of treason.

To Okuma (who had now retired from office) Tagore spoke less passionately of 'this canard' linking their names which had 'greatly pained' him. To Chelmsford he spoke of 'the unscrupulous manufacture of lies employed against myself.' But to Harriet Moody and to another friend in Chicago, he was scalding: 'There is something which is so undignified in this affair that it fills me with disgust . . . I hate to be put in the same category with politicians and diplomats' – he meant the revolutionaries, Indian and German – 'who deal with secret lies and found their schemes upon filth pits of iniquity.'

Okuma replied that he had circulated Tagore's letter in the Japanese press and showed it to the prime minister. Chelmsford accepted that there was 'no foundation whatever' for the allegations. Wilson did not respond; the intended reply apparently fizzled out somewhere between the State Department and the Justice Department in Washington DC, buried by the exigencies of war and bureaucratic inertia. Harriet Moody maintained comfortingly, 'I do not think the slightest credence was given by anyone whose judgement could count for a moment, to that sensational newspaper story.' She obviously believed this, because she repeated it several years later.

In fact the allegations did tremendous damage to Tagore in the USA. They virtually killed the sales of his books for several years and made it almost impossible for him to get a fair hearing from foundations and financiers when he visited the United States again in 1920–21. This would be amply confirmed by, among others, George Brett and James B. Pond. Tagore the realist had been thoroughly perceptive about the wartime American public's likely reaction to charges of 'disloyalty'.

Tagore the idealist was less perceptive. It seems that he *did* meet a German diplomat during his US tour; very likely he also had some social contact with Bengali revolutionaries in New York – the flimsy basis for the stories. In Japan he may also have met the self-confessed terrorist Rashbihari Bose, who was living under the protection of ultra-Right Japanese nationalists and the blind eye of the Japanese government, including Okuma. In 1924 Tagore unquestionably met Bose in Japan and even – staggeringly – offered a post in his university to an associate of Bose who had been indicted (unsuccessfully) at the San Francisco trial and was wanted in India for acts of terrorism. Tagore cannot but have been aware of the belief in violence held by Rashbihari Bose and his circle. Bose was no better than Sandip, the politician in *The Home and the World*; and some of his associates were as rough as the Indian revolutionaries in California. Either Tagore treated all these contacts with saintly naivety – like Nikhil in the earlier part of his novel – or he shared some of their beliefs. The former possibility is by far the more likely, though it must be said that Tagore did show a perverse admiration for authoritarian political systems (especially

Communism) at certain times during his later life, and a converse distrust of democracy. Perhaps there was a hint of this attitude in the scornful language of his letter to President Wilson.

To the majority of British officials in India in 1918–19, the second possibility was by far more likely to be the truth. In their eyes Tagore was probably a revolutionary sympathizer. His actions at the time of the Amritsar Massacre would only confirm their suspicions.

The killing of at least 379 unarmed people and the wounding of 2,000 more by troops under British command at Amritsar's Jallianwala Bagh occurred on 13 April 1919. Tagore was then in Shantiniketan with C. F. Andrews. Neither of them knew what had happened for some time because of press censorship. But Tagore had been expecting trouble from Gandhi's protest against newly-introduced government repression (the Rowlatt Acts). On 12 April, at Gandhi's request, he had sent him a message of support and addressed him for the first time as Mahatma. But he also warned him presciently:

I know your teaching is to fight against evil by the help of the good. But such a fight is for heroes and not for men led by impulses of the moment. Evil on one side naturally begets evil on the other, injustice leading to violence and insult to vengefulness. Unfortunately such a force has already been started, and either through panic or through wrath our authorities have shown us their claws whose sure effect is to drive some of us into the secret path of resentment and others into utter demoralization.

As news of the massacre began to filter into the press he became more and more agitated. Between 23 and 26 April he wrote Andrews, who had rushed off to Delhi, five ringing letters, alternately denouncing official callousness and Indian cowardliness.

Of one thing our authorities seem to be unconscious – it is that they have completely lost their moral prestige. I can recall the time when our people had great faith in [the] justice and truthfulness of British Government . . . It was almost ludicrous to find how our masses during the late war refused to accept as true every news of success of the allies that came to them from the English source.

Andrews had gone to Simla to see government officials. On 1 May he wrote to Tagore:

I said to one of them that never in this century had the moral prestige of the Indian Government been lower. He answered me on the next day 'I thought over what you said and I would wager a considerable sum that it has never been *higher*.' He simply did not know what moral prestige meant.

On 14 May Andrews wrote that the viceroy had been 'cold as ice with me and full of racial bitterness – referring again and again to the murders of English people at Amritsar, but resenting it when I spoke of the intolerable wrongs from which Indians had suffered.' After that Andrews gave up and returned, via Gandhi, to Shantiniketan.

Rabindranath now went to Calcutta. From Andrews he had gathered the dimensions of the brutality, still concealed by press censorship. He also knew that Gandhi was not willing to make forthright public protest. He therefore felt that he *must* act. His idea was to call a public meeting in Calcutta at which the political leaders would speak under his presidency. But when he went to see C. R. Das, one of the firebrands in 1905, he found him cagey. As in 1917 at the time of Annie Besant's internment, no leader would commit himself in public. Tagore returned to Jorasanko feeling that there was a thorn in his chest.

He could not sleep. That night, 30 May, he sat up and wrote a letter to Lord Chelmsford that is now celebrated. At the end of it he asked to be relieved of the knighthood conferred on him four years before by Lord Hardinge, 'for whose nobleness of heart I still entertain great admiration'. Giving his reasons for this public gesture of solitary defiance he wrote:

The enormity of the measures taken by the Government in the Punjab for quelling some local disturbances has, with a rude shock, revealed to our minds the helplessness of our position as British subjects in India . . . Considering that such treatment has been meted out to a population, disarmed and resourceless, by a power which has the most terribly efficient organization for destruction of human lives, we must strongly assert that it can claim no political expediency, far less moral justification. The accounts of the insults and sufferings undergone by our brothers in the Punjab have trickled through the gagged silence, reaching every corner of India, and the universal agony of indignation roused in the hearts of our people has been ignored by our rulers – possibly congratulating themselves for imparting what they imagine as salutary lessons . . . The time has come when badges of honour make our shame glaring in the incongruous context of humiliation, and I for my part wish to stand, shorn of all special distinctions, by the side of those of my countrymen who for their so-called insignificance are liable to suffer a degradation not fit for human beings.

Over a year later, after a government inquiry, in the House of Commons Winston Churchill called the shootings at Amritsar 'without precedent or parallel in the modern history of the British Empire . . . It is an extraordinary event, a monstrous event, an event which stands in singular and sinister isolation.' Churchill was no lover of freedom for India: Tagore had reacted with formidable restraint.

His letter was widely read in India, having been printed in the press on 2 June. But it did not catch the public imagination in the way that, say, Gandhi's picking up salt at Dandi in 1930 did. It did not have the mass appeal of that gesture, despite its courage and nobility. Not one political leader, including Gandhi, congratulated Tagore. Whatever impact the gesture made – and this was hard to measure – it achieved in more subtle ways.

Chelmsford's first instinct was no doubt to ignore Tagore's letter altogether. He took advice on the unknown protocol for repudiating a knighthood from his officials, one of whom minuted: 'The insolence of resigning an honour conferred by the King for literary attainments on the ground of disagreement with the policy of the Government is patent.' Then he cabled Montagu, the secretary of state:

I propose to reply, in view of the advertisement that would be given to Tagore and of the fact that grant of his request might be interpreted as admission of mistaken policy in the Punjab, that I am unable myself to relieve him of his title and, in the circumstances, do not propose to make any recommendation to His Majesty on the subject.

The liberal Montagu took advice too. One of his officials in the India Office noted that 'degradation' of a knight bachelor had been done in the case of Sir Roger Casement. 'It would be quite inapplicable in the present case. The Viceroy's proposed action is right.' King George V, when consulted, concurred. Montagu cabled the viceroy agreeing to his proposal. Officially Tagore would remain Sir Rabindranath.

'I still have it. I have eaten my pudding and must keep it', Tagore told Edward Thompson in 1921. He was correct. And in nationalist India his title remained a handle with which occasionally to beat him. In 1925, even Gandhi, piqued by some particularly acid and effective criticism from Tagore, deliberately referred to him as 'Sir' Rabindranath. Tagore felt obliged to issue a statement:

I have not the overweening conceit discourteously to display an insincere attitude of contempt for a title of honour which was conferred on me in recognition of my literary work. I greatly abhor to make any public gesture which may have the least suggestion of a theatrical character. But in this particular case, I was driven to it when I hopelessly failed to persuade our political leaders to launch an adequate protest against what was happening at that time in the Punjab.

He concluded characteristically: 'I confess to an idiosyncrasy . . . that I do not like any addition to my name – Babu or Sriyut, Sir or Doctor, or Mr, and, the least of all, Esquire. A psycho-analyst may trace this to a sense of pride in the depth of my being and he may not be wrong.'

Outside India he continued to be a knight more often than not – even in the *New York Times*. At Macmillan in London there was considerable indecision in the title pages of his books in the early 1920s. When he died in 1941, almost every obituary in Britain gave him his title. Like it or not, Tagore could never entirely escape the penalties of his unique fame.

22 The Founding of a University (1918–1921)

Beggary is a profitable profession in our country under certain conditions, but my temperament and training are against me.

> letter to W. W. Pearson,
> Shantiniketan, December 1918

In April 1921 an editorial in the London *Nation*, 'A league of spirit', commented:

While the whole world is at war, it is some comfort to hear even one voice, however still and small, persistently murmuring of peace. Amid the turmoil and shouting one may still catch the quiet words of an Indian pleading the cause of understanding, friendliness, and forbearance, as though they, and not devastating conflicts, were the most natural things in the world. In such a spirit it is that Rabindranath Tagore has been moving, almost silently, from country to country, and from hemisphere to hemisphere, insinuating his conception of an International University . . . Suspected as a seditious agitator, dogged by Government spies, impugned by official detraction, or, at the best, scornfully tolerated as an impracticable dreamer, he has trodden the well-worn and dolorous path of the spirit.

The university's conception took place, as we know, in the fragrant orange groves of southern California in October 1916. Its execution would be quite another matter. From 1918 until his dying day Tagore would bear his university on his shoulders almost like the cross on the way to Calvary.

In late 1917 he welcomed at Shantiniketan the members of the Calcutta University Commission. The head was (Sir) Michael Sadler, a well-known educationist and art collector, who soon formed a deep admiration for Tagore. Sadler had come to Calcutta to grapple with the failings of Indian higher education analysed by Rabindranath in numerous lectures and essays since the 1890s, including 'Indian students and western teachers' in 1916. Tagore's discussions with Sadler and others seem to have provoked Tagore to further thinking and writing on education in 1918, culminating in the foundation ceremony of his university in December. He wrote, for instance, *Tota Kahini* (*The Parrot's Training*), a pointed fable about an ignorant bird that receives such a 'sound schooling' from the pundits on the orders of the Raja that it ends up stuffed with the paper of its textbooks, choked to death by education. (Abanindranath supplied some original and amusing illustrations.) And on the subject of the Bengali language having at last been accepted into Calcutta University at MA level – a prospect that might have been expected to please Rabindranath – he wrote dubiously:

> I have found that the direct influence which the Calcutta University wields over our language is not strengthening and vitalizing, but pedantic and narrow. It tries to perpetuate the anachronisms of preserving the Pundit-made Bengali swathed in grammar-wrappings borrowed from a dead language [i.e. Sanskrit]. It is every day becoming a more formidable obstacle in the way of our boys' acquiring that mastery of their mother tongue which is of life and literature. The artificial language of a learned mediocrity, inert and formal, ponderous and didactic, devoid of the least breath of creative vitality, is forced upon our boys at the most receptive period of their life. I know this, because I have to connive, myself, at a kind of intellectual infanticide when my own students try to drown the natural spontaneity of their expression under some stagnant formalism.

His own university would go to the opposite extreme. He called it Visva-Bharati, a compound made from the Sanskrit word for the universe and Bharati, a goddess in the *Rig Veda* associated with the Hindu goddess of learning, Saraswati. 'If an English university wanted a name of the same kind it would call itself Minerveum Universalis', wrote a playful Nirad Chaudhuri. The motto for the university was from Sanskrit and meant 'Where the whole world meets in one nest'. Tagore also wrote: 'Visva-Bharati represents India where she has her wealth of mind which is for all. Visva-Bharati acknowledges India's obligation to offer to others the hospitality of her best culture and India's right to accept from others their best.'

The foundation stone was laid on 22 December 1918 at a special meeting of students, staff, ex-students and well-wishers of the ashram held in the mango grove at Shantiniketan. Rabindranath explained his hope that Shantiniketan would become a rendezvous for western and Asian scholars and a conduit between Asia's past and present, so that the ancient learning might be rejuvenated through contact with modern thinking. Three years later, on 22 December 1921, Visva-Bharati was formally inaugurated in the presence of its chancellor Sir

Brajendranath Seal, India's foremost living scholar, and its first western visiting scholar, Sylvain Lévi. Just before this Seal wrote confidentially to Tagore:

I hope our savants will take this opportunity to establish contact with Sylvain Lévi at [Shantiniketan]. But I do not lay much store by the more famous of them. Some of them are easier to understand and appreciate from a respectable distance than from close up. My fear is that Professor Lévi will notice our lack of hospitality and a certain poverty of spirit, and will begin to doubt the essential greatness of India. The saving grace is that you are there and so is the peasantry, and lastly there is the ever-loving mother Bengal.

The three years before this event, 1919–21, were filled with Tagore's attempts at fund-raising for Visva-Bharati in India, in Europe and in the USA. The first was in south India in early 1919. Rabindranath had been invited by James Cousins, an Irish poet, Theosophist and friend of Yeats who had settled north-east of Bangalore as a college principal. From Bangalore Tagore toured the south and was much sought after. He was disturbed by the sight of fabulous wealth stored away in the great temples instead of being used for educating the young, and conversely excited by his hearty reception from students. Speaking extempore outdoors under the trees he told them disarmingly of the youth hidden in his heart, despite 'witnesses who bear false evidence against this – I mean my grey beard and hair, which, like professional witnesses in the law courts, whose profession it is to give false evidence, contradict my inner youthfulness.' Young people knew he liked their company better than the company of most men of his own age, he said with a laugh.

I find that most of the old men of my age have *opinions*. That is a great nuisance – I can tell you. I have not got any *opinions* till now; and, sometimes, people come to me and they think that I am old enough to give them advices and to tell my 'opinions' about things; and I have to look very grave and wise. But unfortunately I have to disappoint them.

His prepared speech was 'The centre of Indian Culture', his first major effort to define Visva-Bharati to the world. 'The trouble is that as soon as we think of a university, the idea of Oxford, Cambridge, and a host of other European universities rushes in and fills our mind', he said. Then he made a statement that was really a manifesto for his entire life:

Let me state clearly that I have no distrust of any culture because of its foreign character. On the contrary, I believe that the shock of outside forces is necessary for maintaining the vitality of our intellect . . . European culture has come to us not only with its knowledge but with its speed. Even when our assimilation is imperfect and aberrations follow, it is rousing our intellectual life from the inertia of formal habits. The contradiction it offers to our traditions makes our consciousness glow.

What I object to is the artificial arrangement by which this foreign education tends to occupy all the space of our national mind and thus kills, or hampers, the great opportunity for the creation of new thought by a new combination of truths. It is this which makes me urge that all the elements in our own culture have to be strengthened; not to resist the culture of the West, but to accept and assimilate it. It must become for us nourishment and not a burden. We must gain mastery over it and not live on sufferance as hewers of texts and drawers of book-learning.

Tagore's statement acquires added resonance and courage when one recalls that Indo-British friendship was at a low ebb in late 1918/early 1919 and would shortly plunge into a chasm with the shootings at Amritsar in April. It spoke volumes for his strength of character or (if one is a pragmatist) his naivety – for he never abandoned this basic view.

Later in 1919 he took his first steps towards making Visva-Bharati a reality. He signed, along with leading European thinkers and artists including Einstein, 'La déclaration pour l'independence de l'esprit'. This was the brainchild of Romain Rolland, novelist, essayist and pacifist, winner of the 1915 Nobel prize for literature, who had approached Tagore. Rolland, like Tagore, had become enamoured of the idea of the synthesis of East and West; in due course he would write four books on India – studies of Gandhi, Ramakrishna and Vivekananda – without visiting India, without knowing its history and without knowing any of its languages, including English! ('I believe the case is unique in the history of modern culture', noted Mircea Eliade in 1961.) In October 1919 Tagore wrote to Rolland: 'It hurts me very deeply when I think that there is hardly a corner in the vast continent of Asia where men have come to feel any real love for Europe. The great event of the meeting of the East and the West has been desecrated by the spirit of contempt on the one side and a corresponding hatred on the other.'

In Shantiniketan Rabindranath founded three departments, the nucleus of his university, which remained its strongest sections during its subsequent development. There was the department of fine arts (Kala Bhavan) under Nandalal Bose, the most gifted pupil of Abanindranath. There was the department of music (Sangit Bhavan), concentrating on Tagore's own songs. This was run by Dinendranath Tagore, the grandson of his eldest brother

Dwijendranath. Dinu had a powerful voice (it was he who had sung Tagore's patriotic songs best in 1905) and an unrivalled musical memory: often he would be called to stand outside Rabindranath's bathroom window and listen to a new song before the composer forgot the tune. Rabindranath called him the *kandari* (helmsman) and the *bhandari* (storekeeper) of his songs. And lastly there was the department of Indology, founded for the study of Buddhist literature, Vedic and Classical Sanskrit, Pali, Prakrit and later on Tibetan and Chinese. Most foreign scholars would be attached to this department.

To house these departments, to pay the teaching staff and to house and pay the anticipated visiting lecturers would obviously require money. Furthermore Tagore's son Rathindranath had begun to build a house for his father, which would gradually grow into a substantial and elaborate structure as funds became available. And of course, apart from money, Tagore needed to persuade some leading European scholars to spend time in the middle of nowhere, living in fairly primitive conditions. For many reasons therefore the time seemed ripe for another visit to Europe, the first since before the Great War.

He departed in mid-May 1920, but only after vacillating for months. Both his ashram and the political fall-out of the Amritsar Massacre conspired to keep him in India. At Gandhi's request, he presided over a literary conference at Ahmedabad and paid his first call on Gandhi's ashram nearby, where he stayed overnight. Both men kept conspicuously quiet about the visit in public. Then he toured western India, hoping to raise money from minor princes. On 13 April, the first anniversary of the Amritsar Massacre, he sent a message to the Congress meeting in Bombay, at the desire of Mohammed Ali Jinnah. (This was ironic, given the nature of the message and Jinnah's lead in dividing India in 1947.) There had been a move in the Congress to build a memorial to the dead where they had fallen in Amritsar. Tagore opposed it:

Let those, who wish, try to burden the minds of the future with stones, carrying the black memory of wrongs and their anger, but let us bequeath to the generations to come memorials of that only which we can revere – let us be grateful to our forefathers, who have left us the image of our Buddha, who conquered self, preached forgiveness, and spread his love far and wide in time and space.

Tagore was not in tune with mass feeling. The construction of a memorial had Gandhi's active support; and during Tagore's absence abroad Gandhi launched the non-cooperation movement that was anathema to Tagore. Probably Rabindranath sensed the national mood and was torn about leaving India, for he wrote C. F. Andrews two letters before he boarded the ship at

Bombay: 'I wish I had not been leaving India just now but I am certain that the
call is for me to go'; and 'I feel we shan't be long in Europe – I am not in a mood
to face the world and answer its questions.'

In the event he was away from India for fourteen months, almost as long as in
1912–13. Once again, in London William Rothenstein found him and his party
accommodation, this time in South Kensington, and helped him generally. But
the two friends had diverged in the intervening seven years despite keeping in
touch through letters. The war had drawn Rothenstein further into the
mainstream of English thinking; on Tagore it had had the opposite effect.
Rothenstein had become a war artist. In June 1919, just after Tagore wrote his
lacerating letter to the viceroy, Rothenstein wrote from Ypres in Belgium:

> the beauty of places like Ypres is beyond words. I am constantly reminded of
> Chitor and Amber [great abandoned Rajput forts in Rajasthan] – will you
> not some day write an essay on the beauty of desolation? Where hands and
> voices were once busy, all is still, and nature seems to assimilate and take to
> her own bosom the work of our hands when it is shattered and make it her
> own, as though she refused it when it was a nest for our plots and schemes
> against her will, but accepted it when purified from our presence.

Tagore did not reply, but when *he* visited the trenches of northern France in
1920, he wrote an essay in fundamental contradiction to Rothenstein's feeling:

> The awful calm of desolation, which still bore wrinkles of pain – death-
> struggles stiffened into ugly ridges – brought before my mind the vision of a
> huge demon, which had no shape, no meaning, yet had two arms that could
> strike and break and tear, a gaping mouth that could devour, and bulging
> brains that could conspire and plan . . . Something of the same sense of
> oppression in a different degree, the same desolation in a different aspect, is
> produced in my mind when I realize the effect of the West upon Eastern life
> – the West which, in its relation to us, is all plan and purpose incarnate,
> without any superfluous humanity.

Amritsar had divided the two friends, and it would dominate Tagore's entire
visit to England, during which the House of Commons furiously debated the
enquiry into the massacre, with Tagore watching from the Visitor's Gallery.
Most of Tagore's English friends appear to have avoided any reference to his
repudiation of his knighthood. Rothenstein was the only one who actively

approved – and even his praise was brief and muted. Lowes Dickinson wrote awkwardly: 'Dear Sir Rabindranath Tagore I call you so because I understand you have not yet succeeded in getting relieved of your unwelcome title!' Robert Bridges, the Poet Laureate, apologized for his long silence and expressed himself anxious to meet Tagore in Oxford: 'I began a long letter but I feared that you could misinterpret my silence, and in England we could not at first rely on press reports of events.' When, however, Tagore visited Oxford to speak to the students, Bridges excused himself from presiding over the event. In a further letter he regretted missing Tagore in Oxford for a private talk. Their relationship never recovered.

With W. B. Yeats the problem was different, nothing to do with politics. Tagore did not really like Yeats' poetry, despite wanting to, while Yeats, as we know, had by 1920 cooled off on Tagore's poetry. He told Tagore that of his recent works, *My Reminiscences* and *The Home and the World* had impressed him most. He wished that Tagore had carried on the memoirs until his mature years and he thought that the novel was very true of Irish society: had it not stirred up strong feelings in Bengal as it would have done in Ireland if written by an Irish writer? At a party at Rothenstein's Yeats requested Tagore to sing some *Gitanjali* songs. 'Yeats first recited the poem in English in his usual dignified manner; then Father sang in Bengali', Rathindranath noted in his diary. The meetings were pleasant ones – but the old excitement was missing.

Of Tagore's new contacts, two were particularly interesting. The first was a Russian painter, Nicholas Roerich. He is probably best known for his historical stage paintings for Diaghilev's Ballets Russes. Though an aristocrat, Roerich is said to have been asked to be the first minister of culture after the October 1917 revolution, and to have declined. After travelling for many years in the West and in Asia, he settled in India. His mystical paintings are still admired; when, in 1961, Yuri Gagarin was asked what the earth looked like from space, he reportedly said it looked very much like the paintings of Nicholas Roerich. Tagore told Roerich in London: 'When I tried to find words to describe to myself what were the ideas which your pictures suggested I failed . . . When one art can fully be explained by another then it is a failure. Your pictures are distinct and yet are not definable by words – your art is jealous of its independence because it is great.'

The second contact was T. E. Lawrence, who told Tagore he was ashamed to return to Arabia because of the treacherous behaviour of the British government. According to Rathindranath,

When Father told him that he found there was a brutality in the Western people which the Indian people did not have and could never really imbibe from their rulers – temperamentally they were so different – he [Lawrence] replied that the only remedy lay in striking back at the Englishman harder than he hits, for then he would come to his senses and recognize others as worthy brothers.

This story must be treated with some caution, since Tagore himself never described his meeting with Lawrence. He may have admired Lawrence's idealism and freedom from convention – after all, he himself had often spoken of being at heart an Arab Bedouin – but he could hardly have shared Lawrence's stance, as reported by his son, which was that of the terrorists in Bengal.

All this was before the House of Commons debate on Amritsar. Here Tagore was exposed to the full violence of reactionary opinion, which was ready to defend General Dyer, the officer responsible for the massacre, to the hilt, and to disembowel the Jew Edwin Montagu, secretary of state for India. There was much support in the House for the view that the man on the spot had to be trusted, particularly in the difficult conditions of India. One Conservative MP, a brigadier-general, asserted bluntly: 'If we do not hold India by moral suasion, we must hold it by force, possibly thinly veiled, but undoubtedly by force.' When Winston Churchill, the secretary of state for war, rose to speak he knew that the government's survival was in jeopardy. We know part of his speech already; he also said, 'Our reign in India or anywhere else has never rested on a basis of physical force alone, and it would be fatal to the British Empire to try to base ourselves only upon it.' There was a sullen silence. Ultimately defeat for the government was narrowly avoided – but a large number of Conservatives had abstained. Tagore, watching, was shocked by the virulence of the personal attack on Montagu. He wrote him a few lines of congratulation for his tenacity and later supported a move – foredoomed to fail – to have Montagu made viceroy after the retirement of Lord Chelmsford.

A fortnight later Tagore had a most revealing encounter with that formidable Fabian Beatrice Webb, who had toured India, including Bengal, in 1911–12 with her husband Sidney. In her diary she noted:

whilst he [Tagore] resents any criticism of Hindu tradition or of Hindu rites, still more of Hindu mysticism, he is a bitter and uninformed critic of western government, of western industrial organization and of western nationalism, of western science. 'All governments are evil,' he dogmatically asserts: 'The intellect solves no problems' is his constant implication. He is not content to be the seer and the poet – the man who attains wisdom through intellect; he must needs condemn the man of action, the lawyer, the administrator and the politician, and even the scientific worker. This quite unconscious and spiritual insolence, this all-embracing consciousness of his own supreme righteousness (compared to men of action) is due, I think, to the atmosphere of adulation in which the mystic genius lives and has his being.

But in her admitted anger 'at Tagore's quite obvious dislike of all that the Webbs stand for', Beatrice Webb nevertheless added:

I fail to do justice to Tagore as a unique person. He has perfect manners and he is a person of great intellect, distinction, and outstanding personal charm. He is beautiful to look at: he clothes himself exquisitely: the rich, soft grey ribbed silk wrap, in which his tall and graceful figure is enveloped, tones into his iron-grey hair and beard; a finely wrought, thick gold chain, winding in and out of the grey garment, tones into the rich brown hue of his skin. His speech has the perfect intonation and slow chant-like moderation of the dramatic saint. He is indeed an almost too perfect personification of his part in the world's history. Unwittingly one's practical imagination sees a great pageant, staged without limit of cost at Delhi, with Tagore the magnificent saint, standing in the centre in statuesque stillness, personifying Immortal India, and poor little ugly Lloyd George in shabby khaki furtively shifting about in a far off corner, representing dethroned western civilization.

Webb, in her fierce ambivalence, truly was speaking on behalf of western culture. And the general thrust of her criticisms was to a great extent justified. But dwelling in her own variety of 'quite unconscious and spiritual insolence' she was oblivious of two crucial facts. Nowhere did she give the slightest indication of understanding the callousness of the recent debate in the House of Commons that had undoubtedly hardened Tagore's feelings towards imperialism. More important still, despite having travelled in Bengal, she betrayed not the faintest hint of knowledge of Tagore's practical activities – his school, his fledgling university, his agricultural projects – and of his quarter century of involvement in India's public life, culminating in the repudiation of his knighthood the year before.

Even Rothenstein wrote that 'the strong wine of praise, and the weak wine of worship' had gone 'to this good man's head', in a letter to Max Beerbohm. 'At any rate, he is turning his back on the thin stream he can wash his feet in here, for the great gushing river he can bathe in in the new world' – a reference to Tagore's wish to revisit the USA.

In fact, on 6 August, after writing disenchantedly to the social reformer Edward Carpenter, that 'I fear this is going to be my last visit to the West',

Tagore departed not for the United States but for the Continent. He had made little progress with his university in England; in France and elsewhere he hoped for a better reaction. He was not disappointed: in 1920 there was definite interest and when he returned the following year after visiting the USA, the response was phenomenal.

In France he stayed at the country house in Boulogne-sur-Seine on the outskirts of Paris owned by the wealthy but ascetic French-Jewish banker Albert Kahn, who ran the Cercle Autour du Monde. There he first met Sylvain Lévi of the Collège de France. 'He is a great scholar as you know,' Tagore wrote enthusiastically to C. F. Andrews, his chief correspondent during this tour of the West (who was in charge at Shantiniketan), 'but his heart is larger even than his intellect and his learning'. He went further: 'His mind has the translucent simplicity of greatness and his heart is overflowing with trustful generosity which will never acknowledge disillusionment.' The misjudgement was typical of a Tagore clouded by disillusionment with Britain. Lévi was a great scholar, no doubt, but he was by no means a saintly figure nor uncritical of Tagore – as would become painfully clear to both men in the years following Lévi's stay at Shantiniketan. (Even in 1920–21 Lévi discreetly avoided introducing Rabindranath to Romain Rolland, whom Tagore wanted to meet in person, because Lévi disapproved of Rolland's pacifism and his unscholarly approach to India.)

Tagore also met Henri Bergson – but with less rapport; and the flamboyant poetess Countess Anna de Noailles, friend of André Gide, Georges Clemenceau and many others. Introduced by her devoted admirer Albert Kahn, the countess came to conquer Tagore but, according to her own admission to him, she left his presence as his worshipper. She told him that on the day war was declared in 1914, Clemenceau had sent for her and together they had read from Gide's translation of *Gitanjali* to relieve his feeling of depression. In 1930 de Noailles would help to launch Tagore's paintings in Paris.

After six weeks in France Tagore visited Holland at the invitation of his Dutch translator, a well-known writer, Frederik van Eeden. He spoke in Amsterdam, Rotterdam, The Hague, Leiden and Utrecht. Then he went to Brussels, where he addressed a 'heaving sea of faces' at the Palais de Justice. A French writer described the impact:

A face like that of Christ, bronzed, serene and superb, came into view. Now there were no more rows of judges, no more individual men; there was one common humanity, all attentive. High over them was the commanding form of the Poet, with his white beard and his white flowing hair . . . His courtesy had a scrupulous exactness that made it almost religiously refined.

His subject was 'The meeting of the East and the West'.

Meanwhile in London, Willie Pearson had been negotiating with the J. B. Pond Lyceum Bureau for another tour of the United States. Despite the unhappy events of 1918 – the allegations against Tagore and the consequent collapse of his reputation – Rabindranath could not shake off the hope of making another triumphal tour to raise a large sum of money for his university. In his letters to C. F. Andrews in the second half of 1920 there are sardonic references to 'five million dollars', which he called his 'mantra', i.e. a word or phrase such as *Om* that in the Hindu tradition, if constantly repeated, aids meditation and inner peace. Tagore, with his finely-tuned sense of irony, knew the falseness of his appealing for 'big bucks' in America to build a spiritual and intellectual utopia in the Indian *mofussil*. Yet he could not help himself; he had to make the attempt. It would be the bitterest disappointment of all his travels in the West.

He could not say that he had not been warned. Initially Pond had been most enthusiastic. 'I never enjoyed any time in my life so much as I did those days when we were together in the West', Pond told Pearson in late June. But after trawling his contacts across the USA, Pond wrote in mid-September (while Tagore was being lionized in Holland):

So successfully has the propaganda against Tagore been spread that the average person believes that he was an anti-Ally agitator during the war. They will not touch him. This does not mean defeat, but it means that all the usual lecture channels are closed, and that a great popularity need not be expected until the Poet arrives here and once again is interviewed, photographed, and takes the center of the stage as is his custom.

Four days later Pond added: 'I personally think there is a big battle to fight, and my opinion is that the best way is to have Tagore come and to book the tour . . . en route as you go.'

Rabindranath arrived in New York City with Pearson and Rathindranath on 28 October and stayed at the Algonquin Hotel. The USA was in the throes of another presidential election. On 2 November the Republicans won, and the Wilsonian era of plain living and high thinking gave way to a new era of plain thinking and high living. 'Tagore was no longer the exotic novelty he had been in 1916; the fickle public had already turned to new fads, preferring bobbed hair to long grey beards, and short flapper skirts to flowing Oriental robes', wrote the American scholar Stephen Hay.

Tagore remained cooped up in Manhattan (with three brief trips to other places) for more than three months, lecturing inconsequentially, organizing committees and holding meetings, spending money rather than raising it, writing agonized letters to Andrews in Shantiniketan, and getting more and more depressed. In mid-December he fell out even with the faithful Pearson, who seems to have gone off for a while, having reached the point of suicide. In a pained letter dated 13 December but not actually sent to Pearson, Tagore revealed some candid self-analysis:

> You have got into some conventional habits, such as calling me 'Gurudev' and making 'pranam' to me [i.e. touching his feet]. Drop them. For I know there are occasions when they hurt you and for that very reason are truly discourteous to me. You know I never care to assume the role of a prophet or teacher; I do not claim homage from my fellow-beings, I only need love and sympathy and I am merely a poet and nothing else.

On 22 December, writing home to his daughter Mira, he was even more candid: 'I have always been attacked by political groups, religious groups, literary groups, social groups and so on. If I belonged to the opposition camp, each group would have forgiven me. That I do not belong to any group makes them all angry. No one will be able to put a chain on my feet.'

The nadir was plumbed at Christmas in a grand log-house known as Yama Farms in the Catskill Mountains north of New York City. This was a kind of retreat for industrialists where they could enjoy the company of the outstanding intellects of the day without any of the fuss surrounding their millions. The first guests had been Thomas Edison, Henry Ford, Harvey Firestone and the long-bearded naturalist John Burroughs. It was the kind of place where if you were introduced to Mr Waterman, it would be the fountain pen; Mr Colgate, the soap; Mr Eastman, the Kodak. Here Tagore met J. D. Rockefeller – or at least so the story goes, as reported sixty years later in the *New Yorker*. Two émigré Russian artists had captured Rabindranath and were sketching him in a house on the estate when he pulled out a handkerchief and out fell a dime. 'Isn't it odd,' he said. 'An old gentleman gave me this as he was waiting for his car. Do I look like a tramp?' That evening, the owner of Yama Farms identified the donor as Rockefeller, who had mentioned giving a dime to 'an old Negro'!

'We got to know many of the millionaires,' Tagore's son wrote somewhat bitterly to his friend in Chicago from the ship taking them back to Europe in late March 1921. There was a dinner in New York, for instance, where Tagore read *Gitanjali* 'much against his inclination.' The head of the Morgan

Company was present and he effectively banished any hope of funds from the diners. Rathindranath wrote:

> The Morgan Co. is intimately connected with the British Govt . . . After having been in America we began to realize the immense power that England exercises in that country. The financial control is astonishing. Political and cultural propaganda is constantly at work, very cleverly managed, so subtle and underground that it is difficult to fight against it or even to expose it. Wilson's regime had made England's hold over American supreme. We found it safer to criticize the English in England than in America.

Rathindranath was not being paranoid; as in 1917–18 with (Sir) William Wiseman, so in the 1920s British officials in the USA gave a discreet thumbs-down to the recalcitrant Tagore and his university. His repudiation of his knighthood in 1919 only made their task easier. (In 1925, for instance, a British official in New York ensured – no doubt to his complete satisfaction – that an American woman was dissuaded from donating $50,000 to Visva-Bharati.)

But there was another side to the conflict for which Tagore was partly to blame. The dinner in question had been organized by Dorothy Whitney Straight, the New York heiress who later handsomely supported Tagore, married his British friend Leonard Elmhirst in 1925 and co-founded the Dartington Trust. In the months after the dinner she felt bad about not helping Tagore. When Elmhirst, a young Cornell graduate of agricultural science, became passionate about the Shantiniketan ideal after meeting Tagore in New York in March 1921, Dorothy Straight decided to give her money to Elmhirst, to spend on Tagore's project as he saw fit. The point was, she did not want to give it to Tagore directly – not because she distrusted his politics but because she was not convinced by the philosophy behind Shantiniketan. Many other western liberals felt the same. 'In your recognition of the drawbacks of government by an impersonal system do not overlook the necessity of a sound impersonal element with a view to the permanence and stability of an institution like the Shantiniketan', a British missionary acquaintance advised Tagore. Rabindranath was not persuaded. And so, whenever he tried to raise money in the West for Visva-Bharati, especially in the USA, there was a tug-of-war: the money would be made available, *if* he was willing to accept a board of trustees (generally European). Tagore always refused this condition: he would not allow anyone to 'put a chain on his feet'.

Thus came the rupture with William Rothenstein. Tagore had met him briefly in London in April 1921 and then headed for France – by aeroplane. (At the aerodrome in London he was asked, 'Is this your first flight, poet?' and he replied, 'The first of its kind' – which set everyone laughing.) From the Kahn guesthouse outside Paris, he wrote reminding Rothenstein of their conversation in London; Rothenstein had agreed to begin planning Visva-Bharati with the help of Edwin Montagu, Lord Carmichael, (Sir) Michael Sadler and others, official and unofficial. Then, a week later, Tagore changed his mind and wrote asking Rothenstein to desist:

> Very likely I shall never be able to work in harmony with a board of trustees, influential and highly respectable, for I am a vagabond at heart. But the powerful people of the world, the lords of the earth, may make it difficult for me to carry out my work. I know it, and I had experience of it in connection with my Santi Niketan and also in my tour in America. But am I afraid of failure? I am only afraid of being tempted away from truth in pursuit of success. The temptation assaults me occasionally I admit, but it comes from the outside atmosphere – my own abiding faith is in light and life and freedom, and my prayer is: 'Lead me from the unreal to Truth.' [a quotation from the *Upanishads*]
>
> This letter of mine is only to let you that I free myself from the bondage of help and go back to the great Brotherhood of the Tramp, who seem helpless, but who are recruited by God for his own army.

Rothenstein was exasperated. He knew Tagore's moods, but this was too much. He replied with some warmth that he was 'neither a believer in machines, nor an Inspector of Schools, nor an enemy of freedom; yet you write as though I were all these things.' Some home truths about Tagore's impracticality, anti-British/pro-European feeling and love of adulation followed, though sensitively expressed. But Tagore was not to be shifted. He replied from Geneva that he would much rather allow Shantiniketan to be 'strangled' by official mistrust than 'fettered' by official help. Rothenstein drafted a response but did not send it. There was silence between them for a year.

Paris probably influenced Tagore, reminded him of his primary vocation as a poet and sharpened his frustration with the British. He at last met André Gide, his translator, who had no interest in Tagore the ambassador of India. ('He is EXQUISITE', Gide wrote to a friend.) And he met Romain Rolland, who was seriously interested in the proposed university. Later in 1921 Rolland wrote to Hermann Hesse:

> I must say I was somewhat prejudiced against him [Tagore], especially when I saw the snobbery surrounding him. But I had the great pleasure of seeing him privately in Paris last spring. I have become deeply attached to him and

have a profound respect for him. He is highly intelligent and has an acute understanding; he is by no means taken in by people. And now in his independence in the midst of numerous difficulties which arise from his admirers as well as from his enemies, he suffers intensely under the European brutality which he hates. He radiates an astonishing harmony that has grown out of his rich experiences and anguish. Tagore is keenly interested in having some Europeans come to his University, and I would consider it for later on, if my health were not too impaired now. But Tagore comes up against so many obstacles – put up by his compatriots as much as by the English!

The two-and-a-half months Tagore spent in Europe did much to restore his bruised pride, as well as helping his university. 'I only regret that the seven barren months I spent in America' – in fact it was five months – 'cannot be refunded to me by my destiny for my use in the present tour', he wrote to Thomas Sturge Moore from Stockholm in late May, just before delivering his belated Nobel prize acceptance speech. Altogether he visited France, Switzerland, Germany, Denmark, Sweden, Austria and Czechoslovakia. For lack of time he cancelled a visit to Spain, where his translators Juan Ramón Jiménez and wife Zenobia Camprubi had arranged an elaborate reception, including a performance of one of Tagore's plays with Federico García Lorca and Luis Buñuel in the cast.

In Stockholm Tagore witnessed a production of *The Post Office* in Swedish, was received by King Gustavus V and formed a friendship with Sven Hedin, the explorer of Asia. In Copenhagen the students staged a torch-light procession in front of his hotel and sang national songs till late at night. In Prague Leoš Janáček was inspired to set one of Tagore's poems to music, after hearing him lecture. He wrote:

Rabindranath Tagore entered the hall quietly. It seemed to me as if a white sacred flame flared up suddenly over the thousands and thousands of heads of the men and women present . . . But Tagore did not speak. He sang – his voice sounded like a nightingale's song – smooth, simple, without any clash of consonants . . . There is no doubt that the famous Bengali poet has a deep inborn feeling for music. Every syllable sounds as if its tone wings were expanded – very much like our own way of singing.

Rabindranath Tagore descended from the rostrum and made his way towards the exit. On his face you could trace indescribable grief. He spoke to us in his native language – we did not understand – but from the sound of his words, from the melodies of his poetry I could recognize and feel the bitter pain of his soul.

But it was in Germany that Tagore was almost swept off his feet. 'Scenes of frenzied hero worship marked a public lecture given by Sir Rabindranath Tagore today at Berlin University. In the rush for seats many girl students fainted and were trampled on by the crowd', a London newspaper reported on 3 June. And this was confirmed by the British ambassador in Berlin Viscount D'Abernon, whose wife tried to attend and could hardly get into the street, let alone the hall, so great was the crush. The following day Tagore called on the ambassador, who wrote about him in his diary, noting that he was 'more impressive in appearance than most of the conceptions of Christ':

Tagore says that he has talked with most of the intellectuals here and finds the German mind looking about for some new philosophy to replace militarism. He appeared surprised when I told him that the Universities – both professors and students – were considered very monarchistic and bellicose. His experience with the philosophers had been rather that of weariness with the old pre-war conceptions . . . He gave it as his opinion that the result of the war had been a great coarsening of feeling throughout Europe, a greater indifference to disorder and human suffering.

To him all Europe is alike; one European is like another European; our culture and our characteristics are similar: no European realizes how much identity there is, nor how small are the divergences between countries whose main stock-in-trade consists of nationalistic antipathies.

Tagore's own reaction to D'Abernon, given in a letter to C. F. Andrews, was ferocious:

While alluding to the enormous appreciation of my works in Germany he [D'Abernon] expressed his feeling of gratification at the possibility of my supplying some philosophy which may bring consolation to these people. He was glad, I am sure, from his British point of view. He thought that philosophy was a drug which would lull the restless activity of the German Nation into sleep affording the victors a better security in their enjoyment of material benefits. He would gladly concede the possession of soul and God to these unfortunate people only keeping for the share of his own nation the sole possession of worldly good[s]. He smiled up his sleeves and thought his people were going to be the gainers in this bargain. Well, let them laugh and grow fat; only let us have the good sense not to envy them.

No doubt Tagore had a good point. He was speaking, after all, in the immediate aftermath of the Treaty of Versailles that in its short-sightedness helped to precipitate the collapse of the German currency (wiping out Tagore's large earnings in Germany) and the rise of the Nazi Party. Furthermore he had seen and felt the haunting faces of Germans young and old, 'pale and haggard and yet glowing with the intensity of some inner vision and expectancy of a great realization', as he would later write to Walther Rathenau's sister Edith Andreae, with whom he had stayed in Berlin. However, he greatly underestimated the strength of militarism in Germany. He also misunderstood the reactions of writers and intellectuals. Some of them – notably Brecht, Hesse, Stefan Zweig and the philosopher Count Hermann Keyserling – genuinely admired Tagore's writings. Others, such as Rainer Maria Rilke (actually Austrian not German), were curious but unconvinced. A large number, including Thomas Mann, Oswald Spengler and Franz Kafka (who wrote in German), were indifferent or privately dismissive. Spengler declined to meet Tagore, sharing the opinion of a Munich wag who had called Tagore 'Gangeshofer' (Ludwig Ganghofer being a writer of *kitsch*).

Part of the blame for the impression that Tagore's work was lightweight belonged to the German translations, which were of course based on the English versions of Tagore. Unlike in France, Spain or Holland, no major writer translated Tagore into German. (Rilke was invited to, after praising Gide's translation, but did not, after due reflection.) Keyserling, the least substantial of the names mentioned above, also deserves some blame. He had tried to monopolize Tagore for his School of Wisdom at Darmstadt. Here, in June, thousands converged to hear Tagore discourse in the grounds of the palace of the Grand Duke of Hesse, interpreted by Keyserling. Here, particularly, for many Germans Tagore moved beyond the magical name mentioned by the playwright Carl Zuckmayer in our Introduction; he became a living legend, what Zuckmayer called 'almost an oriental fairy tale'.

This was all highly gratifying for Tagore but, as he keenly knew, it had nothing to do with oriental actuality. He had gone so far as to tell the Swedish Academy in Stockholm: 'I do not think that it is the spirit of India to reject anything, reject any race, reject any culture.' In reality, India was in ferment, led by Gandhi, for whom rejection was bred in the bone. While Tagore had been preaching East–West cooperation in Europe, contemporary India's other great voice had been preaching the opposite at home. Despite his long absence from India Tagore knew this only too well, knew what a struggle awaited him on his return. His university plan was not much further along – apart from promises to visit by various Continental scholars. Still Tagore wanted to return. 'All the same my longing is to go back to my own people, to the atmosphere of continual revilement', he wrote to Andrews from Berlin.

On 1 July 1921 he sailed from Marseilles. On board was the twenty-four-year-old Subhashchandra Bose, fresh from Cambridge, having just resigned a coveted position in the Indian Civil Service on a matter of principle. Bose planned to join the political struggle – but how he was uncertain. Tagore's future in India was obscure too. Together, as the ship ploughed on to Bombay, the two Bengalis – poles apart in their attitudes to violence and non-violence – discussed the new political movements sweeping India.

23 Anti-Non-cooperator
(1921–1924)

Poems I can spin, Gandhiji, songs and plays I can spin, but of your precious cotton what a mess I would make!

comment to Mahatma Gandhi,
Calcutta, September 1921

Conflict between Tagore and Gandhi was inevitable. It was latent in 1915 during Gandhi's first visit to Shantiniketan, open at the time of the Amritsar Massacre and its aftermath, and public from mid-1921 onwards. In the 1930s the two men drew nearer again, but only at the intuitive level, hardly at all intellectually. Respect was there on both sides, even love – but not much understanding.

Tagore versus Gandhi was the cherisher of beauty versus the ascetic; the artist versus the utilitarian; the thinker versus the man of action; the individualist versus the politician; the elitist versus the populist; the widely-read versus the narrowly-read; the modernist versus the reactionary; the believer in science versus the anti-scientist; the synthesizer of East and West versus the Indian chauvinist; the internationalist versus the nationalist; the traveller versus the stay-at-home; the Bengali versus the Gujarati; the scholarly Brahmin versus the merchant Vaishya; and, most prominently of all, the fine flowing robes and beard versus the coarse loincloth and bald pate. 'No two persons could probably differ so much as Gandhi and Tagore!' wrote Jawaharlal Nehru. Theirs was one of the great debates of the twentieth century. Gandhi has dominated it in the history books, in the universities and on the movie screen. But India has espoused Tagore's ideas far more than it has Gandhi's, whether Indians and the rest of the world know it or not. Tagore has given India ways to assimilate the West without becoming a mockery of it; Gandhi was not interested in such assimilation, he thought the West should become more like (ancient) India. (This of course was not the picture of Gandhi presented by the film *Gandhi*, which largely 'westernized' its hero.) 'Mr Gandhi, what do you think of western civilization?' the western reporter asked him. 'I think it would be a good idea!' Gandhi famously replied. He wanted everyone to throw away high technology and abandon urban living, to spin their own cloth, go back to the villages and live there austerely. 'I doubt if the steel age is an advance upon the flint age', he told Tagore in 1921. Although Tagore had deep reservations about modern civilization, machines and cities, at bottom he accepted them. Fundamentally Tagore was humble, willing to learn as well as to teach until the day he died; whereas Gandhi, for all his compelling public self-analysis, thought he knew better than anyone else in all matters of importance.

Tagore fired the first salvo from the USA. C. F. Andrews, friend of both Tagore and Gandhi, had been keeping Rabindranath fully informed of the excitement all over India, not excluding Shantiniketan. (Indeed Andrews had been gripped by it – to the alarm of the absent Tagore, who asked him not to involve the ashram in politics.) In March 1921 Tagore wrote Andrews a letter that was published in the Calcutta *Modern Review*:

Non-cooperation appear[s] to me to be the progeny of the union of rejection from one party and dejection from the other party and therefore though I tried to shed upon it my best smile, I long hesitated to welcome it to my heart . . . It is like the exclamation of a malcontent dog to its neglectful master: I was willing to guard your door and beautifully wag my tail at you, if you had provided me with the remnant of your dinner, but as you never cared to do so, I go to join my own species.

Gandhi responded in June:

In my humble opinion, rejection is as much an ideal as the acceptance of a thing. It is as necessary to reject untruth as it is to accept truth. All religions teach that two opposite forces act upon us and that the human endeavour consists in a series of eternal rejections and acceptances . . . *Neti* [not this] was the best description the authors of the *Upanishads* were able to find for Brahman [God].

I therefore think that the Poet has been unnecessarily alarmed at the negative aspect of Non-cooperation. We had lost the power of saying 'no' to the Government. This deliberate refusal to cooperate is like the necessary weeding process that a cultivator has to resort to before he sows. Weeding is as necessary to agriculture as sowing.

Tagore reached India in mid-July 1921. In early September Gandhi came to Calcutta to recruit him for the movement. They met at Jorasanko behind closed doors; only Andrews was present. Their conversation was never published but a few months later Tagore gave an account of it to Leonard Elmhirst, who had recently arrived in Shantiniketan to begin work on the 'institute for rural reconstruction'. The dialogues that follow are therefore Tagore's reconstruction of this momentous talk, noted by Elmhirst.

'Gurudev, you were yourself a leader and promoter of the Swadeshi Movement some twenty years ago', said Gandhi. 'You always wanted Indians to stand on their own feet as Indians and not to be poor copies of westerners. My "Swaraj" [home rule] movement today is the natural offspring of your own "Swadeshi". Join me now and fight with me for Swaraj.'

'Gandhiji, the whole world is suffering today from the cult of a selfish and short-sighted nationalism. India has all down her history offered hospitality to the invader of whatever nation, creed or colour. I have come to believe that, as Indians, we not only have much to learn from the West but that we also have something to contribute. We dare not therefore shut the West out.' The West's ideas and achievements would help Indians to learn how to collaborate among themselves, Tagore implied.

'Gurudev, I have already achieved Hindu–Muslim unity.' Tagore dissented: 'When the British either walk out, or are driven out, what, Gandhiji, will happen then? Will Hindu and Muslim then lie down peacefully together? You know they will not!'

'But, Gurudev, my whole programme for the winning of Swaraj is based on the principle of non-violence. That is why, as a poet, who believes in peace, you can feel free to ally yourself with this peaceful movement and work for it.'

'Come and look over the edge of my veranda, Gandhiji, look down there and see what your so-called non-violent followers are up to.' The non-cooperators had stolen pieces of foreign-made cloth from the bazaar in Chitpur Road and lit a bonfire with them in the courtyard of Jorasanko. 'You can see for yourself. There they are howling around it like a lot of demented dervishes. Is that non-violence, Gandhiji? We Indians are, as you well know, a very emotional people. Do you think you can hold our violent emotions under firm control with your non-violent principles? No! You know you can't. Only when the children of our different religions, communities, and castes have been schooled together can you hope to overcome the violent feelings which exist today.'

So Gandhi appealed to Tagore to support his new programme of national education. 'Hundreds of young teachers and students are now, at my suggestion, leaving the government schools and colleges. They are enlisting in my scheme.'

'Yes, but, Gandhiji, I notice that you first pick out the brightest of the young men and enlist them in your political organization. The less bright you allow to open schools that can offer only a travesty of education.' These new schools, Tagore said, had too limited an objective. 'This is why I am inviting scholars from all over the world to come and help and at the same time to learn something from the creative aspects of our own culture.' (The first, Sylvain Lévi, was about to arrive in Shantiniketan.)

Tagore went on to accuse Gandhi of manipulating the people with symbols instead of substance. 'But Indians by nature have always been worshippers of symbols, of images', Gandhi countered. When talking of economic wrongs, Gandhi said, it was legitimate to refer to foreign-made cloth as 'impure'. Only a word such as this would induce people to sacrifice the cloth and burn it. For Tagore such hypnotism was a matter for shame.

'Well,' said Gandhi, 'I see my request for your help is almost hopeless. If you can do nothing else for me, at least you can put these Bengali *bhadralok* to shame by getting them to do something practical. Gurudev, you can spin. Why not get all your students to sit down around you and spin?' They both laughed. 'Poems I can spin, Gandhiji, songs and plays I can spin, but of your precious cotton what a mess I would make!'

Spinning and the spinning wheel, the *charka*, would become a focus of irreconcilable disagreement between Tagore and Gandhi. Tagore detested Gandhi's diktat that all true Indians must spin; Gandhi as resolutely insisted on spinning's profound symbolic significance. After the meeting Tagore published a powerful essay, 'The call of truth'. Gandhi replied equally powerfully with 'The great sentinel' – his name for Tagore. The up-and-coming Jawaharlal Nehru read both essays in 1921 and found himself agreeing more with Gandhi. 'But the more I have read what Tagore wrote then, the more I have appreciated it and felt in tune with it', he wrote in 1961, as prime minister. Their exchange, in Nehru's view, represented 'two aspects of the truth, neither of which could be ignored.'

Both essays are densely and picturesquely argued. They cannot be summarized, but perhaps the kernel of the argument can be extracted. Tagore said:

Sparta tried to gain strength by narrowing herself down to a particular purpose, but she did not win. Athens sought to attain perfection by opening herself out in all her fullness – and she did win. Her flag of victory still flies at the masthead of man's civilization. It is admitted that European military camps and factories are stunting man, that their greed is cutting man down to the measure of their own narrow purpose, that for these reasons joylessness darkly lowers over the West. But if man be stunted by big machines, the danger of his being stunted by small machines must not be lost sight of. The *charka* in its proper place can do no harm, but will rather do much good. But where, by reason of failure to acknowledge the differences in man's temperament, it is in the wrong place, there thread can only be spun at the cost of a great deal of the mind itself. Mind is no less valuable than cotton thread.

Gandhi responded:

It was our love of foreign cloth that ousted the wheel from its position of dignity. Therefore I consider it a sin to wear foreign cloth. I must confess that I do not draw a sharp or any distinction between economics and ethics. Economics that hurt the moral well-being of an individual or a nation are immoral and therefore sinful. Thus the economics that permit one country to prey upon another are immoral. It is sinful to buy and use articles made by sweated labour. It is sinful to eat American wheat and let my neighbour the grain dealer starve for want of custom. Similarly it is sinful for me to wear the latest finery of Regent Street, when I know that if I had but worn the things woven by the neighbouring spinners and weavers, that would have clothed me, and fed and clothed them. On the knowledge of my sin bursting upon me, I must consign the foreign garments to the flames and thus purify myself, and thenceforth rest content with the rough *khadi* made by my neighbours. On knowing that my neighbours may not, having given up the occupation, take kindly to the spinning wheel, I must take it up myself and thus make it popular.

Gandhi's article was published in mid-October 1921. On Christmas Day C. F. Andrews, though easily swayed by Gandhi, admitted to Tagore: 'every non-cooperator knows (in his heart of hearts) that the plunge over the precipice [into violence] may come at any moment.' On 3 February 1922 Tagore published a clear statement in the Bengali press warning against the violence latent in the movement. Two days later twenty-two policemen who had fired on a crowd of non-cooperators were burnt alive or hacked to death by the mob at Chauri Chaura (a dramatic scene in *Gandhi*). The Mahatma was profoundly shocked. About a week later he suspended the civil disobedience movement. On 10 March he was finally arrested on charges of sedition, tried and sentenced to six years' imprisonment. In Calcutta Tagore cancelled plans to stage his latest play, a kind of tribute to Gandhi and the philosophy of non-violence.

It was Tagore's deep reservations about the non-cooperation movement that had triggered him to tell Leonard Elmhirst the details of his September meeting with Gandhi. He knew that Elmhirst would run into severe problems in trying to establish a cooperative project near Shantiniketan when non-cooperation was both the fashion and the passion of the time.

Really one marvels that Elmhirst, then aged twenty-eight, was willing to make the attempt at all. Besides his degree in agriculture from Cornell and a degree from Cambridge, he was the son of a well-to-do clergyman father, and could easily have slipped into a life of landowning and farming in England.

Only his strange blend of Yorkshire grit and plain-speaking with an almost feminine sensitivity to the contrary moods of Bengalis, fired by the devotion (and the dollars) of Dorothy Whitney Straight in New York, with whom he was in love, and backed to the hilt by Tagore, whom he revered, could have kept Elmhirst going in such intractable conditions. [pl.38] In 1955, speaking in Shantiniketan, he articulated the underlying philosophy: 'It is by research, by activity of thought, by sensitivity to beauty and to humane feeling that the new day for the village will be born.'

All he had at his disposal in 1921 was the large house in Surul, the village close to the ashram – bought by Rabindranath in 1912, occupied by his son and others for a few years, and then more or less abandoned (except for visits by Rabindranath when in hermit mood). Around the house lay a decaying village, once-prosperous, piecemeal lands belonging to some distinctly unidealistic zamindars, and malaria, monkeys and mutual mistrust – the four 'M's, Elmhirst called them. He had to start from scratch with the villagers and zamindars, while training a group of students and teachers offered to him by Tagore. Over the next three years, in Bengal, Britain, the USA and the Far East, Elmhirst became a mediator between different groups interested in Tagore's experiment: British officials high and low, public figures and politicians, potential donors, educationalists, Christian missionaries, artists and writers, agricultural scientists, zamindars, Tagore's family, Tagore's staff at Shantiniketan, non-cooperators and Gandhians, amongst others. With entrées into many camps, but never wholly accepted by any one camp, Elmhirst tried to develop the 'institute for rural reconstruction' – now renamed Shriniketan, 'Abode of Plenty', by an ever-optimistic Rabindranath – according to Tagore's inspiration. 'If we could free even one village from the shackles of helplessness and ignorance,' said Tagore in 1939, 'an ideal for the whole of India would be established.'

Elmhirst gave an almost blow-by-blow description of his struggle to the far-distant Dorothy Straight. Here he is, writing to her on 13 April 1922, the third anniversary of the Amritsar Massacre, with Gandhi now locked away in jail:

I went up to the Ashram walking with Goura and Buddha Das [two students] – but I was unhappy, and a little sad. We were to have had a picnic today, but Dhira, the captain, came to me and said 'we can't have a picnic, some of the boys are going to fast, it is the anniversary of the massacre at Jallianwala Bagh [Amritsar].' . . . No village fires were lit today, no shops were open, Gandhi's festival was observed and, if ever a man was condemned by his legacy, it is Gandhi. Here are we a supposedly International Institution celebrating hatred, commemorating a thing that divides and appeals to baser passions. I felt the boys had built a wall between myself and them. But I said nothing, I knew it would be no use. So I left Goura and went across to the poet's bungalow and found him with Andrews and Morris, the Parsi – he insisted on my sharing the tea and then I told him how sorry I was about this fasting business. He burst out in indignation, saying how ashamed he was that his own students and staff should mutilate his ideas in this way and then, turning to Andrews, he said point-blank, 'And Andrews, it is you who are responsible.' He wasn't far wrong, though there are others who are more to blame perhaps.

Sometimes Elmhirst was critical of Tagore too. He knew that Dorothy Straight had some strong reservations about Tagore, dating from his visit to the USA in 1920–21 when she had failed to back him financially. Leonard's letters to Dorothy therefore alternate between accepting her reservations as valid, and attempting to convert her to his own devotion to Tagore. She appeared, at times, to be won over by his persuasion, but the effects did not last. At bottom, she was not really interested in India or Tagore; it was Leonard who attracted her. As she wrote to him on 27 November 1921:

Every morning in the newspapers I read something about India – the Prince of Wales [then visiting India], or the Moplahs [violent Muslims in Kerala], or the riots in Bombay, or Gandhi's fast in penitence for the use of force by his followers. But all these incidents give me no real picture of you – and India, I'm afraid, in the last analysis, is only a background for you.

Their letters debating the custom of touching the feet of an elder in greeting (*pranam*) – which Tagore had discouraged in Pearson in New York – were particularly revealing. They swung back and forth in mood like Tagore himself in his attitude to the West. In Leonard's first letter after arrival in Shantiniketan he mentioned Pearson's having touched Tagore's feet. He termed it 'a delightful custom but one which should only be adopted when there is sheer conviction behind it', adding, 'Remember that here dwells the greatest of Eastern aristocracy in the best sense of the word . . . so the atmosphere here is not in the least oppressive to the lover of democracy at its best.'
Dorothy replied:

Your letter . . . I love it all myself – every bit of it – except the obeisances to Tagore – brushing dust from his feet! I don't see how he can set himself above the others in this way, and accept these marks of reverence. I'm afraid I'm a terrible rebel against aristocracy – even 'at its best'. St Francis never allowed anything of this kind . . . and Jesus did the same! Perhaps the Indian philosophy is different and demands outward signs of distinction.

To which Leonard responded:

Now let me correct you on the matter of obeisance to Tagore. It shocked me
at first but now I see it is all very different from what I thought . . . It is
politeness mingled with respect. Do not mistake it for refusal 'to wash the
disciples' feet', no one, I think, in the Ashram feels that Gurudev would ever
refuse to do such a thing. Daily he does it in his teaching and in his life,
metaphorically if not actually . . . No, I have never seen him set himself
above others. I know he has his faults, but I believe the world outside has
never yet been introduced to the greatness of the man. It is partly his fault,
partly theirs.

In the meantime, before receiving this letter, Dorothy had revised her
opinion. She wrote again: 'All your friends are fast becoming my friends and
soon I shall be metaphorically brushing the dust from Tagore's feet and begging
your pardon for ever having risen in rebellion . . . I am at last beginning to see it
as the center of which Tagore himself spoke [in New York], though at the time
it seemed to my unenlightened eyes, merely fanciful.' Leonard, however, before
receiving this second letter, had revised *his* opinion. He now wrote:

I've been thinking over your letter [the first one] again, and I think I
overstated my case for the salutation by touching the feet. It is of course only
a salutation, but it does imply something more. Of course I don't deny that
Tagore's weakest spot is his own egotism – the egotism of all subjective
people, artists and poets and prophets for that matter – but it is far more
obvious abroad, I think, than here. Last night, for instance, I was not there
but I heard that he addressed a group of newcomers, some of whom are not
taking their studies or the University seriously. His . . . appeal was partly to
the personal effort and sacrifice involved in building up the institution, but
mainly to the ideals which he holds for the future. 'If ye love me, ye will keep
my commandments.' I am not excusing him, but I am saying that his services
to his own country are inestimable and the recognition of them is at present
almost negligible.

This was Elmhirst's view to the end of his life. As a man of substance himself
with a scientific training, and as the westerner who saw Tagore at closer quarters
and from more angles than any other westerner, Elmhirst's opinion is nonpareil
if not definitive. (No one person's view of Tagore could be definitive.) Elmhirst
summed it up beautifully in late 1923, when fund-raising with Tagore in
western India among the small princely states:

I don't mind what the world says of his spiritual egotism, of his this and that, he is the real prophet . . . What men take for his egotism is but a protecting cloak. He has given them all that he had, he has sacrificed his greatest desire, the longing for a poet's dreamy solitude, and put his pride in his pocket to become a beggar.

24 China and Japan (1924)

In the meanwhile I go to China, in what capacity I do not know. Is it as a poet, or as a bearer of good advice and sound common sense?

letter to Romain Rolland,
Shantiniketan, February 1924

The debates between Tagore and Gandhi over non-cooperation and between Elmhirst and Straight over the touching of Tagore's feet were part of of a wider debate framed by the concepts of East and West, Orient and Occident. Since the 1920s various attempts have been made to kill off this ancient dichotomy and replace it with economic, political, social, racial and religious divisions – the most obvious being those between the former colonizers and the former colonized, between the Communist and the non-Communist worlds, and between the Islamic and non-Islamic worlds. (Thus South Asia, Africa, South America and Indonesia have been lumped together as the ex-colonized Third World.) But culture has proved stronger than all these supposed links, if harder to define. In the words of Satyajit Ray, on receiving an Oscar for lifetime achievement in the cinema in 1992 (the equivalent of Tagore's Nobel prize): 'The most distinctive feature of my films is that they are deeply rooted in Bengal, in Bengali culture, mannerisms and mores. What makes them universal in appeal is that they are about human beings.' The overwhelming majority of Ray's western viewers respond readily to the universal elements but are seldom able to catch the Bengali ethos.

Tagore was hypersensitively aware of this chasm in western understanding of his own work and of India in general. Hence his insistence on the polarities of East and West, and the need to build bridges between them. Here he was both perspicacious and perspicuous. But when he came to fill out the East–West concept with specific ideas, he was often vague, inconsistent and contradictory. Sometimes he would call the West materialistic and aggressive and the East spiritual and non-violent; almost as frequently he would appear to reverse the materialistic/spiritual labels. Or he would drop the dichotomy altogether and make a statement such as this one in Beijing (Peking) in 1924: 'The impertinence of material things is extremely old. The revelation of spirit in man is modern. I am on its side, for I am modern.'

China and Japan showed him both the strength and the weakness inherent in the East/West dichotomy. When Tagore visited Japan in 1916 its prime minister had spoken of a parting of the ways in the country's inner life: in the 1920s Tagore believed that Japan had taken the wrong path and been infected by the virus of western nationalism. He hoped China would avoid this path and adhere to the 'Ideals of the East' set out by his late friend Okakura Kakuzo in his eponymous book, with its rousing opening words, 'Asia is one'. (Naturally the book was published in English and in London!)

Sylvain Lévi, in China and Japan researching his noted dictionary of Buddhism following his year's stay at Shantiniketan (1921–22), was anxious to correct Tagore's misapprehensions about the East, as he saw them. In February 1923 Lévi read in a Japanese newspaper Tagore's plaudits for Germany's spiritual *Zeitgeist* following the Great War (particularly riling for Lévi as a French Jew), and this sparked him to write to Shantiniketan from Tokyo. His letter (hitherto unpublished) was important, not only for what it said but also for who its author was. Lévi was the most distinguished foreign intellectual who worked with Tagore for a prolonged period. He was among the leading orientalists of the time, the same age as Tagore and, what mattered most to Rabindranath, he had dedicated himself to the cause of Shantiniketan: the meeting in Bengal of the best minds of the East and West. [pl.51] Lévi had the right – or so he felt – to be really frank with Tagore:

Ah, Gurudev! whatever you are born, you are not a prophet! You believe that West is waiting for a message of peace from East. East is lacking peace more than West. About India I shall not say anything; you know enough of it. China is a hell, a paradise of looting, fighting, killing; soldiers and robbers are one big company living on poor peasants and merchants. Japan is passing through a tremendous crisis, social as much as financial; peasants and [even] more peasant-women are revolting against landlords; the young students are poisoned with Bolshevism, that is despise [*sic*] of all recognized and settled values. The rate of living here has become over-American . . . Yes, you are a dreamer, and the most delightful of dreamers, the whole of the world appears to you not only as a dream, the maya of your old rishis, but in a dream which you enjoy as a perfect artist, open to all forms of beauty . . . You are a rishi, but you are also what they used to call *bhumideva* or *bhudeva*, a God on earth. But look down to ordinary men, and then you will not sneer any more at our passion for liberty; you will have to recognize that, for an ordinary man at least, dignity of life cannot [exist] without liberty. A man who does not enjoy legal freedom has to wear a mask of complacency, submission, and all grimaces of servility; gradually, his intimate features become also vitiated. But you will answer me that [it is] no matter if millions of men have to live as slaves, if some hundreds can reach moksha, and here is the deep difference between West and India; Brahman India is built on an aristocracy, Buddhist India, which tried to build up a democracy, has been defeated and annihilated. And West is more and more democratic; we believe in the 'Rights of Man', whoever be the man. *I do not say that we are right and you are wrong,* because I do not at all know what is the final goal of man, [or] even if there is any. We may both be right, both wrong; nobody can tell. But let us try to come to a fair understanding of each other. This is, I believe – and you know this is my faith – the aim of all our search in philosophy, history, sciences and so on; and now I am trying to impress the same good idea on my Japanese audience. [our emphasis]

The shafts went deep: Lévi's letter marked the beginning of a decline in his relationship with Tagore that eventually foundered altogether in unbridgeable mistrust. Lévi had put his accusing finger on two of Tagore's most sensitive spots: his sympathy for Brahminism, and his distrust of democracy. Similar criticism from certain intellectuals in China would be so scathing that he would cancel three of his lectures in Beijing.

In Rabindranath's mind his 1924 visit to China was an opportunity to revive the historic impulse that had taken Buddhism from India to China in the first millennium AD. According to Tagore, this impulse had nothing to do with trade, empire-building or curiosity: 'It was a purely disinterested effort to help mankind forward to its final goal.' By Chinese tradition, the earliest missionaries, ten in number, had been sent by the Emperor Asoka (in the third century BC) and killed by the Chinese emperor who built the Great Wall. Between AD 67 and AD 789, thirty-seven Indian Buddhist missionaries had made the perilous journey. The last recorded visit was in AD 1036, before the Mongol curtain fell. Thus Tagore, though not a Buddhist, was reviving Sino-Indian contacts after nine centuries of silence – a fact that he and his party would be reminded of time and again in China.

They were a varied and lively group. There were two notable Bengali scholars (one a student of Lévi), the artist in charge of the Visva-Bharati art school (Nandalal Bose) who was a student of Chinese sculpture and painting, an American nurse from Shriniketan, Gretchen Green (a friend of Dorothy Straight), and Leonard Elmhirst as the group's organizer and secretary. Tagore told Elmhirst that he was not really interested in the details of Chinese politics, antiquities or ancient history: the others could study those. 'But you and I,

Elmhirst, will try and meet their students, their literary men, their actors, painters, poets, musicians and playwrights. We must try to find out what the men and women, who will build the new China, are feeling and thinking.' [pl.40]

At Hong Kong Tagore received an invitation from Sun Yat-sen, the father of the 1911 revolution and leader of the Kuomintang, delivered by his private secretary:

I should greatly wish to have the privilege of personally welcoming you on your arrival in China. It is an ancient way of ours to show honour to the scholar. But in you I shall greet not only a writer who has added lustre to Indian letters but a rare worker in those fields of endeavour wherein lie the seeds of man's future welfare and spiritual triumphs.

May I then have the pleasure of inviting you to Canton?

Tagore preferred not to delay his progress northwards. After speaking in Shanghai and Hangzhou (Hangchow), he went to Nanjing (Nanking). First he called on General Ch'i, the military governor and warlord of the area. He begged him to desist from fighting 'for the sake not only of China but of Asia and of all humanity.' The general, having served champagne to all present, assured Tagore that he was in full accord with his message of peace. Five months later, he renewed his attack on another warlord, was routed, and fled into exile in Japan. His subordinate, the elderly civil governor, a Buddhist scholar, was genuinely enthusiastic for Tagore's ideals. 'For seven hundred years we have waited for a message from India,' he declared. 'And here you are. This, Dr Tagore, is a great anniversary.' But he cautioned Tagore that his message would likely be misunderstood by the 'modern generation' in China.

Three thousand students and others turned out to hear Tagore. There were so many in the balcony above his head that it groaned audibly and seemed in danger of collapse. Regardless, Rabindranath launched calmly into his speech, which Elmhirst thought the best speech he ever heard from Tagore. Despite the confusion the poet made a substantial and favourable impression, though he himself noted afterwards that less than a hundred of his audience could both hear and understand his words. (He spoke in English.)

Then the party boarded a special private car on the Blue Express luxury train to Beijing, provided by General Ch'i, furnished with a military guard provided by the Beijing government. (The year before, thirty-five European and American passengers had been kidnapped by bandits and held hostage for over a month in a mountain redoubt.) There were no bandits, but plenty of tourists who invaded the compartment. An American leaned over to Gretchen Green, fingered her cape of camel's hair and whispered audibly, pointing to the Poet, 'Did *he* give it to you?' 'Tell her,' Rabindranath replied for himself, 'I killed for you my last and favourite camel.' Having broken the journey to pay homage at the tomb of Confucius, they arrived in Beijing on 23 April.

Tagore mixed widely in the capital, as he had intended. At a 'banquet of scholars', a younger scholar jumped up to embrace Tagore across the supper table on realizing their common aim, in Chinese and in Bengali, of breaking away from the rigid classical language of the literati and using the language of common speech. At a grand and colourful meeting of the heads of the nine major religions in Beijing, the Indian party, suitably robed, was solemnly led in by Tagore from the back of the hall – while the Chinese band struck up a raucous version of the most popular American song of the day: 'Yes, We Have No Bananas'! A performance of one of Tagore's plays in English was staged by Chinese actors – which prompted Mei Lan-fang, China's leading actor (and female impersonator), to arrange a performance of a Chinese play for Tagore. Rabindranath was also presented with a pair of seals and a stone tablet inscribed with Chinese characters chosen to form his Chinese name, Chu Chen Tan, 'Thundering Dawn of India'. One delightful invitation – to the famous Buddhist 'Temple of the Origin of the Law' – gave Rabindranath particular pleasure:

> Now You – the great Buddhist poet – come from the original
> country of the Buddha to our sister-country with all your milk of
> thought; surely as a result we realize your flowerly givings all
> world round where your elephant-like steps reach; and therefore we
> are greatly glad for this . . . You – as a star of great love,
> perfect gladness unlimited goodness & continuous newness as well
> as a representative of the Buddhistic civilization – may kindly
> accept our request as we think.
> Hopis [hoping] your flowerly words with a reply.
>
> Yours respectively
> Young Men's Buddhist Association
> (Y.M.B.A.)

Most sensational of all, Tagore was invited to meet the ex-emperor P'u-i in the Forbidden City – the first foreigner to have the honour. [pl.39] The moving spirit behind this was (Sir) Reginald Johnston, P'u-i's English tutor, an admirer of Tagore. He escorted the poet and party from the Shen Wu Men (Gate of Divine Military Genius) through courtyard after courtyard of the old imperial palace, one official after another falling away as he reached a gate that his rank did not entitle him to pass through. Rabindranath and the two ladies in his party were carried in sedan chairs. Finally they reached the inner apartments where the eighteen-year-old ex-emperor was waiting with his two wives.

Elmhirst presented him with a set of the poet's English works, Tagore offered the queens some conch-shell bangles, symbolizing prosperity. Then, according to Nandalal Bose, 'The poet conveyed to the imperial party the greetings of India and gave them their blessings. He spoke of the ancient bonds of friendship between China and India and said that we wanted to re-establish old relations again.' Meanwhile Miss Lin, the delectable young interpreter, fluttered around the poet like a small bird in bright plumage. As Rabindranath told her later in an epigram:

The blue of the sky fell in love with the green of the earth.
The breeze between them sighs 'Alas!'

His public lectures were marred by opposition, however. Leaving the hall after the second lecture, Tagore noticed a leaflet in Chinese. His hosts were unwilling to translate it all, but Tagore obtained a full translation, apparently from some Japanese he had met. He was shocked by its virulence, and forthwith decided to drop some of his lectures. Later a summary of the Chinese opposition was printed in the Calcutta *Bengalee*, as follows:

1. We have suffered much from the ancient Oriental civilizations, which include discrimination between the sexes, the worship of Emperors, oppression of the people, the feudal system, caste distinctions and the blind observance of ceremony. We cannot but oppose Dr Tagore, who tries to uphold these useless and dead aspects of our civilization.

2. We feel a great shame when we come into contact with modern civilization. We should improve these conditions: Man-power farming, hand manufacturing, inefficient vehicles and ships, poor printing, poor roads and lack of sanitation. We oppose Dr Tagore so that we may reap the benefits of modern civilization.

3. The so-called spiritual civilization of the Orient is nothing more than civil wars, selfish occupations, hypocrisy, fraud, rapacity, vicious royalty, wicked filial respect and the contemptuous habit of foot-binding. How can we help but oppose these things which are so ruinous to us?

4. The Chinese have been indifferent towards encroachments by foreign powers and oppression by their own militarism, and their safety and lives are endangered. Dr Tagore would have nationality and politics abolished, replacing them with the consolation of one's soul. These are a refuge and a source of aesthetic joy for the sluggards, but not for us. We cannot but oppose Dr Tagore, who upholds these things which would shorten the life of our nation.

5. Dr Tagore shows a hearty sympathy with the Tung Shan Spiritual Society, a contemptuous and vicious organization in China which combines

Taoism and Buddhism. Dr Tagore speaks of the 'Heavenly Kingdom', 'Almighty God' and 'soul'. If these could remove us from misery what would be the use of man's endeavour to reform the world? We oppose Dr Tagore, who tries to stunt the growth of self-determination and the struggle of the oppressed classes and races.

Part of the hostility must be put down to Tagore's failure to communicate his true beliefs, values and Indian experience clearly, part to the widespread impact in Beijing of Communist ideology; but at root the leaflet pinpointed the gulf between Chinese and Indian civilization – as opposed to the supposed similarity that Tagore cherished. 'I can imagine no greater contrast than that between [the Chinese] character, their institutions, their habits, and those of the Indians', wrote Lowes Dickinson in 1914, after travelling in both lands. Rabindranath reacted angrily to the leaflet, 'These people are *determined* to misunderstand me.' He was wrong – as the triumph of Communism in China (and the comparative failure of Communism in India) would later prove. Asia was *not* one. The West might be said to be a homogeneous entity; the East could not be lumped together coherently.

Tagore knew it really, and knew he was out of step with national feeling, in China and Japan as in India. But he defended his view vigorously, if illogically. Speaking in Tokyo about a month after visiting Beijing, he replied to the charges laid against him by Sylvain Lévi and the Chinese leaflets:

Often have my western friends almost sneeringly said to me that we in the East have no faith in Democracy, and thereupon they have asserted the superiority of their own mind over ours. [In fact Lévi had *not* concluded this in his letter.] Not being combative, I did not want to argue the matter and contradict them in their deep-rooted illusion . . . We, who do not profess democracy, acknowledge our human obligations and have faith in our code of honour. But are you also going to allow yourselves to be tempted by the contagion of this belief in your own hungry right of inborn superiority, bearing the false name of democracy? . . .

I have come to warn you in Japan, the country where I wrote my first lectures against Nationalism at a time when people laughed my ideas to scorn. They thought that I did not know the meaning of the word and accused me of having confused the word Nation with State. But I stuck to my conviction and now after the war, do you not hear everywhere the denunciation of this spirit of the nation, this collective egoism of the people, which is universally hardening their hearts?

25 Argentina
(1924–1925)

Only individuals matter, never the race or the nation.
comment to Leonard Elmhirst,
Argentina, December 1924

While in Japan, Tagore received an official invitation to visit Peru. The government in Lima was planning a celebration of the centenary of Peru's defeat of the Spanish colonial power. Rabindranath agreed to attend, and afterwards to visit Mexico. In discussions with Leonard Elmhirst, as Tagore's secretary, the representatives of Peru and Mexico pledged themselves to donate not less than $100,000 each towards Visva-Bharati.

Meanwhile Tagore and Elmhirst had parted after three months of adventuring in the Far East: Tagore had gone to Shanghai, on his way back to India, Elmhirst was about to sail for the USA and thence to England. From Shanghai, Rabindranath wrote with heartfelt thanks for Leonard's service, and made a significant confession:

I carry an infinite space of loneliness around my soul through which the voice of my personal life very often does not reach my friends – for which I suffer more than they do. I have my yearning for the personal world as much as any other mortal, or perhaps more. But my destiny seems to be careful that in my life's experiences I should only have the *touch* of personality and not the *ties* of it. All the while she claims my thoughts, my dreams and my voice, and for that [,] detachment of life and mind is needed. In fact, I have constantly been deprived of opportunities for intimate [long-lasting] attachments of companionship. Then again I have such an extreme delicacy of sensitiveness with regard to personal relationship that even when I acknowledge and welcome it I cannot invite it to the immediate closeness of my life. This deficiency I acknowledge with resignation knowing that it is a sacrifice claimed of me by my Providence for some purpose which he knows.

Tagore was now sixty-three years old, an old man by Indian standards. Inevitably death had claimed many of his contemporaries in Bengal. Of those remaining, hardly any were capable of offering Tagore intellectual stimulation – though a few of his younger friends did. Among his foreign friends in Bengal, Pearson was dead (killed falling from a train in Italy), Andrews was for the time being semi-estranged, busy with Gandhi and forever on the move, Edward Thompson – never as close as Pearson and Andrews – had left Bengal for Oxford, and now Elmhirst, after two and a half years' proximity, was thinking of leaving India for England. (The idea of Dartington was stirring in his mind.) In Tagore's immediate family, apart from his wife and three children, Rabindranath had lost five brothers (Satyendranath died in 1923) and three sisters. Over the next two years, Jyotirindranath and Dwijendranath would also die, leaving him no intimates of his own generation. His closest family contact would now be with his nephew and niece, Suren and Indira, apart from his two surviving children, Rathindranath and Mira. Partly by necessity and partly by choice – as he had confessed to Elmhirst – Rabindranath had become a lonely man.

His visit to South America would bring him into contact with a remarkable aristocratic Argentine woman who for a brief interval would fill some of the gaps in his life. Today Victoria Ocampo is known chiefly as the publisher of *Sur* (South), the international literary magazine that launched Jorgé Luis Borges (among others); and who also was an author of essays, memoirs and critical studies, and the translator and friend of several well-known European writers and intellectuals. (As a publisher, Ocampo was something like a South American Harriet Monroe, the editor of *Poetry* in Chicago.) But when Tagore met her in Buenos Aires, *Sur* lay some years in the future: Ocampo was effectively unknown outside Argentina. In 1924, she was simply a strikingly beautiful woman in her mid-thirties, wealthy, somewhat spoilt, intelligent, impulsive, with wide literary tastes in French, Spanish and English (less in English), a disastrous marriage to a tyrannical husband in the old Spanish mould, and an ongoing clandestine affair with a cousin of her husband. She adored European culture, knew next to nothing about India, and yearned to break free of the stifling patriarchal and philistine atmosphere in which she had been reared.

At this time Tagore – or rather Tagoré – was a major literary figure in South America, thanks to the translations into Spanish by Juan Ramón Jiménez. These were in fact the work of two translators: Juan Ramón, who supplied the poetry but had minimal English, and his wife, Zenobia Camprubi, who was bilingual in Spanish and English. (Born in Barcelona, she had been raised in the United States.) Their joint translation of *The Crescent Moon* in 1914–15 had been part of their courtship. First Zenobia Camprubi prepared a literal rendition in Spanish; then she and Juan Ramón laboriously went over this literal version in consultation with the English original, Juan Ramón interrogating his wife as to the meaning of certain English phrases (he was frustrated that he could not hear the Bengali); finally he alone 'rewrote' the revised rendering as Spanish poetry. In this way, between 1914 and 1922, husband and wife translated twenty-two books by Tagore, consisting of poetry, plays and short stories, but not, it is worth noting, essays, novels, letters or memoirs. At the same time Jiménez wrote some of his most celebrated poetry (and also translated Yeats). During this period, not coincidentally, Jiménez conceived the idea of *poesia desnuda*, 'naked poetry', now celebrated in the annals of Spanish literature.

The effect of his Tagore translations on a leading Spanish intellectual, José Ortega y Gasset, was interesting. In three essays addressed to an imaginary *señora* (probably Zenobia) in 1918, Ortega argued (to quote the American scholar Howard Young),

that Tagore's wide appeal could be accounted for by the fact that he speaks of longings for perfection that we all have. There is none of us, says Ortega, who like Amal [in *The Post Office*] is not waiting for a letter from the King. In addition, claims Ortega, Tagore awakens a dormant sense of childish wonder, and he saturates the air with all kinds of enchanting promises for the reader, who receives only this message and pays little attention to the deeper import of Oriental mysticism.

In Chile, Gabriela Mistral and Pablo Neruda were both openly influenced by Tagore in Spanish translation. In Mexico, according to Octavio Paz in 1967, 'The young men read [Tagore's] poems with the same fervour with which their grandfathers had, a hundred years back, read the great romantic poets.' Around 1920, free editions of universal classics were published in Mexico, including an anthology of Plato, Dante, Cervantes, Goethe, Greek drama, Tolstoy – and Tagoré. (Robert Bridges had done something similar in *The Spirit of Man* in 1915.) 'Through those books', said Paz, 'we Mexicans of our generation discovered that all great poets, although expressing themselves in separate languages and affirming different truths, spoke in a universal language . . . The paradox of poetry lies in the fact that it is, at one and the same time, universal and untranslatable.' Some of this outpouring of feeling for Tagore lives on today in several countries of South America. In Nicaragua, for instance, in 1986, a visiting Salman Rushdie was surprised to find Tagore much admired.

Victoria Ocampo had read the Spanish translations of Tagore, though she preferred the French translations by Gide that had been her introduction to Tagore in 1914. What brought her in touch with Tagore in person was her spontaneous offer to find him a villa in Buenos Aires where he could convalesce after falling seriously ill on the ship from Europe to Peru. Tagore and Elmhirst, who was again accompanying the poet as secretary (for the last time), accepted Ocampo's offer gratefully. Rabindranath badly needed rest; and already he was tiring of the superficialities and materialism of Argentine high society. Within a week of arrival in Buenos Aires on 6 November, Tagore and Elmhirst moved out of their hotel and into the Villa Miralrío at San Isidro outside the capital, with a beautiful view of the River Plate and not far from the Villa Ocampo.

They remained there, with one brief holiday in a house on the pampas a hundred miles south of Buenos Aires, for over a month and half, until they sailed for Italy in early January 1925. The visit to Peru was cancelled. The paramount reason was doctor's orders, but word had also reached Tagore from various sources – among them Romain Rolland and C. F. Andrews – that the Peruvian government was a dictatorship likely to use him as a pawn in its own schemes. (In 1926, exactly this would happen in Italy with Mussolini.) Tagore was both disappointed and somewhat embarrassed at breaking his promise to attend. To avoid diplomatic embarrassment with Peru, the Argentine government offered to send the poet by Dreadnought via Cape Horn to avoid the journey over the Andes – but even this was apparently vetoed by the doctors. On 16 November Elmhirst wrote to Dorothy Straight, who was by now his fiancée:

> Chile is probably pleased – for she is not on good terms with Peru. The Argentine folk are delighted, and have played the game, given him real consideration at the time of his illness and insisted that it is enough if he will settle in the country and be amongst them for a little, without fulfilling any public engagements. So here we are in a little house of our own, new but in the old Spanish style, very simple and the outlook over the river delightful.

But the next month or two would prove anything but relaxing and delightful for Elmhirst, Tagore and their spirited 'hostess', Señora Victoria Ocampo de Estrada (to use her full married name). After escaping Ocampo and Argentina in January, Elmhirst wrote to his beloved Dorothy from on board ship:

> Our hostess [he never used Ocampo's name in these letters] was quite – next to the poet himself – the most difficult person I have ever come across – I felt now and then as if I was in charge of a madhouse . . . I have seen much that throws light upon the middle ages, the inquisition, the mentality of Spain and the power of the Church of Rome. I am the more astonished at the way in which our own island managed to rid itself of the shackles. The cruelty that was once practised in the open has now been pushed under the

surface and shows itself in odd places and quite ghastly ways. Besides having a keen intellectual understanding of his books, she was in love with him – but instead of being content to build a friendship on the basis of intellect, she was in a hurry to establish that kind of proprietary right over him which he absolutely would not brook. The more she strove and suffered, the further away she seemed to be. She seemed so completely lacking in just those womanly capacities with which she might have given a service that would have been welcome, and in fact she was a bundle of prides, intellectual, aristocratic and physical, against which, and their ferocious hold upon her nature, she was constantly at war. For her, then, I was either bridge or barrier, obstacle or convenience as occasion turned out. Being her guests didn't make matters easier, nor the fact that at [that time] he was ill and needed just the refuge that she was able and delighted to give.

On board too, as the physical distance between himself and Ocampo widened, Tagore wrote letters to her about *his* feelings. He sat, while writing, in a comfortable armchair from Miralrío that Ocampo had insisted he take with him on the ship; she even had the cabin door hinges removed so that the chair could be squeezed into the cabin. (The chair eventually reached Shantiniketan.) Tagore's first letter was slightly frivolous, as if he was still not free of her spell – but his second was a serious, even moving, restatement of his 1924 letter to Elmhirst about loneliness and his recurrent sense of destiny:

I am deeply sorry that it has not been possible for me to have an acquaintance [with] your complete personality – the difficulty having been enhanced owing to the literary character of your mind. For such a mind has its aristocratic code of honour . . . [,] choosing to remain dumb [rather] than to send out its thoughts dressed in rags. But never for a moment imagine that I failed to recognize that you had a mind. To me it was like a star that was distant and not a planet that was dark. When we were together we mostly played with words and tried to laugh away our best opportunities to see each other clearly . . . My mind must have a nest to which the voice of the sky can descend freely . . . Whenever there is the least sign of the nest becoming a jealous rival of the sky[,] my mind, like a migrant bird, tries to take . . . flight to a distant shore . . . I tell you all this because I know you love me . . . I believe that your love may, in some way, help me in my fulfilment. [This] will sound egoistic, only because the voice of our ego has in it the same masterful cry . . . as the voice of that which infinitely surpasses it. I assure you, that through me a claim comes that is not mine. A child's claim upon its mother has a sublime origin – it is not a claim of an individual, it is

that of humanity . . . Your friendship has come to me unexpectedly. It will
grow . . . when you know and accept my real being and see clearly the deeper
meaning of my life. I have lost most of my friends because they asked me for
themselves, and when I said I was not free to offer away myself – they
thought I was proud. I have deeply suffered from this over and over
again – and therefore I always feel nervous whenever a new gift of friendship
comes in my way. But I accept my destiny and if you also have the courage
fully to accept it we shall ever remain friends.

Years later, during the Tagore birth centenary in 1961, Ocampo herself said
of her relationship with Rabindranath at Miralrío: 'Little by little he partially
tamed the young animal, by turns wild and docile, who did not sleep, dog-like,
on the floor outside his door, simply because it was not done.'

Elmhirst, Tagore and Ocampo: the triangle was a fascinating tangle of
mutual attraction and repulsion. Elmhirst was certainly sexually attracted to
Ocampo (though he did not let on to his fiancée in America); and she recipro-
cated, though not physically. All three were strong individuals, of course, and
also in a definite sense representatives of their utterly disparate cultures, compelled to communicate the subtlest ideas and emotions in English, a language
native only to one of them. They remained friends, though Ocampo never visited Tagore in India. Long after Tagore's death she stayed with Elmhirst for a
few days in Dartington: they were bound together by their shared, aromatic
memories of Rabindranath in Argentina.

One incident is worth mentioning for the light it throws on the problem of
translating Tagore. Unusually for him when he was out of India, Rabindranath
wrote a number of poems in Argentina; these were later published in a celebrated collection dedicated to Ocampo under the title *Purabi* – which signifies
both 'Easterner' and an evocative twilight raga in Indian classical music (a
favourite raga of Rabindranath). One of the poems in *Purabi*, 'Kankal' (A
Skeleton), was written at the house on the pampas, the day after the trio had
been for a walk and come across the bleached bones of some bovine creature, a
common sight on the plains of Argentina. In the morning Tagore read the
poem to Ocampo and Elmhirst in Bengali, and she begged him to translate
it – which he did orally. But when he wrote down the translation and she read
it that afternoon, she could not suppress her disappointment: he had omitted
the most valuable part of the poem, she said accusingly. Rabindranath admitted
the charge. 'He replied that he thought *that* would not interest Westerners',
wrote Ocampo in 1961. 'The blood rose to my cheeks as if I had been slapped.'
Her strong objections had a result: at dinner the poet gave her another version
of the poem, this time unmutilated. It was among the finest translations he did

(though still it suffered, especially its final verse). It is also a reminder of the limits and perils of biography.

Here is Tagore's final translation:

A Skeleton

A beast's bony frame lies bleaching on the grass
       by the meadow path, –
the grass that once had given it strength and tender rest.
The dry white bones seem like the hard laughter of Time
       which cries to me:
'Thy end, proud man, is one with the end of the cattle
       that graze no more,
for when thy life's wine is spilt to its last drop
       the cup is flung away with a final unconcern.'

'Hollow is thy mockery, Death,' said I in answer,
Mine is not merely the life that pays its bed and board
       at close of day
with its bankrupt bones and is made destitute.
Never can my life contain to the full all that I have thought
       and felt, gained and given, listened and uttered.
Often my mind has crossed time's border,
Is it to stop at last for ever at the boundary of
       crumbling bones?

Flesh and blood can never be the measure of the truth that is
       myself;
the days and moments cannot wear it with kicks at every step
       as they pass on;
the wayside bandit, dust, dares not rob it of all its
       possessions.
Know that I have drunk the honey of the formless
       from the lotus of endless forms;
in the bosom of sufferings I have found the secret path
       of delight;
I have heard in my being the voice of Eternal Silence;
have seen the tracks of light across the empty desert of the dark.
Death, I accept not from thee
       that I am a gigantic jest of God,
that I am the annihilation built with all the wealth
       of the infinite.

26   Arguing with Gandhi
(1925–1926)

One thing is certain, that the all-embracing poverty which has overwhelmed our country cannot be removed by working with our hands to
the neglect of science.

'The Cult of the Charka',
Calcutta, September 1925

In Buenos Aires Victoria Ocampo had noticed that Tagore's bad moods often
coincided with the arrival of the post from India. In fact letters reached him
from India on the very day he composed 'Kankal' (A Skeleton), and he forthwith dictated to Elmhirst an anguished statement about the misguidedness of
his countrymen in general and the dubiousness of Gandhi's ideas in particular.
Tagore was incensed by the moral tyranny intrinsic in the spinning movement:
the cult of the *charka*, or spinning wheel, and the Congress directive to wear
khadi, hand-spun cloth. In November 1924, Gandhi and other leaders had
recommended – and the Congress had accepted – that all Congress members
must wear *khadi* at political and Congress functions or while engaged in
Congress business, and each must contribute 2,000 yards of evenly-spun yarn
per month 'of his and her spinning or in case of illness, unwillingness or any
such cause a like quantity of yarn spun by any other person.' Not only would
this make India self-supporting regarding her clothing requirements, they said,
but it would establish a 'visible and substantial bond' between the masses and
the Congress members.

To Tagore the decision was like the proverbial red rag. It roused all those
instincts that in 1921, after his return from the West, had produced his clarion
essay, 'The call of truth'. In 1925, as before, Gandhi came to see him after his
return from abroad – this time at Shantiniketan rather than Jorasanko – and
again tried to convert him to the cult of spinning. But the two men found almost
no common ground.

In a brilliantly ironic story he wrote at this time, Rabindranath stabbed at
the fatuity, hypocrisy and suppression of human nature fostered by the non-
cooperation movement and its symbols. His hero, or rather anti-hero, is a jaded

one-time revolutionary, who had his glory in the days of the Swadeshi Movement and who, fifteen or twenty years on, has become 'non-violent'. He attends the 'Gandhian' picketing of milled cloth in favour of handloom *khadi* in the bazaar 'as a mere spectator', with no intention of taking part. But – 'just then a police sergeant shoved a Bengali lady supporter of *khadi*. The next instant my non-violent non-cooperating condition was converted into furious sedition.' The hero is promptly picked up, roughed up and jailed – not for the first time in his life. Meanwhile patriotism afflicts a brilliant college girl in the hero's family. Abandoning her studies, she decides to open a home for destitute females, and tries to persuade her widowed aunt-cum-guardian to supply her with suitable girls from among the adopted village girls living in their house. 'Her aunt replied,' – and clearly Tagore too was speaking – '"What do you mean? They're not waifs and strays. What am I here for? Destitute or not, the girls need a home. Why must they be stamped and stuffed into bales in an institution? If you feel so compassionate, why not give up your room?" '

But the full fire of Rabindranath's scorn was reserved for his essay, 'The cult of the Charka', published in September 1925. It was a coruscating critique of what would now be called 'political correctness'. So devastating was it that Gandhi waited some two months before replying, presumably so that he could calm down and marshal his arguments; even then he showed himself to be severely stung. Gandhi did not emerge well from the exchange. This was apparent even in the strongly pro-Gandhian atmosphere of 1925: reading the debate now, Gandhi's reasoning appears debilitated beside Tagore's. (No wonder Nehru came to agree more with Tagore as he grew older.) In order to evade the force of Tagore's argument Gandhi took refuge in most unMahatma-like sarcasm and in what can only be described as 'economy with the truth' on the crux of their disagreement: the true stature of Rammohun Roy, the great reformer and founder of the Brahmo Samaj.

'I am not ashamed – though there is every reason to be afraid – to admit that the depths of my mind have not been moved by the *Charka* agitation', Tagore stated.

> In Bengal we have a nursery rhyme which soothes the infant with the assurance that it will get the lollipop if only it twirls its hands. But is it a likely policy to reassure grown-up people by telling them that they will get their Swaraj – that is to say, get rid of all poverty, in spite of their social habits that are a perpetual impediment and mental habits producing inertia of intellect and will – by simply twirling away with their hands? No! If we have to get rid of this poverty which is visible outside, it can only be done by rousing our inward forces of wisdom[,] of fellowship and mutual trust which make for cooperation.

'Carlyle may have proclaimed the dignity of labour in his stentorian accents, but a still louder cry has gone up from humanity, age after age, testifying to its indignity', Tagore continued. 'One thing is certain, that the all-embracing poverty which has overwhelmed our country cannot be removed by working with our hands to the neglect of science.' Then, to drive home the point about mental inertia, Tagore gave another down-to-earth analogy.

In my childhood, I had an up-country servant, called Gopee, who used to tell us how once he went to Puri on a pilgrimage, and was at a loss what fruit to offer to [Lord] Jagannath [Juggernaut], since any fruit so offered could not be eaten by him any more. After repeatedly going over the list of edible fruits known to him he suddenly bethought himself of the tomato (which had very little fascination for him) and the tomato it was which he offered, never having reason to repent of such clever abnegation. But to call upon man to make the easiest of offerings to the smallest of gods is the greatest of insults to his manhood. To ask all the millions of our people to spin the *Charka* is as bad as offering the tomato to Jagannath. I do hope and trust that there are not thirty-three crores [330 million, i.e. the population of India] of Gopees in India.

Tagore followed with a direct hit at Gandhi:

There are many who assert and some who believe that Swaraj can be attained by the *Charka*; but I have yet to meet a person who has a clear idea of the process. That is why there is no discussion, but only quarrelling over the question . . . If any true devotee of our motherland should be able to eradicate the poverty of only one of her villages, he will have given permanent wealth to the thirty-three crores of his countrymen.

And then he concluded:

It is extremely distasteful to me to have to differ from Mahatma Gandhi in regard to any matter of principle or method. Not that, from a higher standpoint, there is anything wrong in so doing; but my heart shrinks from it. For what could be a greater joy than to join hands in the field of work with one for whom one has such love and reverence? . . . [However] the difference in our standpoints and temperaments has made the Mahatma look upon Rammohun Roy as a pygmy – while I revere him as a giant. The same difference makes the Mahatma's field of work one which my conscience cannot accept as its own. That is a regret which will abide with me always . . . I feel sure that Mahatmaji himself will not fail to understand me, and keep for me the same forbearance which he has always had . . . As for my countrymen the public – accustomed as they are to drown, under the facile flow of their minds, both past services and past disservices done to them – if today they cannot find it in their hearts to forgive, they will forget tomorrow.

Even if they did not forget, he finished, he knew that in due course others who felt as he did would come to his aid.

There could be no doubt from this article, from Tagore's 1921 articles and from his other writings, that Rabindranath resented the fact that hardly a soul, including Gandhi, bothered to understand his genuine but unsung work on his estates and, later, at Shriniketan with Elmhirst and coworkers. Nor was he given his due for his hard-won experience of politics during the Swadeshi Movement: most of his criticisms in the 1920s had grown out of his 1907 disillusionment with mass movements. The truth was, if Tagore had been a better self-publicist, a better politician – as Gandhi was – he would not have been dismissed by the majority of Indians as an impractical poet. But of course if he had been those things, Tagore would not have been the poet, writer and creative figure he was.

This last fact gave Gandhi the chance to dismiss Tagore's criticism. Temporarily forgetting his own grudging epithet of 1921, the 'Great Sentinel', Gandhi wrote in *Young India*: 'The fact is that the Poet's criticism is a poetic licence and he who takes it literally is in danger of finding himself in an awkward corner.' Gandhi bluntly accused Tagore of living in an ivory tower: 'If the Poet span half an hour daily, his poetry would gain in richness. For it would then represent the poor man's wants and woes in a more forcible manner than now.'

Ironically, and sadly, Gandhi seems to have looked at Tagore's writing through western eyes, regarding it as principally mystical, in the mould of *Gitanjali*. Gandhi seems not to have acquainted himself with even Tagore's best essays in English translation – let alone his many short stories. Either that, or he was pretending publicly that Tagore was something he privately knew him not to be. Probably there was both ingenuous ignorance and ingenious insincerity in the Mahatma's response. Gandhi was never much of a reader of literature, true, but it is hard to believe that by 1925 he was not aware of Tagore as an acute and trenchant critic of the rich and powerful, with a concomitant deep sympathy for the common man and woman.

In any case, Gandhi unquestionably knew that Tagore had repudiated his knighthood. So why did he begin his reply with a gratuitous reference to 'Sir Rabindranath', repeated later in the article with a sly twist? He also said, 'Dame Rumour has whispered that jealousy is the root of all [the] criticism' – and then went on to dismiss this 'cruel charge' as a 'baseless suspicion'. Tagore's criticism had riled Gandhi sufficiently for him to descend to a level of innuendo that was beneath Rabindranath, whatever his private feelings.

The smear about the knighthood – implying that Tagore was tarred with undesirable western influence and given to making empty gestures – was reminiscent of Gandhi's attack on Rammohun Roy in 1921, to which Tagore referred, and would continue to refer, during the 1930s. It was a pivot of controversy between them. Was Rammohun – the so-called 'Father of Modern India' – elevated by his knowledge of the West, or diminished? In 1921, Gandhi was asked in a public meeting: was not English education in India a 'mixed evil'? His chauvinistic answer was later printed in *Young India* (his own newspaper):

Tilak [the Bombay nationalist leader] and Rammohun would have been far greater men if they had not had the contagion of English learning [*clapping*] . . . I am opposed to mak[ing] a fetish of English education. I don't hate English education. When I want to destroy the Government, I don't want to destroy the English language but read English as an Indian nationalist would do. Rammohun and Tilak . . . were so many pygmies who had no hold upon the people compared with Chaitanya [the founder of Vaishnavism], Sankara [the Hindu philosopher], Kabir [the medieval mystic poet] and Nanak [the founder of Sikhism] . . . It is my conviction that if Rammohun and Tilak had not received this [English] education but had their natural training they would have done greater things like Chaitanya.

But in November 1925 Gandhi conveniently forgot what he had said in 1921 and claimed:

I have never anywhere described that great reformer [Rammohun] as a pygmy much less regarded him as such . . . I remember having said that he was a pygmy compared to the unknown authors say of the *Upanishads*. This is altogether different from looking upon [Rammohun] as a pygmy. I do not think meanly of Tennyson if I say that he was a pygmy before Milton or Shakespeare. I claim that I enhance the greatness of both. If I adore the Poet as he knows I do in spite of differences between us, I am not likely to disparage the greatness of the man who made the great reform movement of Bengal possible and of which the Poet is one of the finest of fruit.

The different attitudes to Indian and western learning were obviously basic and could not be resolved by any amount of discussion and professions of mutual respect and love. Gandhi thought the knowledge of the West at best of secondary importance in the revival of India, at worst positively harmful, to be shunned; whereas Tagore was in thrall to the idea of synthesizing the knowledge of the East and West. While the nationalists, led by Gandhi, stoked up Indian xenophobia, Tagore proceeded to receive at Shantiniketan a series of European scholars, willing to share their knowledge of ancient India and eastern philology with Indian students. The mental strain on Tagore was intense. In September 1925, after publishing 'The cult of the Charka', he wrote to Romain Rolland, who admired Gandhi without understanding him:

It is the moral loneliness which is a constant and invisible burden that oppresses me most. I wish it were possible for me to join hands with Mahatma Gandhi and thus at once surrender myself to the current of popular approbation. But I can no longer hide it from myself that we are radically different in our apprehension and pursuit of truth. Today to disagree with Mahatma and yet to find rest in one's surroundings in India is not possible and therefore I am waiting for my escape next March with an impatient feeling of longing. I know I have friends in Europe who are my real kindred and whose sympathy will act as a true restorative in my present state of weariness.

Doubtless Tagore fully meant this when he wrote it in Calcutta in September. But, Tagore being Tagore, as soon as he got away to Europe in mid-1926, he would start to pine for India. He was about to launch himself into the least edifying episode of his world odyssey: his visit to Mussolini's Italy. Here his passion for international cooperation would prove quite as prejudicial to clear thinking as the Mahatma's obsession with non-cooperation.

27   Italy, Mussolini and After
(1926)

Moral judgement and the interest evoked by a dramatic personality are
two entirely different things.

> comment to Signora Salvadori,
> Vienna, July 1926

In the mid-1920s many distinguished people admired Benito Mussolini and
Italian Fascism. They included writers such as T. S. Eliot, Ezra Pound,
George Bernard Shaw and W. B. Yeats; and politicians such as Austen
Chamberlain, Winston Churchill, Ramsay MacDonald – and (later) Gandhi.
The London press was generally benevolent too, as witness this 'diary' item
from June 1926, headed 'Mussolini's motor feat':

I wonder if any contemporary holder of Ministerial office can equal the
driving feat performed by Signor Mussolini a few days ago. Leaving Rome in
a powerful car he drove himself 280 miles, at an average of forty miles an
hour, without a stop of any kind. There followed a return journey the next
day after lunch under similar conditions, work into the small hours, and the
office again at his usual early hour on the following day, during which the
only break of any importance was to hear Sir Rabindranath Tagore lecture in
English on 'The Meaning of Art'.

If there was any lingering anxiety about the Duce's health this, at any rate,
ought to dispel it.

Tagore, at first, was antipathetic to Fascism. On the way back from Argentina
in January 1925, he had stopped in Italy, with the intention of staying for some
weeks. There were enthusiastic crowds. But he found a current of criticism
directed against him by the Fascist press, and he heard about the brutality of the
Fascists from a man he respected, the Duke of Milan, Gallarati Scotti, scholar,
writer and scion of an ancient family. He soon cancelled the rest of his Italian
visit, ostensibly for health reasons, and sailed for India. In an essay published in
July, he remarked *inter alia* that Fascism was the 'exact counterpart' of extreme

Hindu orthodoxy. He compared the callous treatment of the Untouchables by the Brahmins to 'Lynching, Fascism, Ku Klux Klanism, and the like'.

In the meantime, his guide in Italy, the professor of Sanskrit at the University of Rome, Carlo Formichi, had persuaded Mussolini to support Tagore and his Visva-Bharati. In November 1925, Formichi arrived in Shantiniketan as a visiting lecturer; soon after, he was joined by Giuseppe Tucci, also from Rome (and today still a name in oriental studies). Formichi brought with him a grand gift of Italian classics for the university library. Rabindranath was duly grateful. He cabled Mussolini that the gift and the presence of the two scholars would 'open up a channel of communication for exchange of culture between your country and ours having every possibility of developing into an event of great historical significance.' (The draft of the cable read ' . . . into a great historical incident' – an interesting premonition.) Mussolini now extended an invitation to visit Italy, and hoped for the 'reblooming of the cultural relations between Italy and India.'

With some doubts, Tagore accepted. The gift of books had influenced him, as had the interest in him of many Italians during his brief stay. As for Fascism, he knew that opinions of it differed strongly; many were hailing Mussolini as a saviour. And Tagore was curious about his personality. Years earlier, in a somewhat dubious essay on the Indian body politic, Tagore had written: 'If society realizes its unity as embodied in a particular person, then its power will be invincible.' Perhaps Mussolini was such a person?

Despite being the subject of a colonized country, Tagore was a catch for the Italian dictator, and he gave him royal treatment. The poet and his party were met in Naples on 30 May 1926 by Formichi and the chief officials of the city. From now on Formichi, while interpreting, would try not to let Tagore out of his sight. The next day, in Rome, he introduced Tagore to Mussolini, who greeted him with the statement: 'Allow me to tell you that I am one of those who have read every one of your books in Italian'. He insisted that Tagore should stay a fortnight in Rome. After the interview Rabindranath told the *Tribuna*, the leading organ of Fascism: 'His Excellency Mussolini seems modelled body and soul by the chisel of a Michelangelo, whose every action showed intelligence and force.' Asked for some words about Italy, he gushed: 'Let me dream that from the fire-bath the immortal soul of Italy will come out clothed in quenchless light.' But he avoided any statement on Fascism.

There was a formal reception in the historic Capitol. The following day Tagore gave a public lecture, attended by Mussolini. Towards the end, a newspaper noted, 'when the sonorous voice of the poet mingled with the pealing of bells from a nearby church, the audience, perceiving a symbolic blending of the voice of Rome with that of mystic India, was deeply moved and broke into warm and persistent applause.' Then there was a reception at the university. Formichi said: 'These are days of great strain for you. But you, O eagle, know where your nest is; and when you go back home, and climb into your nest, there the echo of our applause, which is a strain on you today, will be soothing, and, as we hope, a source of inspiration.' Earlier that day, in the Colosseum, a choir of 1,000 school children and an audience of some 25–30,000 people, rose from their seats to greet the arrival of the Poet. He was visibly moved, and raised his arms to bless the children with all his heart.

After meeting the king and witnessing a performance of one of his own plays in Italian, Tagore met Mussolini again on 13 June. Here he asked to meet Benedetto Croce, the philosopher. Formichi cried out, 'Impossible! Impossible!' Mussolini calmly said: 'Indeed, he is not in Rome.' 'Yes,' Tagore said, 'but he is in Italy. I am ready, wherever he is, to go to him.' Mussolini regretted that he did not know where Croce was (a lie if ever there was one). Tagore insisted he could not leave Italy without meeting the man who was regarded as the highest living incarnation of Italian thought. So Mussolini instructed Formichi to arrange a meeting. As an opponent of Fascism Croce was in fact practically under house-arrest in Naples. It was unlikely, Tagore knew, that Formichi would pursue the matter (though he later claimed the credit for the meeting), so he turned for help to a young Italian army officer who knew Croce and disliked Il Duce. The officer brought the philosopher to Rome by overnight train. By dawn he and Tagore were sitting down to talk in the hotel. When Formichi later turned up, 'It was amusing to witness the tearing of hair and gnashing of teeth', Tagore's son wrote in his diary. As for the conversation, it went well but did not even touch on Fascism. Croce said much later that he could not mention the subject, knowing that Tagore had sought permission from Mussolini to meet him: 'it was a question of good taste.'

There were comparable incidents in Milan and Venice. In Milan Duke Scotti was a changed man, unable, as he plainly said in the presence of Formichi, to speak openly. Instead he sent his near relative, a sister of the king, to Tagore in Turin; she explained how the family and other intellectuals had suffered under the Fascists, and showed him documentary proof. In Venice, Rabindranath slipped out early one morning with his son and the others for a gondola tour of the canals unbothered by his fame or his chaperone. (In Florence he told the Leonardo da Vinci Society: 'I wish I had not been preceded by my fame. I could then have come close to you, like the English poets, Browning, Shelley, Keats and Byron.') When the group returned from the trip, they found the Grand Hotel in uproar. The manager had collected the entire staff to make enquiries about the poet's disappearance, and Professor Formichi was utterly desperate, 'running about the hotel shouting and gesticulating as only an Italian can', noted an amused Rathindranath.

Thus by the time he left Italy on 22 June, Rabindranath was in a peculiar state of mind: thrilled by his reception, intrigued by Mussolini, but disturbed by the growing picture of repression and violence underpinning the Fascist state. He was unwilling to believe he had made a mistake in coming to Italy, but his conscience was pricking him. Now he would be placed in an anguish of indecision.

For some days he settled in Switzerland, at Villeneuve near Montreux, in the very room at the Hotel Byrone where Victor Hugo had once lived. Nearby was the villa of Romain Rolland: it was Rolland whom Tagore had come to see. He admired Rolland, almost as much as Rolland revered Rabindranath. But Rolland was extremely critical of Italian Fascism: he personally knew several Italians who had been forced into exile by the Fascists. He was determined to shake Tagore out of his ambivalence.

It proved to be exceedingly difficult. Rolland recorded his efforts and Tagore's responses in lengthy and candid diary entries published after Rolland's death as *Inde: Tagore Gandhi Nehru et Les Problèmes Indiens.* They talked extensively about Gandhi and Tagore's dislike of his authoritarianism. Rolland wanted Tagore to see the Italian situation as he did: freedom of thought was being suppressed in both countries, he said, in the name of national progress.

Rolland invited his friend Georges Duhamel, novelist and essayist, to come from Paris, and together they requested Rabindranath give an interview on Fascism that could be published in a major French journal – so as to clear the air. Duhamel would ask the questions, Tagore would respond. Tagore agreed but said he preferred to write his views rather than giving them orally. In the event, he shut himself up in his hotel room and produced an article without reference to Duhamel's questionnaire. Having read the questionnaire, he told Rolland that he had covered the essentials, and that evening after dinner they all met in the hotel room to hear the article read by Tagore and translated into French by Rolland's sister. (She was Rolland's interpreter for everything written or spoken in English.)

Rolland and Duhamel listened, appalled. Tagore's article, Rolland noted in his journal, was vague and diffuse. He mentioned the 'love' and admiration lavished upon him in Italy. At the same time he noted discreetly that as a guest of the Fascist government he had been able to see Italy only through the government's eyes. He indicated his disapproval of the abstract principles of Fascism – but in such a polite and anodyne manner, Rolland felt, that it lacked any connection with real life. Then Tagore quickly added that he neither wished to judge nor was capable of judging the reality of Fascism: 'he had seen nothing, heard nothing, learnt nothing and knew nothing, he washed his hands of

it.' Finally he referred abruptly to his two interviews with Mussolini. Here his portrait was flattering: he described the formidable energy in the upper portion of the
dictator's face, the humane gentleness in the lower; he compared him to Alexander
and Napoleon; and he concluded with a few lines to the effect that, platonically
speaking, he preferred the heroic man of action to his intellectual equivalent.
There was not one line in the piece about the sufferings of individual Italians.

Duhamel had to leave the room; he felt like crying. He was so incensed that he
wanted to expose Tagore in public. But Rolland, better informed about
Rabindranath's courage and more sympathetic to him personally – especially given
his weak state of health – eventually calmed Duhamel down. Rolland had realized
that only eyewitness accounts of Fascist violence might break Tagore's spell. He
therefore asked some of his Italian dissident friends to contact Tagore in Vienna.

During July Tagore received graphic written accounts of brutality from two
Italian exiles, Salvemini and Salvadori (who was unable to travel after his beating in Italy); from an Italian lawyer Modigliani who had worked on the
infamous case of Matteoti, the Socialist politician murdered by Fascists in 1924;
and from Angelica Balabanoff, who had worked with Mussolini, become disillusioned with him and subsequently published interviews and articles attacking
him. She accompanied Modigliani as an interpreter in Vienna, and later wrote
about her encounter with Tagore (from memory):

Tagore was staying at a fashionable hotel, where he was obviously an object
of idolatry among the wealthy patrons.

'There is no need to tell me the details of what is going on in Italy,' he said.
'I have been there and I do not know anything I could say or do about it.'

I would have left immediately had not Modigliani begun to speak in
Italian. As I started to translate his remarks, Tagore interrupted me. 'Are you
the person who gave the interview about Mussolini that was published a few
months ago?'

His secretary answered before I could speak, 'Yes, this is the lady whose
interviews and articles have interested you so much.'

The whole atmosphere changed and Tagore became an understanding and
even apologetic human being.

'Your interpretation of Mussolini's character', he said, 'coincides with the
impression he made upon me – a coward and an actor. When I asked the English
ambassador if he thought my impression was correct, he said it was not – that
Mussolini was a great and courageous man. However he did not convince me'.

On 20 July Tagore decided to speak out. He wrote a lengthy statement in the
form of a letter to C. F. Andrews in India, which was widely published. It

appeared as a letter in the *Manchester Guardian* (whose editor C. P. Scott was a keen admirer of Tagore) on 5 August, followed by his interview with Salvadori's wife on 7 August and an editorial, followed by a pained, defiant and mendacious reply from Formichi on 25 August (and another editorial), and ended with Tagore's reply to Formichi on 20 September.

According to Rolland, Tagore's published position 'did not satisfy anyone'. Undoubtedly Tagore was unhappy at biting the hands of his Italian hosts. But the real sticking point was the character of Mussolini. He told Salvadori's wife, who came to see him in Zurich: 'I did not support Fascism, though I did express my admiration for Mussolini as possessing the personality which alone can effect the miracles of creation in human history.'(!) Rabindranath simply could not make up his mind about the dictator. In his first letter (20 July) he wrote: 'There have been times when history has played tricks with man and through a combination of accidents has magnified the features of essentially small persons into a parody of greatness. Such a distortion of truth often finds its chance not because these men have an extraordinary power in themselves but because they represent some extraordinary weakness in those whom they lead.' But in his second letter (20 September), replying to Formichi, 'one of my best friends in Europe', Tagore wrote: 'it may be because of the great attraction that we have in the East not so much for an efficient organization as for some living genius in all departments of society that I was naturally drawn to the vision of a creative mind, working in the person of Mussolini, moulding the destiny of Italy, infusing life into her from his own abundant life when she showed any sign of feebleness . . . '

Whatever Tagore's waverings, the Fascist press was in no doubt about Tagore. (No opposition paper dared to print a translation of his statements.) An editorial appeared in *Popolo d'Italia*, edited by Mussolini's brother. Without even mentioning what Tagore had said outside Italy, it abused him as the 'Poet of Flowers, Stars and Pounds Sterling', 'this dishonest Tartuffe' who had 'profited by Italy's traditional and lordly hospitality towards her guests, Italy who saw in him the symbol of the great Indian people and its terrifying dilemmas.' The writer concluded: 'Who cares? Italy laughs at Tagore and those who brought this unctuous and insupportable fellow in our midst.'

The Italian episode was a sharp reminder to Rabindranath of the fragility of his enormous reputation in Europe. However it did not stop his progress. Between July and the end of November, he visited Austria, England, Norway, Sweden, Denmark, Germany, Czechoslovakia, Austria (again), Hungary, Rumania, Bulgaria, Greece and Egypt. Everywhere he was received at the highest level, and almost always attended by crowds. Everywhere too there were translations of his works, good, bad and indifferent (even into Bulgarian). Most of his friends assumed that he loved the adulation; Rolland privately criticized him, and more particularly his Bengali companions, for their 'tourist-like attitudes'. But for Tagore it was more like a sense of duty than a love of adulation that propelled him from one country to another. He wrote to C. P. Scott in mid-October from Prague, where he had watched a production of *The Post Office* in Czech:

> I have often wondered whether such rapid flashes of communication which are allowed me can leave any impression upon the minds of my hearers, whether the cost is not too great for me and the recompense too meagre. But what urges me to accept this task is the thought that the mere fact of the welcome which I receive from the different peoples of the West is valuable in itself. That they can express such a genuine enthusiasm in their recognition of a poet from the East is something which could never have been possible fifty years ago – and this is one of the signs of the age which has a positive significance.

He had just come from a tour of Germany where, as in 1921, his welcome had been phenomenal. On successive days in Berlin, for instance, he delivered a lecture at the city's largest concert hall that was sold out days in advance; he had tea with Albert Einstein, who later wrote a most cordial letter, marking the beginning of a friendship; and he was granted an interview with President von Hindenburg. But his German readership was not what it had been five years previously – at least partly because of the collapse of the German economy in between his visits. By September 1922, 800,000 copies of Tagore's works were said to have been sold in Germany. Then came the hyperinflation of 1923; by mid-1923 the currency was losing value by the minute. In October, Tagore's German publisher Kurt Wolff had decided to put 50,000,000,000 German marks, instead of the 5,000,000 marks due him in royalties, at the disposal of a Munich institution for feeding poor children – without waiting for Tagore's permission (if they had, the sum would have been literally worthless). The fund was known as the 'Tagore-Spende'.

In Bucharest he was shamelessly lionized by the Rumanian aristocracy, especially the ladies. Many curtsied and kissed his hand. While he was speaking in the parlour of the capital's most luxurious hotel, there was a sudden cry of horror and a woman's voice was heard: 'He's wounded! The poet's hands are bleeding!' This was all the more dramatic because Tagore had just declared to his reverent audience: 'the blood of our fellow-mortals should never stain our hands.' 'A miracle,' someone murmured.'The blood on the hands is a sign from heaven.' There was a tense hush while Rabindranath looked over his beard and studied the red blotches on his hands. Then he smiled, understanding: his hands had been stained by the multiple kisses of over-rouged female lips.

In Athens his celebrity took on an even more ludicrous form. The weather was wonderful and in the distance the white marbles of the Acropolis were silhouetted against the deep blue of the sky. 'But the enjoyment we should have derived from this pilgrimage was entirely marred', wrote Tagore's son to a friend, 'by a crowd of uninteresting and vulgar modern Greeks who escorted us to a nearer view.' Tourist or not,

Father got so disgusted that he remained in the car and would not be persuaded to see anything. When we returned – we found he had been kidnapped to some unknown destination. After some investigation we found him angrily sitting in an atelier, while a lady utilized the time in making as many exposures as she could with her camera. On our arrival she was not at all ashamed of herself! She had told Father that it was all arranged between her and myself.

Rabindranath had been characteristically trusting, obliging and uncomprehending, because he was out of his own setting. In Bengal or in the rest of India, he would have behaved quite differently. The same had happened to him in Italy – but at a different level. The man who had mordantly and publicly dissected Gandhi's moral tyranny in 'The cult of the Charka' was incapable of doing the same to Mussolini and Fascism. 'He is abdicating his role as moral guide of the independent spirits of Europe and India', a critical Romain Rolland told his diary. 'He does not have the calibre for the role. His nature is too poetic and affectionate for his mission.' Perhaps. But to Rabindranath, these were the very qualities – creative abundance and love of humanity – that defined his mission in nationalistic and technocratic Europe: to abandon them would be to abandon his crowning hope for the meeting of the East and the West.

28 Nationalism versus Internationalism (1927–1930)

It is foolish to think that the country can be awakened by the inanity of ignorant minds.

letter to Rani Mahalanobis,
Shantiniketan, October 1929

The experience in Italy and its troubling aftermath demonstrated to Tagore the gulf between the reality of human affairs and his ideals. An incident in Delhi just after his return from Europe in December reminded him, if he needed reminding, of the even wider gulf in India. On 23 December 1926, a Hindu reformer was assassinated by a Muslim fanatic. Speaking at Shantiniketan (which had not admitted its first Muslim student until 1921), Rabindranath said: 'The greatest calamity which afflicts us in this country is that different communities should be dwelling side by side and yet have no real relations with one another'.

He refused to blame the killing entirely on politics and politicians, a favourite exculpation of Indians then – as it remains now. Relations were *not* better 'in the old days', he said, speaking from deep experience. Politicians, rather than creating dissension, had manipulated a long-standing antipathy. On his estates, he recalled, in the early days of his management, he used to find part of the floor covering in the estate office rolled up by the tenants – to clear a space for the more respectable Muslims. This religious apartheid had long been accepted by Hindu and Muslim alike. 'Then', he said,

all of a sudden there came a day when we [i.e. Hindus] called upon the Mussalmans to join us in our political campaign, saying: You are our brothers; you must take your share of the loss, and join us in braving jail and oppression. To our dismay we found them sporting new blood-red fez caps, asserting that they too desired to maintain their distance! What is the obstacle – we asked, wonder-struck – to our standing shoulder to shoulder in the field of politics? The obstacle was nothing more or less than that same old gap between the carpeted and uncarpeted portions of the floor. By no means a trivial gap – not, at all events, a gap which can be bridged by calls for unity made from public platforms.

Shantiniketan, too, was riven with dissension – though here Rabindranath was less willing to admit the problem. He found that Tucci, the second Italian scholar (more distinguished than Formichi, almost on a par with Lévi), had suddenly left the university, not long before his return, after a year of continuous residence. It was reasonable to suspect that Italian politics were partly responsible for his departure – but disenchantment with Visva-Bharati was a far more potent cause. In Tagore's absence his institutions tended to go to pieces; Tucci had found Tagore's staff, excepting a few brilliant scholars, intolerable as coworkers. He wrote to Rabindranath on 29 December: 'there is something in the atmosphere of Shantiniketan which does not agree with your main idea, to make of it a meeting place of the East and the West.'

Tagore replied immediately and pleasantly, accepting the existence of many obstacles to realizing his ideals in Shantiniketan, but adding that they were not unique to his institution or to India. In Europe, he said, he had seen new education experiments, well funded and efficiently organized, 'struggling with the same moral difficulties as ours which are inherent in the materials they must use and surroundings that they cannot alter.' (Probably he was thinking of Dartington, amongst other places, where he stayed briefly in August 1926.) He felt that Tucci had been unduly influenced by 'scurrilous calumny repeatedly whispered to you behind our back[s] against some of our important members who, at that moment, had no opportunity to defend themselves.'

No, Tucci replied firmly but respectfully, 'I changed my opinion not because somebody whispered some calumny to my [ear] but only because I myself have seen and noted many details which compelled me to judge rather severely some of those who are connected with the institution.' His enthusiasm for the ideal was unchanged, he said; but he hoped that Rabindranath would manage to find someone to run the institution who was both in love with the ideal and competent to boot. (In later life, Tucci looked back on his time at Shantiniketan with reverence for Tagore personally, but kept largely silent about his institution.)

This was Tucci's last communication with Rabindranath, it appears from today's files at Shantiniketan. But Tagore probably saw a copy of a devastating letter, now in the same file, that Tucci had written to someone else – identity unknown – who was closely connected with the ashram. It read in part:

I was glad to leave a place which represents one of the greatest disappointments of my life. You know the enthusiasm with which I went there . . . I tell you frankly that if there is a place where East and West cannot meet [it is]

Santiniketan. And the fault is neither of the ideal nor of the poet, but only of those men who are responsible for its direction and organization. But can we speak of any direction or organization? . . .

. . . a scholar or even a student according to me cannot be judged by a clerk . . . But I ask you, those who are responsible for Santiniketan have [they] really any interest in its life, or rather in its death? I am rather inclined to the second hypothesis . . .

. . . They say that in Santiniketan there is freedom and *Ananda* [bliss]. *Ananda* may be, but certainly no freedom; if somebody wishes to speak frankly, he is very often compelled to go. And therefore you find that everybody in Santiniketan knows how things are going, but *out of fear nobody speaks* [Tucci's italics] . . .

. . . My Dear friend, this is not a confidential letter; I have written to you only a few things which I shall write *in extenso* in an article soon to be published in Europe. I myself do not wish that those who are connected with Santiniketan and whom I have had to criticize repeat about me what my country said about the poet who began to speak against Fascism after he left Italy and had accepted its hospitality. In Santiniketan everybody knows already my ideas. I hope that you will not be surprised. In fact Santiniketan in the mind of the poet was an international institution and as such it must be criticized. Moreover I came to Santiniketan full of enthusiasm and you know that we are in general particularly hard against those men who we loved sincerely but who have disappointed us.

In March and April 1927 Tagore expressed his own frustration in two written outbursts against the West. At the invitation of Ellery Sedgwick, his admirer and editor of the *Atlantic Monthly*, he flayed the United States, acridly denouncing the millionaires and the propagandists who, as he felt, had ruined his fund-raising visit in 1920–21. And, having just read Edward Thompson's biography of him, *Rabindranath Tagore: Poet and Dramatist*, he let fly at what he saw as English imperial arrogance. He wrote William Rothenstein (who admitted to admiring the book) a much-quoted letter:

It is one of the most absurd books that I have ever read dealing with a poet's life and writings. All through his pages he [Thompson] has never allowed his readers to guess that he has a very imperfect knowledge of [the] Bengali language . . . He has been a schoolmaster in an Indian school and that comes out in his pages too often in his pompous spirit of self confidence even in a realm where he ought to have been conscious of his limitations. The book is full of prejudices which have no foundation in facts, as for instance when he insinuates that I lack in my admiration for Shakespeare – or that I have an antipathy against Englishmen. Of course I have my grievances against the British Government in India, but I have a genuine respect for the English character which has so often been expressed in my writings. Then again, being a Christian Missionary, his training makes him incapable of understanding some of the ideas that run all through my writings . . . On the whole, the author is never afraid to be unjust, and that only shows his want of respect. I am certain he would have been much more careful in his treatment if his subject were a continental poet of reputation in Europe. He ought to have realized his responsibility all the more because of the fact that there was hardly anyone in Europe who could judge his book from his own first hand knowledge. But this has only made him bold and safely dogmatic, affording him impunity when he built his conclusions upon inaccurate data.

How I wish you had known Bengali!

Rabindranath roundly condemned the book to Bengali friends too. One of them, the well-known editor Ramananda Chatterji, felt similarly infuriated and published a series of pieces in English and Bengali attacking both the book and Thompson. They included a scathing pseudonymous review in Bengali – written by Rabindranath himself! Altogether, from Tagore-lovers in Bengal the unfortunate Thompson received a 'multiple hatchet-job' (in the phrase of Harish Trivedi, who in 1991 introduced an Indian edition of Thompson's biography).

The circumstances and the details of this fissure between subject and biographer are too complex to discuss here. (E. P. Thompson's *Alien Homage* is devoted to them.) Personal, political, literary and cultural differences in the widest sense all played a part. Overall we can say that Tagore's criticisms had much justification behind them, but that they were too vehement. He ought to have shown more understanding of Thompson's poignant predicament: that he wished to present a poet whom he knew to be of eternal stature to western readers in the 1920s who knew virtually nothing about Bengali culture, leave aside the scepticism generated by the feebleness of most existing Tagore translations. But instead of sympathizing with Thompson, Tagore, like the disillusioned Tucci with Shantiniketan, blasted the biography from which he had expected much.

In mid-July 1927, Rabindranath escaped Shantiniketan and its perplexities again, and sailed not west but east – to Malaya, Java and Bali, islands then part of the Dutch East Indies. He had wanted to tour 'Greater India' ever since his visit to Holland in 1920, when he came into contact with Dutch scholars of the ancient Hindu and Buddhist culture of the region. Indian colonists had settled in Java in the early centuries AD. Tagore therefore saw himself as a pilgrim to the roots of his own civilization, rather as he had visualized his visit to China in

1924. In a poem, 'Shagarika' (Sea-maiden), originally entitled 'Bali' and written during his tour, he imagined Bali as a gorgeous sea-maiden to whom ancient India had journeyed across the ocean bringing treasures in homage, adorning her with flowers and jewels. Then came the shipwreck, the rupture between the motherland, now dying, and her still-vibrant overseas offspring:

When the day faded I did not note,
Twilight found me floating again in the boat.
Suddenly the wind became adverse,
A wave washed up from the deep like a curse.
Salt-water filled the boat
And it sank, jewel-filled, in the dark of night.

The tour was an intriguing one, often exciting, occasionally depressing. Signs of ancient India were everywhere. On Bali Rabindranath found himself in a car with a local chief and no interpreter. Unable to communicate, he looked out of the window at the luscious beauty of the island. Suddenly there was a glimpse of the ocean through a gap in the forest, and the chief uttered the word *samudra* – Sanskrit for 'sea'. Seeing that his eminent guest was both surprised and pleased, the chief went on to repeat the Sanskrit synonyms, following them with *sapta-samudra* (the seven seas), *sapta-parvata* (the seven mountains), *sapta-vana* (the seven forests) and *sapta-akasha* (the seven skies). Then he pointed to a hill and, having given the Sanskrit for 'hill', recited the names of mountains: Sumeru, Himalaya, Vindhya, Malaya, Rishyamukha. When they came to a river, he continued: Ganga, Yamuna, Narmada, Godaveri, Kaveri, Saraswati (all except the last being names of modern rivers in India).

Of the famous Javanese shadow theatre, with its ever-popular stories from the Indian epics *Ramayana* and *Mahabharata*, Tagore noted:

When we first entered the part of the hall facing the lighted side of the screen, the effect was somewhat disappointing. Then we were taken over to the dark side where the women were seated. Here the cut-outs and their manipulators were no longer visible, there were only the shadows dancing on the screen, like the dance of the demon Mahamaya on the body of the prostrate Shiva. We see creation only when the Creator, who abides in the region of light, conceals himself. He who knows that creation and the Creator are indissolubly bound, knows the truth. But he who sees creation as separate from the Creator, sees only maya. There are seekers of truth who would tear away the screen and go over to the other side – so as to see the Creator apart from his creation: nothing can be emptier than the maya of their illusion. This is what I felt as I watched this show.

The great Buddhist temple at Borobudur, which he saw in the company of two admirable Dutch scholars, disappointed him as a whole. [pl.41] He had seen many photographs but hoped that the temple would impress him more in reality. Still, the details in the sculpted pictures of the *Jatakas* delighted him with their loving depiction of everyday life. He commented: 'I remember having seen in my childhood a cow with its tender eyes, coming up and licking a washerman's donkey tied to a peg – and how I was wonderstruck! The *Jataka* writer would have had no hesitation in asserting that the Buddha in one of his births was such a cow . . . Thanks to Buddhism, the whole course of life on earth has been invested with glory.'

Even signs of commerce and industry did not call forth Rabindranath's usual jeremiad – perhaps because the exploitation was Dutch, rather than British. On the way from Batavia (Jakarta) to Singapore, the boat anchored off the island of Billiton, sparsely inhabited except for tin miners and mine managers. Tagore uncharacteristically marvelled at the spirit motivating the European colonists of recent centuries as they sailed forth into unknown waters. He wrote: 'The history of these enterprises bristles with difficulties and dangers. I sometimes try to imagine the feelings of trepidation mixed with hopeful anticipation with which they must have furled their sails on first sighting islands such as these in distant seas. The vegetation, the animals and the men were all unknown. And today – how thoroughly studied and *possessed*.'

But he could not escape the coils of colonial politics entirely. In Malaya, the local jingo press, British-run, published a statement by him, taken from a report in a Manila paper that had published quotations from a statement alleged to have been made to the *Shanghai Times*. (This was curious since Tagore had not been in Shanghai.) In it Tagore criticized British policy in China and said: 'Asia prepare her weapons in her armories for a target which is bound to be the heart of Europe.' Rabindranath was forced to issue a statement in Malaya explaining that the report derived from a distorted interview with an Indian newspaper, which had apparently been picked up by 'unscrupulous editors' in America, further distorted, and then found its way into the Malayan press. But his position was somewhat weakened by his having accepted government hospitality in Malaya (shades of the Italian débâcle). For this he was criticized both by the Malayan press and the press in Calcutta.

While in Bali, he came across a copy of the London *New Statesman* and encountered for the first time a book that would anger him for the next two or three years. It was *Mother India* by Katherine Mayo, an American travel writer.

Published in 1927 (at the same time as Tagore's excoriation of the US in the *Atlantic Monthly*), it became a huge bestseller and had a significant impact on western perceptions of India. It purported to lift the lid on the dark Indian reality through a mixture of eyewitness reportage, official statistics and quotations from sources both British and Indian. Arnold Bennett called it 'a shocking book, in the honourable sense.' Gandhi said it was a 'drain inspector's report', which no westerner but every Indian might profitably read. 'If Miss Mayo had confessed that she had gone to India merely to open out and examine the drains of India, there would perhaps be little to complain about her compilation. But she says in effect with a certain amount of triumph, "The drains are India." '

Tagore was incensed by the way Mayo had deliberately misquoted him on the subject of child marriage, a misquotation gleefully echoed by the *New Statesman* reviewer. (Gandhi said Mayo had 'violated all sense of propriety' in this instance.) By omitting two words, 'said India', from an article Tagore had written in 1925 on marriage in India, Mayo implied that Tagore himself (rather than India in general) supported child marriage in order to control female sexuality. In Mayo's words, Tagore believed 'a woman must be married before she knows she is one.'

He wrote two letters about the book, one to the *Manchester Guardian* from Bali, the other to the *Nation* in New York from Shantiniketan. In the first he said that the accusation against him was like accusing the late President Wilson of 'having expressed his pious conviction that the lynching of Negroes was a moral necessity in a superior civilization for cultivating Christian virtues'. In the second he quoted a strong (Indian) critic of India's social evils who had written that Mayo 'might have asked anyone in Calcutta what the age of marriage of girls is in Tagore's own family.'

This last was an ill-judged, almost purblind defence by Tagore. He was perhaps fortunate that Mayo had *not* turned her attention to his marital arrangements for his daughters. Obviously Rabindranath did not support child marriage, but neither was his record on it an unblemished one. Mayo had misrepresented his essay on marriage, but the essay was nevertheless full of the conflicting feelings about women that had characterized him in his personal life. Tagore's later comments on *Mother India* – which *was* a shocking, if mercenary and malicious book – during his visit to America in 1929, would be more telling than his immediate fury in 1927.

The cumulative weight of foreign criticism, sincere and insincere, made Tagore super-sensitive to any attack on himself or his institution. In late 1927, now back in Shantiniketan, he received from someone in Java a report taken from a

Dutch newspaper in which Sylvain Lévi had apparently been uncomplimentary about Visva-Bharati. Tagore wrote to Lévi and received a pained reply: 'I am deeply sorry that you have taken *au sérieux* some miserable reports the author of which I do not even guess . . . Shall I refer you to the book [on Shantiniketan] published by my wife, about which old friends used to tease her as being in love with you?' It was not clear what Lévi may or may not have said, whether intended for public consumption or not, but Tagore knew from Lévi's several letters to him that he was critical of some aspects of Shantiniketan and of himself. Although he met Lévi again in Calcutta in 1928 (who then paid a farewell visit to Shantiniketan), Rabindranath nursed a feeling of hurt about Lévi and avoided any subsequent contact. Probably Lévi did speak contemptuously of Shantiniketan as an academic institution, perhaps in private, while Tagore, for his part, allowed a genuine grievance to be inflated by 'calumnies' of the kind that he thought had influenced Tucci. Shantiniketan was always rife with rumour: sometimes its founder took note of it, sometimes he did not.

There was conflict too in Bengali literature. 'Modernism' and 'realism' were beginning to thrust their way into Bengali poetry, stories and novels, however crudely and unconvincingly. A younger group of writers were trying to escape from the penumbra of Rabindranath, often by tilting at him and his work. In 1928 he decided to call a meeting of writers at Jorasanko and hear them debate the issues. It was, as might have been expected, an inconclusive occasion. Tagore did not speak; he had already set out his views in an essay the previous year. Although he would make many experiments in his poetry in the 1930s that would liberate it from any charge of Victorianism, he remained a devotee of classical restraint and order in literature. He gave an example of his attitude which is still a good one. The spring festival of Holi traditionally involved, all over India, the scattering of red powder (washable), the spraying of rose-coloured perfumes, laughter and song. But among the riff-raff in the Chitpur Road near the Tagore house, said Rabindranath, Holi meant rolling long pieces of wet cloth through the mud in the street, spattering each other and any passers-by 'to the accompaniment of unearthly yells'. (Nowadays permanent dyes and muck of all kinds are common.) This propensity, this love of soiling, was perfectly natural, Tagore admitted; and psychoanalysts were welcome to revel in its study – Freud was just then entering the Bengali consciousness. Tagore's objection to importing it into the festival of Holi, or by analogy into Bengali literature, was 'not because it is not true, but because it is not appropriate.'

As a painter he had fewer inhibitions. In late 1928, painting took hold of him in earnest, and a flood of strange works came forth, as if Rabindranath were giving vent to all the tensions, including sexual tensions, that had been pent up for so long. He had dabbled in art as far back as the 1890s but never pursued it seriously, certainly never taken lessons in his adult life: maybe he was partly put off by the success of his nephews, Abanindranath and Gaganendranath, and the painters of the Bengal School. In 1924, in Argentina, he produced some remarkable doodles out of his erasures on the poems of *Purabi*. Victoria Ocampo and Leonard Elmhirst encouraged him. A year or so later, Rabindranath wrote from Shantiniketan to Elmhirst, who had sent him a new pen:

You have expressed your hope that this pen of yours will help me in my cult of frenzied drawing. You had the opportunity of observing me in the flowering season of my eccentricity which comes from an excess of dream energy. I have hardly enough left of it even for writing poems. Of late I have occasionally been compelled to write prose compositions with tracks across them of scratches – the hasty burial places of errors – but they remain there undisturbed like a maze of deserted trenches in a shell-ravaged battlefield. Pages full of them rebuke me in pathetic silence claiming for some harmony in this anarchy of forms. But my mind is too weary to respond. It has lost its enthusiasm for all kinds of aristocratic works that are supremely useless.

This was the beginning. Three years later, in November 1928, he told a Bengali friend:

I am hopelessly entangled in the spell that the lines have cast upon me . . . I have almost managed to forget that there was a time when I used to write poetry. It is the element of unpredictability in art that seems to fascinate me. The subject matter of a poem can be traced back to some dim thought in the mind. Once it leaves the matted crown of Shiva, the stream of poetry flows along its measured course – well-defined by its two banks. With painting, the process adopted by me is quite the reverse. First there is the hint of a line, then the line becomes a form. The more pronounced becomes the form the clearer becomes the picture in my imagination. This creation of form is a source of endless wonder. If I were a trained artist I would probably have a preconceived idea for a picture. That is no doubt rewarding. But it is more fun when the mind is seized by something outside of it, some surprise element that gradually evolves into a comprehensible shape. I am so taken with this new game that all my various responsibilities, external to myself, peep in from outside my door – only to withdraw the next moment with much shaking of the head. If I were a free agent as of old, unburdened by cares, do you know what I would do? I would live by the Padma and gather a harvest of pictures, nothing but pictures, with which to load the Golden Boat of Time.

At just this time Rabindranath received two distinguished visitors in Shantiniketan, one German, the other English. Arnold Sommerfeld was professor of theoretical physics at Munich, well known for his work on atomic spectra, and the teacher of, among others, Werner Heisenberg (who would visit Tagore in Calcutta the next year). Sommerfeld was on a world lecture tour. In a later article, translated from German, he described Rabindranath:

He is to India perhaps the same as old Goethe was to the Germany of his time. Like Goethe he is infinitely diligent: he works from early in the morning till night. Even his interest in craft-work was shared by Goethe. His image is known to all, but his actual appearance is much more beautiful than his picture, a pure type of Aryan stock, with a lightness in the colour of the skin resembling that of an elephant's tusk. With his patriarchal beard he looks older than his sixty-eight years. His English is like music. The evening with him on the upper terrace of his house next to his studio is unforgettable.

Lord Irwin, later Lord Halifax, the second important visitor, was the first (and only) viceroy to visit Shantiniketan. Tagore interested Irwin, as did Gandhi: the one with his emphasis on cooperation, the other believing firmly in non-cooperation. While parleying with Gandhi, Irwin also tried to assist Tagore's institutions.

By the late 1920s, Rabindranath's condemnation of non-cooperation had, if anything, become sharper than it was a few years earlier. In late 1929 he told a Bengali friend:

I believe that the cult of the *Charka* could spread easily in India only because the temptation to extort concessions from a merchant nation by putting pressure on Lancashire is strong within us . . . In the days of the Swadeshi Movement the boycott had the same external objective. In all our plans we are constantly thinking of the effect on our masters, of forcing our rulers to come to terms. All this is entirely superficial . . . It is foolish to think that the country can be awakened by the inanity of ignorant minds.

As part of his fight against the perpetuation of such ignorance, Tagore went to Canada and spoke at an international conference on education in Vancouver in April 1929. It was his first visit to the country and he was gratified by his reception. When he spoke in Victoria, the capital of British Columbia but nevertheless only a small town (pop. 40,000), 2,000 people attended the lecture while 3,000 waited outside in pitiless rain for a chance to hear him. This was all the more remarkable, given that Canadian anti-Asiatic feeling was at its most intense in British Columbia.

Asked for a farewell message to Canada at the conference, he said that such a brief visit hardly gave him the right to speak about the country. Travel between nations had become easy, he said, 'the epic age of travelling [had] passed away' – but this did not mean that the races had come to know each other better. He was thinking of *Mother India*, by then in its twenty-second reprint over the border in the USA.

He had not intended to visit the United States again on this trip. But in Canada he received invitations from American universities, including Harvard, Columbia and Southern California, and he changed his mind. Unfortunately his passport had been mislaid. At the immigration office in Vancouver, a US official, aware of who he was, nevertheless kept him standing for half an hour and then asked him the stock questions: who had paid his passage, had he been to jail, was he going to settle permanently in the USA? (A London paper claimed that Tagore was even asked if he could write.) Not surprisingly, Tagore's anti-American hackles rose. After giving one lecture in southern California, he abruptly cancelled his visit and sailed for Japan.

At San Francisco, on the way out, he was asked for interviews. He was reluctant, having come to suspect all American journalists of sensationalism. After some preliminary remarks about individual Americans he knew 'who are gifted with an intellect that can combine wisdom in practical matters with a genuine faith in idealism', he mentioned the immigration incident and then linked it to *Mother India*. What did he think of the book? was the first question he had been asked on arrival in the US, he noted bitterly. 'I suppose you realize that the publication of this book has done more in poisoning our mutual relationship than anything in recent happenings. It almost has the same effect as your immigration regulations in creating a barrier against American lady visitors who try to come to our homes.'

He detested Mayo's hypocrisy. She had dedicated the book 'To the peoples of India', and claimed that she was inflicting on them the 'faithful wounds of a friend'.

Curiously enough she offers [as] her justification for erecting such a skyscraper of calumny, a tender partiality for those whom she knows or imagines to be underdogs! She must have laughed in her sleeve when she made such a statement, for she was perfectly aware that . . . India is one of the underdogs of the world who could be molested with impunity for the delectation of all superdogs; and these superdogs have enjoyed her performance and amply rewarded her.

The *San Francisco Chronicle* editorial was apologetic and sympathetic to

Tagore: 'He is a man of broad education, and it may be because of this rather than despite it that Western civilization seems to him all of a piece in certain respects. He is painfully aware that it is too likely to miss the distinction between Tagores and coolies.' Adverting to the controversy over *Mother India*, the newspaper said:

> There is undoubted beauty in life here as there. Tagore found it in India, expressed it in native poetry, translated that poetry into rarely beautiful English which one does not have to be a reincarnated Bengali to understand. East is East and West is West, but the twain do meet sometimes. Tagore has supplied a common ground for such a meeting . . . We would like to assure him that the experiences which distressed him at our ports of entry do not really reflect the American idea of good manners.

Back in Tokyo, Tagore warned the Japanese about their mistreatment of fellow-Asiatics. Students from Korea, annexed by Japan in 1910, had briefed him on his arrival in the capital. Rabindranath's suspicions about Japan, voiced as far back as 1915, were coming true with a vengeance. When he met the ultra-Right arch-samurai Toyama Mitsuru, godfather of Indian revolutionaries in Japan, Tagore exploded: 'You have been infected by the virus of European imperialism!' He announced hotly that he would never visit Japan again. (But he invited to Shantiniketan a leading Japanese expert in judo, Takagaki – thus introducing the martial art into the subcontinent.)

In India he was now a peculiarly isolated celebrity. To the average British official, especially the police and the intelligence department, he was virtually a non-cooperator; to the average Indian official he did not 'play the game' of Anglo-Indian back-scratching; to the average Indian nationalist he was unpatriotic for not supporting Gandhi's movement; to the average Bengali writer he was a natural object of envy; and to the average Bengali in general he was an aloof, unconventional, critical presence, however much honour he might have brought upon Bengal abroad and in the rest of India. Rabindranath knew it all so well. At the end of 1929 he told one of his closer young Bengali friends, the scholar Suniti Chatterji, that he would have to accept the slander calmly. For, unlike Gandhi, he had no widespread support: 'many are pleased at my being censored and most of the rest are completely indifferent.' He no longer expected his friends and those supposed to be his flatterers to defend him, he said – for he knew that they did not have the support of their countrymen. Thus when, around this time, Tagore announced the first government aid for his 'institute for rural reconstruction' (hitherto reliant upon Elmhirst money), he expected criticism from nationalists – and duly received it. By not joining any group, and refusing to temper his criticisms, Rabindranath had become the target of all groups.

The late 1920s had been a stressful period for him, his ideals and his institutions. No wonder, on Founder's Day 1929 (22 December), Tagore sent a poignant card to his friends worldwide. Illustrated with one of his intriguing rhythmic designs, it bore the following message in his forceful handwriting: 'My salutation is to him who knows me imperfect and loves me.'

29 Farewell to the West
(1930–1931)

My poetry is for my countrymen, my paintings are my gift to the West.

statement to the press,
Munich, July 1930

By early 1930, Tagore had become restless to escape India and its entanglements. A standing offer from Oxford University to give the Hibbert lectures was reason enough to go west again. As important to him, probably more so, was his intense curiosity to know the western response to his paintings.

From the outset as a painter he had distrusted the judgement of Indian artists and audiences. Indeed he had kept the fact of his painting as private as possible. In December 1929 he told Suniti Chatterji: 'Dead or alive I will never make public this creation of mine in my country. My pictures will not be allowed to commit the same offence as my other creations.' He asked permission to tear out of Chatterji's scrapbook a picture he had drawn in it as a favour. The picture was unsigned: 'I did not sign it and I will not.' For a long time Tagore had an aversion for signing his works of art.

His diffidence about exhibiting them was gradually overcome by the warm responses of various foreign artists visiting Shantiniketan. One was a well-known Japanese artist, another a Paris-trained sculptress, Marguerite Milward (a student of Emile Bourdelle), who had come to do a bust of Tagore – perhaps the best one there is. One evening at sunset, she recalled, when the light 'cast a glory over the fine features and snow-white hair of the aged poet', she was talking to him about sculpture and was amazed to learn of his latest craze. She cajoled him into bringing out a portfolio of paintings which together they spread all over the room. Excitedly she told him: 'You must exhibit these in Paris, there the artists will understand and appreciate them.' Rabindranath greatly demurred. (Sixty years later the photographer and painter Henri Cartier-Bresson would feel similarly excited seeing Tagore's art for the first time.)

On 30 March 1930, Tagore wrote seriously about the paintings to William Rothenstein, by now principal of the Royal College of Art in London, where he championed new artists such as Henry Moore. Unknown to Rothenstein, Tagore had just arrived in the French Riviera, carrying with him some 400 works. One is reminded of an earlier arrival, in London in 1912, when Rabindranath carried a manuscript instead of a portfolio. He commented shrewdly to his old artist-friend: 'I still feel misgivings and I want your advice. They [the paintings] certainly possess psychological interest being products of untutored fingers and untrained mind. I am sure they do not represent what they call Indian Art, and in one sense they may be original, revealing a strangeness born of my utter inexperience and individual limitations.' Would Rothenstein be able to join him at the villa near Monte Carlo where he was staying, once again as a guest of Albert Kahn?

This time Rothenstein declined. At such short notice he was unable to get away, and he surely wished to avoid being put in the position of judge, for in his reply he did not mention the paintings. To his credit, however, when he saw the paintings in London two months later, Rothenstein genuinely admired them. '[They] are extraordinarily vital: they show none of the weakness of the revivalist schools which stand for modern Indian art', he told Sturge Moore. Some other western friends, more literary-minded and less open-minded, were unimpressed. Like almost everyone Tagore knew in Bengal, they felt he was making a fool of himself by showing the works; this new creative departure did not at all conform to their vision of India's poet. Among these critics were Albert Kahn, Romain Rolland and C. F. Andrews, the latter ever alert to bolster the saintly image of Gurudev created in the West by *Gitanjali*.

Tagore's faith in himself as a painter was strong enough to ignore such opposition. But it could do nothing to find him an art gallery in Paris in 1930. The credit for this went to Victoria Ocampo. By happy chance she had come to France from Argentina in December. A cable from Tagore brought her south on 15 April. Just two weeks later, on 2 May, an exhibition of Tagore's works opened in Paris at the modernist Galerie Pigalle. Ocampo's friends had rallied round the idea, among them Georges Henri Rivière and Paul Valéry. So had Tagore's admirer Countess Anna de Noailles, who had hoped to conquer Rabindranath ten years previously. She wrote the catalogue introduction: intelligent but surpassing even Yeats' introduction to *Gitanjali* in ecstasy. Henri Bidou, a critic, wrote a major and more reasoned review. The opening was a crowded, cosmopolitan and chic occasion.

At the urging of the countess, Rabindranath wore pure white. She wore a long black skirt to make a striking contrast. A photograph [pl.45] catches the atmosphere of the exhibition wonderfully well. Seated stage centre, a serenely radiant Rabindranath gazes with infinite confidence into the eye of the camera, majestically poised, and apparently without the slightest pose. On his left sits

Ocampo, coolly elegant and faintly sexy, eyes lowered towards the catalogue, the very picture of a Parisian blue-stocking; while behind her stands a tall aristocratic-looking figure, uninvolved, who seems to have stepped out of the weekend house-party in Jean Renoir's *La Règle du Jeu*. On Tagore's right stands Anna de Noailles, all shiny black and white satin drapery and bold buckles, eyes demurely closed, whether in adoration of Rabindranath or to avoid the flash bulb we must decide for ourselves; while just behind her – closer than necessary – stands the minister of fine arts, dapper, moustachioed, half-leering, a Menjou-like caricature of a French cad. And there, behind them all, hangs a haunting Tagore painting, figurative but anonymous, a melancholy beast-hulk with a peculiar bird perched upon its haunch (or is it the shoulder?) – a weird and alien image, yet somehow in tune with the stark clash between its creator and the fashionable people around him. From this photograph it is easy to believe that immediately after the fuss of the gallery opening Tagore was once more immured in painting: when a French artist-friend called at his hotel she found him 'all white and calm like a Hymalaya peak', already generating new 'dream figures' on sheets of white paper.

'Twice I went back to the exhibition to gaze on these strikingly original pictures, full of poise and balance, and refinement, and of such profound psychology', wrote Marguerite Milward. 'No collection has ever interested and moved me so deeply.' Henri Bidou commented perceptively:

Only those who have never recognized those mysterious currents of thought and feeling, the outcome of the age itself, which penetrate all souls as by osmosis ... will be surprised that this pure painting, absolutely sincere and wholly uninfluenced by our studio customs, should resemble now and then the most recent researches of the painters of the West. There can be no question of imitation, but the convergence of spirit is remarkable.

This *succès fou* in Paris seems to have given Rabindranath, who was now in his seventieth year, a remarkable access of energy during the months that followed. During 1930 it is difficult to keep track of where he went in Europe, let alone what he did, said and thought. He moved in at least five overlapping worlds apart from that of painting (his works being shown wherever he went): religious, educational, philosophical, political and literary. If we take just the month in Britain following the Paris opening, we find Tagore staying in a Quaker settlement near Birmingham while the City Art Gallery showed his paintings; protesting strongly in print, speeches and in a private meeting with the secretary of state for India against the arrests of Gandhi and the Congress leaders following the Salt March; lecturing three times at Oxford on *The*

Religion of Man (the Hibbert lectures) before large audiences; being the guest of honour at a P.E.N. Club dinner in London; attempting to raise money for his university from, amongst others, the Aga Khan; and finally settling at Dartington with Leonard Elmhirst for a much-needed rest. By 1930, India was prominent in British minds, as compared with its position during Tagore's previous visits to Britain; Tagore was much in demand.

His relationship with the Quakers was recent, dating from a visit paid to Shantiniketan in 1928 by Horace Alexander, who also knew Gandhi. The hope was, on each side, that the Quakers might support Shantiniketan, both financially and through Quaker staff, Indian and British. But from the start there were problems. Although the Quakers had dropped their commitment to Christian conversion, they were deeply committed to efficiency. In the warning words of Elmhirst to Tagore, 'their background has a Puritan strain which implies an interest in Health work rather than in Cultural enterprise.' Tagore, for better or worse, always refused to compartmentalize his activities at Shantiniketan in this way.

The Quaker settlement was at Woodbrooke in Selly Oak, Birmingham. All had agreed in advance that Tagore would be left in peace to write. He worked hard on his Hibbert lectures, rising at 5 a.m., sleeping at midnight and only occasionally taking part in devotional meetings. Once he was taken for an afternoon drive to the Forest of Arden to see carpets of bluebells. On his return a local Quaker took a photograph of him, of biblical beauty; it makes an interesting contrast with the one taken in Paris two weeks before. The prophet and the poet-artist: the two chief images of Tagore while in the West. [pl.57] But there was a mundane element in the Quaker reaction too. They were somewhat surprised to learn that Tagore was not a vegetarian and relished cold tongue. He told them he regretted not having what he called an 'international stomach'. His late friend Pearson, he said, had been 'famous for this very desirable possession': once Pearson had worked his way through all twenty-five dishes of a Chinese dinner given in Tagore's honour.

Soon Indian politics intruded. On 16 May, twelve days after the arrest of Gandhi, the *Manchester Guardian* printed a lengthy statement by Tagore, the first of many in 1930 during the run-up to the Round Table Conference in London. He made his familiar point to begin with, that in his youth he and others like him had been inspired by English literature, especially Shelley and Wordsworth. 'We believed with all our simple faith that even if we rebeled against foreign rule we should have the sympathy of the West.' This faith, he said, had now gone:

Those who live in England, away from the East, have now got to recognize that Europe has completely lost her former moral prestige in Asia. She is no longer regarded as the champion throughout the world of fair dealing and the exponent of high principle, but rather as the upholder of Western race supremacy and the exploiter of those outside her own borders.

As an instance of this contemptuous attitude he quoted press cables from India stating that under martial law the military were going about the streets flicking the 'Gandhi caps' off the heads of Congress supporters. His proposed solution was of course idealistic: 'a radical change of mind and will and heart.' He continued to believe, he said, in 'a meeting between the best minds of the East and the West in order to come to a frank and honourable understanding.' The failure of such a meeting in his own institution at Shantiniketan and indeed in his own contacts with most of the best minds of the West had still not destroyed his confidence in the essential rightness of the idea.

A week later Tagore became the first non-Quaker in Quaker history to address the annual meeting in London. The atmosphere was electric, Tagore's tone much more bitter than many had expected. Though his approach was the same as in his press statement, he was more brutal in his imagery, speaking of British rule as rule 'by a machine', the existence of 'a dark chasm of aloofness' and a 'disease' in political conditions. Most of those who responded seemed chastened by his tone, but one older Quaker with experience of India strongly dissented. 'It [is] not idealists like Rabindranath Tagore, C. F. Andrews or Mahatma Gandhi that we [have] to deal with,' he said, 'but a very difficult people indeed, whose politics [are] childish . . . India [is] so divided horizontally and perpendicularly by unsympathetic and hostile barriers, personal barriers, of race and religion that it [is] almost impossible to have a united India.' Tagore of course knew this better than almost any other Indian, which was perhaps why, without admitting as much, he felt constrained to add before leaving the meeting, 'I must express my regret for causing some sense of irritation, my only object was that the interest you have in the Indian nation led me to say what I have felt.' He finished with a telling plea: 'I ask you for your cooperation and that you may realize yourselves in our place and recall the time when your own brothers in America wanted to secure their freedom with blood . . . Give us the right to serve our own country.'

Or, to restate the challenge in its widest sense, as Tagore did at Oxford that same week in the Hibbert lectures (foretelling the desperate decade to come): 'The vastness of the race problem with which we are faced today will either compel us to train ourselves to moral fitness in the place of merely external efficiency, or the complications arising out of it will fetter all our movements and drag us to our death.'

These Oxford lectures, unlike Tagore's talk to the Quakers, did not directly concern politics. Their avowed subject was 'the idea of the humanity of our God, or the divinity of Man the Eternal'. Like *Sadhana* in 1913, they are beguiling and brilliant in some parts, tedious and confused in others, but superior to *Sadhana* because they are more personal. 'For it is evident that my religion is a poet's religion . . . Its touch comes to me through the same unseen and trackless channel as does the inspiration of my songs.' Partly for this reason, all three lectures had standing room only, in spite of beautiful summer weather and the counter-attraction of Eights Week in Oxford.

The *Manchester Guardian* ran full reports and remarked on the 'gleams of humour and remarkably lucid illustrations' of Tagore: 'the personality of the poet as he spoke with the sunshine falling on his white head and lighting up his beautiful face made comparatively easy even his most difficult thoughts.' At the end, his friend Sir Michael Sadler, now the master of University College, Oxford, said: 'We wish to tell you that the spirit of the word that has fallen from you has united us together.' When Tagore preached in Manchester College chapel, the congregation was so great that many had to remain standing around the walls and others found seats on the steps leading to the pulpit.

After such warmth, a rebuff that immediately followed was galling for Tagore. It came from the Aga Khan, who, Tagore had been led to believe by an Indian business friend, was willing to fund a chair in Persian studies at Shantiniketan. Having dragged himself out of bed with flu, Tagore tracked down his quarry. As he wrote to his friend immediately afterwards, 'I talked and talked about all kinds of subjects, about the other world and this world, about poetry and pictures, about medieval India and India that is yet to be – till at the end of the last chapter it came out that the . . . whole world was suffering from penury and privation . . . I feel miserably tired and humiliated. I have lost my caste'. In a second letter sent from Dartington he added, a little unfairly: 'It has been my ill-luck to meet with such treatment only from my own countrymen.'

Dartington Hall was one place calculated to provoke such reflections in Tagore. Not only had its owners the Elmhirsts generously donated large sums to Tagore's institute at Shriniketan, the conception of the Dartington Trust was of course inspired by Tagore. Yet the scale, solidity and antiquity of Dartington's buildings, dating back to the fourteenth century, must have bothered Tagore. He would not have been human if he had not felt jealous, sometimes, of Dartington's prodigal resources compared to those of his impoverished institution. Why, otherwise, did he keep almost perversely silent about the glories of the place in his letters to family and others in Bengal, many of whom knew and liked Elmhirst? As with his wealthy grandfather, he wrote barely a word. [pl.38]

He stayed there more than a month, happily painting and recuperating. Then he headed for the Continent again. Between mid-July and mid-September, when he went to Russia, he travelled in Denmark, Switzerland and, most of all, in Germany, where he and his paintings were received with keen appreciation in Berlin, Munich and Dresden. At Oberammergau, as he was leaving after witnessing the Passion Play, a hushed whisper went round the audience: 'How like our Prophet!' Tagore reacted to the play by writing in a single night his only poem in English, *The Child*. The German Youth Movement, then flourishing, appealed to his imagination too and he spent some time visiting one of its camps near Coblenz; the idealism and romanticism he saw there probably made it harder for him to grasp the meaning of Nazism a few years later.

His Danish visit, apart from an opportunity to exhibit his paintings in Copenhagen, included a lecture on education in Krönberg Castle, Elsinore. A visitor from Scotland happened to hear it and compared Rabindranath to a Jewish patriarch, remarking that there was 'something strange in an Oriental lecturing in perfect English to a Danish audience, in a Danish castle which owes its fame to the greatest Englishman of all time.' (Regrettably Tagore did not write about the experience, perhaps because *Hamlet* was not among his favourite Shakespeare plays.)

From Geneva he gave his own estimate of his looks, tailored to suit his eight-year-old granddaughter Nandini, the adopted child of Rathindranath and Pratima, back at Shantiniketan.

Grandad's in a mess. His papers are scattered all over the table. His inkpots are all mixed up. His pens and pencils have all gone missing. His glasses are on his nose, yet he searches for them. He's got a big loose robe on, stained with reds, blues and yellows. His fingers and hands are stained too, and when he eats with them like that, people smile to themselves. Despite seeing his loose robe everyday, people are still amused by it.

When not painting, he was meeting a wide range of people, some of them connected with the League of Nations, an organization he had once welcomed but increasingly regarded with suspicion. He renewed his contact with Romain Rolland after a long gap following his disaster in Italy in 1926, and he met H. G. Wells again after an even longer gap. Neither meeting was really satisfactory, and when their conversations were later published by an American magazine without Wells' permission, Wells severed his link with Tagore.

Tagore's most celebrated meeting of this period was with Albert Einstein. [pl.50] They had had almost nothing to do with each other since Einstein's cordial letter of 1926. Now, in the second half of 1930, they met each other four times or more, in Berlin and in New York. Two of these conversations were published. Both are still of interest, but the first one, that appeared in the

New York Times in August 1930 and in 1931 as an appendix to *The Religion of Man*, is of significance in the history of physics and even to today's science. (In 1992, the physicist Brian Josephson, a Nobel laureate, remarked that 'Tagore is, I think, saying that truth is a subtler concept than Einstein realizes.')

As he aged, Einstein's commitment to realism had hardened. Like Descartes and Newton, he had faith in the existence of a world 'out there', of truth independent of man: the moon *was* there, whether one looked at it or not, as he later famously queried. And the same was so, he believed, in the sub-atomic world. This brought him into conflict with quantum theorists such as Werner Heisenberg and Niels Bohr. They believed that it was 'wrong to think that the task of physics is to find out how nature *is*. Physics concerns what we can say about nature' (to quote Bohr). Their arguments with Einstein over quantum theory, which began around the time of Einstein's first meeting with Tagore in 1926, lasted until Einstein's death in 1955.

Tagore fundamentally disagreed with realism of the Einsteinian kind. 'We can never go beyond man in all that we know and feel.' This was from *The Religion of Man*, and it summarized Tagore's position *vis-à-vis* Einstein's.

They met at Einstein's summer villa at Caputh, outside Berlin. One of those present, Dmitri Marianoff, a journalist who later married Margot Einstein, noted the conversation and probably acted as interpreter. (Einstein understood English but spoke in German.) 'It was interesting to see them together – Tagore, the poet with the head of a thinker, and Einstein, the thinker with the head of a poet', Marianoff commented in the *New York Times*. 'Neither sought to press his opinion. They simply exchanged ideas. But it seemed to an observer as though two planets were engaged in a chat.' This is from the published account:

Einstein: There are two different conceptions about the nature of the universe – the world as a unity dependent on humanity, and the world as reality independent of the human factor . . .
Tagore: This world is a human world – the scientific view of it is also that of the scientific man. Therefore, the world apart from us does not exist; it is a relative world, depending for its reality upon our consciousness.

A little later, Einstein took up the point again:

Einstein: Truth, then, or beauty, is not independent of man?
Tagore: No.
Einstein: If there were no human beings any more, the Apollo Belvedere no longer would be beautiful?

Tagore: No.

Einstein: I agree with regard to this conception of beauty, but not with regard to truth.

Tagore: Why not? Truth is realized through men.

Here, according to a later account by Marianoff, there was a long pause. Then Einstein spoke again very quietly and softly: 'I cannot prove my conception is right, but that is my religion.'

After some further discussion – in which Einstein asserted, 'I cannot prove, but I believe in the Pythagorean argument, that the truth is independent of human beings', and Tagore, for his part, countered with a reference to Brahman, 'the absolute truth, which cannot be conceived by the isolation of the individual mind or described by words' – Einstein became concrete.

Einstein: The mind acknowledges realities outside of it, independent of it. For instance, nobody may be in the house, yet that table remains where it is.

Tagore: Yes, it remains outside the individual mind, but not the universal mind. The table is that which is perceptible by some kind of consciousness we possess.

Einstein: If nobody were in the house the table would exist all the same, but this is already illegitimate from your point of view, because we cannot explain what it means, that the table is there, independently of us. Our natural point of view in regard to the existence of truth apart from humanity cannot be explained or proved, but it is a belief nobody can lack – not even primitive beings. We attribute to truth a superhuman objectivity. It is indispensable for us – this reality which is independent of our existence and our experience and our mind – though we cannot say what it means.

Tagore: In any case, if there be any truth absolutely unrelated to humanity, then for us it is absolutely non-existing.

Einstein: Then I am more religious than you are!

Here, wrote Marianoff later, Einstein 'exclaimed in triumph'.

'A complete non-meeting of minds', Sir Isaiah Berlin said of this exchange. 'I do not believe that, apart from professions of mutual regard and the fact that Einstein and Tagore were both sincere and highly gifted and idealistic thinkers, there was much in common between them – although their social ideals may well have been very similar.' This is true, and is supported by the fact that Einstein in later years referred to Tagore punningly (and no doubt ironically) as 'Rabbi' Tagore. But equally true is that Einstein's basic view of sub-atomic nature has been abandoned by most quantum physicists, who have adopted a position that bears considerable resemblance to the one taken by Tagore.

About two months later, Marianoff, Margot Einstein and several others, including Tagore's Communist great-nephew Saumyendranath, accompanied Rabindranath to Moscow. He had wanted to visit the Soviet Union in 1926, despite warnings from western friends and the mess he had got himself into with Mussolini, but he had fallen ill. In 1928 he had written to his great-nephew (then in Moscow) that he wanted to come, health willing, primarily to understand how Russia was educating its peasantry. 'We will die if we cannot save our villages.' It remained his chief motive in September 1930.

On the Russian side, political advantage apart, there was a genuine demand for Tagore. We already know of Nicholas Roerich's admiration. As early as 1917, there were several Russian translations of *Gitanjali* (from English), one of them edited by Ivan Bunin, the first Russian Nobel laureate in literature. Leo Tolstoy's second son Ilya Tolstoy had translated Tagore; in 1918 he described him as one of the world's greatest living men. Konstantin Stanislavsky had wanted to produce Tagore's *King of the Dark Chamber* (the play that Wittgenstein admired), telling his actors, 'Rabindranath; Aeschylus – well, that's the real thing. This we cannot play but must attempt.' By the late 1920s most of Tagore's poetry and prose in English had been translated into Russian.

He reached Moscow at the moment when forty-eight professionals were executed without trial for supposed sabotage of the meat supply. Naturally, to welcome him 'there were speeches about abundance and the new humanism, and a splendid official reception', in the later sarcastic words of the revolutionary Victor Serge, who in 1930 was living in Moscow in precarious opposition to Stalin. Over the next two weeks, while his paintings went on show, Tagore was taken to many institutions in Moscow, educational, artistic and otherwise. A Pioneer Commune made a particular impression; photographs show him surrounded, grandfather-like, by a crowd of eager children. [pl.46] At the Moscow Arts Theatre, he saw a production of Tolstoy. At the Cinema Union, he asked to see Eisenstein's *Battleship Potemkin*. The director himself was away (in Hollywood), so his assistant and future wife Pera Atasheva acted as interpreter. This meant often looking at Rabindranath – which embarrassed her. His eyes shone 'with white fire' and it was 'simply impossible to resist his glance'. The film gripped him, Atasheva recalled. During the sailors' mutiny, Tagore turned to her and asked: 'Do they rise against the officers?' When she said yes, he remained silent for a minute and then pronounced 'firmly and with inner conviction': 'They are right.' During the Odessa steps sequence, when the czarist troops shoot the people, his face was tense and he clenched and unclenched his hands with excitement.

But he had little direct contact with party leaders, unlike in Italy in 1926, and unlike many western writers (such as Russell, Shaw and Wells). The most senior leader he met was the first deputy minister of foreign affairs. Perhaps Stalin and his cronies knew that they would not get from Tagore an unqualified endorsement of Bolshevism. No doubt they were aware of his very public change of mind about Mussolini's totalitarianism.

Immediately after he left Russia and in his 1931 *Russiar Chithi* (*Letters from Russia*), and also during his final years when he should certainly have known better, Tagore made some painfully misguided statements praising aspects of Russian Communism. He suppressed the memory of the doubts he had felt during his visit and forgot how little of the country he had seen, and, under-standably, he felt obliged to defend the Russian experiment as a counterweight to western propaganda against it and the Indian struggle.

His true views were given – courageously – on the spot and while his impressions were fresh, in an interview with *Izvestia* on the day he left Moscow. Here is a fair selection of extracts.

I wish to let you know how deeply I have been impressed by the amazing intensity of your energy in spreading education among the peasant masses, the most intelligent direction you have given to this work, and also the variety of channels that have been opened out to train their minds and senses and limbs . . . You have recognized the truth that in extirpating all social evils one has to go to the root . . . But I find here certain contradictions to the great mission which you have undertaken . . . I must ask you: Are you doing your ideal a service by arousing in the minds of those under your training anger, class-hatred, and revengefulness against those whom you consider to be your enemies? . . . Freedom of mind is needed for the reception of truth; terror hopelessly kills it . . . For the sake of humanity I hope that you may never cre-ate a vicious force of violence, which will go on weaving an interminable chain of violence and cruelty . . . You have tried to destroy many of the other evils of [the czarist] period. Why not try to destroy this one also?

The interview was published in the *Manchester Guardian*, three weeks later. It did not appear in *Izvestia* until mid-1988, nearly sixty years after it was given. Alexander Dubček read it and wanted to quote the passage about 'arousing class-hatred' in a speech in Italy, along with his own comment: 'These wise, profound – and, yes, prophetic – words retain their value today if one is talking about Czechoslovakia.' But in the end he was overcome by prudence. His words were printed instead in a British newspaper which remarked that Dubček's choice of thoughts from 'philosophers, sages and saints' constituted 'a think-ing-man's elegy for the dreams of the Prague Spring.'

Quite how deeply Tagore had been stirred by Russia is clear from a letter he wrote to his son from the USA on 31 October. Rathindranath had raised some estate matters. Invoking the dead Maharshi's name, Rabindranath replied that the family should no longer think of depending on income from the zamindari. For a long time, he said, he had felt 'ashamed' of being brought up as a 'parasite'; what he had just seen in Russia had strengthened his aversion. He went on to encourage Rathindranath to sell his share of No. 6 Dwarkanath Tagore's Lane. 'It will make us lighter', he wrote. Needless to say, nothing came of this suggestion.

This was plainly not the right frame of mind in which to raise funds in the United States. Once again, as in 1920–21 and 1929 – but unlike in 1916–17, the time of his outstanding lecture tour – Tagore and the USA were rubbing each other the wrong way. In 1930, however, there was huge interest in his activities. Apart from his striking looks and personality, India was in the news because of Gandhi, and Tagore's attitude to Soviet Russia had aroused curiosity; probably too, editors realized that this would be Tagore's last visit. In the sixty-seven days Tagore was in the USA, the *New York Times* ran twenty-one reports on him, including two interviews and a beautiful photograph of him with Einstein, captioned 'A mathematician and a mystic meet in Manhattan'. He was given a private interview with President Hoover, introduced by the British ambassador (a strange contrast with American and British official behaviour in 1917–18). When Tagore once more spoke at Carnegie Hall in New York, which held 4,000 people, thousands had to be turned away. A dance performance was given at the Broadway Theater by Ruth St Denis as a benefit for Shantiniketan; Tagore appeared on stage introduced by his admirer Will Durant. There were exhibitions of his paintings in New York and Boston, to which Ananda Coomaraswamy wrote an interesting introduction. But as a poet and writer, Tagore's stock had fallen low.

Before his ship had even docked, reporters invaded his cabin. 'To each question he gave full thought and bowed his head', wrote one of them. 'Then his very large, deep brown eyes would search out his questioner and the answer would be given in his high, resonant voice, each word clearly enunciated.' According to the *New York Times* on 10 October, under the headline 'Tagore, Here, Hails Advance in Russia' (with the sub-head, 'Scorns Home Rule Theory'),

> He recalled that ten years ago Russia and India were similarly situated, so far as the peasant classes were concerned, while today Russian peasants are bright and answer questions quickly. That is not so in India he said, and education is what must be given to her people before she can stand upon her own feet.
>
> Sir Rabindranath told of conditions among his people and scorned the theory of home rule or independence in the present state of illiteracy. No

country, he said, is capable of governing herself that has so long been in a state of subjugation.

Three days later the *Times* printed Tagore's correction:

Let it be definitely known that according to me it is the opportunity for self-government itself, which gives training for self-government and not foreign subjection, and that an appearance of peace superficially maintained from outside can never lead to real peace, which can only be attained through an inevitable period of suffering and struggle.

One has some sympathy with the reporters. The correction was still not the clearest of statements, and by no means a tasty 'sound-bite' of the kind that Gandhi sometimes produced. As Tagore wrote privately and piteously to his friend Ellery Sedgwick, editor of the *Atlantic Monthly*:

I do not know the technique of your public life and it tires me to be always on my guard. I am beginning to feel like a pedestrian from my country trying to walk in his own absent-minded manner in some busy street in New York . . . I only wish I could laugh at my misadventure, but that has become impossible even for an oriental philosopher owing to its extremely mischievous nature. I have come to the conclusion that the only place which is safe for the eastern simpleton is his own remote corner of obscurity.

The problem was not just that Tagore and the reporters were speaking two different languages. The misreporting of his statement reflected Tagore's own conflict about Indian home rule in late 1930. He had never emphasized the need for political freedom in India before: from 1931 onwards he did. Most likely it was his September exposure to Russia, where political changes in 1917 had made possible rapid progress in education in the 1920s, that had altered Tagore's thinking. Education *always* mattered more to him than politics, but now he recognized that he would have to behave more expediently to attain his real goal.

His unsettled mind was evident in a long letter he sent from the USA to the *Spectator* in London, published in mid-November. Tagore was responding to Gandhi's decision not to attend the Round Table Conference on India's future. Tagore wanted to regard the conference as a moral forum as much as, if not more than, a political one. He regretted that 'an opportunity had been lost' to stir the world's conscience. 'I believe that it would have been worthy of Mahatma Gandhi if he could have accepted unhesitatingly the seat offered to himself.' However, he said, he could not deny the voices of those in India, inspired by Gandhi's courage, who cried angrily to him: 'Stop that discussion about the future . . . let us, unarmed and resourceless, stand and defy the mighty power and say: "We fear thee not. We *do* need redress of our wrongs, but we need even more our self-respect which nobody outside our own selves can restore to us."' He concluded: 'Let me believe in his [Gandhi's] firmness of attitude, and not in my doubts.'

The same ambivalence appeared in an interview he gave to a Jewish newspaper on Zionism and the problem of Palestine. Here he downplayed the role of politics and emphasized that of culture, as he usually did – but without convincing the interviewer:

> I understand Zionism in the same sense as my great friend Einstein. I regard Jewish nationalism as an effort to preserve and enrich Jewish culture and tradition . . . I see that there is scepticism in your eyes and you think these the ramblings of a naive poet . . . The success of Zionism depends entirely upon Arab-Jewish cooperation. This can be obtained in Palestine only by means of a direct understanding between the Arabs and the Jews. If the Zionist leadership will insist on separating Jewish political and economic interests in Palestine from those of the Arabs ugly eruptions will occur in the Holy Land.

The Arab–Israeli clash was still to come, not so Communist repression. Tagore's praise for aspects of Soviet Russia upset Russian émigrés in the USA. Three of them, including Sergei Rachmaninoff and Ilya Tolstoy, Tagore's erstwhile admirer, wrote a long letter to the *New York Times*. Stating that Tagore 'is considered among the great living men of our age' whose 'voice is heard and listened to all over the world', they expressed their deep regret at his statements on Soviet Russia, just as the Italian dissident Salvadori had privately done in 1926 after Tagore had praised aspects of Mussolini's Italy. 'By his evasive attitude toward the Communist grave-diggers of Russia, by the quasi-cordial stand which he has taken toward them, he has lent strong and unjust support to a group of professional murderers.' They conceded, though, that Tagore might not be in possession of all the facts.

In lambasting American society and western civilization in general, Tagore had in the past used language of almost equal ferocity – in, for instance, *Nationalism*. Now, once more, he let fly, though with greater discrimination. At a dinner in New York in his honour arranged by Henry Morgenthau, in the presence of Franklin Roosevelt, the governor of New York, Sinclair Lewis, the latest Nobel laureate in literature (and the first American to win), and five hundred others, Tagore said: 'The age belongs to the West and humanity must be grateful to you for your science. But you have exploited those who are helpless and humiliated those who are unfortunate with this gift. A great portion of the world suffers from your civilization.' At Carnegie Hall a week later, he went even further. As always he expressed admiration for the ideals of liberty and self-expression of the West at the close of the nineteenth century, but he deplored its failure to live up to them in the East, in particular the failure of Americans to recognize the appeal of India to be free. 'Our appeal does not reach you, because you respond only to the appeal of power. Japan appealed to you and you answered because she was able to prove she would make herself as obnoxious as you can.' This remark 'elicited considerable laughter and hand-clapping', according to the *New York Times*.

It was his final message to the West in person. A month later, back in London getting ready to return to India, Tagore spoke to an influential gathering including George Bernard Shaw, organized by the *Spectator*. The League of Nations, he said, was well conceived in theory but mismanaged in practice because the national representatives were politicians. 'It is like organizing a band of robbers into a police department. I have travelled in different countries lately, and everywhere I have seen these very politicians – how they have bungled their peace conference and to what an end they have brought this great civilization.' Afterwards Tagore had a long talk with Shaw and they posed together – the two most renowned living writers – for a photograph showing off their distinctively different beards. [pl.52] Shaw appreciated Tagore better now; no longer did he see in him an Oriental Bluebeard. He told Tagore: 'We are the voices crying in the wilderness, you and I . . . I've always been telling my people not to listen to politicians. I have tried to do this in my own writings. But you know what uphill work it is to convince people against their own will.'

30   Against the Raj
(1931–1932)

Every individual Englishman in India, . . . whatever may be his character,
culture and capacity, cannot help being strongly obsessed by a sense of
almost personal ownership with regard to India.

Modern Review,
Calcutta, January 1933

Before he left New York in December 1930 Tagore had been given a copy of
a new book, *The Case For India*, that had been banned in Bengal. Its author
Will Durant had signed and inscribed it, 'You alone are sufficient reason why
India should be free.' Immediately he returned to India, Rabindranath published his review in the Calcutta *Modern Review*. It summarized his recent
experiences in the West and expressed his growing antipathy for British rule in
concise and forceful language.

'I have more than once had occasion to notice an outburst of irritation even
from some Americans at the idea of India ever dreaming of political severance
of [its] British connection', he wrote. 'It costs them nothing to think that we
Indians are innately and immutably different from themselves and that it would
be annoyingly absurd for us to aspire after the same human rights for which
they once had fought against their own brothers.' But Will Durant was different, Tagore said. Unlike other travellers such as Katherine Mayo – whom
Tagore did not name – Durant had treated Indians like fellow human beings.
'This has come to me as a surprise, for such courtesy is extremely rare today to
those people who have not the power to make themselves obnoxious.' (An echo
here of his speech at Carnegie Hall.) 'I am specially thankful to him [Durant]
for the service he has rendered to the English nation by largely quoting from its
own members the condemnation of British policy where it has cruelly betrayed
its responsibility to India; for after my recent disillusionment I sadly need con-
firmation of the faith I still wish to maintain in the rare magnanimity of soul in
those who are the true representatives of this great race.'

The sincerity of this faith – unfashionable as it was in nationalist India – was
clear from Tagore's interesting letter to the *Spectator* a few months later on the

C. F. Andrews, M. K. Gandhi and W. W. Pearson, in South Africa, 1914

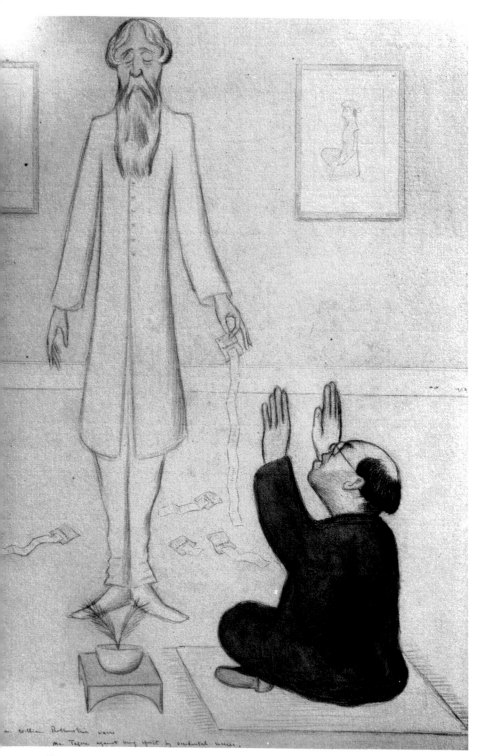

'Mr. William Rothenstein warns Mr. Tagore against being spoilt by occidental ccess.', 1913 (*Max Beerbohm*)

31 Rabindranath, August 1912 (*William Rothenstein*)

Rabindranath, in Calcutta, probably 1915 (*Johnston and Hoffmann*)

When I leave from hence let this be my parting word that what I have seen is unsurpassable. I have tasted of the hidden honey of this lotus yonder that expands on the ocean of light and thus am I blessed, let this be my parting word. In this playhouse of infinite forms I have had my play and here have I caught sight of him that eludes all forms. All my living body and limbs have thrilled with his touch who is beyond touch — and if the end comes here let it come — Let this be my parting . word.

33 *Gitanjali*, verse ninety-six:
top – original translation by Rabindranath in his hand
below – published verse revised by W. B. Yeats, pencilled on the back of a message form by Wilfred Owen, on the Somme, January 1917

Rabindranath, in Japan, 1916

Rabindranath, in the USA (Illinois), December 1916

subject of 'The colour bar'. Here he compared the insularity of Englishmen and Bengalis, thereby also shedding light, unintentionally, on his own aloof image when in Britain. On the Continent, he claimed, no one ever smiled at his costume as they did in London. As for mispronunciation of English by foreigners through no fault of their own, Englishmen felt 'not merely amused but positively irritated' by it. In the same way in India, he said, 'we in Bengal suffer from this imperfect adaptability of imagination which causes arrogance.' He put it down, not altogether convincingly, to Bengalis having lived in a remote corner of India for centuries – somewhat like the British in their island. 'The Bengali people are prone to keep themselves isolated when in unaccustomed surroundings, and they have an unenviable talent [for] making themselves unpopular with the people of other provinces of India.' Differences of colour only accentuated such mental rigidities, he said – as they had earlier in Indian history, during the Aryan invasions.

Though India desperately tried some kind of mechanical race adjustment, she has failed in giving birth to a living political organism owing to this abnormal caste consciousness that obstructs the stream of human sympathy and spirit of mutual cooperation. This is the reason why, in spite of the fact that India has produced a series of great minds, she has not produced a great organic history.

More and more in the 1930s Tagore would be concerned with this 'abnormal caste consciousness', both in Bengal and in India as a whole. With his acute sensitivity and worldwide experience, he perceived its insidiousness with greater clarity than any other Indian, Gandhi included. But for all his efforts he could do little to remove it – least of all in the area of religious differences. During mid-1931 there were more Hindu–Muslim atrocities, this time in many parts of Bengal, to the horror of Tagore. He appealed in the Calcutta press, 'to all God-fearing Mohammedans, for the sake of their own great religion and culture and for the sake of our bleeding humanity, to join hands with us in checking the evil which may grow . . . into a permanent source of futility bringing upon our unfortunate country the disgust and derision of the whole world.'

It was, however, the British–Indian relationship that preoccupied Tagore most during 1931–32. The 'dark chasm of aloofness' that he had mentioned to the Quakers in London stood starkly revealed in September 1931. Two Bengali political prisoners were shot dead and twenty others injured in disturbances at a detention camp in Hijli. The government stated that the prisoners had attacked their guards; nationalists assumed that the guards had attacked the prisoners. In the words of (Sir) Robert Reid, an Indian Civil Service officer in

Bengal at that time who wrote his memoirs in the 1960s, 'Those detained there were known by us to be terrorists, but intimidation of the public had become so effective and widespread that no one dared give evidence against them. They became violent, the camp guard had to fire, and two were killed.' Tagore's biographer Krishna Kripalani, by contrast, called the incident 'murder in cold blood'.

Rabindranath reluctantly agreed to appear at two public meetings about Hijli, one of them a huge outdoor rally of the kind frequent in Calcutta but which he had avoided since 1905. Rabindranath supported the nationalists unequivocally, referring to the 'homicidal callousness' of the guards and the 'humiliations and sufferings' of the 'victims'. 'Sheer rodomontade' replied the *Civil and Military Gazette* (Kipling's old paper), which was normally respectful of Tagore. Nehru, on the other hand, wrote to Gandhi, 'It has really been a terrible affair', after reading Tagore's speech. The outcry compelled the Bengal government to hold an inquiry, which found in favour of the guards. The truth of what happened will never be known.

Tagore's new public tone brought him closer to Gandhi after a decade of virtual estrangement. Though he would continue to disagree with Gandhi periodically in private, there were relatively few open conflicts between the two men in the last ten years of Tagore's life. They reached instead a kind of mutually beneficial accommodation. To what extent each was sincere is doubtful, but it was definitely useful to India as the political struggle intensified. At the very least each regarded the other as a giant, towering above any other living Indian. In Gandhi's case, this was proved by his actions in raising money to preserve Shantiniketan, both while Tagore lived and after he died.

On Gandhi's birthday, 2 October 1931, Tagore told a gathering at Shantiniketan (in Bengali):

This spirit of Mahatmaji's life has been infused into the whole country. It is chasing away our faintness . . . He has not allowed obstacles and dangers to stand in his way; his own mistakes have not dwarfed him; being in the midst of the excitement of the hour, his mind, rising above it yet retains its calm power of judgement. The man in whom resides this vast strength of character – it is him we salute on his birthday.

Gandhi for his part sent a fine message for Tagore's seventieth birthday, given here in full:

In common with thousands of his countrymen I owe much to one who by his poetic genius and singular purity of life has raised India in the estimation of the world. But I owe also more. Did he not harbour in Santiniketan the inmates of my Ashram who had preceded me from South Africa? The other ties and memories are too sacred to bear mention in a public tribute.

This was printed as the first contribution to *The Golden Book of Tagore*, a global anthology sponsored by Gandhi, Einstein, Romain Rolland, the scientist Sir Jagadishchandra Bose and the Greek poet Kostes Palamas, edited in Calcutta by Ramananda Chatterji. Most of the famous people who had personally known Tagore contributed, though often very briefly. In Bengal, money was collected – which Rabindranath requested be given to Bengali flood victims – and a fortnight's festival was arranged in his honour in Calcutta, at which his paintings were first seen in India. (The government churlishly refused to permit the use of the city's Eden Gardens, which were reserved for Europeans.)

On 4 January the celebrations were cut short: Gandhi, returning from the second Round Table Conference in London, had promptly been arrested. His request to meet the viceroy had been refused; the Indian government had decided to be tough with him and his movement.

Tagore felt profoundly frustrated. He cabled the prime minister Ramsay MacDonald protesting against 'the sensational policy of indiscriminate repression . . . causing permanent alienation of our people from yours'. To Indians he issued an emotional statement that censorship prevented from being fully published. It appeared in London instead, in a letter to the *Spectator*, that referred to a 'panic-stricken Government' and the 'primitive lawlessness of the lawmakers'. Tagore appealed to his countrymen for solidarity *and* restraint: to prove themselves 'morally superior' to the 'physically powerful'. The *Spectator*'s editor noted blandly that the government was not acting in panic and that it had a duty to keep order, and anyway Gandhi had welcomed his arrest – thus entirely missing Tagore's wood for Anglo-Indian trees.

He wrote a poem too, 'Prashna' (The Question):

God, you have sent messengers, life after life,
    To this callous earth;
They have said 'Forgive all sins', they have told us 'Love –
    From your heart all malice remove.'
They are venerable men, worthy of reverence, but we
In these dark days reject them with ritual futility.
I see secret violence under cover of darkness
    Slaughtering the helpless,
I see the just weeping in solitary silence,
    No power to protest, their only offence;

I see tender youths hitting out blindly
Cracking their heads against stones in their agony.
Today my voice is choked, my flute is without note,
    The prison of the no-moon night
Has extinguished my world, given me nightmares;
    And this is why I ask, through my tears –
Those who poison your air and blot out the sun,
Do you truly forgive them, do you truly love them?

There was no change in the Indian political situation for months. Gandhi
remained in prison; meanwhile Tagore left India for the last time in order to
visit Persia. Then, in early August, the London government announced the so-
called Communal Award: Hindus, Muslims and some other communities,
including Europeans and Untouchables, were to have separate electorates in the
constitutional reform of India. This was the demand of the Untouchable leader
B. R. Ambedkar. But to Gandhi (and to Tagore) it was anathema: Untouchables
– Harijans, as Gandhi called them, 'People of God' – were Hindus and must be
treated as such. Britain, with the connivance of Indians, must not be permitted
to divide the nation. In protest Gandhi announced that from 20 September he
would fast 'unto death' if the decision was not revoked.

Death was much on Rabindranath's mind at the time. On 8 August he heard
that he had lost his only grandson Nitindranath in Germany to tuberculosis.
Though he had been expecting it, the blow was most bitter. Among the letters of
sympathy were two from Britain: from Lord Irwin, the former viceroy, and from
Ramsay MacDonald. Thanking the prime minister from Shantiniketan on 24
September, Tagore added a PS: 'though I keep away from politics . . . I appeal to
you for the sake of humanity – do nothing to help the alienation of our country
[from] yours, to embitter the memory of our relationship for good.' That same
day, though in poor health, he set off on the long journey across India to Poona,
where Gandhi lay. The Mahatma's great fast was now entering its fifth day and
he was already frighteningly weak. The whole of India was tense.

When Tagore arrived, he was deeply stirred. 'I could hardly have fully realized how great is the strength of this frail man had I not come near to him like
this.' The jail authorities too were affected, and relaxed the usual regulations.
That afternoon a telegram finally arrived giving the British Cabinet's acceptance of a new arrangement between Gandhi, Ambedkar and other leaders, the
so-called Poona Pact. Gandhi agreed to break the fast by taking some orange
juice. But first Rabindranath was asked to sing one of his Bengali songs, the
Mahatma's particular favourite. It was from *Gitanjali*: 'When the heart is hard
and parched up, come upon me with a shower of mercy . . . ' Tagore duly sang

it, but not correctly, for he discovered he had forgotten the melody. Then followed a favourite Vaishnava hymn sung by members of Gandhi's ashram – and after that the Mahatma drank the orange juice. And then, at last, wrote the fifteen-year-old Indira Nehru, the squeezer of the oranges, in a letter to her jailed father Jawaharlal, 'we all went home – happy after an anxious day.'

31 The Great Sentinel
(1932–1933)

You ask others actively to devote their energy to extirpate the evil which
smothers our national life [Untouchability] and enjoin only upon yourself
an extreme form of sacrifice which is of a passive character.

letter to Mahatma Gandhi,
Shantiniketan, May 1933

Despite Tagore's active support for Gandhi's fast, their earlier differences
were not resolved, only suppressed in the interests of Indian unity. In
1921, as we know, Gandhi had dubbed Tagore 'The Great Sentinel'; now he
repeated the title in a letter to Boyd Tucker, an American missionary who knew
both men.

I do not regard my judgements as infallible and even though I may be right in
99 cases out of 100, I do not want to trade upon it and assume or expect other
people to assume that the 100th judgement is also right. I have for that reason
called Gurudev [Tagore] the great sentinel, and I have always appreciated his
warnings even when I have not been able to depart from my course by reason
of his warnings.

The root of the differences was twofold. Tagore believed educational and
cultural progress to be more worthwhile than political work. Secondly, he had
faith in cooperation with the West so that Indians might absorb its best aspects,
including its scientific knowledge. He instinctively rejected rejection.

These were the threads running through his multifarious activities during
the year that followed the fast. In September 1932, for instance, he wrote to
Leonard Elmhirst about a problem with one of the staff at Shriniketan, and
articulated his philosophy of village development:

I remember how you came fresh from your university and you were absurdly
young but you were not in the least academic or aridly intellectual. With your
instinctive humanity you came into the closest touch with the living being

which is the village . . . I who am no scientist, set more value upon this human side of our service than upon anything which is academic . . . The function of specialists . . . should be to serve the makers of history, the guides and lovers of men who, possessing the gift of imaginative understanding, can vitalize knowledge and make it acceptable to others.

In November he again took up the cudgels against Untouchability: what Gandhi now called 'this white ant' which must be 'touched at its source'. The Poona Pact between Gandhi and Ambedkar had changed nothing on the ground. If Hindu temples were not thrown open to Untouchables the Mahatma vowed a further fast. He focused on one major temple at Guruvayur in Kerala (south-west India), and appealed to Tagore to support him. But Rabindranath believed another fast too extreme an act, given that the September fast seemed to be taking effect nationwide. He tried to discourage Gandhi, yet he also wrote an impassioned appeal to the Zamorin of Calicut, a leading trustee of the Guruvayur temple. Untouchability, Tagore told him, was 'one of the darkest evils which degrade us in the estimation of the civilized world'. Gandhi's life simply could not be lost. 'Everlasting shame and ignominy will be our deserved fate if we fail . . . to uphold all that is pure and just in the great religious traditions of our country . . . We must not, we cannot fail to establish our spiritual integrity before the tribunal of world conscience'. (Soon after, and not by coincidence, George Bernard Shaw, calling at Bombay on a world cruise, remarked to Tagore in a letter: 'I step ashore for a few hours and wander about the streets and such temples as are open to European untouchables.')

The problem occupied Tagore for months (as it did Gandhi, who postponed the threatened fast for various reasons). In February 1933 he contributed a translation of a poem to the first issue of *Harijan*, Gandhi's new journal on Untouchability. The poem was by Satyendranath Datta, its title was 'Scavenger'.

Why do they shun your touch, my friend,
      and call you unclean
Whom cleanliness follows at every step . . . ?

Later that year he wrote *Chandalika* (The Untouchable Maid), a drama based on an old Buddhist legend. It was staged in Calcutta in September.

He also spoke twice in February on the 'untouchability' of Rammohun Roy; 1933 being the centenary of Roy's death. As ever, Rabindranath's reverence for Rammohun tended to get the better of his judgement. Nevertheless he made some powerful observations that also applied to himself: 'Rammohun was . . . rudely rejected by his country which refused to be reminded of the responsibility of its great inheritance while clinging with desperate infatuation to its degeneracy . . . It was a lonely life, but it had for its comrades the noble path-seekers who preceded him in India . . . We have the right to hope for the best when we know that Rammohun has been born to us.'

In March he gave one of his best speeches – this time in Bengali not English – on the subject closest to his heart: education. Here too the idea of untouchability found its way in. The so-called educated classes had come to regard themselves as a completely separate caste, he said, by virtue of having been taught only in English; they looked down upon the rest of India as 'untouchables'. To them, the word 'country' had come to mean the educated classes only, 'as if a peacock were all feathers or an elephant all tusks.' At one time, he reminded his audience, a wife could not go about in society in a sari without loss of prestige. 'Similarly, even now many of us think that our "prestige" will suffer if the goddess of education is clothed in a sari, though it is well known that she will find it comfortable to move about our homes in this dress and that she will very probably stumble at every step if she has to put on high-heeled shoes.' Around this time, in cooperation with Calcutta University, Tagore began to collect synonyms for English scientific words in the major Indian languages. He published a letter in the *Times of India* appealing for information from readers throughout India.

He appealed too, in April, for the establishment of 'fully equipped Information Centres' in the West, to counteract propaganda about India. He had already experienced plenty of misquotation of his interviews and writings, both unintentional and deliberate (as in *Mother India*). Now two books, in French and Italian, had been drawn to his notice by European friends, in which he had been made to belittle Gandhi with invented quotes. At a less subtle level he recalled a photograph of a Parsee Tower of Silence he had seen in a newspaper in Argentina, with a caption saying that in these towers living bodies of heretics were offered to kites and vultures by Hindus – a practice that the British government was trying to suppress, the caption-writer said. To fight these lies, Tagore concluded, 'mere sporadic oratorical displays or casual visits in foreign lands by gifted individuals can never have any lasting effect.'

And Tagore was drawn directly into politics for a brief period in mid-1933, as he had been during the Hijli shootings two years earlier. This time the issue was convicted terrorists (many of them Bengalis) held in the Andaman Islands – the Indian equivalent of Devil's Island. They began a hunger strike in protest against their conditions. Tagore requested them by cable to desist while he and others made efforts to have their grievances considered. They did not, and three of them subsequently perished. Tagore and some sixty other prominent

Indians including Nehru now signed a reasoned statement requesting more humane treatment of the prisoners. The request was refused by a government determined to stamp out terrorism; Tagore and the others were referred to sarcastically as 'miscellaneous signatures'.

But of all the aspects of Tagore's life in the year or so following Gandhi's 1932 fast, the most fascinating was his reaction to Gandhi's second fast in May 1933. The first fast Tagore had faith in, albeit with a trembling heart; the second, which lasted twenty-one days (though not in prison), he felt to be misguided. He supported it only under great duress. Most of those around Gandhi, including his long-suffering wife, agreed with Tagore.

Why this switch in attitude? The answer lay in Gandhi's stated purpose for each fast. In September 1932, Gandhi wanted to move the hearts of millions of Hindus who clung to an immoral belief; in May 1933, he said: 'The fast is intended to remove bitterness, to purify hearts and to make it clear that the movement [against Untouchability] is wholly moral, to be prosecuted by wholly moral persons . . . Whether I survive the fast or not, is a matter of little moment. Without it I would, in all probability, have been useless for further service of Harijans, and for that matter, any other service.'

This seemed wrong to Rabindranath. Both he and Gandhi were inspired by the *Isopanishad*, but whereas Gandhi believed in 'renounce and rejoice', Tagore put the phrase the other way round. Gandhi's second fast, entirely ascetic and cathartic in principle, therefore made little appeal to Tagore: he saw it, at root, as life-denying not life-affirming. And its potentially disastrous consequences for India frightened him.

On 11 May, three days into the fast, after reading Gandhi's reasons in the press, Tagore wrote him a rational and heartfelt letter, so masterly it is worth quoting *in toto*.

Dear Mahatmaji

I am trying clearly to find out the meaning of this last message of yours which is before the world today. In every important act of his life Buddha preached limitless love for all creatures. Christ said 'Love thine enemies' and that teaching of his found its final expression in the words of forgiveness he uttered for those who killed him. As far as I can understand, the fast that you have started carries in it the idea of expiation for the sins of your countrymen. But I ask to be excused when I say that the expiation can truly and heroically be done only by daily endeavours for the sake of those unfortunate beings who do not know what they do. The fasting which has no direct action upon the conduct of misdoers and which may abruptly terminate one's power further to serve those who need help, cannot be universally accepted and therefore it is all the more unacceptable for any individual who has the responsibility to represent humanity.

The logical consequences of your example, if followed, will be the elimination of all noble souls from the world leaving the morally feeble and downtrodden multitude to sink into the fathomless depth of ignorance and iniquity. You have no right to say that this process of penance can only be efficacious through your own individual endeavour and for others it has no meaning. If that were true you ought to have performed it in absolute secrecy as a special mystic rite which only claims its one sacrifice beginning and ending in yourself. You ask others to actively devote their energy to extirpate the evil which smothers our national life and enjoin only upon yourself an extreme form of sacrifice which is of a passive character. For lesser men than yourself it opens up an easy and futile path of duty by urging them to take a plunge into a dark abyss of self mortification. You cannot blame them if they follow you in this special method of purification of their country, for all messages must be universal in their application and if not they should never be expressed at all.

The suffering that has been caused to me by the vow you have taken has compelled me to write to you thus – for I cannot bear the sight of a sublimely noble career journeying towards a finality which, to my mind, lacks a perfectly satisfying justification. And once again I appeal to you for the sake of the dignity of our nation which is truly impersonated in you, and for the sake of millions of my countrymen who need your living truth and help to desist from any act that you think is good only for you and not for the rest of humanity.

With deepest pain and love
Rabindranath Tagore

The Great Sentinel had sent his message. The Mahatma, however, was deaf to all pleas.

Early next year, they clashed again. On 15 January 1934, a huge earthquake struck Bihar, the state adjacent to Bengal, in the area north of Patna. There were high casualties and massive destruction. Tagore was in Shantiniketan, Gandhi on tour in south India fighting Untouchability. (Nehru at Allahabad could hardly keep his balance). On 24 January, after calm reflection, Gandhi stated publicly that the earthquake and Untouchability were linked. 'You may call me superstitious if you like. A man like me cannot but believe that this earthquake is a divine chastisement sent by God for our sins.'

Tagore read the statement in the newspapers and immediately wrote to Gandhi enclosing his response for publication – if, that is, Gandhi truly held the view reported. Almost by return Gandhi sent his 'considered opinion'. If after reading it Tagore still wanted to print his piece, it could be published at once, he said. He admitted that 'we have come upon perhaps a fundamental difference. But I cannot help myself. I do believe that super-physical consequences flow from physical events. How they do so, I do not know.'

On 16 February both pieces appeared in *Harijan*. It was an exchange between these two Himalayan personalities that ranked with that of their classic 1921 exchange on non-cooperation. There is a compelling quality similar to that of the Tagore–Einstein conversations in 1930. But, ironically, in 1934 Tagore seemed to take a position close to that of Einstein, who in his contribution to the 1931 *Golden Book of Tagore* wrote objectively: 'Man defends himself from being regarded as an impotent object in the course of the Universe. But should the lawfulness of happenings, such as unveils itself more or less clearly in inorganic nature, cease to function in front of the activities in our brain?' Gandhi said yes, it must; Tagore said no, it cannot.

Tagore wrote:

If we associate ethical principles with cosmic phenomena, we shall have to admit that human nature is morally superior to Providence that preaches its lessons in good behaviour in orgies of the worst behaviour possible. For, we can never imagine any civilized ruler of men making indiscriminate examples of casual victims, including children and members of the Untouchable community, in order to impress others dwelling at a safe distance who possibly deserve severer condemnation . . . The law of gravitation does not in the least respond to the stupendous load of callousness that accumulates till the moral foundation of our society begins to show dangerous cracks and civilizations are undermined . . . We feel perfectly secure in the faith that our own sins and errors, however enormous, have not enough force to drag down the structure of creation to ruins. We can depend upon it, sinners and saints, bigots and breakers of convention.

Gandhi replied:

Knowledge of the tallest scientist or the greatest spiritualist is like a particle of dust . . . I have not the faith which Gurudev [Tagore] has that 'our sins and errors, however enormous, have not enough force to drag down the structure of creation to ruins.' On the contrary I have the faith that our own sins have more force to ruin that structure than any mere physical phenomenon. There is an indissoluble marriage between matter and spirit. Our ignorance of the results of the union makes it a profound mystery and inspires awe in us, but it cannot undo them. But a living recognition of the union has enabled many to use every physical catastrophe for their own moral uplifting.

With me the connection between cosmic phenomena and human behaviour is a living faith that draws me nearer to my God, humbles me and makes me readier for facing him. Such a belief would be a degrading superstition, if out of the depths of my ignorance I used it for castigating my opponents.

Nehru read Gandhi's response to the earthquake 'with a great shock'. He called it 'a staggering remark'. 'Anything more opposed to the scientific outlook it would be difficult to imagine', he wrote in his *Autobiography* in 1936. He welcomed Tagore's response and 'wholly agreed' with it.

Gandhi suffered vilification in India after his statement, though for reasons far more to do with his unflinching criticism of Hindu orthodoxy than for his unscientific outlook. Tagore knew the experience only too well. Despite his irreconcilable opposition to Gandhi on the earthquake, he immediately issued a statement supporting him. 'To one really great, the ready adulation as well as the cheap sneers of the mob mean very little and I know Mahatmaji carries that greatness with him.' Though as an artist and a Bengali Tagore would never be able to acquire Gandhi's thick skin, the words were as true of the Great Sentinel as they were of the Mahatma.

32   Last Travels
(1932–1937)

Do not dismiss me off cheaply with promises of memorial meetings when I
am no longer amongst you, offer me succour even now when I sorely need it.
reply to the Citizens' Address,
Delhi, March 1936

Tagore's halcyon days of travelling were over. He was more than seventy
years old and by no means in strong health, battered by the rigours of the
Bengal climate. But a combination of *Wanderlust* – a word that might have been
coined for Rabindranath – and a crying need of funds for his university Visva-
Bharati, kept him on the move. In 1932, he visited Persia and Iraq; in 1934
Ceylon; in between and after he toured India with his Shantiniketan dance
troupe. As late as 1937, aged seventy-six, he still contemplated a return to the
West: a New York theatrical agent wanted him to lecture in the USA.

The invitation to Persia came from Reza Shah Pahlavi, the modernizing ruler
who had seized power in 1925. Tagore felt inclined to accept for several reasons.
The language and literature of Persia was part of the heritage of Bengal,
courtesy of the Muslim and later Mughal conquest of the region; a significant
proportion of Bengali words, some 3,000, were of Persian origin; Rammohun
Roy, Rabindranath's mentor, and other Hindus of that time had been fluent in
Persian. Though Tagore did not know the language, he had some familiarity
with Persian legends and poetry, especially Hafiz, both in translation and in the
original. (His father Debendranath knew Persian and read Hafiz to the boy
Rabi.) Undoubtedly he was susceptible to the atmosphere of desert life, witness
his early poem about being an Arab Bedouin and his subsequent references to
it, his love of *The Arabian Nights*, and his translation in 1932 of T. S. Eliot's
'The Journey of the Magi'. He was curious to see how Persian tradition was
mixing with the westernizing impulse of Reza Shah. At a practical level, he
hoped that the Persian ruler would endow the chair in Persian studies at Visva-
Bharati that the miserly Aga Khan had failed to endow in 1930. (This time he
would not be disappointed.)

But there remained the problem of how to get to Persia during April, the hot part of the year. Trains and steamers were too stressful for an old poet. Instead of these he went by the Dutch Air Mail, hopping from Calcutta to Allahabad to Jodhpur to Karachi to Jask on the Makran Coast and finally landing at Bushire after two days, fussed over all the way. At Jodhpur the maharaja, a well-known aviator, installed Tagore at his hotel specially built for air-passengers; at Karachi there were Bengali dishes specially prepared by a Bengali lady resident in the city. It was his second flight by aeroplane; the first was from London to Paris in 1921. 'But then I had no special ties with the place from which the ascent was made, so that nothing in the land and water there held me down. This time I had to snap the bonds of my own Bengal, and my heart felt the wrench.'

Despite the 'intolerable din' of the propellers, and the cotton wool stuffed in his ears, Rabindranath enjoyed the experience. It sprang from him a rare tribute to technology, stated, of course, in Tagorean terms. The aeroplane made him feel inferior, he said. It seemed a divine creation, like the air-chariot of Lord Indra in the epics on which mortals like King Dushyanta were occasionally given rides. 'The inventors of the aeroplane belong to a different race', he asserted. 'Had their achievement been merely a matter of superior skill, I would not have been so affected, but it denoted superior force of character – an indomitable perseverance, unflagging courage – things to be really proud of. For these I salute them.'

But he was also quick to grasp the dark side of flying. The aloofness of the slayer from the slain horrified him more than most men. At Baghdad he met a Christian chaplain to the British air-force, which was engaged in bombing operations against some Iraqi villages. Tagore commented grimly: 'So dim and insignificant do those unskilled in the modern arts of killing appear to those who glory in such skill!' When the official priest of the Iraqi air-force asked him for a message he wrote (in part):

From the beginning of our days man has imagined the seat of divinity to be in the upper air, from which comes light, and blows the breath of life, for all the creatures of this earth. The peace of its dawn, the splendour of its sunset, the voice of eternity in its starry silence, have inspired countless generations of men with a sense of the ineffable presence of the infinite, urging their minds away from the sordid interests of daily life . . . If, in an evil moment, man's cruel history should spread its black wings to invade that realm of divine dreams with its cannibalistic greed and fratricidal ferocity, then God's curse will certainly descend upon us for such hideous desecration, and the curtain will finally be rung down upon the world of Man, for whom God feels ashamed.

Tagore had read up on the imperial games of power being played in Iran and Iraq, but they did not much interest him. What touched him in Persia was the warmth of his reception and the artistic glories. At Bushire the crowds accepted him as a poet, even though, unlike in Europe, they knew nothing of his poetry: 'nothing stands in the way of their clothing me with their own idea of what a poet should be.' At Shiraz, the home of Hafiz, he spent a week and paid homage at the poet's tomb. From Shiraz he was driven via Persepolis and Isfahan to Teheran. There he told an audience that the great ruins and the great mosques he had just seen, with their paintings and frescoes, were 'the homage of humanity to the Great Poet; the answer of man to God's call of love.' He was hailed in Teheran as 'the greatest star shining in the eastern sky' and his seventy-first birthday (6 May) was celebrated with oriental lavishness. He, for his part, composed a poem in honour of Reza Shah Pahlavi.

In Baghdad, after meeting King Feisal, he had his chance, at long last, to be a Bedouin: he spent a day in a Bedouin encampment in the desert. In his diary he commented that his own life 'as a son of riverine Bengal' and the life of an illiterate Bedouin chief, 'his every moment a struggle for existence', were as far apart as two lives could be. Then the chief told him, 'Our Prophet has said that a true Muslim is he by whose words and deeds not the least of his brother-men may ever come to any harm.' Tagore noted: 'I was startled into recognizing in his words the voice of essential humanity.' However he told his host that his taste of Bedouin hospitality was incomplete; to round it off, he must see something of the Bedouins operating as highwaymen. The chief smiled and said courteously: 'Ah, there is a snag. Our robbers do not lay hands on the old and the wise. That is why when merchants pass through our regions with their loads of precious merchandise, they often dress up a wise-looking man of advanced years as the leader of the caravan.' [pl.42]

The cumulative result of Rabindranath's Persian experience was a sensuously coloured poem-painting, signed 'Baghdad May 24 1932'. [pl.43] The poem appears, genie-like, inside an orange-and-red puff of smoke that hovers beside a dark and enigmatic shrine (or is it a lamp?) crowned with a glowing sun-like disc. The poem is written first in Bengali, then in English:

> The night has ended.
> Put out the light of the lamp
>   of thine own narrow corner
>   smudged with smoke.
> The great morning which is for all
>   appears in the East.
> Let its light reveal us to each other
>   who walk on the same path
>   of pilgrimage.

Tagore's visit to Ceylon in May 1934 was likewise part-pilgrimage and part-fund-raising tour. He had been there twice before, in 1922 and 1928, attracted by the Buddhist heritage of the island, but now he travelled with a group of Shantiniketan students trained to dance by himself and his daughter-in-law Pratima (wife of Rathindranath). They were to perform *Shapmochan* (Redemption), Tagore's dance-drama on a mythological theme: the misadventure of Urvashi, celestial dancer at the court of Indra, the lord of the gods. In the late 1920s and 1930s, Tagore wrote a number of dance-dramas that remain popular in Calcutta and have also been appreciated in the West. The dancing was based on various north Indian styles, notably Manipuri dance. (Manipur is the Indian state wedged between Bangladesh and Burma.) 'Rabindrik' dance was bright-hued, soft, willowy and feminine to the point of feebleness. As a contemporary Bengali critic noted approvingly, Tagore's dance-dramas were 'entirely free from voluptuousness and sensuality'. To some extent this was Tagore's personal wish, the way he visualized the ideal woman; to some extent it was his pragmatic response to what Bengali society would accept from a respectable girl who appeared on stage; to a great extent it was part of a widespread public reaction to the debasement of dancing into prostitution (the nautch girls of notoriety). For centuries until the 1920s no Indian woman danced in public who was not also a prostitute. Tagore changed that in Bengal with his dance-dramas. Unfortunately he did not go further and draw upon the richness of classical Indian dance, especially south Indian *Bharata Natyam*, as he had done with classical music. This was in contrast to Uday Shankar, the pioneer of modern Indian dance, whose performances, both in India and in the West, had vigour and strength, as well as colour and charm. Tagore's dance-dramas were the weakest part of his artistic achievements.

Nevertheless, when danced by beautiful Bengali girls and rehearsed by Tagore himself, the dance-dramas had considerable grace and refinement. (Among the western admirers of dancing in Shantiniketan was (Sir) Oswald Mosley, who visited the ashram in the 1920s.) *Shapmochan* was a hit in Colombo in 1934. The Oxford-educated cosmopolitan S. W. R. D. Bandaranaike, later prime minister of Ceylon, managed to get a seat at the performance on the Buddha's birthday, and reviewed it for the *Ceylon Daily News*. He was not expecting much, not being one of Tagore's admirers, but he wrote:

> The curtain went up, and my first impression was one of aesthetic satisfaction at the setting and the grouping, which had the simplicity and the beauty which Greek drama alone has yet been able to achieve. There was Tagore seated at one end, appropriately garbed in a yellow robe, a typical bard and seer with his flowing grey hair and beard. The first thing that struck me

was the beauty of his shapely hands and the long tapering fingers: only a great artist could have hands like that . . .

Love and wrath and sorrow and joy and chivalry – all human emotions find their place in this play, and the delicate and sure touch with which they are conveyed by the music and dancing is a revelation of art at its highest . . .

It is interesting to note that W. B. Yeats, to whom perhaps Tagore owes more than to any other individual for the recognition of his art, has himself published a volume of plays, *Four Plays for Dancers*, of a similar type. They possess a strange beauty of their own . . . But anyone reading them will be struck by the great superiority of Tagore.

Bandaranaike mentioned his special admiration for Tagore at the moment in the singing when a waiter suddenly dropped a tray with a great clatter – 'Beyond a slight twitch, he remained immobile, although it must have been torture to him' – and closed his review by supporting the idea of sending pupils to Shantiniketan to train in music and dancing.

The link had been made already. Tagore had come to Colombo at the invitation of Wilmot Perera, a Ceylonese who had stayed in Shantiniketan in 1932. Returning home inspired, like some Ceylonese Leonard Elmhirst, Perera had founded an institute for rural reconstruction, the first in Ceylon. On his 1934 visit Rabindranath named it Sri Palee ('Where beauty reigns'). The institution, now supported by the government, still functions.

Financially, though, Tagore's visit was a disaster. And the same was true of his tours in India. He received, in his own words, 'casual donations collected at the risk of my health and of an utter neglect of my vocation as a literary man.' Visva-Bharati was a difficult animal to make appealing to donors – more like a mythical beast, a white elephant, than a creature of recognizable pedigree – and Rabindranath loathed fund-raising. His letters of the 1920s and 30s were littered with piteous comments on his failures in this area. In 1935, he told Nehru: 'It is a hateful trial for me – this begging business either in the guise of entertaining people or appealing to the generosity of those who are by no means generous. I try to exult in a sense of martyrdom accepting the thorny crown of humiliation and futility without complaining.' His son told an amusing story that summed up the whole sorry business. In Geneva, in 1930, a business friend of Tagore (the same person who knew the Aga Khan) introduced him to the Gaekwad of Baroda, one of India's richest princes. Over lunch an absorbing conversation got underway – so absorbing that Tagore forgot all about money. Rathindranath wrote:

At last Father noticed the look of alarm in our faces and abruptly told the maharaja of his mission, and wound up his appeal for funds with the advice that if the maharaja did decide to give any money to him, he should do it as though he were throwing it into the water. On hearing this my friend gave me a hard kick under the table. The maharaja kept silent and left without making any promise.

By mid-1935, the situation was desperate. Only one person seemed capable of rescuing Visva-Bharati. At the insistence of C. F. Andrews, Tagore put his pride in his pocket and wrote to Gandhi. Owing to some 'deficiency' in himself, he said, his appeals did not find 'adequate response in the heart of my people'. His health was being wrecked by 'constant begging excursions with absurdly meagre results'. Gandhi replied immediately: 'You may depend upon my straining every nerve to find the required money . . . It is unthinkable that you should have to undertake another begging mission at your age. The necessary funds must come to you without your having to stir out of Santiniketan.' He pleaded for time.

In March 1936, they met in Delhi, where Rabindranath had come with his troupe 'to hunt the golden stag' (as he put it in a joky letter to an American friend). At seventy-five, he was truly exhausted by the travelling and performing. Gandhi, moved by his plight, persuaded the businessman G. D. Birla to provide an anonymous donation of Rs. 60,000, Visva-Bharati's outstanding debt. (This was roughly the same amount Tagore had raised in just *one* meeting in 1905 for the National Fund, much less than that in real terms. If only Tagore had permitted himself to become a 'patriot'!) Gandhi sent the cheque to Tagore with a note:

Dear Gurudev
    God has blessed my poor effort. And here is the money. Now
you will relieve the public mind by announcing cancellation of the
rest of the programme. May God keep you for many a year to come.
                                        Yours with love,
                                        M. K. Gandhi

But of course that was by no means the end of the matter. Not only did Visva-Bharati continue to need money, but Tagore felt humiliated by his dependence on Gandhi. He would not let anyone, not even the Mahatma, 'put a chain on his feet' (the phrase he used to his daughter at the lowest point of his American visit in 1920–21). The conflict burst into the open in February 1937 when Tagore asked Gandhi to be a trustee of Visva-Bharati, and Gandhi felt obliged to refuse for lack of time, adding, with a touch of sternness, that he had heard that

Rabindranath was about to go 'on a begging expedition' to Ahmedabad (Gandhi's home territory) 'in spite of your promise to me in Delhi'. Both men had employed the word 'begging' before, but now Gandhi's use of it was like a spark to gunpowder. Tagore wrote heatedly:

Allow me to be frank . . . and to tell you that possibly your own temperament prevents you [from understanding] the dignity of the mission which I am glad to call my own – a mission that is not merely concerned with the economic problem of India, or her sectarian religions, but which comprehends the culture of the human mind in its broadest sense. And when I feel the urge to send abroad some poetical creation of mine, which according to me carries within it a permanent standard of beauty, I expect, not alms or favour, but grateful homage to my art from those who have the sensitiveness of soul to respond to it. And if I have to receive contribution in the shape of admission fees from the audience, I claim it as very much less than what is due to me in return for the rare benefit conferred upon them. Therefore I must refuse to accept the term 'begging expedition' as an accurate or worthy expression coming from your pen.

Gandhi had never much cared for Tagore's artistic creations, just as Tagore could never appreciate Gandhi's utilitarian approach to education. In almost every department of life they differed profoundly. Yet something held these two giants together, something higher than the patriotic duties of the time, some universal human affinity akin to that which Tagore had intuited when talking to the Bedouin chief near Baghdad. In the final analysis it transcended their vast differences. Within a few weeks they made up; later in 1937 Gandhi procured some more funds for Visva-Bharati; and in 1940, he agreed to Tagore's request that he take on the needs of the institution after the poet's death.

Though Tagore's lofty manifesto to Gandhi was a bit pompous, it was achingly sincere. When the urge to create was upon him, he *had* to indulge it: it was his *jiban-debata* ('life-god'). If he did not, his health took a turn for the worse. This put his long-suffering son Rathindranath in a quandary. It was he who had planned the visit to Ahmedabad mentioned by Gandhi, in order to raise money for the music and dance departments at Visva-Bharati. The idea was to go *without* Rabindranath. 'But you know how it is with him', Rathindranath told C. F. Andrews, almost pathetically.

Whenever we try to render one of his plays or operas he will begin composing new songs or write a new play, attend the rehearsals and insist on accompanying the players. Is there anybody who can suppress the artist in him? In consideration of his health we have sometimes stopped rehearsals of these performances or seasonal festivals – but the results have been disastrous. There is nothing that keeps up his spirits (and his health) at Santiniketan as the atmosphere of art and music. Can we deprive him of this sustenance? I have been brutally attacked in the press – but what is the use of explaining? Who, in our country, will understand the life of an artist?

33 Shantiniketan in the Thirties (1931–1940)

That education is a living, not a mechanical process, is a truth as freely admitted as it is persistently ignored.

lecture,
Calcutta, February 1936

In February 1940, Mahatma Gandhi paid his last visit to Shantiniketan while Tagore lived, a quarter century after his first. There were long and sympathetic talks between the two men, a special ceremony in the mango grove with Rabindranath present, followed by a tour of the institution without him. In all the visit lasted two days. As Gandhi came to depart, Tagore placed a letter in his hands. It read, in part:

> Accept this institution under your protection, giving it an assurance of permanence if you consider it to be a national asset. Visva-Bharati is like a vessel which is carrying the cargo of my life's best treasure, and I hope it may claim special care from my countrymen for its preservation.

In his reply, written on the train to Calcutta, Gandhi affectionately accepted the responsibility. He added: 'Though I have always regarded Santiniketan as my second home, this visit has brought me nearer to it than ever before.' [pl.48]

What kind of institution was it that Tagore had created after nearly forty years of effort? Did it deserve such an accolade from its founder, seemingly ranking it as high as his artistic achievements ('a vessel which is carrying the cargo of my life's best treasure')? On the basis of what has been said of it so far, one might think – surely not.

Shantiniketan and its institutions in Tagore's time are not easy to assess. Much can be said against them, backed by solid evidence. Evidence in their favour is harder to quantify. It is interesting, therefore, to know the views of the university's two most distinguished alumni, Satyajit Ray and Indira Gandhi.

Ray was in Shantiniketan from 1940 to 1942, studying fine art. In 1982, he said in a lecture in Calcutta:

To be quite honest, I had no wish to go [there] at all. The few Santiniketanites that I got to know – usually painters and musicians – all had long hair, and spoke Bengali in a strange affected sing-song. One took this to be the Santiniketan accent. Well, such accent and such people put me off, and I thought – if this is what Santiniketan did to you, I had no use for that place.

It was his mother, constantly encouraged by Tagore, who persuaded him to go. 'I think [she] believed that proximity to Rabindranath would have a therapeutic effect on me, such as a visit to a hill station or health resort has on one's system.'

But in his final testimony on Shantiniketan, the last English writing he published before his death in 1992, Ray said simply:

I consider the three years I spent in Santiniketan as the most fruitful of my life. This was not so much because of the proximity of [Rabindranath] . . . It was just that Santiniketan opened my eyes for the first time to the splendours of Indian and Far Eastern art. Until then I was completely under the sway of western art, music and literature. Santiniketan made me the combined product of East and West that I am. As a film maker I owe as much to Santiniketan as I do to American and European cinema. And when I made my first film *Pather Panchali* and embellished it with rural details which I was encountering for the first time, Tagore's little poem in my autograph album came back again and again to my mind.

This eight-line poem, written for the eight-year-old Satyajit on an earlier visit to Shantiniketan in 1929, is untranslatable. Ray paraphrased it thus: 'I have spent a fortune travelling to distant shores and looked at lofty mountains and boundless oceans, and yet I haven't found time to take a few steps from my house to look at a single dew drop on a single blade of grass.' [pls55, 56]

Indira Gandhi spent less than a year at Shantiniketan, in 1934–35, when she was in her mid-teens. She would have stayed longer, but she had to accompany her ailing mother for treatment abroad. She, like Ray, was western-oriented in outlook, and was sent there somewhat against her will by her father Jawaharlal Nehru. Nehru had visited and talked to Tagore in January 1934, during one of his spells out of jail. [pl.49] Some relatives and family friends had warned Indira's mother against the university's accommodation, the food, the summer heat and the exclusive Bengali atmosphere – but, Indira noticed, they had not visited the place: others who had stayed there, seemed to love it. One of the devotees offered her an empty cottage in Shantiniketan; if she took a servant with her, Indira wrote to her father (who was now back in jail), she could live in the cottage and avoid the hostel and its food. Nehru was strongly disapproving:

'It is better not to go to a place than to go as a superior person . . . Do not be prejudiced before even you go to S.N. It has its faults but it has its good points also and I think the latter far outweigh the former.' She must join in with the other girls, he said; it would be good for her. He cited his own experience of public school in England (sublimely inapposite though it was in the context of Tagore's ashram!):

> Do you know what I had to put up with at Harrow? We never had a full meal at school unless we bought it for ourselves. As junior boys we had to wait on the seniors as fags, get their goods, clean their places up, sometimes clean their boots, carry messages for them, etc., and be continually sworn at by them and sometimes beaten.

On her very first day in Shantiniketan Indira was horrified that some of the non-Bengali girls in her dormitory had not had anything to eat. They told her that whenever they asked about food, the older girls deliberately replied in Bengali, even though they knew English and Hindi. So the new arrivals did not know where the dining room was or when meals were served. Indira, being a Nehru, rushed straight to Tagore's house and brought fruits and other things to tide these girls over till the next mealtime. [pl.54]

Her letters to her father from Shantiniketan contain other criticisms; the food, in particular, was never satisfactory. But overall Indira was happy there, pleased to escape the topsy-turvy existence of her family life for a while. (One of the staff, a German, fell in love with her, which she did not tell her father.) Looking back not long after she left the place, she already believed that Shantiniketan had influenced her deeply. In later years, when she was prime minister of India and chancellor of Visva-Bharati, she adhered to this without finding clear words to describe the influence. Unlike Satyajit Ray, Indira Nehru was affected more by Tagore the man than by his works (and the same was true of her father). In 1982 she said:

> I was so interested in all the aspects of Gurudev's personality, not just as a poet – he was even painting at that time – but in his vision in general. So many things are fashionable today but were unheard of in those days, were all there in Gurudev. For example, the environment and concern over the environment . . . Gurudev was working for it at Shantiniketan and Sriniketan [the 'institute for rural reconstruction']. I was absorbing all those things when living there. They became a part of me. Now whether they were already in me and the place helped to bring them out or whether I had got them from the place itself I cannot tell . . . I think what I learnt most at Shantiniketan

was the ability to live quietly within myself no matter what was happening outside. This has always helped me to survive.

Such inner development – confined to a handful of sensitive individuals – was not easy to detect from the outside. Calcuttans in the 1930s generally felt about Shantiniketan as Ray first had: that Visva-Bharati students did little besides singing, acting, dancing and listening to musical performances, while gossiping in precious tones about 'Gurudev'. Rabindranath had intended the place as a rendezvous of the East and the West; but Tucci, the Italian scholar, had said that if there was a place where East and West could not meet, it was Shantiniketan. Bengali observers of Visva-Bharati emotionally reflected this clash of ideal and reality. Thus Buddhadeva Bose, a leading literary critic, by no means gullible, wrote in ecstasy after a fortnight's stay in Shantiniketan:

> It is remarkable how the place absorbs foreigners, at the same time teaching them true national pride: to be a true Englishman, a true Chinese or, for that matter, a true Indian one must come to Santiniketan . . . The spirit of India is here, as incarnated in the life and works of Rabindranath . . . India is an enigma not to foreigners alone but also to ourselves . . . The peasant who, himself hungry, gives us our food is, in a sense, the symbol of India, the symbol that the Mahatma has taken upon himself. But misery is never meant to be worshipped, it is a thing to be fought against . . . Come to Santiniketan to see India in her glory. Between the misery and the glory lie our decaying middle classes, the sham culture of the cities, the crookedness of village life and the craft of self-advancement that passes by the name of politics. And none of these is India.

While Nirad Chaudhuri, a contemporary of Bose, who deliberately avoided Shantiniketan, wrote bluntly that, 'This place with its counterfeit cosmopolitanism became the centre of all that was false, affected and weak in contemporary Bengali culture.' In 1987 he amplified this humorously:

> It [Visva-Bharati] was a curious assortment, materially, of European bric-a-brac and Hindu archaistic tinsel. In its functioning it was almost a vaudeville. Its personal composition was even worse. Besides some serious scholars from Europe, there came to it all types of eccentrics and adventurers, and some were absolutely feeble-minded enthusiasts in the specialized sense of being obsessed with some unpractical idea. Even Tagore at times lost patience with them. As to the Bengalis who went there, as a class they were men who wanted to achieve importance by being epiphytes on Tagore. As there was

very little money going in Santiniketan that had to be compensated for by an artificial idea of personal importance.

Yet it was Shantiniketan that helped to make Satyajit Ray what he was, one of the greatest artists of the twentieth century. The conflicting interpretations of Shantiniketan are like the conflicting attitudes to Dr Aziz and the events of his calamitous picnic at the Marabar Caves. On the circumstantial evidence, Aziz looks unquestionably guilty to those who were not present at the caves; but to Fielding, who was present, Aziz, despite his patent tendency to embroider and exaggerate, is indubitably innocent. Nirad Chaudhuri, looking at Shantiniketan from Calcutta, convicted it of insincerity; Satyajit Ray, though initially sceptical, seeing the place from the inside, intuited that the ideal was sound. East and West at their best *could* coalesce in Shantiniketan, if only rarely and in the privacy of the individual mind.

There was undoubtedly magic in the setting and in the presence of Rabindranath Tagore in that setting. C. F. Andrews was foolish in very many ways, but he understood rightly the landscape of Shantiniketan. In 1939, a year before he died, Andrews recalled his first impressions in 1913:

There was a beauty in every single thing, that went home to me at once – the open country on every side of the Ashram; the scattered palm trees on the far horizon; the vast dome of sky overhead with the dark blue monsoon rain clouds to be followed by great white clouds after the storm had passed over; the long line of palm trees standing like sentinels above the water of the *bandh* [embankment] where they were reflected; the Santhal villages nestling under the trees; the glorious picnic walks when we took our meal to the banks of the Kopai River; the splendour of the sky at dawn and the red after-glow at eventide; the moonlight shining through the clouds after rain; the deep mystery of those still evenings when I sat out on the terrace at Santiniketan and heard the gentle rustling of the leaves as a sudden breeze broke the silence – all these things carried me into a new region of beauty to which I responded as if expecting each day some fresh surprise.

And here is Kshitimohan Sen, probably the most distinguished Indian scholar on the staff at Shantiniketan, recalling the day in 1908 he arrived in the place to which he would dedicate the rest of his life. He had reached Bolpur station after dark and monsoon rain was falling heavily. So he decided to spend the night at the station and go on foot at dawn.

Bolpur then was sparsely populated and I had not proceeded far when the strains of a distant melody came floating on the morning breeze. The Poet, seated on the balcony of his cottage, Dehali, was welcoming the rising sun with his beautiful song, 'Lift me up from slumber, my Lord . . . '. His voice was exceedingly rich and powerful in those days and in the quiet of an early morning his song could be heard more than a mile away. The grateful memory of that voice which greeted me, has remained with me to this day.

Rabindranath of course wrote many poems on the eye-filling delights of nature in Shantiniketan. He had just turned seventy when he produced 'Kopai', about the small river wiggling its way through the eroded lands beside the ashram, where picnics were held. Here is part of it:

> She speaks in homely language –
>   it cannot be called literary.
> Water and land are caught up in her rhythm,
>   There's no friction between stream and green,
>   Her slim shape twists and turns
>   Passing through light and shadow
>   Dancing and clapping with simple steps.
> Monsoon makes her mad, loosens her limbs
>   Like a village girl drunk on *mahua* wine
>   – but she does not burst, she does not drown,
> She only twirls her eddies
> Like a dancer in a long *ghaghra*,
>   Playfully pushes at her banks
> And glides along laughing loudly.

In 1939, when he was nearly eighty and more or less confined to his house and its immediate surroundings, Tagore wrote the superb 'Mayurer Drishti' (In the Eyes of a Peacock). Again, this is an extract (the poem's opening):

> Screened from the sunshine of a midsummer's morning
>   I sit out on the terrace.
>   The break is benign;
>   Dull work is not yet pressing me,
>   No crowd is leaning on me,
>   Trampling my time underfoot.
>   I sit and write,
>   A little juice collecting in my pen-nib this free morning
>   Like a slit made in the bole of a date-palm.

Our peacock comes and sits, tail downwards
    On the railing beside me.
It feels secure in my corner,
    No harsh keeper here, shackles in hand.
Just outside in the branches unripe mangoes hang,
    Lime trees are loaded with limes
    A lone *kurchi*-tree, flowering,
    Somehow looks astonished at its own abundance.
    With pointless vitality
The peacock darts its neck this way and that.
    It stares beadily
Without a speck of interest at my writing-book;
If, by chance, the squiggles had been insects,
Then it would not have thought the poet so trifling.

Tagore loved the setting of Shantiniketan, there was no question (though he loved Shelidah and riverine East Bengal more). But towards its inmates, sheltering there beneath his benign umbrella, he was acutely ambivalent.

He knew their weaknesses: over and over again he made this clear in letters and other writings. Writing from abroad to Andrews in Shantiniketan in 1921, he told him: 'Curiously enough the idea of this huge Institution threatens me with a prospect of loneliness – it will give me responsibility, but no companionship.' A decade later, writing from Munich in 1930, he told Andrews (who was now in Europe too) that he had received a 'piteous' letter from Shantiniketan, from the Indian scholar in charge of arrangements for foreign scholars. Bogdanov, the émigré Russian professor, had had his salary stopped by the clerks in the administration and he and his wife were suffering miserably. Despite the fact that Bogdanov had been holding regular classes, 'our people are cultivating an illusion that he is living on charity. While Prof. Germanus [Professor of Islamic Studies] is drawing four hundred rupees a month for doing nothing, [and] our people are profoundly satisfied . . .' And in 1935, writing to his son (who now had the thankless task of running the university administration), he said he was not quite happy to hear that Leonard and Dorothy Elmhirst were prepared to continue funding Shriniketan. Their support, he said, 'indulges the lazy tendency in the Bengali race.' The people in charge at Shriniketan would never understand, 'until they became unstuck', that a major part of education involved the planning and securing of an income.

Had he been in Shantiniketan instead of in Munich, Tagore would have sorted out the matter of Bogdanov's salary himself. He was not impractical by nature, as he had demonstrated on his estates over nearly twenty years. But by the 1920s and 1930s, he was constantly travelling and not as energetic as he had been. Why then did he not appoint an efficient vice-chancellor of Visva-Bharati and a competent director of Shriniketan who could work under his guidance? Lack of money for salaries was certainly one reason, a dearth of practical idealists in Bengal was another. Neither problem was insuperable however. The real difficulty lay within Rabindranath's mind: though capable of organizing people, he was essentially anti-organization. In 1922 he told the planner (Sir) Patrick Geddes, as quoted in our Introduction: 'If I had in the commencement a definite outline which I was merely to fill in, it would certainly bore me'. His writing and his institutions were all of a piece to him. 'I need, for keeping up my own interest in writing, fresh shocks of surprise in the growth of my story,' he told a British translator of one of his novels in 1920, 'and therefore I never think of a plot but only a central situation which has psychological possibilities.' At the deepest level Shantiniketan was just that: a 'central situation' – the meeting of East and West – with no plot but with intense 'psychological possibilities' for the right individual (such as Satyajit Ray).

Of course by 1940, when Mahatma Gandhi visited, Visva-Bharati also had a substantial physical infrastructure. For a start there was the complex of buildings and gardens in which Rabindranath, Rathindranath, his wife Pratima and their adopted daughter lived, located only a few hundred yards from the original house built by the Maharshi in the nineteenth century. It was a complex because it catered both for Rabindranath's whims, which were simple, and for Rathindranath's tastes, which tended to the luxurious. The main house was started in 1921 and continuously extended until 1938, as funds became available. It was designed by Rathindranath and Surendranath Kar, a painter on the staff with a talent for inexpensive and somewhat fanciful architecture; Kar designed most of the buildings in Shantiniketan, borrowing elements from Hindu temples, Mughal and Rajput palaces and from Java and Japan. The elaborate interior was the work of Rathindranath and Pratima, who together had a special interest in carpentry and textiles. (They pioneered *batik* in India, for instance, following Rabindranath's tour of Java in 1927.) But Rabindranath preferred not to live in this house, indeed apparently disliked it for its size, lack of straightforwardness, and ostentation. [pl.53] During the 1930s he asked Suren Kar to build, one after the other, three small, comparatively simple, houses together in the grounds of the main house. As Rabindranath became bored with a house, he moved into a new one. The first was a mud hut, Shyamali (The Dark One, built in 1935). He wrote a poem about it:

I have built with mud a shelter for my last hours
and have named it Shyamali.

I have built it
on the dust of this earth
which buries in it
all sufferings
and cleanses
all stains.

The first monsoon made the roof leak, as Suren Kar had feared. It had to be covered with a tarpaulin and tarred: nevertheless Gandhi stayed there in 1940 and loved it. The next house, Punascha (Postscript, built in 1936), single-storey like Shyamali but more solid, was where the poet was living when he wrote his poem about the peacock. The last house, Udichi (To the North, built in 1939), was the most satisfactory. Its pseudo-Rajput style had a nice sense of proportion, a grace and a charm, and its elevation gave Rabindranath the sense of light and space that he cherished. [pl.53] (Recall his love of the East Bengal estate house in which he wrote 'The Postmaster'.)

All this was the home of the Founder-President, his family and guests. The buildings of the university itself now included centres for the study of China and of Hindi, paid for by donations from China and from the Marwari community in Calcutta (the Birlas and others); and an attractive hostel, principally for foreign scholars, paid for by the great Parsi industrialists, the Tatas. But buildings apart, not a single department of Visva-Bharati was securely endowed academically, with the exception of Islamic Studies, paid for by the nizam of Hyderabad. The art school, the university's oldest department and its most notable – headed by Nandalal Bose and staffed by, among others, the brilliant, half-blind painter Binodebihari Mukherji – struggled along, inadequately equipped. Even in the study of Bengali, there were no funds to support a Chair, despite Rabindranath's efforts. At Shriniketan, almost the entire financial burden continued to be borne by the Elmhirsts. An imaginative idea supported by Tagore – to have Zionists from Palestine settle around Shriniketan and collaborate with Bengalis in rural reconstruction – never took off. 'I am so alone; my cry for help seems to fall on deaf ears', Tagore sadly told an industrialist supporter (non-Bengali) in 1939. [pl.57]

Why were Bengalis so miserly in their support for Visva-Bharati? One of them, the level-headed Ramananda Chatterji, India's greatest editor and journalist pre-Independence, set out the reasons in his monthly magazine, the *Modern Review*. Although Chatterji was one of Tagore's most committed Bengali admirers, he had on occasions been critical of him. (He had even worked in Shantiniketan in the 1920s, and resigned his post.) Now he wrote from forty years' experience:

Had Tagore been orthodox in his religious, social, political, educational and cultural ideas and ideals – uttering popular catch-phrases, had he been an educational megalomaniac instead of being India's greatest educational genius who thinks independently, he would have probably got plenty of big donations. Probably the fact of his being the grandson of 'Prince' Dwarkanath Tagore has also stood in the way of his being adequately financed by his countrymen, few of whom know that personally he has given unstintedly not only his time and physical and intellectual energy but his material resources also to his university. There may be other causes which it will do no good to state.

This was all true, including the suggestion at the end that Bengalis were jealous of Rabindranath. Even so, some of the blame must be borne by Tagore. He had established an institution aiming at high intellectual standards, among other qualities, physically far from the best minds of Calcutta, without adequate accommodation, food, water, electricity, health treatment or salaries, in a place that was scorchingly hot for nearly half the year and also suffered badly from mosquitoes and malaria. Having himself a strong constitution and a genuine indifference to discomfort – notwithstanding his staying in the best hotels and using the highest-class transport in the West – Tagore did not mind these spartan conditions. But others did. Not surprisingly, like the postmaster of his story, they preferred to stay in Calcutta.

The effect was (as Nirad Chaudhuri said), that the majority of the teachers at Shantiniketan in the 1930s were 'epiphytes on Tagore' with 'an artificial idea of personal importance'. This fact, coupled with the philosophy of individual freedom espoused by Rabindranath, produced an insidious and repellent atmosphere of adulation, cynicism and hypocrisy. A small number of gifted individuals – teachers such as Binodebihari Mukherji and students such as Ray – could make themselves impervious and do worthwhile work, but most became, if anything, more parochial in outlook than if they had stayed in Calcutta. To escape from their society was a major reason behind Tagore's frequent absences from Shantiniketan.

As he aged and was compelled to spend more time there, Rabindranath came to depend on some of these decidedly unreliable people, whose basic characteristics he had earlier pilloried in his writings (especially in his short stories). He was never as good a judge of his associates as he was of his fictional characters. As a man he had a lamentable talent for trusting the untrustworthy and incompetent. Among the worst culprits was his one-time secretary Amiya Chakravarty, a mediocre, pretentious and devious man. In the mid-1930s, with Tagore's help, he was sent to Balliol College, Oxford, to write a thesis on

English literature. While in England, besides shamelessly flattering Tagore in letters, he was partly responsible for the disastrous *Collected Poems and Plays* published by Macmillan in 1936. On his return to Bengal, he mistranslated some of Tagore's poetry into English and began writing 'modernist' poetry in Bengali of astonishing fatuity. In later life, he latched on to Tagore's name, went to the USA as a professor, edited and translated some of Tagore's works, and became a counterfeit 'world citizen'. Chakravarty and others like him bear a large burden of responsibility for today's distortion of Tagore's legacy both within and outside Bengal.

Although Rabindranath saw through the literary pretensions of Chakravarty, he continued to believe in his good qualities. Perhaps his flattery had gone to Tagore's head: more likely Tagore deluded himself. As part of his ideal for Shantiniketan, Tagore felt obliged to give his associates the benefit of the doubt, and more. In 1934, he was tackled on this point by the social worker Muriel Lester, Gandhi's friend and hostess in the East End of London in 1931. Lester had visited Shantiniketan and been taken aback by the cynicism and lack of belief in non-violence among the younger teachers. One of them had even said to her, 'another Amritsar would do good'. Working in the East End she was used to such views, she said, but not to the 'hot air' of the teachers on being asked what their plans for rebuilding society were. When she pressed them, they said, 'Go and ask the Poet. Tell him what we say.' 'I told them' – she wrote privately to Rabindranath – 'if I were asked by friends of Santiniketan for news of it, I should not find it easy to answer.'

> Would I be expected to give them news of what I *saw*, which was good – or of what I heard? The lovely serenity and worship of a Bengal New Year's eve [i.e. mid-April] or the numerous talks with teachers and the elder students who are only too ready to imbibe these cynical and bitter ideas? In fact is Santiniketan what you make it or what the teachers make it?

It was a highly pertinent question, the same one that Indira Gandhi asked herself in 1982. Tagore replied to Lester at length privately, and a year or so later published his response in the *Visva-Bharati News*. Obviously he hoped to provoke reflection among the teachers and students Lester had criticized. He wrote movingly from more than thirty years' heart-searching:

> you must know that those persons are extremely rare who have the genius to construct anything worth building, in an environment where things have to be begun from the very beginning, very often with meagre means and in unsympathetic circumstances. The burden of poverty in our country has

been cruelly heavy and widespread, the training to fight it is absent, and on top of it the depression of spirit that causes inertia finds its shelter in a body whose vitality has been run down owing to the want of nourishment and the consequent series of illnesses amidst surroundings devoid of proper medical help. It hurts me very deeply to find the best of our young minds indulging in a militant form of cynicism which is all the more virulent because of its blankly negative character, destitute of all true vision. Because they have grown callously incapable of the deeper enjoyment of spiritual life they helplessly become addicted to cheap political sensationalism. I understand them, I suffer for them and I can never keep myself away from their wounded selves. I can only nourish a pathetic hope in my mind that in the end the wisdom which is of our own soil will find its way into their life, and if my own inspiration fails them I shall ever blame my own feeble power.

34 The Self-destruction of Bengal (1934–1940)

I was born too early for this post-war age of disillusionment.

speech,
Calcutta, July 1936

If the ageing Rabindranath was keenly divided about Shantiniketan, the Abode of Peace, his inner conflict about Calcutta was agonizing. He had never felt affection for the city; more and more he felt an aversion. In 1930 we know that he urged his son to find a buyer for his part of the family mansion at Jorasanko. Yet he could not keep away from the place: throughout the 1930s he went to Calcutta frequently to lecture, to preside over meetings, to open new institutions, and to keep in touch with his city friends, supporters and associates. It was the place of his birth, childhood and adolescence; whether he liked it or not, he was attached to it and its people by an unsnappable umbilical cord.

He even tried, in 1928, to reform the aggravating street-numbering of the metropolis. He published a letter in the *Calcutta Municipal Gazette* suggesting a more rational system. This was provoked by his failure to find a certain address after much searching and many blank responses from policemen and local people. 'I sometimes wonder if Livingstone himself would not have found exploration in Darkest Africa easier than fruitful exploration in the City of Palaces.'

The image may seem overblown, with the exaggerated whiff of the regular writer of public letters. But to anyone who knows north Calcutta, and has tried to find a tricky address there, Tagore will not seem to have indulged in hyperbole. Calcutta, from the point of view of the municipal planner, is really Kipling's City of Dreadful Night. Unlike most Calcuttans, Rabindranath saw this with the clear vision of the disinterested outsider. But at the same time, as a native of Calcutta, he could see it with the eye of love too.

In 1932 he published a poem about the city imbued with this double vision. Into less than a hundred lines of informal, unrhymed verse, he compressed a world of Bengali feeling, the distillation of his seven decades of life in urban and rural Bengal. The setting is a shabby – in places squalid – lane, perhaps one of

those behind the Jorasanko house; the central figure is a humdrum clerk from a
village in riverine East Bengal, perhaps not dissimilar to those who kept the
account books in the Tagore household; but his fantasies are as soaring and
extravagant as his circumstances are cramped and impoverished. Taken as a
whole, the poem calls to mind almost inescapably that grimy garret above a
smoky, noisy railway yard to which Apu, the dreamy, impecunious would-be
writer, brings his blooming, bejewelled, veiled village bride in Satyajit Ray's
emotionally wrenching *Apur Sansar* (*The World of Apu*, 1959). With this poem
(and others), Tagore lit the path for Ray to follow. Its title is 'Banshi' (Flute-
Music). Extracts would ruin its cumulative power, so here is the entire poem:

Kinugoala Lane
    A two-storey house
    Ground-floor room, bars for windows
    Next to the road.
    On the rotting walls patches of peeling plaster,
    The stains of damp and salt.
    A picture label from a bale of cloth
    Stuck on the door shows
    Elephant-headed Ganesh, Bringer of Success.
Apart from me the room has another denizen,
    Living rent-free:
    A lizard.
    The difference between it and me is simple –
    It never lacks food.

I earn twenty-five rupees a month,
    As a junior clerk in a trading office,
    Eat at the Duttas' house,
    Tutor their boy in exchange.
Then it's off to Sealdah Station
    To spend the evening.
    Saves the expense of lighting.
Engines chuffing,
    Whistles screeching,
      Passengers rushing,
        Coolies yelling,
          It's half-past ten
    When I head for my lonely, silent, gloomy room.

My aunt's village on the Dhaleshwari River.
    Her brother-in-law's daughter
Was all set for marriage to my unfortunate self.
Surely the signs were auspicious, I have proof –
    For when the moment came, I ran away.
The girl was saved from me
    And I from her.
She never came to this room, but she's never away from my mind,
    Wearing a Dacca sari, vermilion in her parting.

Monsoon lours,
    Tram fares go up,
    Often my wages get cut.
In nooks and corners of the lane
There pile up and rot
    Mango skins and stones, jackfruit peelings,
    Fish-gills,
    Corpses of kittens,
    And who knows what other trash!
The state of my umbrella is like
    The state of my wage packet,
        Full of holes.
My office clothes resemble
    The thoughts of a pious Vaishnava,
    Oozing and lachrymose.
The dark presence of the rains
    Hangs in my moist room
    Like a trapped beast
        Stunned and still.
Day and night I feel that the world
    Is half-dead, and I am strapped to its back.

At a bend in the lane lives Kanta Babu,
    Long hair nattily groomed,
        Wide-eyed,
            Refined of manner.
    He loves to play the cornet.
Frequently the notes come floating
    Through the lane's stinking air.
    Sometimes at dead of night

Or in the half-light before dawn,
Sometimes in the afternoons
When light and shadow coruscate.

Suddenly one evening
He begins to play in *Shindhu Baroa* raga,
    And the whole sky rings
    With the yearning of the ages.
Then in a flash I grasp
    That the entire lane is a dreadful lie,
    Insufferable, like the ravings of a drunk.
Suddenly my mind sees
    That Akbar the emperor
    And Haripada the clerk are not different.
    Torn umbrella and royal parasol fuse
    In the pathos of the fluting melody
    Pointing towards one heaven.

    The music is true, the key
To that endless twilit witching
    Where flows the River Dhaleshwari
    Its banks fringed with dark *tamal* trees,
    Where
    In a courtyard
    She is waiting,
    Wearing a Dacca sari, vermilion in her parting.

Rabindranath's last decade saw some of his finest poems, songs and paintings. (He also continued to write novels, stories, plays and dance-dramas.) Yet at the same time Tagore felt compelled to adopt a public role, out of distress at the decline of Bengal in the mid-to-late 1930s. As he saw it, Bengal was fast losing her soul, all the self-destructive tendencies he had inveighed against since the failure of the 1905 Swadeshi Movement were coalescing to make a tragedy. And with hindsight one can see that he was only too accurate in his diagnosis: since his death in 1941, Partition in 1947 and its accompanying bloodshed, Bengal has indeed gradually lost her leadership of India in every field, political, commercial, intellectual and artistic. (This despite the prominent gifts of individual Bengalis, in Bengal, in India generally, and abroad.)

The crux of the political problem was the Hindu–Muslim divide in Bengal.

As part of the machinery of political reform in India leading to the Government of India Act of 1935, the government in London, after consultations with Indian leaders, had announced the Communal Award in August 1932 – against which Gandhi had started his 'fast unto death', stopped by the conclusion of the Poona Pact in late September. Under the original plan, before the Pact, the future legislature in Bengal was to have 250 seats, of which the Muslims were to get 121 seats and the Hindus 78 seats (25 seats were to go to the Europeans, the remaining twenty-six seats to other 'special interests', including the Untouchables or 'Scheduled Castes'). Each block of seats was to have a separate electorate. The implications for Hindus – 45 per cent of Bengal's population – were catastrophic: from having 60 per cent of the elected seats, they were to be reduced to having 39 per cent or less. Correspondingly the Muslims – with 55 per cent of the population – were to have more than 48 per cent of the seats. And for the high-caste Hindus worse was to come with the Poona Pact: in deference to Gandhi as the acknowledged leader of the Congress, Ambedkar, the leader of the Scheduled Castes (Untouchables), reluctantly agreed to renounce separate electorates and merge the Scheduled Castes with the rest of the Hindus, in exchange for having 30 'reserved seats' out of the 78 seats allotted to all Hindus. Thus, in a 250-seat legislative assembly, high-caste Hindus, the undoubted leaders of Bengali society for nearly two centuries, were to be guaranteed just 48 seats, a mere one-fifth of the total.

They had acquiesced at the time of the fast in 1932, Tagore included – but within months they began a long agitation against both the Communal Award and the Poona Pact, with Tagore's support. He admitted he had made a mistake, out of concern for Gandhi's life, and he wrote to Gandhi that the Pact would cause a 'fatal break in the spirit of mutual cooperation in our province.' Shortly after he added: 'You know that I am not a politician, and I look upon the whole thing from the point of view of humanity which will cruelly suffer when its claim to justice is ignored.' But Gandhi and other Congress leaders were not convinced that there had been an injustice. The Mahatma advised Tagore that he should convene a meeting of all the parties in Bengal and try to persuade them to alter the seat allocation. He was opposed to making appeals to the British, as Tagore appeared to want: Bengalis, Gandhi felt, must first resolve the problem by mutual agreement.

No agreement was feasible. Three years later, in 1936, Rabindranath joined other prominent Bengali Hindus in sending a memorial to the secretary of state for India in London, asking for a modification of the Communal Award; he also presided over an impassioned mass meeting on the subject in Calcutta. In his speech he reiterated his usual disclaimer that he was no politician. Events had forced his hand, he said: 'I found it painfully impossible to ignore the sinister threat of a bisecting blade hissing while being sharpened, ready to divide the one vital sensitive cord that is to bind our people into a nation.' But for all that, Tagore put his signature to the following politically explosive statement in the memorial:

> the Hindus of Bengal, though numerically a minority, are overwhelmingly superior [to the Muslims] culturally, constituting as much as 64 per cent of the total literate population and more than 80 per cent of the total school-going population, while their economic preponderance is equally manifest in the spheres of the independent professions and commercial careers . . .

The secretary of state replied that nothing could be done without the consent of all those concerned. A Bengali Muslim newspaper commented with some acidity that even if the above facts were fully correct, 'we are rather surprised to find that in these days of democracy claims have been put forward on grounds which are totally anti-democratic. How far such claims are consistent with Dr Rabindranath's professed ideas we are unable to say.'

The Muslim commentator had hit the nail on the head. While Tagore's speech had been an honourable effort at reminding both Hindus and Muslims of the risks they were running, he had placed the major share of the blame on the British for 'divide and rule' and on the Muslims for accepting the British 'offer of an intoxicant'; he gave scarcely a nod to the hubris shown by many Bengali Hindus towards the Muslims, of which he had long been aware. Furthermore he had to some extent given way to his distrust of democracy. As always, Tagore believed that politics should be the art of the noble, rather than of the possible. The ideals of ancient India reinterpreted by Bengali Hindus such as Rammohun Roy and the ideals of nineteenth-century European liberalism, were in Tagore's mind infinitely superior to any democratic ideal based purely on numerical calculations of the size of the different communities. 'I was born too early for this post-war age of disillusionment', he said. 'I still feel inclined to appeal to the chivalrous humanity of the Englishman representing the best ideals of western culture.' He hoped that 'this pathetic faith which dies hard' was not an illusion.

The Communal Award, damaging and unfair as it was to Bengal, was not rescinded; the new provincial legislature came into operation in 1937; and the confusion and bitterness in Bengal escalated. By 1938, there was a new stridency in Rabindranath's public pronouncements on British rule. He told the *Manchester Guardian* that the new constitution was worthless to Indians:

It was made by politicians and bureaucrats, who, even as it was being framed, were sending some of our best men and women to prison, mainly without trial. It therefore embodies all their narrow caution and miserly mistrust . . . I want to tell the British people quite plainly: So long as you hold us in your grip, you can never have either our trust or our friendship. We know that, in your own homes, you have many kindly virtues, and are admirable for your sense of fair play and human justice. Perhaps for that very reason you find it difficult to understand how the same English people out here can betray your best traditions. But then you have to remember that possession of empire always corrupts, and it has corrupted you.

However he wrote privately to a clergyman, who had written to him from England after reading his article: 'It was more in sorrow than in bitterness that I wrote the [piece] and I hope my English friends will not understand its moral appeal as mere political propaganda.'

His feelings of despair helped to push him into supporting Bengal's only outstanding political leader, Subhashchandra Bose. Until now the two had not had much to do with each other, in fact Tagore's admiration for Gandhi and Bose's critical attitude to the Mahatma had divided them. In early 1939, when Bose was president of the Congress, they had two meetings at Shantiniketan and Tagore hailed Bose as Deshanayak ('The Leader of the Country'). 'At such a juncture of nationwide crisis, we require the service of a forceful personality, the invincible faith of a natural leader, who can defy the adverse fate that threatens our progress', he wrote. 'More than anything else Bengal needs today to emulate the powerful force of your determination and self-reliant courage . . . Let Bengal affirm in one united voice that her deliverer's seat is ready, spread for you . . . ' It almost seemed that Tagore had found a Bengali Mussolini. (Subhash Bose was notably sympathetic to Fascism, and had considerable contact with Mussolini in the 1930s.) However, Tagore's enthusiasm for Bose was not shared by Gandhi, Nehru and most of the influential Congress leaders. During 1939, they compelled Bose to resign as president. Rabindranath's several efforts to reunite the Congress leadership went in vain. 'I am quite clear that the matter is too complicated for Gurudev to handle', Gandhi warned C. F. Andrews in January 1940.

Bose was courageous, if misguided, but he was unable to unify his countrymen. Soon he was arrested and went his own way following the paths of secrecy and violence that were anathema to Rabindranath. (He joined forces with the Axis Powers and founded the Indian National Army, which fought the British in Burma.) Bengal was left politically rudderless. It was a bad blow for the aged Tagore. In April 1940 he lashed the people most responsible,

the Hindus of Calcutta (and by extension Shantiniketan), with some anguished
language.

> People here do not combine to build up anything bit by bit but they flock
> together to enjoy the unholy glee of pulling down what has already been built.
> Even this might have been condoned if it had not been inspired by hideous
> self-interest . . . For this long life of mine I often curse myself. I do not even
> entertain the hope that out of this orgy of destruction, life will emerge
> somehow or other . . . This will not happen here. The seed of truth cannot
> germinate in the rubbish-heap of untruth.

He had said similar things many times before – which did not make his
criticism one jot less true. What was new was the note of despair. Not only had
Bengal taken virtually no notice of his practical works and his warning words,
now the West was busy tearing itself apart. Rabindranath had been closely
following political developments in Europe with the help of his many friends
and contacts there. By the time the Second World War began in September
1939, he had already sensed the horror of what was to come.

35   War, Tagore and the West
(1939–1940)

I shall cherish the fact to the end of my days that my life has been linked
with the memory of one of the greatest poets of modern Europe.

statement on the death of W. B. Yeats,
Shantiniketan, February 1939

Tagore had been warning both the West and Japan about the militarism
inherent in their politics since the time of *Nationalism*, his lectures during
the First World War. Coming down to specifics in the 1930s, he was less perceptive – though still much more far-sighted than the majority of western
democratic statesmen, and indeed many western writers and intellectuals. It
took him several years to make up his mind about German Fascism. He could
not bring himself to accept the grotesque contradiction it presented with his
first-hand experience in Germany as recently as 1930; his idealism revolted at
the thought. Furthermore, as we know, he was attracted to strong leadership.
Nevertheless, by the later 1930s Tagore had rejected Fascism in Italy, Germany
and Japan. In 1937, in a stirring appeal for the republican side in the Spanish
civil war, he wrote: 'This devastating tide of International Fascism must be
checked . . . come in your millions to the aid of democracy, to the succour of civilization and culture.' About Soviet Communism he would remain ambivalent
until the day he died, over-impressed by its achievements in mass education.

Tagore was not, in general, naive about politics; the Soviet Union was his one
serious blind-spot. As early as 1931 he wrote to his grandson in Germany: 'I
don't like the attitude of Bavaria. Just as weak people struck by poverty can be
gripped by epidemics, the spread of famine in Europe is enabling Fascism and
Bolshevism to get a strong hold. Both are symptoms of unhealthiness.'

In August 1933, seven months after Hitler became chancellor, a German
consular official gave a lecture on 'Elements of New Germany' at Visva-Bharati
under the presidency of Tagore. Much of the speech, as printed in a Calcutta
journal in October, was innocuous, but there were some passages of anti-
semitism that must have made Rabindranath very uneasy. In print and in
writing he said nothing however. When the journal reached his Communist

great-nephew in Paris (who had been with him in Moscow in 1930), he wrote robustly to Rabindranath:

> You have expressed your opposition to Italian Fascism. If you have not changed your views, you cannot possibly support German Fascism, which is now being called Nazism . . . Wise men from all corners of the world have loudly voiced their views, only you have remained silent. Nobody expects anything from Gandhi but they do from you. You have spoilt a great opportunity for India.

To drive home his point he said that someone in Paris had asked him if the Nazis were financing Shantiniketan.

Tagore did not much respect the opinions of his great-nephew. But in this instance he probably did take note, knowing that as a Communist he had been arrested in Germany in April and, according to his statements to the French press, had only narrowly escaped a savage beating by virtue of his being a British subject. The Nazi press had accused him of planning to assassinate Hitler.

More significant to Rabindranath was the Nazi vilification of Einstein, who had fled Berlin, never to return to Germany, in December 1932. A few months after, brownshirt thugs raided Einstein's villa at Caputh where he and Tagore had talked, supposedly searching for arms. In June 1934, Tagore made a public statement on racial hatred and referred to this incident, at the request of a Zionist newspaper in Shanghai, whose editor he had met in 1924. What he wrote was by no means an unqualified indictment of the Nazis.

> As regards the Hitler regime in Germany, we read different versions of it. And certainly it cannot be denied that the German people were goaded to many acts of desperate folly by the humiliations imposed on them by the victorious nations of the War. Nevertheless, if the brutalities we read of are authentic, then no civilized conscience can allow compromise with them. The insults offered to my friend Einstein have shocked me to the point of torturing my faith in modern civilization. I can only draw consolation from the hope that it was an unhappy act done in a drunken mood and not the sober choice of a people so gifted as the Germans.

Tagore said hardly anything more on the subject of Nazi Germany directly, though he apparently rejected an offer of a degree from Berlin University in 1937 as a protest against Nazi oppression of Einstein and other Jewish intellectuals and writers.

Mussolini's invasion of Abyssinia in 1935 provoked him to a poem on Africa, almost his only writing about that continent. It was remarkable less for what it said about Africa than for its view of modern civilization as a form of savagery. This is the last verse:

Today when on the western horizon
   The sunset sky is stifled with dust-storm,
      When the beast, creeping out of its dark den
      Proclaims the death of the day with ghastly howls,
Come, you poet of the fatal hour,
   Stand in the dying light before nightfall,
      At the door of that ravished woman
      And beg her, 'Forgive, forgive.'
      In the midst of violent delirium,
Let that be your civilization's last great word.

At the suggestion of an African prince then in Oxford, Tagore translated the poem, and told him: 'I shall feel richly compensated if I know it will reach my friends in Africa and let them realize how an Indian poet feels about the despoliation of a whole continent in the name of civilization.' (The translation was published in the *Spectator*.)

In 1936, he succinctly articulated his philosophy of international relations in a message to the World Peace Congress at Brussels:

If peace is to be anything more than the mere absence of war, it must be founded on the strength of the just and not on the weariness of the weak. The groan of peace in Abyssinia is no less ghastly than the howl of war in Spain. If then we are to strive for that true peace, in which the satisfaction of one people is not built on the frustration of another, then the average peace-loving citizen of the successful nations of today must extricate himself from the obvious anomaly of wishing for peace whilst sharing in the spoils of war – which exposes his wish to the charge of mere pretence. He must not let himself be bribed on the promise of prosperity and honour and call it patriotism. We cannot have peace until we deserve it by paying its full price, which is, that the strong must cease to be greedy and the weak must learn to be bold.

If the aggression of first Italy and then Germany was disillusioning for Tagore, the policy of appeasement pursued by France and Britain was devastating. He had many friends and admirers in Czechoslovakia, including President Masaryk. The closest was an Indologist at Prague, Vincenc Lesny, a lecturer at Visva-Bharati in the 1920s and a biographer of Tagore in the 1930s. In mid-October 1938, some two weeks after the Munich Agreement, Tagore wrote to Lesny in real agony:

I feel so keenly . . . the suffering of your people as if I was one of them. For what has happened in your country is not a mere local misfortune which may at the best claim our sympathy, it is a tragic revelation that the destiny of all those principles of humanity for which the peoples of the West turned martyrs for three centuries rests in the hands of cowardly guardians who are selling it to save their own skins. It turns one cynical to see the democratic peoples betraying their kind when even the bullies stand by each other.

I feel so humiliated and so helpless . . . My words have no power to stay the onslaught of the maniacs . . . I can only remind those who are not yet wholly demented that when men turn beasts they sooner or later tear each other.

The situation in the Far East was much worse, though not as hard a psychological blow for Rabindranath because he had long distrusted the Japanese leaders. But he was stunned to receive a letter from a Japanese poet whom he knew and respected, arguing vociferously for Japan's spiritual and moral role in sending its army to China. Yone Noguchi is now almost forgotten in the West (certainly as compared to his son, the sculptor Isamu Noguchi), but in the first two or three decades of this century he was among the best-known Japanese writers, and the associate of Yeats and Pound. His poetry was, if anything, more romantic and devoid of martial spirit than Tagore's poetry: yet here Noguchi was, in mid-1938, a spokesman – and, it seems a convinced spokesman – for carnage on a grand scale. His hope was to enlist Tagore's support in India.

The two poets exchanged long letters twice in public. Noguchi bluntly accused Tagore of being ignorant of the real China, the China of rapacious warlords, rural oppression and Kuomintang atrocities, which Japan, he said, was in the process of sweeping away. (It was the old argument of Sylvain Lévi – given a new twist in Japan's favour.) Noguchi argued: 'if you take the present war in China for the criminal outcome of Japan's surrender to the West' – which was exactly how Tagore had viewed Japan's depredations in Korea –

you are wrong, because, not being a slaughtering madness, it is, I believe, the inevitable means, terrible [as] it is, for establishing a new great world in the Asiatic continent, where the 'principle of live-and-let-live' has to be realized. [sic] Believe me, it is the war of 'Asia for Asia' . . .
. . . I believe that you are versed in Bushido. In olden times soldiery was

lifted in Japan to a status equally high as that of art and morality. I have no doubt that our soldiers will not betray the tradition. If there is a difference [between] Japanese militarism [and] that of the West, it is because the former is not without moral element.

A shocked Tagore responded:

You are building your conception of an Asia which would be raised on a tower of skulls. I have, as you rightly point out, believed in the message of Asia, but I never dreamt that this message could be identified with deeds which brought exaltation to the heart of Tamer Lane [Timur, the Mongol conqueror] . . .

. . . It is true that there are no better standards prevalent anywhere else and that the so-called civilized peoples of the West are proving equally barbarous and even less 'worthy of trust'. If you refer me to them, I have nothing to say. What I should have liked is to be able to refer them to you. I shall say nothing of my own people, for it is vain to boast until one has succeeded in sustaining one's principles to the end . . .

. . . Wishing your people whom I love, not success, but remorse.

After war in Europe was finally declared, Tagore wrote a song, which he translated into English on Christmas Day, 1939. Here is the last stanza in his own translation:

Those who struck Him once
in the name of their rulers
are born again in the present age.
They gather in their prayer halls in a pious garb,
they call their soldiers,
'Kill, kill,' they shout.
In their roaring mingles
the music of their hymns,
while the Son of Man
in His agony prays,
'O God, fling, fling far away
this cup filled with the bitterest of poisons.'

And a week or two later he produced a disturbing poem about the war as seen from far-off Bengal. This is the complete poem, 'Apaghat' (Injury):

The late afternoon glow is fading towards dark.
　　The drowsy wind is slack.
A cart full of paddy-straw for far-off Nadia market plods
　　Across the desolate fields.
　　Behind the sheaves,
　　Following, tied-on, a calf.
In the low-caste quarter on a bank
　　Beside the tank
　　Pundit Banamali's eldest son
　　Sits all day with a fishing line.
High above him wild geese honk
　　Flying from the river's dried-up bank
　　To the lake, the Black Beel,
　　In search of snails.

The sugar-cane is cut; beside its stubble
　　Two friends indolently amble
　　inhaling the scent as they pass
　　Of rain-washed forest and grass.
　　　They are on holiday –
Met each other by chance in some village by-way,
　　One of them being newly-wed;
Their delight in talking seems to have no end.
All around, the *bhati* flowers are in the bloom of youth;
　　In the maze of forest paths
　　　Their soft fragrance has wings
　　　　Scattering the ecstasy of late Spring.
While nearby in a *jarul* tree
　　A cuckoo hammers its note dementedly.

　　A telegram comes:
'Finland pulverized by Soviet bombs.'

'I tremble to think of the future,' Tagore told a Jewish friend living in Palestine, on 7 January, 'if the year 1940 ends as it has begun, with slaughter on every side, with history being made only in terms of outrage and violence.'

Few outside India would have been aware of these poems. Very little of Rabindranath's poetry of the 1930s had appeared in the West. What had been published had appeared chiefly in magazines; the only book by Tagore from Macmillan in this decade was the *Collected Poems and Plays*, in which the fact of translation was not disclosed. Tagore's western reputation as a writer had taken a nose-dive. Introducing a novel by the new Indian writer R. K. Narayan in 1937, Graham Greene wrote: 'As for Rabindranath Tagore, I cannot believe that anyone but Mr Yeats can still take his poems very seriously.' (Yeats had just brought out *The Oxford Book of Modern Verse*, that included poems by Tagore.) 'One associates him with what [G. K.] Chesterton calls "the bright pebbly eyes" of the Theosophists.'

Of course the plunge in Tagore's literary reputation, and the cynical and brutal politics of the 1930s, were connected. But much more damaging had been the translations done by himself and by other hands after *The Crescent Moon*. They were 'a velation – a cloud between his poetry and the western public', Edward Thompson perceived. In the 1920s Thompson had attempted a revelation of Tagore by retranslation. He failed.

Rabindranath was understandably dismayed by all this, and it certainly deepened the gloom of his last years. To fail in influencing Indian or western politics was bearable, but to fail in the correct propagation of one's own writing was bitterly disappointing. Yet Tagore did not shirk his own responsibility. Even at the height of his literary fame in English, in 1915, he had told Robert Bridges: 'If there be any excellence in my translations it is unconscious, it is like correctly walking in dreams in places which it is not safe to attempt when wakeful.' By 1921, he had become even more humble. Writing to Thompson from New York, he admitted:

You know I began to pay court to your language when I was fifty. It was pretty late for me ever to hope to win her heart. Occasional gifts of favour do not delude me with false hopes. Not being a degree-holder of any of our Universities I know my limitations – and I fear to rush into the field reserved for angels to tread. In my translations I timidly avoid all difficulties, which has the effect of making them smooth and thin. I know I am misrepresenting myself as a poet to the western readers. But when I began this career of falsifying my own coins I did it in play. Now I am becoming frightened of its enormity and I am willing to make a confession of my misdeeds and withdraw into my original vocation as a mere Bengali poet.

In 1935, the year before the publication of the *Collected Poems and Plays*, he made the most interesting of his numerous statements and remarks on translation. He was writing to Thomas Sturge Moore, the poet who had proposed him for the Nobel prize and helped him with revisions in 1913 (and whom Yeats described as 'one of the most exquisite poets writing in England'). The very vividness of Tagore's language in his letter to Sturge Moore (whatever its minor grammatical solecisms) underscored the poignancy of his literary predicament. He could handle English words with Nobel-winning brilliance – had not Harriet Monroe written in her memoirs that his English in person was 'more perfect' than hers? – and yet the English language as a whole eluded him. But if he had never followed the urge to translate his works into English, then Tagore would never have known Sturge Moore: and as a result both he, Sturge Moore and the whole world would have been the poorer. Tagore's letter is reproduced here in full.

I am no longer young, and I have had ample time to realize the futility of going out of one's own natural sphere for winning recognition. Languages are jealous sovereigns, and passports are rarely allowed for travellers to cross their strictly guarded boundaries. What is the use of my awkwardly knocking my head against their prohibitions, specially when I have the cause to feel sure of having contributed something acceptable to the world literature through my own mother tongue. I ought to remain loyally content with her limitations that are inevitable and yet which afford the only reliable means I have of offering my hospitality to the larger world.

In India circumstances almost compel us to learn English, and this lucky accident has given us the opportunity of an access into the richest of all poetical literatures of the world. Otherwise it would have remained to us like a mine of wealth unknown, unclaimed and unregretted, concealed for all time in an alien planet. Translations, however clever, can only transfigure dancing into acrobatic tricks, in most cases playing treason against the majesty of the original. I often imagine apes to be an attempt by the devil of a translator to render human form in the mould of his own outlandish idiom. The case may be to some extent different in European languages which, in spite of their respective individual characteristics, have closely similar temperaments and atmosphere, the western culture being truly a common culture.

As for myself, I ought never to have intruded into your realm of glory with my offerings hastily giving them a foreign shine and certain assumed gestures familiar to you. I have done thereby injustice to myself and the shrine of Muse which proudly claims flowers from its own climate and culture. There is something humiliating in such an indecent hurry of impatience clamouring for one's immediate dues in wrong time and out of the way places.

That is why I asked my young friend [Amiya Chakravarty], who is in Oxford now, not to participate in perpetuating my offence of transgression by arranging a collected edition of my own translations which they [Macmillan] had planned. Inadequate though these translations may be in their representation they have helped to introduce me to your people with some success. I was lured to a risky adventure when I submitted my manuscript to my English publishers only because of my great admiration for your literature which tempted me to seek the precious courtesy of its acknowledgement for my own things. But casual visitors must not overstay their welcome and I feel that it is time for them to leave the stage withdrawing themselves from a too prolonged stare of the critical footlight.

But the fact was, despite his (absolutely genuine) reservations, Tagore could not bring himself to follow his self-denying ordinance. His letter to Sturge Moore was written on 11 June 1935. Almost a month before, on 17 May, he had written to Macmillan agreeing to a selection of his poems being made by the ambitious Chakravarty 'with the help of my English literary friends'. He added: 'But I shall of course myself revise the final selection.' During 1935–36, C. F. Andrews played a role, but most of the work was done by Ernest Rhys, the editor of Everyman, who had never lost his admiration for Tagore even though they had fallen out of touch. In late 1936, the *Collected Poems and Plays* appeared. Writing to Rhys and Macmillan Tagore declared himself pleased; he did not mention the omission of any note that the works were translations.

There was minimal interest from the critics (though the book was subsequently reprinted many times). But in August 1939, reviewing Vincenc Lesny's biography of Tagore in English translation, the BBC's journal, the *Listener*, called Tagore 'the most famous of living poets; his renown is worldwide'. So while Tagore's literary stock among English writers was extremely low, his personal reputation was Olympian.

For instance, in 1937 there was a press rumour that he was to play the Buddha in a film, which he had to deny. In 1938 *Life* magazine ran a full-page photograph of Tagore being lip-read by Helen Keller in 1930. [pl.47] At the Nazi Party's biggest-ever rally, at Nuremberg in September 1937, Joseph Goebbels denounced Tagore by name as part of the 'world liberalism' that was supporting the republican government in Spain. (Ironically, as a student in 1918, Goebbels had read the love songs of *The Gardener* with delight.) A few months later, at Christmas 1937, Lesny and the Czech novelist Karel Čapek tried to arrange an exchange of goodwill messages via the Czechoslovak Broadcasting Corporation between Tagore in India and Einstein in the USA. Unfortunately, owing to technical difficulties in Calcutta, the poet's message could not be recorded in time for broadcast. And, as we know, in June 1940, the evening before Paris fell, *The Post Office* in André Gide's translation was broadcast over French radio. A French friend of Rabindranath caught it in far-away India, while staying at Kalimpong near Darjeeling in the shadow of the

Himalayas. 'We could listen clearly . . . and marvel at this heroic display of spiritual resistance to despondency by Parisians at the most fateful moment of their destiny.'

From Britain, at the same time, came an appropriate accolade of a different kind: the conferring of an honorary doctorate on Tagore by Oxford University. It was the second such doctorate to be given to an Indian; the first had been given to Sourindromohun Tagore in 1896, as mentioned in Chapter 1. (Oxford's three subsequent Indian doctorates in the humanities would be given to Bengalis too.) However, the award came with a history that reflected the general western ambivalence to Tagore. In mid-1912, *before* his arrival in England, Arthur Fox Strangways had proposed Tagore to Oxford. Lord Curzon, as chancellor, had been uncooperative for fairly obvious reasons, given the events of 1905 in Bengal. Curzon wrote for advice to a British orientalist friend, commenting, 'I question whether he [Tagore] is up to the standard.' In the mid-1920s, Robert Bridges, with the encouragement of Edward Thompson, had pursued the idea – and met with a mixed response. (Thompson admitted to Yeats that Tagore's poetry was regarded with 'extreme contempt' in Oxford at this time.) But by the late 1930s, British opinion had moved some way towards India, politically and academically, even though it was still dismissive of Tagore's poetry. Moreover Lord Halifax, the former viceroy Irwin who admired Tagore, was now chancellor at Oxford.

There was no question of Tagore coming personally to Oxford, for both reasons of health and war, and so the university agreed, most unusually, to confer the degree in Shantiniketan. As *The Times* neatly put it on 8 August 1940, the day after the ceremony: 'In Gangem Defluit Isis.' The chief justice of India, Sir Maurice Gwyer, an Oxford graduate, presided and read the speech traditionally given by the public orator. 'Gurudev replied to this volley of Latin by a volley of Sanskrit, so India held its own; and all agreed that our Sanskrit and Bengali music was an acceptable addition to the traditional ceremony', wrote an English resident of Shantiniketan, the Quaker (and Cambridge graduate) Marjorie Sykes.

It was a good speech, with a noble and touching reply by Rabindranath. (Only Tagore's paintings were omitted; they were no doubt considered too incongruous.) Rabindranath was described in a happy phrase as 'most dear to all the muses', a writer who had 'touched nothing that he has not adorned'.

Let it also be said that he has not valued a sheltered life so far above the public good as to hold himself wholly aloof from the dust and heat of the world outside; for there have been times when he has not scorned to step down into the market-place; when, if he thought that a wrong had been done he has not feared to challenge the British raj itself and the authority of its magistrates; and when he has boldly corrected the faults of his own fellow-citizens . . . Here before you is the myriad-minded poet and writer, the musician famous in his art, the philosopher proven both in word and deed, the fervent upholder of learning and sound doctrine, the ardent defender of public liberties, one who by the sanctity of his life and character has won for himself the praise of all mankind.

Rabindranath responded:

In honouring me, an Indian poet, your ancient seat of learning has chosen to express its great tradition of humanity . . .

. . . In an era of mounting anguish and vanishing worth, when disaster is fast overtaking countries and continents, with savagery let loose and brutal thirst for possession augmented by science, it may sound merely poetic to speak of any emerging principle of worldwide relationship. But Time's violence, however immediately threatening, is circumscribed, and we who live beyond it and dwell also in the larger reality of Time, must renew our faith in the perennial growth of civilization towards an ultimate purpose.

I accept this recognition from Oxford University, as a happy augury of an Age to come, and though I shall not live to see it established, let me welcome this friendly gesture as a promise of better days.

36   The Myriad-Minded Man (1937–1941)

As I look around I see the crumbling ruins of a proud civilization strewn like a vast heap of futility. And yet I shall not commit the grievous sin of losing faith in Man.

Crisis in Civilization,
Shantiniketan, April 1941

Tagore's last years were a torture to him in many ways, but they were artistically fecund. Relatively few artists produce work of the highest standard as death approaches – Rabindranath was an exception. In the teeth of man's mounting inhumanity to man, he clung to humanism. The tremendous tension between the mayhem of the external world and the stillness in Tagore's heart was the source of his creative spurt. Instead of dulling his sensibility, the Indian struggle and the wars in Europe and the Far East sharpened it. The years of heart-breaking failure to stir up either his countrymen or the British rulers had not been entirely wasted; they had distilled and enriched his poetry and songs. (The effect on his paintings is hard to gauge, since they started only in 1928 and are insufficiently dated for chronological analysis.) Lyricism and irony were still there in the poems of the 1930s – along with a new economy and astringency. Many Bengalis preferred, and prefer still, the younger Tagore, especially the Tagore pre-*Gitanjali* (1910); others, such as Satyajit Ray, admired the later years more. Indeed a comparison with Ray's films is illuminating: the younger Tagore is reminiscent of the big-hearted Apu Trilogy (1955–59); the older Tagore of Ray's last film, *Agantuk* (*The Stranger*, 1991), with its sublime synthesis of wit and profundity.

To what extent the constitutionally restless Rabindranath consciously understood his inner transformation is unclear. In July 1937, he joked to the American wife of a Bengali scientist that he would try to follow her husband's 'clever' advice: 'that I should no longer strive and strain myself with the impossible task of benefiting humanity and improving the world. He says I should just keep to my chair and emanate a sort of spiritual electricity of a high voltage' - Tagore was then immersed in writing his science primer *Visva-*

Parichay (*Our Universe*) – 'which will successfully do the trick. The suggestion has my full approval and would suit admirably my own temperament. I shall try to live up to the ideal.'

It was wishful thinking. On 10 September, while preparing to leave for Gwalior at the invitation of the maharaja, he was struck down by an attack of erysipelas. For nearly sixty hours he was in a coma, much of the time without medical help, since there was no telephone in Shantiniketan with which to summon medical help from Calcutta. He almost died.

On 19 September, in a shaky hand, he wrote to Gandhi: 'The first thing which welcomed me into the world of life after the period of stupor I passed through was your message of affectionate anxiety and it was fully worth the cost of sufferings which were unremitting in their long persistence.' A week later, his handwriting now stronger, he told Leonard Elmhirst:

Returning from this my first and latest voyage to the limitless dark I seem to realize in a brighter light a clearer vision of all the precious gifts of life that [have] come to my share. One of these which appeared to my mind was your friendship for which let me offer you my thanks with a renewed freshness and fervour.

Leonard replied: 'At one point I nearly cabled you to the effect that the heart that successfully defied the Peruvian militarists and the opposition forces in Milan might once again be demanding its right measure of peace and quiet, but was not nearly ready yet to leave your service.' Two weeks after that, Tagore told Ernest Rhys: 'I am slowly recovering from [an] illness which had nearly handed me over to your classical ferryman. I am still weak and shirk all intellectual labour, and sit and amuse myself with painting.'

His very first creative act on regaining consciousness had been to paint. Propped up on pillows, he noticed a piece of plywood, a table top, lying in the room; he asked for colours and a brush and painted on it a landscape: dark trees outlined against a ghostly twilight beneath which glimmered irregular patches of white light with a hint of the palest yellow. Dark trees silhouetted against burning orange and yellow skies had been a favourite image of Tagore the painter, now this image subtly suggested the returning of his mind from the place of no return; the miracle of his recovery.

He wrote a number of poems on the same subject, published as *Prantik* (The Borderland), as well as letters. But the painting speaks the most vividly. This is often the case with Tagore for non-Bengalis. As he had said in Germany in 1930: 'My poetry is for my countrymen, my paintings are my gift to the West.' It would barely be exaggerating to say that the best of Rabindranath's paintings – several hundred out of more that 2,000 – are, for the non-Bengali, the best way to understand his mind. No one could look at the 'twelve faces of Tagore' or even at just one of those bizarre self-portraits and not comprehend something of Tagore's mercurial complexity. They are about as far from the saintly, tedious image of him engendered by insipid translations of his poetry as one can get. Here, one feels, is a man who recognizes the savage in himself and is grappling with it; here Rabindranath is as much Old Bluebeard (as Shaw quipped) as Wise Man from the East. Other paintings and drawings cover a huge gamut of moods, subjects and styles, with a correspondingly bold but harmonious palette. Altogether Tagore's paintings prove, if proof is needed, that Rabindranath Tagore speaks to those with no particular interest in India.

This was demonstrated in 1930 by the reactions of critics and artists in France, Germany and Russia, and to a lesser extent in Britain and the United States. (In Britain Tagore's art was admired by Sir Michael Sadler, the leading collector of contemporary art, who in 1933 'discovered' Francis Bacon; and Dorothy Elmhirst, an art-lover and collector who was no great admirer of Tagore's poetry, was excited by his paintings.) In recent years there have been major exhibitions in Britain, Japan and Russia, among other countries. The paintings definitely intrigue people who may barely have heard of Tagore. But while critics and audiences may be free of the old preconceptions – the mystical halo that wreathed anything Tagore touched in the West – they lack new points of reference. Which painters, Indian and non-Indian, influenced Tagore? In what sense are the paintings 'Indian'? Are they essentially figurative or abstract? Why did Tagore generally refuse to name them? How does his lack of training affect their significance? Where is the chronological 'development' expected in an artist? How does one organize and come to grips with such a disparate and prolific body of work?

Much ink has been lavished on the first and second of these questions. With a world traveller like Tagore, who also had a library of art books, it is tempting to assign particular 'influences', eastern and western, to his art, in proportions that vary with the sympathies of the critic. But the most competent critics, who know both Tagore's art, Indian art and world art, such as the painter K. G. Subramanyan, have been chary of this procedure. Satyajit Ray wrote: 'It is important to stress that [Tagore] was uninfluenced by any painter, eastern or western. His work does not stem from any tradition but is truly original. Whether one likes it or not, one has to admit its uniqueness.'

Ananda Coomaraswamy, the best-known critic of Indian art, who had been among Tagore's first translators, tried to respond to some of the problems raised by the paintings in his 1930 catalogue introduction for the Boston exhibition. (Coomaraswamy was a research fellow at the Museum of Fine Arts.)

It is said that he wrote the piece reluctantly, as was evident in its tone. Nonetheless, he was perceptive:

Because Rabindranath is a great and sophisticated poet, a citizen of the world, acquainted with life by personal experience, and by familiarity with the history of culture in Asia and Europe, it must not be inferred that these paintings . . . are sophisticated or metaphysical. It would be a great mistake to search in them for hidden spiritual symbolisms; they are not meant to be deciphered like puzzles and code messages. Nor do they bear any definite relation to the contemporary Bengali school of painting led by his nephews Abanindranath and Gogonendranath Tagore, or to the contemporary movement elsewhere [i.e. in the West]. It is obvious that the poet must have looked at many pictures in the course of his long life; but there is nothing in his own work to show that he has seen them. This is genuinely original, genuinely naive expression; extraordinary evidence of eternal youth persistent in a hoary and venerable personage.

Childlike, but not childish. It is perfectly legitimate to be amused by, to laugh at, or with, some of these creations, as one is amused by a child's vision of the world; it is not legitimate to ridicule them . . .

. . . Rabindranath . . . has no contempt for training or virtuosity; he simply does not possess it, and knowing this he puts before us in all simplicity, certainly not cynically, the creations of his playful vision, for us to use as we will . . .

. . . The poet gives no descriptive titles to his pictures – how could he? They are not pictures about things, but pictures about himself . . .

. . . any method of [painting] is employed that may be available or that may suggest itself at the moment. The artist, like a child, invents his own technique as he goes along; nothing has been allowed to interfere with zest. The means are always adequate to the end in view: this end is not 'Art' with a capital A, on the one hand – nor, on the other, a merely pathological self-expression; nor art intended to improve our minds, nor to provide for the artist himself an 'escape'; but without ulterior motives, truly innocent, like the creation of a universe.

'Like the creation of a universe': it was a shrewd judgement. Perhaps Coomaraswamy had in mind, or half in mind, the universe Tagore had created at Shantiniketan, where Coomaraswamy had visited in pre-Nobel-prize days, when it was truly a childlike projection of Rabindranath's ideals. There is an intimate but mysterious connection between Rabindranath's art and the landscape, light, people and creatures of Shantiniketan and its surrounding villages, many of them tribal (Santhal) villages. To have seen Shantiniketan, to have lived in it, to have fallen for it – all these experiences tune one to the same wavelength as Rabindranath's paintings. And yet by themselves they are not enough: one must also know the world outside Shantiniketan, as the artist did. Rabindranath's portraits, particularly his haunting images of women (including his long-dead sister-in-law Kadambari), are instinct with his sympathy for people, yet simultaneously detached from them. 'Are those goblin faces the cooks in his kitchen and those sad, poker-faced, wide-eyed women the maids in his back yard?' Subramanyan speculated. 'These women are recognizably Bengali, portrayed in an infinity of moods and expressions', wrote Satyajit Ray (of whose films the same may be said). To the connoisseur who knows both eastern and western art, the portraits seem to hover between the here and now and the eternal, the familiar and the alien. By the same reasoning, to the Shantiniketan-dweller who does not know the West or to the unprepared western art critic, the portraits can seem unsatisfying, lacking in depth or technique. Very few of those around Tagore admired his portraits; even now there is little genuine feeling for them in Shantiniketan. While in London, in 1986, most art critics called the portraits 'expressionless', 'often stylized and imaginary', 'repetitive and uniformly non-committal'. Almost without exception, they preferred Tagore's landscapes.

Coomaraswamy's emphasis on the child's vision was significant too. Rabindranath's paintings are capable, sometimes, of reawakening our early sense of wonder. They are full of fantastic metamorphoses and frolicking grotesques, as in fairy tales and legends, and in our childish imaginations. But one has to be willing to suspend one's sophistication, so as to marvel. Perhaps the most striking fact of all about the paintings is how susceptible they are to the mood of the viewer. One day they can seem gorgeous and magical, another day lifeless and crude. There are few painters so reticent as Rabindranath. He rarely beards a viewer with one of his works and says, 'Look, look at me!' In this sense his paintings are like the mask he adopted when travelling in the West or in translating his works into English; for the receptive foreigner, who is open-minded and curious for the unfamiliar, they offer a whole world awaiting discovery.

In Tagore's music, *Rabindrasangit*, the same is true – but the secret is harder to penetrate. The first non-Bengali to discover it and tell the western world was Arthur Fox Strangways, founder of *Music and Letters* and music critic of the London *Observer*. In 1914, Fox Strangways published *The Music of Hindostan* based on his extensive travels in the subcontinent, a book still admired by Indian musical connoisseurs. In it he noted the words and melodies of several Tagore songs and had this to say of *Rabindrasangit*:

To hear him [Rabindranath] sing them is to realize the music in a way that it is seldom given to a foreigner to do. The notes of the song are no longer their mere selves, but the vehicle of a personality, and as such they go behind this or that system of music to that beauty of sound which all systems put out their hands to seize. These melodies are such as would have satisfied Plato. 'I do not know the modes,' said Socrates, 'but leave me one that will imitate the tones and accents of a brave man enduring danger or distress, fighting with constancy against fortune; and also one fitted for the work of peace, for prayer heard by the gods, and for the successful persuasion or exhortation of men.'

For Bengalis, *Rabindrasangit*, properly sung, does all these things. It has a beauty combined with strength that surpasses Rabindranath's poetry. In 1932, the *Modern Review* noted matter-of-factly that 'There is in Bengal no cultured home where Rabindranath's songs are not sung or at least attempted to be sung . . . Even illiterate villagers sing his songs.' Today most of his great songs have been lifted for use in Bombay cinema – either just the tunes or both the tunes and the words (translated into Hindi) by film composers such as the immensely successful S. D. Burman (a member of the princely family of Tripura that was close to Rabindranath). In 1991 Ravi Shankar, another Bengali (though born outside Bengal), said: 'Tagore had the genius of composing ten different tunes from whatever he heard. . . I don't think his creativity ever knew any bounds.' Satyajit Ray, a composer steeped in the classical music of the West and the East (whose music was admired by, among others, Mstislav Rostropovich), said simply: 'As a Bengali I know that as a composer of songs, Tagore has no equal, not even in the West – and I know Schubert and Hugo Wolf'.
 This is extremely unlikely ever to be understood in the West, let alone accepted. (Nevertheless, a Tagore song made a wonderful opening for the film of *The Mahabharata* by Peter Brook.) History, culture and language all bar the way; and Tagore's songs cannot be translated into English literature. Period. The truth is that unless one can understand the words of Tagore's songs, they quickly begin to sound monotonous – though a small selection, carefully made, is usually convincing of his melodic gift and its range. (The songs from his first opera *Valmiki Pratibha* are probably sufficient alone.) Another way to understand is from Ray's films, in which *Rabindrasangit* appears time and again in various forms, vocal and instrumental. The Tagore songs in *Monihara* (*The Lost Jewels*, 1961), *Kanchenjungha* (1962) and *Agantuk* (*The Stranger*, 1991), are especially moving; the use of *Rabindrasangit* in the soundtrack of *Charulata* (1964) and *Ghare Baire* (*The Home and the World*, 1984) particularly imaginative.
 Rabindranath understood the barriers very well and had no illusions that they might easily be removed. He had never admired western orchestral music

and operatic singing in the way that he had western literature and western art (remember his amused teenage reaction to the cadenzas of Victorian prima donnas); in his later years he moved even further away from them. He told Edward Thompson in the early 1920s:

> it is nonsense to say that music is a universal language. I should like my music to find acceptance, but I know this cannot be, at least not till the West has had time to study and learn to appreciate our music. All the same, I know the artistic value of my songs. They have great beauty. Though they will not be known outside my province, and much of my work will be gradually lost, I leave them as a legacy. My own countrymen do not understand. But they will.

In 1967, Satyajit Ray commented valuably (in Bengali) on Tagore's attitude to musical tradition:

> Though as a child he was nourished by classical Indian music in his household at Jorasanko, and even lovingly composed some songs in that tradition . . . he was never keen on the rigidity of raga-based music. He was quite fond of *ustadi* songs, but he never cared much for their prescriptive basis. This suggests that Rabindranath did not consider the evidence of flexibility in ragas carefully: for the fact is that a raga may sound much more satisfying when rendered by an imaginative *ustad* than by a lesser *ustad*. The raga is only a basic formula, not a composition. Unlike in Europe, where if a composition is weak the conductor expresses the weakness, in India the weakness or strength of a piece of music is one hundred per cent the responsibility of the *ustad*. Thus we cannot call the mere existence of ragas stagnant or outmoded.
>
> No doubt Rabindranath began to compose his songs in a spirit of rebellion. He wanted to break with convention, break new ground. Though he did not abide by the prescribed forms, he did not consider them to be unnecessary either. His aim was the perfect union of word, tune and rhythm, but because he was as fine a writer as he was a composer, he had difficulty in creating this union in a song without compromising either the words or the tune. Sometimes his words are too dominant, enfeebling the tune . . . Personally, I believe his musical genius achieved full play only after he came away from the direct influence of his family. The songs he composed later still contain snatches of ragas but they are no longer classically based like his earlier [hymns]. They are his own creations, in which his poetic skills have come in to increase the beauty of the song, to generate an interplay between word, mood and beat.

As a poet, Rabindranath broke more and more with convention over the years. His final four collections of verse were nearly all unrhymed, free in rhythm and with a straight margin. He showed a deepening concentration on immediate concrete experience – but not in any trite or limiting way, rather as a reflection of something lying beyond the poet (like the reflection in a dewdrop). In this sense he stayed true to his best youthful work, 'to the subject on which all my writings have dwelt: the delight of attaining the infinite within the finite', as he had written in *My Reminiscences*.

> Here rolls the sea
> And even here
>   Lies the other shore
> Waiting to be reached
>   Yes here
> Is the everlasting present
>   Not distant
>   Not anywhere else

– he wrote in *Sadhana*, his philosophical lectures, given at Harvard University and in London in 1913. The same idea was evident in the story 'The Postmaster', and in his letters to his niece Indira, *Chhinnapatra* (Torn Leaves); in the play *Dak Ghar* (*The Post Office*), and in the poems of *Gitanjali* ('Thou art the sky and Thou art also the nest'); in the poem 'Shah Jahan' and in the novel *Ghare Baire* (*The Home and the World*); in the poem 'Kankal' (A Skeleton) and in the small poem about the dewdrop he wrote for the eight-year-old Satyajit. Now, in late 1940, convalescing after another brush with death, Rabindranath found similar inspiration in two common-or-garden sights: a sparrow knocking at his door, and a rose on his bedside table. This is the last verse of the sparrow poem, which was written in his Jorasanko house:

> Whenever I pass the night sleepless and sore,
> I await your first beak-tap at my door.
> How fearless, how nimble you are.
> The simple message of your life,
> I need it –
> The light that bathes all creatures
> Is calling me,
> O my day-break sparrow.

And here is the rose poem in its entirety, written after he had returned to

Shantiniketan for what would be the last time:

Awakening this morning
In my vase I saw a rose:
The question came to my mind –
Through the cycling of time over aeons
This power that made you a thing of beauty
Shunning all distortion into uncouth imperfection,
Is it blind, is it abstracted?
– Like an ascetic who renounces the world,
the beautiful and the unbeautiful without distinction –
Is it just logical, just physical?
Does not consciousness play its part?
There are those who argue and maintain
That in the court of Creation
Form and formlessness have equal rank,
No guards restrain them.
I am a poet, I do not debate,
I look at the world in its wholeness –
At the millions of planets and stars in the sky
Revolving in grandeur and harmony
Never losing the beat of their music
Never slipping into derangement.
When I look at the sky I see spreading petalled layers,
A vast and resplendent rose.

These poems, untitled, were from a collection entitled *Rogashajyay* (The Sick-bed). In January 1941, Rabindranath composed a poem, also untitled, published shortly after in a collection with the hopeful title *Arogya* (Recovery). It brilliantly captured the suffering and the faith underlying his final year of existence.

Brutal night comes silently,
Breaks down the loosened bolts of my spent body,
Enters my insides,
Starts stealing images of life's dignity:
My heart succumbs to the assault of darkness.
The shame of defeat,
        the insult of this fatigue,
Grow intense.

Suddenly on the horizon,
Dawn's banner laced with rays of gold;
From a distant centre of the sky a shout:
    'It's a lie, a lie!'
Against the tranquil light of morning
I can see myself as a conqueror of sorrows
Standing on top of my fortress, my ruin, my body.

Musing nostalgically, he thought of Victoria Ocampo and her celebrated chair
that he had brought back all the way to Shantiniketan from Argentina:

One more time, if I may,
I would like to find that seat
In the lap of which is spread
A caress from a foreign land. . .
. . . It will keep for ever unsleeping
That message, so sad, so tender,
Of that woman whose language I did not know
But whose eyes were eloquent.

He no longer cared to live, such was the unrelenting pain. When Gandhi sent
a telegram on the eve of his eightieth birthday, 'Four score not enough. May you
finish five', Rabindranath replied: 'Thanks message. But four score is
impertinence. Five score intolerable.'

Yet for all his physical and mental distress – the former at the state of his
body, the latter at the state of the world – Rabindranath's mind and heart
remained acutely, wondrously active and feeling. He could no longer move in
the world, but his interest and concern for its affairs did not dim. There was no
'Indian' retreat into indifference; if anything his delight, his sorrow and, yes, his
rage, burned more brightly than ever before. Photographs of him at eighty show
a man of radiant, almost incandescent beauty. It was how he must have looked
when Eisenstein's wife, Pera Atasheva, had sat next to him in Moscow in 1930
and watched *Battleship Potemkin*: his eyes, she had said, shone 'with white fire',
to resist his glance was 'simply impossible'.

On 14 April, the Bengali New Year, Tagore's final testament was read out at
Shantiniketan in his presence; Rabindranath was too weak to read it himself. Its
title was 'Shabhyatar Shankat' (*Crisis in Civilization*). It was a *cri de coeur*, a
passionate and uncompromising statement of Tagore's loss of faith in western
civilization, encapsulated in its closing quotation, a favourite of Rabindranath,
from Sanskrit: 'By unrighteousness man prospers, gains what appears desirable,

conquers enemies, but perishes at the root.' Or, in the words of Jesus in the Gospel According to Mark (a comparison not drawn by Tagore, who mentioned neither Christ nor, surprisingly, the Buddha): 'What shall it profit a man, if he shall gain the whole world, and lose his own soul?'

Tagore's respect for individual Englishmen – he mentioned the late C. F. Andrews by name – remained. 'Without the slightest hesitation I may say that the nobility of their character was without parallel – in no country or community have I come across such greatness of soul. Such examples would not allow me wholly to lose faith in the race which produced them.' But his indictment of British rule in India was severe and without mitigation:

The wheels of Fate will some day compel the British to give up their Indian Empire. But what kind of India will they leave behind, what stark misery? When the stream of their two centuries' administration runs dry at last, what a waste of mud and filth will they leave behind them! I had at one time believed that the springs of civilization would issue out of the heart of Europe. But today, when I am about to quit the world, that faith has deserted me.

He concluded the address:

And yet I shall not commit the grievous sin of losing faith in Man. I would rather look forward to the opening of a new chapter in his history after the cataclysm is over and the atmosphere rendered clean with the spirit of service and sacrifice. Perhaps that dawn will come from this horizon, from the East where the sun rises. A day will come when unvanquished Man will retrace his path of conquest, despite all barriers, to win back his lost human heritage.

Reading his words one thinks almost inevitably of his lovely, sensuous 'poem-painting' created in Baghdad in 1932. [pl.43]

There was barely a word of his usual unsparing criticism of his own people; no attempt to distinguish between Fascism and imperialism; and ample ill-judged praise of the utopia in the Soviet Union. 'Her civilization is free from all invidious distinction between one class and another, between one sect and another.' He contrasted the Soviet Union's progress with India's 'disorder of barbarism' and described the two systems of government, 'one based on cooperation' (the Soviet Union), 'the other on exploitation' (India). For Rabindranath, it seemed that no amount of evidence of Stalin's hideous crimes against his own people, culminating in the Nazi–Soviet Pact of 1939 – still in force at the time of Tagore's writing – was capable of shaking his faith in his own experience of the Soviet system in 1930. Here was the greatest blunder of his life.

Crisis in Civilization is easy to dismiss. It is definitely not among Tagore's finest and most lasting essays. Hardly anyone, looking at the state of either India, China or Japan today, can have any confidence that they will create a more humane civilization as Rabindranath hoped. But the very forcefulness of the essay's language, coming from a man of Tagore's worldwide experience, sensitivity and imagination, compels a response. V. S. Naipaul, a great writer of the late twentieth century, wrote of it in *India: A Million Mutinies Now* (1990):

It was an old man's melancholy farewell to the world. Five years later the war was over. Europe began to heal; in the second half of the century Europe and the West were to be stronger and more creative and more influential than they have ever been. The calamity Tagore hadn't seen was the calamity that was to come to Calcutta.

Bold words, words of faith – almost as bold as Tagore's hopes for the East. Undoubtedly the years since 1945 have seen a strengthening of western power, wealth and welfare. Maybe too the West has become more influential in the rest of the world than before, even though the colonial empires no longer exist. But more *creative?* Apart from science (and even there the great conceptual advances chiefly predate 1945), is there a single field of post-war artistic and intellectual endeavour that is indubitably superior to that which preceded it? Really only in the cinema – and even there the golden age seems to be over.

To Rabindranath, British rule in India was, in the final analysis, uncreative: and that was why he condemned it. The chasm of aloofness between ruler and ruled, of which he had spoken with bitterness to the Quakers in London in 1930, deprived the *Pax Britannica* of any glory in Tagore's eyes. It was a machine, not a living organism. And machines not controlled by humanity – whether they were regimental rifles under British command at Amritsar, or the spinning wheels of the Congress Party – were hateful to Rabindranath.

Perhaps a small incident in September 1940 best illustrated the attitude Tagore was fighting. While staying at Kalimpong near Darjeeling, he again lost consciousness. As in September 1937 at Shantiniketan, no medical help was immediately available. Indian doctors were sent for from Calcutta, and in the meantime the British civil surgeon at Darjeeling was frantically appealed to. He came, reluctantly, and, after examining the patient, enquired gruffly – did (Sir) Rabindranath Tagore understand English? 'No sadder instance can be cited of the rapidly increasing alienation of the British ruling class from the people they governed', wrote Krishna Kripalani. Half a century earlier, at Ghazipur in

1888, it was the local civil surgeon at whose request Tagore had first translated one of his poems into English.

Crisis in Civilization was not Rabindranath's absolutely final pronouncement on British rule. In June 1941, he received a letter from Foss Westcott, the bishop of Calcutta (and head of the Anglican Church in India) who had made India his home, pleading for more sympathetic Congress understanding of Britain's peril in the war. Tagore replied in measured words that may stand for his ultimate verdict on this deeply contentious subject:

> I have neither the right nor the desire to judge the British people as such; but I cannot help being concerned at the conduct of the British Government in India, since it directly involves the life and well-being of millions of my countrymen. I am too painfully conscious of the extreme poverty, helplessness and misery of our people not to deplore the supineness of the Government that has tolerated this condition for so long. . . I had hoped that the leaders of the British nation, who had grown apathetic to our suffering and forgetful of their own sacred trust in India during their days of prosperity and success, would at last, in the time of their own great trial, awake to the justice and humanity of our cause. It has been a most grievous disappointment to me to find that fondly cherished hope receding farther and farther from realization each day. Believe me, nothing would give me greater happiness than to see the people of the West and the East march in a common crusade against all that robs the human spirit of its significance.

The ideal was a noble one – most people would today feel that the fight against Fascism was 'a common crusade against all that [robbed] the human spirit of its significance'– but the psychology had a fatal flaw: nations cannot be appealed to like individuals. Rabindranath always maintained that they could be and must be. History, however, has not supported him. As the bishop pragmatically replied: 'Is there any nation in the world which, when involved in a life and death struggle, would tolerate active propaganda against cooperating in the fight for freedom. . . ?'

Tagore's letter had been sent on 16 June. By then he was obviously sinking. But his sense of humour remained with him to the last. He could not get over his amusement at being fed on Glaxo, referring to himself as a 'Glaxo baby'. Having once been told that he was receiving the dose prescribed for a two-month-old baby, he liked to enquire from his nurses: 'How many months old am I today?' In addition to allopathy, he now received ayurvedic treatment based on Indian treatises. There was some improvement, but by mid-July his doctors

37 Rabindranath as the Fakir in *Dak Ghar* (*The Post Office*), with Gaganendranath as Father, in Jorasanko, 1917

38 Agricultural economist Leonard Elmhirst, founder of the Dartington Trust, and Rabindranath: *top* – in Bengal, 1920s/30s; *below left* – in Dartington, England, 1930; *below right* – 'Poet and Plowman', mural in Shriniketan, 1920s (*Nandalal Bose*)

Rabindranath and P'u-i, last emperor of China, in the Forbidden City, Beijing, 1924 (Reginald Johnston)

Rabindranath and party, in Beijing, 1924: interpreter Lin Hui-yin, scholar Kalidas Nag, Leonard Elmhirst, scholar Kshitimohan Sen, nurse Gretchen Green (*with hat*), artist Nandalal Bose (*Reginald Johnston*)

41 Rabindranath, at Borobudur, Java, 1927

42 Rabindranath, in a Bedouin encampment near Baghdad, Iraq, 1932

অবসান হোলো রাতি।
নিবাইয়া ফেলো কোণের – জ্বলিত
ধূর্ত কোণের বাতি।
নিখিলের আলো শুদ্ধ আকাশে
জ্বলিল শুধাদিনে
একপথে যারা চলিবে তাহারা
সকলেরে নিক চিনে।

The night has ended.

Put out the light of the lamp
of thine own narrow corner
smudged with smoke.

The great morning which is for all

appears in the East.

Let its light reveal us
to each other
who walk on
on the same
path of pilgrimage.

Rabindranath
Tagore

Baghdad
May 24
1932

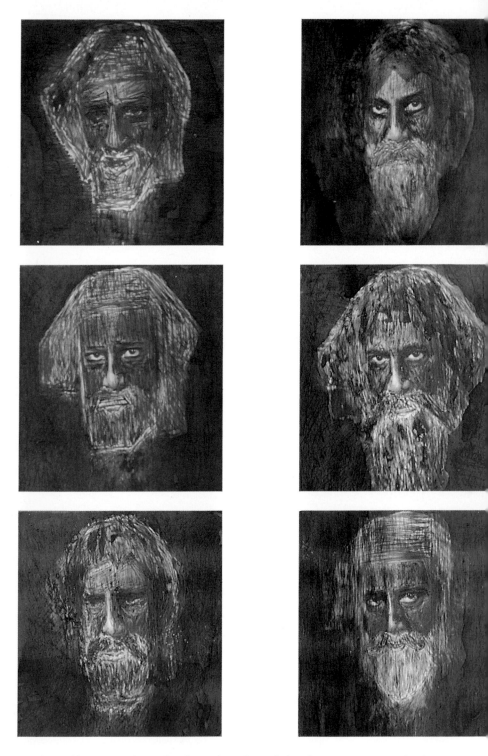

Twelve self-portraits by Rabindranath, coloured doodles on a black-and-white photograph

45 Rabindranath and companions at the exhibition opening of his paintings, Galèrie Pigalle, Paris, May 1930: Countess Anna de Noailles, the French minister of fine arts, Victoria Ocampo

46 Rabindranath at a Pioneer Commune, in Moscow, 1930

were convinced that an operation in Calcutta was necessary. Rabindranath would have preferred to avoid it, not to leave Shantiniketan – he was plainly ready for death – but his doctors explained that without the operation he would suffer frightfully. Finally he consented.

On the morning of 25 July, Tagore left Shantiniketan for the last time. The whole ashram had gathered at his house from early on and quietly waited for him to be taken down from his room upstairs on a specially constructed stretcher to the ashram's bus. (During the previous day, the pot-holes in the short stretch of road from Shantiniketan to Bolpur station had been filled up to give him a bearable ride.) Rabindranath was too exhausted even to address a few words to his workers and students and they did not take the dust of his feet, lest they disturb him. His secretary described the moment of farewell: 'In deep silence and with mute salutations they bade him goodbye but as the bus began to move they could not contain themselves any longer. Spontaneously from a thousand throats broke out the ashram song "Amader Shantiniketan". It reached Gurudev's ears and there were tears in his eyes.'

Two weeks later, around noon on 7 August 1941, in north Calcutta, in an upstairs room of the house where he was born, Rabindranath Tagore expired. But not before he had dictated three more poems, published posthumously as *Shesh Lekha* (Last Writings). They were untitled, brief and utterly direct. On 27 July he said:

The sun of the first day
Put the question
To the new manifestation of life –
Who are you?
There was no answer.
Years passed by.
The last sun of the last day
Uttered the question on the shore of the western sea,
In the hush of evening –
Who are you!
No answer came.

And on 30 July, just before the operation, he produced his very last poem, which he was unable to correct. Translation, as ever, fails to do justice to Tagore's Bengali; this is Nirad Chaudhuri's précis:

Sorceress! You have strewn the path of creation with
    your varied wiles. . .

With a cunning hand laid the snares of false trust for
    a simple soul. . .
But his glory is that, however devious outside, he is
    still straight at heart. . . . .
He who had yielded so easily to manifold deceptions
    has received from you
The inviolate right to peace.

Sixty years before, the poet had written to his young niece Indira: 'In my life I may have done many things that were unworthy, with or without knowing, but in my poetry I have never uttered anything false; it is the sanctuary for the deepest truths I know.' He had kept his promise to himself.

He also told her: 'How I cherish light and space! Goethe on his death-bed wanted "more light". If I am capable of expressing my desire then, it will be for "more light and more space".'

His last wish was not fulfilled in death – as his deepest wishes had seldom been fulfilled in life. Instead of passing on among the trees of Shantiniketan that he loved, beneath the open sky and breezes of Bengal, he died in a house he disliked in the most congested part of a city he detested. It was a mercy he could not see his own funeral. While he might have been moved by the ocean of Bengali faces – comparable in size to the funeral of Gandhi in 1948 – he would have been disgusted by the chaos and indiscipline, as he had scorned the crowd that had descended on Shantiniketan from Calcutta after the Nobel prize announcement in 1913. As the funeral cortège moved haltingly along, hairs were plucked from the famous head; and at the cremation ghat itself, beside the Ganges, before the body was completely burnt, the crowd invaded and began searching for bones and other relics of the Poet's mortal being. (The fire had to be lit by a great-nephew of Rabindranath, not by his son, as is customary – Rathindranath could not get near the ghat.) There was much shouting and cursing, for little was left among the ashes. 'It was a disconcerting, indeed a mind-boggling spectacle', wrote Alex Aronson, the Jewish-refugee teacher from Shantiniketan who witnessed the macabre scene. [pl.58]

Jawaharlal Nehru was in prison when he heard the news. His daughter Indira happened to be visiting. In his jail diary for 7 August Nehru wrote:

So Gurudev is dead – An age seems to be over. Perhaps it is as well that he died now and did not see the many horrors that are likely to descend in increasing measure on the world and on India. He had seen enough and he was infinitely sad and unhappy. He seemed to have little faith left in his people, especially in Bengal. Eighty was a noble age to die after the magnificently full and creative life he had lived. Why live longer and submit to slow decay?. . .

. . . Gandhi and Tagore. Two types entirely different from each other, and yet both of them typical of India, both in the long line of India's great men. How rich and extravagant is India to produce two such men in a generation – just to show what she can do even in her present distress and lowly state. Judged as types of men, I have felt for long that they were the outstanding examples in the world today. There are many of course who may be abler than them or greater geniuses in their own line. Einstein is great. There may be greater poets than Tagore, greater writers . . . It is not so much because of any single virtue but because of the *tout ensemble*, that I felt that among the world's great men today Gandhi and Tagore were supreme as human beings. What good fortune for me to have come into close contact with them.

In India, the chief memorial ceremony for the dead, the *shraddha*, is performed on the tenth day after death. Rathindranath Tagore had publicly appealed for people to observe the occasion in their own homes, not to come to Shantiniketan. Only a few intimate friends came to the ashram on the 17th. A temporary platform of bamboo poles and matting, beautifully decorated with leaves and lotus flowers, was erected near the place where Maharshi Debendranath had first meditated eighty years before.

The service was a simple one, beginning, naturally, with a song by the deceased. It had never been sung before. Rabindranath had composed it in December 1939, intending to sing it himself, in the role of Fakir, at a new production of *The Post Office*, after the death of the boy Amal. When the production was called off, he expressed a wish that the song be sung after his own death. Even in translation, bereft of its melody, far away from Shantiniketan, it suggests that 'interpenetration of human life with the cosmic life of the world' of which the poet spoke: the quintessence of Rabindranath Tagore.

The ocean of peace lies ahead of me.
Sail the boat, O pilot
You are my constant companion now.
Take me in your lap.
Along our journey to the infinite
The pole star alone will shine.

Giver of Freedom
Set me free.
May your forgiveness and compassion
Be my eternal resources for the journey –
May the mortal ties fall away,
May the vast universe
Hold me in embrace,
And with an undaunted heart
May I come to know the Great Unknown.

Postscript

Dear Leonard

Letters from across the sea have become painfully scarce. Now, when we crave mutual touch with distant friends with such hunger, your letter this morning gave me a complete surprise of delight. As for the condition of my body it is very similar to that of world politics today. It has stood eighty years of buffeting and yet is not unseaworthy. My organs are in perfect harmony with each other, only some intolerable hooligans come to deliver sudden blows from unexpected directions. But still I have not lost my courage and am pretty nearly in the same mental condition as your Great Churchill. I have decided to win at the last. But when I speak like this I must take into account the paucity of the numbers of years still left to me, however friendly their attitude may be.

Our breakfast table remains still unaffected by war unlike yours. The meagreness of its fare is not owing to any miserliness of human agency but owing to scarcity of rain which is holding off its ministrations with unseasonable persistence. But you know we are used all through our days to half rations and are reconciled to such further curtailments of our needs. Our Visva-Bharati just now has had the good luck to receive a pecuniary grant from our central government for a year which will help us to tide over to some extent our difficulties for the present season. I believe you have heard about the visit of the Chinese Ambassador of Goodwill Mission to our Ashram and we have been greatly impressed by the old world graciousness beaming out of his countenance. His presence has been a real source of inspiration to our people.

Please give my love to Dorothy and share it yourself with her. My pen is helplessly lame and therefore I have to borrow help from others when I write letters which have become necessarily scarce.

Ever yours
Rabindranath Tagore

Lisbon
24 July 1941

Dear Gurudev

I found your cheering letter waiting for me on my return from America in early June. And now the United States Department of Agriculture has asked Dorothy and me to return to America to work for them for two months. This is why I write you from Lisbon. On Monday we fly on to New York.

I was happy to find everyone in England in such good spirits, and in spite of all the pounding their cities have had, so detached, so kindly, so lacking in bitterness and in so many ways so considerate to one another.

Russia coming in aroused no undue hopes of an early release from Hitler's pressure upon us, but it gave us all a feeling of not being alone in the world any longer, and more strangely still, a feeling of no longer being separated from the Russian people by an 'ism' that in the face of German dive bombers and monster tanks no longer seems to have any *reality*. I often think of your continuous emphasis upon that word. 'Help us to distinguish the real from the unreal' – you used to say. Did those Hindu wisemen of old ever give a hint of their having been able to discover and define 'the real' – or must each seeker achieve through experience and intuition his own sense of reality?

You, Sir, have had a longer and a more many-sided life of search and research in your effort to pin down reality than perhaps anyone else in our day. If you are not ready to tell us just what reality is, perhaps you can now say, without undue hesitation, what it is not.

I wish we could sit together in your little porch, watching the rain clouds roll in from the Dumka hills and discuss this question of all questions.

I met a Dr Kuo last week who reminded me that you and I nearly perished under the balcony of his gymnasium in Nanking – and I remembered pushing you out to the front of the platform so that if the gallery did fall it might not be upon us both. Do you remember that charming Civil Governor at Nanking – a Buddhist scholar – who said for him India meant Heaven and that undoubtedly you had come from there, renewing the broken connection after 700 years, a successor to those early Buddhist missionaries from over the Himalayas. The Military Governor on the other hand gave us champagne at 11.00 a.m. – we needed it. Our deepest love to you and all our friends.

Yours affectionately
Leonard

APPENDIX 1

Tagore Family Tree
(Jorasanko Branch)

'PRINCE' DWARKANATH (b. Calcutta, 1794; d. London, 1846)

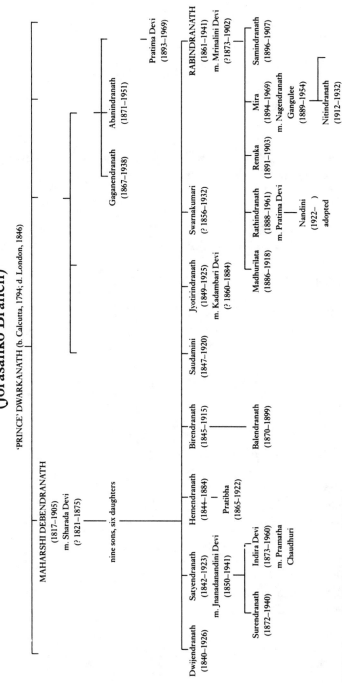

MAHARSHI DEBENDRANATH
(1817–1905)
m. Sharada Devi
(? 1821–1875)

nine sons, six daughters

Dwijendranath
(1840–1926)

Satyendranath
(1842–1923)
m. Jnanadanandini Devi
(1850–1941)

Surendranath
(1872–1940)

Indira Devi
(1873–1960)
m. Pramatha
Chaudhuri

Hemendranath
(1844–1884)

Pratibha
(1865–1922)

Birendranath
(1845–1915)

Balendranath
(1870–1899)

Saudamini
(1847–1920)

Jyotirindranath
(1849–1925)
m. Kadambari Devi
(? 1860–1884)

Swarnakumari
(? 1856–1932)

Gaganendranath
(1867–1938)

Abanindranath
(1871–1951)

Pratima Devi
(1893–1969)

RABINDRANATH
(1861–1941)
m. Mrinalini Devi
(?1873–1902)

Madhurilata
(1886–1918)

Rathindranath
(1888–1961)
m. Pratima Devi

Nandini
(1922–   )
adopted

Renuka
(1891–1903)

Mira
(1894–1969)
m. Nagendranath
Gangulee
(1889–1954)

Samindranath
(1896–1907)

Nitindranath
(1912–1932)

NB Only those mentioned in the text appear in this Tree.

APPENDIX 2

Tagore's Travels: A Chronology

Only the dates of Tagore's travels beyond the mainland of India are listed. Some less important visits have been omitted.

1878
October–December   Britain

1879
January–December   Britain

1880
January–February   Britain

1890
September–October   Britain

1912
June–October   Britain
November–December   USA

1913
January–April   USA
May–September   Britain

1916
May   Burma
May–September   Japan
September–December   USA

1917
January   USA
February   Japan

1920

June–August	Britain
August–September	France
September	Holland
September–October	Belgium
October	Britain
October–December	USA

1921

January–March	USA
March–April	Britain
April	France
April –May	Switzerland
May	Germany, Denmark, Sweden
May–June	Germany
June	Austria, Czechoslovakia

1922

October–November	Ceylon

1924

April –May	China
June–July	Japan
November–December	Argentina

1925

January	Argentina
January–February	Italy

1926

May–June	Italy
June–July	Switzerland
July	Austria
July–August	Britain
August	Norway
August–September	Sweden
September	Denmark
September–October	Germany
October	Czechoslovakia, Austria
October–November	Hungary

November	Bulgaria, Romania, Greece, Egypt

1927

July	Singapore
July–August	Malaya
August–September	Java, Bali
October	Thailand

1928

May– June	Ceylon

1929

March	Japan
April	Canada, USA
May–June	Japan
June	Indo-China

1930

March–May	France
May–July	Britain
July–August	Germany
August	Denmark
August–September	Switzerland
September	Russia
October–December	USA
December	Britain

1931

January	Britain

1932

April –May	Persia
May–June	Iraq

1934

May–June	Ceylon

Exact dates are given in *Rabindranath Tagore: A Centenary Volume, 1861–1961* (Sahitya Akademi, New Delhi, 1961).

Notes

A Note about References

The references in the Notes to Rabindranath Tagore's writings are bilingual (English and Bengali), wherever the work cited already exists in translation and we have decided to quote the translation, rather than making our own translation. The English source is given first, followed by a slash·/, then the Bengali source. However, the Bengali sources are presented in a more abbreviated form than the English sources. Translators are credited, where known.

For unpublished material – mainly letters in English – the library or individual holding the material is given at the end of the reference in square brackets, e.g. [RB], [Dartington]. Details of these sources are given in the Bibliography under Manuscript Sources.

Where a Bengali date is given in the Notes, the English date appears in square brackets (year only). The Bengali months (generally not converted) are as follows: Magh (mid-January to mid-February); Phalgun (mid-February to mid-March); Chaitra (mid-March to mid-April); Baishakh (mid-April to mid-May); Jaishtha (mid-May to mid-June); Asharh (mid-June to mid-July); Shraban (mid-July to mid-August); Bhadra (mid-August to mid-September); Ashwin (mid-September to mid-October); Kartik (mid-October to mid-November); Agrahayan (mid-November to mid-December); Paush (mid-December to mid-January).

The following abbreviations are used:

RT	Rabindranath Tagore
CMG	*Calcutta Municipal Gazette* (Tagore Memorial Special Supplement), 13 Sept. 1941
CWMG	*Collected Works of Mahatma Gandhi*
GB	*Gitabitan* (collected songs of RT)
Glimpses	*Glimpses of Bengal*
MR	*Modern Review*
My Rem	*My Reminiscences*
RR	*Rabindra Rachanabali* (collected works of RT)
RR(AS)	*Rabindra Rachanabali (Achalita Shangraha)* (addenda to collected works)

TUM	*Towards Universal Man*
VBN	*Visva-Bharati News*
VBQ	*Visva-Bharati Quarterly*

The Bibliography contains only manuscript sources and books. Articles are fully referenced in the Notes. All books cited in the Notes only by author's name (or equivalent) are fully referenced in the Bibliography. Some other books, not cited but also consulted, are included in the Bibliography, but we have made no attempt to compile a full-scale bibliography. A useful, though incomplete and sometimes inaccurate, bibliography of writings by and about RT (in English only), exists (see Katherine Henn, *Rabindranath Tagore: A Bibliography*, Metuchen, New Jersey and London, 1985). Our Bibliography should provide an extra guide to English sources, both for the scholar and for the general reader, for the second of whom we have given a list of significant English translations of RT, past and current.

Introductory epigraphs
Rabindranath Tagore: letter to Thomas Sturge Moore, 11 June 1935 [RB]
Satyajit Ray: written interview, 1982 (Robinson, *Satyajit Ray*, p. 10)
E. P. Thompson: Thompson, p. 51

Introduction
Epigraph   RT to E. J. Thompson, 20 Sept. 1921 [Bodleian]
p. 1   'Europe's power' 'On the eve of departure', *TUM*, p. 167/*RR*, *26*, p. 468. The speech was given in Shantiniketan in May 1912.
p. 1   'Christ' For instance, Frances Cornford, granddaughter of Charles Darwin, met Tagore in Cambridge and wrote to Rothenstein on 15 July 1912: 'I can now imagine a powerful and gentle Christ, which I never could before.' (Lago, p. 19) RT was constantly compared to Christ during his western travels between 1912 and 1931.
p. 2   'Susan Owen' 1 Aug. 1920. The complete letter is printed in Rathindranath Tagore, p. 111. Susan Owen offered RT a copy of Wilfred Owen's first book of poems, which was about to be published. Whether RT replied is not known.
p. 2   'message form' In Edmund Blunden's memoir of Owen written in 1931 and published in his edition of Owen's poems (*The Poems of Wilfred Owen*, p. 35), Blunden (who also admired RT) noted that Owen 'repeated à favourite passage of Rabindranath Tagore' on his last day with his mother in August 1918. The verse is *Gitanjali* (96).

The same verse was pencilled on the back of a message form he received on 30 Jan. 1917 while fighting on the Somme. It is preserved in Owen's papers at the English Faculty Library in Oxford. The pocketbook to which his mother referred is not extant. Dominic Hibberd (*Wilfred Owen: The Last Year, 1917–1918*) suggested that Owen's brother Harold may have destroyed it in the 1950s. (Hibberd to Authors, 8 Feb. 1993) There are two brief references to RT by Owen in *Wilfred Owen: Collected Letters.*

p. 2   'Carl Zuckmayer' 'Rabindranath Tagore and Germany', paper presented by Carl Zuckmayer to an 'international literary seminar' in New Delhi, 1961, published as 'The splendour of a name', *Statesman*, Calcutta, 7 May 1994 (information courtesy Martin Kämpchen). 'I don't think that my friend the medical sergeant had known much more than the name of Rabindranath Tagore, and I doubt if the Indian soldier knew more about him,' Zuckmayer commented.

p. 3   'Bettelheim' p. 206. Bettelheim added:

> After World War II, Janusz Korczak – his work and his life – became a legend, and not only in Poland. He and his work are now well known among European educators, and in many countries outside of Europe. His work is studied at European universities, and symposia are devoted to it. Many monuments have been erected to honour him; a play, *Korczak and the Children*, has been widely performed. Books have been written on his work; his own writings have been republished and translated into many languages. He was posthumously given the German Peace Prize. The hundredth anniversary of his birth, 1978–79, was declared Korczak Year by UNESCO, and in Poland and many other countries. Pope John Paul II said once that for the world of today, Janusz Korczak is a symbol of true religion and true morality.

Korczak's diary was hidden during the war and eventually published as *Ghetto Diary*. The performance of *The Post Office* is described on p. 168, and in *The Ghetto Years, 1939–1942*, pp. 79–81.

p. 3   'Michael Tolstoy' 8 Sept. 1935 [RB]. Michael Tolstoy wanted help from RT for a plan to settle in Paraguay with a group of Russian émigrés. He died, however, in Rabat in 1944. (Nikolai Tolstoy to Authors, May 1993) Leo Tolstoy's second son, Ilya, greatly respected RT and translated him into Russian, though he was critical of RT's visit to Russia in 1930. (See pp. 296, 300.)

p. 3　　'no particular affinity' RT tried to read *Anna Karenina* but could not finish it. He did read *What is Art?*, but disagreed with it. He wrote to Nicholas Roerich, who knew Tolstoy and who had written an essay, 'Tolstoy and Tagore': 'It is indeed most kind of you to associate my name with that of Tolstoy, but I feel sure you were more guided by your affection for me than anything else.' (11 March 1937 [copy at RB])

p. 3　　'these prose translations' Introduction to *Gitanjali*, pp. vii, xiii

p. 4　　'After *Gitanjali*' 28 Jan. 1917, Nowell-Smith, p. 291

p. 4　　'Damn Tagore' ?7 May 1935, Yeats, pp. 834–35

p. 4　　'*Oxford Book of Modern Verse*' This covered 1892 to 1935 and appeared in 1936, with Yeats as editor. RT's poems, five from *Gitanjali* and two from *The Gardener*, are on pp. 63 – 67. Probably Yeats' outburst to Rothenstein was provoked by his having reread RT's English works while making a selection for *The Oxford Book*.

p. 4　　'Gide . . . Jiménez . . . Pasternak' Gide's relationship with RT is discussed by Michael Tilby in Pollard, pp. 67 – 77. Jiménez and RT are discussed in Howard T. Young, 'Juan Ramón, traductor alerta', *Bulletin of Hispanic Studies*, 1992, pp. 141–51 and, more fully, in Young's 'The invention of a Spanish Tagore' (forthcoming: information courtesy Howard T. Young); also by Graciela Palau de Nemes ('Tagore and Jiménez: poetic coincidences') in Sahitya Akademi, pp. 187 – 97. Pasternak's translations of RT are mentioned by his cotranslator Olga Ivinskaya in her book *A Captive of Time: My Years with Pasternak*, pp. 32 – 34.

Other non-English-speaking Nobel laureates in literature who have a published interest in RT include Ivan Bunin (Russia), Hermann Hesse (Germany), Yasunari Kawabata (Japan), Halldor Laxness (Iceland), Pablo Neruda (Chile), Octavio Paz (Mexico), Saint-John Perse (France) and Romain Rolland (France).

p. 4　　'These are Tagore's ashes' Rabindranath Tagore, *Obra escojida*, p. 1287

p. 4　　'Akhmatova' Nayman, p. 153

p. 5　　'I had my misgivings' 5 Feb. 1913 [Yale]

p. 5　　'André Gide' Introduction to *L'Offrande Lyrique (Gitanjali)*, pp. ix–x

p. 5　　'*The Post Office*' Gide's translation was entitled *Amal et la Lettre du Roi*.

p. 5   'But that Indian Orient' 17 Jan. 1918, Gide, p. 223

p. 5   'most valuable and rich' Yeats first expressed his interest to
            Macmillan in April 1916, subsequently to RT himself in 1918, 1920
            and 1931, to Rothenstein in 1935, and to others. Considering how
            greatly *My Reminiscences* differed from *Gitanjali*, Yeats' penchant
            for *both* books proved his deep attraction to RT's writing.

p. 6   'the sixth Briton' Ackroyd, p. 289. Strictly speaking, RT was a Briton,
            since he was a subject of the British Empire. But he never referred to
            himself as such, and certainly never thought of himself as a Briton.

p. 6   'Kipling' Kipling won the Nobel prize in 1907, six years before RT.
            According to a surprised Thomas Pinney, the editor of Kipling's
            letters, there is 'nothing in the letters, nothing in print, nothing in
            anyone's recollections of what Kipling thought and said',
            concerning RT. (Pinney to Authors, 26 Jan. 1993) Given Kipling's
            scorn for Bengalis, frequently expressed, he must have had acutely
            conflicting feelings about sharing the Nobel honour with a 'Briton'
            like Tagore. RT, by contrast, commented on Kipling a number of
            times, mostly unfavourably.

p. 6   'Joyce . . . Tagore . . . Hemingway' Lord Renfrew of Kaimsthorn,
            Hansard, 24 March 1993, p. 407

p. 6   'Old Bluebeard' Rothenstein, *Men and Memories*, p. 265

p. 6   '*Gitanjali*' The original line from *Gitanjali* (10) is: 'Here is thy
            footstool and there rest thy feet where live the poorest, and lowliest,
            and lost.' It was quoted in 1975 by Indira Gandhi in her foreword to
            Doig, *Mother Teresa: Her People and her Work*.

p. 6   'Epstein' p. 92

p. 6   'Beerbohm' Preface to Rothenstein, *Six Portraits of Sir Rabindranath
            Tagore*, p. ix

p. 6   'acerbic Epstein' 'No artist owed more to William [Rothenstein] than
            Epstein; none repaid him more scurvily.' (Speaight, p. 187)

p. 6   'self-portraits' The twelve self-portraits appear in Dutta and
            Robinson, *Purabi*, pp. 201–03. They were probably painted around
            May 1934.

p. 7   'Thompson' Letter to Prasanta Mahalanobis, 6 Nov. 1920, in E. P.
            Thompson, p. 49

p. 7   'Larkin' Letter to Robert Conquest, 29 November 1956, in Larkin,
            p. 270

p. 7   'But why should the West care?' Ray, *Our Films Their Films*, p. 161

p. 7   'the cultural gap' Robinson, *Satyajit Ray*, p. 322

p. 7   'Dwarkanath replied' Max Müller, pp. 7–8. In 1835, Thomas

Babington Macaulay, a contemporary of Dwarkanath in Calcutta, asserted in a famous 'minute on education in India' that 'a single shelf of a good European library is worth the whole native literature of India and Arabia'. Probably Macaulay, among others, was in Dwarkanath's mind.

p. 8   'Oriental Croesus' The sobriquet is mentioned in a footnote to an article about Dwarkanath's son Debendranath published in Charles Dickens' journal *All the Year Round*, 5 April 1862, p. 80. Very likely the note was written by Dickens himself.

p. 8   'written out . . . by Bengalis' This attitude is changing now – see Siddhartha Ghosh, 'Dwarkanath Thakur', *Desh*, 12 Feb. 1994.

p. 8   'burned . . . correspondence' This is alleged in a letter written by Kshemendranath Tagore on 11 Nov. 1939, in Kling, p. 256. See also Kling, 'Rabindranath's bonfire', in *Rabindranath Tagore in Perspective*, pp. 41–52.

p. 8   'references to Dwarkanath' There are hardly more than a dozen references to Dwarkanath in RT's entire writings. All are cursory, neither laudatory nor critical.

p. 8   'We all live' 'The Master's will be done', *TUM*, pp. 176, 181, 186–87 (translation slightly modified)/ *RR, 18*, pp. 546, 549, 553

p. 9   'mounted police' Rathindranath Tagore to Mayce Seymour, 28 August 1917 [RB].

p. 9   'alleged . . . syphilis' The article alleged RT had contracted a sexually transmitted disease when young. RT read the piece and complained bitterly to Prasanta Mahalanobis on 1 Oct. 1928 that no other celebrity in India had to tolerate such vilification. His son Rathindranath remarked in 1958: 'One obvious reason for the persistence of such vituperations appearing regularly in a section of the Bengali press, was that the editors had early discovered that slandering Father paid handsomely.' (Rathindranath Tagore, pp. 152–53) Unlike others, RT never sued.

p. 9   'Few writers . . . abused' *Thy Hand*, p. 607

p. 9   'Chaudhuri claimed' ibid, p. 606

p. 9   'prominent Bengali scholar' Niharranjan Ray, pp. 354–55

p. 9   'another Bengali scholar' Sibnarayan Ray, 'Rabindranath Tagore and modern Bengal', *Quest*, Bombay, May 1961, p. 58

p. 9   'holy mascot' *Thy Hand*, p. 596

p. 10   'institutions . . . seriously' Nemaisadhan Basu, vice-chancellor of RT's university in the 1980s, called it, on retirement, a 'distorted shadow' of RT's intentions. (Basu, p. 110)

p. 10 'I do not put my faith' *Creative Unity*, p. 153 (translation slightly modified)

p. 10 'I find it rather difficult' 9 May 1922, 'The Poet's town planner: remembering Patrick Geddes', Supriya Roy, *Rabindra-Bhavana*, Shantiniketan, summer 1990, pp. 12–13

p. 11 'white man's burden' *VBN*, Dec. 1945, p. 24

p. 11 'less shriney' Forster to Robert Trevelyan, 26 Nov. 1945, Forster, *Letters*, 2, p. 217. Alex Aronson, a Cambridge graduate and lecturer at Shantiniketan from 1937 to 1944, sought advice from Forster before taking the job. Forster sent a postcard 'warning me against inflated expectations but advising me to go.' (Aronson, *Brief Chronicles*, p. 22)

p. 11 'In the very atmosphere' 15 Nov. 1936, in Sonia Gandhi, p. 296

p. 11 'Nehru almost never quoted' Nehru often mentioned RT in letters and speeches, both before and after he became chancellor, as did his daughter. Indira Gandhi quoted RT's poetry and his prose writings. In a speech on Martin Luther King, she said: 'As if he too had envisaged the martyrdoms of Mahatma Gandhi and Martin Luther King, Rabindranath Tagore once sang:

> In anger we slew him,
> With love let us embrace him now,
> For in death he lives amongst us,
> The mighty conqueror of death.

(24 Jan. 1969, *Selected Speeches* (1966–1969), p. 312). And in a speech to the UN Conference on Trade and Development, she said: 'Years ago Rabindranath Tagore wrote, "Power has to be made secure not only against power but also against weakness" . . . The question before the advanced nations is not whether they can afford to help the developing nations, but whether they can afford not to do so.' (1 Feb. 1968, *Selected Speeches* (1966–1969), p. 370)

p. 11 'Indo-Chinese unity' Like RT, Nehru backed Chiang Kai-shek in the late 1930s and 40s, and had little idea of the strength of the Communists in China.

p. 11 'If democracy' *VBN*, Jan. 1968, p. 144. She was speaking at the beginning of the violent Naxalite movement in West Bengal, which had already affected Shantiniketan.

p. 11 'he had few friends' RT's correspondence with his son Rathindranath and daughter Mira makes constant reference to guilty feelings about his family. In June 1932 he wrote to Rathindranath: 'I have made wrong decisions over and over again concerning my dearest ones'. (Sharadiya *Desh*, 1396 [1989], p. 13) In a letter of 1927, when he was sixty-six, RT regretted that he had kept only one friend through the decades: 'there must be some terrible lack in me.' (RT to Ramananda Chatterji, *Chithipatra*, *12*, pp. 106–10)

p. 12   'ferociously egocentric individualist' *Thy Hand*, p. 599

p. 12   'Satyajit Ray' Interview with Julian Crandall Hollick, 1987 (partly published in Robinson, *Satyajit Ray*, p. 48). Ray said many times that he found RT unapproachable, and that he had learnt from his work, not directly from the man.

p. 12   'remarked in Germany' 'Rabindranath Tagore in Munich', *MR*, Oct. 1930, p. 370

p. 12   'William Radice' Introduction to *Selected Short Stories*, William Radice trans., p. 25

p. 13   'E. P. Thompson' Introduction to *Nationalism*, p. 14. In 1993, Edward Said called *Nationalism* 'great lectures'. (*Culture and Imperialism*, p. 259)

p. 13   'Great Sentinel' *CWMG*, *21*, p. 288 (*Young India*, 13 Oct. 1921)

p. 13   'Tagore chided Elmhirst' 3 Sept. 1932, Dutta and Robinson, *Purabi*, p. 109

p. 14   'talking to . . . Einstein' 'Note on the nature of reality', *Religion of Man*, p. 222

p. 14   'Prigogine' *Order out of Chaos*, p. 293

p. 14   'Dwelling on Shakespeare' *Creative Unity*, p. 61

p. 14   'letter to . . . Indira' 20 Aug. 1892, *Glimpses*, pp. 76–77/*Chhinnapatra*, pp. 139

p. 14   'No biography' Rathindranath Tagore, p. 160

p. 14   'reviewing . . . Tennyson' 'A poet's biography', *MR*, June 1936, pp. 604–05/ *RR*, *8*, pp. 452–55. RT expressed the same idea, famously in Bengal, in a poem in 1914 (*Utsharga* (21), *RR*, *10*, p. 36).

p. 15   'allowed [Thompson] to propose' E. J. Thompson, p. 304

p. 15   'E. P. Thompson' p. 34

p. 15   'harmonious and noble' Kripalani, *Rabindranath*, p. 6

p. 16   'Ordinarily research scholars' 'Dr. P. K. Acharya on Indian architecture', *VBQ*, May–July 1935, p. 115 (book review)

1 The Tagores and 'Prince' Dwarkanath

p. 17   'My ancestors . . . Victorian manners' *Religion of Man*, p. 170

p. 17   'I came to a world' 'A Poet's school', *TUM*, p. 290

p. 17   'widely accepted story' Other stories are discussed in Kripalani,
             Dwarkanath, pp. 6–10.
p. 18   '50,000 rupees' Shib Chunder Bose, p. 167
p. 18   'expelled from his family' *Bengal Hurkaru and India Gazette*, 1 May
             1852
p. 19   'On a plot of land at Jorasanko' The name derived either from twin
             (*jora*) wooden or bamboo bridges (*sanko*) that spanned a small
             stream, or from two temples devoted to Sankar, Lord Shiva.
p. 19   'Rashmani's Son' *Selected Short Stories*, Dutta and Lago trans.,
             pp. 200–38/ *RR*, *22*, pp. 371–407
p. 19   'What is materialism' 'Our materialism', *MR*, April 1925, p. 484
p. 19   'disinherited' Furrell, p. 147. Prosunno Coomar Tagore
             disinherited Ganendramohun, who settled in England.
p. 20   'great in the annals' Governor of Bengal, 1866, in Furrell, p. 163.
             He was honouring Jotendramohun Tagore.
p. 20   '*Victoria-Gitika*' ibid, pp. 170–71
p. 20   'British commentator' *Friend of India*, 12 Feb. 1876, in Sumanta
             Banerjee, p. 197
p. 20   'he informed Curzon' Prodyot Coomar Tagore to Curzon, 22 Aug.
             1905, [Curzon], *Letters and Telegrams*, p. 42. There is a copy of this
             rare compilation in the library of the Indian Institute at Oxford.
p. 20   'deleted from his citation' The draft of the citation written by the
             public orator at Oxford mentions that the university conferred a
             degree on the 'father' of RT '44 years ago', i.e. in 1896. In the final
             citation many Tagores were mentioned, but not one was a
             Pathuriaghat Tagore. The antipathy continues – see the memoirs of
             a Pathuriaghat Tagore, Sandip Tagore (in the Bibliography).
p. 20   'nothing of the flunkey' Mittra, p. 67
p. 21   'She was like a . . . doll' 'Match-Making', *Selected Short Stories*,
             Dutta and Lago trans., pp. 263–64/ *RR*, *23*, pp. 339–40
p. 21   'late father's estates' Strictly speaking, adoptive father. (Kripalani,
             Dwarkanath, p. 21)
p. 21   'two guineas' ibid, p. 28
p. 21   'In 1830 and 1834' Kling, p. 31
p. 21   'one-fifteenth . . . of the revenue' ibid, p. 90
p. 22   'stoney-hearted zamindar . . . piteable condition' ibid, p. 33
p. 22   'As a zamindar' ibid, p. 34
p. 22   'the bank was the keystone' ibid, p. 43
p. 22   'chief of Calcutta's business world' For a discussion of these
             ventures, see Kling, especially pp. 114, 155, 195.

p. 23   'Emily Eden' pp. 215–16, 234. There was a doggerel current among
             Bengalis in Calcutta (here translated): 'Knives and forks are
             clanking in the Belgatchia garden house; what fun with all that food
             around! But what do we know of it? It's all an affair of Tagore
             Company.' (Sumanta Banerjee, p. 87)
p. 23   'he was kind to . . . officer' Kripalani, *Dwarkanath*, pp. 90–91
p. 23   '*Friend of India*' 6 Jan. 1842, in Kripalani, *Dwarkanath*, p. 140
p. 24   'Colosseum' Mittra, p. 82
p. 24   'many-bladed knife' ibid, p. 95
p. 24   'Hill Coolies' Letter to Debendranath Tagore in Kripalani,
             Dwarkanath, p. 171
p. 24   'animated occasion' Mittra, pp. 113–14. The guests had some link
             with India: Thackeray was born in Calcutta, though sent home at
             the age of five; Mayhew had visited India as a young man, after
             running away from home.
p. 24   'Dwarkanaught Tagore' 5 Aug. 1842, Dickens, *Letters*, *3* (1842–43),
             pp. 304–05. Dickens had misspelt the name, though more than one
             spelling was current in India in 1842.
p. 25   'thanked him heartily' Dickens to the countess of Blessington, 31
             Oct. 1845, Dickens, *Letters*, *4* (1844–46), p. 421
p. 25   'I saw the Baboo' 31 Oct. 1845, ibid, pp. 421–22
p. 25   'Oriental Croesus' See p. 8–note.
p. 25   'Blair Kling' p. 174

2 Maharshi Debendranath

Epigraph   *Visva-Bharati Patrika*, Kartik-Paush 1350 [1943], p. 120
p. 27   'letter to. . . Debendranath' 22 May 1846, in Debendranath Tagore,
             Atmajibani, p. 224 (the letter is in English)
p. 27   'Married' It is said that the girl was selected and taken off without
             the knowledge of her mother, who died when she discovered her
             daughter gone. (Jnanadanandini Devi, 'Smriti katha', Sharadiya
             Ekshan, 1990, p. 11)
p. 27   'height of fashion' *My Rem*, p. 79/*RR*, *17*, p. 323
p. 27   'Raja Rammohun Roy' Debendranath Tagore, *Auto*, pp. 54–56/
             Atmajibani, pp. 12–13
p. 27   'the best friend' 'Ideals of education', *VBQ*, April–July 1929, p. 72
p. 28   'Father of Modern India' For a discussion, see Killingley, especially
             pp. 2, 17.
p. 28   'Indira Gandhi' 20 May. 1972, *Selected Speeches*, 1969–1972, p. 811
p. 28   'Mahatma Gandhi' *CWMG*, *19*, p. 477 (*Young India*, 13 April 1921)

p. 28 'out-and-out Bengali' This and other remarks on Rammohun are from 'Vidyasagar-charit', *RR*, *4*, p. 480.

p. 28 '*sati*' However, ten years after the banning, the British, bowing to Bengali public opinion, made a legal distinction between voluntary and involuntary *sati* – see Karlekar, p. 39.

p. 28 'a strange sense of the unreality' *Auto*, p. 38/ *Atmajibani*, p. 2

p. 29 'Brahma Sabha' Debendranath Tagore, *Auto*, pp. 57–58/ *Atmajibani*, p. 14

p. 29 'All that is changing' 'Rabindranath Tagore on his father Debendranath Tagore', *VBQ*, No. 1, 1961, p. 1. The verse is the first verse of the *Isopanishad*. Juan Mascaró translated it as follows: 'Behold the universe in the glory of God: and all that lives and moves on earth. Leaving the transient, find joy in the Eternal: set not your heart on another's possession.' (*Upanishads*, p. 49)

p. 29 'The flower says' 'Moods', John Boulton, *VBQ*, Feb.–April 1975, pp. 314–15 (trans. by Boulton)/ *GB*, *3*, p. 716. The song was written for the play *Chandalika* in 1933.

p. 30 'said of the *Upanishads*' Foreword to Macnicol, p. vi

p. 30 'Debendranath's reply' *Auto*, p. 120/ *Atmajibani*, p. 57

p. 31 'So thriftily . . . threefold.' Kling, p. 241; Debendranath Tagore, *Auto*, p. 142/ *Atmajibani*, p. 71

p. 31 'legacy to the blind' 'Rabindranath Tagore on his father Debendranath Tagore', *VBQ*, No. 1, 1961, p. 4

p. 31 'E. M. Forster' *Daily News and Leader*, 11 Nov. 1914

p. 31 'I know, but I won't tell you' Chaudhuri, *Autobiography*, p. 215

p. 31 'Nirad Chaudhuri . . . wrote' ibid, p. 221

p. 31 'Brahmos of that time' Robinson, *Satyajit Ray*, p. 15

p. 32 '*All the Year Round*' 5 April 1862, p. 80

p. 32 'greatly embittered' Debendranath Tagore, *Auto*, p. 28

p. 32 'police' Paul, *1*, p. 47

p. 32 'stab himself' Debendranath Tagore, *Auto*, p. 83/ *Atmajibani*, p. 114

p. 32 'Keshub insisted' Debendranath Tagore, *Auto* (Calcutta, 1909), p. 148 – this edition has appendices omitted from the London edition.

p. 32 'You must remember' ibid, p. 149

p. 32 'Low Church . . . High Church' For a discussion of the schisms in the Brahmo Samaj, see Kopf.

p. 33 'Until the right man' *My Rem*, p. 78/ *RR*, *17*, p. 322

3 The House of the Tagores

Epigraph   *My Boyhood*, p. 6/ *RR*, *26*, p. 590

p. 34   'much painted by British artists' Historical views of the Chitpur Road appear in Losty, pls. 9, 17, 23; and in Chaudhuri, *Calcutta*, *1*, p. 29.

p. 34   'when the day was over' *My Boyhood*, p. 21/ *RR*, *26*, p. 598

p. 35   'brothel' S. N. Mukherjee, p. 101

p. 35   'The church clock chimed' Kaliprasanna Sinha, in Sumanta Banerjee, p. 179 (trans. by Banerjee)/ *Hutom Pyanchar Naksha*, p. 39. The novel was first published in the early 1860s.

p. 36   'Times have changed' Karlekar, p. 50

p. 36   'lightening her complexion' Jnanadanandini Devi, 'Smriti katha', Sharadiya *Ekshan*, 1990, p. 12

p. 36   'kidnapped' *My Boyhood*, p. 57/ *RR*, *26*, p. 615

p. 36   'backbiting' RT never wrote openly about this atmosphere, but he gave hints in his letters to his wife, children and others. In old age he gave a talk to a society for uplifting women at which he was less guarded. Referring to the many destitute women who sheltered in the Jorasanko house throughout his life, he said: 'as a result of them there was no peace in the house and it became a place of constant bickering and strife.' ('Agranthita Rabindranath', *Pakshik Bashumati*, 1 May 1993)

p. 36   'the Tagore women' According to RT's niece, 'All my aunts, although they were daughters of rich men, were not generous. Their in-laws, the wives of their brothers, though coming from poor families, were generous.' (Indira Devi, 'Jiban katha', Sharadiya *Ekshan*, 1992, p. 24)

p. 36   'letter in English' *My Rem*, p. 105/ *RR*, *17*, p. 348

p. 36   'Hindu Mela' ibid. The Hindu Mela was closed down after 1880.

p. 37   'figure of Britannia' Mitter, p. 222 (trans. by Mitter)/ Gupta, p. 298. Dwijendranath told the story to Gupta a few years before his death in 1926.

p. 37   'If Bara Dada' Nagendranath Gupta, 'Dwijendranath Tagore', *MR*, May 1927, p. 541

p. 37   'In *My Reminiscences* he recalled' pp. 93–94/ *RR*, *17*, p. 337

p. 38   'Gandhi's leadership' Kripalani, *Rabindranath*, pp. 35, 257

p. 38   'definitely did not approve' Satyendranath to Jnanadanandini, 'Prabashir patra 1863–64', Sharadiya *Desh*, 1363 [1956], pp. 41–45

p. 38   'nothing gave Satyendranath' Indira Devi, 'In memoriam Dwijendranath Tagore', *VBQ*, Nov. 1944–Jan. 1945, p. 129

p. 38   'fiery ordeal' Satyendranath to Estlin Carpenter, 24 Feb. 1910 [Manchester College]

p. 38   'Pirali pugree' Nagendranath Gupta, 'Satyendranath Tagore', *MR*, May 1927, p. 542

p. 38   'real literary achievements' 'Satyendranath Tagore', *MR*, Feb. 1923, pp. 277–78 (obituary)

p. 38   'mental illness' The two brothers were Birendranath and Somendranath.

p. 39   'My brother . . . pan-Indian garb' *My Rem*, p. 107/ *RR*, *17*, pp. 350–51

p. 39   'book of . . . pencil portraits' *Twenty-five Collotypes From the Original Drawings by Jyotirindra Nath Tagore*, Hammersmith (London), 1914. The book is rare: there is a copy in the Rabindra Bhavan library, but none in the major libraries in London. In his preface, Rothenstein, whose forte was portraiture, wrote: 'The drawings of Indian ladies are especially remarkable . . . one has almost to go back to Dürer and Holbein to find such frank and sincere portraits as these.' The originals, running into many hundreds, are kept by the Rabindra Bharati Society in Calcutta; regrettably, no larger book of them has been published.

p. 39   'Satyajit Ray' *Rabindranath Tagore*, 1961 (documentary film)

p. 39   'fiery summer' *My Rem*, p. 97/ *RR*, *17*, p. 340

p. 39   'Bankimchandra Chatterji' For an outline of Bankim's literary works, see J. C. Ghosh, pp. 152–64. For a discussion of his life and ideas, see Raychaudhuri.

p. 40   'Swarnakumari' RT was crushing about his elder sister's writing. He told Rothenstein: 'She is one of those unfortunate beings who has more ambition than abilities but just enough talent to keep her mediocrity alive for a short period of time.' (Feb. 1914, Lago, p.147) A note on her life and two chapters of a novel by her appear in Tharu and Lalita, pp. 235–43.

p. 40   'J. C. Ghosh' p. 12

p. 40   'Bengali vocabulary' J. C. Ghosh, p. 4

p. 40   'Kalidasa' *My Rem*, pp. 62–63/ *RR*, *17*, p. 307

p. 41   'J. C. Ghosh's phrase' p. 58

p. 41   'worthwhile attempts' For example, Dimock and Levertov

p. 41   'Let my body' J. C. Ghosh, p. 59 (trans. by Ghosh)

p. 41   'oozing and lachrymose' 'Banshi', *Punashcha*, *RR*, *16*, pp. 84–87 (25 Asharh 1339 [1932])

p. 41   'Gaganendranath Tagore' Four of these caricatures appear in Dutta and Robinson, *Purabi*, pp. 206–07.

p. 41   'films of Satyajit Ray' The satire is most pointed in *Mahapurush* (*The Holy Man*, 1965), *Jana Aranya* (*The Middle Man*, 1975) and

Joi Baba Felunath (*The Elephant God*, 1978).

p. 42   'wrote Nirad Chaudhuri' *Thy Hand*, p. 612

p. 42   'Our literary gods' *My Rem*, pp. 130–31/*RR*, *17*, p. 374

4 Rabi

Epigraph   *My Rem*, p. 29/*RR*, *17*, p. 274

p. 43   'most valuable and rich' See p. 5–note.

p. 43   'Inaccuracies' Leonard Elmhirst to Dorothy Straight, 23 Sept. 1921 [Dartington], after overhearing Yeats in Ireland

p. 43   'memory pictures' *My Rem*, p. 18/*RR*, *17*, p. 263

p. 43   'I do not know . . . respected' ibid, p. 17/p. 264

p. 44   'We were too young' ibid, pp. 91–92/ p. 335

p. 44   'From our place . . . extraordinary antics' ibid, p. 92/ p. 335

p. 44   'In our boyhood . . . vanished' ibid, p. 95/pp. 338–39

p. 45   '*Addas*' For instance, the *adda* and its decline is pivotal in Satyajit Ray's last film *Agantuk* (*The Stranger*).

p. 45   'Luxury was a thing' pp. 21–22/*RR*, *17*, p. 268

p. 45   'We wore the very simplest' p. 15/*RR*, *26*, p. 595

p. 45   'lack of love' Paul, *1*, pp. 91–93

p. 45   'they were . . . kept apart' *My Boyhood*, p. 23/*RR*, *26*, p. 599

p. 46   'if the Russians' *My Rem*, p. 60/ *RR*, *17*, p. 305

p. 46   'image of white stone' *My Boyhood*, p. 49/ *RR*, *26*, p. 611

p. 46   'Beyond my reach' *My Rem*, p. 25/ *RR*, *17*, p. 270

p. 47   'A mysterious Shape' *My Boyhood*, p. 6/ *RR*, *26*, p. 590

p. 47   'All those musty . . . creeps' ibid, pp. 6–7/ p. 590

p. 47   'servocracy' *My Rem*, p. 31/ *RR*, *17*, p. 276. Nirad Chaudhuri preferred 'servantocracy'. (*Thy Hand*, p. 600)

p. 47   'most gratify' *My Rem*, p. 35/ *RR*, *17*, p. 279

p. 47   'Whether the danger' ibid, p. 23/ p. 269

p. 48   'stories of dacoity' *My Boyhood*, pp. 30–31/ *RR*, *26*, p. 603

p. 48   'to grasp him . . . citizens' ibid, p. 31/ p. 602

p. 49   '*sutras* of the grammarian' *My Rem*, p. 41/ *RR*, *17*, p. 286

p. 49   'wrote in English very rarely' For instance, in 1913 RT wrote to his niece Indira (in Bengali): 'That I cannot write English is such a patent fact, that I never had even the vanity to feel ashamed of it. If anybody wrote an English note asking me to tea, I never felt equal to answering it.' (6 May 1913, *Tagore Reader*, p. 20/ *Chithipatra*, *5*, p. 19)

p. 49   'The discovery of fire' *My Rem*, p. 41/ *RR*, *17*, p. 286

p. 49   'The Familiar Black Umbrella' The illustration appeared in *MR*, Feb. 1916, opposite p. 141, as part of the Calcutta serialization of

My Rem, but was omitted from the 1917 Macmillan edition. It was published in *Gaganendranath Tagore*, pl. 8.

p. 49   'It is evening' ibid, p. 42/ p. 287

p. 50   'The main object' ibid, p. 62/ p. 307

p. 50   'Like a young deer' ibid, p. 39/ p. 283

p. 50   'Well done!. . . stuck in position' ibid, pp. 39–40/ p. 284. The editor was Nabagopal Mitra, who had started the Hindu Mela. Twenty-five years later, RT referred to some bees in his houseboat in East Bengal in a way that recalled this boyish encounter. 'They visit me generally between nine and ten in the morning, patrol my table, dive under my desk, bang against the coloured-glass window, circle my head, and shoot off in a whizz.' He often imagined them to be 'dissatisfied spirits' that had returned from the next world and were calling upon him in passing to give him 'the once-over'. 'But I know better really. Actually they are mere bees, honey-suckers: what we occasionally call in Sanskrit twin-proboscideans.' (23 Feb. 1895, *Glimpses*, p. 117/ *Chhinnapatra*, p. 265)

5 A Journey to the Himalayas

Epigraph   *My Rem*, p. 78/ *RR*, *17*, p. 322

p. 52   'first major expedition' *My Rem*, p. 44/ *RR*, *17*, p. 309

p. 52   'budding Brahmins' ibid, p. 61/ p. 306

p. 52   'I am convinced' ibid, p. 62/ p. 307

p. 53   'some idea of How!' ibid, p. 65/ p. 310

p. 53   'newly sacred-threaded' Paul, *1*, p. 150

p. 53   'Sinha' The Sinhas were Brahmos, based at Raipur, a village south of Shantiniketan. One of the family, Srikantha Sinha, was an early admirer of RT. (*My Rem*, pp. 49–51/ *RR*, *17*, pp. 294–96) He was the uncle of Satyendra's Prashanna Sinha, later Lord Sinha, the first Indian member of the viceroy's council and the first Indian to receive a peerage. (Kopf, pp. 110–11) In 1912, the Sinhas sold RT the house at Surul that became the headquarters of his 'institute for rural reconstruction'.

p. 53   'Shantiniketan . . . small hut' Paul, *1*, p. 155

p. 53   'possible . . . impossible' *My Rem*, p. 66/ *RR*, *17*, p. 312

p. 53   'ray of sun . . . drop of rain' ibid, p. 67/ p. 312

p. 53   'What I could not see' ibid, p. 68/ p. 312

p. 54   'I do not find anything' RT to Mahadev Desai (secretary of Gandhi), 4 Jan. 1937 [copy at RB]

p. 54   'his first song' Paul, *1*, p. 151

p. 54   'I can see the moon' *My Rem*, p. 72/ *RR*, *17*, pp. 316–17

p. 55   'science of the heavens' In 1937, RT published *Visva-Parichay* (*Our Universe*), a science primer. He was influenced by the popular astronomy of Sir Arthur Eddington. When he mentioned this to Eddington in a letter, the latter replied: 'I think it is true as scientific thought goes deeper it finds much in common with Indian philosophy.' (7 Feb. 1938 [RB])

p. 55   'calculated morality' *My Rem*, p. 73/ *RR*, *17*, p. 318

p. 55   'That is the great advantage' ibid, p. 75/ p. 319

p. 56   'excruciatingly wintry' ibid, p. 76/ p. 320

p. 56   'old practice of Debendranath' See, for instance, Debendranath Tagore, *Auto*, p. 250/ *Atmajibani*, p. 150.

p. 56   'This was more than flesh' *My Rem*, p. 77/ *RR*, *17*, p. 321

p. 56   'He held up a standard' ibid, p. 78/ p. 322

p. 56   'The impression on my mind' *Statesman*, Calcutta, 22 Jan. 1936. The quotation is from the *Svetasvatara Upanishad*, 3:9. (See *Upanishads*, p. 89.)

6 Adolescence

Epigraph   *My Boyhood*, p. 65/ *RR*, *26*, p. 619

p. 57   'I at once disclosed it' *My Rem*, p. 82/ *RR*, *17*, p. 326

p. 57   'Rabi was in a fix' ibid, pp. 83–84/ p. 327

p. 58   'one appealing verse' *Swapnaprayan*, 3:27

p. 58   'old nurse' Indira Devi, 'In memoriam Dwijendranath Tagore', *VBQ*, Nov. 1944–Jan. 1945, p. 131

p. 58   'Tagore, Nubindronath' Paul, *1*, p. 193

p. 58   'Are you not well, Tagore?' *My Rem*, p. 85/ *RR*, *17*, p. 329

p. 58   'DePeneranda' The information about him came from two letters to RT, one from H. W. B. Moreno, a Calcuttan of Spanish descent (9 March 1931 [RB]), the other from Zenobia Camprubi Jiménez, wife of Juan Ramón (13 Aug. 1918 [RB]).

p. 59   'Saudamini' *My Rem*, p. 84/ *RR*, *17*, p. 328

p. 59   'gust of suppressed laughter' *Hindu*, Madras, 17 Feb. 1937/ *Shiksha*, p. 254

p. 59   'In 1936 Tagore told an audience' 'Asrama education', *VBQ*, Winter 1957–58, p. 173/ *Shiksha*, p. 248. The article was first published in 1936.

p. 59   'claimed in his memoirs' *My Rem*, p. 86/ *RR*, *17*, p. 330

p. 59   'My heart thumped' ibid, pp. 86–87/ p. 330

p. 60   'J. C. Ghosh', p. 150

p. 60   'Bengali heart by storm' *My Rem*, p. 89/ *RR, 17*, p. 333

p. 60   'moulded myself' 'Atma parichay', *Prabasi*, Magh 1338 [1932], p. 511

p. 60   'At the end of the day' *My Boyhood*, p. 58/ *RR, 26*, p. 616

p. 61   'Showers of melody' *My Rem*, p. 98/ *RR, 17*, p. 341

p. 61   '*jatra*' See Sumanta Banerjee for details of such songs and their
            singers.

p. 61   'Mr. Shelley' Paul, *1*, p. 228

p. 61   'Tagore pondered' *My Boyhood*, pp. 63–64/ *RR, 26*, p. 618

p. 62   'Dwarkanath' Kling, p. 86

p. 62   'engineering' *My Boyhood*, pp. 69–70/ *RR, 26*, p. 622

p. 62   'Queen Victoria' Paul, *1*, p. 254

p. 62   'self-mockingly' *My Rem*, p. 105/ *RR, 17*, p. 349

p. 63   'long "a" sounds' ibid, p. 100/ p. 344

p. 63   'Hesitantly I tried' 'Kancha Am', *Akashpradip*, *RR, 23*, p. 125 (8
            April 1939)

p. 64   'melodramatic element' *My Rem*, p. 103/ *RR, 17*, p. 347

p. 64   'wryly amused words' ibid, p. 104/ p. 347

p. 64   'PhD was . . . awarded' RT named the Bengali scholar in *My Rem*
            as Nishikanta Chatterji (who died in 1910, the year before RT
            wrote). There is no reference to Bhanu Singh in Chatterji's *The
            Yatras* (Zurich, 1882), a book presumably based on his PhD thesis,
            but it does refer to *Bharati* (p. 26) and clearly Chatterji read *Bharati*
            regularly. Possibly, Bhanu Singh appeared in the original thesis,
            which was perhaps read by Dwijendranath, the editor of *Bharati*
            – and was deleted before publication when the embarrassing
            mistake became known to Chatterji.

p. 64   'base metal' *My Rem*, p. 104/ *RR, 17*, p. 348

p. 64   'impudent' *My Rem*, p. 111/ *RR, 17*, p. 354. RT's essay on
            Madhushudan appears in *RR(AS)*, *2*, pp. 75–79.

p. 65   'the conceit inspired' *My Boyhood*, p. 80/ *RR, 26*, p. 627. A recent
            translation of 'The Hungry Stones' appears in *Selected Short
            Stories*, William Radice trans., pp. 236–45.

p. 65   'inarticulate cooings' *My Rem*, p. 114/ *RR, 17*, p. 357

p. 65   'Poet, I think' *My Boyhood*, p. 82/ *RR, 26*, p. 629

p. 66   'I could never insult' Dilip Kumar Roy, pp. 173–74

7 England

Epigraph   Dutta and Robinson, *Purabi*, p. 40/ *Yurop Prabashir Patra*, pp.
            20–21. Quotations from this Bengali book are taken partly from
            'Letters from Europe', in Dutta and Robinson, pp. 39–53, a

selection translated by William Radice, some of which was broadcast on BBC radio in 1987.

p. 67 'all our simple faith' *Manchester Guardian*, 16 May 1930

p. 68 'beyond my power' *My Rem*, p. 115/ *RR, 17*, p. 358

p. 68 'He would start singing' Sahitya Akademi, p. 5

p. 69 'European music' *My Rem*, p. 136/ *RR, 17*, p. 379

p. 69 'told Romain Rolland' Aronson and Kripalani, p. 85

p. 69 'give us a song . . . tame birds' *Selected Poems*, p. 54 (trans. by William Radice)/ *Kahini, RR, 7*, pp. 93–95 (24 Asharh 1300 [1893])

p. 69 'In our country' *My Rem*, p. 135/ *RR, 17*, p. 379

p. 69 'cousins . . . in Tunbridge Wells' They were the two daughters of Ganendramohun Tagore. They teased him for being shy (he recalled much later), telling him, 'Why can't you flirt a little?' (Paul, *2*, p. 27) There is no proof that they lived in Tunbridge Wells, but references by RT to Tunbridge Wells strongly suggest that they did.

p. 70 'Indians would come' *My Rem*, p. 117/ *RR, 17*, p. 361

p. 70 'Once Mrs Barker' Dutta and Robinson, *Purabi*, p. 49/ *Yurop Prabashir Patra*, p. 141

p. 70 'fancy-dress ball' ibid, p. 42/ p. 29

p. 71 'amusing short story' 'Atonement', *Selected Short Stories*, Dutta and Lago trans., pp. 103–19/ *RR, 19*, pp. 235–48

p. 71 'He wrote chirpily' Dutta and Robinson, *Purabi*, p. 53/ *Yurop Prabashir Patra*, p. 211

p. 71 'I really cannot . . . Bengali girls' ibid, pp. 41, 43–44/ p. 35

p. 71 'complete ignoramus' ibid, p. 41/ p. 27

p. 71 'He is so lacking . . . Shakespeare!' ibid, pp. 45–46/ pp. 89–91

p. 72 '*ingabangas*' The word was coined by Dwijendranath Tagore, according to Indira Devi. ('In memoriam Dwijendranath Tagore', *VBQ*, Nov. 1944–Jan. 1945, p. 130)

p. 72 'To know the *ingabanga*' *Yurop Prabashir Patra*, pp. 61–62

p. 73 'National Indian Association' *Journal of the National Indian Association*, March 1879, pp. 102–03 (Satyendranath's speech)

p. 73 'Sir William Muir' ibid, p.104. Muir was the archetypal administrator-scholar of nineteenth-century Anglo-India: Mutiny veteran, governor of a province, member of the viceroy's council, Arabic scholar and historian of Islam, later principal of Edinburgh University.

p. 73 'Conservatives' *Yurop Prabashir Patra*, p. 42

p. 74 'his last lecture' *Crisis in Civilization*, p. 12/ *RR, 26*, pp. 636–37

p. 74 'Gladstone' *Yurop Prabashir Patra*, p. 45

p. 74 'Nirad Chaudhuri claimed' 'There is not a word of praise for [the glorious landscape of England] in his writings.' (Chaudhuri, *Thy Hand*, p. 605) There is, for instance, a passage of praise in *Yurop Prabashir Patra*, pp. 188–90, and in *Pather Shanchay*, *RR*, *26*, pp. 539–47.

p. 74   'a seam of coal' Dutta and Robinson, *Purabi*, p. 49/ *Yurop Prabashir Patra*, p. 183

p. 74   '*Antony and Cleopatra* . . . *Religio Medici*' E. J. Thompson, p. 31

p. 74   'the remote *mofussil*' *My Rem*, p. 128/ *RR*, *17*, p. 371

p. 75   'reproachful blue eyes' ibid, p. 127/ p. 370

p. 75   'force of habit . . . transgressions' ibid, p. 128/ p. 371

p. 75   '10 Tavistock Square' RT did not mention the address in *My Reminiscences*; the information comes from a letter written to him by a descendant of the family (S. G. Scott to RT, 2 Feb. 1929 [RB]).

p. 75   'I was harmless' *My Rem*, p. 120/ *RR*, *17*, p. 363

p. 75   'Mrs Scott . . . Indian wife' ibid

p. 75   ' he confessed to . . . a friend' Dilip Kumar Roy, p. 171

p. 75   'And O the regret' Kripalani, *Rabindranath*, p. 90 (trans. by Kripalani)/ 'Du Din', *Sandhya Sangit*, *RR*, *1*, pp. 32–33 (1288 [1881]). The two lines quoted do not appear in the published poem.

p. 76   'Satan' *My Rem*, p. 121/ *RR*, *17*, p. 364

p. 76   'Lucy' 'My Aunt Lucy has often told me of the enjoyable evenings spent with reading aloud, music and singing, and the enjoyment your singing always gave . . . She played and sang a great deal, and always accompanied your songs.' (S. G. Scott to RT, 2 Feb. 1929 [RB])

p. 76   'doleful poem' *My Rem*, p. 122/ *RR*, *17*, p. 366

p. 76   'Dr Scott's girls' ibid, p.126/ p. 369

p. 77   'The European idea' 'The origins of Tagore's message to the world', Stephen Hay, *Quest*, Bombay, May 1961, p. 51 (trans. by Hay)/ *Bharati*, Magh 1284 [Jan.–Feb. 1878]. There is some doubt about whether RT is the author of the article, which is unsigned. (Paul, *1*, pp. 279–80)

p. 77   'East and West' *My Boyhood*, p. 87/ *RR*, *26*, p. 631

8 Renaissance in Bengal
Epigraph *My Rem*, p. 141/ *RR*, *17*, p. 384

p. 78   'first published book' This was *Kabi Kahini*.

p. 78   'Rubbish' Paul, *2*, p. 136

p. 78   'When I began' *My Rem*, p. 129/ *RR*, *17*, pp. 372–73

p. 78   'Tripura' For an account of the Tagore–Tripura relationship, see *Tripura's Ties with Tagore* (a compilation of selected speeches, letters and songs of Tagore), which is an abridged edition of *Rabindranath o Tripura.*

p. 79   'Byron' He was Nabinchandra Sen. (E. J. Thompson, p. 16)
p. 79   'insulting to Shelley' *My Rem*, p. 173/ *RR*, *17*, p. 417
p. 79   'My attainments were few' ibid, pp. 173–74/ p. 417
p. 80   'Your voice shall resound' Kripalani, *Rabindranath*, p. 95 (trans. by Kripalani)/ *Valmiki Pratibha*, *RR*, *1*, pp. 225–26
p. 80   'master jeweller . . . ornaments' 'Simplicity and elaboration in music', Dilip Kumar Roy, *VBQ*, July 1928, p. 235
p. 80   'freedom from intricacy' ibid, p. 236
p. 80   'follow the example of wives' *My Rem*, p. 146/ *RR*, *17*, p. 389
p. 81   'The death traffic' *MR*, May 1925, pp. 504–07/ 'Chine maraner byabshay', *Bharati*, Jaishtha 1288 [1881]
p. 81   'cloven-footed commerce' 'The rule of the giant', *VBQ*, July 1926, p. 103
p. 81   'raga *Purabi*' *My Rem*, p. 149/ *RR*, *17*, p. 391
p. 82   'words of Satyajit Ray' Robinson, *Satyajit Ray*, p. 160
p. 82   'Night of the Moonless Light' This is Ray's translation of *amabyashar chand*, in place of (the correct) *amabyashar alo.*
p. 82   'Suicide of a Star' The version translated by RT's friend Loken Palit makes the star male, not female. ('The Death of a Star', *MR*, Aug. 1911, p. 201)
p. 82   'attempted suicide' Prabhat Mukherji, *1*, pp. 118–19
p. 83   'The wreath to him' *My Rem*, p. 151/ *RR*, *17*, p. 394
p. 83   'bigwigs' ibid, p. 161/ pp. 403–04
p. 83   'As I gazed' ibid, pp. 153–54/ pp. 396–97
p. 83   'My mother had . . . centrality' Sahitya Akademi, p. 6
p. 83   'Ingabanga Samaj' Rathindranath Tagore, p. 7
p. 84   'flung out its arms' *My Rem*, p. 164/ *RR*, *17*, p. 406
p. 84   'Then the sannyasi' ibid, pp. 166–67/ pp. 409–10
p. 84   'I was married' ibid, p. 167/ p. 411

9 Marriage and Bereavement
Epigraph   *My Rem*, p. 179/ *RR*, *17*, p. 424
p. 85   'marriage between Ana and Rabi' Paul, *2*, p. 41
p. 86   'hunting party' ibid, p. 233
p. 86   'Dearest Rabi' 7 Sept. 1883, ibid, p. 233
p. 86   'he wrote obliquely' n.d., *Chithipatra*, *8*, p. 8
p. 87   'eyeing his . . . bride' Paul, *2*, p. 246
p. 87   'To . . . Priyanath Sen' n.d., *Chithipatra*, *8*, p. 9

p. 87   'You make the flowers bloom' *GB*, *3*, p. 776

p. 87   'gossipy sister-in-law' Hemalata Tagore, in Paul, *2*, p. 250

p. 88   'I am your companion' Kripalani, *Rabindranath*, p. 113 (trans. by
             Kripalani)/ *Chabi o Gan*, *RR*, *1*, pp. 140–44

p. 88   'Expenses' Paul, *2*, p. 272

p. 88   'Kübler-Ross' *On Death and Dying* has quotations from *Fruit-
             Gathering*, *Stray Birds*, *Gitanjali*, *The Fugitive*. Her comment on
             RT is taken from a report in the Calcutta *Statesman*, 29 May 1993
             (information courtesy Dipankar Home). At the memorial service
             for Dorothy Elmhirst in 1968, Leonard Elmhirst read, at his wife's
             request, a passage from RT inspired by a conversation about *The
             Post Office*. ('Rabindranath Tagore on death', *VBQ*, Winter
             1963–64, pp. 284–88)

p. 88   'That there could be any gap . . . revelation' *My Rem*, pp. 179–80/
             RR, *17*, p. 424

p. 89   'glowing eyes' The artist-friend was Nandalal Bose; the story is
             reported in Hiranmoy Banerjee, p. 154.

p. 89   'dampen speculation' Indira Devi, 'Jiban katha', Sharadiya *Ekshan*,
             1992, p. 44

p. 90   'letter . . . in his pocket.' Paul, *2*, pp. 268–69

p. 90   'Indira recalled' 'Old Memories', *VBQ*, May–Oct. 1941, p. 64

p. 90   'party at the steamer' Indira Devi, 'Jiban katha', Sharadiya *Ekshan*,
             1992, p. 44

p. 91   'one or two other cases of suicide' ibid

p. 91   'When clouds gather' *Bharati*, Shraban 1291 [1884], p. 154, in
             Paul, *2*, p. 278. This is the uncut version of the account published in
             RR(AS).

10 Peripatetic Littérateur

Epigraph *My Rem*, p. 186/ *RR*, *17*, p. 431

p. 92   'efficiency and foresight' 7 Dec. 1883, Paul, *2*, p. 247

p. 92   'second novel' *Rajarshi*, *RR*, *2*, pp. 375–501. RT wrote about it in
             My Rem, p. 170/ *RR*, *17*, p. 413.

p. 93   'found a school' Paul, *3*, p. 8

p. 93   'Bankim Babu wrote me a letter' *My Rem*, p. 175/ *RR*, *17*, p. 419

p. 94   'Rammohun Roy' RT's first essay appears in *RR*, *4*, pp. 511–23.

p. 94   'Swami Vivekananda' Paul, *2*, pp. 125–26

p. 94   'erotic venom' The phrase occurs in a letter written by
             Sister Nivedita (Margaret Noble) on 12 March 1899. (Paul, *4*,
             p. 229)

p. 94   'This world is sweet' *My Rem*, p. 184/ 'Pran', *Kari o Komal, RR,
         17*, p. 428
p. 94   'Tagore told Edward Thompson' E. J. Thompson, p. 56
p. 95   'a morass of conceits' ibid
p. 95   'Leaving their homes' ibid, p. 56/ 'Chumban', *Kari o Komal, RR, 2*,
         p. 78
p. 95   'Throw off your robe' 'Bibashana', *RR, 2*, pp. 78–79
p. 95   'did not mention the event' Paul, *3*, p. 50
p. 95   'Hindu marriage' 'Hindu bibaha', *RR, 12*, pp. 413–49
p. 95   'child marriage' In 1911, Ramananda Chatterji, the progressive
         Brahmo editor of Calcutta's *Modern Review* – i.e. one of the most
         progressive men in India – editorialized that for a bride sixteen was
         in practice still regarded as a 'safe maximum' age, 'though it is
         mentioned in pledges and resolutions as the minimum'. (*MR*, Aug.
         1911, p. 219)
p. 96   'an interesting vignette' Nagendranath Gupta, 'Rabindranath
         Tagore', *MR*, May 1927, p. 543
p. 96   'Grand Trunk Road' *My Rem*, p. 77/ *RR, 17*, p. 321. The idea pops
         up in RT's novel *Gora*, p. 109/ *RR, 6*, p. 248.
p. 97   'my twenty-seventh year' RT to Shrishchandra Majumdar, 27 July
         1887, in *Glimpses*, pp. 24–25/ *Chhinnapatra*, p. 21
p. 97   'civil surgeon' Paul, *3*, p. 98
p. 98   'When the sun sets' 28–30 Nov. 1889, *Glimpses*, p. 26/
         Chhinnapatra, pp. 32–33
p. 98   'he wrote to his wife' 29 Aug. 1890, 'Letters to his wife', *VBQ*,
         Summer 1953, pp. 2–3 (trans. by Lila Majumdar)/ *Chithipatra, 1*, p. 3
p. 99   'deleted from the published version' *Yurop Jatrir Diary*, as
         published in 1961, contains both the version RT published in
         1891/93 *and* his original uncut diary.
p. 99   'While the show went on' 28 Sept. 1890, *Yurop Jatrir Diary*, p. 181
p. 99   'female nude' 26 Sept. 1890, ibid, p. 182
p. 99   'If we black chaps' 5 Oct. 1890, ibid, p. 186
p. 99   'When a mind is inert' ibid, p. 109

11 Manashi, The Lady of the Mind
Epigraph *My Rem*, p. 183/ *RR, 17*, p. 428
p. 101   'Sudhin Datta' Sudhindranath Datta, 'Tagore as a lyric poet', *Quest*,
         Bombay, May 1961, p. 25
p. 102   'book's dedication' This is in the form of a poem, 'Upahar' (Gift),
         the last line of which dedicates the 'poetic outbursts of a restless

heart' to 'you', 'in memory of our happy moments'.

p. 102   '735 pilgrims' Paul, *3*, p. 68

p. 102   'grandest sea-storm' E. J. Thompson, p. 74

p. 102   'On the breast of the shoreless sea' ibid, pp. 71–72 (trans. by Thompson)/ *RR*, *2*, pp. 157–61 (Asharh 1294 [1887]). (We have altered one word of Thompson's translation.)

p. 103   'A. L. Basham' p. 419

p. 103   'As Dante looked' E. J. Thompson, p. 66

p. 103   'Master Poet' *RR*, *2*, pp. 258–62 (7–8 Jaishtha 1297 [1890])

p. 104   'The wedding night' *RR*, *2*, pp. 242–45 (23 Asharh 1295 [1888])

p. 104   'Playing our flutes' E. J. Thompson, p. 82/ *RR*, *2*, pp. 226–30 (28 Jaishtha 1295 [1888])

p. 105   'lives . . . needlessly sacrificed' E. J. Thompson, p. 78

p. 105   'Listen, Brother Bishu!' *RR*, *2*, pp. 236–42 (32 Jaishtha 1295 [1888]). (This is our translation with help from E. J. Thompson's.)

p. 106   'beat and kick their wives' This behaviour does not appear in the published version today. 'In later editions, the poet remitted this part of the castigation.' (E. J. Thompson, p. 81)

p. 106   'His scorn has wings' E. J. Thompson, p. 76

p. 106   'While in our hearts' *RR*, *2*, pp. 197–201 (18 Jaishtha 1295 [1888])

p. 106   'But I am a Bengali' 2 June 1892, *Glimpses*, p. 67/ *Chhinnapatra*, p. 117

p. 107   'Tagore's reply' 29 Jan. 1891, Kripalani, *Rabindranath*, pp. 132–33 (trans. by Kripalani)/ *Chithipatra*, *5*, pp. 150–51. The letter was addressed to Pramatha Chaudhuri, who married RT's niece Indira in 1899.

12 The Shelidah Years

Epigraph   24 June 1894, *Glimpses*, p. 102/ *Chhinnapatra*, p. 211

p. 108   'Jyotirindranath' E. J. Thompson, p. 95

p. 108   'Whoever wishes to' 'Tatvajnanhin', *Chaitali*, *RR*, *5*, p. 36 (27 Chaitra 1302 [1896])

p. 109   'Chaudhuri later observed' *Thy Hand*, p. 602

p. 109   'documentary' For a discussion of the film, see Robinson, *Satyajit Ray*, pp. 277–79.

p. 109   'fifty-nine short stories' This figure includes 'Nashtanirh' ('The Broken Nest'), which is really a novella.

p. 109   'world's great short stories' E. J. Thompson to RT, 28 April 1935: 'I am sure that there is no greater short story writer in the world's literature than you.' (E.P. Thompson, p. 24)

p. 110   'This river has no current' 'Letters to his wife', *VBQ*, Summer 1953, pp. 4–5/ *Chithipatra*, *1*, pp. 9–10

p. 110   '*Padma*' Rathindranath Tagore, p. 33

p. 110   'firing of guns' ibid, p. 36

p. 111   'footpath in my life history' 17 June 1918 [Michael Yeats]

p. 111   'All of a sudden . . . entered my writing' 5 Sept. 1894, *Glimpses*, pp. 108–09/ *Chhinnapatra*, pp. 239–40

p. 112   'earliest stories' RT contributed six stories to a new weekly magazine *Hitabadi* from 30 May 1891; 'The Postmaster' was one of them.

p. 112   'the most improbable things' ?9 Feb. 1891, *Glimpses*, p. 38/ *Chhinnapatra*, p. 60

p. 112   'real postmaster . . . recognized himself' 29 June 1892, *Glimpses*, p. 74/ *Chhinnapatra*, p. 132. In 1936, RT told an interviewer: 'There was a postmaster. He used to come to me. He had been away from his place for a long time and he was longing to go back. He didn't like his surroundings. He thought he was forced to live among barbarians. And his desire to get leave was so intense that he even thought of resigning from his post.' (*Forward*, Calcutta, 23 Feb. 1936)

p. 112   'Every few minutes' June 1891, *Glimpses*, p. 41/ *Chhinnapatra*, p. 75

p. 112   'place for pity . . . sorrow' 4 July 1893, ibid, p. 90/ p. 178

p. 113   'half-English' 'Jiban katha', Sharadiya *Ekshan*, 1992, p. 86

p. 113   'For a moment . . . soles of his feet' 25 Jan. 1890, *Glimpses*, pp. 28–30/ *Chhinnapatra*, pp. 40–41

p. 114   'lost track of time' 24 June 1894, ibid, p. 102/ p. 211

p. 114   'The day-world' 10 August 1894, ibid, pp. 105–06/ pp. 230–31

p. 115   'I am a lamp' Arthur A. Bake, 'Indian music and Rabindranath Tagore', *Indian Art and Letters*, London, second issue for 1931, p. 86 (the example of *bhatiali* came from Kshitimohan Sen.) For a photographic view of the life of the boatmen of Bangladesh, see Jansen.

p. 115   'Goethe' 12 August 1894, *VBN*, Dec. 1966, p. 77 (trans. by Kshitis Roy)/ *Chhinnapatrabali*, p. 216

p. 116   'No sign of my servant' 'Karma', *Chaitali*, *RR*, *5*, p. 16 (18 Chaitra 1302 [1896])

p. 116   'Nirad Chaudhuri' Letter to Authors, 13 Aug. 1990

p. 116   'The rain-soaked foliage' *Selected Short Stories*, Dutta and Lago trans., pp. 27–28/ *RR*, *15*, pp. 413–14

p. 117   'The lamp flickered' ibid, p. 29/ p. 415

p. 117 'Ratan, I've never' ibid, p. 31/ p. 416. In the story, Ratan clasps the postmaster's feet before running away; in the film her reaction is more restrained. See Robinson, *Satyajit Ray*, pp. 128–31.

p. 117 '*New York Times*' 5 May 1963 (Bosley Crowther)

p. 117 'the rain-swollen river' *Selected Short Stories*, Dutta and Lago trans., p. 31/ *RR*, *15*, pp. 416–17

p. 117 'Alas' ibid, pp. 31–32/ p. 417

p. 118 'Loaded with my gold paddy' *Selected Poems*, p. 53 (trans. by William Radice)/ *RR*, *3*, pp. 7–8 (Phalgun 1298 [1892])

p. 118 'Outside on the doorstep' 'Moods', John Boulton, *VBQ*, Feb.–April 1975, pp. 326–27 (trans. by Boulton)/*RR*, *3*, pp. 49–55 (14 Kartik 1299 [1892]). (We have considerably modified the translation.)

p. 119 'Under a tattered canopy' 'The philosophy of our people', *VBQ*, Jan. 1926, p. 301

p. 119 'syncretic religious traditions' See, for instance, 'Rabindranath on Baul songs', *MR*, Oct. 1928, p. 448.

p. 120 'This system prevailed' Rathindranath Tagore, p. 29

p. 120 'Durbuddhi' *Selected Short Stories*, Dutta and Lago trans., pp. 133–38/*RR*, *22*, pp. 181–85

p. 120 'It was so difficult . . . inconveniences' 'City and village', *TUM*, pp. 318–20/*RR*, *27*, p. 554

p. 121 'Abanindranath recalled' 'Jorasanko way', *VBQ*, Feb.–April 1948, p. 327 (trans. by Lila Majumdar)/ *Abanindra Rachanabali (Gharoa)*, *1*, p. 69

p. 121 'Rabi Babu' Rathindranath Tagore, p. 17

p. 121 'The moment he set foot' Dutta and Robinson, *Noon in Calcutta*, p. 11/*RR*, *21*, p. 248

p. 122 'It is hard to see . . . of the time' 'Vidyasagar-charit', *RR*, *4*, pp. 501–02

p. 122 'British in India' Little of RT's most scathing criticism of the British in India has been translated. *Glimpses of Bengal* contains a sample:

> He was an Englishman of the worst sort: beak-nosed, wily-eyed, big-chinned, thick-necked – a fully developed bull of a man. At present the government is under pressure to curtail our right to trial by jury. This fellow dragged in the subject by the ears and insisted on arguing it out with our host, poor Bihari Lal Babu. He said that the people of this country had a low moral standard; that they had no real belief in the sacredness of life; and so they were unfit to serve on juries.

For a man like this to accept hospitality from a Bengali and feel no shame in talking thus when seated at his host's table, how great his contempt for us must be! (10 Feb. 1893, p. 79/ *Chhinnapatra*, p. 148). See also 6 March 1893, ibid, pp. 81–82/ pp. 155–56. In 1893, RT wrote four essays criticizing the British in India, published in *RR*, *10*.

p. 123   'Kantharodh' *RR*, *10*, pp. 424–31

p. 123   'two British barristers' Tahmankar, p. 87

13 Family Life

Epigraph   December 1900, 'Letters to his wife', *VBQ*, Summer 1953, p. 12 (trans. by Lila Majumdar)/ *Chithipatra*, *1*, p. 43

p. 124   'At midnight' *Gardener* (75), p. 130/ 'Bairagya', *Chaitali*, *RR*, *5*, p. 11 (14 Chaitra 1302 [1896])

p. 125   'Our teacher of English' Rathindranath Tagore, p. 20

p. 125   'silly stuff' ibid, pp. 20–21

p. 125   'difficult for Mother' ibid, p. 21. It is surprising that RT did not introduce his children to the graphic children's versions of the *Ramayana* and *Mahabharata* written by his friend Upendrakishore Ray – see Robinson, *Satyajit Ray*, pp. 17–18.

p. 126   'dived into the river' Rathindranath Tagore, p. 31

p. 126   'The husband was sent for ' ibid, pp. 32–34

p. 126   'scorpion' 29 Aug. 1899, *Chithipatra*, *1*, pp. 32–34

p. 126   'a lady from Calcutta' Rathindranath Tagore, p. 12. She was the sister of C. R. Das.

p. 126   'after a hurried dinner' ibid, p. 26

p. 127   'Once I lived' 'Kopai', *RR*, *16*, pp. 1–10 (1 Bhadra 1339 [1932])

p. 127   'crystal-clear lake . . . grew up' Rathindranath Tagore, pp. 23–24

p. 128   'Oriental life' Geddes, p. 223. Geddes' biography is still the best book on J. C. Bose.

p. 128   'The moment a new discovery' 31 Aug. 1900, 'One friend to another', *VBQ*, Spring 1959, pp. 260, 263 (trans. by Somnath Maitra)/ *Patrabali*, Calcutta, 1958, pp. 31–32

p. 128   'There I was . . . lap it up' 17 Sept. 1900, *Chithipatra*, *6*, p. 7. This is our translation; the full letter appears in 'One friend to another', ibid, pp. 263–66. The remarkable range of subject-matter in RT's letter to Bose indicates their intimacy at this time; RT even mentions an early attempt to be a painter, and makes a dismissive remark: 'the pictures are not intended for any salon in Paris'.

p. 128   'a sum of money' RT raised Rs. 5,000 for Bose from the maharaja of

Tripura. See his letter, 9 Aug. 1901 in *Tripura's Ties with Tagore*, pp. 31–33/ *Rabindranath o Tripura*, pp. 409–11.

p. 129   'mumbo-jumbo' A physicist who knew Raman well wrote: 'Raman once referred me to one of Bose's scientific papers and remarked: "He did some very clever physics before he started on all his mumbo-jumbo".' (Siv Ramaseshan to Authors, 23 Nov. 1992)

p. 129   'The Sunset of the Century' E. J. Thompson, p. 183 (trans. by Thompson)/ *Naivedya* (64), *RR*, *8*, pp. 51–52

p. 129   'After fifty' *I Won't Let You Go: Selected Poems*, p. 122 (trans. by Ketaki Kushari Dyson)/ *Kshanika*, *RR*, *7*, pp. 213–14

p. 130   'luxuries of European life' 7 April 1902, *Tripura's Ties with Tagore*, p. 44/ *Rabindranath o Tripura*, p. 437

p. 130   'I have just come . . . primal mother' July 1901, 'Letters to his wife', *VBQ*, Summer 1953, pp. 17–19 (trans. by Lila Majumdar)/ *Chithipatra*, *1*, pp. 61–63

p. 131   'tolerant Rathindranath remarked' Rathindranath Tagore, p. 148

p. 131   '*jiban-debata*' Much (too much) has been written on this concept. To quote RT's own definition: 'the limited aspect of divinity which has its unique place in the individual life, in contrast to that which belongs to the universe.' (RT to Rothenstein, 20 April 1927, in Lago, p. 321) Significantly, Nirad Chaudhuri made no reference to the *jiban-debata* in 'Tagore's Religious Life' (*Thy Hand*, pp. 614–19).

p. 131   '*Nashtanirh*' *Selected Short Stories*, Dutta and Lago trans. pp. 139–99/ *RR*, *22*, pp. 207–63. The first instalment was published in mid-April 1901, the last in mid-November.

p. 132   'unconditional blessing' Paul, *5*, p. 44

p. 132   'I find it very poignant' *Selected Short Stories*, William Radice trans., p. 10/ *Chithipatra*, *1*, p. 68

14 Small Beginnings in Shantiniketan

Epigraph   7 April 1902, *Tripura's Ties with Tagore*, p. 44/ *Rabindranath o Tripura*, p. 437

p. 133   'gathering of Tagores' Paul, *3*, p. 101

p. 133   'Mandir' RT often preached in the Mandir, but in 1933 he told Gandhi:

Our religious service could as well take place under the trees, its truth and sacredness would not at all be affected but perhaps enhanced by such a natural environment. Difficulties of climate and season intervene, otherwise I do not think separate buildings are really necessary for prayer and communication with the Divine.

(March 1933, 'Letters to Mahatma Gandhi', *Rabindra-Biksha*, Dec. 1991, p. 20)

p. 133   'sacred thread' Rathindranath Tagore, p. 42

p. 134   'first and deepest love' ibid, p. 34

p. 134   'Satyajit Ray' 'My life, my work' *Telegraph*, Calcutta, 28 Sept. 1982

p. 134   'full of paradoxes' 2 May 1892, *Glimpses*, p. 60/ *Chhinnapatra*, p. 108

p. 134   'the storm . . . false' 24 May 1892, ibid, pp. 62–63/ pp. 111–13

p. 135   'five pupils' The other four came from a school in Calcutta established by Brahmabandhab Upadhyay. See Animananda, pp. 93–94; *MR*, Aug. 1933, pp. 225–26.

p. 135   'opening ceremony' Rathindranath Tagore, p. 44

p. 135   'Hitlerian type' ibid, p. 50. The Catholic Bengali was Brahmabandhab Upadhyay. His later activities and death are described in Kopf, p. 213, and in Nandy, pp. 51–79.

p. 135   'Gurudev' Kshitimohan Sen, *VBN*, June 1939, p. 91

p. 135   'disciplinarian' Rathindranath Tagore, p. 44

p. 135   'non-Brahmin teacher' Paul, *5*, p. 98

p. 136   'surreptitious raids' Rathindranath Tagore, p. 45

p. 136   'watching the constellations . . . under a tree' ibid, pp. 48–49

p. 137   'Thou comest' *Spectator*, 10 Jan. 1931, p. 50 (trans. by RT)/ *Kalpana*, *RR*, *7*, pp. 184–88 (30 Chaitra 1305 [1899])

p. 137   'nephews' Balendranath died in 1899, Nitindranath in 1902.

p. 137   'death rate' The death rate (per thousand) in Britain was 17 in 1893, 15.4 in 1903 and 14.4 in 1906, as compared with 31.3, 33.3, and 36 respectively in Bengal. (*MR*, May 1909, p. 454)

p. 137   'nurse Mrinalini' Rathindranath Tagore, p. 52; Kripalani, *Rabindranath*, p. 203; and Paul, *5*, pp. 95–96.

p. 137   'Who will provide them' *Smaran* (14), *RR*, *8*, pp. 90–91 (2 Paush 1309 [1902])

p. 138   'miss his wife' There are very few posthumous references to Mrinalini by RT, the most notable being those in the Visva-Bharati anthology, *Mrinalini Devi*, pp. 46–47. There are *no* significant references to her in RT's letters to his children, where one would most expect to find them, even with a man as reticent about his marriage as RT.

p. 138   'Supposing I became . . . Ma?' *The Crescent Moon*, p. 29

p. 138 'When, come evening' 'Lukochuri', *Shishu*, *RR*, *9*, pp. 54–55

p. 138 'A poet who was truly' 'Cheleta', *Punashcha*, *RR*, 16, pp. 39–44 (28 Shraban 1339 [1932])

p. 139 'When Amala's mother died' 'Shesh Chithi', *Punashcha*, *RR*, *16*, pp. 49–52 (31 Shraban 1339 [1932])

p. 139 '*Bengalee*' 20 Jan. 1905, in *VBN*, Feb. 1978, p. 103

p. 139 'charge of fifteen rupees' Prasanta Mahalanobis, 'The growth of the Visva-Bharati, 1901–1921', *VBQ*, April 1928, p. 83 (quotes Ajit Kumar Chakraborty)

p. 140 'Rs. 2,000' This is the generally accepted figure, but the family cashbook mentions only Rs. 1,500. (Paul, *5*, p. 151)

15 The Swadeshi Movement

Epigraph 'Two folk-tales of Bengal', *VBQ*, Feb.–April 1952, p. 324 (trans. by Lila Ray, modified by us)/ Introduction to Dakshinaranjan Mitra Mazumdar, *Thakumar Jhuli*, p. 10

p. 141 'If we begin to rate' 6 March 1893, *Glimpses*, p. 81/ *Chhinnapatra*, p. 155

p. 142 'Dickinson' For RT's reaction to this, see Paul, *5*, pp. 74–75.

p. 142 'Curzon' On 15 Feb. 1902 Curzon, as chancellor of Calcutta University, told the Convocation: 'If I were asked to sum up in a single word the most notable characteristic of the East – physical, intellectual and moral – as compared with the West, the word "exaggeration," or "extravagance," is the one that I should employ.' (*Speeches*, *2*, (1900–1902), p. 432)

p. 142 'Badshahs' 'Atyukti', *RR*, *4*, p. 446

p. 143 'The way of the East' *TUM*, pp. 56–57/ *RR*, *3*, p. 535

p. 143 'invest a strong personality' ibid, p. 59/ p. 543

p. 143 'British officials' Curzon's correspondence leaves no doubt as to his enthusiasm for Partition as a way of controlling the Bengali babu – see Sumit Sarkar, pp. 19–20.

p. 144 'Kindly convey' 17 Nov. 1905, [Curzon], *Letters and Telegrams*, p. 284

p. 144 'twenty-three songs' Paul, *5*, pp. 259–61

p. 144 'Nirad Chaudhuri . . . wrote' *Autobiography*, pp. 225–26

p. 144 'Let the soil' *GB*, *1*, p. 255. This translation appears in Sumit Sarkar, p. 292. The second and third songs mentioned are in *GB*, *1*, pp. 266, 244.

p. 145 'On the way to the river . . . smiled' Abanindranath Tagore, 'Jorasanko way', *VBQ*, Feb.–April 1948, p. 328 (trans. by Lila Majumdar)/ *Abanindra Rachanabali (Gharoa)*, *1*, p. 72

p. 145   'Rs. 50,000' Rathindranath Tagore, p. 62

p. 145   'five meetings up to 16 October' Paul, 5, p. 270

p. 145   *The Home and the World* pp. 149–53/ *RR*, 8, pp. 235–36

p. 145   'fundamentally creative' Sahitya Akademi, p. 53

p. 146   'anarchy of emptiness' RT to C. F. Andrews, 5 March 1921, *Letters to a Friend*, pp. 131–32

p. 146   'affiliating his school' Prasanta Mahalanobis, 'The growth of the Visva-Bharati', *VBQ*, April 1928, p. 87

p. 146   'bias towards technical education' Rathindranath Tagore, p. 61

p. 146   'government of East Pakistan' Rathindranath Tagore in Sahitya Akademi, p. 57

p. 147   'there was one problem . . . tenants' ibid, p. 55

p. 147   'two students from Indiana' Rathindranath Tagore, pp. 68–69

p. 148   'forewords' *The Russian Horizon* (foreword by H. G. Wells); *Thoughts for Meditation* (foreword by T. S. Eliot). Both are anthologies: the former contains an extract from RT's *Crisis in Civilization*, the latter includes a translation of Kabir by RT.

p. 148   'I dealt the first blow' n.d., Sharadiya *Desh*, 1396 [1989], p. 24. The most likely date is 1919–20, since RT mentions a stay in Madras that took place in March 1919.

p. 148   'When his last moment' RT to Maharajkumari Vidyabati Devi, 27 Dec. 1935, *VBN*, Dec. 1942, p. 67

p. 149   'a recognized hallmark' 26 Aug. 1907, *Chithipatra*, 2, p. 5

p. 149   'drum-beating' 7 April 1910, ibid, p. 14

p. 149   'I cannot take responsibility' Sahitya Akademi, pp. 57–58/ *RR*, 27, p. 558

p. 150   'wrote Nirad Chaudhuri' *Thy Hand*, p. 610

16 The Voice of Bengal

Epigraph   4 Jan. 1909, 'The problem of India', *MR*, Aug. 1910, p. 187

p. 151   'greatest man ever born' 'Buddhadeva', *VBQ*, Winter 1956/57, p. 169/ *Buddhadeva*, p. 1 (speech delivered on 18 March 1935). 'The mode of self-expression in Christian life is in love which works, in that of a Hindu it is in love which contemplates, enjoys the spiritual emotion as an end in itself.' (RT to C. F. Andrews, 2 Aug. 1932, *VBN*, March 1933, p. 81)

p. 152   'just because Bengalis' *RR*, 10, p. 447

p. 152   'Many of us' ibid, p. 463

p. 152   'Some of us' ibid, pp. 464–65

p. 152   'men from all quarters' ibid, p. 467

p. 153   'At every turn' *TUM*, pp. 139–40/ *RR, 12*, pp. 272–73

p. 153   'The government was prosecuting' Paul, *6*, p. 34. The writer in question was a teacher at Shantiniketan; after he was released from jail, RT found him a job in Shelidah.

p. 153   '*Bengalee*' 26 March 1909, in Paul, *6*, p. 60

p. 154   'Blessed is my birth' *GB, 1*, p. 257

p. 154   '[genesis of] *Gora*' RT to W. W. Pearson, 1922, 'Letters to W. W. Pearson', *VBQ*, Aug.–Oct. 1943, p. 179

p. 154   'Sister Nivedita' For an account of her life, see Foxe. RT wrote an introduction to the second (posthumous) edition of Nivedita's *The Web of Indian Life*.

p. 154   'angry with his story' E. P. Thompson, p. 147 (remark by RT to E. J. Thompson)

p. 155   'The translation . . . corrected' W. W. Pearson was the translator. After his death in 1923, RT wrote to Thomas Sturge Moore: 'Pearson did not know enough Bengali to be able to give a correct rendering of the story in English. My nephew Suren revised it comparing it with the original. Macmillans in their haste only had half of the corrected version and the latter half remains untouched with its ludicrous mistakes and crudities.' (20 May 1924 [London])

p. 155   '*Uncle Tom's Cabin*' *Nation and Athenaeum*, 9 Feb. 1924, p. 669

p. 155   'an event in 1873' The launching of *Bangadarshan* by Bankimchandra Chatterji (*Gora*, p. 174/ *RR, 6*, p. 323)

p. 155   'They want to sever' ibid, p. 89/ p. 222

p. 156   'It has ever been India's lot' 4 Jan. 1909, 'The problem of India', *MR*, Aug. 1910, pp. 185, 186

p. 156   'visited Shelidah' Rathindranath Tagore, p. 74

p. 156   'Successive bereavements' ibid, pp. 73–74

p. 156   'training in the sciences' ibid

p. 157   'Pratima' She was the daughter of Binayini, the sister of Gaganendranath and Abanindranath.

p. 157   'no children' In the 1920s, Rathindranath and Pratima adopted a girl from Gujarat, whom they called Nandini or La Poupée.

p. 157   'difficult not to suspect' This speculation is also made by the English Buddhist Sangharakshita, who met Pratima Devi in the early 1950s. (Sangharakshita, p. 169)

p. 157   'In other parts of the world' *My Rem*, p. 186/ *RR, 17*, pp. 431–32

p. 157   'The Institution of Fixed Beliefs' RT suggested this title to Thompson. (E. J. Thompson, p. 215)

p. 157   '*The Post Office*' For an account of a recent production in Europe, see Martin Kämpchen, 'The flowering of Rabindranath on European soil', *Statesman*, Calcutta, 9 May 1993.

p. 158   'coming down the hillside' *The Post Office*, p. 68/ *RR*, *11*, p. 398 (translation slightly amended)

p. 158   'When will he be awake?' ibid, p. 88/ *RR*, *11*, p. 406

p. 159   'in the presence of Gandhi' Rathindranath Tagore, p. 91

p. 159   'Amal represents' 4 June 1921, *Letters to a Friend*, p. 172

p. 159   'Asia is one' These are the opening words of Okakura, *The Ideals of the East* (1903). There was a second edition in 1904, with an Introduction by Sister Nivedita, which was reprinted in 1905. The book remains in print today in Japan.

p. 160   'Coomaraswamy translated' The very first English translations of Tagore's poetry to be published in book form are those in Roby Datta, *Echoes from East and West* (1909), where RT is referred to as Roby Tagore. Coomaraswamy's versions appear in *Art and Swadeshi*, pp. 112–24; there are eleven poems taken from *Shonar Tari* (1894), *Chaitali* (1896), *Kanika* (1899), *Kalpana* (1900), *Shishu* (1902) – none from *Gitanjali*.

p. 160   'remarkable men of his time' *Men and Memories*, p. 249

p. 160   'Yourself I shall always allow' 21 Feb. 1911, Lago, p. 35

p. 160   'short story . . . *Modern Review*' *Men and Memories*, p. 262. Rothenstein later gave a somewhat different account: 'on the way home [i.e. on board ship], in a copy of the *Modern Review*, I read a striking story and some poems, signed "Rabindranath Tagore".' (*Indian Art and Letters*, London, second issue for 1941, p. 65)

p. 160   'offered his hospitality' Abanindranath Tagore to William Rothenstein, 21 March 1912 [IOL]: 'It was so very kind of you to have offered him [RT] your hospitality. I have shown him your kind letter.'

p. 160   'highly mystical' *Men and Memories*, p. 262

p. 160   'as far back as 1901' Several translations of short stories were published in *New India* in 1901–02, translated by various Bengalis. The first translation of all was almost certainly one by Sister Nivedita ('The Cabuliwallah'), completed in 1900 but not published until Jan. 1912 in the *MR*: it was this translation that J. C. Bose offered to *Harper's Magazine*.

p. 160   'piles' Paul, 6, p. 234. Piles were not specifically mentioned at this time, but it was for piles that RT had surgery in London in 1913.

p. 160   'forced him to cancel' Paul, 6, p. 238. On 10 Oct. 1911, Rathindranath told his American friend Mayce Seymour that his father would leave for Europe on 26 Oct. 'This voyage is being taken mostly on account of Father's health, and also because he wants to come in closer contact with present-day Europe and America'. [RB]

p. 161 'this great lie' 'Atmaparichay', *RR*, *18*, p. 466

p. 161 'altogether unsuitable' Sehanobis, p. 28

p. 161 'education officials . . . refused' Paul, *6*, p. 272

p. 161 'surveillance by the police' RT told E. J. Thompson that he had requested a man to leave Shantiniketan on the grounds that he was a government spy. (E. P. Thompson, p. 117)

p. 161 'they were disappointed' Paul, *6*, p. 256. See also 'Jana Gana Mana: its occasion and date', *VBN*, Dec. 1948, pp. 40–41. Ironically, the official version of 'Jana Gana Mana' as a national anthem was played by the London Philharmonic Society. Nehru commented to the Cabinet: 'In order that it may not become too western in conception an expert Indian musician is advising them.' (*Selected Works*, *6* (second series), p. 278)

p. 161 'The national committee came' Jan. 1913, Pound, p. 49

p. 162 'sit in a deck-chair' RT to Indira Devi, 6 May 1913, in *Tagore Reader*, p. 21/ *Chithipatra*, *5*, p. 9

17 England and the USA

Epigraph 2 Sept. 1912, Finneran *et al.*, *2*, p. 251

p. 163 'Left Luggage Office' Rathindranath Tagore, p. 100

p. 163 'comparatively brief and superficial' See, for instance, Rathindranath Tagore to Mayce Seymour, 26 June 1909 [RB].

p. 163 'a moored boat' 'A friend', *VBQ*, Feb.–April 1945, pp. 157–58 (trans. by Kshitis Roy)/ *RR*, *26*, p. 517

p. 164 'Speaight wrote' p. 253

p. 164 'What the poems are he is' 18 Aug. 1912, Finneran *et al.*, *2*, p. 249

p. 164 'the vision to see truth' RT to E. Speight, 14 July 1916 [RB]

p. 164 'told Thompson airily' Thompson, pp. 221–22. Rothenstein must have been irritated to read this in Thompson's biography in 1927 – which may account for the tone of *Men and Memories* (1932) on this particular point.

p. 165 'rented house in Hampstead' Upon arrival in Hampstead, RT and party stayed at Holford Road, NW3. They shifted from there to the nearby 3 Villas on the Heath in the Vale of Health, between 21 and 28 June, where they remained until the end of July/beginning of August. Today the house bears a commemorative blue plaque.

p. 165   'Oxford doctorate' Lago, pp. 38–39

p. 165   'two Brahmo friends' Brajendranath Seal and Promothalal Sen

p. 165   'He begged' *Men and Memories*, p. 262. In 1941, after RT's death, Rothenstein said: 'he [RT] presented me with a small manuscript book . . . saying in that modest way our Indian friends have: "You were good enough to be interested in my poetry. On my way to your country I made for you a few translations."' (*Indian Art and Letters*, London, second issue for 1941, p. 66)

p. 165   'Rothenstein told Yeats' 11 July 1912, Finneran *et al.*, 2, p. 247

p. 165   'Fox Strangways' 10 July 1912 [IOL]. Fox Strangways added: 'I'm glad to think the old fellow [i.e. RT] will go back to his country with warm feelings in his heart.'

p. 165   'unofficial literary agent' Fox Strangways and Rothenstein negotiated for RT a generous royalty agreement for *Gitanjali*. But Fox Strangways became disenchanted with the position in 1913, especially after the Nobel prize, because it took up too much time and because of·'the unpleasantness in which I am involved when you say one thing to me and another to someone else.' (Fox Strangways to RT, 28 Nov. 1913 [RB]) In early 1914, Macmillan took over as RT's literary agent. There are many letters from Fox Strangways to RT in RB; Fox Strangways' personal papers have not been traced, despite exhaustive efforts by the Authors.

p. 166   'first little chapter' 7 Sept. 1912, *Men and Memories*, p. 267

p. 166   'I have carried . . . image' Introduction to *Gitanjali*, pp. xiii, xiv, xvi–xvii

p. 166   'painted pict' 4 Oct. 1912, Pound and Litz, p. 163. Pound's friend at that time, Richard Aldington, later wrote: 'he [RT] hit Yeats bang in the Blavatsky. Ezra too had a streak of superstition . . . I wasn't allowed to see Tagore as being too profane; but I could always tell when Ezra had been seeing him, because he was so infernally smug.' (Aldington, pp. 108–09) For a full discussion of Pound and RT see Bikash Chakraborty, 'Incomplete dialogue: Tagore and Ezra Pound', *VBN*, May–June 1986, pp. 307–13. It is worth emphasizing that Pound was *not* present at the soirée on 7 July when Yeats read, since several writers, including Kripalani, have stated that he was.

p. 166   'Pound . . . boldly asserted' 'Rabindranath Tagore', *Fortnightly Review*, March 1913, p. 575

p. 167   'Dante' ibid, p. 576

p. 167   'Nash' 12 December 1912 [RB]. Presumably, Rothenstein passed Nash's letter on to RT, hence its present location.

p. 167   *'Times Literary Supplement'* 7 Nov. 1912, p. 492

p. 167   'verse ninety-six' *RR, 11*, p. 111

p. 167   'verse sixty-three' *RR, 11*, pp. 6–7

p. 167   'telegram' 'I beg to convey to the Swedish Academy my grateful appreciation of the breadth of understanding which has brought the distant near, and has made a stranger a brother.' (*The Nobel Century*, p. 210 – no author; some other statements about RT in this book are incorrect.)

p. 167   'verse sixty' *RR, 9*, p. 1

p. 168   'verse seventy-three' *RR, 8*, p. 30

p. 168   'verse thirty-nine' *RR, 11*, p. 48

p. 168   'verse thirty' *RR, 11*, p. 79

p. 168   'verse one hundred and two' *RR, 10*, p. 14

p. 168   'verse sixty-seven' *RR, 8*, p. 63. Bridges, *The Spirit of Man* (38); Yeats, *The Oxford Book of Modern Verse, 1892–1935*, p. 67

p. 169   'ineffective dreamer' See p. 7. Nevertheless E. J. Thompson admitted: 'It was through the English *Gitanjali* that I got my first introduction to his poetry, and I confess myself to this day so under its spell that I cannot appraise it with any degree of accuracy.' (p. 218)

p. 169   'fashionable to say so' For example, Amit Chaudhuri, *London Review of Books*, 23 Sept. 1993, pp. 10–11: 'The whole idea, propagated by the poet's Indian and western admirers alike, of Tagore as a "world poet", was a harmful falsification.' It all depends what one means by 'world poet'.

p. 169   'Larkin' See p. 7. Larkin was surely the archetypal 'jealous sovereign', strictly guarding the boundaries of the English language against foreign adulteration (to borrow Tagore's image from the epigraph at the beginning of this book). Larkin's finest poetry would no doubt be as untranslatable into Bengali as Rabindranath's best poems are into English.

p. 169   'Saint-John Perse' 'Homage à la mémoire de Rabindranath Tagore', *Nouvelle Revue Française*, Nov. 1961, pp. 868–71

p. 169   'Edward Thomas' See reviews by Thomas in *Daily Chronicle*, 15 Nov. 1913, 12 Dec. 1913. (Kundu *et al.*, pp. 39–40, 45–47)

p. 169   'Hart Crane' Weber, pp. 10–11, 105–06

p. 169   'Robert Frost' 'Remarks on the occasion of the Tagore centenary', *Poetry*, Nov. 1961, pp. 106–19; also, less significantly, Frost, p. 72

p.169   'enormous condescension' *The Making of the English Working Class*, London, 1963, p. 12

p. 169   'New Testament' RT rarely referred to specific passages of the

Bible, but he spoke regularly about Christ and he wrote several poems about Christ. *RR, 27,* contains his main talks, collected by himself. He was not much interested in the Old Testament. (RT to Theodore Dunn, 4 July 1918 [Cambridge])

p. 169 'Cornford' 15 July 1912, Lago, p. 19

p. 169 'others felt similarly' For example, May Sinclair to RT, 8 July 1912, in Rathindranath Tagore, pp. 102–03

p. 170 'Nirad Chaudhuri explained' *Thy Hand,* p. 627

p. 170 'wealthy Edwardian Englishmen' Nirad Chaudhuri (*Thy Hand,* p. 627) made some interesting comments on RT and the Edwardian summer. Harold Macmillan remained curious about RT to the end of his life, as one of the Authors (AR), who met Macmillan in 1986, can testify.

p.170 'bitter poetry' Owen first recorded his interest in *Gitanjali* in Jan. 1917, and spoke the same line to his mother in Aug. 1918: in between he wrote almost all his worthwhile poetry – see p. 2 – note. A vivid memoir of the war as seen by a gunner, as yet unpublished, read by the Authors, begins with a quotation from the *The Crescent Moon*: 'Death is abroad and children play.' (information courtesy Adrian Bishop-Laggett)

p. 170 'From the words of the poet' Verse 75/ *RR, 8,* p. 39

p. 170 'Rhys . . . mentioned' Rhys, *Rabindranath Tagore,* p. 96. This remark makes an interesting contrast with Wilfred Owen's attitude towards *Gitanjali.* The verse selected by Owen celebrates *this* world, not the next, for which Owen seems nevertheless to have been yearning.

p. 170 'Sturge Moore' Letter to Robert Trevelyan, n.d., in Lago, pp. 17–18

p. 170 'Bertrand Russell' 16 Nov. 1912 [RB]

p. 171 'Gloucestershire' It was while RT was staying with him in Gloucestershire that Rothenstein wrote passionately to Yeats on 18 August – see p. 164.

p. 171 'wrote to . . . Bela' 19 Feb. 1913, 'Letters to his daughters', *VBQ,* Spring 1957, p. 266 (trans. by Lila Majumdar)/ *Chithipatra, 4,* p. 7

p. 171 'wrote to . . . Monroe' ?24 Sept. 1913, Pound, p. 44

p. 171 'he trumpeted' Oct. 1913, Monroe, p. 262

p. 171 'R. N. Tagore Jr.' 9 Dec. 1912 [Chicago]

p. 171 'editorial in *Chicago Tribune*' Monroe, p. 320

p. 171 'I feel great reluctance' 25 Dec. 1912 [Chicago]

p. 172 'inertia' 4 Jan. 1913 [Chicago]

p. 172 'chanting . . . Buddha' Monroe, p. 321

p. 172   'those sacred songs' ibid, p. 294

p. 172   'satirical-humorous observations' ibid, p. 321

p. 172   'serenely noble Laureate' ibid, p. 320

p. 172   'well-known American poets' For example, Robert Frost

p. 172   'machinery of her life' Dunbar, p. 94

p. 172   'Tagore himself wrote to Rothenstein' 14 Feb. 1913, Lago, p. 99

p. 172   'Lowell' Paul, 6, p. 365

p. 172   'Vivekananda's triumph' Isherwood, pp. 319–22

p. 173   'Woods . . . wrote . . . to Tagore' n.d. [RB]

p. 173   'at his own expense' Lago, p. 100

p. 173   'Ellery Sedgwick' 21 Dec. 1926 [RB]

p. 173   'article on Shantiniketan' 'An evening in July', *Atlantic Monthly*, July 1913, pp. 58–61

p. 173   'anthology' See p. 148 – note.

p. 173   'he did attend' Kripalani, *Rabindranath*, p. 245

p. 173   'R. F. Rattray' 22 March 1940 [RB]. See also Rattray's 'With Tagore in 1913', *Inquirer*, London, 16 March 1940, p. 82.

p. 173   'Mr. T. S. Eliot' 3 May 1940 [RB]

p. 174   'Bridges . . . wrote' 7 June 1914, Lago, p. 177

p. 174   'Suhrawardy' He became professor of fine arts at Calcutta University.

p. 174   'vivid portrait' 'Tagore at Oxford' in *CMG*, p. 40

p. 174   'One day I was out . . . existence' *Sadhana*, pp. 110–11. This passage was read by Dame Peggy Ashcroft at the opening of an exhibition of RT's paintings and drawings at the Barbican Art Gallery, London, in Aug. 1986.

p. 175   'Inge . . . noted' 19 June 1913 (wrongly noted 17 June), Inge, p. 20

p. 175   'Lowes Dickinson' *Appearances*, p. 233

p. 176   'respect and ridicule' This attitude is also revealed in Winsten, pp. 148–50. However, Winsten's book is not reliable.

p. 176   ' dinner in Rothenstein's house'. See p. 6; and also Crow, p. 164.

p. 176   'I am Bernard Shaw' Rathindranath Tagore, p. 106

p. 176   'Shaw wrote . . . to a friend' 22 Aug. 1913, Shaw to Grace Rhys (wife of Ernest Rhys) [RB]

p. 176   'ripped-up Rabindranaths' 19 April 1919, Shaw, *Letters*, 3, p. 602

p. 176   'Stupendranath Begorr' 'A Glimpse of the Domesticity of Franklyn Barnabas', Shaw, *Short Stories, Scraps and Shavings*, p. 159 (information courtesy Amartya Sen)

p. 176   'Kenneth Clark' 'Tagore's portraits', in *CMG*, p. 55. Reuter reported on 13 Sept. 1941:

In accordance with a suggestion made by Mr. Bernard Shaw, the Director of the National Portrait Gallery in London has agreed to hang portraits of Dr. Rabindranath Tagore painted by Sir William Rothenstein and Sir Muirhead Bone. Sir Kenneth Clark, Director of the National Gallery, made this move on behalf of the Tagore Society.

p. 176   'Lowes Dickinson' 'A personal impression of Tagore', *New Leader*, London, 23 Feb. 1923, pp. 11–12

p. 176   'I do not remember a word' *Nation and Athenaeum*, 18 July 1925, p. 490 (book review by Lord Olivier). In 1941, Rothenstein said of RT: 'I remember his remark, after a visit to Cambridge, where he had met Lowes Dickinson and Bertrand Russell: "Such nice men; and they would so much like to believe in God, but they want a receipt first!"' (*Indian Art and Letters*, London, second issue for 1941, p. 67)

p. 177   'One more visitor' Rathindranath Tagore, pp. 104–05

p. 177   'Tagore visited me three times' Russell to N. Chatterji, 16 Feb. 1960 [copy at McMaster University]

p. 177   'I recall the meeting' Russell to N. Chatterji, 16 Feb. 1963, in Feinberg and Kasrils, p. 189

p. 177   'factually incorrect on three counts' RT visited Cambridge in July 1912, May 1913 and late June 1920. Lowes Dickinson was not in Cambridge in May 1913 (he was in the Far East). Russell was not in Cambridge in late June 1920. Therefore Tagore, Lowes Dickinson and Russell met in Cambridge only once, in July 1912. That Russell met Tagore twice in 1913, once in Cambridge and once in London, is proved by his letters to Ottoline Morrell. His last meeting (in Cornwall) is mentioned by his daughter Katharine Tait (Tait, p. 11). The London meeting was at Russell's own initiative, as he told Morrell.

p. 178   'The essence of religion', *Hibbert Journal*, Oct. 1912, pp. 46–62

p. 178   'Wittgenstein felt' Russell, *Letters*, *1*, pp. 437–38

p. 178   '*Upanishads*' *Taittiriya Upanishad*, 2:9 (*Upanishads*, p. 110), quoted in RT to Russell, 13 Oct. 1912, in Russell, *Autobiography*, p. 221

p. 178   'talk about the infinite' Russell to N. Chatterji, 26 April 1967 [copy at McMaster University]

p. 178   'humbug like . . . Radhakrishnan' Anyone who doubts this description of Radhakrishnan should read the *MR*, Jan., Feb., March, April 1929, in which Radhakrishnan stands accused of plagiarizing the work of a doctoral student in his major work on Indian philosophy.

p. 178   'Wittgenstein . . . devotee' Ray Monk, 'Seeing in the dark:

Wittgenstein and Tagore', in Dutta and Robinson, *Purabi*, pp. 142–44; also various references in Monk, *Ludwig Wittgenstein: The Duty of Genius*.

p. 179	'your lovely little play' 12 July 1913 [RB]
p. 179	'What a crew!' *Men and Memories*, p. 269
p. 179	'last letter to Yeats' 16 July 1935 [Michael Yeats]
p. 179	'Rhys wrote' 17 Sept. 1913 [RB]

18 The Nobel Prize

Epigraph	22 Jan. 1914 [Chicago]
p. 180	'The boys went mad . . . public show of me there.' E. P. Thompson, pp. 114–15
p. 181	'touch his feet' In the *MR* (Aug. 1912, p. 222), it was reported – sensationally for the time – that 'a retired English member' of the ICS (Indian Civil Service) had touched RT's feet. In fact, it was W. W. Pearson who did so. The mistake was never corrected in print.
p. 181	'MacDonald' He wrote 'Mr. Rabindranath Tagore's school', *Daily Chronicle*, 12 Jan. 1914 (Kundu *et al.*, pp. 53–55).
p. 181	'Will Lawrence' Stock, p. 132
p. 181	'a now notorious letter' 18 Nov. 1913, Lago, p. 140. In Feb. 1914, speaking at Pabna in East Bengal, RT diplomatically modified the image of the dog and the tin can. In *England*, he said, naughty boys sometimes tied an object to a dog's tail; now the same had been done to him, with the award of the Nobel prize. (*RR, 10*, pp. 496–522)
p. 181	'my days are riddled all over' 10 Dec. 1913, Lago, p. 143
p. 182	'My ordeal' 16 Dec. 1913, ibid, pp. 143–44
p. 182	'Subhashchandra Bose' 17 Sept. 1912, Subhash Bose, pp. 133–34. Bose also said: 'I am almost stung with self-reproach when I think how indifferent Bengal has been in showering laurels upon him'.
p. 183	'extracts of the speech' Chaudhuri, *Thy Hand*, p. 623/ *Sanjivani*, 28 Nov. 1913, in *CMG*, p. 80
p. 183	'a Bengali present' Mohitlal Majumdar, a teacher of Nirad Chaudhuri – see *Thy Hand*, p. 622.
p. 183	'Bipinchandra Pal' *CMG*, p. 79
p. 183	'At Home' Tinker, p.70. Among those present was Sir Michael O'Dwyer, the tough new lieutenant-governor of the Punjab, who in April 1919 helped to provoke the Amritsar Massacre.
p. 183	'Hardinge overruled it.' 20 Oct. 1913, in Nanda, pp. 400–01
p. 183	'retiring disposition' *CMG*, p. 80
p. 183	'chaste and elegant Bengali' Chaudhuri, *Thy Hand*, p. 608

p. 183   'E. M. Forster' 6 Nov. 1919, Forster to Florence Barger, in Forster, *Letters*, *1*, p. 312

p. 183   'Naturally such rumours' Feb. 1914, Lago, p. 147

p. 184   'Yeats . . . told Macmillan' 28 Jan. 1917, Nowell-Smith, p. 291

p. 184   'Rothenstein specifically discounted' *Men and Memories*, p. 301

p. 184   'Yeats amended', Paul, *6*, p. 323

p. 184   'Tagore . . . wrote to Thompson' 18 Nov. 1913 [Bodleian]

p. 184   'Prince William' 'The prince and the poet', *Truth*, London, pp. 1502–03 (comment on the book with translated excerpts)

p. 184   'mentioned it to Thompson' 18 Feb. 1914 [Bodleian]

p. 185   'Robert Bridges' 7 June 1914, Lago, p. 177

p. 185   'defective translation of . . . stories' *Glimpses of Bengal Life*, Rajani Ranjan Sen trans., Madras, 1913. RT had promised Sen in 1909 that he could translate some of the short stories. When Sen saw Tagore's fame in 1913, he promptly went ahead with his translation, despite RT's attempt to dissuade him. RT wrote to Macmillan: 'his translation is very inaccurate, and as far as I am able to judge, his English is poor.' (28 Dec. 1914 [BL])

p. 185   'a Swedish academic' Anders Osterling, 'Tagore and the Nobel prize', in Sahitya Akademi, p. 204. On 14 Nov. 1913, the day after the award was made public, the chairman of the Nobel committee, Harald Hjarne, wrote to Macmillan asking for a set of RT's works in Bengali. He said: 'of course we are acquainted with his principal works in English translations (and to some extent of his Bengali books also)'. [RB]

p. 185   'Anarchist' Espmark, pp. 4, 174

p. 185   'von Heidenstam' ibid, pp. 28–29

p. 186   'haunting the newspaper columns' ibid, p. 29

p. 186   'Per Hallström' ibid, p. 182

p. 186   'exotic Buddhistic fashion' *Neue Freie Presse*, Nov. 1913, in Aronson, *Rabindranath*, p. 5

p. 186   'le Rabbin Tégoro' J. D. Anderson to RT, 9 Dec. 1913 [RB]

p. 187   *'Punch'* 'Mr. Punch's Indian poet', 10 Dec. 1913, p. 494. A sample: 'When the soul is young it sings like a bird in the topmost branches of the tree. Sing, thou careless bird, and my soul shall sing too. But my soul can do more than sing. My soul can fly, bearing a message. My soul can skim along the river and can kiss the moist toes of her dipped foot.'

p. 187   *'New Statesman'* 13 Dec. 1913, p. 309

p. 187   'Sturge Moore' 22 Jan. 1914 [RB]

p. 187   'sacrificed my Nobel prize' 17 Feb. 1914 [copy at RB]

19 Never at Rest
Epigraph   15 Feb. 1914 [Bodleian]
p. 188   'a little rest' 1 Jan. 1914 [Bodleian]
p. 189   'the magic garment' 18 Sept. 1914 [Bodleian]
p. 189   'boat to Japan' RT to Rothenstein, 29 Dec. 1914, in Lago, p. 175.
            'I may reach your door some sunny day of summer.'
p. 189   'Rothenstein told . . . Rhys' 8 May 1915, Rhys, *Letters from Limbo*,
            p. 213
p. 189   'highly perceptive letter' *Tagore Reader*, p. 23
p. 190   'It has added . . . passing moments' ibid, pp. 23–24
p. 191   'Oxford University Press' Gollancz, pp. 320–21
p. 191   'When you arose' *Balaka* (39), *RR*, *12*, p. 65 (13 Agrayahan 1322
            [1915])
p. 191   'conflicting interpretations' *RR*, *12*, p. 594
p. 191   'Great poets raise' *VBN*, Aug. 1961, p. 31 (trans. by Jitendranarayan
            Sen)/ Paul, *6*, p. 55. The poet in question was Nabinchandra Sen.
p. 191   'I say to Shah Jahan' Brittain, p. 139. The visitor was William
            Pethick-Lawrence.
p. 192   'Tagore's own version' *Lover's Gift*, pp. 1–2
p. 192   'This fact you knew' *Balaka* (7), *RR*, *12*, pp. 14–20 (14 Kartik 1321
            [1914])
p. 193   'admired by Rothenstein' Rothenstein to RT, 11 July 1919, in Lago,
            pp. 255–56
p. 193   'You simply *must* read it' Hedwig Born (wife of Max Born) to
            Einstein, 8 Sept. 1920, in Born, p. 34
p. 193   'Hermann Hesse' Nov. 1920, Kämpchen, p. 41
p. 193   'Bertolt Brecht' 26 Sept. 1920, Brecht, p. 55
p. 193   'Georg Lukács' pp. 8–11
p. 193   'Russian scholar' S. D. Serebriany, 'F. Dostoevsky and R. Tagore:
            artists in search of identity for their cultures' (unpublished
            translation of an article in Russian: courtesy Serebriany).
            Serebriany identifies similarities between both the plots and the
            characters in *The Possessed* and *The Home and the World*.
p. 193   'Anita Desai' Introduction to *The Home and the World* (1985),
            p. 12
p. 193   'During the day' *The Home and the World* (1919), p. 204/ *RR*, *8*,
            pp. 265–66
p. 194   'E. M. Forster' Forster, *Abinger Harvest*, p. 321

p. 194   'he defended himself' 'The object and subject of a story', *MR*,
          Sept. 1918, pp. 221

p. 195   'poem in July' 'The Destroyer', *Letters to a Friend*, p. 37/ *Balaka*
          (2), *RR*, *12*, pp. 3–4 (5 Jaishtha 1321 [1914])

p. 195   'Andrews . . . concluded' ibid, p. 37

p. 195   'told Thompson' 25 Feb. 1914 [Bodleian]

p. 195   'under abuse' Chaudhuri, *Thy Hand*, p. 610/ 'Boshtami', *RR*, *23*,
          p. 234

p. 195   'I am ashamed . . . family and country.' n.d., *Chithipatra*, *2*, pp.
          27–32. A possible date for this letter is Sept.–Oct. 1914.

p. 196   'Pearson . . . wrote a book' See Bibliography.

p. 196   'Pearson wrote to Tagore' 16 July 1913, 'W. W. Pearson and
          Santiniketan', Tarasankar Banerjee, *VBQ*, May 1982–April 1983,
          p. 105

p. 196   'Andrews wrote to . . . Tagore' 15 Dec. 1914 [RB]

p. 197   'my misgivings' 18 Nov. 1914 [RB] On 15 Nov. RT had written to
          Andrews: 'These boys are in danger of forgetting to wish for any-
          thing, and wishing is the best part of attainment. However they are
          happy, though they have no business to be happy.'

p. 197   'wrote Gandhi' *My Experiments*, p. 302

p. 197   'scavenger's work' ibid, p. 319

p. 197   'Tagore remarked in 1937' RT to Gertrude Emerson Sen, Nov.
          1937 [copy at RB]

p. 197   'someone who was losing his mind' Devabrata Mukerjea, who had
          translated *The Post Office*. Mukerjea had become friendly with
          Yeats, Maud Gonne and especially her daughter Iseult – see various
          references in MacBride White and Jeffares. In 1918, Yeats wrote to
          RT enquiring about Mukerjea's fate. RT replied: 'What you have
          heard about Devabrata is true. He has completely lost his mind'. (17
          June 1918 [Michael Yeats])

p. 197   'Carmichael . . . wrote' 5 May 1915 [RB]

p. 198   'Oaten' In 1925 Oaten, as director of public instruction, wrote a
          remarkably fair-minded report on Visva-Bharati. (Sanat Kumar
          Bagchi, 'The poet and the Raj', *VBQ*, May 1984–April 1985; pp.
          115–21 refer to this report.)

p. 198   'Subhashchandra' Gordon, pp. 48–49

p. 198   'Both . . . received it coolly' Tinker, p. 145

p. 198   'Let us . . . frankly acknowledge' *MR*, April 1916, p. 419

p. 198   'a mere adjective to the Englishman' ibid, p. 422

p. 198   'Chelmsford . . . objected strongly' Sukumar Bhattacharya, 'Lord

Carmichael in Bengal; proposal for his recall', *Bengal Past and Present, 80*, July–Dec. 1960, pp. 67–70

p. 199   'a poet's licence' Lord Chelmsford to Austen Chamberlain, 30 Aug. 1916 [IOL] (partly quoted in Tinker, p. 145)

p. 199   'indignation of the British' Dignan, p. 188

p. 199   'even Rothenstein' For example, Rothenstein to RT, 4 Aug. 1914, in Lago, p. 172 (on the outbreak of war with Germany); also Rothenstein to C. F. Andrews, 24 Aug. 1914 [RB]: 'Perhaps the dear poet will write a poem too – Binyon, Bridges and many others have found noble voices and I hope Rabindranath may feel inspired to say something which will touch our people's hearts.' RT detested this brand of poetry – see his 'Sunset of the Century', p. 129.

p. 199   'D. H. Lawrence' 24 May 1916, Lawrence, pp. 451–52. Lawrence continued: '"Better fifty years of Europe" even as she is. Buddha-worship is completely decadent and foul nowadays: and it *was* always only half civilized. *Tant pour l'Asie*: it is ridiculous to look to the East for inspiration.'

20 Japan and the USA

Epigraph   22 Oct. 1916, *Chithipatra, 4*, pp. 40–42

p. 200   'request Okakura made' Hay, p. 48

p. 200   'shortage of funds' RT to C. F. Andrews, 16 July 1915 [RB]

p. 200   'famine' RT to William Rothenstein, 22 July 1915, in Lago, p. 206

p. 200   'I have given up Japan' 11 June 1915 [RB]

p. 200   'I gave up Japan' 12 July 1915 [RB]

p. 201   'Keedick' C. F. Andrews to George Brett, 28 April 1916 [New York]

p. 201   'George Brett' George Brett to RT, 22 March 1916 [New York]

p. 201   'told his daughter' 'Letters to his daughters', *VBQ*, Spring 1957, p. 270 (trans. by Lila Majumdar)/ *Chithipatra, 4*, p. 71

p. 201   'Rangoon' RT disliked the British-built city but was thrilled by the Shwedagon Pagoda. During the 1930s, his poetry was perhaps the chief influence on Burmese writers; today interest in his works remains strong, with many new translations of his poems and short stories into Burmese. Among his admirers is Aung San Suu Kyi, who won the Nobel prize for peace in 1991. See her *Freedom from Fear and Other Writings*; also U Thein Han (Zawgyi), 'The impact of Rabindranath Tagore on modern Burmese poetry', *Guardian*, Rangoon, Oct. 1979.

p. 201   'we know this from his travel diary' 'On the way to Japan', *VBQ*, Aug. 1938, pp. 102–04 (trans. by Indira Devi)/ *RR, 19*, pp. 307–10

p. 202   'greeted at the station' W. W. Pearson to Rathindranath Tagore, 11 June 1916 [RB]

p. 202   'tears of joy' Kawabata, p. 57

p. 202   'The contrast is so striking' 11 June 1916 [RB]

p. 202   'Kawabata' pp. 56–57

p. 202   'It is the responsibility . . . the world' ibid, p. 53

p. 202   '[Japan] has given rise' ibid, p. 55

p. 202   'We may rejoice' ibid, p. 54

p. 203   'Okuma' Hay, p. 66

p. 203   'Official invitations . . . soon ceased' ibid, pp. 72–77

p. 203   'told the Indian community' *VBQ*, April 1925, p. 73

p. 203   'Pond informed Macmillan' W. W. Pearson to Rathindranath Tagore, 8 July 1916 [RB]

p. 203   'Frost' Letter to Frederic G. Melcher, 24 Nov. 1923, in Frost, p. 297

p. 204   '*Minneapolis Tribune*' 15 Nov. 1916, in Sujit Mukherjee, p. 81

p. 204   'Pond . . . seemed to expect' W. W. Pearson to Rathindranath Tagore, 8 July 1916 [RB]

p. 204   'San Francisco *Examiner*' n.d., Stephen N. Hay, 'Rabindranath Tagore in America', *American Quarterly*, Fall 1962, p. 446

p. 204   'One . . . published a letter' His name was Gobinda Behari Lal. ('The German-Indian conspiracy trial', *MR*, June 1918, p. 675)

p. 204   'fell out in the lobby' 'Gahdr party and Dr. Tagore', *Statesman*, Calcutta, 9 July 1933. The newspaper reported the allegations of a Sikh who had just returned to India from a ten-year stay in California. The exact story of the assassination attempt will never be known, but the Sikh's allegations appear extremely probable.

p. 205   'Hindu Savant' *Minneapolis Tribune*, in Sujit Mukherjee, p. 77

p. 205   'Californian women' *Examiner*, Los Angeles, 7 Oct. 1916, in Stephen N. Hay, 'Rabindranath Tagore in America', *American Quarterly*, Fall 1962, p. 447

p. 205   'to his son . . . he dreamed' *Chithipatra*, 2, pp. 55–56

p. 205   'earliest recorded glimmering' However, RT spoke of his 'world university' in July 1916 in Japan to Paul Richard, who mentioned it to Romain Rolland – see Rolland, *Inde*, pp. 48–49. This was probably the earliest mention of what became Visva-Bharati.

p. 205   'American . . . reporter' *Rocky Mountain News*, 17 Oct. 1916, in Sujit Mukherjee, p. 77

p. 205   'vice-consul' *Telegram*, Salt Lake City, 15 Oct. 1916, in Sujit Mukherjee, p. 77. The 'vice-consul' gave himself away by addressing RT as 'Your Lordship', and was helped out of the room by Pearson. (*MR*, Feb. 1917, p. 217)

p. 205   'Master of Seventeen Languages' Denver newspaper, 16 Oct. 1916 [copy at RB]

p. 206   'halve his efficiency' W. W. Pearson to Rathindranath Tagore, 27 Sept. 1916 [RB]

p. 206   'Boston Baked Beans' ibid

p. 206   'over-tired' 9 Nov. 1916 [RB]

p. 206   'real crisis' 27 Sept. 1916 [RB]

p. 206   'Pond remarked' *Daily Mail and Empire*, Toronto, 16 Sept. 1932

p. 206   'wrote to Harriet Monroe' 4 Oct. 1916 [Chicago]

p. 206   'To . . . Harriet Moody' 23 Nov. 1916 [RB]

p. 206   'furore' 11 June 1919 [copy at New York]

p. 207   '*New York Times*' The ten volumes, published as The Bolpur Edition, were *Chitra, The Crescent Moon, The Gardener, Gitanjali, The King of the Dark Chamber, Songs of Kabir, Sadhana, The Post Office, The Hungry Stones and Other Stories, Fruit-Gathering.*

p. 207   '*Nation*' 'Rabindranath Tagore', 30 Nov. 1916, pp. 506–07

p. 207   'particularly admired the *Nation*' RT to George Brett, 3 Sept. 1919 [New York]: 'I prize this paper very highly because of its staunch love of justice, its fearless advocacy of unpopular causes.'

p. 207   'J. B. Yeats' 23 Nov. 1916, Finneran *et al.*, 2, p. 329

p. 208   'Ezra Pound' Letter to Iris Barry, 25 Jan. 1917, in Pound, p. 159. See also Pound, *The Little Review*, pp. 16, 56, 58, 128, 131–32.

p. 208   'Hart Crane' Weber, pp. 10–11, 105–06

p. 208   'Orson Welles' mother' Leaming, p. 57

p. 208   'Pearson said' 11 Nov. 1916 [RB]

21 Anti-Imperialist

Epigraph   6 March 1918, 'Letters to W. W. Pearson', *VBQ*, May–July 1943, p. 80

p. 209   'Vichitra Club' Rathindranath Tagore, pp. 76–81

p. 209   'Ronaldshay' p. 124

p. 210   'caricatures . . . by Gaganendranath' Four of them appear in Dutta and Robinson, *Purabi*, pp. 206–07. They are taken from the portfolio *Adbhut Lok* (The Realm of the Absurd), Calcutta, 1917.

p. 210   'falling like bombshells' Rathindranath to Mayce Seymour, 28 Aug. 1917 [RB]

p. 210   'He spared neither the Government' ibid

p. 210   'National self-respect' See p. 8-note.

p. 210   'The weak' 'The Master's will be done', *TUM*, p. 194/ *RR*, *18*,
           p. 560

p. 210   'Indira Gandhi' See p. 11 – note.

p. 211   'distrust of Theosophy' In 1913, RT told E. J. Thompson that he had
           never met Annie Besant and had no wish to. (E. P. Thompson, p. 110)

p. 211   'embroiled in a mess' A few months later, RT agreed to be chairman
           of the reception committee of the Congress in Calcutta, as a
           compromise candidate. He withdrew when the Congress politicians
           settled the matter among themselves. A year later, in Oct. 1918,
           Besant, the outgoing Congress president, asked RT to become the
           next president. He refused, saying: 'one of the very few things that I
           know for certain about myself is that I am wholly unfit for politics.'
           (RT to Besant, 15 Oct. 1918 [Adyar])

p. 211   'that most desperate of creatures' 'The small and the great', *MR*,
           Dec. 1917, p. 601/ *RR*, *24*, p. 288. RT also referred specifically to
           the 'Punjab Lieutenant Governor' who, he said, sneered at
           upholding moral values in India. This was O'Dwyer, the power
           behind the Amritsar Massacre in 1919.

p. 211   'Writing to . . . Montagu' 6 April 1918 [copy at RB]

p. 211   'he told an English editor' RT to G. R. S. Mead, 18 Sept. 1917
           [copy at RB]. This letter was published in the Indian press.

p. 212   'Wilson . . . to Macmillan' Wilson, *42*, p. 21

p. 212   'a raid on Indian plotters' Dignan, p. 131

p. 212   'Wiseman . . . to House' House to Wilson, 6 April 1917: 'Wiseman
           has investigated the Tagore matter and advises that you decline to
           have his book dedicated to you. His reason is that when Tagore was
           here he got tangled up in some way with the Indian plotters'.
           (Wilson, *41*, p. 554) House had himself advised against the
           dedication after reading Tagore. (30 March 1917, Wilson, *41*, p. 502)

p. 212   'von Bernstorff' *New York Times*, 8 Aug. 1941 (obituary of RT)

p. 212   'Chandra was shot dead' Dignan, p. 133

p. 212   'Chandra . . . denied it' *Evening Telegram*, Portland (Oregon), 21
           Oct. 1916, in Horst Krueger, 'Rabindranath Tagore and the Indian
           revolutionary-terrorist movement during World War I', *Proceedings
           of the Indian Historical Records Commission*, Poona, 1962, p. 92

p. 212   'prosecuting attorney' Stephen N. Hay, 'Rabindranath Tagore in
           America', *American Quarterly*, Fall 1962, p. 450

p. 213   'favourite child' Rathindranath Tagore, p. 55

p. 213   'letters to Wilson' 9 May 1918, Stephen N. Hay, 'Rabindranath
           Tagore in America', *American Quarterly*, Fall 1962, p. 451

p. 214 '[letter to] Okuma' 9 May 1918 [copy at RB]

p. 214 '[letter to] Chelmsford' 12 May 1918 [copy at RB]

p. 214 '[letter to] Moody' 13 May 1918 [Chicago]

p. 214 'I hate . . . iniquity' RT to Mayce Seymour, 14 May 1918 [RB]

p. 214 'Okuma replied' 10 July 1918 [RB]. The Japanese prime minister was Count Terauchi, who had also been named in the allegations.

p. 214 'Chelmsford accepted' Maffey (secretary to Chelmsford) to RT, 17 June 1918 [RB]

p. 214 'Wilson did not respond' Stephen N. Hay, 'Rabindranath Tagore in America', *American Quarterly*, Fall 1962, pp. 451–52

p. 214 'Moody maintained' 12 Sept. 1918 [RB]

p. 214 'she repeated it' Moody to Rathindranath Tagore, 22 Sept. 1924 [RB]

p. 214 'Brett and . . . Pond' For instance, Brett to RT, 18 April 1919 [New York]: 'This slump in the sale of some of your books . . . was occasioned, I think, by some reports which crept into the American papers in regard to Indian affairs'. Brett and Pond made several references to the allegations, both to RT and to others.

p. 214 'he *did* meet a German diplomat' Horst Krueger, 'Rabindranath Tagore and the Indian revolutionary-terrorist movement during World War I', *Proceedings of the Indian Historical Records Commission*, Poona, 1962, p. 91. Krueger cites the German archives of the Indo-German conspiracy, but gives no details. RT is likely to have met German diplomats at one or other of his lectures in the US, even though he himself never mentioned a meeting.

p. 214 'contact with Bengali revolutionaries' RT met Basanta Koomar Roy, then living in New York, the author of a (bad) biography of RT, who knew the Bengali revolutionaries. RT was wary of the contact, as shown by a letter written to George Brett of Macmillan by C. F. Andrews (10 July 1914 [New York]). Brett had asked for RT's reaction to Roy's proposed biography of him; Andrews replied on RT's behalf: 'There should be nothing . . . in any sense implicating him [RT] directly or indirectly with the anarchist movement.' So, even in 1914, before visiting the USA again, RT was sensitive on this issue.

p. 214 'an associate of Bose' He was Kesho Ram Sabarwal. RT's letter to Sabarwal, written in Japan in June 1924, is reproduced in Sanat Kumar Bagchi, 'The poet and the Raj', *VBQ*, May 1984–April 1985, p. 113.

p. 214 'Bose and his circle' In the late 1930s, Rashbihari Bose tried to persuade RT to come to Japan again, to promote Indo-Japanese friendship. By then, RT had seen the naked face of Japanese violence and he refused, though not without much heart-searching. When Japan joined the war against the British in 1941, Bose sided enthusiastically with the Japanese.

p. 215   'he . . . warned [Gandhi]' 'Letters to Mahatma Gandhi', *Rabindra-Biksha*, Dec. 1991, p. 12

p. 215   'he wrote Andrews' RT to Andrews, 24 April 1919 [RB]

p. 215   '[Andrews] wrote to Tagore' Andrews to RT, 1 May 1919 [RB]. The official in question was probably Sir John Maffey – see Tinker, p. 154.

p. 216   'cold as ice' Andrews to RT, 14 May 1919 [RB]

p. 216   'thorn in his chest' RT made this remark to Prasanta Mahalanobis. (Nepal Majumdar, *2*, p. 35)

p. 216   'letter to Lord Chelmsford' E. J. Thompson, pp. 259-60

p. 217   'Churchill' Draper, p. 231

p. 217   'Whatever impact' British press-reporting of RT's gesture was extremely limited. *The Times* ran only two very brief reports (19 June and 2 Aug. 1919); the *Manchester Guardian* printed the text of RT's letter to the viceroy (9 July 1919); the *Daily Telegraph* enquired from Montagu, the secretary of state for India, if there was any truth in the report that RT had reconsidered his decision. (7 July 1919 [IOL]) RT's friends in Britain did not refer to the incident, with the solitary exception of Rothenstein, who seems to have learnt about it from Andrews (not from the British press) and wrote only, 'How can I not approve of it? You have not put off, but have put on dignity.' (11 July 1919, Lago, p. 256) The matter was also raised twice in Parliament, with inconsequential results.

p. 217   'The insolence' Quoted in Somendranath Bose, 'Sarkari Filey Rabindranath', *Rabindra-Bhavana*, Baishakh 1384 [1977], p. 26

p. 217   'cabled Montagu' 11 June 1919 [IOL]

p. 217   'Sir Roger Casement' Witt to Montagu, 13 June 1919 [IOL]

p. 217   'Montagu cabled the viceroy' 16 June 1919 [IOL]

p. 217   'Tagore told [E. J.] Thompson' E. P. Thompson, p. 152

p. 217   'In 1925, even Gandhi' 'The Poet and the Charka', *CWMG, 28*, p. 429. It is worth noting that Gandhi did not return his official awards until 1 Aug. 1920. He referred to RT by his title several times in the first part of 1920 (see *CWMG, 17*). Once he commented directly on RT's gesture: 'I still believe that for the moment I consider that I am alone capable of offering *satyagraha* in its fine form . . . [When] Sir Rabindranath Tagore asked to be relieved of his distinction [he] did not do so as a [*satyagrahi*].' (*Young India*, 17 March 1920, *CWMG*, *17*, p. 92) Overall, it is hard to avoid concluding that the up-and coming Gandhi felt RT might upstage him; he certainly never praised RT's gesture in the fine spirit in which it was made. As for the rest of the Congress leadership, they seem to have treated the gesture with keen ambivalence, not to say hostility. An attempt by a Bengali (Amal Home) to have a congratulatory motion passed by Congress was silently quashed by the Congress president Motilal Nehru, father of Jawaharlal; nor would any Bengali leader, C. R. Das included, support it. (Nepal Majumdar, *2*, pp. 47–48) A standard history of India, written by three Bengalis and published in 1946, just prior to Independence, failed to mention RT's gesture. (R. C. Majumdar, H. C. Raychaudhuri, Kalikinkar Datta, *An Advanced History of India*, London.) In a way, the repudiation of the knighthood was symbolic of RT's treatment both by the West and by Indians: by acting alone, true to himself, he alienated the elite of both cultures.

p. 217   'statement' 'Rabindranath Tagore and knighthood', *MR*, Feb. 1926, p. 158

p. 218   'almost every obituary' *The Times* commented with myopic euphemism: 'In the summer of 1919 his indignation regarding the maintenance of martial law in the Punjab led him to surrender his knighthood, but such a course is not permissible.' (8 Aug. 1941) The very difficulty of finding a suitable word to describe RT's act – 'surrender', 'resign', 'renounce', 'return', 'revoke', 'repudiate' – was an indication of the complex emotions it aroused.

22 *The Founding of a University*
Epigraph   12 Dec. 1918, 'Letters to W. W. Pearson', *VBQ*, May–July 1943, p. 85

p. 219   '*Nation*' Nation and Athenaeum, 9 April 1921, p. 49

p. 219   'discussions with Sadler' There are significant letters between Sadler and RT at RB; notably Sadler to RT, 24 May 1918, RT to Sadler, 27 June 1918, RT to Sadler, 26 Jan. 1920.

p. 220   'he wrote dubiously' 'Vernaculars for the M.A. degree' *MR*, Nov. 1918, pp. 462–63

p. 220   'Minerveum Universalis' *Thy Hand*, p. 633

p. 220   'motto . . . from Sanskrit' The Sanskrit verse is 'Yatra visvam bhavati ekaniram.' It is from a commentary on the *Rig Veda*. The parallel with *Gitanjali* (67) is patent.

p. 220 'Visva-Bharati represents' *Visva-Bharati Bulletin*, Feb. 1929. RT may have written this statement earlier, but this date was its first publication (information courtesy Uma Das Gupta).

p. 221 'Seal wrote' 24 Nov. 1921, *VBQ*, No. 3, 1964–65, p. 156 (trans. by Kshitis Roy)/*Visva-Bharati Patrika*, Baishakh–Asharh 1880 [1958], pp. 263–65

p. 221 'fabulous wealth' Cousins, p. 341

p. 221 'Speaking extempore' "'This Youth which lies hidden in my heart'", *MR*, Feb. 1919, p. 190

p. 221 'The centre of Indian Culture' *TUM*, pp. 222–23

p. 222 'Mircea Eliade' Eliade, 11 July 1961, p. 134

p. 222 'Tagore wrote to Rolland' 14 Oct. 1919 [copy at RB]

p. 223 '*kandari . . . bhandari*' 'Dinendranath Tagore', *MR*, Aug. 1935, p. 237

p. 223 'first call on Gandhi's ashram' For Gandhi's ambivalent reaction, see his letter to Maganlal Gandhi, 4 May 1920, in *CWMG*, *17*, p. 386.

p. 223 'Let those, who wish' Chander, p. 17. C. F. Andrews read the message in RT's absence. In a second statement, not made to the Congress, RT was much blunter in criticizing the advocates of a memorial.

p. 223 'Gandhi's active support' Gandhi helped to collect money for the memorial. He claimed that its building 'would succeed in further cementing Hindu–Muslim unity which was strengthened on April 13, 1919.' But in the same breath he claimed to agree with RT: 'What Sir Rabindranath Tagore has said is perfectly true, that we shall certainly not advance by keeping alive the memory of General Dyer's cruelty.' (*Navajivan*, 18 April 1920, *CWMG*, *17*, p. 322) The debate is reminiscent of the recent debate in India about the proper way to treat the ruined mosque at Ayodhya, after it was destroyed by a Hindu mob in 1992.

p. 224 'I wish . . . to go' 14 May 1920 [RB]

p. 224 'I feel we shan't be long' n.d. [RB]

p. 224 'wrote from Ypres' 10 June 1919, Lago, p. 255

p. 224 'awful calm of desolation' *Creative Unity*, pp. 96–97

p. 224 'Rothenstein . . . approved' See p. 217 – note.

p. 225 'Lowes Dickinson' 19 June 1920 [RB]. In 1921 there was an interesting contretemps between RT and Lowes Dickinson: RT wrote a pained and somewhat unfair article in the *MR* objecting to Lowes Dickinson's praise for the British in India. E. M. Forster, then in India, tried to defend Lowes Dickinson, and commented to him, not very perceptively: 'T. has gone to bits since Amritsar, I gather.' For details see Forster, *Letters*, 2, pp. 5, 10–11, and related references.

p. 225   'Bridges . . . apologized' 15 June 1920 [RB]

p. 225   'Bridges excused himself' Sanat Kumar Bagchi, 'Montagu, Rabindranath and Visva-Bharati', *VBQ*, Nov. 1990–April 1991, p. 311

p. 225   'regretted missing Tagore' 1 July 1920 [RB]

p. 225   'Rathindranath noted' Rathindranath Tagore, p. 117

p. 225   'Yuri Gagarin' The comment appears in Gagarin's *Road to the Stars* (Moscow, 1961), 'as told to' two special correspondents of *Pravda*, and is therefore not wholly reliable.

p. 225   'Tagore told Roerich' July 1920 [copy at RB]

p. 225   'T. E. Lawrence' Rathindranath Tagore, p. 115. W. H. Hudson met RT and, separately, Lawrence at this time too, and wrote: 'He [RT] is the finest specimen of an Indian gentleman I have ever met, and has a wonderful charm in his manner. But yesterday I met exactly his opposite.' (16 June 1920, Hudson, pp. 204–05)

p. 226   'One Conservative MP' Brigadier-General Surtees, in Draper, p. 233

p. 226   'Churchill . . . said' ibid, p. 231

p. 226   'Tagore . . . was shocked' Sanat Kumar Bagchi, 'Montagu, Rabindranath and Visva-Bharati', *VBQ*, Nov. 1990–April 1991, p. 310. RT addressed a letter to Lloyd George suggesting Montagu as viceroy (reproduced in *MR*, Sept. 1920, pp. 348–50). This was reported in *The Times*, 11 Aug. 1920 (Kundu *et al.*, p. 112)

p. 226   'Beatrice Webb . . . noted' 20 July 1920, Webb, pp. 184–85

p. 227   'letter to Max Beerbohm' 5 Aug. 1920, Lago, *Max and Will*, p. 113

p. 227   'writing . . . to . . . Edward Carpenter' [Sheffield]

p. 228   'wrote enthusiastically to . . . Andrews' 28 Aug. 1920 [RB]

p. 228   'Romain Rolland' Rolland, *Inde*, pp. 39–40. Mircea Eliade, reading Rolland's remarks on Lévi in 1961, commented: 'All these details must be carefully read and meditated upon to understand the sectarianism of scholars and teachers.' (Eliade, p. 133) See also Rathindranath Tagore, p. 128.

p. 228   'Henri Bergson' Bergson found RT's knowledge of the West 'somewhat superficial'. (Chevalier, p. 147)

p. 228   'Countess de Noailles' Rathindranath Tagore, p. 126

p. 228   'Clemenceau' There is doubt about this story. Rathindranath
           Tagore wrote: 'I have been told that Clemenceau sent for the
           Comtesse de Noailles to read out to him poems from *Gitanjali* on
           the evening the armistice was declared after the First World War.'
           (p. 110) Kripalani claimed that the Countess told RT she read
           Gitanjali with Clemenceau on the day war was declared.
           (*Rabindranath*, p. 293) This is more probable, since Clemenceau
           was prime minister in Nov. 1918, and less likely to have had time to
           read poetry. Three authorities, one on Clemenceau and two on de
           Noailles, consulted by the Authors, agreed that the story is
           plausible, but it cannot be confirmed. 'It is very likely that she read
           Gitanjali with her friend Clemenceau, but I don't know if it was in
           1914 or 1918.' (Claude Mignot-Ogliastri, editor of de Noailles'
           letters, to Authors, 9 Nov. 1993) The fact that *The Post Office* was
           broadcast on French radio the evening before Paris fell in June 1940
           lends credence to the story.

p. 228   'A French writer' Gaston Denys Revier, 'Rabindranath Tagore in
           Brussels', *VBN*, June 1943, p. 159

p. 229   'mantra' On 3 Oct. 1920, RT told Andrews that the US tour was off,
           and 'The atmosphere of our mind has been cleared, at a sweep, of the
           dense fog of contemplation of five million dollars.' On 12 Oct.,
           having decided to go after all, his tone had completely changed. [RB]

p. 229   'Pond had been . . . enthusiastic' 29 June 1920 [RB]

p. 229   'Pond wrote in mid-September' 17 Sept. 1920 [RB]

p. 229   'Four days later Pond added' 21 Sept. 1920 [RB]

p. 229   'Stephen Hay' Hay, 'Rabindranath Tagore in America', *American
           Quarterly*, Fall 1962, p. 453

p. 230   'cooped up in Manhattan' In early 1921, however, at Pond's
           organizing, RT undertook a fairly successful lecture tour in Texas.

p. 230   'candid self-analysis' 13 Dec. 1920, Taransankar Banerjee, 'W. W.
           Pearson and Santiniketan', *VBQ*, May 1982–April 1983, p. 128

p. 230   'writing home to . . . Mira' Sharadiya *Desh*, 1397 [1990], p. 42

p. 230   'Yama Farms' The irony of the name Yama cannot have escaped RT;
           in Hinduism Yama is the god of Death. In 1923, RT wrote to Upton
           Sinclair about his book *The Brass Check*, praising 'your viewpoint of
           the humiliation that worship of money brings, its stifling quality, its
           empty arrogance, its insidious undermining of self-respect, its
           valuelessness, all the attributes which are its curse when dollars own
           the man'. (4 Sept. 1923, Sinclair, p. 293) Was he thinking of Yama
           Farms?

p. 230   'Do I look like a tramp?' *New Yorker*, 3 May 1982, p. 75. Not to spoil a good story, it must be said that J. D. Rockefeller loved to give dimes to all and sundry. His great-grandson Richard Rockefeller said of this particular story: 'I don't know whether it actually happened, but it certainly might have. In my lifetime I have met many people, many of them perfectly well off, who remember getting dimes from JDR.' (information courtesy Anne Row, 1992)

p. 231   'The Morgan Co.' Rathindranath Tagore to Mayce Seymour, 30 March 1921 [RB]. 'Last year Rabindranath Tagore did not come anywhere near making the success that the memory of his previous visit should have helped to bring him. This was because he was supposed to advocate – not in public – Indian independence.' (Padraic Colum, 'An American letter', *Nation and Athenaeum*, 17 Dec. 1921, p. 472)

p. 231   'British official' Sanat Kumar Bagchi, 'The poet and the Raj', *VBQ*, May 1984–April 1985, p. 96. The official was Angus Fletcher.

p. 231   'her money to Elmhirst' Dorothy Straight told Elmhirst: 'It would be such fun to work it out in that way – and so much more satisfactory to me than to hand it over bodily to Tagore.' (28 June 1921 [Dartington])

p. 231   'British missionary acquaintance' R. Gordon Milburn (a missionary friend of W. W. Pearson) to RT, 19 Oct. 1920 [RB]

p. 231   'your first flight' W. B. Yeats told this story to Abinash Chandra Bose in 1937. (*Rabindranath Tagore and W. B. Yeats: The Story of a Literary Friendship*, New Delhi, 1965, p. 23 (booklet))

p. 232   'planning Visva-Bharati' RT to Rothenstein, 17 April 1921, in Lago, pp. 279–80

p. 232   'vagabond at heart' 24 April 1921, ibid, p. 284

p. 232   'Lead me from the unreal' *Brihad-aranyaka Upanishad*, 1:3:28 (*Upanishads*, p. 127)

p. 232   'believer in machines' 28 April 1921, in Lago, pp. 284–85

p. 232   'replied from Geneva' 8 May 1921, ibid, p. 286

p. 232   'drafted a response' ibid, pp. 287–88

p. 232   'silence between them' Rothenstein broke the silence, and RT apologized. (13 July 1922, Lago, pp. 292–93)

p. 232   'Gide wrote' Gide to Dorothy Bussy, 26 April 1921, Tedeschi, p. 67

p. 232   'Rolland wrote to . . . Hesse' 22 Nov. 1921, Hesse, pp. 63–64

p. 233   'wrote to . . . Moore' ? May 1921 [London]

p. 233   'visit to Spain' The play was *Visarjan* (*Sacrifice*). There are documents in the handwriting of Juan Ramón Jiménez, showing his careful preparations for the visit, kept in the National Archives in Madrid (information courtesy Howard T. Young). No doubt RT's cancellation, and the end of the Jiménez translations of RT, which coincide, were linked: Jiménez must have been very disappointed.

p. 233 'Janáček' 'Leoš Janáček and Rabindranath Tagore' in Sahitya Akademi, p. 162

p. 234 'frenzied hero worship' *Daily News*, 3 June 1921

p. 234 'D'Abernon' 3 June 1921, pp. 179–80

p. 234 'Tagore's own reaction to D'Abernon' 10 June 1921 [RB]

p. 235 'wrote to . . . Edith Andreae' 27 Oct. 1921 [copy at RB]

p. 235 'Brecht . . . Keyserling' For the reactions of these and other German writers and intellectuals, see Kämpchen. In 1957 Hesse wrote:

> Tagore's partial eclipse in the West at the present time is a phenomenon based on a universal historical truth. Today's man of fame falls into oblivion after his death, and only after a lapse of time – sometimes prolonged – does the world take the trouble to re-examine and reappraise both his former fame and his present neglect. Indeed, the greater the fame the more obdurate the oblivion that follows . . .
>
> . . . Although I had no close relationship with Tagore, I contemplate his memory – that of a noble and venerable presence in the intellectual world of his time – with affection and delight. And I would be happy if I lived to see his triumphant re-emergence after a testing period of temporary oblivion.

(translated in Kämpchen, p. 43). See also Kämpchen's *Hermann Hesse and Kalidas Nag: A Friendship* (Calcutta, 1994).

p. 235 'Thomas Mann' 8 June 1921, Mann, p. 117: 'At eleven went with Katia to Kurt Wolff's for the Tagore lecture. Select audience. Confirmed my impression of him as being a refined old English lady. His son brown and muscular, a virile type.' Ironically, Vladimir Nabokov dismissed Mann in the same breath as Tagore: 'Why should we continue to mislead students by teaching them that Mann, Galsworthy, Faulkner, Tagore and Sartre are "great craftsmen"?' (Nabokov, p. 242)

p. 235 'Spengler' Kotanek, p. 461

p. 235 'Rilke was invited to' Kurt Wolff invited Rilke; Rilke's reply, dated 7 Jan. 1914, appears (translated) in Kämpchen, pp. 31–32. Some confusion surrounds the first publication of RT in German. It is

Rabindranath, lip-read by Helen Keller, in New York, 1930

48 Rabindranath and Mahatma Gandhi, in Shantiniketan, 1940

49 Jawaharlal Nehru and Rabindranath, in Shantiniketan, 1939

Albert Einstein and Rabindranath, in New York, 1930 (*Martin Vos*)

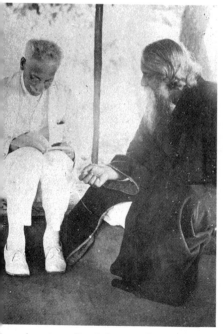

French orientalist Sylvain Lévi, and Rabindranath, in Shantiniketan, 1921/22

52 George Bernard Shaw and Rabindranath, in London, 1931

53 Two of the houses of Rabindranath, in Shantiniketan:
top – Udayan, completed in the 1930s (*Samiran Nandy*)
below – Udichi, completed in 1939, his final house (*Samiran Nandy*)

Indira Nehru (*extreme right*), later Indira Gandhi, as a student in Shantiniketan, ▪34/35

55 Satyajit Ray, as a student in
Shantiniketan, 1940/41 (*Sambhu Shaha*)

56 Rabindranath in later life
(*Satyajit Ray*)

57 Rabindranath in old age:
top – at the Quaker Woodbrooke Settlement, Birmingham, 1930
below – with a boy in Shantiniketan, 1938/39 (*Sambhu Shaha*)

) – in Shantiniketan, 1938 (*Raymond Burnier*)
low – in Shantiniketan, 1941 (*Jitendra Pratap Singh*)

58 The funeral of Rabindranath Tagore in Calcutta, 1941

said that Wolff had decided to return *Gitanjali* to Macmillan in London, as being of no interest to German readers, and that the package had already been taken to the post office when Wolff heard the news of the Nobel prize for RT. The parcel was hastily retrieved, and a translation by Marie Luise Gothein was published in early 1914. (Kämpchen, pp. 12, 27) This is a good story, but it is contradicted by another story told in a letter written by Karl Jaspers to Hannah Arendt. According to Jaspers, Gothein had sent Wolff her translation of *Gitanjali* much before the news of the Nobel prize. After some time Wolff tried to buy her out at a low price, having learnt secretly about the coming Nobel award. When the award was announced, Max Weber, outraged, compelled Wolff to offer Gothein better terms. (15 Nov. 1957, Kohler and Saner, p. 365) Neither story is entirely credible.

p. 235 'School of Wisdom' See Kämpchen, pp. 72–81 and Kämpchen, 'The poet and the philosopher', *Statesman*, Calcutta, 29 Dec. 1991.

p. 235 'Zuckmayer' See p. 2 – note.

p. 235 'Swedish Academy' Nobel prize acceptance speech [RB]

p. 235 ' he wrote . . . from Berlin' 28 May 1921 [RB]

p. 236 'the two Bengalis . . . discussed' Mihir Bose, p. 20

23 Anti-Non-cooperator

Epigraph Elmhirst, p. 22

p. 237 'Nehru' Letter, 27 Aug. 1941, in Kripalani, *Rabindranath*, p. 455

p. 238 'steel age' 'The great sentinel', *CWMG*, *21*, p. 289 (*Young India*, 13 Oct. 1921)

p. 238 'not to involve the ashram in politics' 4 Nov. 1920, *Letters to a Friend*, p. 102. In a passage cut from the letter by Andrews, RT was more emphatic.

p. 238 'Non-cooperation appear[s] to me' 'Rabindranath Tagore on constructive work', Chander, p. 23 (*MR*, March 1921)

p. 238 'In my humble opinion' 'The poet's anxiety', *CWMG*, *20*, p. 163 (*Young India*, 1 June 1921)

p. 239 'noted by Elmhirst' Elmhirst, pp. 20–22

p. 240 'When talking . . . "impure" . . . shame' Rabindranath Tagore, 'The importance of the individual in the history of India', *VBQ*, No. 2, 1962–63, p. 99

p. 240 'The call of truth' This was first delivered as a lecture in Calcutta on 29 Aug. 1921, *before* RT's meeting with Gandhi.

p. 240 'Nehru . . . read' Introduction to Sahitya Akademi, p. xiv

p. 240   'Sparta' 'The call of truth', *TUM*, p. 267

p. 241   'our love of foreign cloth' *CWMG*, *21*, p. 290

p. 241   'C. F. Andrews . . . admitted' [RB]

p. 241   'statement in the . . . press' *Bengalee* in Nepal Majumdar, *2*, p. 159

p. 241   'his latest play' *Muktadhara* (The Free Current), *RR*, *14*, pp. 185–240. A translation by Marjorie Sykes appears in *Three Plays*.

p. 241   'severe problems' See Elmhirst, pp. 29–30, for Gandhi's attitude to Shriniketan.

p. 241   'Elmhirst . . . was willing' On 28 July 1921 he told Dorothy Straight: 'don't you see that you were the first person to help to buckle the sword on to a thin-legged, knock-kneed pseudo-knight surrounded by sceptics – everyday this is what I get: "Isn't Tagore rather dangerous, isn't he a traitor, didn't he speak disparagingly of the British Government?" (Holy, holy, holy, Lord God Almighty.)'

p. 242   'humane feeling' 'Sriniketan', *VBQ*, Autumn 1955, p. 132

p. 242   'If we could free even one village' 'City and village', *TUM*, p. 322

p. 242   'I went up to the Ashram' [Dartington]

p. 243   'Every morning in the newspapers' ibid

p. 243   'a delightful custom' 29 Nov. 1921, ibid

p. 243   'Your letter . . . I love it all' 11 Jan. 1922, ibid

p. 244   'Now let me correct you' 22 Feb. 1922, ibid

p. 244   'All your friends' 19 Feb. 1922, ibid

p. 244   'I've been thinking' 5 March 1922, ibid

p. 244   'summed it up beautifully' 30 Nov. 1923, ibid

24 China and Japan

Epigraph   28 Feb. 1924 [copy at RB]

p. 246   'Satyajit Ray' *Time* (international edn), 6 Jan. 1992, p. 84

p. 246   'materialistic/spiritual labels' See p. 19.

p. 246   'statement . . . in Beijing' 'Tagore as a revolutionary', *MR*, Nov. 1924, p. 550

p. 247   'most distinguished foreign intellectual' The only other candidate might be the Czech orientalist Moritz Winternitz, who also spent a year at Shantiniketan, in 1922–23.

p. 247   'Ah, Gurudev!' 7 Feb. 1923 [RB]. The Authors are unable to locate Sylvain Lévi's papers.

p. 248   'purely disinterested effort' *VBQ*, Jan. 1924, p. 383

p. 248   'thirty-seven Indian Buddhist missionaries' Leonard Elmhirst in Sahitya Akademi, p. 20

p. 248 'two notable Bengali scholars' Kshitimohan Sen and Kalidas Nag (Nag had studied with Lévi)

p. 249 'you and I, Elmhirst' Elmhirst in Sahitya Akademi, p. 19

p. 249 'Sun Yat-sen' *VBN*, Dec. 1949, p. 50; also Hay, p. 147

p. 249 'military governor . . . civil governor' Hay, p. 153

p. 250 'my last and favourite camel' Green, p. 84

p. 250 'grand and colourful meeting' This was organized by Dr Gilbert Reid, a foreign missionary. (Hay, p. 177)

p. 250 'Mei Lan-fang' ibid, pp. 167, 178

p. 250 'Chu Chen Tan' ibid, p. 166

p. 250 'Y.M.B.A.' ibid, p. 159

p. 250 'Johnston' Johnston wrote:

Tagore came to China at a time when alien influences were at work in academic and other circles which caused his message to fall on stony ground; and his appeal to Young China to cherish what was noble and beautiful in the cultural heritage of the race met with a cold and even hostile reception by some of his student-audiences. I was anxious that Tagore should not leave Peking without catching a glimpse of the courteous and dignified China that has never failed to rouse the homage of foreign visitors, and I therefore spoke of him to the emperor and requested permission to bring him to the Forbidden City. I also showed the emperor some English and Chinese translations of Tagore's poetry. The permission asked for was most readily granted, and the meeting, when it took place in my pavilion in the imperial garden, gave pleasure certainly to the emperor and I think also to the poet.

(Johnston, p. 347)

There are copies of Tagore's works signed by Johnston in the library of the School of Oriental and African Studies in London.

p. 251 'According to Nandalal Bose' Kalidas Nag, p. 54. See also *MR*, Sept. 1924, p. 294.

p. 251 'Miss Lin' The image came from one of RT's Chinese companions. (Hay, p. 161).

p. 251 'The blue of the sky' Hay, p. 165 (trans. by Hay)/ *Lekhan* (34), *RR*, *14*, p. 163. At a large dinner in Beijing, RT suddenly threw down his chopsticks, gave 'a languishing sigh' and, when questioned, stated that he was 'so overcome with the beauty and charm of some of the

Chinese ladies present, he could not eat.' (Letter from 'Impressed but not Converted', *Peking & Tientsin Times*, 6 Dec. 1924 – possibly written by Gilbert Reid, according to Hay, p. 378)

p. 251   '*Bengalee*' 11 July 1924; see also Hay, pp. 170–71.

p. 252   'Communist ideology' Leo Karakhan, the Soviet Union's official representative in China, was very popular with radical Chinese students. Karakhan and RT met and agreed that their educational ideals were similar. But when Karakhan boasted that a decision in Moscow would be implemented in thousands of villages, RT objected, 'No! That's just the opposite of my own approach to the village.' (Leonard Elmhirst's diary, 13 May 1924 [Dartington]; Hay, pp. 173–74) It is a pity that RT did not take more careful note of this clash when he visited Russia in 1930. In Moscow he was a guest of Karakhan, ironically, who was by then first deputy minister of foreign affairs.

p. 252   'Lowes Dickinson' *India, China and Japan*, p. 43

p. 252   'Rabindranath reacted angrily' Hay, p. 171. The influence of Tagore on Chinese intellectuals, even Communists, was nevertheless considerable, e.g. Guo Moruo, a scholar and official who was highly influential in China after 1949. Guo Moruo's attitude to RT appears to have been misunderstood by Hay and Jonathan D. Spence (*The Gate of Heavenly Peace*) who both represent Moruo as hostile to RT after an initial period of attraction. In fact, Guo Moruo remained favourably inclined to RT's writings and ideas. The point is discussed at length in 'The Rabindranath thunder of oriental dawn: a Sino-Indian perspective of Tagore', paper presented by Tan Chung in Simla, 1986 (?unpublished: information courtesy Peter Cox). In 1957, Chou En-lai accepted an honorary degree from Visva-Bharati conferred by Nehru as chancellor. (*VBN*, Feb. 1957, pp. 86–89)

p. 252   'Tagore knew it really' In Tokyo, in 1929, he said: 'When we talk about European civilization, we use a term which is real in its meaning, it is an undoubted fact. But when they [Europeans] talk glibly of the Oriental mind and culture, they do not realize that we have not yet been able to develop a universal mind, a great background of Oriental cultures. Our cultures are too scattered.' (*On Oriental Cultures and Japan's Mission*, pp. 14–15)

p. 252   'he replied to the charges' 'International relations', *VBQ*, Jan. 1925, pp. 314–15

25 Argentina

Epigraph 'The importance of the individual in the history of India', *VBQ*, No. 2, 1962–63, p. 97 (opening sentence)

p. 253 'not less than $100,000 each' Leonard Elmhirst to Rathindranath Tagore, 11 July 1924, in Dyson, p. 67

p. 253 'I carry an infinite space' 26 June 1924, Dutta and Robinson, *Purabi*, pp. 83–84

p. 254 'The idea of Dartington' This was first mentioned in a letter from Elmhirst to Straight, 19 May 1923; there are many references to the idea in 1923–24 in their correspondence kept at Dartington.

p. 254 'European writers and intellectuals' See Meyer. There is some controversy about how close these friendships really were.

p. 254 'or rather Tagoré' In a letter to RT, 25 May 1920 [RB], Zenobia Camprubi Jiménez specifically raised the question of how to spell Tagore's name in Spanish – with or without an accented 'e'. RT had already sailed for Europe, so he probably never replied.

p. 254 'part of their courtship' Young, 'Juan Ramón, traductor alerta' *Bulletin of Hispanic Studies*, 1992, p. 141

p. 255 'frustrated' Zenobia Camprubi Jiménez to RT, 12 Dec. 1919 [RB]

p. 255 '*poesia desnuda*' See Graciela Palau de Nemes, 'Tagore and Jiménez: poetic coincidences' in Sahitya Akademi, pp. 187–97.

p. 255 'Ortega argued' Introduction to *Obra escojida*. The essays were originally published in *El Sol* (information courtesy Howard T. Young).

p. 255 'Mistral and . . . Neruda' For Mistral and RT, see Dyson, pp. 65–66; for Neruda and RT, see Teitelboim, pp. 190–92.

p. 255 'said Paz' Dyson, p. 65 (trans. by Dyson)/ 'Los manuscritos de Tagore', *El Tiempo*, Bogota, 2 April 1967

p. 255 'Salman Rushdie' Rushdie, *Jaguar Smile*, pp. 55–56, 143, 167, 169. Tagore was of course pronounced to Rushdie with an accented 'e'. See also Rushdie, *Imaginary Homelands*, p. 69.

p. 256 'Argentine high society' RT's reaction was evident from Elmhirst's letters to Straight, also from his strong criticism of Argentina in a letter to Romain Rolland, 29 Jan. 1925 [copy at RB].

p. 256 'dictatorship' RT received a local warning too. (Dyson, pp. 90–91)

p. 256 'Dreadnought' The Dreadnought was already planned by the Argentine government to assist in the Peruvian celebrations. (Dyson, p. 89)

p. 256 'Chile is probably pleased' [Dartington]

p. 256 'Our hostess' 6 Jan. 1925, Dyson, p. 198

p. 257   'I am deeply sorry' 13 Jan. 1925, Dyson, pp. 390–92 (full letter)

p. 258   'Ocampo herself said' 'Tagore on the banks of the River Plate' in Sahitya Akademi, p. 34

p. 258   'certainly sexually attracted' Leonard Elmhirst to Rathindranath Tagore, 9 Sept. 1956, in Dyson, p. 277

p. 258   'they were bound together' Ocampo 'needed Elmhirst to interpret Tagore', wrote Ketaki Kushari Dyson, a Bengali scholar who studied the Argentinian episode in detail. (Dyson, p. 288)

p. 258   'Rabindranath admitted the charge' 'Tagore on the banks of the River Plate' in Sahitya Akademi, p. 44

p. 258   'at dinner' Dyson, p. 163

p. 259   '*A Skeleton*' *VBQ*, April 1925, pp. 36–37. RT's 'mutilated' version appears in *VBQ*, Winter 1954–55, p. 186. The original poem is 'Kankal', *Purabi*, *RR*, *14*, pp. 130–31 (17 Dec. 1924).

26 Arguing with Gandhi

Epigraph Chander, p. 71 (*MR*, Sept. 1925)

p. 260   'an anguished statement' 'The importance of the individual in the history of India', *VBQ*, No. 2, 1962–63 (dictated to Elmhirst on 17 Dec. 1924)

p. 260   'visible and substantial bond' Tendulkar, *2*, p. 218

p. 261   'a police sergeant' 'The Rejected Story', *Selected Short Stories*, Dutta and Lago trans., p. 280/*RR*, *24*, p. 205

p. 261   'Her aunt replied' ibid, p. 289/pp. 211–12

p. 261   'apparent even in . . . 1925' Gandhi was severely criticized by one of his admirers, K. Natarajan. The criticism is reproduced in 'The poet and the charka', *MR*, Dec. 1925, pp. 725–28, which also discusses Gandhi's other criticisms of RT.

p. 261   'I am not ashamed' 'The cult of the Charka', Chander, pp. 67–68

p. 261   'In Bengal' ibid, pp. 69–70

p. 262   'Carlyle' ibid, p. 70

p. 262   'One thing is certain' ibid, p. 71. In 1936, RT *supported* the use of a simple machine for husking rice (as opposed to factory husking) on scientific grounds – i.e. better nutrition – among other reasons. ('The rice we eat', *VBN*, Jan. 1936, p. 51)

p. 262   'In my childhood' 'The cult of the charka', Chander, p. 72

p. 262   'There are many who assert' ibid, p. 76. Gandhi responded:

Round the Charka, that is, amidst the people who have shed their idleness and who have understood the value of cooperation, a national servant would build up a programme of anti-malaria campaign, improved sanitation, settlement of village disputes, conservation and breeding of cattle and hundreds of other beneficial activities.

('The poet and the wheel', *CWMG*, *28*, p. 429 (*Young India*, 5 Nov. 1925))

p. 262   'It is extremely distasteful' 'The cult of the Charka', Chander, p. 79

p. 263   'poetic licence' 'The poet and the wheel', *CWMG*, *28*, p. 427

p. 263   'Gandhi . . . not . . . acquainted' Gandhi referred fleetingly to *Sadhana* and the short stories (*CWMG*, *17*, p. 73) when introducing RT to Gujarat in March 1920 – but never to *Nationalism*, *The Home and the World*, and other openly political writings.

p. 263   'sly twist' ibid, p. 429. Gandhi wrote: 'A Sir Gangaram may give us a model farm which can be no model for the penniless Indian farmer who has hardly two to three acres of land which every day runs the risk of being further cut up.' This was an obvious innuendo about RT's Shriniketan experiment. (Gangaram is a well-known figure of fun in Bengal, a ne'er-do-well.)

p. 263   'Dame Rumour' ibid, p. 426

p. 264   'Tilak and Rammohun' *CWMG*, *19*, p. 477 (*Young India*, 13 April 1921)

p. 264   'I have never anywhere described' 'The poet and the wheel', *CWMG*, *28*, p. 429. C. F. Andrews shared RT's indignation, tackled Gandhi on this point and wrote with dubious conviction to RT on 10 Nov. 1925: 'he was very emphatic that he had not meant to run down the founder of Modern Bengal [i.e. Rammohun Roy] . . . I think the thing may drop from your mind and this was rather a lapse on his part than a genuine opinion.' [RB]

p. 265   'wrote to Romain Rolland' 23 Sept. 1925 [copy at RB]. Rolland admired Gandhi and had already written a book about him.

27 Italy, Mussolini and After

Epigraph 'A conversation with Tagore', *Manchester Guardian*, 7 Aug. 1926

p. 266   'Yeats' Richard Ellmann commented, in a sentence that could have applied as well to RT as to Yeats: 'Fortunately he did not go so far as to accept Fascism explicitly, but he came dangerously close.' (Ellmann, p. 244) Richard Griffiths discusses the admiration for Mussolini of the other writers and politicians mentioned. Gandhi's admiration may be found in his letter to Romain Rolland, 20 Dec. 1931, *CWMG*, *48*, pp. 429–30. In Calcutta, the press, even including the *MR*, was full of admiration for Mussolini.

p. 266 'London press' *Evening Standard*, 14 June 1926

p. 266 'cancelled the . . . visit' Rathindranath Tagore claimed that Mussolini sent his 'trusted mistress' to stay at the hotel in Milan where RT was staying, to keep an eye on RT's relationship with the (anti-Fascist) duke of Milan. (Rathindranath Tagore, p. 138)

p. 267 'Lynching' 'The Indian ideal of marriage', *VBQ*, July 1925, p. 96; also published in Keyserling

p. 267 'cabled Mussolini' The text is printed in *MR*, Dec. 1925, p. 742. The draft, in RT's handwriting, is in RB.

p. 267 'reblooming' Italian Consul in Calcutta to RT, 6 April 1926 (enclosing translation of Mussolini's message) [RB]

p. 267 'somewhat dubious essay' 'Communal life in India', *MR*, June 1913, p. 658 (trans. by Jadunath Sarkar)/ *RR*, *3*, p. 543

p. 267 'Allow me to tell you' 'Our founder-president in Italy', *VBQ*, Oct. 1926, p. 280. Needless to say, this was almost certainly a bare-faced lie by Mussolini.

p. 267 'His Excellency' 2 June 1926, ibid, p. 281

p. 267 'fire-bath' ibid

p. 267 'sonorous voice' *Il Resto del Carlino*, 10 June 1926, ibid, p. 285

p. 268 'Formichi said' *Popolo di Roma*, 10 June 1926, ibid, p. 287

p. 268 'Mussolini instructed' Rolland, *Inde*, p. 117

p. 268 'Tagore's son wrote' Rathindranath Tagore, p. 137

p. 268 'question of good taste' Croce, p. 98

p. 268 'documentary proof' Rathindranath Tagore, pp. 138–39

p. 268 'English poets' 16 June 1926, 'Our founder-president in Italy', *VBQ*, Oct. 1926, p. 294

p. 269 'an amused Rathindranath' Rathindranath Tagore, p. 140

p. 269 '*Inde*' pp. 87–136 deals with RT in Europe in 1926. The diary has not been translated into English.

p. 269 'Rolland noted in his journal' *Inde*, p. 115

p. 270 'Angelica Balabanoff' pp. 312–14

p. 271 '*Manchester Guardian*' The newspaper published the following items solely about RT and Fascism: RT, 'The philosophy of Fascism', 5 Aug. 1926; RT (interview with Salvadori), 'A conversation with Tagore', 7 Aug. 1926; editorial, 'Dr. Tagore on Fascism', 7 Aug. 1926; Formichi (letter), 'Dr. Tagore in Italy', 25 Aug. 1926; editorial, 'Dr. Tagore and Italy', 25 Aug. 1926; RT (letter), 'Dr. Tagore and Fascism', 20 Sept. 1926.

p. 271 'According to Rolland' *Inde*, p. 135

p. 271   'miracles of creation' 'A conversation with Tagore', *Manchester Guardian*, 7 Aug. 1926. The transcript of this interview, edited by RT, shows that before publication he *strengthened* his praise for Mussolini at this point in the interview. [RB]

p. 271   'There have been times' 'The philosophy of Fascism', *Manchester Guardian*, 5 Aug. 1926

p. 271   'it may be because' 'Dr. Tagore and Fascism', *Manchester Guardian*, 20 Sept. 1926. In 1930, in New York, RT again met Formichi, who seems to have persuaded him to write to Mussolini in an attempt to mend fences. The letter was not sent, on the advice of Rathindranath Tagore, but the draft survives at RB, dated 21 Nov. 1930. RT wrote (in part): 'The politics of a country is its own, its culture belongs to all humanity. My mission is to acknowledge all that has eternal value in the self-expression of any country.'

p. 271   *'Popolo d'Italia'* Quoted in translation in *Manchester Guardian*, 15 Sept. 1926

p. 272   'tourist-like attitudes' Rolland to Kalidas Nag, 6 Dec. 1926, in Rolland, *Letters*, p. 81

p. 272   'wrote to C. P. Scott' 12 Oct. 1926 [Manchester]

p. 272   'Albert Einstein' 25 Sept. 1926 [RB]. 'If there is anything in Germany that you would like and which could be done by me, I beg you to command me at any time.' (translated) Einstein's step-daughter Margot treated RT as a sort of father-figure. (Margot Einstein to RT, 20 Sept. 1926 [RB]) The positions of Einstein and RT in the public mind worldwide were remarkably similar at this time. To quote an Einstein biographer's words, which could apply to RT too: 'The speed with which his fame spread across the world, down through the intellectual layers to the man-in-the-street, the mixture of semi-religious awe and near hysteria which his figure aroused, created a startling phenomenon which has never been fully explained.' (Ronald Clark, p. 246)

p. 272   '800,000 copies' Laurence Clarke, 'What Germany is reading', *John O'London's Weekly*, 30 Sept. 1922, p. 800. 'No German novelist, dramatist, or poet is in it with the Indian gentle dreamer.' This figure may be exaggerated, judging from a letter written by Kurt Wolff Verlag to Macmillan on 14 Sept. 1921, correcting an earlier over-excited newspaper report. [BL]

p. 272   'Tagore-Spende' Kurt Wolff Verlag to RT, 17 Oct. 1923 [RB]

p. 272   'blood on the hands' *New York Morning Telegraph*, 27 March 1927 (quoting UP, Berlin)

p. 273 'Father got so disgusted' Rathindranath Tagore to Mayce Seymour, 25 Nov. 1926 [RB]

p. 273 'a critical Romain Rolland' *Inde*, p. 133

28 Nationalism versus Internationalism

Epigraph *VBQ*, Oct. 1929, p. 310/*Desh*, 13 May 1961, p. 227

p. 274 'greatest calamity' 'Swami Sraddhananda', *VBQ*, Jan. 1927, p. 405/*RR*, *24*, p. 433

p. 274 'all of a sudden' ibid, p. 406/p. 434

p. 275 '[Tucci] wrote to Rabindranath' [RB]

p. 275 'Tagore replied' 31 Dec. 1926 [copy at RB]

p. 275 'our important members' RT probably meant Prasanta Mahalanobis, who had clashed with Tucci in May 1926, concerning the number of passages to Italy to be provided to RT and his party by the Italian government.

p. 275 'No, Tucci replied' n.d. [RB]

p. 275 'Tucci looked back' 'Recollections of Tagore', speech delivered in Rome, 9 April 1960 (information courtesy Gherardo Gnoli)

p. 275 'I was glad to leave a place' n.d. [copy at RB]. The recipient of this letter from Tucci cannot have been Kshitimohan Sen or Vidusekhar Shastri, since both are mentioned in the letter.

p. 276 '*Atlantic Monthly*' 'East to West', June 1927, pp. 729–34 (also in *VBQ*, April 1927, pp. 85–92). Sedgwick felt obliged to preface the article with a warning to Americans not to react defensively to RT's criticism.

p. 276 '[Tagore] wrote William Rothenstein' 20 April 1927, Lago, pp. 321–22. Rothenstein told RT (15 March 1927) only that he admired some of Thompson's translations, but, as RT must have realized, he also admired the biography – see Rothenstein, *Since Fifty*, pp. 44–46, in which E. J. Thompson's interesting 1931 letter about RT is reproduced.

p. 277 'pseudonymous review' Shri Banibinod [i.e. 'Banter'] Bandyopadhyaya', *Prabasi*, Shraban 1334 [1927], pp. 513–18. The other pieces attacking Thompson's book are discussed in Harish Trivedi's Introduction to E. J. Thompson's biography; 'multiple hatchet-job' appears on p. a14.

p. 277 'poignant predicament' E. J. Thompson explained it brilliantly to Yeats in 1924. (Finneran *et al.*, *2*, pp. 451–53)

p. 277 'wanted to tour "Greater India"' RT to C. F. Andrews, 25 Sept. 1920 [RB]

p. 278   'Shagarika' *RR*, *15*, pp. 47–49 (1 Oct. 1927)

p. 278   'Unable to communicate . . . rivers in India' 'Letters from Java', *VBQ*, Jan. 1928, pp. 330–31/*RR*, *19*, p. 485

p. 278   'When we first entered' 'Letters from Java', *VBQ*, July 1928, p. 178/*RR*, *19*, p. 511

p. 279   'I remember . . . glory' 'Letters from Java', *VBQ*, Jan. 1929, p. 375/*RR*, *19*, p. 521

p. 279   'The history of these enterprises' ibid, *VBQ*, p. 377/*RR*, *19*, pp. 522–23

p. 279   'Malayan press . . . press in Calcutta' The original attack on RT appeared in the *Malaya Tribune*, 2 Aug. 1927; his correction in the *Malay Mail*, 5 Aug. 1927.

p. 280   'Arnold Bennett' Quoted in publisher's advertisement for *Mother India*, *Nation*, New York, 12 Oct. 1927, p. x (no source given)

p. 280   'If Miss Mayo' *CWMG*, *34*, pp. 539–40 (*Young India*, 15 Sept. 1927)

p. 280   '*New Statesman*' 'India as it is', 16 July 1927, pp. 448–49. The reviewer ('C. S.') called *Mother India* 'the most important and truthful book that has been written about India for a good deal more than a generation.'

p. 280   'violated . . . propriety' *CWMG*, *34*, p. 541 (*Young India*, 15 Sept. 1927)

p. 280   'omitting two words' RT actually wrote: 'There is a particular age, *said India* [our emphasis], at which this attraction between the sexes reaches its height; so if marriage is to be regulated according to the social will, it must be finished with before such age. Hence the Indian custom of early marriage.' ('The Indian ideal of marriage', *VBQ*, July 1925, p. 100)

p. 280   'Mayo's words' p. 51

p. 280   'letter to . . . *Guardian*' *Manchester Guardian Weekly*, 14 Oct. 1927

p. 280   'letter to . . . *Nation*' 4 Jan. 1928, pp. 53–55

p. 280   'strong (Indian) critic' K. Natarajan, who had criticized Gandhi in 1925 for his reaction to 'The cult of the Charka' – see p. 261 – note.

p. 280   'received from someone in Java' RT to Lévi, 18 Jan. 1928 [copy at RB]. The report from the Dutch newspaper is missing.

p. 281   'pained reply' 16 Dec. 1927 [RB]. Desirée Lévi published a book about her stay in India full of praise for RT – see Bibliography.

p. 281   'Lévi's several letters to him' All Lévi's letters to RT mix praise, affection and criticism, e.g. 17 Oct. 1923: 'I do not know if Santiniketan will ever rank among the most developed institutions of learning in the world, but you can be satisfied that you have built up an abode of unparalleled peace.' [RB]

p. 281   'nursed a feeling of hurt' After Lévi died in 1935, one of his Indian friends in Paris, S. R. Rana, tried to mend fences. Rathindranath Tagore wrote to Rana on behalf of his father: 'You know how dear is the name of Santiniketan to Father and he can never forgive anyone who slanders his efforts, though he is only too glad to have constructive criticism. There are mischief-mongers about and it is quite possible that some busy-body reported against Prof. Levy to him and he had become bitter about the Professor.' (20 July 1937 [copy at RB])

p. 281   'inconclusive occasion' Nirad Chaudhuri was present and described it in *Thy Hand*, pp. 228–29.

p. 281   'an example . . . Holi' 'The principle of literature', *VBQ*, July 1927, pp. 111–12. RT gives some amusing examples of 'realism' in literature in 'The nature of literature', *VBQ*, Spring 1959, pp. 307–14 (trans. by Saroj N. Ray)/ *RR*, *27*, pp. 251–56.

p. 282   'wrote . . . to Elmhirst' 11 Oct. 1925, Dutta and Robinson, *Purabi*, p. 94

p. 282   'told a Bengali friend' 7 Nov. 1928, *RT on Art and Aesthetics*, pp. 89–90 (trans. by Kshitis Roy)/Rani Mahalanobis, pp. 53–54

p. 283   'Heisenberg' Heisenberg expressed an interest in seeing RT and was taken to Jorasanko by the scientist D. M. Bose, a nephew of J. C. Bose. 'We left Heisenberg to have a talk with the poet. I do not remember what was the substance of his talk, but Heisenberg was very much impressed by the poet's illuminatory personality which reminded him of a prophet of the old days.' (Bose Institute, p. 15) Heisenberg spontaneously recalled the encounter at least twice during the late 1960s and early 1970s: once to his doctoral student Helmut Rechenberg (now in charge of Heisenberg's scientific papers), and again to the writer and physicist Fritjof Capra in 1972. 'I remember it quite vividly.' (Rechenberg to Authors, 11 Aug. 1992) 'Heisenberg told me that he had long conversations with Tagore specifically about Indian philosophy, and that this was his introduction to Indian thought.' (Capra to Authors, 13 April 1993) However, according to Heisenberg's wife (who was not a scientist), 'my husband was not too much impressed by his [RT's] thoughts. The mixture of eastern and western philosophy in his thoughts did not really convince him.' (Elisabeth Heisenberg to Authors, 3 Oct. 1990) Since Heisenberg himself wrote nothing on the meeting that has survived, it is hard to know his true impressions. Very likely he became more sympathetic to RT's ideas towards the end of his life; this would tally with the trend in his scientific thinking. In 1975 he told a student of his, the physicist Jagdish Mehra:

> You know, in the West we have built a large, beautiful ship. It has all the comforts in it, but one thing is missing: it has no compass and does not know where to go. Men like Tagore and Gandhi and their spiritual forebears found the compass. Why can this compass not be put in the ship, so that both can realize their purpose? (Mehra to Authors, 1 Aug. 1994)

p. 283   'Sommerfeld' 'Arnold Sommerfeld: his life, work and an impression of his recent visit to India', *MR*, June 1929, pp. 738–39. This article contains translated extracts from an article by Sommerfeld on his Indian visit. (We have modified the translation.)

p. 283   'Irwin' There are letters between Irwin and RT in RB, concerning Irwin's desire to help Shriniketan financially.

p. 283   'the cult of the *Charka*' RT to Rani Mahalanobis, 16 Oct. 1929, *VBQ*, Oct. 1929, pp. 310, 311/*Desh*, 13 May 1961, p. 227

p. 283   '2,000 people' Maitraye [Devi], p. 190

p. 284   'twenty-second reprint' Sujit Mukherjee, p. 96

p. 284   'had he been to jail' *San Francisco News*, 26 April 1929

p. 284   'asked if he could write' *Evening News*, 24 April 1929

p. 284   'faithful wounds' Mayo, p. 363

p. 284   'skyscraper of calumny' 'Interview to the newspaper men at San Francisco', *MR*, Aug. 1929, p. 135

p. 284   '*San Francisco Chronicle*' 'Hoping for beauty in some of Tagore's memories of America', 28 April 1929. Harriet Moody's comment to Mayce Seymour in 1926/7 – one of Moody's rare criticisms of RT was: 'I don't know whether you feel as I do, but to me it always seems that Robi Babu's absolute severance from his exterior environment unfits him for getting the real quality of American life'. (n.d. [RB])

p. 285   'never visit Japan again' Hay, pp. 318–19

p. 285   'Takagaki' See *VBN*, Jan. 1954, pp. 68–69. The young Satyajit Ray briefly took lessons from Takagaki in Calcutta in the mid-1930s. (*Jakhan Chhoto Chhilam*, 1982, pp. 38–39)

p. 285   'virtually a non-cooperator' Sanat Kumar Bagchi, 'The poet and the Raj', *VBQ*, May 1984–April 1985, p. 97

p. 285   'pleased at my being censored' 26 Dec. 1929, *VBQ*, May–Oct. 1990, p. 140 (trans. by Jibankrishna Banerjee)/*Desh*, 28 July 1990, pp. 42–43

29 Farewell to the West

Epigraph   'Rabindranath Tagore in Munich', *MR*, Oct. 1930, p. 370

p. 287   'Dead or alive' 20 Dec. 1929, *VBQ*, May–Oct. 1990, p. 142 (trans. by Jibankrishna Banerjee)/*Desh*, 28 July 1990, pp. 43–44

p. 287   'signing his works' It appears that during the 1930s he signed some of his paintings *en masse*; many remain unsigned, however. The chronology of his art is therefore virtually impossible to establish.

p. 287   'bust of Tagore' This stands in India House, London. A photograph appears as the frontispiece of Milward's *An Artist in Unknown India*.

p. 287   'she recalled' Milward, 'Rabindranath Tagore's paintings', *MR*, Nov. 1930, p. 545

p. 287   'Cartier-Bresson' Letter to Authors, 26 March 1991

p. 288   'manuscript instead of a portfolio' 'If I ever have the opportunity I should like to show you some pictures that I have done myself with the hope of once again being startled with your appreciation as in the case of *Gitanjali*.' (RT to Rothenstein, 22 Feb. 1929, in Lago, p. 325)

p. 288   'commented shrewdly' 30 March 1930, Lago, p. 326

p. 288   'did not mention the paintings' 3 April 1930, Lago, pp. 326–27

p. 288   'told Sturge Moore' 6 June 1930, Lago, p. 329. But in 1941, after RT's death, Rothenstein was less enthused: 'It was touching to find how in his old age Tagore took up drawing in a curious, rather vague and symbolic way; yet he did bring a new vitality into Indian draughtsmanship, leading the way towards a more immediate interpretation of life.' (*Indian Art and Letters*, second issue for 1941, pp. 67–68)

p. 288   'Rolland' Victoria Ocampo in Sahitya Akademi, p. 39

p. 288   'Andrews' RT thought that Andrews wanted to stop him from exhibiting in Britain. (RT to Rathindranath Tagore, 2 June 1930, Sharadiya *Desh*, 1396 [1989], p. 12) Sir Francis Younghusband, a Tagore admirer, saw an exhibition in London and wrote to his daughter: 'Between you and me if you or I had painted them people would have said "What awful monstrosities." But last night we said "What marvellous creations of this amazing many-sided genius."' (French, p. 349)

p. 288   'Rivière and Valéry' Ocampo in Sahitya Akademi, p. 39

p. 288   'catalogue introduction' 'The visible dreams of Rabindranath Tagore' in *CMG*, pp. 176–79 (translation)

p. 288   'Henri Bidou' His review was printed in translation as the

Introduction to the catalogue, 'An Exhibition of Drawings by Rabindranath Tagore (1928–1930)', at the City Museum and Art Gallery, Birmingham in June 1930.

p. 289   'like a Hymalaya peak' Andrée Karpelès in Dyson, p. 238

p. 289   'Milward' 'Rabindranath Tagore's paintings', *MR*, Nov. 1930, p. 545

p. 289   'Bidou' See above note.

p. 290   'Elmhirst to Tagore' 7 May 1930, Dutta and Robinson, *Purabi*, p. 105

p. 290   'international stomach' 'Tagore at Woodbrooke', *Friend*, 6 June 1930, p. 553

p. 291   'The atmosphere was electric' Pickett, p. 91. 'I was surprised by the bitterness in Tagore's voice.' (Diana D. Harriss to Authors, 23 June 1992) RT's speech appears in the *Friend*, 30 May 1930, pp. 490–94.

p. 291   'one older Quaker' John W. Graham, ibid, p. 494

p. 291   'The vastness of the race problem' *Religion of Man*, p. 158

p. 292   'the idea of the humanity of our God' ibid, p. 17

p. 292   'poet's religion' ibid, p. 93

p. 292   'Sadler' *Manchester Guardian*, 27 May 1930

p. 292   'I talked and talked' RT to S. R. Bomanji, n.d. [copy at RB]

p. 292   'second letter . . . from Dartington' 6 June 1930 [copy at RB]

p. 292   'barely a word' His most substantial reference to Dartington's buildings was just one (Bengali) adjective, 'palatial', in a letter to his daughter Mira. (9 July 1930, Sharadiya *Desh*, 1397 [1990], p. 49)

p. 293   'How like our Prophet!' Rathindranath Tagore in Sahitya Akademi, p. 50. *The Child* was published in London in 1931.

p. 293   'lecture . . . in Krönberg Castle' Muriel Morgan Gibbon, *Edinburgh Evening News*, 23 Sept. 1932.

p. 293   'Grandad's in a mess' 21 Aug. 1930, 'Moods', John Boulton, *VBQ*, Feb.–April 1975, p. 310/*Chithipatra*, *4*, p. 215

p. 293   'contact with Romain Rolland' There are very few surviving letters between Rolland and Tagore for the period following the 1926 meeting until RT's death.

p. 293   'Wells severed his link' Lago, p. 330

p. 293   'Two . . . conversations were published' The publishing history is somewhat chequered. The first conversation, on 14 July, was published in the *New York Times* magazine on 10 Aug. 1930 ('Einstein and Tagore plumb the truth'). Neither RT nor Einstein was satisfied with it. RT subsequently edited it, added some new material and published it as an appendix to *The Religion of Man* ('Note on the nature of reality'). His version also appeared in the *MR* (Jan. 1931, pp. 42–43) and in the *American Hebrew* (11 Sept.

1931). The second conversation, on 19 August, was published in the New York-based magazine *Asia*, March 1931, pp. 140–42. In quoting from the first conversation, we have used the *New York Times* version since this was approved by Einstein and, it would appear, by RT. The differences between this and the later version are substantive.

p. 294   'Josephson' Letter to Authors, 11 Dec. 1992

p. 294   'to quote Bohr' Pais, *Niels Bohrs' Times*, p. 427

p. 294   'We can never go beyond man' p. 114

p. 294   'two planets' Preamble to the conversation by Marianoff. Amiya Chakravarty was also present and noted the conversation.

p. 295   'later account by Marianoff' Marianoff, p. 76. Einstein repudiated Marianoff's biography when it appeared in 1944. There is no doubt that it was inadequate scientifically speaking, but there is no particular reason to doubt its account of this conversation. It is certain that Einstein approved the version published in the *New York Times*, judging from a letter written to RT by the *New York Times*: 'At the request of Professor Einstein we are sending you herewith for your private use a transcript of your recent conversation with him, which is to appear exclusively in the *New York Times*.' (Guido E. Enderis (Berlin News Bureau) to RT, 21 July 1930 [RB]). But by October, Einstein had changed his mind and told Romain Rolland: 'My conversation with Tagore was rather unsuccessful because of difficulties of communication and should, of course, never have been published.' (10 Oct. 1930, Nathan and Norden, p. 112) The reason was more complex than Einstein admitted to Rolland; it was connected with his philosophical disagreement with RT (and the quantum theorists such as Bohr and Heisenberg) – as Einstein implicitly indicated in his contribution to *The Golden Book of Tagore*, 'About free will' (Ramananda Chatterjee, p. 12). The Authors propose a full discussion of the Tagore–Einstein relationship in future publications; an inaccurate and incomplete account appears in Pais, *Einstein Lived Here*.

p. 295   'exclaimed in triumph' Marianoff, p. 77

p. 295   'Isaiah Berlin' Letter to Authors, 15 March 1993. See also Berlin's paper, 'Tagore and the consciousness of nationality', presented to an 'international literary seminar' in New Delhi, 1961 (unpublished: information courtesy Martin Kämpchen).

p. 295   'Rabbi' Pais, *Einstein Lived Here*, p. 99 (private communication to

Pais by Helen Dukas, secretary to Einstein). Isaiah Berlin commented: 'I think it ['Rabbi'] was meant to be ironical, in the gentlest way. Einstein did not hold with rabbis much; still less with quantum physics'. (Letter to Authors, 24 May 1993)

p. 296   'written to his great-nephew' RT to Saumyendranath Tagore, 17 April 1928, in Gnatyuk-Danil'chuk, pp. 215–16

p. 296   'Russian translations of *Gitanjali*' Between 1913 and 1917, there were six different translations.

p. 296   'Ilya Tolstoy' 'Chats with Count Tolstoy in America', *MR*, Jan. 1918, p. 34

p. 296   'Stanislavsky' 11 Aug. 1916, Gnatyuk-Danil'chuk, pp. 97–98

p. 296   'Victor Serge' p. 248

p. 296   '*Battleship Potemkin*' Pera Atasheva, 'Tagore and Battleship Potemkin'. This translation is from a booklet prepared by the Eisenstein Cine Club of Calcutta for a festival dedicated to *Battleship Potemkin*, 3–11 April 1987 (information courtesy Aida Sofjan). RT's sense of the expressive possibilities of film was given in a letter in Nov. 1929; an English translation appears in Monk and Robinson, p. 51. He regarded the spoken word as 'crippling' film.

p. 297   'first deputy minister' This was Leo Karakhan – see p. 252 – note.

p. 297   'Stalin' Perhaps one day the Soviet government archives will yield up Stalin's reaction to RT. Lenin is known to have kept RT's *Nationalism* in his personal library. (Gnatyuk-Danil'chuk, p. 97)

p. 297   'statements praising . . . Russian Communism' e.g. 'The Soviet system', *MR*, Sept. 1931, pp. 249–54

p. 297   'I wish to let you know' *Manchester Guardian*, 14 Oct. 1930; also *Friend*, 10 July 1931, p. 642

p. 297   'British newspaper' *Independent*, 14 Nov. 1988

p. 298   'ashamed' *Chithipatra*, 2, p. 102

p. 298   'photograph . . . with Einstein' 21 Dec. 1930

p. 298   'thousands had to be turned away' *New York Times*, 2 Dec. 1930

p. 298   'dance performance' RT asked for the proceeds to be given to New York's unemployed, rather than to Shantiniketan.

p. 298   'To each question' *New York Herald Tribune*, 10 Oct. 1930

p. 299   'Tagore's correction' 13 Oct. 1930

p. 299   'wrote . . . to . . . Sedgwick' 12 Oct. 1930 [copy at RB]

p. 299   '*Spectator*' 'The Round Table Conference', 15 Nov. 1930, pp. 724–25

p. 300   'I understand Zionism' *Jewish Standard*, ?Toronto, 28 Nov. 1930

p. 300   'long letter to the *New York Times*' 15 Jan. 1931

p. 300   'The age belongs to the West' Hay, 'Rabindranath Tagore in America', *American Quarterly*, Fall 1962, p. 459

p. 301   'Our appeal' *New York Times*, 2 Dec. 1930

p. 301   'band of robbers' *Manchester Guardian*, 9 Jan. 1931

p. 301   'voices . . . in the wilderness' *Daily Sketch*, 9 Jan. 1931

p. 301   'not to listen to politicians' *Daily Mail and Empire*, Toronto, ?9 Jan. 1931 (quoting UP, London)

30 Against the Raj

Epigraph   '"Rebel India"' *MR*, Jan. 1933, p. 2 (book review)

p. 302   'Will Durant' Kripalani, *Rabindranath*, p. 378

p. 302   'published his review' 'Will Durant's "The Case for India"', *MR*, March 1931, p. 268

p. 303   'The colour bar' *Spectator*, 9 May 1931, p. 737

p. 303   'appealed in the Calcutta press' *Statesman*, 6 Sept. 1931

p. 303   'Robert Reid' p. 64

p. 304   'Kripalani' *Rabindranath*, p. 383

p. 304   'humiliations and sufferings' *Hindu*, Madras, 26 Sept. 1931

p. 304   '*Civil and Military Gazette*' 28 Sept. 1931

p. 304   'terrible affair' 1 Oct. 1931, Nehru, *Selected Works*, 5 (first series), p. 135

p. 304   'spirit of Mahatmaji's life' 'Mohandas Karamchand Gandhi', *MR*, Jan. 1932, p. 8/ *RR*, *27*, p. 297

p. 304   'Gandhi sent . . . message' Ramananda Chatterjee, p. 1

p. 305   'Most of the famous people' Yeats was reluctant and sent instead a personal letter, which was printed; Wells refused outright; Shaw told Rothenstein; 'To the devil with these Nitwitiketant idiots! I spend half the year telling them to put my name to anything they like that will please Tagore, and the other half telling you to tell them so.' (Rothenstein, *Since Fifty*, p. 178) Nothing by Shaw appeared in *The Golden Book*.

p. 305   'Eden Gardens' *MR*, Dec. 1931, p. 709

p. 305   'request to meet the viceroy' On 10 Jan. 1932, the viceroy Lord Willingdon informed the secretary of state for India, Samuel Hoare: 'while he [Gandhi] may possibly have his saint-like side, on the other he is the most Machiavellian bargaining little political humbug I have ever come across.' (Brown, p. 262)

p. 305   'cabled the prime minister' *MR*, Feb. 1932, p. 226

p. 305   '*Spectator*' 'The issue in India', 30 Jan. 1932, p. 145 (with comment by the editor)

p. 305   'The Question' 'Prashna', *Punashcha*, *RR*, *15*, pp. 196–97 (Paush 1338 [1932])

p. 306   'Tagore added a PS' [copy at RB]

p. 306   'strength of this frail man' 'With Mahatmaji in Poona', *Mahatma Gandhi*, p. 47/*RR*, *27*, p. 309

p. 307   'Indira Nehru' 27 Sept. 1932, Sonia Gandhi, p. 68

31 The Great Sentinel

Epigraph   11 May 1933, 'Letters to Mahatma Gandhi', *Rabindra-Biksha*, Dec. 1991, p. 23

p. 308   'letter to . . . Tucker' 4 March 1933, *CWMG*, *53*, pp. 465–66

p. 308   'fresh from your university' 3 Sept. 1932, Dutta and Robinson, *Purabi*, p. 109

p. 309   'this white ant' 5 Nov. 1932, *CWMG*, *51*, p. 349

p. 309   'wrote to . . . Zamorin' 16 Nov. 1932, *Hindu*, Madras, 6 Dec. 1932

p. 309   'Shaw' 10 Jan. 1933, Shaw, *Letters*, *4*, p. 321

p. 309   'Scavenger' 'The Cleanser', *VBQ*, July 1925, p. 148; also in *Harijan*, 11 Feb. 1933

p. 309   'Rammohun' 'Rammohun Roy', *VBN*, March 1933, p. 77. The second speech appears in *MR*, March 1933, pp. 319–21.

p. 310   'one of his best speeches' 'The diffusion of education', *MR*, July 1939, pp. 25–30 (trans. by Amal Krishna Mukherjee)/*Shiksha*, pp. 214–23

p. 310   '*Times of India*' 17 April 1933

p. 310   'oratorical displays' *Advance*, Calcutta, 16 April 1933

p. 311   'miscellaneous signatures' Comment by Sir Harry Haig, *MR*, Oct. 1933, p. 470. (Jawaharlal Nehru commented on this episode in his *Autobiography*, p. 385.)

p. 311   'long-suffering wife' Tendulkar, *3*, p. 247

p. 311   'The fast is intended' *CWMG*, *55*, pp. 156–57 (8 May 1933)

p. 311   'Gandhi believed in "renounce and rejoice"' Patel and Sykes, p. 65. RT told Gandhi's disciple Miraben (Madeleine Slade): 'According to the *Upanishad* the reconciliation of the contradiction between *tapasya* [austerity] and *ananda* [joyfulness] is at the root of creation – and Mahatmaji is the prophet of *tapasya* and I am the poet of *ananda*.' (19 Dec. 1929, *VBQ*, 1985, p. 23)

p. 311   'Dear Mahatmaji' 'Letters to Mahatma Gandhi', *Rabindra-Biksha*, Dec. 1991, pp. 22–23

p. 312   'You may call me superstitious' *CWMG*, *57*, p. 44

p. 313   'I cannot help myself' 2 Feb. 1934, ibid, p. 95

p. 313   'Man defends himself' Ramananda Chatterjee, p. 12
p. 313   'If we associate ethical principles' Tendulkar, *3*, pp. 306–07
p. 313   'Knowledge of the tallest scientist' *CWMG, 57*, pp. 165–66
p. 314   'staggering remark' *Autobiography*, p. 490
p. 314   'To one really great' 6 Feb. 1934. The statement was published in the Indian press on 8 Feb.

32 Last Travels

Epigraph   *MR*, April 1936, p. 476
p. 315   'New York theatrical agent' I .S. Richter. There are letters between Richter and Rathindranath Tagore from 1934 to 1937. [RB]
p. 315   'Debendranath' Debendranath refers to Hafiz in his *Autobiography*. 'In the case of my father there occurred a . . . synthesis of Hafiz and the *Upanishads*.' (RT to Brajendranath Seal, n.d., *VBQ*, No. 3, 1964–65, p. 154 (trans. by Kshitis Roy)/ *Visva-Bharati Patrika*, Baishakh–Asharh 1880 [1958], pp. 263–65
p. 315   'Journey of the Magi' 'Tirthajatri', *Punashcha, 16*, pp. 95–97. The translation reads as well in Bengali as Eliot's poem does in English.
p. 315   'not be disappointed' See the exchange of messages between RT and the Persian ministry of foreign affairs in *Parashya-Jatri*, pp. 172–75.
p. 316   'no special ties' 11 April 1932, 'Journey to Persia', *VBQ*, Feb. 1937, p. 73 (trans. by Surendranath Tagore)/ *RR, 22*, p. 433
p. 316   'inventors of the aeroplane' 13 April 1932, ibid, pp. 79–80/ p. 441
p. 316   'Iraqi air-force . . . message' ibid, p. 79/ p. 440
p. 317   'what a poet should be' 15 April 1932, *VBQ*, Aug. 1937, p. 112/ *RR, 22*, p. 450
p. 317   'homage of humanity' 9 May 1932, 'Art', *MR*, July 1932, p. 27
p. 317   'a day in a Bedouin encampment' Kripalani, *Rabindranath*, pp. 386–87 (trans. by Kripalani)/ *RR, 22*, p. 502
p. 317   'The night has ended' *Sphulinga, RR, 27*, p. 3. The poem-painting is reproduced in colour in Robinson, *Art of Rabindranath*, pl. 16. RT composed/painted it for the occasion of his arrival in Baghdad and meeting with King Feisal. (*Parashya-Jatri*, p. 148)
p. 318   'contemporary Bengali critic' Ramananda Chatterji (editor of *MR*), 'Visva-Bharati as an educational centre', *MR*, July 1936, p. 108
p. 318   'Oswald Mosley' p. 126
p. 318   '*Ceylon Daily News*' 31 May 1934 (information courtesy S. C. C. Atukorale)
p. 319   'Wilmot Perera' See his article on Sri Palee, *Times of Ceylon*, 26 Jan. 1959.

p. 319   'casual donations' *Hyderabad Bulletin*, 15 Dec. 1933 (letter)
p. 319   'he told Nehru' 9 Oct. 1935 [copy at RB]
p. 319   'Gaekwad of Baroda' Rathindranath Tagore, p. 156
p. 320   'wrote to Gandhi' 12 Sept. 1935, 'Letters to Mahatma Gandhi',
           Rabindra-Biksha, Dec. 1991, p. 26
p. 320   'Gandhi replied' 13 Oct. 1935, *CWMG*, *62*, p. 34
p. 320   'hunt the golden stag' RT to Gretchen Green, 16 Jan. 1936 [copy at
           RB]
p. 320   'Dear Gurudev' 27 March 1936, *CWMG*, *62*, p. 290. An anonymous
           letter from the donor (Birla) accompanied the donation, quoted in
           Nepal Majumdar, 'Visva-Bharati, Rabindranath and Gandhiji',
           VBQ, May 1969–April 1970, pp. 67–68
p. 320   'put a chain on his feet' See p. 230.
p. 320   'Tagore asked Gandhi to be a trustee' 10 Feb. 1937, 'Letters to
           Mahatma Gandhi', *Rabindra-Biksha*, Dec. 1991, p. 32
p. 321   'on a begging expedition' 19 Feb. 1937, *CWMG*, *64*, p. 381
p. 321   'Tagore wrote heatedly' 26 Feb. 1937, 'Letters to Mahatma
           Gandhi', *Rabindra-Biksha*, Dec. 1991, pp. 26–27
p. 321   'Tagore could never appreciate' On 19 Dec. 1937, RT drafted a
           letter to Leonard Elmhirst from which he eventually omitted the
           following portions: 'Mahatma Gandhi has the rare gift of making an
           ideal effective which I cannot claim; nevertheless I cannot help
           feeling sorry that though I took up the cause long before others even
           considered it, lack of true workers should have rendered my ideal
           ineffectual so far.
               'Education specially labelled as rural education is not my ideal –
           education should be more or less of the same quality for all
           humanity . . . '
p. 321   'they made up' RT apologized (his letter is lost); Gandhi replied to
           the apology on 9 April 1937, *CWMG*, *65*, p. 64.
p. 321   'more funds for Visva-Bharati' Gandhi to RT, 6 Nov. 1937, *CWMG*,
           66, p. 289 (fragment of a letter)
p. 321   'Rathindranath told C. F. Andrews' 17 Oct. 1937, Nepal Majumdar,
           'Visva-Bharati, Rabindranath and Gandhiji', *VBQ*, May 1969–
           April 1970, pp. 73–74

33 Shantiniketan in the Thirties
Epigraph   *Advance*, Calcutta, 10 Feb. 1936
p. 323   'Accept this institution' 19 Feb. 1940, 'Letters to Mahatma
           Gandhi', *Rabindra-Biksha*, Dec. 1991, p. 29

p. 323   'Gandhi affectionately accepted' 19 Feb. 1940, *CWMG*, *71*, p. 228

p. 323   'Ray . . . said' 'My life, my work', *Telegraph*, Calcutta, 28 Sept. 1982

p. 324   '[Ray's] final testimony' *Guardian*, London, 1 Aug. 1991

p. 324   'Ray paraphrased it' ibid. The poem appears in *Sphulinga*, *RR*, *27*,
             p. 41 (7 Paush 1336 [1929]); there is a facsimile in RT's handwriting
             in Satyajit Ray's *Jakhan Chhoto Chhilam*, p. 37. Compare RT's
             poem with 'Gratitude to the Unknown Instructors', the four-line
             poem by W. B. Yeats, written in 1931 at almost the same age as RT
             when he wrote his poem:

             What they undertook to do
             They brought to pass;
             All things hang like a drop of dew
             Upon a blade of grass.

p. 324   'others . . . seemed to love it' Indira to Jawaharlal, 7 July 1934, in
             Sonia Gandhi, p. 122

p. 324   'live in the cottage' 28 May 1934, Sonia Gandhi, p. 116

p. 324   'Nehru was . . . disapproving' 15 June 1934, ibid, pp. 119–21

p. 325   'Indira was horrified' Indira Gandhi, 11 April 1976, *Selected
             Speeches* (1972–77), p. 579

p. 325   'German' Frank Oberdorf. See various references in Jayakar.

p. 325   'In 1982 she said' *VBN*, Oct.–Dec. 1984, pp. 29, 32

p. 326   'Visva-Bharati students did little' See *MR*, July 1936, pp. 108–09,
             for Ramananda Chatterji's attempt to combat this common
             conception.

p. 326   'Buddhadeva Bose' 'Land of heart's desire', *VBN*, June 1941, p. 95

p. 326   'counterfeit cosmopolitanism' *Times Literary Supplement*, 27 Sept.
             1974, p. 1031.

p. 326   'curious assortment' *Thy Hand*, p. 633. For amusing accounts of the
             eccentricities of Visva-Bharati in the 1930s, see Aronson, *Brief
             Chronicles*, and the novel by Rózsa Hajnóczy, *Fire of Bengal*, an
             intriguing melange of fact and fiction written by the wife of Julius
             Germanus, the Hungarian professor of Islamic Studies at
             Shantiniketan from 1929. (The dates given in the novel are
             generally wrong.)

p. 327   'Andrews . . . recalled' 'Old memories of the Ashram', *VBN*, May
             1939, pp. 83–84

p. 327   'Kshitimohan Sen' 'Rabindranath and the Ashram of early days',
             VBN, June 1939, p. 91 (trans. by Kshitis Roy). Sen was, among

many other things, the grandfather of Amartya Sen (who was a student at Shantiniketan), and the author of *Hinduism*.

p. 328   'Kopai' *Punashcha, RR, 16*, p. 7 (1 Bhadra 1339 [1932])

p. 328   'Mayurer Drishti' *Akashpradip, RR, 23*, pp. 121–23 (April 1939)

p. 329   'Writing from abroad to Andrews' 28 March 1921 [RB]

p. 329   'Prof. Germanus' n.d. [RB]

p. 329   'writing to his son' 4 June 1935, *Chithipatra, 2*, pp. 110–11

p. 330   'fresh shocks of surprise' RT to J. G. Drummond, 21 Jan. 1920 [Edinburgh: Patrick Geddes collection]

p. 330   'Surendranath Kar' See Raj Kumar Konar, 'Search for an Indian idiom in design' in Som.

p. 330   'I have built with mud' *Uttarayan Rabindra-Bhavana: An Introduction*, Shantiniketan, 1989, p. 7 (booklet: text by Supriya Roy)/ *Shesh Shaptak* (44), *RR, 18*, pp. 97–99

p. 331   'Tatas' The building was named Ratan Kuthi, after Ratan Tata. The inscription on it was agreed as follows: 'This building is erected out of a donation of Rs. 25,000 by Trustees of Sir Ratan Tata to be used as a residence for scholars (primarily of foreign countries) who stay and work at Shantiniketan.' (N. R. Tata to H. Morris, 6 July 1925 [RB]) The Tata donation was triggered by the presence of Sylvain Lévi at Shantiniketan: R. D. Tata married a Frenchwoman and was in love with France.

p. 331   'Bose . . . Binodebihari Mukherji' Both Bose and Mukherji were teachers of Satyajit Ray. In 1972, Ray made a gem of a film about Mukherji, *The Inner Eye*.

p. 331   'Even in the study of Bengali' 'Needs of Visva-Bharati', *VBN*, April 1940, p. 75

p. 331   'Zionists from Palestine' RT to Immanuel Olsvanger (Jewish Agency, Rehavia, Jerusalem), 8 Sept. 1937 [RB]. In 1937 a Jewish refugee, Alex Aronson, came to Shantiniketan, though not from Palestine; he taught English literature rather than farming.

p. 331   'I am so alone' RT to Ramkrishna Dalmia, 24 March 1939 [RB]

p. 331   'Ramananda Chatterji' *MR*, April 1936, p. 476

p. 332   'adulation, cynicism and hypocrisy' 'Some problems of Santiniketan', *VBN*, June 1933, pp. 101–03. Hajnóczy's *Fire of Bengal* captures this atmosphere well.

p. 332   'Amiya Chakravarty' E. P. Thompson mentions how Chakravarty attempted to poison RT's relationship with E. J. Thompson in the mid-1930s, despite Thompson's generous help to Chakravarty when he was in Oxford. (E. P. Thompson, pp. 94–95). In 1945

Chakravarty persuaded a well-known Calcutta publisher, D. K. Gupta of Signet Press, to reject a manuscript concerning RT written by Alex Aronson. Aronson's friend Satyajit Ray, who was working for Gupta as a jacket-designer and illustrator, tried to mediate and was rudely rebuffed. Ray told Aronson in a letter:

> Dr. Amiya Chakravarty, it seems, had done an intensive bit of propaganda against you, and Mr. D. K. Gupta had fallen for it. How a person of normal intelligence can fail to see through the patent hypocrisy of Dr. Chakravarty is beyond me, but it happened.
>
> It is all very unfortunate and disgusting. I know you have had to suffer a lot of humiliation, and if my apologies mean anything to you, please accept them. Let this unpleasant episode be closed, and for my sake at least, *do not* let these dark and shameful dealings of a certain publisher be generally known.

(19 Sept. 1945 – information courtesy Alex Aronson)

p. 333   'Muriel Lester' 9 July 1934 [RB]
p. 333   'replied . . . privately' 15 August 1934, *VBN*, Dec. 1935, p. 43

34 The Self-destruction of Bengal
Epigraph   'The communal decision', *MR*, Aug. 1936, p. 186
p. 335   '*Calcutta Municipal Gazette*' 8 Nov. 1928, 'The poet wants a street-number', in *CMG* (1941), p. 150
p. 336   'Banshi' *Punashcha*, *RR*, *16*, pp. 84–87 (25 Asharh 1339 [1932]). Bibhutibhushan Banerji's classic novel, *Pather Panchali*, was published four years before RT wrote this poem. Banerji came from the same class of society as the clerk in the poem. Nirad Chaudhuri knew him well and said of him:

> His hard life had not embittered him nor made him a cynic. His sympathy for ordinary people was unlimited, and he was not repelled even by the squalor in which such people had to live in our society. *Somehow, he could always make them rise above their surroundings; I would even say – far above the limitations of their world.* [our emphasis]

(*Thy Hand*, p. 90)

p. 339   'Communal Award . . . Poona Pact' The details are discussed in Gordon, pp. 266–67.

p. 339   'wrote to Gandhi' 28 July 1933, 'Letters to Mahatma Gandhi', *Rabindra-Biksha*, Dec. 1991, p. 31

p. 339   'Shortly after he added' 8 Aug. 1933, ibid, p. 24

p. 339   'The Mahatma advised Tagore' 27 July 1933, *CWMG*, 55, pp. 311–12

p. 339   'impassioned mass meeting' The announcement in the *Amrita Bazar Patrika*, 15 July 1936, on the day of the meeting, read as follows:

> All Hindus must now realize how the coming Constitution based on the Communal Award will reduce them to a position of a permanent statutory inferiority in the Legislature, curtail their existing rights, and deprive them of their legitimate place in government and administration, which they had acquired for themselves through long years of service, sacrifice and suffering for the country.

p. 340   'bisecting blade' 'The communal decision', *MR*, Aug. 1936, p. 184

p. 340   'politically explosive statement' Quoted in an editorial, 'An amazing memorial', *Mussulman*, Calcutta, 3 July 1936

p. 340   'secretary of state replied' Lord Zetland to RT, 30 July 1936 [RB]

p. 340   'Bengali Muslim newspaper' *Mussulman*, Calcutta, 3 July 1936

p. 340   'offer of an intoxicant' 'The communal decision', *MR*, Aug. 1936, p. 185

p. 340   'hubris' For an example, see Chaudhuri, *Thy Hand*, p. 466.

p. 340   'post-war age of disillusionment' 'The communal decision', *MR*, Aug. 1936, p. 186

p. 340   'told the *Manchester Guardian*' 10 March 1938 (letter to the editor); also *VBN*, April 1938, pp. 75–76

p. 341   'wrote . . . to a clergyman' RT to Rev. William Riley, 30 March 1938 [copy at RB]

p. 341   'Tagore's admiration . . . Bose's critical attitude' On 3 Aug. 1934, in a letter to RT, Bose wondered if RT might write a preface to his book, *The Indian Struggle*, which was critical of Gandhi, and doubted that he would, since 'you yourself have recently become Mahatmaji's blind admirer – at any rate, people may get this impression from your writings.' (Gordon, p. 289)

p. 341   'Deshanayak' Gordon, pp. 402–03/'Deshanayak' in *Kalantar*, Calcutta, 1962, pp. 371–73. The address was printed as a pamphlet but not delivered at a meeting in Calcutta as originally intended.

p. 341   'considerable contact with Mussolini' Gordon, pp. 278–79

p. 341   'compelled Bose to resign' ibid, pp. 374–440; Chaudhuri, *Thy Hand*, pp. 500–29

p. 341   'Gandhi warned C. F. Andrews' 15 Jan. 1940, *CWMG*, *71*, pp. 113–14. During 1939, RT and Gandhi exchanged several messages about Bose's position – see 'Letters to Mahatma Gandhi', *Rabindra-Biksha*, Dec. 1991 and *CWMG*.

p. 342   'anguished language' 'These squabbles', *Amrita Bazar Patrika*, 26 April 1940 (translation of interview published in *Shanibarer Chithi*)

35 War, Tagore and the West

Epigraph   *VBQ*, May–July 1951, p. 28 (facsimile of RT's original draft)

p. 343   'stirring appeal' 'To the conscience of humanity', *Spain*, Calcutta, 1937. This pamphlet also contained appeals by Romain Rolland and Henri Barbusse.

p. 343   'wrote to his grandson' 31 July 1931, *Chithipatra*, *4*, p. 179

p. 343   'Elements of New Germany' Herbert Richter, *Calcutta Review*, Oct. 1933, pp. 21–32

p. 344   'wrote robustly to Rabindranath' Saumyendranath Tagore to RT, 1 Nov. 1933, in Nepal Majumdar, *Rabindranath o Koikti Rajnaitik Prashanga*, pp. 97, 99

p. 344   'statements to the French press' Saumyendranath gave an interview to *Paris-Soir*, which was published in the *Record* (TUC journal), London, June 1933. There are various references to Saumyendranath in Rolland, *Inde*. He wrote a book attacking Gandhi, which Jawaharlal Nehru showed to André Malraux, asking him to look at the dedication: 'To the masses of India, that they may annihilate Gandhiism which enslaves them to priestly intrigue, to feudal autocracy, to native capitalism, and holds them by trickery under the yoke of British imperialism.' Nehru commented sadly to Malraux (quoting Swami Vivekananda on his master Ramakrishna): 'He was content to live that great life – and left it to others to explain it.' (Malraux, p. 236)

p. 344   'As regards the Hitler regime' *Israel's Messenger*, Shanghai, 3 Aug. 1934, p. 7. In publishing RT's letter, N. E. B. Ezra, the editor, commented prophetically on RT's expressed 'hope' about the German regime: 'Unfortunately, it is not so . . . history will brand the Hitler regime as the most cowardly and infamous that has ever disfigured the annals of our civilization.' (A copy is kept at Jews College in north London.)

p. 344   'rejected . . . Berlin University' *Cavalcade*, London, 30 March 1940, p. 17. There appears to be no surviving official record of RT's refusal.

p. 344   'poem on Africa' *Patraput*, *RR*, *20*, pp. 49–50 (28 Magh 1343 [1937]). The original poem is untitled.

p. 345   'I shall feel richly compensated' RT to Prince Nyabongo, 22 March 1937 [copy at RB]

p. 345   '*Spectator*' 'To Africa', 7 May 1937, p. 858, also in *VBQ*, May 1937, pp. 35–36

p. 345   'message to the World Peace Congress' *MR*, Oct. 1936, p. 442

p. 345   'Masaryk' Masaryk to RT, 25 Dec. 1925 [RB]

p. 346   'wrote to Lesny' 15 Oct. 1938, *VBN*, Nov. 1938, p. 38. On 8 Sept. 1938, RT told C. F. Andrews: 'I am anxious for the fate of Czechoslovakia and I earnestly hope that Chamberlain will not betray that country in the guise of a friend.' [RB]

p. 346   'spokesman' Yone Noguchi changed his mind about Japanese imperialism during the Second World War. In 1942, on the death of RT, he gave a moving speech during which he was 'overcome by emotion many a time' (as reported by Amar Lahiri, *VBN*, Aug. 1947, p. 10). After the war, in 1947, he wrote to his son in the USA, Isamu Noguchi, that he had made a 'terrible mistake' in supporting the Japanese leaders. (Interview with Isamu Noguchi in Noguchi, *1*, p. 42)

p. 346   'you are wrong . . . Asia' 23 July 1938, 'Poet to poet', *VBQ*, Nov. 1938, p. 199. Though despicable, Yone Noguchi's position was not without mitigating arguments. For instance, he cited to RT the Kuomintang's breaching of the dykes of the Huang He (Yellow River) in June 1938, in order to stop the advance of the Japanese army. Perhaps as many as a million Chinese were deliberately drowned. RT did not respond on the point.

p. 346   'if you take . . . moral element' 2 Oct. 1938, ibid, p. 208

p. 347   'You are building' 1 Sept. 1938, ibid, p. 203

p. 347   'It is true . . . remorse' Oct. 1938, ibid, pp. 211–12

p. 347   'Those who struck Him once' *Poems*, p. 186 (trans. by RT)/ 'Baradin', *RR*, *27*, pp. 628–29

p. 348   'Apaghat' *Shehnai*, *RR*, *24*, pp. 132–33 (1 Jaishtha 1347 [1940]). Earlier, RT had written an essay about Russia's attack on Finland – see Nepal Majumdar, *Bharate Jatiyata o Antarjatikata ebang Rabindranath*, *6*, pp. 119–24.

p. 347   'told a Jewish friend' RT to Schlomith Flaum [copy at RB]

p. 349   'Graham Greene' Introduction to Narayan, *The Bachelor of Arts*. For Chesterton's putative fictionalizing of RT, see Dale, p. 191.

p. 349   'Thompson perceived' E. J. Thompson, p. 264

p. 349   'Thompson had attempted' In 1925, he published *Rabindranath Tagore*, twenty poems in his own translations in Benn's Sixpenny Poets (later the Augustan Books of Modern Poetry), a series of which E. J. Thompson was general editor that otherwise consisted entirely of English poets of the previous two centuries.

p. 349   'told Robert Bridges' 18 Nov. 1915 [Bodleian]. RT and Bridges disagreed over Bridges' wish to alter one of the poems in *Gitanjali* ('Thou art the sky' – see p. 168) for inclusion in Bridges' anthology, *The Spirit of Man* (1915). RT for some months refused all attempts at persuasion, but eventually yielded at the request of Yeats. Bridges undoubtedly improved the poem, as may be seen by comparing the two published versions. The whole episode is discussed in Lago, pp. 177–86.

p. 349   'admitted [to Thompson]' 2 Feb. 1921, E. J. Thompson, p. 264 (omitted sentence restored)

p. 349   'Yeats described' Epigraph to Gwynn

p. 350   'I am no longer young' 11 June 1935 [London]. In Sturge Moore's letter to RT, dated 20 May 1935, he had said: 'I could not advise republication without retranslation.' [RB] On receiving RT's reply, he wrote again:

> I had felt both grateful for and saddened by [your] letter, but it struck me dumb as not knowing what to say. I have often speculated about the nature and value of your poetry in Bengali but only to feel baffled. I had felt that you were a great poet but the translations did not altogether strengthen that idea and what I from time to time heard from your countrymen set me wondering whether you were not rather a popular poet the divine part of whose work was more or less drowned in facility. But two long talks with Sudhanshu K. Sengupta whom I liked extremely removed all my doubts and assured me that you were one of the unapproachably excellent and Mr Bake [Dutch scholar and musicologist] held the same opinion adding what only an European who understood Sanskrit and Bengali could to my assurance.

(21 Oct. 1935 [RB])

This was the last exchange of letters between RT and Sturge Moore, who must have been somewhat taken aback to see the *Collected Poems and Plays* the following year. Presumably out of embarrassment, RT did not ask Macmillan to send a complimentary copy to Sturge Moore. (Anil Chanda (secretary to RT) to Macmillan, 3 Nov. 1936 [BL])

p. 351   'writing to Rhys and Macmillan' RT to Ernest Rhys, 31 Dec. 1936 [copy at RB]; RT to Macmillan, 3 Dec. 1936 [BL]

p. 351   'minimal interest' There was no review in the *Times Literary Supplement*, for example, which had reviewed almost all RT's English translations.

p. 351   '*Listener*' 24 Aug. 1939, p. 396 (first sentence of review)

p. 351   'play the Buddha in a film' A number of RT's works were (badly) filmed in India during his lifetime, but there were no foreign adaptations, despite E. J. Thompson's persistent efforts to interest Alexander Korda. (Happily – given Korda's record on India – Thompson failed.)

p. 351   '*Life*' 28 Feb. 1938, p. 21. RT met Keller twice, in 1921 and 1930. She admired him, but in her autobiography, she was gently mocking: 'After the Stately One had seated himself in the centre of a circle of friendly and reverent listeners, he talked of poetry, of India and China and the power of the spirit that alone can bring freedom.' She added: 'I could not help thinking of Gandhi, who not only hears this message of love, but also teaches it and lets it shine in his deeds before all men.' (Keller, pp. 282–83) This representative American comment on RT must actually have been a later thought, since Gandhi was barely known in the USA in Jan. 1921.

p. 351   'Nuremberg' *News Chronicle*, London, 10 Sept. 1937, reporting Goebbels' speech at the rally:

> World liberalism was . . . attacked savagely for having lent its moral aid to the Spanish Government.
>
> 'The marriage between Bolshevism and Democracy is quite strange, revealing perverse characteristics,' said the Minister [i.e. Goebbels].
>
> Rabindranath Tagore, the Dean of Canterbury, the Bishop of Worcester, and the Archbishop of York were all attacked for their support of Madrid.

Presumably, Goebbels was reacting to RT's anti-Fascist message in *Spain* – see p. 343.

p. 351   'Goebbels had read . . . *The Gardener*' Manvell and Fraenkel, p. 11

p. 351   'Čapek' RT admired Čapek too. He told Lesny that he found

Čapek's *Letters from England* 'brilliantly suggestive and full of originality'. (23 Oct. 1926 [copy at RB])

p. 351   'exchange of goodwill messages' Kshitis Roy, *Voice of Rabindranath: A Chronicle of Recordings*, 1973, New Delhi, p. 9 (booklet)

p. 351   'A French friend of Rabindranath' Christiane Bossenec, *Amrita Bazar Patrika*, 22 June 1940

p. 352   'Oxford's . . . doctorates' The three Bengalis were Surendranath Sen, Satyajit Ray and Nirad Chaudhuri. Indira Gandhi also received a doctorate, but of a different kind.

p. 352   'Lord Curzon . . . wrote for advice' E. Denison Ross, *Both Ends of the Candle*, London, 1943, pp. 142–43. Ross's reply is not extant. See also Lago, pp. 38–39, for Fox Strangways' letter to Rothenstein about Oxford's refusal.

p. 352   'Bridges . . . Thompson' E. J. Thompson, pp. 286–87

p. 352   'extreme contempt' 16 April 1924, Finneran *et al.*, *2*, p. 452

p. 352   'by the late 1930s' Oxford University first approached RT about the doctorate on 10 Feb. 1938. [RB]

p. 352   '*Times*' Kundu *et al.*, p. 149

p. 352   'Marjorie Sykes' Sykes to Friends Service Council, 28 Dec. 1940 [Friends House]

p. 352   'most dear to all the muses' *VBN*, Sept. 1940 (special supplement)

p. 353   'In honouring me' ibid

36 The Myriad-Minded Man

Epigraph   *Crisis in Civilization*, p. 23 / *RR*, *26*, p. 640

p. 354   'he joked' RT to Gertrude Emerson Sen, 21 July 1937. She was a journalist and author, the wife of Boshi Sen, a former assistant to Sir J. C. Bose.

p. 355   'he wrote to Gandhi' 'Letters to Mahatma Gandhi', *Rabindra-Biksha*, Dec. 1991, p. 28. A facsimile of his letter is reproduced in Kripalani, *Rabindranath*, opp. p. 393.

p. 355   'he told Leonard Elmhirst' 26 Sept. 1937, Dutta and Robinson, *Purabi*, pp. 112–13

p. 355   'Leonard replied' 8 Oct. 1937, ibid, p. 113

p. 355   'told Ernest Rhys' 9 Oct. 1937 [copy at RB]

p. 355   'His very first creative act' The painting is reproduced as the frontispiece of *VBQ*, Nov. 1937.

p. 356   'reactions of critics and artists' See Robinson, *Art of Rabindranath*, pp. 49–67.

p. 356   'Francis Bacon' Kenneth Clark, p. 201. There are several letters in

RB between RT and Sadler concerning RT's paintings. On 13 Oct. 1934, RT wrote to Sadler: 'It gives me great pleasure to know that you still take an interest in my paintings: I remember so well those days in Oxford [in 1930] when you saw some of my things and liked them.' Shortly afterwards Sadler recommended the paintings to a London gallery. An exhibition was eventually held in the Calmann Gallery in London, organized by the India Society. It was opened by Lord Zetland, the secretary of state for India, on 9 Dec. 1938, and garnered considerable press attention.

p. 356   'Dorothy Elmhirst' She told Leonard (then in India): 'I hope you will tell him [RT] that I enjoyed my second visit [to the Calmann Gallery] even more than the first.' (28 Dec. 1938 [Dartington]) Probably as a result of Dorothy's interest, a small collection of paintings came to be deposited at Dartington in 1939.

p. 356   'K. G. Subramanyan' See 'Tagore – the poet painter' in Monk and Robinson, pp. 55–61.

p. 356   'Satyajit Ray' Introduction to Robinson, *Art of Rabindranath*, p. 13

p. 356   'Ananda Coomaraswamy' According to Roger Lipsey, Coomaraswamy's biographer (who got the story from Dona Luisa Coomaraswamy, the wife of Coomaraswamy), one evening in 1930 Coomaraswamy came heavily down the stairs after having written something, passed it to his wife and said: 'Here, take a look. This is what you sometimes have to do for a friend.' The piece was the catalogue introduction to RT's exhibition. (Lipsey to Authors, 21 May 1992)

p. 357   'a great and sophisticated poet' Foreword to *Rabindranath Tagore*, dated 20 Oct. 1930. American reaction to RT's paintings in 1930 was, on the whole, disappointing for RT. Compare the reaction of the *New York Times* (30 Nov. 1930) with Coomaraswamy's:

> Were it not that Sir Rabindranath Tagore has himself expressly stated that his paintings . . . are 'spontaneous creations and must stand by themselves as they are', the approach to them would be easier. That is to say, it would seem most simple and reasonable to look upon them as spray from the mystic fountain whose major waters have been communicated in words . . .
>
> . . . What are we to make of these curious animal forms, of these hardly less curious human [forms]? Despite Tagore's warning, we cannot help trying to retrace their journey from the subconscious, trying to visualize the mystic concept from which

they spring. But the questions are never answered; and in the end we turn aside, not without impatience, though remembering, in the bustle of the street, certain queer, haunting beauties of light, a kind of fugitive translucence, glimpsed and then gone, suggestive, tantalizing, never really articulate.

p. 358   'Kadambari' See p. 89.

p. 358   'Subramanyan speculated' 'Tagore – the poet painter' in Monk and Robinson, p. 59

p. 358   'recognizably Bengali' Introduction to Robinson, *Art of Rabindranath*, p. 13

p. 358   'expressionless . . . ' ibid, p. 57 (where each source is given)

p. 358   'Coomaraswamy's emphasis on the child's vision' ibid, pp. 58–59

p. 358   'Indian musical connoisseurs' For example, the highly musical Upendrakishore Ray, grandfather of Satyajit Ray, who also admired Fox Strangways' book.

p. 359   'To hear him sing' Fox Strangways, p. 92

p. 359   '*Modern Review* noted' May 1932, p. 588

p. 359   'Bombay cinema' Nirupama and Ajit Sheth, 'Tagore and Indian cinema with special reference to his impact on Indian film music', paper presented in London, May 1986 (?unpublished). These writers described the use of *Rabindrasangit* in Hindi cinema in detail and remarked: 'R. C. Boral, Timir Baran, Anupam Ghatak, Anil Biswas, S. D. Burman, R. D. Burman, Hemant Kumar and even Naushad have often lifted Tagore melodies and introduced them in their Hindi film songs without expressing their indebtedness to Tagore.' They added: 'S. D. Burman has utilized Tagore melodies to the utmost in his compositions. These melodies invariably provided the material for many of his popular tunes' – among them one of Amitabh Bachchan's early hits, *Abhiman* (1973). Translation of Tagore's *words* into Hindi is much less satisfactory. 'When a literal translation of the words is attempted, they sound ponderous or stilted . . . Pankaj Mullick succeeded, to a large extent, in expressing in Hindi both the spirit of the words and the lilt of the melody found in the original Bengali composition.' Most of the Hindi film music composers have failed in this respect, but 'the rendering of Tagore songs into Hindi still presents a temptation and a challenge.' The latest film songs have used less of RT, however.

p. 359   'Ravi Shankar' Interview, *Independent*, Bombay, 17 Feb. 1991

p. 359   'Rostropovich' Nemai Ghosh, p. 114

p. 359   'Tagore has no equal' Robinson, *Satyajit Ray*, p. 47

p. 359   '*Mahabharata*' The song (*GB, 1*, p. 51) was sung by Sarmila Roy. In 1984, a song by ex-Beatle Paul McCartney, 'Pipes of Peace', based on a line of poetry by RT ('In love all of life's contradictions dissolve and disappear') reached No. 1 in the British music charts.

p. 359   'Tagore's songs cannot be translated' Nevertheless, a surprising number of significant western composers, including Janáček, have composed settings for Tagore poems in translation. See Raymond Head, 'The flute and the harp: Rabindranath Tagore and western composers' in Lago and Warwick, pp. 122–40. Head is probably incorrect in suggesting that Arnold Schoenberg was uninfluenced by RT's poetry; it appears that part of a work by Schoenberg was inspired by *Gitanjali* and possibly also *The Gardener* (see Stuckenschmidt, p. 237).

p. 360   'moved . . . away from [western music]' This was the impression of Satyajit Ray and Alex Aronson, who knew RT at Shantiniketan from 1937. (Ray and Aronson to Authors in conversation)

p. 360   'told Edward Thompson' E. J. Thompson, p. 61. E. J. Thompson's notes on this conversation appear in E. P. Thompson, pp. 142–43, and are slightly different.

p. 360   'Ray commented valuably' 'Some reflections on *Rabindrasangit*', Dutta and Robinson, *Purabi*, p. 178. This is a précis/translation of 'Rabindrasangite bhabbar katha', Sharadiya *Ekshan*, 1967, pp. 1–21

p. 361   '*My Reminiscences*' See p. 84.

p. 361   '*Sadhana*' p. 164 (concluding words). They were beautifully carved in limestone by the typographer Ralph Beyer and are reproduced on the back cover of Dutta and Robinson, *Purabi*. We follow Beyer's arrangement.

p. 361   'sparrow poem' *Rogashajyay* (6), *RR, 25*, pp. 10–11 (11 Nov. 1940)

p. 361   'the rose poem' ibid (21), pp. 23–24 (24 Nov. 1940)

p. 362   'Brutal night comes silently' 'Eight poems and songs of Rabindranath Tagore', *VBQ*, 1985, p. 6 (trans. by A. K. Ramanujan and Naresh Guha)/*Arogya* (7), *RR, 25*, pp. 47–48 (27 Jan. 1941). We have altered one word of the translation.

p. 363   'thought of Victoria Ocampo' *I Won't Let You Go: Selected Poems*, p. 221 (trans. by Ketaki Kushari Dyson)/ *Shesh Lekha (5)*, *RR, 26*, pp. 42–43 (6 April 1941)

p. 363   'Four score not enough' 12 April 1941, *CWMG, 73*, p. 438

p. 363   'Five score intolerable' 14 April 1941, 'Letters to Mahatma

Gandhi', *Rabindra-Biksha*, Dec. 1991, p. 33

p. 363   'Sanskrit' Manu 4: 174 (trans. by RT). See also *The Laws of Manu*, Wendy Doniger with Brian K. Smith trans., London, 1991.

p. 364   'Gospel According to Mark' Mark 8:36. RT mentioned that Andrews was a Christian, but did not mention Christ himself.

p. 364   'C. F. Andrews' RT's choice of Andrews as exemplifying the highest type of Englishman is intelligible if deeply flawed. Andrews had a tangled character, as weak in some respects as it was strong in others. No one who commanded the respect of both Tagore and Gandhi over many years can simply be dismissed, nevertheless it is very difficult to point clearly to solid achievements by Andrews – unless one counts the sheer prolificness and length of his letters over several decades! Perhaps Leonard Elmhirst – surely a more typical Englishman than Andrews – described Andrews best when he wrote to RT in 1940 after hearing of Andrews' death:

> You'll miss Sir Charles [RT's nickname for Andrews] – there are some people who the more we curse them the more we express the reverse side only of the true coin of our love. I suppose I was jealous of him, at first. I envied the secure place he had, not without toil, won for himself in India, as I admired the indomitable courage of the man, barefaced non-stop courage. But he could be exasperating.

(19 May 1940, Dutta and Robinson, *Purabi*, p. 118)

p. 364   'Without the slightest hesitation' *Crisis in Civilization*, p. 21/*RR*, *26*, p. 639

p. 364   'The wheels of Fate' ibid, p. 22/p. 640

p. 364   'grievous sin' ibid, p. 23/p. 640

p. 364   'ill-judged praise of . . . Soviet Union' ibid, pp. 16–17/pp. 636–37

p. 365   'V. S. Naipaul', p. 350

p. 365   'Kripalani' *Rabindranath*, p. 434

p. 366   'Tagore replied in measured words' 16 June 1941 [RB]. Westcott was provoked to write by RT's statement on 4 June 1941 in reply to an open letter to Indians sent by Eleanor Rathbone, MP, asking them to cooperate with the British in fighting Fascism. The acerbic tenor of RT's response to Rathbone can be gathered from his statement that,

> The British hate the Nazis for merely challenging their world-mastery . . . It is not so much because the British are foreigners

that they are unwelcome to us and have found no place in our hearts, as because, while pretending to be trustees of our welfare, they have betrayed the great trust and have sacrificed the happiness of millions in India to bloat the pockets of a few capitalists at home.

The entire statement is printed in *CMG*, p. 107. Rathbone's view is explained in Stocks, which also reproduces Jawaharlal Nehru's pungent response to Rathbone's letter as an appendix.

p. 366   'bishop pragmatically replied' 19 June 1941 [RB]

p. 366   'Glaxo baby' 'Last days with Gurudeva', *CMG*, p. 10

p. 367   'His secretary described' Anil Chanda, 'The last ten months', *VBN*, Sept. 1941, p. 36

p. 367   'The sun of the first day' *Shesh Lekha* (13), *RR*, *26*, pp. 49–50 (27 July 1941)

p. 367   'Sorceress!' *Thy Hand*, pp. 635–36/ *Shesh Lekha* (15), *RR*, *26*, pp. 50–51 (30 July 1941)

p. 368   'sanctuary' 8 May 1893, *Glimpses*, p. 83/*Chhinnapatra*, p. 163

p. 368   'Goethe' 22 Sept. 1894, ibid, p. 111/p. 245

p. 368   'Alex Aronson' Aronson, *Brief Chronicles*, p. 88

p. 368   'So Gurudev is dead' 'Prison diary with letters', *Selected Works*, *11* (first series), pp. 671–72

p. 369   'temporary platform' Marjorie Sykes to Friends Service Council, 10 Oct. 1941 [Friends House]

p. 369   'interpenetration of human life' See p. 14.

p. 369   'ocean of peace lies ahead of me' *Shesh Lekha* (1), *RR*, *26*, p. 39 (3 Dec. 1939)

Postscript

The two letters appear in Dutta and Robinson, *Purabi*, pp. 120–21.

Bibliography

1 MANUSCRIPT SOURCES

We have quoted from unpublished papers in the following collections (the abbreviation used in the Notes is given first):

[Adyar] Theosophical Society archives, Adyar, (Madras). (Annie Besant)
[BL] British Library, London. (Macmillan Company, Charlotte Shaw)
[Bodleian] Bodleian Library, Oxford. (Robert Bridges, E. J. Thompson)
[Cambridge] Cambridge University Library. (Theodore Dunn)
[Chicago] The Joseph Regenstein Library, University of Chicago. (Harriet Monroe, Harriet Moody)
[Dartington] The Elmhirst Centre. (Leonard and Dorothy Elmhirst)
[Edinburgh] National Library of Scotland. (Patrick Geddes)
[Friends House] Friends House (Quakers), London. (Friends Service Council, Marjorie Sykes)
[IOL] India Office Library and Records, London. (Viceroys/secretaries of state for India, William Rothenstein)
[London] University of London Library. (Thomas Sturge Moore)
[McMaster University] Mills Memorial Library. (Bertrand Russell)
[Manchester] The John Rylands University Library. *(Manchester Guardian/* C. P. Scott)
[Manchester College] Manchester College, Oxford. (Estlin Carpenter)
[New York] New York Public Library. (Macmillan Company)
[RB] Rabindra Bhavan, Shantiniketan. (This is the chief repository of RT's papers and papers relating to RT.)
[Sheffield] Sheffield City Archives. (Edward Carpenter)
[Yale] Beinecke Rare Book and Manuscript Library, Yale University. (Ezra Pound)
[Michael Yeats] Personal papers of Michael Yeats. (W. B. Yeats)

For holdings in the collections of Rabindra Bhavan, Shantiniketan, the catalogue-in-progress (1982–) is invaluable. A useful list of Tagore papers held in Britain may be found in the *Location Register of Twentieth-Century English Literary Manuscripts and Letters*, published by the British Library and University of Reading, in 1988. In the USA, the Houghton Library at Harvard University holds most of the papers of William Rothenstein dealing with Rabindranath Tagore.

2 BOOKS

Place of publication of all cited books in Bengali is Calcutta. The Bengali date of publication is given in square brackets.

A. *Books by Rabindranath Tagore (including anthologies and compilations)*
Only significant non-Bengali works, and only those Bengali writings cited in the text and not included in the *Rabindra Rachanabali*, are listed. Where no translator is given, the translation is generally by RT.

Amal et la Lettre du Roi, André Gide trans., Paris, 1922 (play)
Binodini, Krishna Kripalani trans., New Delhi, 1959 (novel)
Broken Ties and Other Stories, translated by various hands, London, 1925
Buddhadeva, 1956 [1363] (essays on Buddhism)
Chhinnapatra, 1912 [1319] (letters)
Chhinnapatrabali, 1960 [1367] (letters)
The Child, London, 1931 (poem)
Chithipatra: *1*, rev. edn, 1993, [1400]; *2*, 1942 [1349]; *3*, 1942 [1349]; *4*, 1943 [1350]; *5*, 1945 [1352]; *6*, 1957 [1364]; *7*, 1960 [1367]; *8*, 1963 [1370]; *9*, 1964 [1371]; *10*, 1967 [1374]; *11*, 1974 [1381]; *12*, 1986 [1393]; *13*, 1992 [1399] (letters) [revised editions in progress]
Chitra, London, 1914 (drama)
Collected Poems and Plays, London, 1936
Creative Unity, London, 1922 (essays)
The Crescent Moon, illus. edn, London, 1913 (poems)
Crisis in Civilization, Calcutta, 1941 (essay)
The Curse at Farewell, E. J. Thompson trans., London, 1924 (drama)
Drawings and Paintings of Rabindranath Tagore, New Delhi, 1961 (introduction by Prithwish Neogy)
East and West, Paris, 1934 (two letters: from Gilbert Murray to RT, with RT's reply)
The English Writings of Rabindranath Tagore, Sisir Kumar Das ed., *1*, 1994 [further volumes expected].

Farewell, My Friend, Krishna Kripalani trans., London, 1946 (novel)

Fireflies, New York, 1928 (epigrams)

Four Chapters, Surendranath Tagore trans., Calcutta, 1950 (novel)

Fruit-Gathering, London, 1916 (poems)

The Gardener, London, 1913 (poems)

Gitabitan: 1, 1967 [1374]; *2*, 1968 [1375]; *3*, 1966 [1373] (songs)

Gitanjali (Song Offerings), London, 1913 (introduction by W. B. Yeats) (poems)

Glimpses of Bengal, Krishna Dutta and Andrew Robinson trans., London, 1991 (letters)

Glimpses of Bengal Life, Rajani Ranjan Sen trans., Madras, 1913 (short stories)

Gora, [W. W. Pearson / Surendranath Tagore trans.], London, 1924 (novel)

Greater India, Madras, 1921 (essays)

The Home and the World, [Surendranath Tagore trans.], London, 1919; London, 1985 (introduction by Anita Desai) (novel)

The Hungry Stones and Other Stories, translated by various hands, London, 1916

I Won't Let You Go: Selected Poems, Ketaki Kushari Dyson trans., Newcastle-upon-Tyne, 1991

Kalantar, rev. edn, 1961 [1367] (essays)

The King of the Dark Chamber, Kshitis Chandra Sen trans., London, 1914 (drama)

Letters from Russia, Sasadhar Sinha trans., Calcutta, 1960

Letters to a Friend, C. F. Andrews ed., London, 1928

Lover's Gift and Crossing, London, 1918 (poems)

Mahatma Gandhi, 1963 (compilation in English)

Mashi and Other Stories, translated by various hands, London, 1918

My Boyhood Days, Marjorie Sykes trans., Calcutta, 1940

My Reminiscences, London, 1991

Nationalism, London, 1991 (introduction by E. P. Thompson) (essays)

Obra escojida, Juan Ramón and Zenobia Camprubi Jiménez trans., Madrid, 1963 (collected writings in Spanish translation)

L'Offrande Lyrique (Gitanjali), André Gide trans., Paris, 1913 (poems)

On Oriental Cultures and Japan's Mission, Tokyo, 1929

Our Universe, Indu Dutt trans., London 1958 (science primer)

Parashya-Jatri, 1963 [1370] (travel diary in Persia)

The Parrot's Training, Calcutta, 1918 (fable)

Pathe o Pather Prante, 1938 [1345] (letters)

Personality, London, 1917 (essays)

Poems, Calcutta, 1942 (anthology)

The Post Office, Devabrata Mukerjea trans., London, 1914 (drama)

Rabindra Rachanabali, 1–27, 1939–65 [1346–72] (collected writings)
Rabindra Rachanabali: Achalita Shangraha, 1940–41 [1347–48] (addenda)
Rabindranath o Tripura, Agartala, 1961 [1368] (compilation of speeches, letters and songs)
Rabindranath Tagore, E. J. Thompson trans., London, 1925 (poems)
Rabindranath Tagore on Art and Aesthetics, Prithwish Neogy ed., New Delhi, 1961 (compilation)
Rabindranath Tagore: Pioneer in Education, London, 1961 (essays and exchanges between RT and Leonard K. Elmhirst)
The Religion of Man, London, 1931 (essays)
Sacrifice and Other Plays, London, 1917
Sadhana: The Realisation of Life, London, 1913 (essays)
Selected Poems, William Radice trans., rev. edn, London, 1987
Selected Short Stories, Krishna Dutta and Mary Lago trans., London, 1991
Selected Short Stories, William Radice trans., rev. edn, London, 1994
Shiksha, rev. edn, 1990 [1397] (essays on education)
Songs of Kabir, Rabindranath Tagore trans., New York, 1915
Stray Birds, New York, 1916 (epigrams)
A Tagore Reader, Amiya Chakravarty ed., New York, 1961 (anthology)
Talks in China, Calcutta, 1925
Three Plays, Marjorie Sykes trans., Bombay, 1950
Towards Universal Man, translated by various hands, Bombay, 1961 (essays)
Tripura's Ties with Tagore, Chiranjiv Kaviraj trans., Agartala, 1969 (abridged and translated version of *Rabindranath o Tripura*)
Yurop Jatrir Diary, 1961 [1368] (travel diary in Europe, 1890)
Yurop Prabashir Patra, 1961 [1368] (letters)

B. *Other Books*
Ackroyd, Peter, *T. S. Eliot*, London, 1984
Adhikari, Sachindranath, *Shelidah o Rabindranath*, 1974 [1380]
Aldington, Richard, *Life for Life's Sake*, New York, 1941
Alexander, Horace, *The Indian Ferment*, London, 1929
Animananda, [Swami], *The Blade: Life and Works of Brahmabandhab Upadhyay*, Calcutta, n.d. (after 1923)
Aronson, Alex, *Brief Chronicles of the Time: Personal Recollections of My Stay in Bengal (1937–1946)*, Calcutta, 1991
    Rabindranath Tagore Through Western Eyes, 2nd edn, Calcutta, 1978
Aronson, Alex and Krishna Kripalani eds, *Rolland and Tagore*, Calcutta, 1945
Balabanoff, Angelica, *My Life as a Rebel*, New York, 1965
Banerjee, Hiranmoy, *Rabindranath Tagore*, New Delhi, 1971

Banerjee, Sumanta, *The Parlour and the Streets: Elite and Popular Culture in Nineteenth Century Calcutta*, Calcutta, 1989

Basham, A. L., *The Wonder That Was India*, London, 1954

Basu, Nemaisadhan, *Bhagnanirh Visva-Bharati*, 1991 [1398]

Bettelheim, Bruno, *Recollections and Reflections*, London, 1990

Bhattacharya, Sukhamay, *Shanskritanushilane Rabindranath*, 1991 [1398]

Bibliothèque Nationale, *Rabindranath Tagore 1941–1961*, Paris, 1961

Bisi, Pramathanath, *Rabindranath o Shantiniketan*, 1975 [1382]

Boardman, Philip, *The Worlds of Patrick Geddes: Biologist, Town planner, Re-educator, Peace-warrior*, London, 1978

Born, Irene, trans., *The Born–Einstein Letters*, London, 1971 (foreword by Bertrand Russell)

Bose Institute, *Dr. D. M. Bose: Birth Centenary Commemoration Volume, 1885–1985*, Calcutta, 1985

Bose, Mihir, *The Lost Hero: A Biography of Subhas Bose*, London, 1982

Bose, Shib Chunder, *The Hindoos As They Are*, London, 1881

Bose, Subhas Chandra, *An Indian Pilgrim*, London, 1965

Brecht, Bertolt, *Diaries 1920–1922*, Herta Ramthun ed., John Willett trans., London, 1979

Bridge, Ursula, *W. B. Yeats and T. Sturge Moore: Their Correspondence, 1901–1937*, London, 1953

Bridges, Robert, ed., *The Spirit of Man*, London, 1915

Brittain, Vera, *Pethick-Lawrence: A Portrait*, London, 1963

Brown, Judith M., *Gandhi: Prisoner of Hope*, London, 1989

Calcutta Municipal Gazette (Tagore Memorial Special Supplement), 13 Sept. 1941

Chander, Jag Parvesh ed., *Tagore and Gandhi Argue*, Lahore, 1945 (selected writings)

Chatterjee, Ramananda ed., *The Golden Book of Tagore*, Calcutta, 1931

Chaudhuri, Nirad C., *The Autobiography of an Unknown Indian*, London, 1951
  Hinduism, London, 1978
  Scholar Extraordinary: The Life of F. Max Müller, London, 1974
  Thy Hand, Great Anarch!, London, 1987

Chaudhuri, Sukanta ed., *Calcutta: The Living City*, 1 (The Past), Calcutta, 1990

Chevalier, Jacques, *Entretiens avec Bergson*, Paris, 1959

Chirol, Valentine, *Indian Unrest*, London, 1910

Clark, Kenneth, *Another Part of the Wood: A Self Portrait*, London, 1985

Clark, Ronald W., *Einstein: The Life and Times*, New York, 1971

Coomaraswamy, Ananda K., *Art and Swadeshi*, Madras, 1912

Cousins, J. H. and M. E., *We Two Together*, Madras, 1950

Croce, Benedetto, *Epistolario, 2 (Lettere ad Alessandro Casati, 1907–1952)*, Naples, 1969

Crow, Duncan, *A Man of Push and Go: The Life of George Macaulay Booth*, London, 1965

[Curzon, Lord], *Letters and Telegrams*, Calcutta, 1905
Speeches, 2 (1900–1902), Calcutta, 1902

D'Abernon, Viscount, *An Ambassador of Peace: Pages from the Diary of Viscount D'Abernon, 1*, (1920–1922), London, 1929

Dale, Alzina Stone, *The Outline of Sanity: A Biography of G. K. Chesterton*, Grand Rapids (Michigan), 1983

Das, Anathnath ed., *Rathindranath Thakur*, 1988 [1395]

Das, Suranjan, *Communal Riots in Bengal 1905–1947*, New Delhi, 1991

Das Gupta, Tapati, *Social Thought of Rabindranath Tagore: A Historical Analysis*, New Delhi, 1993

Das Gupta, Uma, *Santiniketan and Sriniketan*, Calcutta, 1983 (booklet)

Datta, Roby, *Echoes from East and West*, Cambridge, 1909

Dewey, Clive, *Anglo-Indian Attitudes: The Mind of the Indian Civil Service*, London, 1993

Dickens, Charles: *The Letters of Charles Dickens, 3* (1842–1843), Madeline House, Graham Storey and Kathleen Tillotson eds, Oxford, 1974; *4*, (1844–1846), Kathleen Tillotson ed., Oxford, 1977

Dignan, Don, *The Indian Revolutionary Problem in British Diplomacy 1914–1919*, New Delhi, 1983

Dimock, E. C. and Denise Levertov trans., *In Praise of Krishna: Songs from the Bengali*, Chicago, 1967

Doig, Desmond, *Mother Teresa: Her people and her work*, New Delhi, 1975 (foreword by Indira Gandhi)

Draper, Alfred, *Amritsar: The massacre that ended the Raj*, London, 1981

Du Bois, W. E. B., *The Correspondence of W. E. B. Du Bois, 1, Selections, 1877–1934*, Herbert Aptheker ed., University of Massachusetts Press, 1973

Dunbar, Olivia Howard, *A House in Chicago*, Chicago, 1947

Dutt, Gurusaday, *Folk Arts and Crafts of Bengal: The Collected Papers*, Calcutta, 1990 (introduction by Samik Bandopadhyay)

Dutta, Krishna and Andrew Robinson eds, *Purabi: A Miscellany in Memory of Rabindranath Tagore, 1941–1991*, London, 1991 (foreword by Javier Pérez de Cuéllar)
Noon in Calcutta: Short Stories from Bengal, London, 1992

Dyson, Ketaki Kushari, *In Your Blossoming Flower-Garden: Rabindranath Tagore and Victoria Ocampo*, New Delhi, 1988

Eden, Emily, *Letters from India, 1*, London, 1872

Eliade, Mircea, *Bengal Nights*, Catherine Spencer trans., London, 1993
No Souvenirs: Journal, 1957–1969, Fred H. Johnson Jr trans., London, 1978

Ellmann, Richard, *Yeats: The Man and the Masks*, rev. edn, London, 1979

Elmhirst, Leonard K., *Poet and Plowman*, Calcutta, 1975

Epstein, Jacob, *An Autobiography*, London, 1955

Espmark, Kjell, *The Nobel Prize in Literature: a study of the criteria behind the choices*, Boston, 1991

Feinberg, Barry and Ronald Kasrils eds, *Dear Bertrand Russell*, London, 1969

Field, Michael, *Works and Days: from the Journal of Michael Field*, T. and D. C. Sturge Moore eds, London, 1933

Finneran, Richard J., George Mills Harper, William H. Murphy, eds, *Letters to W. B. Yeats, 2*, London, 1977

Forster, E. M., *Abinger Harvest*, London, 1936
Selected Letters of E. M. Forster, Mary Lago and P. N. Furbank eds *1* (1879–1920), London, 1983; *2* (1921–1970), London, 1985

Fox Strangways, Arthur H., *The Music of Hindostan*, Oxford, 1914

Foxe, Barbara, *Long Journey Home: A Biography of Margaret Noble*, London, 1975

Frankfurter, M. D. and Gardner Jackson eds, *The Letters of Sacco and Vanzetti*, New York, 1928

Frost, Robert, *Selected Letters of Robert Frost*, Lawrance Thompson ed., London, 1965

Furrell, James W., *The Tagore Family: A Memoir*, Calcutta, 1882

Gandhi, Indira, *Selected Speeches of Indira Gandhi* (1966–1969), New Delhi, 1971; *The Years of Endeavour: Selected Speeches of Indira Gandhi* (1969–1972), New Delhi, 1975; *Selected Speeches and Writings of Indira Gandhi* (1972–1977), New Delhi, 1984

Gandhi, Mahatma, *The Collected Works of Mahatma Gandhi, 1–90*, Ahmedabad, 1958–1984 (especially *15–74*, 1918–1941)
The Story of My Experiments with Truth, 2, Mahadev Desai trans., New Delhi, 1930

Gandhi, Sonia ed., *Freedom's Daughter: Letters Between Indira Gandhi and Jawaharlal Nehru, 1922–1939*, London, 1989

Gangulee, Nagendranath, ed., *The Russian Horizon*, London, 1943 (foreword by H. G. Wells)
Thoughts for Meditation, London, 1951 (foreword by T. S. Eliot)

Geddes, Patrick, *The Life and Work of Sir Jagadis C. Bose*, London, 1920

Ghosh, J. C., *Bengali Literature*, London, 1976

Ghosh, Sankha, *Nirman ar Shrishti*, 1982 [1389]

Ghosh, Nemai, *Satyajit Ray at 70: Photographs*, Brussels, 1991

Gide, André, *The Journals of André Gide*, 2 (1914–1927), Justin O'Brien trans., London, 1948

Gnatyuk-Danil'chuk, A. P., *Tagore, India and the Soviet Union: A Dream Fulfilled*, Calcutta, 1986

Gollancz, Israel ed., *A Book of Homage to Shakespeare*, Oxford, 1916

Gordon, Leonard A., *Brothers Against the Raj: A Biography of Indian Nationalists Sarat & Subhas Chandra Bose*, New York, 1990

Green, Gretchen, *The Whole World and Company*, New York, 1936

Gregory, Lady, *Lady Gregory's Journals*, 1 (1916–1925), Daniel J. Murphy ed., Gerrards Cross (UK), 1978

Griffiths, Richard, *Fellow Travellers of the Right*, London, 1980

Gupta, Bipinbehari, *Puratan Prashanga*, 1966 [1373]

Gwynn, Frederick L., *Sturge Moore and The Life of Art*, London, 1952

Hajnóczy, Rózsa, *Fire of Bengal*, Éva Wimmer and David Grant trans., William Radice ed., Dhaka, 1993

Havighurst, Alfred F., *Radical Journalist: H. W. Massingham*, Cambridge, 1974

Hay, Stephen N., *Asian Ideas of East and West: Tagore and His Critics in Japan, China and India*, Cambridge (Massachusetts), 1970

Henn, Katherine, *Rabindranath Tagore: A Bibliography*, Metuchen (New Jersey) and London, 1985

Hesse, M. G. trans., *Hermann Hesse and Romain Rolland*, London, 1978

Hibberd, Dominic, *Wilfred Owen: The Last Year, 1917–1918*, London, 1992

Hobson-Jobson: A Glossary of Colloquial Anglo-Indian Words and Phrases, and of Kindred Terms, Etymological, Historical, Geographical and Discursive, London, 1994 (introduction by Nirad C. Chaudhuri) (first published 1886)

Hudson, W. H., *Men, Books and Birds*, London, 1925

Hunter, Ian, *Malcolm Muggeridge: A Life*, London, 1980

Huxley, Aldous, *The Letters of Aldous Huxley*, Grover Smith ed., London, 1969

Inge, W. R., *Diary of a Dean*, London, 1949

Isherwood, Christopher, *Ramakrishna and His Disciples*, London, 1965

Ivinskaya, Olga, *A Captive of Time: My Years with Pasternak*, Max Hayward trans., London, 1978

Jansen, Eirik, (photographs by Trygve Bolstad), *Sailing against the wind*, Dhaka, 1992

Jayakar, Pupul, *Indira Gandhi: A Biography*, New Delhi, 1992

Johnston, Reginald, *Twilight in the Forbidden City*, London, 1934

Kämpchen, Martin, *Rabindranath Tagore and Germany: A Documentation*, Calcutta, 1991

Karlekar, Kalyani, *Voices from Within: Early Personal Narratives of Bengali Women*, New Delhi, 1991

Kawabata, Yasunari, *The Existence and Discovery of Beauty*, V. H. Viglielmo trans., Tokyo, 1969

Keller, Helen, *Midstream: My Later Life*, London, 1929

Keyserling, Hermann, *The Book of Marriage*, London, 1927

Killingley, Dermot, *Rammohun Roy in Hindu and Christian Tradition*, Newcastle-upon-Tyne, 1993

Kling, Blair B., *Partner in Empire: Dwarkanath Tagore and the Age of Enterprise in Eastern India*, Berkeley, 1976

Kohler, Lotte and Hans Saner eds, *Hannah Arendt Karl Jaspers Briefwechsel 1926–1969*, Munich, 1985

Koktanek, Anton Mirko, *Oswald Spengler in Seiner Zeit*, Munich, 1968

Kopf, David, *The Brahmo Samaj and the Shaping of the Modern Indian Mind*, Princeton, 1979

British Orientalism and the Bengal Renaissance, Berkeley, 1969

Korczak, Janusz, *Ghetto Diary*, New York, 1978

The Ghetto Years, 1939–1942, [Israel], 1980

Kramrisch, Stella, *Exploring India's Sacred Art: Selected Writings of Stella Kramrisch*, Barbara Stoler Miller ed., Philadelphia, 1983

Kripalani, Krishna, *Dwarkanath Tagore: A Forgotten Pioneer*, New Delhi, 1981

Rabindranath Tagore: A Biography, 2nd edn, Calcutta, 1980

Kübler-Ross, Elisabeth, *On Death and Dying*, New York, 1969

Kundu, Kalyan et al., eds, *Rabindranath Tagore and the British Press (1912–1941)*, London, 1990 [revised and extended edn. forthcoming]

Lago, Mary M., ed., *Imperfect Encounter: Letters of William Rothenstein and Rabindranath Tagore, 1911–1941*, Cambridge (Massachusetts), 1972

Max and Will: Max Beerbohm and William Rothenstein, Their Friendship and Letters 1893–1945, London, 1975

Lago, Mary M. and Ronald Warwick, eds, *Rabindranath Tagore: Perspectives in Time*, London, 1989

Larkin, Philip, *Selected Letters of Philip Larkin*, Anthony Thwaite ed., London, 1992

Lawrence, D. H., *The Collected Letters of D. H. Lawrence*, *1*, Harry T. Moore ed., London, 1962

Leaming, Barbara, *Orson Welles: A Biography*, London, 1985

Lesny, Vincenc, *Rabindranath Tagore, His Personality and Work*, Guy McKeever Phillips trans., London, 1939

Lévi, Desirée, *Dans l'Inde (de Ceylan au Nepal)*, Paris, 1925

Lochner, Louis P., *Fritz Kreisler*, London, 1951

Lodge, Oliver, *Letters from Sir Oliver Lodge: Psychical, Religious, Scientific and Personal*, J. Arthur Hill ed., London, 1932 (foreword by Oliver Lodge)

Losty, J. P., *Calcutta: City of Palaces*, London, 1990

Lowes Dickinson, Goldsworthy, *Appearances: Being Notes of Travel*, London, 1914

    An Essay on the Civilizations of India, China and Japan, London, 1914

Lukács, Georg, *Reviews and Articles*, Peter Palmer trans., London, 1983

MacBride White, Anna and A. Norman Jeffares eds, *The Gonne–Yeats Letters*, London, 1992

Macnicol, Nicol, ed., *Hindu Scriptures*, London, 1938 (foreword by Rabindranath Tagore)

Mahalanobis, Nirmalkumari, *Kabir shange Yurope*, 1969 [1376]

Mahalanobis, Prasantachandra, *Prashanga Rabindranath*, 1985 [1392]

Maitraye [Devi], *The Great Wanderer*, Calcutta, 1961

Maitrayee [Devi], *It Does Not Die: A Romance*, Chicago, 1993

Majumdar, Nepal, *Bharate Jatiyata o Antarjatikata ebang Rabindranath*, 2, rev., edn, 1988 [1395]; 6, 1980 [1387]

    Rabindranath Koikti Rajnitik Prashanga, 1987 [1394]

    Rabindranath o Subhashchandra, 1968 [1375]

Majumdar, Swapan, *Rabindragranthashuchi*, 1988 [1395]

Malraux, André, *Antimemoirs*, Terence Kilmartin trans., London, 1968

Mann, Thomas, *Diaries 1918–1939*, Richard and Clara Winston trans., New York, 1982

Manvell, Roger and Heinrich Fraenkel, *Doctor Goebbels: His Life and Death*, London, 1960

Marianoff, Dimitri, with Palma Wayne, *Einstein: An Intimate Study of a Great Man*, New York, 1944

Mayo, Katharine, *Mother India*, New York, 1927

Meyer, Doris, *Victoria Ocampo: Against the Wind and the Tide*, Austin (Texas), 1990

Milward, Marguerite, *An Artist in Unknown India*, London, 1948

Mira [Devi], *Smriti Katha*, 1975 [1382]

Mitter, Partha, *Art and Nationalism in Colonial India: Occidental Orientations*, Cambridge UK, 1994

Mittra, Kissory Chand, *Memoir of Dwarkanath Tagore*, Calcutta, 1870

Monk, Ray, *Ludwig Wittgenstein: The Duty of Genius*, London, 1990

Monk, Ray and Andrew Robinson eds, *Rabindranath Tagore: A Celebration of His Life and Work*, London/Oxford, 1986

Monroe, Harriet, *A Poet's Life: Seventy Years in a Changing World*, New York, 1938

Mosley, Oswald, *My Life*, London, 1968

Muggeridge, Malcolm, *Chronicles of Wasted Time*, London, 1973

Mukherjee, S. N., *Calcutta: Myths and History*, Calcutta, 1977

Mukherjee, Sujit, *Passage to America: The Reception of Rabindranath Tagore in the United States, 1912–1941*, Calcutta, 1964

Mukherji, Prabhat Kumar, *Rabindrajibani, 1–4*, rev. edns, 1946–64 [1353–71]

Müller, Friedrich Max *Auld Lang Syne: My Indian Friends*, London, 1899

Nabokov, Vladimir, *Selected Letters 1940–1977*, Dmitri Nabokov and Matthew Bruccoli eds, London, 1990

Nag, Kalidas, *Tagore and China*, Calcutta, 1945

Naipaul, V. S., *A House for Mr Biswas*, 2nd edn, London, 1983 (foreword by Naipaul)

    India: A Million Mutinies Now, London, 1990

Nanda, B. R., *Gokhale*, New Delhi, 1977

Nandy, Ashis, *The Illegitimacy of Nationalism: Rabindranath Tagore and the Politics of Self*, New Delhi, 1994

Narayan, R. K., *The Bachelor of Arts*, London, 1937 (introduction by Graham Greene)

Nathan, Otto and Heinz Norden eds, *Einstein on Peace*, London, 1963

Nayman, Anatoly, *Remembering Anna Akhmatova*, Wendy Rosslyn trans., London, 1991

Nehru, Jawaharlal, *An Autobiography*, 2nd edn, London, 1989

    Selected Works of Jawaharlal Nehru, 1–15 (first series), New Delhi, 1972–82; *1–15* (second series), New Delhi, 1984–

The Nobel Century, [no author], London, 1991 (introduction by Asa Briggs)

Noble, Margaret (Sister Nivedita), *The Web of Indian Life*, 2nd edn, Calcutta, 1918 (foreword by Rabindranath Tagore)

Noguchi, Yone, *Selected English Writings of Yone Noguchi, 1 (Poetry)*, Yoshinobu Hakutani ed., London, 1990

Nowell-Smith, Simon, ed., *Letters to Macmillan*, London, 1967

Okakura, Kakasu [Kakuzo], *The Ideals of the East*, London, 1903

Owen, Wilfred, *The Collected Letters of Wilfred Owen*, Harold Owen and John Bell eds, Oxford, 1967

    The Poems of Wilfred Owen, Edmund Blunden ed., London, 1952

The Oxford Book of Modern Verse, 1892–1935, W. B. Yeats ed., Oxford, 1936

Pais, Abraham, *Einstein Lived Here*, New York, 1994

    Niels Bohr's Times in Physics, Philosophy, and Polity, Oxford, 1991

Patel, Jehangir P. and Marjorie Sykes, *Gandhi: His Gift of the Fight*, Rasulia (India), 1987

Paul, Prashanta Kumar, *Rabijibani*, *1*, (1861–1878), rev. edn, 1993 [1400]; *2*, (1878/9–1884/5), 1984 [1391]; *3*, (1885/6–1893/4, 1986 [1393]; *4*, (1894/5–1900/1), 1988 [1395]; *5*, (1901/2–1907/8), 1990 [1397]; *6*, (1908/9–1913/14), 1993 [1399] [further volumes and revised volumes expected]

Pearson, W. W., *Shantiniketan: The Bolpur School of Rabindranath Tagore*, London, 1917

Pickett, Clarence, *For More Than Bread*, Boston, 1953

Pollard, Patrick ed., *André Gide et l'Angleterre*, London, 1986

Pound, Ezra, *The Letters of Ezra Pound 1907–1941*, D. D. Paige ed., London, 1951
    The Little Review: The Letters of Ezra Pound to Margaret Anderson, Thomas L. Scott and Melvin J. Friedman eds, London, 1989

Pound, Omar and A. Walton Litz eds, *Ezra Pound and Dorothy Shakespear: Their Letters: 1909–1914*, London, 1985

Prigogine, Ilya and Isabelle Stengers, *Order out of Chaos: Man's New Dialogue with Nature*, London, 1984

Rabindranath Tagore in Perspective: A Bunch of Essays [no editor], Calcutta, 1989 (foreword by Nemai Sadhan Bose)

Ray, Niharranjan, *Rabindranath Tagore: An Artist in Life*, Trivandrum (India), 1967

Ray, Satyajit, *Jakhan Chhoto Chhilam*, 1982 [1389]
    Our Films Their Films, New Delhi, 1976

Raychaudhuri, Tapan, *Europe Reconsidered*, New Delhi, 1988

Reid, Robert, *Years of Change in Bengal and Assam*, London, 1966

Reynolds, E. E., *Baden-Powell: A Biography*, London, 1942

Rhys, Ernest, *Everyman Remembers*, London, 1931
    Letters from Limbo, London, 1936
    Rabindranath Tagore: A Biographical Study, London, 1915

Robinson, Andrew, *The Art of Rabindranath Tagore*, London, 1989 (foreword by Satyajit Ray)
    Satyajit Ray: The Inner Eye, London, 1989

Rolland, Romain, *Inde: Journal (1915–1943), Tagore Gandhi Nehru et les Problèmes Indiens*, Paris, 1951
    Selected Letters of Romain Rolland, Francis Doré and Marie-Laure Prevost eds, New Delhi, 1990

Ronaldshay, Lord, *'Essayez': The Memoirs of Lawrence, Second Marquess of Zetland*, London, 1956

Ross, E. Denison, *Both Ends of the Candle*, London, 1943

Rothenstein, John, *Summer's Lease: Autobiography, 1901–1938*, London, 1965

Rothenstein, William, *Men and Memories: Recollections, 1900–1922*, London, 1932
  Since Fifty: Recollections, 1922–1938, London, 1939
  Six Portraits of Sir Rabindranath Tagore, London, 1915 (preface by Max Beerbohm)
Roy, Basanta Koomar, *Rabindranath Tagore: The Man and His Poetry*, New York, 1915
Roy, Dilip Kumar, *Among the Great*, 4th edn, Pondicherry, 1984
Rushdie, Salman, *Imaginary Homelands: Essays and Criticism 1981–1991*, London, 1991
  The Jaguar Smile: A Nicaraguan Journey, London, 1987
Russell, Bertrand, *The Autobiography of Bertrand Russell, 1872–1914*, London, 1967
  The Selected Letters of Bertrand Russell, 1, The Private Years (1884–1914), Nicholas Griffin ed., London, 1992
Sadleir, Michael, *Michael Ernest Sadler: A Memoir by His Son*, London, 1949
Sahitya Akademi, *Rabindranath Tagore: A Centenary Volume, 1861–1961*, New Delhi, 1961 (introduction by Jawaharlal Nehru)
Said, Edward W., *Culture and Imperialism*, London, 1993
Saint Denis, Ruth, *Ruth St. Denis: An Unfinished Life*, London, 1939
Sangharakshita (D. P. E. Lingwood), *Facing Mount Kanchanjungha: An English Buddhist in the Eastern Himalayas*, London, 1991
Sarkar, Sumit, *The Swadeshi Movement in Bengal, 1903–1908*, Calcutta, 1973
Savigneau, Josyane, *Marguerite Yourcenar: L'Invention d'une Vie*, Paris, 1990
Seal, Brajendranath, *New Essays in Criticism*, Calcutta, 1903
Sehanobis, Chinmohan, *Rabindranath o Biplabi Samaj*, 1985 [1392]
Sen, K. M. [Kshitimohan], *Hinduism*, London, 1961
Serge, Victor, *Memoirs of a Revolutionary 1901–1941*, Peter Sedgwick trans., London, 1963
Shaha, Gourchandra, *Rabindra Patrabali*, 1984 [1391]
Shaw, George Bernard, *Collected Letters*, Dan. H. Laurence ed., *3* (1911–1925), London, 1985; *4* (1925–1950), London, 1988
  Short Stories, Scraps and Shavings, London, 1934
Sinclair, Upton, *My Lifetime in Letters*, Missouri, 1960
Sinha, Kaliprasanna, *Hutom Pyanchar Naksha*, Arun Nag ed., 1991 [1398]
Som, Shobhan ed., *Rabindraparikar Surendranath Kar*, Calcutta, 1993 [1400] (preface by K. G. Subramanyan)
Speaight, Robert, *William Rothenstein: The Portrait of an Artist in His Time*, London, 1962
Spence, Jonathan D., *The Gate of Heavenly Peace: The Chinese and Their Revolution, 1895–1980*, London, 1982

Stock, Noel, *The Life of Ezra Pound*, London, 1970

Stocks, Mary D., *Eleanor Rathbone: A Biography*, London, 1949

Stuckenschmidt, H. H., *Schoenberg: His Life, World and Work*, Humphrey Searle trans., London, 1977

Suu Kyi, Aung San, *Freedom from Fear and Other Writings*, London, 1991

Tagore, Abanindranath, *Abanindra Rachanabali (Gharoa)*, *1*, 1973 [1379]

Tagore, Debendranath, *Atmajibani*, Arabinda Mitra and Ashim Ahmed eds, Calcutta, 1988 [1395]

    The Autobiography of Maharshi Devendranath Tagore, Satyendranath Tagore and Indira Devi trans., London, 1914

Tagore, Dwijendranath, *Swapnaprayan*, 1914 [1321]

Tagore, Gaganendranath, *Gaganendranath Tagore*, Calcutta, 1964

Tagore, Jyotirindranath, *Twenty-Five Collotypes from the Original Drawings by Jyotirindra Nath Tagore*, Hammersmith (London), 1914 (preface by William Rothenstein)

Tagore, Rathindranath, *On the Edges of Time*, 2nd edn, Calcutta, 1981

Tagore, Sandip, *Peopled Azimuth: Reminiscences and Reflections of an Indian in Japan*, New Delhi, 1987

Tagore, Satyendranath, *Jiban o Shrishti*, Amita Bhattacharya ed., 1986

Tahmankar, D. V., *Lokamanya Tilak: Father of Indian Unrest and Maker of Modern India*, London, 1956

Tait, Katharine, *My Father Bertrand Russell*, London, 1976

Tedeschi, Richard trans., *Selected Letters of André Gide and Dorothy Bussy*, Oxford, 1983

Teitelboim, Volodia, *Neruda: An Intimate Biography*, Austin (Texas), 1991

Tendulkar, D. G., *Mahatma: Life of Mohandas Karamchand Gandhi*, *1–8*, Bombay, 1951–54

Tharu, Susie and K. Lalita eds, *Women Writing in India: 600 B.C. to the Present*, *1* (600 B. C. to the Early 20th Century), New York, 1991

Thompson, E. J., *Rabindranath Tagore: Poet and Dramatist*, New Delhi, 1991 (introduction by Harish Trivedi)

Thompson, E. P., *Alien Homage: Edward Thompson and Rabindranath Tagore*, New Delhi, 1993

Tinker, Hugh, *The Ordeal of Love: C. F. Andrews and India*, New Delhi, 1979

The Upanishads, Juan Mascaró trans., London, 1965

Visva-Bharati, *Mrinalini Devi*, 1974 [1381]

Webb, Barry, *Edmund Blunden: A Biography*, London, 1990

Webb, Beatrice, *Diaries 1912–1924*, Margaret I. Cole ed., London, 1952

Weber, Brom, *Hart Crane: A Biographical and Critical Study*, 2nd edn, New York, 1970

Wells, H. G., *God the Invisible King*, London, 1917

Wilson, Woodrow: *The Papers of Woodrow Wilson*, Arthur S. Link ed., *41*, Princeton, 1983; *42*, Princeton, 1983

Winsten, Stephen, *Jesting Apostle: The Life of Bernard Shaw*, London, 1956

Yeats, J. B., *Letters to His Son W. B. Yeats and Others 1869–1922*, Joseph Hone ed., London, 1983

Yeats, W. B., *The Letters of W. B. Yeats*, Allan Wade ed., New York, 1955

Young, Michael, *The Elmhirsts of Dartington: The Creation of an Utopian Community*, Dartington/London, 1982

Index